THE PAPERS OF DANIEL WEBSTER

CHARLES M. WILTSE, EDITOR-IN-CHIEF

SERIES TWO: LEGAL PAPERS

THE UNIVERSITY PRESS

OF NEW ENGLAND

Sponsoring Institutions

BRANDEIS UNIVERSITY

BROWN UNIVERSITY

CLARK UNIVERSITY

DARTMOUTH COLLEGE

UNIVERSITY OF NEW HAMPSHIRE

UNIVERSITY OF RHODE ISLAND

TUFTS UNIVERSITY

UNIVERSITY OF VERMONT

The Papers of
Daniel Webster

Legal Papers, Volume 2

The Boston Practice

ALFRED S. KONEFSKY AND

ANDREW J. KING, EDITORS

PUBLISHED FOR

DARTMOUTH COLLEGE BY THE

UNIVERSITY PRESS OF NEW ENGLAND

HANOVER, NEW HAMPSHIRE

AND LONDON, ENGLAND 1983

Library of Congress Catalog Card Number 73-92705

International Standard Book Number 0-87451-240-9

Printed in the United States of America

Library of Congress Cataloging in Publication data
will be found on the last printed page of this book.

The edition of the Papers of Daniel Webster, of which this is Volume 2 in the Legal Series, has been made possible by aid from several sources. The editorial preparation of this volume and costs associated with its publication were supported through grants from the Editing and Publication Programs of the National Endowment for the Humanities, an independent federal agency. Continuing support, both administrative and financial, has been given by the National Historical Publications and Records Commission. With specific reference to the Legal Papers, the William Nelson Cromwell Foundation has provided generous assistance. The edition is sponsored and published by Dartmouth College.

Foreword

This second volume of the Legal Papers of Daniel Webster is a continuation of the first, picking up the story when Webster moved his burgeoning practice from Portsmouth to Boston. He was already well acquainted in his new home, both with members of the business community who would be his clients, and with the system of courts. He continued his debt collection and commercial practice, but inevitably as the base of Boston's economy broadened, Webster's professional activities were extended to include transportation, manufacturing, and insurance litigation. At the same time he devoted more of his time to politics, and extended his practice to an increasing number of federal cases, many of which will be considered in volume three of this series.

The present volume, because of its integral relationship to its predecessor, will dispense with some of the usual preliminaries. Acknowledgments have been omitted because they are identical with those for Volume I of the Legal Papers, and there are no prefatory remarks because no more need here be said. The practice selectively discussed in the following pages is that of a better than average lawyer in a large commercial city, during much of the first half of the nineteenth century. Boston remained through Webster's time the cultural center of the country, and her hinterland was rapidly developing into an industrial area. His practice reflects the problems and the aspirations of the city and of her growing number of inhabitants.

CHARLES M. WILTSE

Contents

PLAN OF WORK

From the outset the Papers of Daniel Webster was planned as an integrated project, using both microfilm and letterpress publication. The persistent pressure of time and the steadily rising cost of book publication were important factors in the choice of the dual media, but the overriding consideration was the desire to bring all of Webster together, without abridgment or gloss, for those who were equipped to use it that way, while providing the less dedicated scholar and the general reader with the essential Webster in convenient annotated form. The microfilm edition, in four different groupings, is as complete as the surviving records permit. Webster's correspondence, including letters received as well as letters sent, together with miscellaneous notes, memoranda, briefs, drafts, formal writings, reports, petitions, and business papers have been issued with printed guide and index as *The Papers of Daniel Webster* by University Microfilms, Ann Arbor, Michigan. *The Legal Papers of Daniel Webster*, also to be issued with guide and alphabetical list of cases by University Microfilms, consists of records drawn primarily from the county courts of New Hampshire and Massachusetts and from the state and lower federal courts in New England. Records of the Department of State and of the Supreme Court are available on film from the National Archives and Records Service of the General Services Administration, but the user must select for himself the reels that may contain Webster material.

The value of these films, including as they do virtually all known Webster papers, cannot be overstated; but the very magnitude of the material makes it unmanageable. The films, moreover, are relatively expensive, require special equipment to use, are hard on the eyes, and effectively bury the grains of wheat by mixing them unevenly with an enormous amount of chaff. The user must decipher for himself often difficult or faded handwriting. He must search out the identity of persons and the nature of events alluded to, and finally he must rely upon his own judgment as to the significance of the given document. In the letterpress edition all this has been done for him, even to the selection of documents in terms of their significance, by editors totally immersed in the time and place and almost as familiar with the central characters as was Webster himself.

The letterpress edition in effect complements and renders more useful these various microfilm collections, whose very existence has made it possible to select more rigorously the documents important enough to be offered to the larger audience reached by the printed book. Each volume of correspondence, moreover, includes a calendar of letters written in the same time period but not selected for publication. For each of these the microfilm frame number is cited, as is volume and page citation for any document now available only in a printed version. Footnote references are also made to the film wherever appropriate. Items found subsequent to publication of the appropriate volume will be calendared at the end of the Correspondence Series. For the general reader and for the student of the period rather than of the man, the editors believe the selection of items printed will be ample. The biographer, and the scholar pursuing an in-depth study of some segment of the times, will need the film, to which he will find the printed volumes an indispensable annotated guide.

The letterpress edition is being published in four different series, overlapping in time but not in content, in order to make maximum use of subject matter specialists as technical editors. The edition has been planned in a total of fourteen volumes, of which seven are correspondence, three are legal papers, two are diplomatic papers, and two are speeches and formal writings. The present volume, dealing with Webster's Boston practice, is the second of the Legal Series.

EDITORIAL METHOD

Letters and documents included in this volume are arranged in broad subject categories. Within each appropriate category chronological sequence is maintained. The only exception is for letters that were sent as enclosures in later correspondence. These have been placed immediately after the document they accompanied. Date and point of origin have been placed at the upper right of each letter. If all or part of this information has been supplied by the editors, it appears in square brackets, with a question mark if conjecture. The complimentary close, which in the original manuscripts often takes up three or four lines, has been run continuously with the last line of the text.

All letters are reproduced in full except in rare instances where the only surviving text is incomplete or is from a printed source that did not reproduce it in its entirety. The documents are printed in substantially complete form. The editors, however, have deleted extraneous legal formalities. Occasionally, excerpts from letters and documents of particular relevance to the subject under discussion have been reproduced. Needless to say, texts from printed sources are used only when the original manuscript has not been found but the letter or document is of sufficient importance to warrant its inclusion.

The letters and documents themselves have been reproduced in type as nearly as possible the way they were written. Misspellings have been retained without the annoyingly obtrusive "(sic)"; and abbreviations and contractions have been allowed to stand unless the editors believe they would not be readily understood by a present-day reader—in which case the abbreviation has been expanded, with square brackets enclosing the letters supplied. Punctuation, too, has been left as Webster and his contemporaries used it, save only that dashes clearly intended as periods or commas are so written. Superscript letters in abbreviations or contractions have been brought down, but a period is supplied only if the last letter of the abbreviation is not the last letter of the word abbreviated. In all other cases, periods, apostrophes, dashes, and other forms of punctuation have been left unchanged. The ampersand, far more frequently used than the spelled out "and," has been retained, but diacritical marks over contractions have been omitted even where the contraction itself is retained.

Canceled words or passages that are obvious slips, immediately corrected, have been left out altogether; those which show some change of thought or attitude or have stylistic or psychological implications have been included between angled brackets. Interlineations by the author have been incorporated into the text. Marginal passages also appear in the text, except in a few instances where they have been treated as postscripts.

In order to make these legal materials accessible to the general reader, extensive introductory matter has been included. These general introductions appear both at the beginning of sections and, occasionally, interspersed with the letters and documents that constitute the main text of the volume. Both these formats serve not only to elucidate the nature of the legal materials under consideration, but to indicate what Webster was doing at a particular time. Footnotes are numbered consecutively within major subject categories. They are used to identify persons, places, events, situations, problems, or other matters that should help the reader to understand the context of a particular reference. Individuals and legal decisions are identified only once, generally the first time they are mentioned. For the convenience of the reader who may have missed this first reference, the appropriate index entry is printed in boldface type. Given names and initials in square brackets are added only where the identity of the individual is unclear from the context.

Immediately following each letter or document is an unnumbered note indicating the provenance of the document and, if appropriate, giving some information about the writer or recipient. Symbols used in these provenance notes are the standard descriptive symbols, and the location symbols developed by the Union Catalog Division of the Library of Congress. Those appearing in the present volume are listed below under Abbrevations and Symbols. For the most part, attorney identifications appearing in Volume 1 of the Legal Series are not repeated in the text of Volume 2. They will be found in an appendix at the end, with appropriate index references printed in boldface type.

Abbreviations and Symbols

DESCRIPTIVE SYMBOLS

Abstract	Summary of contents, or a portion thereof, of a letter or document
AD	Autograph Document
AD draft	Autograph Document, draft
ADS	Autograph Document Signed
ADS copy	Autograph Document Signed, copied by writer
ADS draft	Autograph Document Signed, draft
AL	Autograph Letter
ALS	Autograph Letter Signed
ALS copy	Autograph Letter Signed, copied by writer
ALS draft	Autograph Letter Signed, draft
AN	Autograph Note
ANS	Autograph Note Signed
APD	Autograph (in part) Document
APD draft	Autograph (in part) Document, draft
APDS	Autograph (in part) Document Signed
APDS draft	Autograph (in part) Document Signed, draft
Copy	Copy not by writer
DFS	Draft Signed
Extract	Copy of a portion of a letter or document
LC	Letterbook Copy
LS	Letter Signed
(DW)	Autograph in Webster's hand
(DWp)	Autograph partly in Webster's hand

LOCATION SYMBOLS

CSmH	Henry E. Huntington Library
DLC	Library of Congress
DNA	National Archives
MBNU	Northeastern University
MH	Harvard University
MHi	Massachusetts Historical Society
MiU-C	University of Michigan, Clements Library
MWA	American Antiquarian Society

MWalB	Brandeis University
N	New York State Library
Nh-Ar	New Hampshire State Archives
NhD	Dartmouth College
NhHi	New Hampshire Historical Society
NhPoS	Strawbery Banke, Portsmouth, N.H.
NNC	Columbia University
OClWHi	Western Reserve Historical Society, Cleveland
PPINA	Insurance Company of North America, Philadelphia
PU	University of Pennsylvania
RNHi	Newport Historical Society, R.I.
Vi	Virginia State Library
ViU	University of Virginia

COURT ABBREVIATIONS

JP	Justice of the Peace Court
MassCCP,E	Massachusetts Court of Common Pleas, Essex County
MassCCP,M	Massachusetts Court of Common Pleas, Middlesex County
MassCCP,S	Massachusetts Court of Common Pleas, Suffolk County
MassSJC,E	Massachusetts Supreme Judicial Court, Essex County
MassSJC,M	Massachusetts Supreme Judicial Court, Middlesex County
MassSJC,N	Massachusetts Supreme Judicial Court, Norfolk County
MassSJC,S	Massachusetts Supreme Judicial Court, Suffolk County
NHCCP,G–H	New Hampshire Court of Common Pleas, Grafton County—Haverhill Session
NHCCP,G–P	New Hampshire Court of Common Pleas, Grafton County—Plymouth Session
NHCCP,H–A	New Hampshire Court of Common Pleas, Hillsborough County—Amherst Session
NHCCP,H–H	New Hampshire Court of Common Pleas, Hillsborough County—Hopkinton Session
NHCCP,R–E	New Hampshire Court of Common Pleas, Rockingham County—Exeter Session
NHCCP,R–P	New Hampshire Court of Common Pleas, Rockingham County—Portsmouth Session
NHSCJ,G–H	New Hampshire Superior Court of Judicature, Grafton County—Haverhill Session

NHSCJ,G–P	New Hampshire Superior Court of Judicature, Grafton County—Plymouth Session
NHSCJ,H–A	New Hampshire Superior Court of Judicature, Hillsborough County—Amherst Session
NHSCJ,H–H	New Hampshire Superior Court of Judicature, Hillsborough County—Hopkinton Session
NHSCJ,R–E	New Hampshire Superior Court of Judicature, Rockingham County—Exeter Session
NHSCJ,R–P	New Hampshire Superior Court of Judicature, Rockingham County—Portsmouth Session
NHSJC,G–H	New Hampshire Supreme Judicial Court, Grafton County—Haverhill Session
NHSJC,G–P	New Hampshire Supreme Judicial Court, Grafton County—Plymouth Session
NHSJC,H–A	New Hampshire Supreme Judicial Court, Hillsborough County—Amherst Session
NHSJC,H–H	New Hampshire Supreme Judicial Court, Hillsborough County—Hopkinton Session
NHSJC,R–E	New Hampshire Supreme Judicial Court, Rockingham County—Exeter Session
NHSJC,R–P	New Hampshire Supreme Judicial Court, Rockingham County—Portsmouth Session
USCC,DMass	United States Circuit Court, District of Massachusetts
USCC,DMe–Pl	United States Circuit Court, District of Maine—Portland Session
USCC,DMe–W	United States Circuit Court, District of Maine—Wiscasset Session
USCC,DNH–E	United States Circuit Court, District of New Hampshire—Exeter Session
USCC,DNH–Po	United States Circuit Court, District of New Hampshire—Portsmouth Session
USCC,DRI–N	United States Circuit Court, District of Rhode Island—Newport Session
USCC,DRI–Pr	United States Circuit Court, District of Rhode Island—Providence Session
USDC,DMass	United States District Court, District of Massachusetts
USDC,DMe–Pl	United States District Court, District of Maine—Portland Session
USDC,DMe–W	United States District Court, District of Maine—Wiscasset Session
USDC,DNH–E	United States District Court, District of New Hampshire—Exeter Session
USDC,DNH–Po	United States District Court, District of New Hampshire—Portsmouth Session

USDC,DRI–N	United States District Court, District of Rhode Island—Newport Session
USDC,DRI–Pr	United States District Court, District of Rhode Island—Providence Session
USSC	United States Supreme Court

SHORT TITLES

Bell	Charles H. Bell, *The Bench and Bar of New Hampshire* (Boston, 1894).
Blackstone	William Blackstone, *Commentaries on the Laws of England* (4 vols., Oxford, 1765–1769).
Correspondence	Charles M. Wiltse and others, eds., *The Papers of Daniel Webster: Correspondence* (7 vols., Hanover, N.H. and London, 1974–198–).
Curtis	George Ticknor Curtis, *Life of Daniel Webster* (2 vols., New York, 1870).
Fuess, *Webster*	Claude Moore Fuess, *Daniel Webster* (2 vols., Boston, 1930).
Goebel	Julius Goebel and others, eds., *The Law Practice of Alexander Hamilton* (5 vols., New York and London, 1964–1981).
Gould	James Gould, *A Treatise on the Principles of Pleading in Civil Actions* (Boston, 1832).
Horwitz	Morton J. Horwitz, *The Transformation of American Law, 1780–1860* (Cambridge, Mass., 1977).
Kent	James Kent, *Commentaries on American Law* (4 vols., New York, 1826–1830; 2nd edition, 1832).
LPJA	L. Kinvin Wroth and Hiller B. Zobel, eds., *Legal Papers of John Adams* (3 vols., Cambridge, Mass., 1965).
Legal Papers	Alfred S. Konefsky and Andrew J. King, eds., *The Papers of Daniel Webster: Legal Papers* (3 vols., Hanover, N.H. and London, 1982–198–).
mDW	Microfilm Edition of the Papers of Daniel Webster (Ann Arbor, 1971). References are followed by frame numbers.
mDWs	Microfilm Edition of the Papers of Daniel Webster, Supplementary Reel.
Miller	Hunter Miller, ed., *Treaties and Other International Acts of the United States of America* (8 vols., Washington, 1931–1948).
Moore, *Arbitrations*	John Bassett Moore, *History and Digest of the International Arbitrations to which the United States has been a Party* (6 vols., Washington, 1898).

Morison	John Hopkins Morison, *Life of the Hon. Jeremiah Smith* (Boston, 1845).
PC	Fletcher Webster, ed., *The Private Correspondence of Daniel Webster* (2 vols., Boston, 1856).
Smith, *Reports*	Jeremiah Smith, *Decisions of the Superior and Supreme Courts of New Hampshire* (Boston, 1879).
Speeches	Charles M. Wiltse, ed., *The Papers of Daniel Webster: Speeches and Formal Writings* (2 vols., Hanover, N.H. and London, 198–).
W. Story	William W. Story, *Life and Letters of Joseph Story* (2 vols., Boston, 1851).
Van Tyne	Claude H. Van Tyne, ed., *The Letters of Daniel Webster* (New York, 1902).
W & S	James W. McIntyre, ed., *The Writings and Speeches of Daniel Webster* (18 vols., New York, 1903).

In citing cases we have used the nominative reporters. Citations to Wheaton, Peters, Howard, and Wallace refer to cases decided by the United States Supreme Court. Citations to Gallison, Mason, Sumner, Story, Ware, and Sprague correspond to cases reported, alphabetically, in *Federal Cases*. Citations to Tyng, Pickering, Metcalf, and Cushing refer to cases from the Massachusetts Supreme Judicial Court reported in *Massachusetts Reports*. We have frequently used the abbreviation BUS for Bank of the United States.

SERIES TWO: LEGAL PAPERS

VOLUME TWO: THE BOSTON PRACTICE

CHAPTER 1. Relocating the Practice of Law

1. INTRODUCTION: FROM PORTSMOUTH, NEW HAMPSHIRE TO BOSTON

The War of 1812 accelerated Portsmouth's slide into economic stagnation. Unable to stem the decline in the carrying trade or to withstand the competition from Boston, the merchants and shipowners of Portsmouth, like their counterparts in other small New England seaports, watched as their economic strength slowly ebbed. Webster, too, soon became aware that Portsmouth could not provide an adequate setting for his ambition. Before making the decision to leave, however, he embarked on the path to success followed by many lawyers; he accepted nomination to political office. While Americans of Webster's generation accepted public office in the spirit of civic duty, lawyers especially gravitated toward politics to further their professional careers. Political office bolstered reputations and thereby gained the lawyers new clients.[1]

When the Portsmouth voters elected Webster to Congress in 1812, the business community already counted him among the state's leading lawyers. Being in Washington gave him the opportunity to begin his Supreme Court practice. It also put him in contact with other young men of similar ambition. By his third year in Congress (December 1815) he realized that even though his New Hampshire practice had reached a peak, "its results were not competent" to support his family.[2] Influenced by his Washington friends, he decided to leave Portsmouth. To his brother Ezekiel he wrote:

> I have settled my purpose to remove from New Hampshire in the course of the summer. I have thought of Boston, New York, and Al-

1. For example, Philadelphia lawyer Horace Binney wrote:

> After being admitted to the Bar in 1800, I continued, an unrewarded drudge until the year 1806, when I was chosen to represent this city in the State legislature. I had in the meantime married . . . and was prevailed upon to leave my family merely as a professional experiment. . . . The experiment succeeded. On my return I found several persons of consequence in the city disposed to patronize me, and I declined a re-election.

Binney to John Pickering, February 13, 1815, printed in Mary Orne Pickering, ed., *Life of John Pickering* (Boston, 1887), p. 255. Binney used politics as a springboard. Political ambition, on the other hand, seduced Webster. Had he left political office after he made his Boston reputation, he would have had much greater financial success.

2. "Autobiography," *Correspondence*, 1: 23.

> bany. On the whole I shall, probably, go to Boston; although I am not without some inducements to go into the State of New York. Our New England prosperity and importance are passing away. This is fact. The events of the times, the policy of England, the consequences of our war, and the Ghent Treaty, have bereft us of our commerce, the great source of our wealth. If any great scenes are to be acted in this country within the next twenty years, New York is the place in which those scenes are to be viewed. More of this hereafter.[3]

Although he deprecated Boston's future, his integration into its legal community would be relatively easy. Since he was already a member of the Suffolk bar, the friend of several Boston lawyers, and the attorney for some local mercantile firms, he would not be an unknown.

In the summer of 1816 Webster moved to Boston. He attended the short session of the Fourteenth Congress, December 1816 to March 1817, still representing Portsmouth, New Hampshire; but for the next six years he would be out of Congress. During this time he established his Massachusetts practice while gaining national renown before the bar of the United States Supreme Court. At the outset he attended the nearby state courts, on circuit, much as he had done in New Hampshire. He also established an extensive federal practice in the United States circuit and district courts.

As his reputation in Massachusetts commercial and legal circles grew, he left behind the remnants of his New Hampshire debt collection practice. Commercial interests now retained him in major litigation, for which they paid him fees far greater than any he had received before.[4] Other lawyers, too, began to call on him for advice in the preparation of their own cases and for assistance in handling appeals. In common with other leading lawyers of his time, Webster had the ability to perceive quickly the basic legal issue in a case. Once he had isolated the legal question, he could advise the other attorney how to draft the pleas and where to look for precedents. As a counsellor and appellate lawyer, Webster often appeared in cases only when a court heard the appeal. When his political ambition reached its height in the 1830s, he practiced chiefly in this appellate capacity. Often hired on an annual retainer, he entered cases at the last moment and formulated his argument after a quick perusal of his co-counsel's brief.

Although Webster participated to some extent every winter in the United States Supreme Court term, for practical reasons he always maintained a Boston office in association with another lawyer. These

3. March 26, 1816, *Correspondence*, 1: 196. In his "Autobiography" DW attributed to Theodore Dwight the decision to choose Boston.

4. See Chapter 3, below, for examples of DW's fees for this period.

relationships were not partnerships. Generally, each man had his own clients and kept his own accounts. The Boston associate saw to the day-to-day business of running the office, supervising the law students, assisting in routine legal matters, and handling Webster's financial affairs when he was out of the city. In one instance, however, that of Webster's first associate, Alexander Bliss, the relationship verged on a closer association. In many of Webster's SJC cases both their names appear on the pleadings and other documents. This indicates that Bliss took an active part with Webster in preparing the cases. They also worked closely together in the Spanish claims affair.[5] Indeed, the Webster-Bliss connection was tinged with affection, and Bliss's tragic death deeply affected Webster. His relationship with the two lawyers who followed Bliss never reached the same level of intensity. The following three sections, organized in terms of Webster's associates, cover through selections from his correspondence the entire period of his later career. They illustrate the nature of his multi-jurisdiction practice, the rhythm of his life, and his perception of his career in the law.

a. A Note on the Massachusetts Judicial System

The Massachusetts courts and their procedure were familiar to Webster. As a law student he had spent six months in 1805 in Christopher Gore's Boston office. In addition, both Massachusetts and New Hampshire had similarly structured judicial systems and followed a comparable law of procedure. Like their New Hampshire counterparts the Massachusetts CCPs were organized on a county basis. During his first few years in Boston, Webster built his practice by traveling the circuit of the common pleas courts in Suffolk (Boston), Essex, Middlesex, and Norfolk counties. These CCP courts had a general civil and criminal jurisdiction. In an attempt to limit the number of cases appealed to the SJC, the legislature had enacted a statute which barred an appeal from a full CCP trial unless the amount in controversy exceeded $100. In cases that exceeded this amount, the parties would use a sham demurrer to move the case to an SJC trial.[1] In CCP cases with a jurisdictional amount below $100, the losing side might seek a review of points of law in the SJC by a writ of error. Single judges held SJC trials at nisi prius terms. By a bill of exceptions attorneys could reserve for argument before the full SJC bench questions of law relating to the evidence or instructions.[2] Removing

5. See Chapter 4, below.

1. This brief discussion draws on William E. Nelson, *Americanization of the Common Law: The Impact of Legal Change on Massachusetts Society, 1760–1830* (Cambridge, Mass., 1975), pp. 165–169. For an examination of the sham demurrer see *Legal Papers*, 1: 64.

2. Arguments on reserved questions of law usually took place at the law terms in Suffolk County. This fol-

consideration by the full SJC bench of run of the mill cases allowed this highest Massachusetts court to develop through its reported appellate opinions a jurisprudence of both procedural and substantive law. The consequent elevation of appellate review in both status and importance made it possible for lawyers like Webster to make a career out of appellate advocacy.

2. THE SCOPE OF THE PRACTICE

a. Alexander Bliss: 1816–1827

Before he moved to Boston, Webster rented office space and selected an associate. From his relationship with Timothy Farrar, Jr., in Portsmouth, he had learned the importance of having someone attend to routine office business while he himself might be absent for long periods of time. It was especially important if the business was to grow. Sometime, probably in the early summer of 1816, Alexander Bliss, recently admitted to the Suffolk bar after reading law in Webster's office, agreed to become Webster's associate. On June 27, 1816, Webster wrote to Bliss:

> I see nothing to prevent me from being in Boston in next month, & think the Offices which we examined in Court Street should be prepared, as soon as may be, unless you should find better rooms.
>
> I shall send my library up in a week or two, directed to your care. I must trouble you to see cases provided for the books, but it will be in season perhaps to order them when the books come, & when it can be better seen what is wanted.[1]

With no distracting official responsibilities, Webster could devote his energies to building the practice. In January 1818 he wrote to Connecticut congressman David Daggett in an optimistic vein.

> We have nothing new here at all. The weather is fine, & every body busy in his own concerns. I think the Commercial property of this place, like others, is rapidly encreasing, & every body seems satisfied with the prospects of trade & business. If you keep us out of a Spanish war, & all other wars, a few years will make the Country too rich to contain itself.[2]

Shortly thereafter Webster left for Washington to argue the *Dartmouth College* case. His successful defense of the College gave him a national reputation. In those years a lawyer's reputation often rested on two traits: first, the ability to handle a jury, and second, facility in making a legal

---

lowed the model of the English Court of King's Bench.

1. *Correspondence*, 1: 200. For a catalogue of DW's library see Document 1, printed below.

2. January 9, 1818, mDW 2134.

argument.[3] In both Webster became highly regarded, and put himself in a position to earn large fees as an appellate advocate.[4]

Webster developed a practice in which he spent three months or so a year attending the United States Supreme Court and the rest of the time cultivating a local clientele. This forced him to rely on Bliss to keep his engagements in order. Fortunately for Webster, the Massachusetts lawyers accommodated one another in the same manner as those of the New Hampshire bar.[5] As the letters printed below show, Bliss proved indispensable in keeping track of Webster's schedule and commitments. Webster could always count on Bliss to appear for him in court and to get a continuance if necessary.

Webster spent his time moving between the various jurisdictions in which he practiced. For example, in the fall of 1819 he attended the October terms of the state and federal courts. In February 1820 he left for Washington, where he argued four cases at the Supreme Court. In March he returned to Boston and immediately attended cases at the spring SJC term. He wrote to Justice Joseph Story in April:

> I have been uncommonly occupied since I came home. Our Court has had a law term of four weeks, & is to assemble, in full bench, again, today week. I believe I shall tax you for an opinion on one case, which I have the charge of. It turns on N.E[ngland] Law, which I am heartily sick of.[6]

Then, before the SJC finished, the USCC began its May session. Finally, at the end of May, both court sessions ended. "Our courts are thro. Judge Story adjourned on Saturday, & Chief Jus Parker on the Saturday before."[7]

While Webster was developing his Boston practice, he was faced with a number of competing concerns. First, as the pace of his practice indicates, he was anxious to build a secure financial base. Business meant fees. But he was also concerned with his reputation, for increased reputation meant increased business. His busy schedule, however, occasionally

3. In this regard DW remained faithful to his earlier Boston role models. See *Legal Papers*, 1: 33–34, 41–42.

4. For a discussion of DW's fees, see Chapter 3, below.

5. Massachusetts lawyer and judge Samuel Putnam recalled the experience of the Essex County bar: "The habit of that bar was to disclose freely to the adverse counsel the points which were to be controverted or admitted, *whereby much expense to clients was saved*. What out of court was agreed to be admitted was always admitted on trial. . . . These agreements were uniformly verbal, but always performed." *Massachusetts Law Quarterly*, 8 (November, 1922): 8.

6. April 3 [1820], *Correspondence*, 1: 271–272. The case has not been identified.

7. DW to Jeremiah Mason, May 30, 1820, *Correspondence*, 1: 273.

meant that he risked being unprepared because he was overcommitted. This was a serious problem for a lawyer on the rise.

DOCUMENT 1. WEBSTER'S LAW LIBRARY

Catalogue of Books in the Law library
of D. Webster.

Boston Aug 12.th 1816

Abbott's law of shipping 1 vol. 8vo.[8] 2 setts.
Adye's Courts martial 1 vol. 12 mo.[9]
Admiralty decisions 2 vol. 8vo. 2d missing
Anstruther's Reports 1 vol. 8vo
Andrews Rep. 1 vol. 8vo
Atkins Rep. 3 vols 8vo

Bacon's abridgement 7 vos. 8vo. Guillim Ed.
Bailey on bills 1 vol. 8vo
Burrow's Rep. 5 vos 8vo
Butler's Horae juridicae 1 vol. 8vo.
Brown's Rep. 4 vol. 8vo.
Blackstone's Rep. 2 vol. 8vo
H. Blackstones Rep 2. 8vo.
Blackstone's Commentaries 4 vols. 8vo
Bosanquet & Puller's Rep. 3 vol 8vo
Ditto New Rep. 2 vol. 8vo
Booth on Real Actions 1 vol 8vo
Brown's Civ et Adm. law 2 vols. 8vo
Burn's dig. Mod. Rep. 1 vol 8vo
Binney's Rep. 1 vol. 8vo
Barnes Cases 1 vol. 8vo
Barrington on the Statutes 1 vol. 4to.[10]
Buller's Nisi prius 1 vol. 8vo.

Cranch's Reports 6 vols. added
Coke on Lyttleton 1 vol. Folio
Cruise on Real property 5 vols. 8vo
Chitty on bills 1 vol. 8vo. 2 setts 1 in boards
Cooper's opinion on Foreign decisions in Adm[iralty] 1 vol 8vo
Constitutions Smiths 1 vol 4to.
Clarks praxis 1 vol. 12 mo.

8. Octavo, a measure of the size of the page in a book, approximately 9 by 6 inches.

9. Duodecimo, a page approximately 7 by 5 inches.

10. Quarto, a page approximately 12 by 9½ inches.

Clerks' assistant 1 vol. 8vo
Complete Justice 1 vol. 8vo
Corpus Juris Civilis 1 vol. Royal 8vo.
Cases in equity 1 vol. Fol[io]
Chitty on pleadings 2 vol. 8vo
Comyn on contracts 2 vol. 8vo.
Comyn's Digest 6 vols 8vo.
Comyn's Rep 2 vols 8vo.
Cases in Equity abridged 2 vol. 8vo
Cases Temp. Hardwicke 1 vol. 8vo
Croke's Rep. 3 vol. 8vo
Campbell's Rep. 2 vols. 8vo
Cooper's Justinian 1 vol. 8vo

Day's Rep. 2 vol. 8vo.
Douglas Rep. 2 vol. 8vo
Douglass' Elections 4 vols in 2. 8vo
Dyer's Rep. 3 vols. 8vo
Durnford & East's Rep. 8 vols. 8vo.
Dagge on crim law 3 vols. 12 mo.
Doctor and Student 1 vol. 12 mo.

Emerigon 1 vol. 8vo
Espinasse's Nisi prius 4 vols. 8vo Walpole Ed.
Ditto 2 vols. 8vo Gould's Ed.
Do. Rep. 5 vols. 8vo in 3 Day's Ed.
Easts Rep. 15 vols. 8vo. plus 1 vol.
East's Crown Law 2 vols. 8vo
Every man his own lawyer 1 vol. 8vo
Espinasse's Nisi prius 2 vols. 8vo 1st missing

Fonblanque's Equity 2 vols. 8vo
Finch's Chancery 1 vol. 8vo
Fearne on Remainders 2 vols 8vo 2d. missing
Francis maxims 1 vol 8vo.

Gilberts devises 1 vol. 8vo
Grotius de jure belli ac pacis 1 vol. 8vo

Hughe's abridgment 3 vol. 4to. 1 & 2d missing
Hawkins pleas of the Crown 1 vol. Fol.
Hargrave's State Trials 3 vols. 4to. paper
Hawkins abridgt of Coke. 1 vol. 12 mo.
Hale's Common Law 2 vol. 8vo.
Historical Law tracts 1 vol. 8vo.
Hardres Rep. 1 vol. 8vo.

Interrogatories in equity 1 vol. 12 mo

Jones on Bailments 1 vol. 8vo.
Johnsons Rep. 11 vol. 8vo.
Johnsons Cases in Er. 2 vol. 8vo.

Kidd on awards 1 vol. 8vo

Loft's Rep 1 vol 8vo
Latch's Rep. 1 vol 8vo
Laws of Massachusetts 4 vol. 8vo. 1 n. series. 1 ancient charter
Laws of Virginia 1 vol. Fol.
Laws of Mass. prov. 1 vol. 4to
Laws of N. Hampshire 1 vol. 8vo. 8 setts
Lawes on pleading 1 vol. 8vo 2 setts
Laws of Vermont 1 vol. 8vo
Law of Partnership 1 vol. 8vo
Landlord & Tenant 1 vol. 12 mo.
Leach's Crown Law 2 vols 8vo
Lilly's Entries 2 vol. 8vo.

Massachusetts Term Reports 11 vol. 8vo
Modern Rep. 12 vols 8vo in 9 vols.
Macomb on Courts martial 1 vol. 8vo
Marshall on Insurance 1 vol 8vo. Amer[ica]n Edn by Conde
MacNally on evidence 2 vols. 8vo.
Montesquieu's spirit of Laws 2 vols. 8vo.
Mitford's pleadings 1 vol 8vo.
Montagu on Set-off 1 vol. 8vo.
Molloy de jure maritimo 1 vol. 8vo

Newland on contracts 1 vol. 8vo.
Nisi Prius Law abridged Farrand Ed. 3 vols. 8vo.
Noy's maxims 1 vol. 12 mo.
Nelson's Justice 1 vol. 8vo.
Natura brevium 1 vol. 8vo.
New York Term Reports 3 vols. 8vo. Caines
New York cases in Error 2 vols. 8vo

Peere Williams' Rep. 3 vols 8vo.
Powell on devises 1 vol 8vo
Peake's evidence 1 vol. 8vo.
Precedents of declarations 1 vol. 8vo.
Perkins' conveyancing 1 vol. 12 mo.
Powell on contracts 1 vol. 8vo
Practical Forms 1 vol. 8vo
Pothier on obligations 2 vols. 8vo

Robinson's admiralty Rep. 5 vol. 8vo
Runnington's practice 1 vol. 8vo.
Reeves law of shipping 1 vol 8vo boards
Raymonds Rep. 3 vols 8vo.
Rep. 1 circuit U. States. 1 vol. 8vo.
Roberts on Frauds 1 vol. 8vo.
Re[g]istrum Brevium 1 vol. Fol.
Rutherfor[d]'s institutes Nat[ural] law. 2 vols. 8vo.

Sheppard's assurance 1 vol. Fol.
Sanders on uses 1 vol. 8vo.
Saunders Rep. 1 vol. Fol.
Strange's Rep. 2 vol. 8vo.
Sullivan's lectures 2 vols. 8vo. boards
Smiths Rep. K[ing's] B[ench] 3 vols 8vo.
Salkelds Rep. 3 vols. 8vo.
Saunders Rep. 3 vols 8vo
Storys pleadings 1 vol. 8vo.
Sugden's law of vendors 1 vol 8vo
Sellon's practice 2 vols 8vo
Swinburne on wills 3 vols 8vo
Swift's system 2 vols 8vo
Sayers law of damages 1 vol 12 mo
Schiefer's practice 1 vol. 8vo
Sullivan's Land Titles 1 vol. 8vo
System of universal law Turnbulls 2 vols 8vo

Toller's law of Executors 1 vol. 8vo
Tidd's practice 2 vols 8vo
Trials per pais 1 vol 8vo
Tauntons Rep. 8vo. only 1st vol of sett present plus 3 vols
Tomlin's Index 1 vol. 8vo

Vattels Law of Nations 1 vol. 8vo.
Vesey's Jun. Rep. 15 vols 8vo 10, 11 & 12th. missing
Vesey's Reports 2 vols. 8vo
Ventris' Rep. 1 vol. Folio
Vinnius 1 vol. 4to

Williams' Statute laws 2 vols 4to
Wilkins Leges Anglo Saxon 1 vol Folio
Wooddeson's Lectures 3 vol 8vo.
Willes Reports 1 vol. 8vo.
Wilson's Rep. 3 vols 8vo.
Wills 1 vol. 12 mo. Meritons

Yelverton's Rep 1 vol 8vo Total 330 vols.

Books Lent

Dec	15	E. Cutts Chitty & Bailey on bills
Jan	4	Register to Mr [Peyton Randolph] Freeman
	7	2d vol. Ferne on Rem[ainders] Esqr Humphries
	25	4 vols Vezy Jun Mr Cutts
Feb	5	1 & 2d vol Campall's Rep E. Cutts Esq
	12	Sugden E. Cutts
	13	1st Vezy, 6 & 12th Modern Rep Mr [Nathaniel Pierce] Hoar

AD. NhD.

TO ALEXANDER BLISS

My dear Sir Washington Feb. 27. [1820] (Sunday)

The Court here has made unusually slow progress, & at present the prospect is that I must leave most of my business unfinished. The docket is to be called Tomorrow morning, for the purpose of ascertaining what causes can be tried this term, & what cannot. My belief is, that I shall be able to do little more, & that I shall get away in season to be in Boston the first week of the [MassSJC] Court. I wish you would mention this to Mr [William] Prescott, & also, perhaps, to the Chief Justice, unless I should write you again in a day or two. The [Supreme] Court is yet only *at No. 16*. I have looked over your engagement in Lazarus' cause. If the Court should call that on, before my arrival, please give them your argument.[11] I presume however it will lie till my arrival. I do not know that I have any other cause which stands early on the docket, except the case of Foster's Ex[ecuto]rs vs the Essex Bank, con[tinue]d nisi[12] from Essex. Mr. [John] Pickering, of Salem, is my colleague, in this cause, Mr. Prescott is agt. us. I understood Mr. Pickering that the 2nd day of the Term was agreed on, for the Argument. I suppose it would be equally agreeable to all parties that it shd. be fixed for a later day—say to the second Wednesday. I wish you would speak to Mr Prescott about it, & then write to Mr Pickering.

I shall write you again in a day or two.

Remember me to the family at the house—as I do not write Mrs W. today Yrs. D. Webster

ALS. DLC. Alexander Bliss (1792–1827; Yale 1812), Boston lawyer, studied with DW, admitted in July 1816, and became DW's associate.

11. Case not identified.

12. MassSJC,E, October 1821, and 17 Mass. 479 (1821). DW had also argued the case on an earlier procedural question: MassSJC,E, March 1819, and 16 Mass. 245 (1819). See pp. 530–533, below. DW meant the case had been taken from the nisi prius (i.e., jury trial) stage for the argument of a question of law before the full bench.

TO DUDLEY ATKINS TYNG

[November 1820]

It is not in my power to do any thing in this Dedham cause by way of notes of an Argument.[13] I am *tired of thinking of it*;—as I am of thinking of any thing else, that has gone *wrong*, & cannot be helped.

Mr Metcalf[14] has sent me the accompanying loose notes. I do not think you can make much of them. I believe the best way is to omit the Arguments altogether, & let the Ch. J.[15] stand alone.

Excuse my late answer to your note. I have been in the Com. Pleas two days in an *11 c[oun]ts* cause;[16] & have not found time to attend to *minor* matters. Yrs truly D Webster

ALS. NhD. Misdated November 1819 in *Correspondence*, 1, Calendar: 432. Dudley Atkins Tyng (1760–1829; Harvard 1781), Massachusetts lawyer, studied with Judge Mercer in Virginia, admitted to the Essex bar in 1784, appointed reporter, MassSJC in 1805. His reports cover volumes 2–17 of the Massachusetts Reports.

TO ALEXANDER BLISS

Dr Sir Washington Feb. 9. [1821]

I recd yrs, thro the hands of Mr. Gorham.[17] I am willing to take the new Offices,[18] especially as Mr [William] Prescott is going over head. I confess I have been unwilling to remove, but as you seem to prefer it, I am disposed to submit. I must have a room—& there must be accomodations also for you & the Students. I shall leave the matter entirely with you. If we move, I hope you will have the job over, before I return.

13. *Baker* v. *Fales*, 16 Mass. 147, 488 (1820), known as the *Dedham Church* case. The case was argued in October 1820, but the court did not announce its decision in favor of DW's opponents until November.

14. Theron Metcalf (1784–1875; Brown 1805), Massachusetts lawyer and judge, studied at Litchfield Law School, admitted to the Norfolk bar in 1808, Norfolk county attorney (1817–1829), state legislator, opened a law school in 1828, reporter, MassSJC (1838–1847), judge, MassSJC (1848–1865). DW and Metcalf unsuccessfully argued the plea in abatement at the first hearing; DW alone argued the appeal that followed the February 1820 trial.

15. Isaac Parker (1768–1830; Harvard 1786), studied with William Tudor, admitted in 1789, state and federal representative, U.S. marshal (1797–1801), judge, MassSJC (1806–1814; chief justice, 1814–1830), Royall professor of law, Harvard Law School (1816–1827).

16. We have not identified this case.

17. Benjamin Gorham (1775–1856; Harvard 1795), Boston lawyer, U.S. representative (1820–1823, 1827–1835). Letter not found.

18. Probably DW's second office on the ground floor of a building on the northern corner of Court and Tremont Streets.

Pray let me hear from you often, respecting our business in Court. What causes are tried, & how decided. We are now trying the cause from R. Island, in which Mr Greene[19] was concerned. It looks well, for our side. In a day or two Mr [George] Blake's case[20] will be on.

As to news, here, there is none. My opinion is, it is more probable than otherwise that Missouri will come in, on some terms or other.

I wrote Mrs W.[21] yesterday. It is now mild & fine weather here. Yrs truly D. Webster

ALS. DLC. Published in *Correspondence*, 1: 281–282.

TO ALEXANDER BLISS

Dear Bliss, Feb. 14 [1821]

I cannot say that I remember any specific agreement that the Action of Messrs C. D. & Co. vs Cns. Coolidge, in Suffolk, should be tried, before his action against them in Norfolk.[22] Of course we expected to try it first, because the Court was expected to sit first. Mr Aylwyn[23] has been m[ore?] part[icu]larly conversant with the course of the causes than I have been. Tell Mr S. F. C. that he need be under no fear of trying the cause at Norfolk, with Mr Aylwyn for Counsel. I am fully persuaded C. C. can make out no sort of a case; & yet, I apprehend, Mr [William] Prescott would not press a trial very rigorously, if Mr S. F. C. preferred a delay. Mr. Aylwyn is entirely competent to keep off harm, in any event. I recd the comm[ission] in Haven v Holland.[24] Yrs D Webster

ALS. DLC. Postscript on back of a cover addressed to Mrs. Webster. Misdated February 14, 1820, in *Correspondence*, 1, Calendar: 432.

19. Richard Ward Greene (1792–1875; Brown 1812), Rhode Island lawyer and judge, studied at Litchfield Law School and with Ebenezer Rockwell, admitted 1816, U.S. district attorney, Rhode Island (1826–1845), state legislator, chief justice, Rhode Island supreme court (1848–1854); *The Bello Corrunes*, 6 Wheaton 152 (1821). DW successfully represented the Spanish consul in this prize case.

20. *Hughes* v. *Blake*, 6 Wheaton 453 (1821). DW had also argued the lower court case with George Blake, USCC,DMass, October 1818, and 1 Mason 515 (1818).

21. Grace Fletcher Webster (1781–1828), DW's first wife.

22. Samuel F. Coolidge, George Deblois, and William Skinner, Boston merchants doing business as Coolidge, Deblois & Company, sued Cornelius Coolidge in Suffolk County in January 1820 (*S. F. Coolidge et al.* v. *C. Coolidge*, MassSJC,S, November 1821). In March 1821 attorneys for both sides agreed to refer both the Suffolk and Norfolk cases to arbitration.

23. William Cushing Aylwin (d. 1851), Boston lawyer, admitted in 1807, appointed clerk, MassSJC,S, in 1825.

24. *N. A. Haven et al.* v. *Holland*, USCC,DMass, May 1821, and 2 Mason 230 (1820). See pp. 418–438, below.

TO GEORGE BLISS

Boston April 28 [1821]
Saturday

Dear Sir

I recd yrs this morning, & also a letter from Mr. Ely, who seems disposed to have me at Springfield.[25] If it be true that the creditors in these cases did prove their claims, & receive a dividend, under the assignment, I think a case exists, which has not yet been decided, & that the Insolvent Law of N York[26] ought now, under these circumstances, to be pleaded. I think it an important fact, that the creditor has proved under the Commission.

On Monday I shall go to Ipswich, to return home the latter end of the week. Mr. Bliss will forward, to Springfield, by Tuesday's mail, a copy of the Pleas in the case agt. Mr Crowningshield, in the Circuit Court.[27] These pleas were drawn with care, &, *mutatis mutandis*, will probably answer for a guide. I suppose Mr Ely's discharge was under the same law, viz the law of 1811.

I should be exceedingly glad to be excused from going up, if I can. To this plea of the discharge under the N. York law, the Plf can of course do nothing but demur. It must be a mere question of law. The other issues, & the probable course the trial will take, in regard to them, we have already talked about and considered. Mr. Mills[28] I learn is on the other side. I think you should give him notice immediately that you shall wish to plead the discharge, & I wish you would tell him I should take it as a great favor if he could make such an arrangement with you as to save all the points, & leave me at home, till the law term. I have made up my mind, however, to go, unless I get a dispensation from you, which I yet hope to receive. After seeing what you can do, be kind eno. to write me again. Your letter must get here Saturday or Sunday, to be in season, as the mail, if any comes on Monday, probably comes too late to deliver letters that Evening, & I shall go in the Stage on Tuesday Morning, too early to receive letters that morning.

25. Letters not found. Ely has not been identified.

26. The New York law, enacted on April 3, 1811, discharged the debts of debtors who took the poor man's oath. The USSC held the statute unconstitutional and therefore decreed that it did not provide a good defense to a suit for collection of a pre-existing debt. *Sturges* v. *Crowninshield*, 4 Wheaton 122 (1819). Evidently DW, who had participated in the *Sturges* case at the circuit court level (USCC,DMass, May 1819), believed he could distinguish Sturgis and bring Ely's case under the still valid part of the statute.

27. Richard Crowninshield, Danvers merchant. The pleas are in the case file; see note 26, above.

28. Elijah Hunt Mills (1776–1829; Williams 1797), Northampton, Massachusetts lawyer, admitted to the Suffolk bar in 1807, state senator (1811), U.S. representative (1815–1819), U.S. senator (1820–1827).

We shall send up the Plea, & can probably s[end the] *Act*, if you have it not. I shall writ[e] to Mr Ely, tomorrow, & ask him to see you, as early as Wednesday or Thursday, that you may make a final decision, as to my going up. I still incline to think that you can make such arrangements with Mr. Mills, as to dispense with my presence; if not, I shall go up to Springfield in the Stage, on Tuesday the 8th. Will thank you to make my respects to Mr. Mills, & tell him I will thank him to let me stay at home if he can. I shall hear from you, I trust, at the latter end of the week. Yours with respect Danl. Webster

I shall ask Mr E[ly to go] to N. Hampton, Wednesday or Thursday.

ALS. DLC. George Bliss (1764–1830; Yale 1784), Springfield lawyer and legislator, delegate to the Hartford Convention.

TO GEORGE BLISS

Dear Sir, Boston Sep. 7. 1822

I recd yours, some days ago, respecting Mr. Ely's case. I intend to be at the Court, on the evening of the first day of the session, (if that will be in season, otherwise earlier) if Mr. Ely supposes my attendance important to him. It has occurred to me that we might save considerable expense, by presenting our arguments in this case, *in writing*. That course is frequently adopted, & perhaps is as good as any other mode of arguing causes. If we were to argue this case, *ore tenus*, the Court would no doubt take time for advisement; and in cases where time is taken to advise, there is an advantage in having the full argument before the Court in writing.

I suggest this, for the consideration of yourself, & Mr. Ely. If it could be arranged to have a written argument, I could send up to you such an argument as I might make, in ten days, or a fortnight;—or if the other side opens, within a similar period after seeing theirs. This would save a good deal of expense to Mr. Ely, & would in my sincere opinion, give him the utmost benefit of every thing in my power to do for him.

I shall leave the matter for his determination, under your advice. If he, after all, think my presence necessary, I shall endeavor to be at the Court, in season for the argument.

Let me hear from you, in the course of next week, if convenient. Yours with regard Danl. Webster

ALS. Dr. Williams's Library, London.

Webster made his formal entry into Massachusetts politics in October 1820, when he was elected to the Massachusetts Constitutional Convention. His leadership there helped lay the foundation for his future political career. In 1821 Webster added to his other legal business the preparation and presentation of claims to the Spanish Claims Commission.[29] Attempting to coordinate both the claims and his usual Supreme Court practice put Webster under a great physical strain. In February 1822 he wrote to Bliss:

> I am almost tired to death; & have come nearer giving up in despair, than ever before. I have written some *cords* of arguments such as they are; & have fortunately got thro far the greater part of this sort of labor, before the Court came.[30]

Even after he returned to Boston, he found little time to relax. In September he complained to Justice Joseph Story:

> For two or three days I have not been much in Town, not having been very well, & being willing to sit down a while, without the sight of a client. I find I am growing rusty, in general knowledge, & unless I can find, or make, some leisure from my office, I shall shortly be neither more nor less than an *attorney*.[31]

At the beginning of 1823 he returned to Washington to devote his energies to the claims. Again the work proved so tiring that he felt constrained to call on Bliss to relieve him.

> I begin to be tired of staying here, & feel as if I must beg of you to come, by & by, to my relief. Most of my cases will be decided, in the course of a fortnight, I think, but all will not, & I fear there will be complaints, if some body be not here so long as the Commissioners stay. I left my affairs in such state as to make it necessary to go home some time next month, even if I should be obliged to return. . . . I must try to persuade you to come, & *spell* me. You shall name your own compensation, & I will try to take care of your affairs at home.[32]

TO ALEXANDER BLISS

Dear Bliss, Washington, Sat. March 8 [1823]

My affairs have pressed so much for some time past, that I have not written you, thro want of time. Some cases have come on, in the Court, & our anxiety to get at the Steam Boat cause, keeps me constantly on the watch. Our present prospect of reaching the cause is not great, the intervening causes being ready, & every body pressing for trial.[33]

29. See Chapter 4, below.

30. February 4, 1822, p. 231, below.

31. September 27, 1822, *Correspondence*, 1: 315.

32. March 20, 1823, pp. 236–237, below. Five days later he wrote to Bliss that he would probably not need him in Washington (March 25, 1823, pp. 237–238, below).

33. *Gibbons* v. *Ogden*, 9 Wheaton 1 (1824). DW was right; the case

In the meantime the Commissioners are at work very hard, & preparation for them occupies some time.[34] I have prepared Mr Coolidge's Pet[ition] for rehearing of the Bell Savage. It will be presented in a day or two. I have also assisted Mr Lloyd[35] to arrange all the proofs, in the Washington, & we mean to get a final decision next week. I have examined and presented most of Mr Brooks'[36] cases; & some few of them have been decided. I write this without my docket before me, & add the following from recollection. Mercury, Brooks—*allowed.* Diana, Freeman, *allowed*: Snow Sisters, *Adamson, allowed.* Hannah, (Griste); *allowed.* Charles, Butler *not allowed; William* (Holbrook) allowed; *Washington* (Hedge Cl[aiman]t) *allowed.*

Say to Mr Brooks that I have recd his, & shall write him soon; & that I have *squeezed in* Kennedy's Memorial; as I have also that of Jona. Mason[37] & als, in the Sea Flower.

I suppose you have the [MassSJC] Court, now with you. I do not know whether there is any thing, in which I am expected. At any rate, there is nothing which I can attend to. That case of Assurance on the *Tobacco,* bound to Mediterranean (Mr Snelling's[38]) you must argue—if you make a good Argument, you will beat the adversary. There is a little case, argued at Cambrige, last fall on mot[ion] for new trial—Golding v Skinner.[39] I am for plf, & hold the Verdict. I suppose the Court will give a judgt. this term, in Boston. If so, you must take the necessary care of the case, till my return—as there is no other Counsel, now, on our side.

Tell William H. that by the aid of his excellent brief, I got up an argument, in Gracie v Palmer, which I think will reverse Judge Washington; —tho' we have no decision, yet.[40]

Mr Gray expects to set out for home by the 12 or 15—& Mr Gardiner

---

was not argued until the next session.

34. For the Spanish claims litigation, see Chapter 4, below.

35. James Lloyd (1769–1831; Harvard 1787), Boston merchant, state legislator, U.S. senator (1808–1813, 1822–1826).

36. Peter Chardon Brooks (1767–1849), Boston merchant and marine insurance broker (1789–1803), president, New England Insurance Company, one of the Spanish claimants.

37. Jonathan Mason, wealthy Bostonian, director of the Massachusetts Fire & Marine Insurance Company. See note 6, p. 201, below.

38. Probably *Clark* v. *Massachusetts Fire & Marine Insurance Company,* MassSJC,S, March 1824. Nathaniel G. Snelling was the company president. DW's client won the case.

39. *Goulding et al.* v. *Skinner et al.,* 18 Mass. 162 (1822). Contrary to DW's apparent confidence, the court ruled favorably on the defendant's motion for a new trial in March 1823. Neither party, however, appeared at the October 1823 term (MassSJC,M, October 1823).

40. William Townsend Haddock (1798–1835), nephew and former student of DW's who had been in practice a year. *Gracie* v. *Palmer,* 8 Wheaton 605 (1823); DW argued for Gracie and won. Bushrod Washington (1762–1829; William and Mary 1778), Virginia lawyer and judge, studied with James Wilson, associate justice, USSC (1798–1829).

also, I believe. Mr Hunter is to join our Mess, & he, & Mr Cowper & Mr Jaudon,[41] & myself shall be left to watch the Comm[issione]rs. I shall not go home, while any thing remains to be done here.

Tell Master Danl. that I have recd. a very good letter from him, which I shall shortly answer, & let Mrs. W. know of my health & happiness (as far as she will allow me to be happy so far from home) at the date hereof. Mr & Mrs Blake[42] set out for home tomorrow. Yr D Webster

ALS. DLC.

TO JEREMIAH MASON

Dear Sir, Washington, April 10, 1823.

Mr. John D. Williams of Boston informs me that he has written requesting you to go to Portland, at the Circuit Court, and argue his cause against Mr. Reed.[43] I hope you will be able to go. He is a very worthy man, and an exceeding good client. He will satisfy you well; and his case you will easily understand. Mr. Greenleaf,[44] who is in the cause for the plaintiff, Williams, is a very correct and able lawyer of his age, and

41. Either Horace or his brother Francis C. Gray; see pp. 166, 214, below. William Howard Gardiner (d. 1882; Harvard 1816), Boston lawyer, admitted in 1819; William Hunter (1774–1849; Brown 1791), of Newport, Rhode Island, studied law at Inner Temple, London, admitted in 1795, state legislator, U.S. senator (1811–1821), U.S. envoy, Brazil (1834–1843); John Cowper, agent of the Marine Insurance Company of Norfolk, Virginia; Samuel Jaudon (1796–1874; Princeton 1813), cashier of the BUS, New Orleans for some years before his appointment as cashier in Philadelphia (1832), the bank's agent in England (1837–1841), and a director (1841) for the remainder of the bank's short existence. All five represented claimants under the Spanish treaty. A "mess" was the collective term for those who shared the accommodations of a Washington boarding house—generally congressmen and other transients in the city on business.

42. DW's son, Daniel Fletcher, born in 1818. Sarah Olcott Blake, née Murdoch (1789–1826).

43. John Davis Williams (1769–1848), Boston businessman and banker; Isaac G. Reed, Maine attorney. This letter came after DW had written to Story of his difficulty:

I am in some trouble in relation to the case of *Williams* vs *Reid*, in the Maine Circuit Court. It will not be possible for me to g[et home] in season to be there, especially as the Court is bro[ught] forward a week. I have written to Mr. Williams, to that effect, & he & Mr. Greenleaf must manage as well as they can.

DW to Joseph Story, April 6, 1823, *Correspondence*, 1: 326. Williams' letter has not been found. DW prepared the bill in equity for Williams. *Williams* v. *Reed*, USCC,DMe–Pl, May 1824, and 3 Mason 405 (1824). Williams sued Reed for fraudulent misconduct in collecting debts.

44. Simon Greenleaf (1783–1853), Maine lawyer, teacher, and author, studied with Ezekiel Whitman, admitted in 1806, reporter, Maine SJC (1820–1832), Royall professor of law (1833–1846), and Dane professor of law (1846–1848), Harvard Law School.

will have the case duly prepared. It is a case of some importance and some expectation; and I would not for a good deal, as we say, that any thing should prevent your attention to it. I cannot be home in season to rest and then go to Portland. I have no other engagements there, and do not intend practising in that court. You are sixty miles nearer the court than I am, and I am sure you would find it much to your advantage to attend regularly.

When you see Judge Story, ask him to show you a letter which I wrote him about the appointment of a judge.[45]

I grow very anxious to get home. The commissioners are here yet, and will remain probably ten days longer.

I have got through the bulk of all the cases committed to my care, and hope now to have a little repose. I shall be ready for any scheme of play which you can get up. Yours very sincerely, D. Webster.

Text from *PC*, 1: 324–325. Original not found.

TO ALEXANDER BLISS

Dear Bliss, Washington April 12. [1823]

I have recd. yours of Tuesday, detailing all your "griefs," public & private.[46] As to the public griefs, I was prepared for them—never having, for one moment expected any other result. As to losing Mason v Rider & als, that is a bad little business, & we must try to remedy it by another suit.

The case of the Genl. Washington (Perkins & Lloyd) is *continued.*[47] That winds up my concerns here, & I depart on Monday.

I do not expect to go home in a hurry—having stops to make at different places. The Court I learn sits to try causes on *Tuesday*—there are one or two I should like to be present to try, *& one or two I should not.* The principal of this last class is Com[monweal]th v Rider.[48] *Inter nos*, if it should so happen that this case should be disposed of before my return, I should be *very particularly* glad of it.

The Comm[issione]rs will now probably rise in three or four days—having but three or four more cases to examine, & a little clearing off to do. They made the application for Capt. Rich,[49] sometime ago.

45. DW to Story, April 6, 1823, *Correspondence*, 1: 325–326. The death of Henry Brockholst Livingston on March 18, 1823 created a vacancy on the USSC. DW correctly anticipated the appointment of Smith Thompson of New York.

46. Letter not found.

47. *Mason* v. *Rider et al.*, MassSJC,S, March 1823. DW's client, Mason, was nonsuited. *The General Washington* was a Spanish claims case.

48. No additional information has been found respecting this case.

49. Boston merchant, former shipmaster.

Mr Meade's[50] case is not yet decided. I imagine he will be told that his case must be examined, like all others; & that the auditing of the Spanish Govt. will not be recd as conclusive. Yrs D. Webster

I shall write Mrs W. Tomorrow—take good care of the boys.

ALS. DLC.

TO ALEXANDER BLISS

Dear Sir Washington May 9th. [1824]

It is now certain I shall not be home, till near or quite the end of the Court, at soonest; & perhaps not till after it is finished. You must do the best you can with the cases. Where there is other Counsel, they can get along without me. Where there are none, you must beg for continuance. Of this last class is United States vs Downes.[51] There is no other Counsel, nor time to instruct any, on the part of Mr. Whitney.[52] The United States needs not to press very hard, & I hope the Counsel on that side will not object, under existing circumstances to a continuance. At any rate, you must move the Court, & if you cannot obtain a continuance, try to get the facts into the case, & let judgment go, & *appeal*. Messrs Appleton & Paige,[53] who are the correspondents of Mr Whitney, will give any Appeal Bond. Time, however, would doubtless be given for that. But it is much more desirable to have a real trial before the Circuit Court, which, in all probability, would end the suit.

As to other causes, I leave them to your discretion. Do not consult *my* interest in any of them. Whatever can be done, without real injury to parties, assent to; & ask for as little indulgence as possible.

The Commissioners are going on with the Rehearing cases; but we

50. Richard Worsam Meade (1778–1828) moved from Philadelphia to Cadiz in 1803, where he was a merchant and shipowner for twenty years, U.S. naval agent (1805–1816). In 1819 the Spanish government approved Meade's claim for damages to his business incurred during the Napoleonic wars. When Meade presented his claim to the Spanish Claims Commission, the commissioners rejected it for want of evidence. Meade's heirs pressed the claim from 1866 into the present century in the courts and in Congress. See Frank Warren Hackett, *The Meade Claim* (Washington, 1910).

51. DW is referring to the May term of the USCC,DMass. *U.S.* v. *John Downes et al.*, USCC,DMass, October 1824.

52. Reuben Whitney. Whitney appealed; *U.S.* v. *Whitney*, unreported USSC case.

53. Appleton, Paige & Company, Boston mercantile partnership; William Appleton (1786–1862), president of the Boston branch of the BUS (1832–1836), U.S. representative (1851–1855, 1861); James William Paige (1792–1868), Grace Fletcher Webster's half brother.

do not know results. If, however, you should meet with Mr I. P. Davis, you may whisper "Minerva" in his ears, with a hopeful accent.[54] Yours

D. Webster

I have so written this letter, that you can shew it to the Court. You will get continuance, if you can—if not, you must *appeal*—such are my orders from Mr Whitney. Perhaps you can give a judgment, with liberty to put in evidence, if the evidence is not now complete.

Get time for claiming the Appeal, till I come home. Yrs D. W.

I have recd some *powers*[55]—hasten on the rest. I fear I shall not see you till after the 8th June.

ALS. DLC. The postscript is listed as a separate item under date [May] 1824 in *Correspondence*, 1, *Calendar*: 468.

By the summer of 1824 Webster had completed most of the Spanish claims work. Boston voters had elected him to the House of Representatives in the fall of 1822, and when he took his seat in December 1823, he resumed his national political career. Although now a congressman, he was still able to devote a large share of his time to the Supreme Court once the bulk of the Spanish claims litigation was behind him. At the 1826 term he appeared in fifteen cases, almost half of them unreported. In May he commented to Story,

> From the first day of December [1825], I have not been an inch from my place till Saturday, when I rode a few miles on horseback. I need motion and air, more than a court.[56]

At the 1827 term he again had a hectic session, with sixteen cases. That year he won election to the Senate, where he found more extensive duties than he had experienced in the House. As a result, he was forced to reduce his Supreme Court practice.

TO ALEXANDER BLISS

My D Sir Washington May 8. 1826

I have already mentioned to you my intention to leave here this day week. We propose to send the horses ahead, by some days, & to take, ourselves, the quickest conveyance to Philadelphia. We do not intend stopping, any where; & I hope to be home in 7 or 8 days from the time of setting out. This will enable me to be at the Circuit Court, the second

54. Isaac P. Davis (1771–1855), Boston manufacturer and businessman, a close friend of DW. The *Minerva* was a Spanish claims case.

55. A reference to the powers of attorney which DW requested his Spanish claims clients to send to him authorizing collection of their awards. See pp. 253–260, below.

56. May 8, 1826, *Correspondence*, 2: 114.

week. I suppose there will be no difficulty in deferring, to that time, any thing in which I am concerned. But I have a *strong wish* to continue every thing, as far as possible, to next term. I hardly recollect what causes I am engaged in, but none occur to me as likely to be pressing, in their nature. After the second week of the Court comes Election; a time not suited to Judge Story's Court, tho' well adapted to a Court holden occasionally by me & Judge Isaac Davis![57] Soon after the first of June, I must go to N. Hampshire, to be gone a fortnight. I am unluckily the proprietor of some lands in the North part of that State, which I must give some attention to. It will be my purpose to get thro. this, so as to be home to attend the Sup[reme Judicial] Court in July, if any one should need me there. August is not a working month.

This is my present plan for the Summer, which I mention that you may answer inquiries. For the present, the object is, as far as practicable, to continue the Circuit Court business to the next term. If any thing occurs to keep me here longer than I now expect, I shall give you due notice. Yrs always, D Webster

ALS. DLC. Published in *Correspondence*, 2: 112–113.

Webster had achieved a close working relationship with Bliss. When in July 1827 the younger man died suddenly, Webster moved quickly to form a new association. Again he chose a former student, Henry Willis Kinsman.

> The death of poor Bliss is a dreadful thing to us all. I ought hardly to speak of my own loss, when that of his wife & child are to be considered; but he was very dear to me. We have been together eleven years, in entire harmony, & to mutual benefit.
>
> Mr Bliss' death will probably confine me more at home, for the summer, than I could wish. I have taken, in his stead, Mr. Henry W. Kinsman, a young Gentleman who read Law with me, has been in practice two years, & whom I can recommend for fidelity & capacity.[58]

TO JOSEPH STORY

Boston Thursday Morning

My Dear Sir [July 17, 1827]

You will be shocked to hear of the death of Mr. Bliss. He died at 10 OClock, on Sunday Evening, at Plymo. after one week's illness, of a fever. Mrs W. & myself go down today to attend his funeral, & shall return tomorrow at noon.

57. A jocular reference to Davis as a drinking companion.

58. DW to Samuel Jaudon, July 25, 1827, *Correspondence*, 2: 233.

It is a dreadfull calamity. I should feel that it fell heavily on me, if I did not see how it must crush others.

The bearer is Mr Hopkins,[59] of Philadelphia, whom you may remember to have seen last winter at W. He is a highly respectable Gent. of our profession, & as he goes today to look at Salem, I give him this introduction to you Yrs always D Webster

ALS. DLC. Published in *Correspondence*, 2: 231.

b. Henry Willis Kinsman: 1827–1837

Webster spent much of the period of his association with Kinsman actively engaged in politics. From his base in the Senate (where he remained until 1841) he helped organize the Whig party and pursued its presidential nomination. With less time for a broad local practice, he preferred to devote his energy to the Supreme Court and major federal cases. Even then his Senate duties frequently forced him to decline cases.[1] To maintain a minimum level of income, he accepted annual retainers of one hundred dollars from several Boston insurance offices. Kinsman did not have as close a relationship with Webster as had Bliss. He served more as a business manager, taking care of the office and Webster's finances. In only one instance did they engage in a closer working relationship. In 1833 and 1834 Webster became the attorney for the claimants in a series of cases similar to the Spanish claims of the 1820s.[2] Upon the conclusion of these claims, Kinsman left Webster and moved to Newburyport.

FROM HENRY WILLIS KINSMAN TO HARVEY C. MACKAY

No. 136. June 2d. 1829.

Sir—Mr. Webster desires me to inform you, that he has examined the will of the late Mr. William Dane[3] of Gloucester, a copy of which was left with him by yourself. Upon consideration, & an examination of authorities upon the subject, Mr. Webster has come to the following opinion—viz—That the certificates of the Bank stock, & certain notes of hand, being contained in a trunk & desk in his house, that clause in Mr.

59. Possibly Howell Hopkins, designated an attorney in the Philadelphia directories for 1825 and 1828; or either of two others, Joseph R., listed in 1825, David in 1828.

1. In 1835 he wrote to William Sullivan: "As I am circumstanced, at present, I cannot practise extensively in the Sup. Court, because I cannot leave the Senate, long enough to go thro' an important cause." February 23, 1835, *Correspondence*, 4: 32.

2. See pp. 325–343, below.

3. William Dane (1746–1820), a Gloucester shopkeeper and state representative (1812). In 1772 he married Mary Kinsman, not further identified.

Dane's will, giving to his wife, her heirs & assigns, all the personal property of every description now in the house &c, which I occupy, entitles Mrs. Dane to the absolute & entire property of said stock & notes of hand forever. I return you Enclosed, the copy of the will, & the other papers which were left at our office. I am Respy, your obt. svt.

Henry W. Kinsman

LC. NhD. Kinsman letterbook. Henry Willis Kinsman (1803–1859; Dartmouth 1822), studied with DW, admitted in 1826, state representative, moved to Newburyport in 1837, collector, port of Newburyport (1841–1845, 1849–1853). Captain Harvey C. Mackay, born Joshua Gee Whittemore in Gloucester in 1762, had his name changed by the Massachusetts legislature in 1813.

FROM HENRY WILLIS KINSMAN

No. 17. Jany. 18. 1830

Dr. Sir I have received this morning a notice of a note, *not on my minutes*, for $600. which, upon inquiry, I find to be one indorsed by Isaac P. Davis, whether it is a collection note, or not, I cannot tell. It is at the City Bank & becomes due 18/21st.[4] I have now three notes to pay in three or four days.

The one above mentioned—$600
Mr. Hales at Am. Bank 750
Mr. Welles[5] at Br[anch] B. 700 $2050. These notes, unless I receive some assistance from you, in the meantime, will more than exhaust all your funds at the Bank, & I shall be obliged to draw it all when the first becomes due, because I have only one check. In making up my accounts for the last year, I charged you $150. for general services, being the same <amount> sum which you told me to charge last year; if this is more than you think right, I will alter it to suit you. I am Respectfully Yrs. Henry W. Kinsman.

LC. NhD. Kinsman letterbook.

TO [HENRY WILLIS KINSMAN]

D. Sir Washington feb. 25. 1831

I write, at this time, to give you a little intimation, respecting my projects, for the next three months.

4. A note presented on the 18th would be paid by the 21st, after the customary three-day grace period.

5. Nathan Hale (1784–1863; Williams 1804), Boston lawyer and journalist, studied with Peter Oxenbridge Thacher, state legislator, member, Massachusetts Constitutional Convention (1820), president, Boston & Worcester Railroad; John Welles (1764–1855; A.M. Harvard 1782), Boston merchant, state legislator, a director of the BUS, Boston branch. Mention of these notes is also made in DW to Kinsman, January 1830, *Correspondence*, 3: 14–15.

I have long contemplated a tour to the West, as far as Ohio & Kentucky;—& know not when I can better put that purpose into execution, than this Spring. My plan, at present, is this.

To get away from this place, so soon as my Court business will allow—say, abt. Mar. 15. To stay a day or two in Philadelphia—as many in N. York—leave Mrs W.[6] there, & proceed straight to Boston—to be in Boston, say, a little before April 1. Stay in & about Boston three weeks, or 4. Then return to N. York, take Mrs W.—go up by way of her brothers, in the western District of N York—pass into Ohio, &c, go over to Kentucky, & then home by way of Pittsburg & Philadelphia.

The whole journey occupying May, & a considerable part of June.

To arrange this, I must have the C[ircui]t Court p[ost]p[one]d till after the session of the same Court at New York. That is, I mean, so far as I am concerned in that Court. I imagine there will be no difficulty in this. There is no important case, as I [see] at present, except Mr Balchs—& the one I lately wrote you about.[7] Any professional business, which can be performed in April, I shall be willing to attend to, probably.

At present, I would not have you mention this project, to any one. I have written to Mr Paige, on the matter—& shall give the necessary notice to our domestics.

Many things may occur, to defeat or vary this project—& for this, as well as other reasons, I wish little, indeed nothing, said about it.

We are now in the neighborhood of the Bridge cause.[8] Yrs truly

D. Webster

ALS. NNC. Published in *Correspondence*, 3: 102–103.

TO HENRY WILLIS KINSMAN

Dr Sir Thursday P.M. [April 4, 1833]

I intend going home on Saturday, or Monday, at farthest.—as to the Worcester cause, the day of trial, April 23rd, suits me.[9] I can be at home, for aught I know, almost any intervening day, on a little notice.

6. Webster's second wife, Caroline Le Roy Webster (1797–1882).

7. Letter not found. Joseph Balch was an officer of the Merchants' Insurance Company. *Carrington* v. *Merchants' Insurance Company*, unreported USCC,DMass case. DW argued the USSC appeal, 8 Peters 495 (1834), and appeared in the later USCC trial, USCC,DMass, October 1837. The second case has not been identified.

8. *Charles River Bridge* v. *Warren Bridge*, argued in 1831 without a decision; reargued in 1837, 11 Peters 420. This case will be discussed in *Legal Papers*, 3.

9. Kinsman noted in his letterbook that on April 1, 1833 he wrote to DW in New York "about Mr. Lawrence's case Worcester S.J.C." He also wrote that day to "Samuel Barrett, P[ost] M[aster] Ashburnham Mass" about the case, and again to Barrett on April 6 "for Mr. Lawrence to come down 11 or 12 Apr." (mDW 7482).

As the Court sits the 16th, his counsel can probably come to Boston most conveniently before that time. Therefore, let them come down next week, say Thursday or friday, the 11th. or 12th.—or any other day, about that time—but let them give a day or two's notice, lest I should be gone to Marshfield, which I must visit pretty soon. I trust you to send up this word.

If D. A. Hall Esqr,[10] of Washington, draws on me for 5 or 6 hundred Dollars, or not exceeding that, please accept his draft.

I am busy here with two or three professional matters. Yr D. W.

ALS. Dr. Gurdon S. Pulford, Palo Alto, California. The postmark indicates that Webster was writing from New York.

TO NICHOLAS BIDDLE

Private

My Dr Sir Boston April 13. [18]33

I hear nothing yet, from Mr L[ivingston].[11] I am under engagement to go into the interior of this State, toward the latter end of this month, to take part in the trial of a cause, which may require some time.[12] Under existing circumstances, I have felt it my duty to write, & endeavor to obtain a release from the engagement, so that I may be ready to go elsewhere, if called. Yrs truly D. Webster

ALS. DLC. Nicholas Biddle (1786–1844), financier, director, BUS (1819–1822), president, BUS (1822–1839). On April 10, 1833, Biddle had suggested that DW meet with Edward Livingston in New York (*Correspondence*, 3: 242).

TO JOHN DAVIS

Private

My Dr Sir, Boston April 15 [13]. 1833

I write a letter today to Mr Washburn,[13] which he will probably show to you. I write this privately, & for your own eye *alone*.

10. David Aiken Hall (1795–1870; Middlebury 1815), Washington attorney.

11. Edward Livingston (1764–1836; Princeton 1781), lawyer and politician, studied with John Lansing, practiced in New York and then New Orleans, drafted the Louisiana penal code, U.S. representative (1823–1829), U.S. senator from Louisiana (1829–1831), U.S. secretary of state (1831–1833), minister to France (1833–1835).

12. The case mentioned in DW's letter to Kinsman, April 4, 1833, above, and DW to John Davis, April 13, 1833, below.

13. Probably Emory Washburn (1800–1877; Williams 1817), Massachusetts lawyer, author, and teacher, studied at the Harvard Law School, admitted in 1821, state legislator, judge, MassCCP, Massachusetts governor (1854), Bussey professor, Harvard Law School (1856–1876).

The fact is, I am fearful it may be a little inconvenient for me to go to Worcester. I am looking for a call to N. York, on an occasion, which must not be made public, & which I cannot, now, state to you; & which, if I go there, I must disguise under "Professional business," "French claims," &c &c.

If you *really think* my services *necessary*, or likely to be *highly useful*, to our client, so say to him, & I will attend the trial, & forego other calls & occasions. But if you are not of that opinion, I pray you not to let your civility to me, or your own desire to see me, (which I hope is strong) prevail on you to advise my coming. I want to see you, much; but shall want to see you more, a month hence, or after my return from New York, should I go there. Let me off, therefore, from going to Worcester on this occasion, if you can, without injustice to Mr Lawrence.[14] I really do not see what good I can do him. Some prejudice may be created by sending far, for a Lawyer; &, of all men, Mr [Samuel?] Hoar knows best how to make the most of that prejudice.

In short, it does not seem to be a case for me to make my appearance in, in yr good County. Yet I will present myself, if you think justice & the interest of our client require it.

I have come home, in good health; and feel, at this moment, some little spirit of enterprise. Yrs always most sincerely Danl Webster

ALS. MWA. Endorsed in DW's hand: "*April 13th* dated 15, within, by mistake." John Davis (1787–1854; Yale 1812), Worcester lawyer and politician, studied with Francis Blake of Worcester, admitted in 1815, U.S. representative (1825–1834), governor, Massachusetts (1834–1835, 1841–1843), U.S. senator (1835–1841, 1845–1853); at this time Davis was in partnership with Emory Washburn.

Following the Webster-Hayne debate in January 1830, Webster's political ambitions came into even greater conflict with his professional responsibilities. Early in 1831 he toyed with the idea of leaving the Senate.

> I have endeavored, My Dear Sir, to find time to write something on this very important subject;—but, truly, I have not been able to detract sufficient time from my professional labors. If I could afford to study law cases less & some of these great questions more, I should appear, I think, to somewhat more advantage, & do a little more for the advancement of useful objects. I sometimes feel this so strongly, as to be on the very point of relinquishing my situation here to some one who can give better attention to it. The Bank question itself, is enough to occupy the thoughts of a public man, till it shall be settled.[15]

14. William J. Lawrence (1773–1844), a tanner and extensive property owner in Ashburnham, Massachusetts, father-in-law of Samuel Barrett, n. 9 above.

15. DW to Nicholas Biddle, Feb-

In September 1833 Ohio representative Elisha Whittlesey urged Webster to abandon his thoughts of a presidential nomination and instead to consider seeking a seat on the Supreme Court.

> So long as the Judiciary shall remain unpolluted, and shall possess intelligence, the citadel will be defended against the machinations of the Executive, or the sudden convulsions of the people.[16]

Webster wrote back, in a letter printed below, that he had no interest in a judgeship. His ambition continued to focus on the presidency. Though his passion for the law seemed on the wane, it represented his only means of gaining his livelihood. Webster expressed these thoughts to Jeremiah Mason, in a letter printed below, as he contemplated a political swing through the West.

TO ELISHA WHITTLESEY

My Dear Sir Boston, Sep. 25, [18]33

I am quite obliged to you for your letter,[17] tho' sorry you should write, if you did so merely from a sense of obligation. Your suggestion that you would write me, was nothing that I had any right to insist on.

Your letter, My Dear Sir, is, in temper & spirit just such as I should expect from you, & such as is most agreeable to me to receive. It is frank, candid, & at the same time friendly.

In most of your views, of men [and] things, I entirely concur. But in one respect we differ. Between the candidate, whom it is undoubtedly the purpose of those now in power to bring into Office, & that other Candidate,[18] who is, in your opinion, the only one competent to oppose him successfully, I do not discern those grounds of preference, which seem to be apparent to you. Nor do I, at present, see any reason to think that other Candidate can be chosen.

I thank you, My Dear Sir, for the friendly things which you say of myself, & among others, for the suggestion, that I might, perhaps, usefully fill a judicial situation. It is not wise, perhaps, to speak of an intention to decline that, which, in all probability, will never be offered; but since you have made the suggestion, I will say, in the confidence which belongs to all parts of this correspondence, that there is no judicial station which I would accept; &, indeed, that it is not my intention to fill any

ruary 2, 1831, *Correspondence*, 3: 100. DW was deeply involved in the struggle with the Jacksonians over the rechartering of the BUS.

16. September 14, 1833, mDW 11118.

17. Elisha Whittlesey to DW, September 14, 1833, mDW 11118.

18. A reference to Martin Van Buren, the Jacksonian presidential candidate, and USSC Justice John McLean, who also had presidential ambitions.

Office, in the gift of the Govt. of U. S.; tho' I do not know what effect particular circumstances might have, in relation to this last particular. These things it would be foolish to say, except privately, & in confidence. In my opinion, the affairs of the Govt. are approaching a crisis. The question, I think, will soon come to be, the preservation, or the prostration, of the Constitution. No uncertain or undecided man can be fit for such a crisis. It is better that good men remain in a firm & well principled minority, than that they give their support to any Candidate, not known to them to be worthy of all confidence, & all trust.

On all these, & other matters, I hope soon to have the pleasure of personal communication with you; & in the mean time pray you to accept the pledge of my regard & esteem. Danl. Webster

ALS. OClWHi. Elisha Whittlesey (1783–1863), Ohio lawyer and a founder of the Whig party, state legislator (1820–1821), U.S. representative (1823–1838), comptroller of the treasury (1849–1857, 1861–1863).

TO JEREMIAH MASON

Private

My Dear Sir, Washington Feb. 6 1835

It is true that I have looked forward to the events which the approaching election might bring about, as likely to furnish a fit occasion for my retirement from the Senate. I have fixed on no particular time, nor made, indeed, any such determination as may not be changed, by the advice or the wishes of friends. As I am now placed, I shall certainly not leave my place, till the time arrives when I may think that its relinquishment will not be unsatisfactory to *Massachusetts*.

I do not affect, My Dear Sir to desire to retire from public life, & to resume my profession. My habits, I must confess, & the nature of my pursuits for some years, render it more agreeable to me to <follow> attend to political than to professional subjects. But I have not lost all relish for the bar, I can still make something by the practice, & by remaining in the Senate, I am making sacrifices which my own circumstances do not justify. My residence here so many months every year greatly encreases my expenses, & greatly reduces my income. You know the charge of living here, with a family; & I cannot leave my wife & daughter at home, & come here & go into a "mess", at 10 Dollars a week.

I find it inconvenient to push my practice in the Supreme Court, while a member of the Senate; & am inclined, under any view of the future, to decline engagements hereafter, in that Court, unless under special circumstances.

These are the Reasons that have led me to *hope* for a fit occasion of leaving the Senate; and when I can quit, with the approbation of friends,

I shall eagerly embrace the opportunity. In the meantime, I shall say nothing about it.

I ought, this Spring to go to the West, as far at least as Ken. & Indiana. I am fully persuaded it would be a highly useful thing. My friends urge it upon me, incessantly; & I hold back from promising compliance with their wishes only from an unwillingness to lose six weeks more, after the session closes. On this point, however, as nothing is decided, I say nothing at present. There will be no cause in Court, I think, to detain me after the 3rd of March.

We have nothing new here. A base attempt has been made to ascribe the *madness* of Lawrence[19] to the Speeches &c of the Senate. An inquisition, if it may be so called, has been had upon Lawrence, by two physicians, who have signed a report, & returned it to the Marshall. It proves a clear case of insanity. The Report will not be published, so long as its publication can be withheld.

We shall pass thro' the Senate, a pretty good Bill for reorganizing the Post Office.

I saw lately a strange letter from Washington in the Boston Gazette, about an express from the N. Y. Whigs, & a coldness between Mr W. & Mr Clay. Both stories are equally & entirely groundless. There has been no express here from N. Y.—On the contrary, *all* the Whig papers of the City (except Noahs)[20] will soon be out, (or we are misinformed) in the direction you would desire. Yrs truly D Webster

ALS. DLC. Published in *Correspondence*, 4: 26–27.

During the 1830s Webster's oldest son, Daniel Fletcher, embarked on his own legal career. Fletcher's experience was far different from his father's. The letters that follow provide an interesting contrast to Webster's successful entrance into the profession. After graduating from Harvard in 1833, Fletcher read law with a former tutor, Samuel B. Walcott of Hopkinton. Fletcher wrote to his father:

> I have been "tearing the law to pieces" these last *seven months* that I have been at Hopkinton and have arrived to such a degree of proficiency as to be able to take care of almost any business that presents itself at our office.
>
> Mr Walcott was kind enough to say he felt no anxiety about his law affairs when at the Legislature, if I was in the office, and as this is the first thing that sounds any way like a compliment, that I

19. On January 30, 1835, Richard Lawrence, a lunatic, attempted to assassinate Andrew Jackson as the President left the House of Representatives.

20. Mordecai Manuel Noah (1785–1851) was at this time editor of the New York *Evening Star* (Whig).

> ever received upon my attention to study I'm quite proud of it, and hope to give Mr. W. no reason to take it back again. . . . Mr. W. has given up all thoughts of leaving town at present, I believe, at least he never speaks of it. I do not think he will for some years yet; his business is all the time increasing, he is getting well known at Middlesex bar and has no inclination to bury himself at Salem I think.[21]

In 1836 the MassSJC,S admitted Fletcher to the bar. The bar association no longer controlled admission to practice. Three years of reading law qualified a student for automatic admission.[22] Like his father before him, Fletcher began his career in the hinterland. In the mid 1830s Webster had borrowed heavily to invest in western lands. While still riding the upward slope of this speculative venture, he needed agents to superintend his lands. Fletcher agreed to serve his father, first in Michigan and then in Illinois. In the latter state Fletcher decided to settle and establish himself as a country lawyer. Working for his father would give him enough income to live on while he built a practice. At the same time he could enter local politics and make his name known.

In February 1837 Webster sent his son some instructions and advice.

> As to the Gibraltar installments, you will manage them as you think best. For whatever is necessary, you will either draw on me, or give me notice, in season, to enable me to remit. I shall not undertake to keep the run of the several times of payment. You must see to all that.
>
> If on the whole you think it advisable that Harding should join you, I shall not object. You must take care that it does not lead you to neglect Office business. I must give you a similar hint, in regard to business not professional. You must remember that Professional Eminence is the great point to be aimed at. . . . you will find no pursuit permanently gratifying, except your profession.[23]

Fletcher, dutifully, agreed:

> I agree most entirely in what you say about professional matters, & really, although I would like, as every one else, to make money fast, yet I should prefer earning by my profession. As your correspon-

21. February 28, 1835, *Correspondence*, 4: 33–34.

22. The second Boston bar association went out of existence in 1835. The legislature enacted the three-year requirement in 1836. Hollis Bailey, *Attorneys and Their Admission to the Bar in Massachusetts* (Boston, 1907), pp. 57–58. For a further description of change in standards of admission, see Gerald W. Gawalt, *The Promise of Power: The Emergence of the Legal Profession in Massachusetts, 1760–1840* (Westport, Conn., 1979).

23. February 12, 1837, *Correspondence*, 4: 190. Twelve years earlier Caleb Cushing noted DW's advice: "Said practice in a small town was very useful as a means of getting experience. Said I ought always to keep in view the object of a permanent residence elsewhere (out of N[ewbury]port). The defect of young men in the city is lack of experience." Fuess, *Caleb Cushing*, 1: 63.

> dent Williams of Toledo said to me, I took more pleas[ur]e in five dollars earned at law than in fifty or a hundred gained in speculations.[24]

Soon after he arrived in Illinois, in 1839, Fletcher brought his family down from Detroit. Full of hope, they eagerly set about fixing up their new home. But it was not a propitious time to begin a legal career. A change in the land sales policy of the federal government, followed by the Panic of 1837 and the ensuing depression, caused land values to plummet. Speculators like Webster, who had gone into debt to purchase the land grants, found themselves caught short. Webster himself had to begin selling off his shares in a land company to stave off complete ruin.[25]

Fletcher had counted on the completion of the Illinois and Michigan canal to bring agricultural prosperity to the region and opportunity for a young lawyer. But when the depression undermined the state's fragile economy and forced a slowdown in construction, his hopes for success in the West faded. In the spring of 1840 he decided to move back East, and wrote to his father for advice and assistance. Webster's response on May 31, 1840, printed below, revealed the extent to which he still believed that politics represented the surest entrance to success in the law.

Fletcher did return East, but not immediately to a legal career. Webster used his position as secretary of state in the Harrison-Tyler administration to gain the appointment of his son as chief clerk in the state department, and then secretary to Caleb Cushing's mission to China in 1843. Following his return to the United States, Fletcher served one term in the Massachusetts legislature. Then Webster again used his influence in his son's behalf. First, he tried, unsuccessfully, to win him the position of U.S. attorney for Massachusetts. When that fell through, he secured for him the lucrative post of surveyor for the port of Boston.

FROM DANIEL FLETCHER WEBSTER

My dear Father, Salisbury April 26. 1839.

We are yet busily at work cleaning and repairing the house. We shall paper, plaster, and paint it, almost all over. Both chimnies are in a ruinous condition, one of them indeed all down. The Ravine at the Back of the house is full of all uncleanliness and bones & broken dishes. These matters however are better understood by Caroline and Mother than you & me. Warren Kinney was here the day before yesterday (Wednesday the 24th) and gave me up the bond for the Miller Farm, of which I informed

24. February 24, 1837, mDW 14104, Van Tyne, pp. 209–210.

25. In 1838 he wrote: "The idea of getting some relief, even in 4 months, leads me to be willing to make almost any sacrifice." DW to [William A.] Bradley, September 5, 1838, *Correspondence*, 4: 321.

you. I will send it to you in a few days. The title to the land I sold Col. Perkins is good.[26]

I have heard nothing against my title to the Haight & Warren & Miller places. It appears however that Col. Kinney deceived me a good deal as to the terms on which they were let. He told me they were rented to the halves, but I find it was no such thing; on the contrary they have liens on the places for improvements put on them agreeably to contracts made with him. I have not yet learned the exact amount, but Miller claims something like four hundred and fifty dollars and the others one hundred & fifty. I think I can arrange with them by selling them some of the Bureau lands and a lot or so in Peru. The White Hall farm is mortgaged for something like two thousand dollars, which will be due about two years from the present time. This is a serious matter; but I think it can be managed well enough by the time it becomes due. The person who holds it, a widow woman is anxious to sell it out and would take part cash & the rest in Lots in town. I have learned from Cornelius[27] himself that the lease by which he holds White Hall *rent free*, was not made by Col. K. till the very night before he went away although it bears date Aug. 10. so that he has no good claim to the occupancy. The Writing given him by Col. K. estimates the amount due by him to Cornelius at forty six dollars, & for this he gives him all his cattle, thirty head at the least, and the farm for a year. I can turn him out and take all the cattle on attachment if you so direct. It would certainly be a pecuniary advantage and no one could complain against you. We should have I suppose to pay him for the crops he has put in.

I have had letters sent to the Register's offices of Ottawa, La Salle Co. Hennepin Putnam Co. and Princeton Bureau Co. asking for abstracts of all conveyances to & from H.L.K. to be found on the records—and also to the Surveyor at Indian Town to come up & run all the lines. I have all the descriptions except of Salisbury which I would like to have Ray[28] copy from your deed.

Peru lots are selling very fast and I understand from Theron Brewster[29] that there will be some hundreds of dollars coming to you on the division. I must have your full power of Atty. signed also by Mother, to

26. Caroline Story White (1811–1886), married Fletcher on November 27, 1836; Thomas Handasyd Perkins (1764–1854), Boston merchant. Perkins and DW invested in Western lands together, through the agency of Henry L. Kinney. Warren Kinney was probably a brother (see *Correspondence*, 4: 104, 358).

27. Cornelius Cokeley (d. c. 1850), a native of Pennsylvania, went to Peru about 1835 with Henry L. Kinney.

28. Nathaniel Ray Thomas (1812–1840), son of Captain John Thomas from whom DW purchased his Marshfield estate in 1832, was at this time serving as DW's agent in the west.

29. Theron Brewster, settled in Peru in 1835, merchant, grain trader, manufacturer of agricultural implements, mayor (1851).

act for you and make the necessary conveyances for you. This part of your property which, by the way, was not included, I believe, in Thomas' & my estimate of your Illinois property will be worth something handsome I hope.

Please let Ray forward your deed from May to be recorded & mine from you. The affair as I mentioned in my last, requires *despatch.*[30] As soon as I have got my house & office in order and have been to the Court at Ottawa, I shall go down to see Mr. Walker and consult with him on the Lapsly matters.

I hope to have but little trouble in settling Messrs Lyon & Howards business.[31] Warren Kinney pretends to be very friendly. I shall do nothing hastily, but shall allow no threats or promises to deter me from a pretty straight forward course. I hope you will have time to write me your desires upon the matters I have above mentioned to you.

Caroline has just finished a letter to her Sisters. She wrote Mother from on Board the Canal Boat.

With my best love to all I am dear Father Your affectionate Son

Daniel F. Webster.

I wrote you in some haste a day or two since, but find no reason to change my opinions of the necessity of some more funds in our joint account. D. F. W.

ALS. NhHi. Published in *Correspondence*, 4: 356–358. Daniel Fletcher Webster (1813–1862; Harvard 1833), admitted in 1836, practiced briefly in the Midwest (1837–1840), chief clerk, U.S. state department (1841–1843), secretary, China mission (1843–1845), Massachusetts state representative (1845), surveyor, port of Boston (1850–1861).

FROM DANIEL FLETCHER WEBSTER

My dear Father, Peru June 22. 1839

I hardly ever expected to write to you in England, from Peru.[32] We are now almost as far apart as the limited circumference of our little earth will allow, and probably are moving in scenes as diverse as the distance is great. You must now be in London, where I imagine the wilderness of humanity to be as vast as that of the prairies here. I can of course form no idea of the events & occurrences, the sights, sounds & actions that you are acting & suffering, grammatically speaking, but I promise myself bye & bye the great pleasure of seeing a letter from

30. Probably Daniel Fletcher Webster to DW, April 23, 1839, mDW 15463.

31. Walker not identified; Samuel Lapsley (d. 1839), a native of Pennsylvania, settled in La Salle in 1830, where he farmed and ran a sawmill. Lyon and Howard, of New York, otherwise not identified.

32. In the summer of 1839 DW traveled to England.

you, which shall give us some ideas worth having about England & London.

When I last wrote you,[33] I am aware that my letter was full of troubles & embarrassments; I shall endeavour to write more agreeably at present.

I have been very much occupied with the care of the many interests you have here. We have divided the interests in the Brewster estate, so far as Ninawa Lots are concerned and your share is a good one. I have endeavoured to make a division between you & me, which of course will always be subject to your approbation; I believe it to be as equal as can be made.

The farms are all doing pretty well and I hope to be able to clear them from most of the encumbrances left on them by Kinney, without great cost or inconvenience.

I have spent a good deal in fitting up the house at Salisbury and in stocking & improving the farm, which had gone to disorder very much. Caroline & Miss Fettyplace[34] have painted & papered & carpeted & whitewashed with all their might. We enlarged the house, connected the two buildings by a large shed, had a well dug; Lowry has been ditching and draining and Tilden[35] planting & hoeing and making fences—my department was that of finance, in which I have much display of science & tact, worthy a Morris or a Hamilton. I have bought a pair of farm horses; all sorts of farming tools, four nice cows and a great quantity of poultry for Caroline.

I have had some business in my profession and have just got home from Hennepin, where I argued a case the day before yesterday. My office is a nice one & I hope to be able soon to earn enough to pay the rent of it.

I have not yet seen Mr. Walker about the Adams & Lapsly claim; but I have written to him & shall soon have an answer appointing time & place to meet him. The [Illinois] Supreme Court sits soon at Springfield & it will be there & then in all probability.

Kinney's affairs turn out very badly. I have not been able to find any property and of course cannot get a judgment worth having. There may [be] hopes of finding some lands *entered* by him, of which there are no conveyances, & which can be discovered by going to the land office at Galena. The first opportunity I have I shall make an investigation. Peru has improved very much and property is rising in value gradually &

33. Probably Daniel Fletcher Webster to DW, April 26, 1839, printed pp. 33–35, above.

34. Probably a daughter of William Fettyplace of Boston, originally of Salem, who was a near relative of Caroline's father, Stephen White.

35. Lowry, or Lowrie, a former laborer at Marshfield, sent by DW to work at the Salisbury farm in Peru (see DFW to DW, December 28, 1837, mDW 14522); John P. Tilden, a farmer and native of Marblehead, Massachusetts, settled in Peru in the fall of 1837.

surely. I hope you will not sell your four farms in England—if you do, get at the least $50. per acre. They will be worth all that in a few years. They are allowed by every one to be the best farms anywhere in the vicinity of Peru & as good as any in the county—their proximity to town doubles their value. If you can get $10 or 9 1/2 for some of your outlying property it would be as well to sell it: though from all I can learn the selections are generally very good. I have not yet made the tour through Wisconsin & the Northern part of this State. I reserve that for the fall. I believe I have now told you of all our business matters. I keep a strict account of all money paid out which you can examine when you come out to visit me & see lands which only want a small outlay to equal in beauty [any that?] can be in England. Our health has been thus far ve[ry good] Caroline is more than contented and takes great pride in her house and her poultry. Grace is very much grown and talks famously. She is going to be a great songstress as well as very pretty. I need not tell you that we think & speak of you every day and *wonder*, of course, what Mother & Julia & Harriet[36] are about. Please tell Julia that we all desire our love to the Queen & will take it out in any thing. I had a letter from Saml. Appleton[37] the other day. He is anxious enough for August to come. Mother I am sure is pleased and I dare say she and Mrs. P. have been to Randell and Bridges and "to the famed Bazaar."

You find yourself in the midst of great political excitement, & what with Chartists[38] and changes of Administration and Court news, have doubtless food enough for thought and speculation. Pray write me, dear Father, bye & bye a short description of men & things. Caroline depends on a letter from Mother & Harriet & Julia. I have no recent news from Boston. Nothing from Ray Thomas since you left. We all desire our best love to Mother & sisters, and anticipate the greatest pleasure in hearing of the respect & attention which we are sure you must all receive. A *stronger* party we feel, could not have been sent. Caroline is as happy in imagining & picturing to herself the enjoyments of the ladies as if she was herself a participator. For my own part I think it would have a greater appearance of reality if I were with you; Julia must therefore make it up to me by one of her best & longest letters. News from the Eastern cities reaches you as soon as us. You were probably not so long going to London as we were coming here. You will be very sorry to find Sir Charles Vaughan deceased.[39] We heard of it here but a few days

36. Julia Webster (1811–1848); Harriette Story White Paige (1809–1863), wife of James William Paige and sister of Fletcher's wife, Caroline.

37. Samuel A. Appleton (1811–1861), of Boston, married Julia in London on September 24, 1839.

38. A group of political reformers who sought to improve the living conditions for England's industrial working population.

39. Sir Charles Richard Vaughan (1774–1849), English diplomat,

since in a letter from Col. Perkins. Mr. Saml Cabot and his wife[40] & daughter have just left us, after a visit of a week. They were much pleased with the Country & I believe he left directions with his son's partner to buy some of our lots for him, for he has been making some advances. I have spared paper, my dear Father, for I know your frank won't go in England. I have but room to add that you all have our constant prayers for your happiness while absent & your safe return to home and friends. Good bye, my dear Father. God protect you from all accident & bless you always. Your most affectionate Son Daniel F.

ALS. NhHi. Published in *Correspondence*, 4: 371–373.

FROM DANIEL FLETCHER WEBSTER

My dear Father, Peru Mar. 30th. 1840.

I received your last kind letter[41] just as I was leaving home for the Princeton Court. The two cases in which the Mechanics Lien was sought to be enforced against the Miller place, which I sold to you for $600. and against White Hall for $220. were both decided against me. The question now arises whether, these liens having been granted after the lands were sold, they can attach upon the land. This question we will try at the next Court or Court after, and I think it will be decided that a Mechanic after constructive notice of Sale by the recording of the Deed before his work was finished, if he goes on with it, looks to the personal security of the Employer and not to the land. At any rate, unless it shall be decided that on the granting a petition for lien it shall take effect from the time when work was first commenced & hold the lands notwithstanding any sale of the lands, the farms will escape. I did my best, with Kinney's assistance, but the Jury in every case this term seemed to think that the Plaintiff would not sue unless he had a right to recover.

In the case of the suit against me as Indorser on one of Kinney's drafts, I got off on the ground of want of sufficient notice to charge me. I was engaged in one or two other suits, with various success.

I send you a letter which I received the other day from my agent at Mineral Point, in which the Amt. of Taxes, due on your lands there, is stated. You had better send a certificate of deposite for the amount. I hope you have some one in Michigan to look after those there. I want a list of all yours here & the *time* of *purchase*, so that I can know when they are taxed. These taxes will be eating us up soon.

---

envoy to the United States (1825–1835). The report of his death was incorrect.

40. Samuel Cabot, Jr. (1784–1863), Boston merchant, married to Elizabeth Perkins (1791–1885), daughter of Thomas Handasyd Perkins.

41. Probably March 5, 1840, mDW 26194.

We are all alive in politics. I have been speech-making considerably the last fortnight and have a good chance for the legislature I think, if Warren Kinney does not conclude to run. I would try to get the nomination if he was not in the way. They begin to think there is something in me, I learn.

I have moved down to town & have leased Salisbury for the best price I could get. The House and twenty acres of land for one hundred & eighty dollars—twenty acres to the halves, furnishing seed and a team—eight acres for three dollars per acre; twenty five acres to be put into Timothy. The rest is yet on my hands.

The Haight & Warren & Miller Farms are still on my hands. I have let White Hall for $100. to be paid in Carpenter work.

These, dear Father, are the best terms I can make. The farmers are all down; produce brings nothing—there is no money *at all* out here. All my lots in Peru, would not bring five hundred dollars in Cash. Lands have fallen very much—our Rail Road has stopped.

In fact we are all down & prospects are very dull indeed, in *pecuniam*.

Caroline keeps well & the Babe grows. Caroline sticks to "Daniel" for his name, although if we had not fixed on that we would have called him Charles, at your suggestion.

He is very bright & we hope to show him to you one of these days & that you will think him a "pretty copious boy".

There has a great question of title arisen with regard to Peru and Brewster's titles. It seems that L. D. Brewster had a right to a Pre-emption Claim[42] to the land on which the Town stands, & another to a tract of land on the Pekatonika, in the North part of the state, not being able of course to establish both he purchased a floating claim, which be laid on Peru, choosing to prove up his pre-emption on the other place. This float[43] he purchased of a woman then a Minor—paid her for it & also furnished the money for the payment of the lands taken by him under the float, being the lands at Peru. The lands entered under & by virtue of the float were entered in the name of the woman. The patent however was granted to Brewster as assignee. The Woman now avoids her transfer on the ground of infancy & has sold her float to another. The Woman was not known at the time to be a Minor. A Float cannot be laid on a pre-emption claim.

Now, I am going to get a fee in this Case, and you are very much inter-

42. The federal preemption acts authorized settlers who had cultivated land on the public domain to enter as many as 160 acres at the price of $1.25 an acre. See note a., 4 U.S. Statutes at Large 420. Lyman D. Brewster (d. 1835), moved from Nashville, Tennessee to Peru, Illinois in 1834.

43. A *float* was a certificate authorizing the holder to enter an unidentified and otherwise unselected parcel of land.

ested in it, though if Brewster's title fails, Hubbard of N.H. must answer to May & May to you. May is worthless.[44]

We imagine that this is a case of *resulting trust.* Will you let some of the Clerks send me all the Land laws of the U. S. for the last six years. I want to know how Minors come by floats & all about such matters. The Copy of the U. S. Land laws which you gave me come down no later than 1833.

How can the present Claimant proceed? If he commence by ejectment—we have the Patent. If by bill in Equity—we have the equity certainly. Mr. Hubbard has, I have just learned, a full statement of the case from T. D. Brewster, the present owner of most of the property here & the Grantee of the Colonization Society.

Judge Logan has not yet commenced in the Lapsley case. I intend seeing him soon on the subject. Mr. Butterfield will write you himself on the subject of Hubbard & Turner's suit.[45] I believe they have not compromised.

If possible I shall leave here in July and while my family get out of the hot weather here, make you all a flying visit at Marshfield. Mr. White has broken up so badly that I suppose there is no chance of his making his trip to Mackinaw, so I shall leave Caroline at Chicago for a few weeks. I would come on earlier, but I am a Delegate to the Convention at Springfield, and feel that I must go and make a speech.[46] The field is open for me and I must begin my career pretty soon, or never.

I have been requested by the Mortgagee to inform you that the amt. due on White Hall is $2700. This is about the amount according to the Register's certificate, which I enclose.[47] If you could pay him soon, I believe he would make a deduction—say $2000. in cash for the whole amt. due.

You will see by my letter, how troubled we are with claims & law suits, in consequence of the loose manner in which all business out here has been conducted. Kinney left us a world of annoyance.

Please give my best love to Mother & present my best regards to Mr & Mrs Curtis.[48] He has been very obliging indeed to me this winter.

44. Henry Hubbard, see p. 325, below; William L. May (c. 1793–1849), Illinois lawyer, U.S. representative (1834–1839). In 1838 DW agreed to purchase May's share of the Brewster lands, see mDW 39835-247.

45. Stephen Trigg Logan (1800–1880), Kentucky and Illinois lawyer, judge, Illinois circuit court (1835–1839), Abraham Lincoln's partner (1841–1844), state legislator; Justin Butterfield, Illinois attorney; Levi C. Turner (c. 1805–1867), Ohio lawyer, newspaperman, and land agent, employed by DW in the 1830s.

46. A Whig political convention.

47. Enclosure not found.

48. Probably the Edward Curtises; Edward Curtis (1801–1856; Union College 1821), New York lawyer, U.S. representative (1837–1841), collector, port of New York (1841–1844).

Caroline sends you her best love. She hopes you will like your little grandson & namesake. Ever your affectionate Son Danl F. Webster

ALS. NhHi.

FROM DANIEL FLETCHER WEBSTER

My dear Father, Peru April 8th. 1840.

I have just recd your letter of Mar. 22d.[49]

I have been thinking for some time that this would not do for me, & had pretty much determined, after another year, if things did not mend, to remove, somewhere. The business here will not support one. All our hopes have been upon the Canal, and the consequent growth of the place, but when the Canal will be finished is very doubtful, certainly not for some time, which would be to me almost lost time.

These considerations, together with the unhealthiness of the country, have weaned me of my Western fever. If there were any chance here, or any tolerable prospect for the future, I could stay & wait a reasonable time, but every thing is so bad, that really we all feel discouraged.

Caroline is very anxious to come East. She fears for herself and her children. We have to give little Daniel calomel already, he is so bilious.

If it could be so arranged that I could form some connection in New York, which would give me a good start, I would bring on my family this Summer, stay awhile with you myself, come out to settle up all business here during the Winter and then finally come East in the Spring. But, you will agree with me, that I could hardly bring my family East, without some prospect of making a final settlement there & without some previous arrangement or prospect that would justify the expence. I would scarcely like Boston, but would try it there, if I could do no better. I should prefer New York.

I have thought that perhaps Mr. [Edward] Curtis could suggest some connection there for me, if he would not be disposed to make one himself. Could some such plan be effected, the Sale of my effects here would put me in funds for some time, leaving the lands in Peru to await the course of events & I could come on, without being any expense to you. I think I could do something in New York—there is a field for all exertion & I could probably earn a handsome living there, with your influence. It is as you say, precisely. The blight which has fallen upon every thing seems to render it necessary to change our plans of operation.

I leave the first Boat, for Springfield, on business connected with the Miller Farm & the Lapsley place. I shall be absent about a week.

In confidence. Mr. Cabots mercantile establishment here has pretty

49. Letter not found.

much gone down. They have lost a good deal of money. The Farm is kept up by main force.

I have let the Haight & Warren & Miller Farms for $200. for one year, to a very good man. I will at all events, if I am well, come to see you in July. If a good arrangement meanwhile can be made, I will bring on the family & leave them East while I come out to finish & settle up affairs—otherwise I shall take them to Chicago & come on myself.

We are all pretty well today.

The Harrison[50] cause is gaining ground daily. We have just had a famous meeting at Ottawa, the County seat. A slight bilious attack prevented me from attending, which I regret very much, as I wanted to give them a speech. I have made three recently to very respectable audiences.

With much love to Mother & all & many thanks for Edward's letter.[51] I remain dear Father your affectionate Son Danl. F. Webster

ALS. NhHi. Published in *Correspondence*, 5: 38–39.

FROM DANIEL FLETCHER WEBSTER

My dear Father, Peru April 16th. 1840.

Your kind letter of April 1st.[52] has just been received.

There are two chief reasons why I wish to move East and two chief favours which I ask of you in order to enable me to do so advantageously. In the first place, we are very unhealthy here & though I hope in any event, that we might all live through it, yet, in the second place, there is no business here worth living for.

I was unfortunate in coming here. I came here on the *ebb tide* and things have been going backward ever since.

The favours I want you to grant are these. To give me your co[u]ntenance and support in forming a connection in New York,—& to let it be understood that the firm will have the benefit of your advice in all necessary cases. If these can be granted, I shall try to leave here. Otherwise I dare not venture.

I will not boast of my business habits. The great trouble is that as yet I have had very little to do. What little I have I attend to, as well as I know how, & with a good will.

I shall be very glad to go to Wisconsin for you & can take care of all your Illinois business as well as any body. I wrote you about the Lapsley affair in my last. I hope you will be able to get back your money from

50. William Henry Harrison (1773–1841), soldier and politician, U.S. president (1841).

51. Edward Webster (1820–1848; Dartmouth 1841), Fletcher's brother.

52. Letter not found.

Jones,[53] for I do not think the whole concern worth four thousand dollars.

There is nothing new here. Things growing worse & worse every day.

With much love to all I remain yr. affectionate Son

Danl. F. Webster.

ALS. NhHi.

TO DANIEL FLETCHER WEBSTER

My Dear Son Washington May 31, 1840

I have recd. your letter of the 16th. of this month, & also Caroline's, enclosing one to her father.[54] I am glad to see that the Whigs are stirring, in your quarter. Your Senators, I believe are still confident that the vote of the State will be given to Mr Van-Buren; but Mr Stuart thinks otherwise.[55] Our intelligence is encouraging, from all quarters, & I have no doubt, or very little, at present, that Genl. Harrison will be elected.

You seem to be hesitating about coming East. No doubt, it is a subject demanding due consideration. You seem also to think that you prefer Peru to any place East, except N York or Washington. I believe you can get a living in N. York, but there is not a very extensive field of local practice, in Washington. It is, however, a good spot for practice in the Supreme Court, & I believe money is occasionally made by attention to claims pending before Congress. But for political objects, neither N. Y. or Washington is so good as Boston, or Lowell. In either of these last, you would go immediately into the State Legislature, & have a chance to show yourself. And in either of them, you could by diligence & hard labor get a living. Middlesex is not full of talent, & I should esteem Lowell quite a good place, for a promising & resolute young man. With you politics must be subordinate to law. Your first study must be to live.

Perhaps you will not find yourself ready or able to make up your mind, definitely, until I see you. Much ought to depend on what you think of the healthfulness of Peru. My property in the West will want attention from somebody, & since Ray's death[56] I have thought of no way but of

53. George Wallace Jones (1804–1896; Transylvania University, Kentucky, 1825), lawyer, clerk, U.S. courts, Missouri (1826), delegate to Congress (1835–1837, Michigan; 1837–1839, Wisconsin), surveyor of public lands (1840–1841, 1846–1848), U.S. senator (1848–1859).

54. Fletcher's letter of May 16, 1840, mDW 16680; Caroline's has not been found.

55. Martin Van Buren (1782–1862), New York lawyer and politician, U.S. president (1837–1841). Probably John Todd Stuart (1807–1885), U.S. representative from Illinois (1839–1843).

56. Nathaniel Ray Thomas died in March 1840, while on a trip East.

putting it into your management. At any rate, I must see you, in the course of the season, & we must settle upon something. If you could send your family East, at the same or as little expense as you can send them, & support them, at the North, we will find a corner for them at Marshfield till Autumn. I do not know the arrangement of your courts, & therefore cannot say when you yourself can best leave home. Many things depend on the result of the ensuing election. If that should go against us, I should know pretty well what to do myself, & what to recommend you to do. If it should go for us, different questions would arise. I hope you will think of all these things, & write to me often. Yours affectionately Danl Webster

Is there any other place in the West, where you think you can do better than in Peru? Do you know any thing of Madison City, Wisconsin?

ALS. NhHi. Published in *Correspondence*, 5: 38–39.

c. *John Plummer Healy: 1838–1852*

After Kinsman left in 1837, Webster maintained his office under John Plummer Healy, a recent Dartmouth graduate, who was reading law in the office. When Healy was admitted to the bar in 1838, Webster entered into an association with him that lasted to Webster's death in 1852. In 1838 they had to find a new office. Webster wrote to Healy:

> I am sorry we must leave our old office. We must try to get another, tho' I hardly know where to find one, to my mind. I want, for myself, one large room—in which I can place all my Books, except what are in the Study at home. At present, my Library is too much scattered.
>
> Then another room will be wanted, for you or whoever may be with me. I am not particular about the part of the town. Please look round, enquire, & let me know what you can find.[1]

FROM JOHN PLUMMER HEALY

Dear Sir, Boston Jan'y 30. 1839.

The accompanying letter from Mr. Fisk was recd. today.[2] It appears that your claim upon the land referred to, is good for nothing.

Mr. Fisk is a sound Whig, an active & estimable man, & has been several years a member of the N.H. Senate. If you are sending documents &c. into that State, one occasionally addressed to Mr. F. would be well disposed of.

Mr. Peabody[3] wishes to retain your services, in a case now pending in

1. February 12, 1838, mDW 14634.

2. Letter not found. Levi Fisk (1775–1857), of Jaffrey, New Hampshire was a representative to the New Hampshire legislature for three years and a state senator (1835–1837).

3. Possibly Augustus Peabody (1779–1851; Dartmouth 1803), Bos-

the Supreme Court in this State, Bass v. Stevens.[4] Mr. P. is for the Pltf. A trial has just been had, but the jury could not agree upon a verdict. A new trial will be had probably the latter part of March or first of April. The matter of a retainer will be satisfactorily adjusted, Mr. P. says.

Nothing new, but the recent gale & freshet, of which the papers give full accounts. Yours truly, J. P. Healy

P.S. A draft from N. Ray Thomas, for $125, dated at Buffalo. Dec. 10, 1838, & payable at the Merchants' Bank in New York, sixty days after date, has just been presented for acceptance; &, under your general direction to accept all drafts drawn by Mr. T. accepted. It falls due therefore the 8/11th of Feb'y, & must be paid in N. York.

ALS. MHi. John Plummer Healy (1810–1882; Dartmouth 1835), studied with DW and practiced as his associate (1838–1852), Boston city solicitor (1856–1882), state legislator, appointed and confirmed U.S. district judge, southern district of California on September 28, 1850, but after accepting the appointment, declined it because of his father's ill health.

TO JOHN PLUMMER HEALY

Dear Sir Saturday Morning [April 20, 1839]

I do not think I can be relied on to try Mr Bass' case,[5] if it is to come up on Tuesday. Indeed it may be as well to say, that with my present purposes & hopes, I do not expect to find time to try any causes, this Spring. I am engaged in one very important suit here, which perhaps I shall not address the Jury in, but which I must attend to, & which may last to, & thro., Tuesday. Mr. Peabody had better, at once, settle it, that he will rely on his own tongue, to set forth Mr Bass' wounds & bruises, or else to engage that of somebody else, beside me. If I should make up my mind, as I probably shall, to take a sail abt. the middle of May, I shall have matters & things eno. on hand, in the meantime, to keep me busy.[6] Yrs

D. W.

[P.S.] The best way to treat the notion of my going abroad, is to admit that I think of it, but that nothing can be determined for ten or twelve days, after I get home.

ALS. MHi.

TO JOHN PLUMMER HEALY

Dear Sir Washington Jan. 11 [18]41

Your letter respecting the case in Court gives me trouble.[7] I really

---

ton lawyer, studied with Timothy Bigelow, state representative.

4. No further information on the litigants in this case has been obtained.

5. See preceding letter.

6. In the summer of 1839 DW traveled to England.

7. Letter not found; case not identified.

thought you would contrive to get a continuance. I know nothing of the rules, & of course know not what time was allowed for cross Interrogatories. You do not even now mention what the time is. It must be plain & manifest, that I cannot personally attend to this matter, till after March the 3rd. I pray you, see if you cannot get a postponement beyond that time.

It gives me much trouble Yrs D. Webster

ALS. MHi.

Webster had always been available to handle cases in other cities while traveling between Boston and Washington. Writing in 1843 to his friend and fellow attorney Hiram Ketchum, Webster commented on a proposal that he cultivate a small New York practice.

> Will you do me the favor to confer with Mr. Moulton, on this subject.
>
> I could well enough be in N. Y. "at stated times"; but I do not like to make a formal tender of professional service to the public. What I have thought desirable is, that I should be engaged, in some proper case, in the higher Courts, which would lead me to N. Y., into the Courts, & might lead to other cases, & also to some settled arrangement, such as Mr Moulton proposes.[8]

Nothing formal seems to have come of this until 1844, almost a year after Webster resigned his cabinet post as secretary of state. Then the rumors flew thick and fast. In a letter to Healy, printed below, he sought to squelch any stories reaching Boston. To Ketchum he wrote a short note:

> I will write you to-morrow, but for mercy's sake do not let Mr. Moulton put up my name on a sign in New York. I cannot consent to any such thing. What has already occurred and been published, has caused me much annoyance.[9]

The next day he explained his reasons:

> As to Professional business in N. Y., I do not feel at all sanguine. You have a great many competent men at your Bar, as well as several who are eminent; & I do not expect to find more than here & there a case, soliciting my aid. As a general field, I believe Boston is better.[10]

Webster may also have wanted to avoid making more formal ties with a New York clientele for political reasons. It may have occurred to him that his national ambitions might be better launched from New England than from the New York mercantile community.

8. November 25 [1843], mDW 20720.

9. February 14, 1844, *PC*, 2: 184.

10. February 15, 1844, mDW 25683, and *Correspondence*, 6.

TO JOHN PLUMMER HEALY

My Dear Sir Jan: 27 [18]44

The Newspapers will let nobody & nothing alone, public or private. You see how the Commercial speaks of my taking rooms, &c in N. York. The truth is, I have recd three or four retainers, in N. Y. cases, & wished it to be quietly understood that I would see my clients at a room connected with those of Mr Van Winkle & Mr Moulton[11]—but I positively forbad any advertising, or public notice about it. It will now be said, no doubt, that I am to leave Boston. How can such gossip be stopped? I wish no publication about it—as if it were a public affair—but would be glad you would say to friends what is necessary in the case. I am willing to argue causes in N.Y. when convenient, & having already some engagements, thought it might be well to have a calling place, to consult books &c &c.—That is all. Yrs D. W.

ALS. MHi. Published in *Correspondence*, 6.

TO THOMAS BUCKMINSTER CURTIS

My Dear Sir, Washington, Jan. 30, 1844

I am obliged to you for your letter. I have seen your son, for a moment, & shall try to look him up again today, & his friend Clark.[12]

The notice of Mr Choate's resignation is at least premature.[13] He is here yet, & I believe speaks today, in the Senate on the Oregon business.

These Newspaper accounts of my being about to go to N. York have annoyed me exceedingly. I really wish the printers would let private men & private things alone. Let me tell you just what has occurred.

I had a quantity of titles to Western lands, which I placed in the hands of an agent in N. Y. to sell, or exchange for productive property elsewhere, &c. He found a house & a dozen acres of land, the house used as a boarding house, on the Jersey Shore, opposite N. Y. This he took, paying for it some money, & some western lands. And that is all, for rumour No. one. Now for No. 2.—I am retained to argue three or four causes, in N. Y. in the course of the Spring & Summer. Some very respectable

11. Edgar S. Van Winkle (1810–1882), New York lawyer, studied with John P. Jackson and William Slosson, admitted in 1831; Joseph W. Moulton, New York lawyer. On March 8, 1844, DW wrote to Moulton that he expected to spend most of April and May in New York (mDWs).

12. Letter not found; Daniel Sargent Curtis; Clark has not been identified.

13. Rufus Choate (1799–1859; Dartmouth 1819), studied with William Wirt, admitted in Essex County, Massachusetts in 1823, practiced in Danvers, Salem, and then Boston (from 1834), U.S. representative (1831–1834), U.S. senator (1841–1845), Massachusetts attorney general (1853–1854).

Young Gentlemen thought it wd. be convenient for me, & not inconvenient to them, that when in N. Y. on Professional business, I should occupy a room near theirs, with access to their Library &c. And this offer, I of course gladly accepted. And that is all of No. 2. What No. 3 will be, cannot be foreseen. I do not wish to make statements about myself, or my purposes, thro. the press; but I will thank you to say, to all & singular, that I am, & shall be as long as I live, "D. W. of Marshfield, in the County of Plymouth, & Commonwealth of Massachusetts."

It is not likely that I shall long continue to do professional business, any where. And while I continue in my vocation, its principal theatre must of course be Massachusetts; not declining offers, however, which can be conveniently accepted, from other States.

Mr Clay's friends continue to be confident of his success.[14] It is most certain that Mr Van Buren is regarded as a heavy load to carry. Yet, he will be nominated, & you know there is much cohesion in that party. State elections will be taking place throughout the Country at or about the same time as the choice of Electors. These elections will bring out parties, strongly, & party feeling & party action being thus roused, Mr. Van Buren's cause, now apparently cold, may be warmed again, & cherished with more zeal & spirit. So that if the Whigs hope to carry the Country, they ought to be prepared for a vigorous contest. I am, Dear Sir, with great regard, Yours, Danl. Webster

ALS. MHi. Published in *Correspondence*, 6. Thomas Buckminster Curtis (1795–1871), Boston merchant and banker, brother of Charles Pelham Curtis.

Late in 1843 it became known in Massachusetts political circles that Rufus Choate, who had taken Webster's senate seat when the latter went into the cabinet, intended to resign. Several of Webster's friends sounded him out on seeking his former position. Now sixty-two years of age and heavily in debt, he carefully weighed the prospects of national office. In two letters written in February 1844, printed below, he indicated his willingness to accept public office and his view of law practice. In the first letter, to David Sears, he expressed a weariness with practice; in the second, to Jeremiah Mason, he took a more combative stance.

TO DAVID SEARS

My Dear Sir; Washington Feb. 5. '44

Your letter of the 27th of Jany. has been some days before me, & I

14. Henry Clay (1777–1852), lawyer and politician, practiced law in Kentucky, state legislator, U.S. representative and senator for various terms between 1808 and his death, twice Speaker of the House, secretary of state under John Quincy Adams, unsuccessful presidential candidate in 1824, 1832, and 1844.

have reflected on its contents.[15] Indeed, similar suggestions had been previously made to me, from other quarters.

I suppose it is true, that Mr. Choate intends to leave the Senate, sometime in March, or perhaps not till April.

The term for which Mr Choate was elected, will expire, in March 1845. There will, therefore, remain only the remnant of this session, & the short session of next winter. I doubt whether any thing important will be done, or seriously attempted this session, except on the subject of the Tariff; & I hope *that* may not be successfully assailed.

Before next session, a new President will be chosen, & the greater part of a new Congress; so that an expiring Congress, with an expiring Administration, would hardly be likely to venture on great public measures, especially as one house seems an effectual check, on the other.

Under these circumstances, My Dear Sir, I do not see, even supposing me capable of performing an important part in public affairs, that I could be, in any considerable degree useful, in the Senate, for this session or the next. And there are weighty private reasons, which render it desirable that I should not, for some time, be charged with responsible public duties.

I will not affect to deny, that if all other things favored, I should prefer suitable public employment to returning to the Bar, at my age. I have seen enough of Courts of Law, to desire to be in, & among, them no more. But my affairs require attention, & the means of living, you know must be had.

In 1836, by the aid of friends, & my own exertions, I settled up my concerns, & owed no man any thing. I was then desirous of leaving Congress, & resuming professional labors, vigorously. But friends opposed it, & my papers of resignation were sent back to me. It was a day of buoyancy, & great hope, in matters of business; & what money I had, or could get, I laid out in the West, principally in well selected Govt. Lands. But times soon changed, & I have since had nothing but a struggle. If in the Senate, I should have time to attend to affairs *private* & *personal*, but not to affairs *professional*.

I may say to you, in confidence, that I am now earning & receiving $15.000 a year, from my profession, which must be almost entirely sacrificed by a return to the Senate. I am sanguine eno. to hope for better times, & a better state of things, in which I may turn some considerable remnants of property to good account. And if, after this Congress, it should seem to friends desirable that I should be in the Senate, & I should be able to see that I could possibly afford it, I should probably feel it right, to put myself at their disposition. But for the remnant of this year, & until March of the next, I cannot but think it more impor-

15. Curtis, 2: 238–239.

tant to me, that I should remain where I am, than it can be to the Country, that I should return to the Senate.[16]

I have said more, My Dear Sir, than was perhaps necessary. But your letter manifests much kindness, & good feeling on your part. I value your friendship, highly; & have thought it right, therefore, to give you my thoughts, frankly & in full. Yours very truly Danl Webster

ALS. MHi. Published in *PC*, 2: 182–183. David Sears (1787–1871; Harvard 1807), Boston merchant, philanthropist, and state legislator.

TO JEREMIAH MASON

Washington, February 6, 1844.

My Dear Sir,—I have received your letter of January 29th.[17] The story of my being about to remove to New York is quite idle. Having entered into engagements to take part in three or four causes, to be heard in that city, some young gentlemen invited me to take a room near theirs, for my use, when there, with access to their library, etc. This I agreed to as being convenient to me; and probably they supposed it would not be prejudicial to them. The subject of returning to the Senate has been suggested to me, from various quarters. At the present moment I see no great public object to be accomplished, by such a movement, and it might only excite expectations not likely to be fulfilled. No great interest can be felt for what remains to be done, under the present administration. The country is likely to be mainly occupied with the next election. The result of that election may enable us to see what is before us, more clearly. Mr. Choate's term expires in March 1845, and from the proposed time of his resignation to that time, I do not see much that could be done for good. Besides, I think it would be rather awkward to be in the Senate now. I could not probably approve much of what should be done by the administration; and it would be disagreeable to find myself obliged to oppose vigorously, an administration to which I have myself belonged. There being therefore, in my judgment, no great public object to be attained, I feel the more at liberty to consult my private convenience. I am now a little engaged in the law, and need strongly enough what fees I may be able to pick up. To be sure, I should be very glad to be done with the courts; but their atmosphere, if not altogether pleasant, is yet usefully *bracing*, to those whose purses are slender, however it may be with their constitutions. On all accounts, therefore, I think it better that I should, for the present, remain where I am. Let us see what the ensuing election may bring forth. I dare say there is no *very strong* desire that I should return to the Senate. The body of the Whigs might

16. The Massachusetts legislature selected DW to complete Choate's term, but he did not take his seat until March 1845, as he said.

17. Letter not found.

wish it, but there are other candidates, who may like the chance, and there are also some prominent men who have not yet digested the spleen, generated by past events. As to these last, let them indulge themselves, I shall bide my time.

I am, dear Sir, yours very truly, Daniel Webster

Text from *W & S*, 16: 424–425. Original not found.

In March 1845 Webster returned to the Senate. In a letter to George Ticknor, printed below, he indicated his pleasure at being back at the locus of national affairs. In these final years of his life Webster continued to take cases both in state and federal courts. Though now more easily tired by these labors, his financial straits did not permit him to refuse a lucrative offer. From Washington, he wrote to New York attorney Richard M. Blatchford:

> I am overwhelmed with Labor—obliged to study from 5 to 11. A. M.—be in Court from 11 to 3—& all the rest of the day in the Senate till 10 oclock.[18]

When Millard Fillmore became president in 1850, Webster once again entered the cabinet as secretary of state. In March 1852 he journeyed to Trenton, New Jersey, where he made his last courtroom appearance in the patent case of *Goodyear* v. *Day*.[19] In September 1852 he returned to his estate in Marshfield, Massachusetts, where, on October 24, 1852, he died.

FROM NATHAN SELBERT

Dear Sir Philad. March 18—1845

I pen these lines to you for the purpose of inquiring whether you intend to practice law occasionally, and whether you would be at liberty by the 24th. of April to take charge of a suit which is a very heavy one and in which the Parties are desirous of engaging the first talent. If you should take a favorable notice of this letter please answer early, and I will call upon you at Washington for the purpose of closing a bargain with you concerning it. It would be hardly worth while entering into a description of the case until assured that you intend to practice.[20]

By noticing this early you will much Oblige Your Ob't Sv't

Nathan Selbert

ALS. NhD. Nathan Selbert has not been identified.

18. February 27, 1849, mDW 29109 and *W & S*, 16: 508.

19. 2 Wallace Jr. 283 (1852), 10 Federal Cases 678 (1852). This case will be discussed in *Legal Papers*, 3.

20. DW intended to take the case if he could find the time. See DW to John Plummer Healy, March 19, 1845, mDW 26239.

TO JOHN PLUMMER HEALY

Dear Sir N. York Monday Mar: 20 [24] [1845]

I recd yrs yesterday,[21] & had finished a letter to you, saying I would be home this week, when I learn that that will not be possible. You know I have an Albany case,[22] which has been put off from time to time, & which, as I learn this morning, is now *irrevocably* fixed for *Tuesday*, the first day of April. Thus, I cannot be home till the 4th. or 5th. If the Bulfinch Church case[23] cannot be put off, till that time, other counsel must be employed, & I will return my fee. My greater concern is about Mr Gray's case;[24] but as you do not mention that case, I suppose it is not pressing.

If any [thing] shd. happen to disturb my engagement at Albany, I shall go strait home. I will, in the mean time, write you daily.

A note for $500—given to Jno. Taylor—(Worcester Webster &c)[25] will present itself, abt. 25/28. Herewith you will receive the means of taking it up. Yrs D. Webster

ALS. MHi.

TO JOHN PLUMMER HEALY

Dear Sir Saturday 2 o clock [April 12, 1845]

Up to this hour, I got no letter from Boston today, & indeed am not certain that any mail has been recd, or boat arrived.

My cause is now definitely fixed for *Tuesday*,[26] & I think I *must* stay & try it, I wd. readily give up the fees, but it would be dishonorable to abandon clients, when too late to instruct other Counsel.

I hope the letter written to Mr Haven by Mr B. & Mr J. will induce him to take care of all my matters till the 20th.[27] Mr B. will go to Boston with me, & not quit till something is concluded.

21. Letter not found.

22. Case not identified.

23. *Mussey* v. *Bulfinch Street Society*, 55 Mass. 148 (1848); DW did not argue the case.

24. Not identified.

25. John Taylor (1801–1869), overseer of DW's New Hampshire farm, the Elms; Worcester Webster (b. 1794), a Boscawen shopkeeper.

26. DW wrote to Healy on April 7, the day of his return to New York City from Albany, that he had "*one* cause, & *two* consultations to attend to, here" (mDW 26289), and again, on April 10, that he had "engaged to argue a cause in the Circuit Court" the next day (mDW 26293).

27. Franklin Haven (1804–1895), became president of the Merchants' Bank of Boston in 1837; probably Richard Milford Blatchford (1798–1875; Union College 1815), New York lawyer, admitted in 1819, founder and senior member (1819–1855) of "the Blatchford firm," precursor of the present-day Cravath, Swaine & Moore, also financial agent for the Bank of England and the BUS, as well as DW's intimate friend and political adviser. See Robert T. Swaine, *The Cravath Firm and its*

Mr Beals'[28] check of $500, among other things, will be due on Monday, the 15. I devoutly hope Mr H. will pay it. If not pray Mr Beals to keep it till I get home, which will not be later than the 19—or 20th. according to my original plan—if I live. Yrs truly D. Webster

ALS. MHi.

TO GEORGE TICKNOR

My Dear Sir: Washington, January 24, 1846.

The accompanying letter and copy of answer respect a question which has been a great many times asked me.[29] I place them in your hands, to serve if similar inquiries should happen to be made of you.

You see all that is publicly done here. As to personal and domestic matters, we get along pretty well. We have taken a house, *called* ready furnished, about as big as two pigeon-boxes, but pleasantly situated, and some little space and shrubbery about it. Our nearest neighbor is very quiet. It is the Unitarian Church. The ringing of the bell on Sunday is all we hear from it.

My health is excellent. I must say I am surprised to think how well I am, and how little abatement I feel of the disposition for occupation. My affairs in court are as numerous and as important as at any time of my life.[30] But, I would be glad to be relieved from the necessity of attending to these, for two reasons. First, if I remain in the Senate, I wish to be able to fulfill the duties of the place, so far as attention to the business before it is regarded; second, if I should have leisure, there are some things which I would gladly bestow thought and time upon, of more permanent interest than the temporary politics of the day.

I pray you make Mrs. Webster's and my own kindest remembrances to Mrs. Ticknor and your daughter. Yours always cordially,

Dan'l Webster.

Text from Curtis, 2: 295–296. Original not found. George Ticknor (1791–1871; Dartmouth 1807), lawyer and scholar, studied with William Prescott, practiced in Boston (1813–1817), taught at Harvard (1816–1835).

Predecessors 1819–1947 (2 vols., New York, 1946), 1: passim; probably Samuel Jaudon, who established himself as a New York broker shortly after the demise of the BUS in 1841.

28. Not identified.

29. A reference to a letter from Peter J. Becker of Auburn, New York, seeking to know whether a certain part of DW's 1826 speech in commemoration of the lives of John Adams and Thomas Jefferson was "the *very* speech" which Adams gave prior to the adoption of the Declaration of Independence; and DW's answer explaining that the composition was his own. (Curtis, 2: 294–295).

30. DW argued four USSC cases in 1846.

TO [JOHN PAUL] ROBINSON

Boston Thursday Morning
My Dr Sir 9 o.clock [October 15, 1846]

This postponement of Mr Parkers cause[31] is a bad business. I have made other things give way for it, to no small inconvenience, & came up today, to spend the day with you, & be ready for tomorrow.

I know not what time is now fixed, or whether I am expected, now, to have any thing to do with the case. The argument will probably come on, when I shall be at Washington. Probably it is best for Mr Parker to look out for other Counsel (tho' I do not think you need an associate) without further reference to me, as I cd. not well undertake to come from Washington to argue the cause for any such compensation as he could afford to make.

I am afraid you apprehended that I should *not come to time*. You need not have feared that. Mr Choate said *friday* (16th.) wd. be the day; but I resolved to be on hand *this morning*, 15th.

I shall go to N.H. on my ppd. visit next Tuesday, in the 11 oclock train Yrs truly Danl Webster

ALS. RNHi. John Paul Robinson (1800–1864; Harvard M.A. 1845), read law with DW, admitted in 1827, practiced in Lowell, state legislator.

31. Not identified.

CHAPTER 2. The Elements and Style of Practice

Oral advocacy was the hallmark of lawyering in the antebellum period. Though printed briefs became common before the Civil War, a lawyer's reputation depended on his courtroom eloquence. Some lawyers became known as formidable trial practitioners; others won reputations for their appellate abilities. Webster became famous for his proficiency at both. Each of the great lawyers of the period developed his own expository style. A few, like William Pinkney, used classical allusion and rhetorical flourishes to dazzle both the judges and the courtroom audience. Others, like Lemuel Shaw, confined themselves to technical virtuosity to draw the court to their side. Webster appears to have been eclectic in his approach. He fashioned his argument around the strengths of his case, resorting at times to rhetoric, but chiefly relying on the power of an eloquent presentation of the case to draw the judges or jurors to his side. He prepared for his legal arguments by isolating those points that represented the crux of the dispute. He then outlined an argument supporting his position, using both precedents and logic. In his presentation, he would state, as persuasively as possible, his view of the central issue, back off and try to show how his opponents' interpretation and explanations failed to sustain their argument, and then return to his own explanation. If the court or jury had come with him that far, they would be drawn irresistibly to his side.

Although many of Webster's Supreme Court and lower federal court arguments were reported, few of his jury arguments exist. There are, also, only scattered remnants of the notes he used to prepare his presentations. From these limited materials, it appears, he sketched his argument in skeletal fashion, relying on his ability to make an almost extemporaneous presentation. He knew where he wanted to go, and the general route to take him there; the details came during the trip. In researching the legal precedents bearing on a case for argument to a court, he relied on American and English digests of law. There he would find a handful of precedents on the legal aspects of his case. If he could not find a precedent on all fours with it, he proceeded to build his argument analogically. He also consulted treatises on the subject and used them as authority for particular points of law. Thus his citation in court of an earlier English decision may have rested on his reading of the case or simply on its citation in a digest. He trusted that his opponent also lacked access to a more elaborate discussion of the case.

Each of the four sections below illustrates a stage in the trial and appellate process and Webster's style in addressing them. The first shows the complete range and analysis of a case from pretrial investigation to posttrial motion practice. The second is his examination of a witness and summation to a jury in a contested will case which he handled late in his career. The correspondence associated with this case clearly reveals his sensitivity and shrewdness in properly presenting evidence to a jury. Third is the reported summation of Webster's argument to the jury in a complex land title case which he eventually argued in the Supreme Court. The last is a technical appellate oral argument in a losing cause made three years after his arrival in Boston. The chapter is organized in this way in order to give the reader a sense of the stages in the legal process.

I. STAGES IN THE TRIAL PROCESS: PRETRIAL PREPARATION TO POSTTRIAL MOTIONS: *United States* v. *Henry Hatch*[1]

In September and December 1807, in separate actions, the United States successfully sued Boston area merchants John Rose Greene, as principal, and Crowell Hatch and Samuel Blagge, as sureties, on two customs bonds. On the first execution issued under the September judgment, Hatch gave the U.S. marshal $883.56. This left a balance of $913.55.[2] The court clerk issued nine more executions against Hatch. Hatch paid no more money, however, and the marshal never returned the last execution. George Blake, the U.S. attorney, then tried unsuccessfully to collect the balance from Samuel Blagge. On the December judgment the marshal seized property from Greene and Hatch worth $196.13 and $786.22 respectively. The marshal apparently never turned these proceeds over to the U.S. attorney. The clerk issued several more executions on which none of the defendants paid anything more. At the end of 1811, the U.S. attorney took no further action.

In 1814 Crowell Hatch died, leaving an estate worth about $3500. However, Hatch had been one of the Spanish claimants, and when the

1. The documents in this section are taken from the case file and from the Sang collection at Brandeis University. Since it was not always clear to which part of the litigation they belonged, we have arranged them in what appeared to us as the most likely order. Variations between text and footnote citations usually mean the document's author used a different edition of the cited work.

2. The September action against Greene was a trustee suit. The government apparently recovered judgment against Greene's trustee but not against Greene, who turned out to be insolvent.

commissioners announced the awards in 1824 his estate suddenly mushroomed to almost $30,000. Perhaps this sudden increase in the assets of a deceased merchant's estate prompted the U.S. attorney to examine his old cases. In any event, in 1824 someone found the unsatisfied judgments. Blake then brought suit against Hatch's estate to collect $2570.[3]

Henry Hatch, Crowell's son and administrator of the enlarged estate, retained Webster and Bliss to defend the suit. The attorneys continued the case for almost a year as Bliss searched for evidence on which to construct a defense. They faced the problem that although the uncollected judgments were sixteen years old, the federal government was not subject to any statute of limitations or equitable defense of laches. Two strategies presented themselves. First, if they could find evidence proving that Hatch had paid all or most of the judgments, they could win the case. The marshal would be blamed for the disappearance of the funds. Second, barring clear proof of payment, they needed to present the evidence of the government's lack of diligence in such a way that the court would allow the jury to presume that Hatch had paid the judgments.

Bliss examined both Crowell Hatch's business records and those of the federal court. In the former, he discovered an entry for money paid on behalf of John Greene's firm. This seemed to cover the amount of the judgments. It was not conclusive proof of payment, but if admissible, it would be a reasonable basis for a presumption of payment. To construct a clear picture of the case since 1807, Bliss obtained from the court clerk a history of the executions for both judgments (Documents 2 and 3). After learning that someone had challenged the marshal's seizure of John Greene's property, Bliss sent an investigator to Norfolk County to inspect the court records (Document 4). When the time came for Webster and Bliss to prepare their formal answer to the declaration,

3. *U.S.* v. *Hatch, administrator*, USDC,DMass, September 1826. The Congressional bill authorizing the payment of the Spanish claims, 4 U.S. Statutes at Large 33–34 (1824), contained a proviso in its second section requiring the secretary of the treasury, in cases where the claimant was in debt to the U.S., to retain the amount owed by the claimant and withhold the debt from the claim award. Apparently at the time the treasury department made payment to Henry Hatch as his father's administrator, no one in the department was aware of the unsatisfied judgment, so no amount was subtracted from the award. The suit against Henry Hatch may have been an attempt to collect the old debt in light of both the stipulation in the claim award bill and the recently received public word of the sudden increase in the old estate. The neglect in the first instance by the treasury department in not withholding the debt to the U.S. did not prejudice the government claim in any way. See *U.S.* v. *Hunter*, 5 Mason 62 (1828), and 5 Peters 173 (1831). Henry Hatch's lawyer before the Spanish claims commission was DW.

Bliss could place at Webster's disposal the information he had gathered. Webster summarized the facts (Documents 5 and 6) and probably supervised the preparation of the pleadings (Document 7).

DOCUMENT 2. ABSTRACT OF EXECUTIONS

Sept. Term 1807. Judgt vs Crowell Hatch

N E No. 15 — for	1687.98	prin.
No. 14 Same judgt vs Saml Blagge	10.69	Int to 9 Sept. 1807
	1698.67	
	14.29	costs
No. 13 D[itt]o vs John R. Greene of L Chandler adjudged Trustee[4] for $29.7/100	1712.96	

No Ex[ecuti]on vs Greene appeal to C[ircui]t Ct by U States. Appeal never ent[ere]d in Circt. Ct.

Exon issued 11 Sept 1807 vs Hatch & Blagge } returned Decr 1807—unsatisfied not having been in hands of M[a]r[shal]

Alias issd 6 Jany 1808, returnd March 1808, wholly unsatisfied by Attys direction

Pluries[5] issue—4 April 1808—Returnd June 1808, dated 24 June 1808 satisfied for—$883.56 levied on Hatch & unsatisfied as to the remainder viz $913.55. Same return on both Exons. G[eorge] Blake's receipt given to the Mshls is on Hatch's Exon for $883.58 dated 29 Mrch 1809

2d Pluries issue 22 July 1808, retd Sept 1808, unsatisfied by Attys direction

3d Pls. issue 30 Sept. 1808, retd Dec 1808, unsatisfied by Attys direcn

4th Pls. issue 3 Jany 1809, retd March 1809 unsatisfied by Attys directn

5th Pls. issue 14 Apl. 1809, retd June 1809 unsatisfied by Attys directn

6th Pls issue 14 Augt. 1809, retd Sept 1809, unsatisfied by Attys permission

7th Pls issue 16 Oct. 1809, retd. Dec 1809, unsatisfied by Attys direction

8th Pls issue 27 March 1810, retd June 1810 unsatisfied by Attys directn

9th Pls. issue 20 Augt 1810, retd Sept 1810 not satisfied not having been committed to the Mshl.

4. Crowell Hatch (1737–1814), Roxbury merchant; Samuel Blagge, merchant, otherwise not identified; John Rose Greene (d. c. 1812); Chandler has not been identified.

5. A *pluries* is the third or more in a series of writs of execution; the second is called an *alias*.

10th Pls issue 6 Nov 1810, Retd Dec 1810, unsatisfied with assent of U. S. Atty—no further Exon vs Hatch

11th Pls. vs Blagge issue 13 Nov 1811, retd Dec 1811 unsatisfied pursuant to instructions from the U. S. Atty.

1807[6] Sept. 15.	Crowell Hatch	See other side	Exon Satisfied June 1808 & pd to Blake by Marshal
26.	Same	$609.24	Do do do
28.	Same	$653.80	Do do do
Decr. No. 30	Same	$729.45	9th Pls. retd. not Satisfied Decr. 1810. Costs pd to Mr. Blake by M[arsha]l satisfied by taking Greene's property which was replevied
1808 March 9.	Same	$577.01	Satisfied & pd to Mr. Blake by Ml. June 1809
1810 Decr. No. 137.	Same	$740.41	Pluries retd. Sept 1811, not satisfied 2d. Pluries issue Nov. 1811, & not retd.

AD. *U.S.* v. *H. Hatch, administrator*, USDC,DMass, September 1826.

DOCUMENT 3. ABSTRACT OF EXECUTIONS

Dec T[erm] 1807—Judgt vs Crowell Hatch

N. E. No. 30	for	1688.	prin[cipal]
		9.85	int to 12 Decr 1807
		1697.85	
		13.95	costs
		1711.80	

6. The rest of the document was written on the back. Note that the final entry indicates that the last execution issued in November 1811 was never returned by the marshal. Although this conflicts with the 10th

No. 29 same Judgt vs John R Greene
30 Do vs Saml Blagge.

Exons vs Hatch, Greene & Blagge issued 16 Dec. 1807, returned wholly unsatisfied by Attys direction March 1808.

Alias issue 4 April 1808, Retd June 1808, satisfied in part viz for the sum of $982.35,

viz 196.13 from sale of J. R. Greens right in equity in Real Estate
786 22 levied on C Hatchs effects
982.35
& not satisfied for $786.22 bal. due.

Same return on all 3 Exons & receipts written for Mr Blakes signature, but not signed by said Blake. Return dated 24 June 1808

Pl[urie]s issue 22 July 1808, retd Sept 1808, unsatisfied by Attys directn

2d Pls issue 4 Oct. 1808, retd Dec. 1808, unsatisfied by Attys directn

3d Pls issue 3 Jany 1809 retd March 1809, unsatisfied by Attys directn

4th Pls. issue 14 April 1809 retd June 1809, unsatisfied by Attys direction

5th Pls. issue 14 Aug 1809, retd Sept 1809, unsatisfied by Attys permission

6th Pls issue 14 Oct 1809, retd Dec. 1809 unsatisfied by Attys directn

7th Pls. issue 27 March 1810, retd June 1810 unsatisfied by Attys directn

8th Pls. issue 20 Augt 1810, retd Sept 1810 not having been committed to the Mshl, & unsatisfied

9th Pls. issued 6 Nov. 1810, retd Dec 1810, not satisfied. Goods of Greene having been taken, but afterwards replevied by a Sheriff. No further Exons vs. Hatch or Greene.

10th Pls. vs Blagge issue 13 Nov 1811, retd Decr 1811 unsatisfied pursuant to instructions from the U. S. Atty

AD. *U.S.* v. *H. Hatch, administrator*, USDC,DMass, September 1826.

DOCUMENT 4. PRETRIAL INVESTIGATION

Samuel Nicholson in Rep[levin] vs Saml. Prince[7]
Common Pleas, Norfolk, 4 Monday of *April 1811*. New Entries.

pluries mentioned in the abstract, the court accepted the position that the last execution had not been returned.

7. Nicholson has not been identified; this Prince may have been related to James Prince, the marshal, and may have been his deputy.

Ascertain from the clerk what was the final Judgment in that case. If in favor of the Officer, see whether execution issued, & what return made.[8]

Action entrd C. C. Pleas	April Term 1811
Demurred	Sept. Term 1811

but not entered in S. J Court

Judgt. for Costs for Deft in C Pleas taxed at $

<Amt. of Property Replevied $160.32>[9]

Then inquire of Mr Richardson, or ascertain from the clerk office, whether a suit was brought on the replevin bond, or the amount of it paid the Marshall or his Attorney in any manner.[10]

AD. MWalB.

DOCUMENT 5. PRETRIAL NOTES

2 Tuesday Sept 1807

1698.67	838.58 cts pd
15.62	sh[ould] be 883.58

1 Tues Decembr 1807

1697.85	1714.29
15.28	883.58
1713.13	820.71
875.71	
2588.84	1713.13
	982.35
	730.78

exon on *Sept* Judg, issued 11 Sept. 1807, never handed Marshall—
alias 6 Jan 1808 returnd March 1808 by Prince[11] not sat[isfied]—
pluries 4th April 1808—returned sat for 883.58, June 24. 1808.

Exon in Dec Judg issued 16 Decr 1807—returned by the Marshall, March 1808, wholly unsatisfied—alias issued 4 Apr 1808 returned by Marshall June 1808 sat[isfied] in part to wit for 196.13 collected of Greene, and 786.22, from *Hatch*

AD(DW). MWalB.

Prince demurred the case to the SJC, but never entered it there. This left standing the judgment in Nicholson's favor.

8. Bliss wrote these instructions.

9. The investigator wrote this paragraph.

10. Richardson has not been identified. Bliss added this further instruction.

11. James Prince (d. 1821), U.S. marshal.

DOCUMENT 6. PRETRIAL NOTES

James Prince debits Crowell Hatch as paid on executions as follows—
on an execution granted 2d. Tuesday September 1807

in full—	$ 609.24
on execution for J. R. Greens bonds 1—	898.56
" " " " " " 2	786.—
for sundry fees on executions	92.57
	$2366:37

Amount paid by Crowell Hatch for Greens bonds was 2999.59[12]
the 609.24 had nothing to do with it.
What was the sum for?

Amt paid for Green & fees is	1757.53
balance is	1242.06
ballance due in the clerks office	2999.59

on 1 <bond>	786.22
" 2 "	913.55
	1699:77
less for furniture of Green taken by [s]d marshall	196
	$1503.77 amount standing against C. Hatch
	1242. 6 ballance as above
	$ 261.71 which sum is not accounted for.[13]

AD(DW). MWalB.

DOCUMENT 7. PLEADINGS

U.S. District Court
United States vs Henry Hatch admor.

And the said Henry Hatch (as he is administrator de bonis non[14] of the goods and Estate which were of the said Crowell Hatch deceased, comes and defends &c when &c and saith that the United States their action aforesaid thereof against him in his said capacity ought not to have or maintain, because he saith that after the recovery of the said several judgments and before the decease of the said Crowell Hatch, & whilst writs of Execution of said several judgments, duly issued thereon & de-

12. This was the figure entered on Hatch's books.

13. DW appears to be constructing a case for whittling down the Hatch debt from the alleged $2570 to $262.

14. A person appointed by the probate court to administer the effects of a decedent which have not been included in an earlier administration. This plea, first authorized by statute in 1705 (4 and 5 Anne, c. 16), became known as the "plea of payment." Henry Hatch has not been further identified.

livered to the Marshall of the United States for said District to be served and executed according to law, were in the hands of said Marshall, he, the said Crowell, fully paid and satisfied to the plaintiffs and the said Marshall the amount of money due by virtue of said judgments—to wit, at Boston in the District aforesaid—and this, he the said Henry, in his said capacity, is ready to verify. Wherefore he prays judgment if the Plaintiffs their action aforesaid thereof against him ought to have and maintain)—by his Attorneys

D Webster & A Bliss

And the United States by their Attorney say that the said Crowell Hatch did not and never hath paid and satisfied to the said Plaintiffs or said Marshall the amount of money due by virtue of said judgments or either of them in manner and form as the said Henry Hatch the said administrator, hath above in his plea aforesaid alleged and this they pray may be inquired of by the Country

Geo: Blake US. Atty for Massts. Dist

And the said Henry Hatch in his said capacity doth the like by his Attorneys

D Webster & A Bliss

And for another & further plea in this behalf by leave of the Court for that purpose first had and obtained the said Henry saith that the plaintiffs their aforesaid action thereof against him in his said capacity ought not to have and maintain because he saith that after the recovery of the said several judgments namely in the day of November in the year of our Lord eighteen hundred and fourteen the said Crowell Hatch died intestate, at Roxbury in the County of Norfolk within the District aforesaid—and thereupon administration of the goods and estate which were of said Crowell was committed to one John Boit[15] who accepted said trust and then and there entered upon the performance of the duties thereof and continued in the due and faithful performance thereof till the day of December in the year of our Lord eighteen hundred and seventeen when the said Boit removed out of the Country and thereby vacated the said office, having during his performance of said duties collected all the goods, effects, and estate of said Crowell which came to his knowledge, and paid all the debts and outstanding claims which were presented to him for payment or which otherwise came to his knowledge;

15. Boit, Boston merchant. This second plea was known as a *plene administravit.* It alleged that the administrator had administered all the assets and that none remained out of which the plaintiff's claim could be satisfied.

and, moreover, duly rendered to the Judge of Probate and for granting Letters of administration for said County, accounts of his doings as such administrator as by law required; and, by order of said Judge, paid and distributed to and among the legal heirs of said Crowell all the residue of said goods and estate remaining after the paying of said debts and the funeral expenses and other expenses of said administration.

And the said Henry further saith that after the said Boit had ceased to be administrator as aforesaid, the said Judge of Probate committed to him, said Henry, administration de bonis non administratis of the said Crowell Hatch, deceased, to wit, on the day and year last aforesaid —and that he, said Henry, thereupon entered upon the performance of the duties of said administration, having given bonds and in all respects complied with the laws in that behalf made—and in pursuance thereof gave public notice of his appointment and request to all persons having demands on said estate to present the same for payment to him the said Henry—and said Henry further saith that on the day of July in the year of our Lord one thousand eight hundred and twenty four, having fully administered all and singular the goods and estate effects and credits which were of said Crowell Hatch, not before administered, and having paid all debts and claims which had come to his knowledge and collected all the goods effects and credits which had belonged to said intestate, & paid and distributed the residue thereof to and among the legal heirs of said deceased, he, the said Henry rendered to the said Judge of Probate the final accounts of his administration of said estate and his doings in said trust, which said accounts and doings the said Judge thereupon allowed and approved. And said Henry further saith that by reason of such administrations the estate of the said deceased was and now is spent and exhausted in his, said Henry's, hands, and no part thereof remained or now remains therein to be administered.

And said Henry further saith that said Boit and he, said Henry, or either of them, during all the time they were respectively administrators as aforesaid, till, and after, the rendering, by said Henry as aforesaid, of the final accounts of his said administration—namely, till the commencement of said action—had no notice—and none was given them by the plaintiffs of the said judgments mentioned in said writ and declaration, and that he, the said Henry, had no knowledge whatever of the existence thereof, nor reason to suspect the same were in force, and this he is ready to verify: wherefore he prays judgment if the plaintiffs their action aforesaid thereof against him ought to have or maintain by his said Attorneys.

D Webster & A Bliss

ADS. *U.S.* v. *H. Hatch, administrator*, USDC,DMass, September 1826. The plea is in Bliss's hand.

DOCUMENT 8. REPLICATION TO DEFENDANT'S SECOND PLEA

As to the second and last plea of him the said Henry, in his capacity of administrator as aforesaid, inasmuch as the said United States cannot deny the several matters therein contained; and in as much as the said Defendant hath not in, and by this said last mentioned plea and the matters therein contained denied the action of the said United States or the debt therein demanded, the said United States move for Judgement of Assets[16] which shall hereafter come to the said Defendant in his said capacity of Administrator as aforesaid

by Geo: Blake US. Atty for Massts Dist.

ADS. *U.S.* v. *H. Hatch, administrator*, USDC,DMass, September 1826.

In September 1825 the trial took place in district court. Over the objection of George Blake, Judge John Davis admitted two pieces of written evidence. The first was the waste book of Hatch's clerk. It contained an entry that Hatch had paid the marshal and had charged John Greene's father and partner, David Greene, $2999.59.[17] Presumably, this covered the judgment on the bonds. The second was a transcript of the waste book in the form of a memorandum in Hatch's account book (also referred to as his journal).[18] The admissibility of this documentary evidence would form one of the principal issues on appeal. Webster intended to use this evidence to build a case for the presumption of payment. During the course of the trial Webster sent Justice Story a note, printed below. Webster sought a summary of Story's instructions to the jury in an earlier case where Story had addressed the question of when a jury might presume settlements and payments. It is not known whether Story replied, but Webster convinced Judge Davis to instruct the jury that given the lapse of sixteen years and the other circumstances surrounding the case, unless the U.S. could offer a satisfactory explanation for the delay, the jury could presume payment of the debt. Blake ad-

16. When *plene administravit* was pleaded, the plaintiff could pray to have judgment of assets *quando acciderant* (when they shall come in). The plaintiff thereby admitted that the defendant had fully administered the estate to that time, but sought satisfaction from future assets.

17. A wastebook was a record book in which a clerk made rough entries in their order of occurrence prior to posting them in a journal. It was also called a blotter. DW apparently argued that posting the payment to David Greene's firm was the appropriate entry for payment of John Greene's business-related debts.

18. The account book, day book, or journal was a daily double entry record containing items from the waste. Entries in the journal were later posted in the ledger, the merchant's principal record, in two columns of debits and credits.

dressed the jury first. Webster made notes and comments on Blake's argument (Document 9) and then prepared notes for his own summation (Documents 10 and 11). After the attorneys had completed their arguments, Judge Davis commented on the evidence and instructed the jury (Document 12).

TO JOSEPH STORY

Sir friday Afternoon Sep. 17 [1825]

On the trial of a cause, now going on in the District Court, between U.S. & the Representative of the late Crowell Hatch, some reference has been made to your observations to the Jury, in the case of U.S. v Hoar, Admr. of Tuttle.[19] Mr. Blake's recollection & mine do not altogether agree, as to the purport of those remarks; and the object of this is to ask the use of your minutes, or a general abstract of them, if you have preserved them. Mr Blake's idea, if I understand it, is, that the ground, left to the Jury, on which to discharge Col Tuttle's surety, was his supposed robbery, or robbery & murder & loss of vouchers. My recollection is, that there was no competent proof, of *any loss* of vouchers, although some proof, not competent, I believe, was offered; & that it was left to the Jury, generally, on all the circumstances, to presume a settlement, & pay[men]t of any balance, if they could so presume. That this presumption might arise, among other things, from the lapse of time, which, however, was not great, in that case; from the circumstance of his being, then & afterwards, trusted with the disbursement of large sums of money; from the satisfaction of Govt. with his conduct to the day of his death; & also that he being dead, & dying suddenly, some allowance might be justly given to his defense, which it might not be entitled to, if he were alive, & had the power of shewing all things—&c &c &c

I will be greatly obliged to you, to excuse this trouble, & to furnish me, for the use of Judge Davis, with a brief sketch of the purport of your remarks, if you have now the means of giving it.[20] Most truly yrs.

Danl. Webster

I send the bearer with this, as the case will be given to the Jury tomorrow Morning.

ALS. MiU-C. Mistakenly attributed to 1819 in *Correspondence*, 1, Calendar:

19. *U.S.* v. *Samuel Hoar Jr., administrator*, 2 Mason 311 (1821). The U.S. sued a decedent's estate for a debt. Hoar raised several defenses based on state statutes of limitation and the plea of *plene administravit*. Story ruled in favor of the U.S. claim on the grounds that the laws of the states cannot regulate the rights of the national government. Mason's report deals only with a preliminary ruling on Hoar's demurrer and does not indicate the nature of Story's instructions.

20. No record of a reply has been found.

431. We have postulated 1825 on the basis of the internal evidence that the trial was in fact held in September, 1825. Per contra, however, September 17 was on a Saturday rather than Friday in that year.

DOCUMENT 9. NOTES ON GEORGE BLAKE'S JURY ARGUMENT

Mr. Blake

it must happen that claims are overlooked for years.
Hatch & Prince intimate.
non intercourse act[21] kept the Marshall busy from 1807 to 1814
Atty & Marshall, Judges & all too busy to attend to it.

duty to obtain paym[en]t from principal

☞ *What sort of evidence ought to be expected?*
☞ how cd. we have proved the 1.000 now admitted
☞ opportu[ni]ty to offer Mr Waters[22]
yet Waters wd. testify truly

Atty U. S. feels bound to defend the interest of Mr. Prince.
1. Evidence wd. be indorsement—(not always so).
James Prince [illegible] &c.
2. *a r[ec]eipt* from Prince
☞ *20 dollars not paid w[ithou]t a receipt!!*
might be a *promise* to indorse it [i.e. the execution]
☞ *There might have been a receipt*
receipts may be lost in <20> many yrs.
That is the ground of all the Statutes of limitation.

as to waste Book.
☞ Proper evidence wd. be D. Green's[23] testimony!!
There is no doubt D. G. was holden further
Journal too broad for the *waste.*
(this Mr Blake's construction abt. Journals & wastes)
Mr Hobb[24] *vanished* with Exons.

4. *other Exeons*
1. <April 14. 1809.> 551. & costs
April 4. 1808 609.24 cts
Judgt. Sepr. 1807—
June—
2. Exn 22. June, 1808

21. 2 U.S. Statutes at Large 528 (1809).
22. Not identified.
23. David Greene (d. 1812), father and partner of John Rose Greene.
24. Not identified.

☞ why was not the Exons renewed after 1810.

Ex[ecution]s kept alive till Decr. 1810—& then died—
on the pluries, on the second jugt, returned Decr. 1810.

Goods seized—Decr. 1810—agt. Jno. R. Greene.

Mr Frothingham
knows Ritch's hand writing, was Clerk of Hatch,[25]
why in his hand writing.
entry. 2,999.59
Exon issued on Jugt vs Jno. R. Green 729.45
13.63
returnable Decr. 1810.
Decr. 4. 1810

Mr Paltran[?][26]
knew Mr Hatch [17]90
extensive foreign business, great underwriter, wealthy, worth
300.000 Dlls.
Mr. Hatch died in 1814 Mr Prince died in 1821.
Mr Greene in 1812
Jno. R. Greene—1810 or 12

AD(DW). MWalB.

DOCUMENT 10. TRIAL NOTES

U. S. v Henry Hatch, Admr of Crowell Hatch
debt. on two judgts.
1 Sep. 1807 $1712.96
on bond
same judgt, same
time, [a]gt. Jno. R. Greene
& agt. Saml. Blagge
appeal in J. R. G's case
as [a]gt trustee, never presented.
2. Decr. 1807 $1711.80
Bond
Same also vs Blagg & Green
on the 1st. Judgt. various Exns issued.
on June 24. 1808, p[ar]t satisfaction

25. Possibly Samuel Frothingham (1787–1869), cashier of the Boston branch of the Bank of the United States; Ritch [Rich] has not been identified.

26. Not identified.

vid Exon, viz 883.58—
paid to G. B[lake]
on the 2. Judgt. various Exons
on June 24. 1808, pt. satisfaction.
vid Exn viz 196.13. from J. R. G.
786.22. from Hatch
982.35
this last sum not paid to G. B[lake]

AD(DW). MWalB.

DOCUMENT II. WEBSTER'S NOTES FOR JURY ARGUMENT

This suit is in the name of U. S. Certain *prerogatives* belong to U. S. But this suit is admitted to be principally for int[erest] of J[ames] P[rince]—ergo—not exactly right to insist on said certain prerogatives.

D. Greene & son—partners—nature of the origl. debt.

Suppose U. S. had sued Mr. Princes Admr, what defense could *he* make. Mr Hatch &c could prove payment—he had by his having been guilty, as to part—then easy to make him answerable for the whole.

The true object is to have justice done; & all ought to be willing for that.

One other remark, said Mr Prince & Mr Hatch friends, & Mr Prince *indulged* him, this not honorable to Mr. *Prince*, such indulgences hurt all parties.

Mr. Hatch a mere surety—all equity with him.

☞ Plea pay[men]t. We are not called on to *prove* it, *directly*. The real question is, may the Jury, from the circumstances in the case, legally presume payt. Is it allowed to them. If it be, it is equitable & just; & they will do it.

It is all equitable. H[atch] a surety—estate settled. It is just.

First. Because of the lapse of time. This has its effects, not as a strict bar, but as affording presumption of payt. In this view, it has the same effect agt. Govt. as agt. Individuals. Probably it ought to have more. The agents of Govt. have nothing to do but attend to these things. Their particular duty. If they had done it, Mr Hatch wd. have been much better off.

From what circumstances is payt. to be presumed.
1. & principally *From lapse of time.*

There are many cases where payt. is presumed from lapse of time alone

By 20 yrs it must be presumed.

It may be presumed, in a less time

1. Burroughs 434 — 1. Cowper 108–9 (16 yrs)
1. Term — 270 —
7. Jno. 556 —[27]

Nor is there any thing, nor any case, showing that this is not as strong agt. Govts as individuals.

There is as much reason for it, in one case as in the other. Now is it not to be presumed that the Officers of the U. S. did their duty with ordinary diligence? It is the sworn duty of the Atty to sue. It is the duty of the Marshall to collect.

There has always been a Marshall, what has *hindered looking this up for 17. yrs?* We presume he did.

But there are many other circumstances, beside the mere lapse of time.

1. Mr. Hatch always solvent—money to be had any day—why not call.
here it rested, 4 or 5 yrs, till Jno. R. Greene died—say, abt. 1811 or 1812, *why not call then*—but no call. Mr Hatch lived till 1814. Still never called on.

2. In 1814, Mr Hatch died, his estate to be *settld*, this was an *awaking circumstance*. It must have excited Mr Prince's attention. *Yet he did not call.* All that can be said is, *that he had forgot it. Is it not as likely that he remembered the payt.?*

3. All the parties lived here. Mr Prince knew of Mr Hatch's death.

4. In 1817, H[enry] H[atch] appeared in [18]17, why not call then?

27. In *Rex* v. *Stephens*, 1 Burrows 434 (1757), the court refused to grant a *quo warranto* for an act that occurred twenty-nine years earlier, even though no statute of limitations applied. In *Mayor of Kingston upon Hull* v. *Horner*, 1 Cowper 102 (1774), Lord Mansfield (at pp. 108–109) distinguished passage of time as a bar from passage of time as evidence on which a jury might decide that a debt had been discharged. In the latter case no specific period of time need have passed. *Oswald et al.* v. *Legh*, 1 Term Reports 270 (1786), involved a suit on a nineteen-year-old bond. Justice Buller stated that inaction for twenty years raised a legal presumption that the bond had been satisfied. In *Oswald*, therefore, the lapse of time did not raise a legal presumption but could be considered by the jury as evidence of payment. *Thompson* v. *Skinner*, 7 Johnson (N.Y.) 556 (1811), held that after twenty years, no judicial proceeding should be set aside for irregularity.

Mr. Prince lived till 1821—& for this whole period, with the Exon in his desk—*he never called.*
Now, when Mr Hatch's estate settld, Mr Prince if he had had the debt, wd. fear it would be barred—generally thought so.

5. Three yrs after Mr Prince's death—10 yrs after Mr Hatch's death —12 after D. Greene—& 12 after Jno. R.—*U. S. come forth.*

☞ *It is admitted that no* [notice?] *whatever was given of this till 1824, ten years under Administration.* Now, I say, that this length of time, with these circumstances, are enough to presume payt. unless U. S. can give *some reason.*

They give no reason.
They do not shew that H. requested *time*—or that he was *unable*—or *harrassed*—he died rich—always able.

6. A still stranger circumstance—Exons kept alive till the levy on Jno. R. G. *then all suffered to die. vid Abstract*[28]

7. Mr Hatch's subsequent credit at the Custom House.

8. It is quite clear that the Marshall was guilty of negligence—& a defalcation—as to the 9 hund[red] & odd Dollars.
Did he forget to pay this to U. S.? or did he forget also that the residue had been paid

9. Nor ought it to prejudice Deft that he has not receipt to produce. *He may well not be able to find it.* All Stat[ute]s of Limitation rest on this idea, that the party may have paid, & lost his proof.

which is most likely, that a man shd. pay & lose his proof, or that a creditor should forbear for 20 years to collect a debt under his nose, especially where Officers are *bound* by law & their oaths to collect—consider this case, in that view. Mr H being dead ten yrs, & [under?] administration. We are calld on to prove facts *by the dead*—this shews that the claims ought [not] now to be made.

10. It is certain that *no notice* was ever given.

11. Jno. R. Greene may have paid it. Thus far I have only stated *facts*, about which there is no dispute—viz—

That it is now 18 yrs since judgt was recovered.

That Crowell Hatch has been dead	11 yrs
D Creen	12
Jno. R. G	11
J. Prince	4

28. See Documents 2 and 3, above.

That all the parties lived near, & knew one another.
That the estate has been 10 yrs open.
That it is now closed, & all the effects distributed.
That Mr. Prince never called for this money.
That Mr H. was always able to pay it.
That Mr P. has been shewn guilty of negligence, in relation to this.
That he ceased to renew Exeons, when we say the last payt. was made.
That Mr. Hatch had credit at the Custom House.

Then, secondly, there are other circumstances, about which there may be questions.

1. The payt. of 2999.59 June 4. 1808
Was this money paid?—no one can doubt it. Books prove it. And day Book & Waste prove it to have [been] on the 24. The Court had admitted the evidence, & it proves the point.

Then, is <proved that> probable that this money was applied to this debt?

It is probable, & they do not shew it otherwise applied

They attempt to shew it, in two ways—viz 2. Exeons. *As to first it may be* so—& may not—*not proved.* no matter, that other particulars do not appear—genl charges to Greene

As to 2. *cannot be so.*
1. Because sums do not agree.
2. Because time does not agree.
☞ *It is certain this payt. was made on the 24.*

Why was it not indorsed? I can conjecture—just half paid, rest in nature of a deposite[29]—& never applied.

Lastly as to the seizure of Jno. R.'s property—law of that case—fairly payt. of the 350 Dlls—*but it also tends to prove all paid,* it supports the whole hypothesis.

What more can or could defdt prove?

Mr Blake's mode of accounting—
62 *Dlls* to *be* made out
mistake—of Mr Prince—relieves him
recd. 32 Dlls <of Jno. R. G.>
paid by Hatch—as costs

29. DW is suggesting that Prince treated half the money paid as a bailment, and that he never returned it to Hatch or paid it into the court.

in <Marshalls>
20.28—

AD(DW). MWalB.

DOCUMENT 12. NOTES ON JUDGE'S COMMENTS

Judge Davis—there ought to be full & satisfactory evidence of payment as to part there is no doubt.
balance 1623.08 cts dols &c—with interest
deduct levy on J. R. Greene's furniture
as to this balance, Dft. relies on *presumption* from circumstances.

1. The Entry in Dft's books—great endulgence to allow admission of such entry—common course would be to see money endorsed on the exon —or take a receipt. This sum plfs attempt to account for—
   2932 accounted for on
   2999 [tr?]

2. March 1809, 29th, check—they consider may be payment—Jury to consider whether this not a sum *loaned* or paid for loan

Great Ground for observations made by Dft's counsel.

Some reasonable account ought to be given for delay—1. urgency of business—2. favor & friendship of Prince for Hatch—Mr Prince might on this a/c have spared him—no other way to account for it. If so, it was culpable—& could exist no longer than Mr. Prince lived. With regard to levy on J. R. G.'s goods, have doubts whether it ought to be allowed as extinguishment of debt.

AD. MWalB.

The jury returned a verdict in favor of Henry Hatch. Blake immediately moved for a new trial and two days later filed his written motion (Document 13). He enumerated four errors committed by the court: two involved the written evidence, the third, the admission of testimony bearing on the probability that the debt had been paid, and the fourth, the instruction that allowed the jury to infer payment. Nearly two weeks later the attorneys argued the motion. Webster took careful notes of Blake's presentation (Document 14). Blake had not quite concluded when the court adjourned. Since it was Saturday, the court would not reconvene until Monday. Webster may have spent the time preparing his own argument (Documents 15 and 16). Many of the cases cited by Blake appeared in marginal notes in Nathan Dane's *Abridgment*. Webster, too, probably began his preparation by perusing Dane's discussion of precedents. Ironically, Webster now found himself on the other side of an issue he had previously argued in 1819 in *Welsh* v. *Barrett* (see below).

It was Blake who had to attack the liberal New England rule on admitting written evidence.

On Monday Blake completed his argument (Documents 17 and 18). Then, apparently, Bliss spoke, followed by Webster. Only a fragment of Webster's argument, in which he stood on the New England rule, remains (Document 19). The court did not reach a decision that term. Instead, it carried the case from term to term. Finally, a year later, in September 1826, the court denied Blake's motion. Webster had won.

DOCUMENT 13. MOTION FOR NEW TRIAL

United States of America
Masstts. District ss. [September 19, 1825]

District Court of U States for said District Septr. Term 1825.

And now after the return of the Verdict in favor of the Defendant, upon the issue in fact, to wit, on this seventeenth day of September in the year 1825, being the same day as the rendition thereof, the Attorney of the United States for said District, being present here in Court, moves the Court that said Verdict may be set aside, and a new trial upon said issue awarded for the following reasons Viz

Ist Because the Judge, although the same was objected to by the said Attorney of the United States, did admit, on the part of the Defendant, a certain item of charge contained in a certain Book of accounts commonly called a Waste Book, which had been kept by a deceased clerk of Crowel Hatch the deceased Debtor refered to in the declaration, purporting to be a charge of a sum of money being the sum of 2999 Dollars & 59 cents, to James Prince on account of David Green, on the 24th. of June 1808, as evidence to the Jury, that the said sum of money had actually been paid at that time, to James Prince Esqr deceased, late Marshall of said District, & in part satisfaction of the debt sued for in the writ, although the said Charge in said Waste Book contained no reference whatsoever to the debt aforesaid; which said evidence, the said Attorney saith, was wholly illegal & inadmissible.

II. Because the Judge did also, admit in evidence, at the trial, on the part of the Defendant, although the same was duly objected to by the Attorney for the United States, a certain memorandum in writing contained in a certain Book of accounts, of the said Crowell Hatch deceased, commonly called a Journal, purporting to be a transcript from the beforementioned Waste Book, of the same charge of cash paid to James Prince, as aforementioned, on account of David Green, although the statement thereof in said last mentioned Book speaks of said payment to James Prince, as having been made on "*account of Bonds*" whereas there was no reference whatever in the Charge Contained in the Waste Book, specifying the purpose or object to which said payment of money was intended to be applied. Which said last mentioned Book of accounts, for the purposes aforesaid, the said Attorney of the United States doth say, was wholly inadmissible in evidence.

III. For that, whereas the debt demanded in the action was founded on certain Judgements rendered against the said Crowell Hatch the Debtor mentioned in the declaration, in the District Court of the United States, & the evidence of said debt consisted, therefore, of the Records of said Court, so that the payment or discharge of said debt, cou[l]d not, by Law, otherwise, be proved, than by Defendants producing in evidence, some release or discharge of equal weight & solemnity, nevertheless the said Judge, at the trial, although the Attorney of the United States, did then, and there, duly Object thereto, did permit several witnesses to be sworn, on the part of the Defendant, & to testify to the Jury, as to various circumstances, not being matters of record or specialties of any kind, for the purpose of shewing the probability that the debt sued for had been paid, & satisfied. Which permission, the said Attorney of the United States, contends was against Law.

IV. Because the said Judge, in summing up the evidence to the Jury, did instruct them that, inasmuch as sixteen years & a half had elapsed since the rendition of said Judgements or any demand whatever had been made by the United States or any of its Officers, upon the said Crowell Hatch, in his life time, or his legal Representatives since his decease, from the time of the rendition of the several Judgements refered to in the declaration, the said Jury might, if they saw fit, infer from that circumstance, connected with other circumstances which had appeared in evidence at the trial that the debt aforesaid had been paid unless the United States should give some satisfactory explanation of the delay; which said instruction the said Attorney of the United States insists, was wrong & contrary to law.

Geo: Blake U. S. Atty for Mass Dist

ADS. *U.S.* v. *H. Hatch, administrator,* USDC,DMass, September 1826.

DOCUMENT 14. NOTES ON BLAKE'S ARGUMENT

U.S. vs. Hatch *Octor 1. 1825*

On motion for new Trial

Mr. Blake reads the *motion*—& remodels his fourth reason for new trial[30]

30. See Document 13, above.

—thinks shall be able to shew *improper evidence* was admitted, & then that a *misdirection*

1st. complains of *Day-book*.

☞ Cowp. 593[31]—where improper evidence is admitted, however slight, verdict must be set aside.

☞ Practice of admitting books, even in proof of delivery of goods, peculiar in New England, has grown up in Massachusetts—at common law no such evidence is *known*

4 *Mass* 457[32]—book had not been kept in common and ordinary mode. "This mode of proof ought not to be extended by any new precedent"—"*wholly improper to prove payment of cash*"

6. Term Rep. 66[33]

3. *Dane's abridgment*[34]—states usage, not proof of cash exceeding sum of 6.67 cts. (Judge Davis says 40s was the old sum) reads whole *title*

12 Johns 461[35]—Dane 318.

Swifts ev. 81. 91—3. Day Rep. 37—4. Mass. 453

31. *Goodright ex dem. Stevens* v. *Moss et al.*, 2 Cowper 591 (1777). Mansfield actually stated the converse: if the trial court rejected any evidence that ought to have been admitted, there must be a new trial.

32. In *Prince, administratrix* v. *Smith*, 4 Mass. 454 (1808), the court reluctantly upheld the New England practice of allowing the admission of a plaintiff's account book to prove the sale of goods or performance of work. The court restricted such evidence to instances where the entries clearly had been made in the course of business. Although in the *Prince* case the memorandum (an abstract) offered in evidence was not of such a routine character, the court ruled that if the original books had been destroyed, a transcript of the memorandum might be admitted if the plaintiff proved that the entries had been drawn from the original accounts. The quotations in the text are substantially correct. The second one refers to the second point of the *Prince* case: a record of the entry could not be used to prove an allegation of a payment to a third party outside the scope of the decedent's everyday business.

33. In *Griffiths* v. *Brome*, 6 Term Reports 66 (1794), the court ruled that evidence of conduct could not be introduced to prove that the defendant had subsequently promised to compensate the plaintiff where no proof existed of an original promise.

34. Nathan Dane, *A General Abridgment and Digest of American Law* (9 vols., Boston 1823–1829), 3: 318–323. Chapter 81 covered the use of written records as evidence; DW seems concerned with article 4, books of account. Dane discusses the Massachusetts rule that allows introduction of book evidence of goods, services, and the payment of sums of money less than $6.67. Most of the cases cited by DW in his argument appear in this section of Dane.

35. *Vosburgh* v. *Thayer*, 12 Johnson (N.Y.) 461 (1805) held that where there are regular dealings between a butcher and a customer, and it is proved that the butcher kept honest books, his account books are admissible, although he had no clerk. The books cannot serve as proof of money lent but only to support a suit for goods or services.

Warren vs Grenville (2. Strange 1129)—1. Phil. 214)
8 John 211 10 East 109[36]—as to evidence of sum in Day-book.

The journal is objectionable as not being the original Entry—& moreover, did not conform to the *waste*
2 Mass. Rep. 569 Prince Ex vs Swett[37]

Mr G[eorge Blake] goes into a discourse about presumption from lapse of time, intimates that as no *bar* exists against a demand of the Governt so no *presumption* ought to arise against them from mere lapse of time.

☞ This is saying in other words that rules of evidence, as applied to questions in which U. S. are concerned are to be *reversed,* and violence committed on the understandings of mankind.

Why not be affecte[d] by presumption from lapse of time, as well as presumption from the circumstances.

May not a debt of the United States be *paid*? & without a *discharge*? Is not the *thing possible* & if possible, may it not be proved—and if it may be proved, why should it not be proved as any other fact is *proved,* & by the same rules of evidence as apply to other questions.

AD(DW). MWalB.

36. Zephaniah Swift, *A Digest of the Law of Evidence* (Hartford, 1810), pp. 81–91, discusses the instances where written evidence may be admitted under an exception to the general rule barring the evidence of the interested party. DW must have meant *Hinsdale* v. *Eeles*, 3 Day (Conn.) 377 (1820), where the court allowed the plaintiff to show the jury the defendant's receipt, in order to prove that the defendant had promised to repay the money. *Warren* v. *Greenville*, 2 Strange 1129 (1739), was a land title case in which the court used the next best evidence rule to admit a deceased attorney's debt book to prove that he had handled a common recovery for the plaintiff. Samuel March Phillipps, *A Treatise on the Law of Evidence*, 6th ed. (2 vols., London, 1824), 1: 243, discusses declarations against interest as an exception to the hearsay rule. In *Case* v. *Potter*, 8 Johnson (N.Y.) 211 (1811), although the court refused to admit an intestate's book entries as conclusive proof of a debt, it did allow the jury to consider it as part of plaintiff-administrator's entire case. *Higham* v. *Ridgway*, 10 East 109 (1808), involved an entry by a male midwife in a book of delivery stating his charges paid. The court allowed the jury to see the book as evidence of the age of the child.

37. In *Prince's executrix* v. *Swett*, 2 Mass. 569 (1793), the court rejected the offer of the testator's day book, since it appeared that the entries had been transferred to the ledger. The day book, therefore, was not the best evidence of the debt, since it would not contain possible credits to the defendant's accounts. Moreover, no proof had been offered that the ledger was unavailable.

DOCUMENT 15. NOTES FOR ORAL ARGUMENT

—it is obvious that the evidence bore on an admitted fact.

The objections seem to be two.

1. To the manner of the entry in the waste, & Journal, & the use of the Ledger.

   ☞ these are subjects of remark to the Jury

2. The general objection to the use of the Books at all.

examine the cases—read fully Ld. Hardwicke[38]

2. Vesey 42. *same point*
   reasoning of the Court.
Buller 282. *Evans* v Lake
   Smartle v Williams.
      money paid
Welsh v Barrett—
this very case; put to them
8 Wheaton 336[39]

Peake, 21. 24—
1 Salkeld 285 Price v. Torrington
   the Brewer's case—
      coram Holt
same case in Ld. Raymond

2. Salkeld 689. Pitman v. Madox
      Tailors bill
   same case, in principle.
3. *Stra[n]ge 1129, note,* (Nolan's Ed:)
4. *Lafebure v Wordon, 2. Vesey. 54.*
   Belt[40]—

38. Philip Yorke, Earl of Hardwicke (1690–1764), chief justice, King's Bench (1732/3–1736/7), lord chancellor (1736/7–1764). DW refers to the two cases in 2 Vesey's Reports; see notes 39 and 40, below.

39. In *Glynn* v. *Bank of England*, 2 Vesey 42 (1750), Lord Hardwicke rejected the offer of a list of notes to prove lost promissory notes in a chancery proceeding. He did, however, discuss the use of such secondhand evidence in cases at law; and indicated that the passage of time might allow a man to make evidence for himself. On pp. 282–283 Buller discusses the subject of when parties can use written evidence. In *Evans* v. *Lake*, Buller's Nisi Prius 282 (1738), the court admitted the plaintiff's account to prove that the defendant had purchased stock in trust for him. The *Williams* case (1751) held a dead scrivener's book of accounts to be good evidence of the payment of a mortgage. For *Welsh* v. *Barrett*, see pp. 115–118, below. In *Nicholls* v. *Webb*, 8 Wheaton 326 (1823), Justice Story wrote in support of the rule that an official's memorandum made in the ordinary course of duty should be admissible.

40. Thomas Peake, *A Compendium of the Law of Evidence*, from the 3d London ed., with additions (Fredericktown, Md., 1809), pp. 20–25. These pages deal with the role of presumption in the law of evidence. Peake distinguished irrebuttable presumptions from other presumptions which might be rebutted by slight evidence to the contrary. This paralleled Mansfield's distinction between length of time as a bar and as evidence for the jury. In *Price* v. *The Earl of Torrington* (1704), the court accepted the account book entries of a deceased deliveryman; in *Pitman* v. *Maddox* (1699), the court received a shop-book as evidence of a dead clerk's handwriting. DW had examined these cases six years earlier in

2. point—plea of payment—not good to be proved in this way.
Probable ancient—
Statute of Anne. universal practice.
Mr Blake calld for receipt
☞ *a record may be presumed*—Jury must presume a release upon record.
Cowper 102. 214.
☞ read the two cases in Cowper.[41]
as to the length of time—not long enough—two years after Prince's death.
☞ *all this was commentary to the Jury*
I argued this circumstance—Mr. B[lake] agt. it.
said to be difficult to give explanation
time is *essentially* evidence
suppose one of us to be presented with *a bill.*
—*Judge Story.*
☞ *The true inquiry is—has there been more than ordinary delay*
take this first judgt. ordinarily it wd. be paid in Decr. 1807—partly paid in June 8.
—as to presumption agt. U. S. *Time nothing to do.*
Cannot be argued upon. 4 Mass 528. *Stoughton vs Baker*,[42] no laches imputed to Govt.—& agt it no time runs—case of a water right.
length of time in all cases, necessarily bears.
—suppose a case of an *old* murder, or *old smuggling.*
In all these post office cases, no pretense of payment.

Welsh v. *Barrett*, see pp. 117–118, below. "[C]oram Holt" means in the presence of Lord Holt, chief justice of the King's Bench, who heard both *Price* and *Pitman*. The *Price* case is also in 2 Raymond 873. In *Warren* v. *Greenville*, 2 Strange 1129 (1739), the reporter delineated four classes where private records could be admitted as evidence, see p. 117, n. 9 below. In *Lefebure* v. *Wordon*, 2 Vesey 54 (1750), Lord Hardwicke ruled that a master should examine, as evidence of a claim, a decedent's entry in his book of accounts.

41. In an action of debt on a judgment, the statute 4 & 5 Anne, c. 16 (1705) authorized the defendant to plead payment of the judgment. For *Mayor of Kingston upon Hull* v. *Horner*, see n. 27 above. That decision reiterated the distinction between the passage of time as a bar and the passage of time as evidence for the jury. *Eldridge* v. *Knott et al.*, 2 Cowper 214 (1774), held that mere length of time (less than the statute of limitations) was not sufficient by itself to presume a release or extinguishment of a quit rent.

42. *Inhabitants of Stoughton* v. *Baker*, 4 Mass. 521 (1808). In the course of an opinion dealing with the responsibilities of mill dam owners and public rights to river fishery, Chief Justice Theophilus Parsons (at p. 528) stated that although a franchise could be lost by non-user, public neglect would not extinguish a dam owner's obligation to erect a fishway. Neither time nor laches ran against the government.

Locke's case[43] nothing to do with the lapse of time.
on this
Mr Bliss. Tidd. 20. 21. Peake 21. 24.
Precedents—Story—294
Comyn Dig. 639 title Pleader 2. W. 13.
☞ *1 Strange* 638. Flower v Ld Bolingbroke
very strong case
1 Campbell 217.[44]
vid Mr Bliss remark on Mr Blakes point[45]

AD(DW). MWalB.

DOCUMENT 16. NOTES FOR ORAL ARGUMENT

I because entry contains no reference to the judgments

see facts—

1. It appeared that debt was the proper debt of David Greene & Son—that Hatch was surety, had been sued[.] Ex[ecuti]on was then [sued] out & in the hands of James Prince, Marshall

2 further that on the same day at date of this Entry—a payment in part, if not the whole, of this debt was made by Hatch to Prince. This appeared by Prince's endorsement on the exon.
Now—object of Dft was to shew that more money had been paid to Prince than he had end[orse]d[;] as one circumstance tending, with others to make out this point Dft. produced the books of Hatch.

43. In *Locke, in error*, v. *Postmaster General of the U.S.*, 3 Mason 446 (1824), Justice Story held that a delay by the postmaster general in carrying out his duty would not discharge a surety on a postmaster's bond.

44. William Tidd, *The Practice of the Court of King's Bench in Personal Actions*, 3rd ed. (2 vols., London, 1803), 1: 20–21, discusses the use of presumption in actions of debt on a bond; Peake is discussed at n. 40, above; Joseph Story, *Pleadings in Civil Actions* (Salem, 1805), p. 294, sets forth a sample plea of payment; John Comyns, *A Digest of the Laws of England*, 5th ed. (8 vols., London, 1822), 6: 364–403. Section 2 W 13 (p. 376) illustrates pleadings in debt on a judgment and reiterates the position that in this action the defendant may plead payment in bar of the action. In *Flower* v. *Bolingbroke*, 1 Strange 639 (1727), the court upheld a presumption that a judgment recovered twenty years earlier had been satisfied. In *Willaume* v. *Gorges*, 1 Campbell 217 (1808), the court held that the presumption of payment of a judgment from lapse of time could not be rebutted by evidence proving that the defendant had been insolvent at the time the court handed down the judgment.

45. There is no record of what Bliss said.

Hatch was dead—both the persons composing the firm of D G & son were dead[.] Prince was dead—& Rich, who was H's book-keeper at the time was dead. The Books produced were a waste-book, journal & ledger The Entry in the *waste* was as follows—"Boston, June 24, 1808 David Green Dr To cash paid James Prince. 2999.59"

Entry in *Journal* as follows—"Boston June 24 1808. Sundry accounts Dr David Greene, paid James Prince for bonds 2999.59."

Entry in *Ledger* as follows—in the account of *D. Greene*, "1808 Jun. 24. To cash 2999.56."

all these books in regular form as kept by good merchants nor was there any appearance or intimation that they had been fabricated or altered to suit the present purpose.
Proof was offered that these entries were in the handwriting of *Rich*.

Under these circumstances, connected with the death of parties & the lapse of time Court permitted these books to go to the Jury—to have such weight, with other facts and inferences, as the Jury might think them entitled to, to make out the general fact, or presumption of payment.
Peake 21 where mark[ed] & 24
Price vs Torrington, 1. Salk. 285
Pitman vs *Madox*, Salk. 2. 689—whole case
2. Strange. 1129. Nolan's note—
Lefebre vs Worden (2.Vez: 54 as *marked*)—Belt Sub. 270
(*Glyn* vs *Bank. Eng.* 42. Vez 2)
Buller (282—) —Evans vs Lake
Welsh vs Barrett 15. Mass. Rep. 380
Nichols vs Webb 8 Wheaton 336

2. that circumstances not matters of rec[or]d were admitted

1. Tidd 20. 21—(Willaume vs Georges 1. Camp. 217)
Peake—21 & 24
1. Strange. 638
Story's pleadings 294
Com. Dig. 639—657[46]

12 Veazy 261. Hilary vs Waller
as to presumptions
ss. 6 Wheaton, Prevost vs Gratz[47]

AD(DW). MWalB.

46. All these cases are discussed in the footnotes to the preceding document.

47. In *Hillary* v. *Waller*, 12 Vesey

DOCUMENT 17. NOTES OF BLAKE'S ARGUMENT

Monday— [October 3, 1825]

—question whether circumstances *without discharge* can be given in evidence—*Mr. Parsons*, Mr *Prescott* & Thacher[48]

Jacob's Dictionary. Tit[le] *Judgt*—relates to confession—

paymt. Satisfaction—must be entered of *record*

Lilly's abridgement—same[49]—

judgment differs from bond—higher security—Powell on contracts 423—Co. Lit. 250[50]—whole world accessible to *the record*

differs as to *lien* on *real estate*.

admits judgment may be affected by length of time may be presumed. but then Jury ought to have been instructed to *presume* a release by *record*.

4. as to presumption—again—*Time*, as to the U. S. has nothing to do, no time runs against it, or laches imputed t[o it]

4. Mass. 508 Stoughton vs Baker—against Govt no time runs. This a water privilege

[Post office cases, *U. S.* vs *Locke* another in Gazette.]

AD. *U.S.* v. *H. Hatch, administrator*, USDC,DMass, September 1826.

Jr. 239 (1806), the court made two points: (1) title to land could be presumed from adverse possession, and (2) a bond on which no interest had been paid for twenty years could be presumed to have been satisfied. *Prevost* v. *Gratz*, 6 Wheaton 481 (1821), a case argued by DW, held that length of time (in that case forty years) plus death of all the parties supported the presumption that a trust had been discharged.

48. George Thacher (1754–1824; Harvard 1776), Massachusetts lawler and judge, studied with Shearjahub Bourne, state legislator, U.S. representative (1789–1801), judge, MassSJC (1801–1824).

49. Giles Jacob, *The Law Dictionary*, 1st Am. ed. (6 vols., New York and Philadelphia, 1811), see "Judgment," 3: 551–563; "Payment," 5: 111–112; "Satisfaction," 6: 10. John Lilly, *The Practical Register: or a General Abridgement of the Law*, 2nd ed. (2 vols., London, 1745), 2: 495–496, deals with "satisfaction" and notes that after a defendant pays a judgment the plaintiff is supposed to acknowledge satisfaction on the record. Blake seems to be citing these authorities for two purposes: (1) although payment may be pleaded in an action of debt on a judgment, such payment is not satisfaction of the judgment unless entered on the record, and (2) since the U.S. never acknowledged payment, DW's case for the presumption of payment is rebutted.

50. John Joseph Powell, *Essay upon the Law of Contracts and Agreements*, 3rd ed. (2 vols., London, 1790), 1: 423. In a chapter on the recission of contracts, Powell commented that a contract is discharged when one party recovers judgment on it. If the plaintiff neglects to take out an execution, he cannot, thereafter, sue on the same contract a second time. Edward Coke, *A Commentarie upon Littleton* (Lon-

DOCUMENT 18. NOTES OF BLAKE'S AND BLISS'S ARGUMENTS

[October 3, 1825]

Mr Blake in continuation—has done with the Books—can a judgt be discharged, but by entry of satisfaction on the record. *4 D. & E. 669*[51]
Jacob's Dictionary
"Judgt."—last sentence—when satisfied, satisfaction to be acknowledged by party in Court
"Satisfaction", in case of Judgt entered of Record cites—

2. Lilly 495. "Payt."—"money in Court."
Mr. Bliss
2. questions
1. admission of evidence
2. admission of circumstance to found presumption

AD(DWp). *U.S.* v. *H. Hatch, administrator*, USDC,DMass, September 1826.

DOCUMENT 19. NOTES OF WEBSTER'S ARGUMENT

[October 3, 1825]

Mr. Webster. If evidence was irregular, as fact was admitted, new trial ought not to be granted
obj[ection] two fold. First, in the motion for
new [trial] the objection is not so
much to the *admissibility* of the Book as to the
nature of the Entry

The limitation of rule as to proof of money by entries in book, contended for by Dis[trict] Atty. is a limitation of the New England doctrine —which he would impress upon the Common Law—we stand on the Common Law which knows of no such limitation

AD. MWalB.

2: COURTROOM STRATEGY AND THE EXAMINATION OF A WITNESS: THE OLIVER SMITH WILL CASE

Late in his career Webster was asked to assist the beneficiaries in a contest over a will. Oliver Smith, a western Massachusetts farmer and

---

don, 1628); page 250.b. deals with the preservation of certain claims (Littleton, sect. 414).

51. *Stead et al.* v. *Heaton et al.*, 4 Durnford & East 669 (1792), involved a dispute between two townships over contribution to the parish church; the court admitted past entries of receipts as evidence of (1) the fact of payment, and (2) the rate of contribution.

bachelor, had died in 1845 in possession of property worth almost $400,000. In his will he gave his farm to his nephew, several small legacies to his nieces, and left the remainder in trust for disposition to the American Colonization Society, to an agricultural school to be founded in Smith's name, and for poor relief in the surrounding towns. Smith's heirs-at-law (his nephews and nieces) decided to contest the will on two grounds: (1) Smith's sanity, and (2) the mental competency of one of the witnesses to the will. When the heirs lost the first round in probate court, they appealed to the MassSJC, but only on the second ground. The towns that stood to gain from Smith's generosity undertook the defense of the will. One of them, probably Northampton, retained Webster. In a letter of March 1847, printed below, Webster sought the assistance of Lemuel Shaw, then MassSJC chief justice, in getting the trial date delayed. After consulting with his co-counsel in Boston in June 1847, Webster journeyed to Northampton.[1]

The trial began on a sultry July day. The heirs had retained Rufus Choate and two local lawyers to press their case. Choate intended to nullify the will by proving that one of the witnesses, Theophilus Parsons Phelps, had been insane at the time Smith signed it. The Massachusetts statute required three witnesses "competent" at the time of attestation to prove a will. If the jury found Phelps incompetent, the will would fail and the court would order Smith's estate administered in accordance with the intestacy statute.

Although Phelps had a history of mental instability both before and after he witnessed the will, he claimed to have been sane during that period.[2] Webster feared that the other side would use their cross-examination of Phelps to reveal his insanity and thereby discredit his testimony. Faced with this problem, Webster decided to undercut the opposition by directly examining Phelps on his psychiatric problems. If Webster could draw forth lucid and sincere testimony on this subject, the jury might be willing to decide that at the time Phelps witnessed the will, he had been competent. His history of instability both before and after that moment would become irrelevant. Webster's strategy succeed-

1. "We shall have a long cause, & I prescribe to myself patience, moderation, & coolness. We begin tomorrow." DW to Daniel Fletcher Webster, July 5, 1847, mDW 28066; *W & S*, 16: 487.

2. The case also illuminates the diagnosis and treatment of the mentally ill in antebellum America. There is a voluminous literature on this subject. For example, see Norman Dain, *Concepts of Insanity in the United States, 1789–1865* (New Brunswick, N.J., 1964); Gerald N. Grob, *The State and the Mentally Ill: Worcester State Hospital in Massachusetts, 1830–1920* (Chapel Hill, N.C., 1966); and David J. Rothman, *The Discovery of the Asylum: Social Order and Disorder in the New Republic* (Boston, 1971).

ed. Under his questioning (Document 20), Phelps gave a candid account of his mental history. Opposing counsel cross-examined Phelps but could not shake his composure or recollection of the events surrounding Smith's will. That evening Webster wrote a long letter, printed below, in which he recounted his success.

The following day, Choate and his fellow counsel presented their evidence of Phelps's insanity. Webster then recalled several of his witnesses to establish the periods of lucidity in Phelps's past. Both sides then presented expert medical testimony on the subject of insanity. Two of the doctors seemed to be on Webster's side, one hedged, and the fourth stated his belief that Phelps had been insane all along. On Thursday, July 8th, the attorneys summed up their cases. Choate addressed the jury for three hours. He appealed to their sense of family not to allow all of Smith's property to go to charity. He then addressed the crux of the case: the meaning of the term "competent witness." Here Choate argued that the jury must consider the mental ability of the proffered witness, not merely his presence at the signing. He pointed out that Phelps's continuing insanity had never been disproved and that all the causes for his condition had been present when he attested the will.

When Choate had finished, Webster rose and spoke for two hours. He stressed Smith's decision to give his property to charity and the heirs' obvious disappointment. But, he admonished the jury, they must distinguish between rights and expectations. Their task was to decide the question of attestation, not whether the will was a good or bad one. He then discussed the question of competency (Document 21).

When Webster finished that afternoon, Judge Samuel Sumner Wilde charged the jury. He told them that the sole issue was Phelps's competency. He instructed them that if they believed Phelps might have been allowed to testify in court immediately after the attestation, the law considered him a competent witness. The jury retired for one hour, and then returned a verdict confirming the will.

TO LEMUEL SHAW

My Dear Sir Washington Mar: 30 [18]47

I have been requested to attend the trial of Oliver Smiths Will, in the County of Hampshire, which I understand is to come on, at a special term of the Court, now arranged to be holden in May. I am about leaving this place, for a visit to the South, & was obliged to inform Mr Baker,[3] the writer of the enclosed letter, that I could not engage to be

3. Osmyn Baker (1800–1875; Yale 1822), Amherst and Northampton lawyer, state legislator, U.S. representative (1840–1845), president, Smith Charities (1860–1870). Baker served as one of DW's co-counsel.

home, in season to attend the Court, by that time.[4] I added, that I expected to go to Boston, before setting off for the South;[5] & if he thought proper, I would address myself to the Judges, with a view of obtaining, if suitable to their convenience, the assignment of a day, a little more distant, if I should find, at Boston, a letter from him, expressing his wishes, to that effect. In consequence of this, he addressed me the enclosed letter, at Boston.

Meantime, it has so happened, that some affairs have detained me here so long, that I have not time to visit Boston, before commencing my Southern Journey. I shall not, therefore, have the honor of waiting on the Judges, personally; but I enclose his letter, as expressing the wishes of the Party, and my own. I understood, Mr Ashmun, of the other side,[6] to have no objection that the term should be holden, at a later day.

July, as early as the 5th. or 10th, or any later period of the month would suit my convenience.

I have to request that this letter, with Mr. Baker's, may be laid before the Judges; & the term postponed till July, if the convenience of the Judges should permit. Mr. Baker, to whom I write, will apply to be informed of the result. Very respectfully, & truly Yr. Ob. Sert

Danl Webster

ALS. MHi. Lemuel Shaw (1781–1861; Harvard 1800), Massachusetts lawyer and judge, studied with David Everett, admitted in 1804, state representative, member, Massachusetts Constitutional Convention (1820), chief justice, MassSJC (1830–1860).

TO DANIEL FLETCHER WEBSTER

Monday Morning 1/2 past 4.
[June 14, 1847]

Dear F.

Mr Baker, counsel with me in the case to be tried next month at Northampton, is coming down this week to Boston for consultation; but thinks he may not till *Wednesday*; it is possible therefore I may not go up till Wednesday, 10 o clock train, tho I may go tomorrow. Tell Mr Healey to send no more letters. Yrs D. W.

Oliver Smith (1766–1845), Massachusetts philanthropist, member, Massachusetts Constitutional Convention (1820), state legislator.

4. Enclosure not found.

5. At the end of April DW journeyed to Virginia and the Carolinas. He returned to Marshfield on June 8, 1847.

6. At this time the lawyers opposing DW were: George Ashmun (1804–1870), Springfield lawyer, U.S. representative (1845–1851); Reuben Atwater Chapman (1801–1873), Ashmun's partner, judge, MassSJC (1860–1868; chief justice, 1868–1873); Charles Phelps Huntington (b. 1802; Harvard 1822), Massachusetts lawyer, practiced in Northampton until 1855 when he moved to Boston, judge, Suffolk County superior court (1855–1859).

Mrs W. thanks Caroline for her letter. All well, & have had glorious rains. There is more greensward, now, in Marshfield, than in S. C. & Geo

D. W.

ALS. NhHi.

DOCUMENT 20. DIRECT EXAMINATION OF A WITNESS

[July 6, 1847]

Mr. Webster. What is your age?

Theophilus.[7] I was born in 1821.

Mr. Webster. At what college were you educated?

Theophilus. At Amherst.

Mr. Webster. In what year did you graduate?

Theophilus. I entered in 1837 and staid four years, till 1841.

Mr. Webster. Were you out of health the latter part of your college course?

Theophilus. Yes, the last year.

Mr. Webster. What was the nature of your complaint?

Theophilus. I was told by my physicians, that it was of a nervous and dyspeptic character.

Mr. Webster. Did it, or not, oblige you to leave college the last part of your college career?

Theophilus. It did, in the Junior year.

Mr. Webster. You did not attend your commencement?

Theophilus. I did not go through the exercises, the latter part of the Senior year.

Mr. Webster. Had you a part assigned you at commencement?

Theophilus. I had.

Mr. Webster. Did you perform it?

Theophilus, I did not.

Judge Wilde.[8] Do you remember what your part was?

Theophilus. One side of a Disputation.

Mr. Webster. You obtained a Degree, I suppose?

Theophilus. Yes, sir.

Mr. Webster. What course of life did you addict yourself to?

7. Theophilus Parsons Phelps (1821–1899; Amherst 1841), the allegedly insane witness, was an invalid nearly his entire life; his mother, Charlotte Parsons, was a daughter of Chief Justice Theophilus Parsons.

8. Samuel Sumner Wilde (1771–1855; Dartmouth 1789), studied law with Seth Padelford, admitted in 1792, practiced in Maine, judge, MassSJC (1815–1850), member, Massachusetts Constitutional Convention (1820).

Theophilus. I resolved to stay at home and work.

Mr. Webster. Did you take a journey to Boston, or the South?

Theophilus. I did, *the summer after I left college*.

Mr. Webster. How far did you go?

Theophilus. First, to Boston; and, there, I took a Packet for Philadelphia.

Mr. Webster. What effect did it have on your health?

Theophilus. My health was improved.

Mr. Webster. Do you remember when you returned?

Theophilus. The fifth day of July, the *summer but one* after I left college. I made a little mistake. It was not the next summer, nor the next summer but one,—*it was three years after I left college*.

Mr. Webster. From this journey, did you return again to your father's House?

Theophilus. Yes, sir.

Mr. Webster. Do you remember the accident that happened to your father?

Theophilus. I have a general recollection of it, I saw a wagon with my father by a shed, and very soon heard it upset. Father was brought into the house.

Mr. Webster. Can you say whether that event alarmed yourself and other members of the family?

Theophilus. It did, I recollect a great excitement, being much alarmed.

Mr. Webster. What was the nature of the wound your father received, on what part of the body?

Theophilus. An injury to the thigh.

Mr. Webster. Do you remember how long it confined him to his room?

Theophilus. I do not.

Mr. Webster. How long after this, did you go to Worcester?

Theophilus. A few days.

Mr. Webster. What induced you to go to Worcester, at that time?

Theophilus. The fright from my father.

Mr. Webster. Have you heard your brother's statement about your father's[9] calling him in, about your apprehensions?

Theophilus. I have an indistinct recollection, a general, imperfect memory of an apprehension, on my mind, of other persons.

Mr. Webster. Who went with you to Worcester?

Theophilus. My brother Arthur.

Mr. Webster. Whom did you see and consult?

9. Charles Phelps, half-brother of the witness, has not been further identified; their father, Charles Porter Phelps (d. 1857; Harvard 1791), Massachusetts lawyer, studied with Theophilus Parsons. DW may have confused the two in the letter immediately following.

Theophilus. Dr. Woodward.[10]

Mr. Webster. Did he give you medicine?

Theophilus. He gave me a prescription.

Mr. Webster. Did you follow the course prescribed?

Theophilus. I did.

Mr. Webster. How did you find yourself after your return from Worcester?

Theophilus. No better.

Mr. Webster. Are you now conscious, that after your visit to Worcester, you were in a state of excitement?

Theophilus. I was in a state different from any other time.

Mr. Webster. How long did this excitement continue?

Theophilus. Two, or three months.

Judge Wilde. Did it particularly affect your spirits?

Theophilus. It did.

Mr. Webster. After the change, how did you occupy yourself?

Theophilus. It had got to be winter and I was occupied in farm work.

Mr. Webster. Did you feel in better spirits, or were your ideas brighter and clearer?

Theophilus. My ideas were brighter.

Mr. Webster. At these most unhappy periods, are you conscious of loss of your perceptions?

Theophilus. I am conscious of mental delusion, rather than a delusion of sense.

Mr. Webster. Had your experience led you to read on the nature of such diseases?

Theophilus. It had.

Mr. Webster. Was it Hypocondria?

Theophilus. It resembled that, more than any form I have read of.

Mr. Webster. What did you do in the spring of 1844?

Theophilus. Some of the time, I wrote a small book.

Mr. Webster. Is that (*a book was here shown to the witness*) a book of your composition?

Theophilus. It is.

Mr. Webster. In what month did you compose that book?

Theophilus. In March, 1844.

(*Mr. Webster read the title page, and it appeared that the work was a History of the Five Books of Moses, for the use of Sabbath Schools.*)

10. Samuel Bayard Woodward (1787–1850), physician, founder, Connecticut Retreat for the Insane, Hartford, Connecticut (1824), superintendent of the State Lunatic Asylum in Worcester (1832–1846) where, in 1843, he examined Phelps.

Mr. Webster. Do you know to what extent the Sabbath School Committee revised your publication?

Theophilus. They made no substantial alteration; there were one or two verbal alterations.

Mr. Webster. Did the Sabbath School Society pay you for the publication?

Theophilus. Yes, sir, over twenty dollars.

Judge Wilde. Do you remember at what time it was finished?

Theophilus. It was entirely written in March, published three months afterwards, and the money was paid six months after the date of publication, according to the society's custom.

Mr. Webster. Do you remember your occupation in the summer of 1844?

Theophilus. I worked on the farm.

Mr. Webster. Was there any particular allotment of the farm?

Theophilus. A part was called my own, but I worked on other parts of the farm, also.

Mr. Webster. What was the state of your health of mind and body, at the time of the execution of the will?

Theophilus. My bodily health was not much improved, *but my mind was good.* I could occupy myself, so far as bodily health allowed.

Mr. Webster. Do you speak of any change, or improvement, particularly, that summer?

Theophilus. My mind improved much at that time.

Mr. Webster. Did you find, that you could apply your mind steadily, through the summer of 1844, to anything your bodily health allowed you to pursue?

Theophilus. Yes, sir.

Mr. Webster. Did you write anything for publication in 1844?

Theophilus. Two or three short pieces.

Judge Wilde. Were they published in the papers?

Theophilus. Yes, sir.

Mr. Webster. What was the general nature of your reading?

Theophilus. It was of a miscellaneous character.

Mr. Webster. Did you read a good deal?

Theophilus. At times, I did.

Mr. Webster. Have you avoided company at your father's house?

Theophilus. I have, since I left college.

Mr. Webster. How was your habit, when a boy?

Theophilus. I cannot recollect. It was on account of the state of my health.

Mr. Webster. Is your brother a talking man?

Theophilus. He is rather inclined to silence.

Mr. Webster. What did you do with your little crop of broom corn?

Theophilus. I sold it in Northampton.

Mr. Webster. Did you use, yourself, at your discretion, your little gains?

Theophilus. Yes, sir.

Mr. [*Osmyn*] *Baker*.[11] What quantity of broom brush, had you?

Theophilus. From ninety to one hundred pounds.

Mr. Webster. Had you known Oliver Smith by sight?

Theophilus. By no other way.

Mr. Webster. *Have you, now, a distinct recollection of what took place, at the signature of the will?*

Theophilus. *Quite.*

Mr. Webster. Was Mr. Smith an old man, or a young man?

Theophilus. An old man.

Mr. Webster. Was he large or small?

Theophilus. Not remarkably large or small.

Mr. Webster. Had he hair, or was he bald?

Theophilus. Bald, sir.

Mr. Webster. Did you know how he came to your father's?

Theophilus. He sometimes walked, but usually came in a wagon.

Mr. Webster. Had you seen him at your father's house before?

Theophilus. I had, sir.

Mr. Webster. So far as you know, *when you attested the will was your mind as clear and strong, as when you wrote the book?*

Theophilus. *I think it was.*

Mr. Webster. *Do you believe that your mind was as strong and clear, and your memory as good, when you witnessed the signature of the will, as they are now?*

Theophilus. *Yes, sir.*

Extract. James W. Boyden, reporter, *The Evidence of the Validity of the Will of Oliver Smith* (Amherst, Mass., 1847), pp. 12–16.

TO [?]

Northampton, July 6. [18]47
8 P. M.

My Dear Sir

We have had a long session, of nine or ten hours, in very hot weather, & in a crowded Court house, but I feel well. Perspiration is pouring out of me, at every pore.

Our case is somewhat singular. One Oliver Smith, a Bachelor, with

11. DW's co-counsel; DW's other co-counsel was Charles Edwin Forbes (1795–1881; Brown 1815), practiced in Northampton, state legislator, judge, MassCCP (1847–1848), judge, MassSJC (1848).

little original means, son of a farmer, lived in a neighboring town, to the age of 80. Always saving & economical, & loving money, in later life he became shrewd, & skilful, in the management of large sums; & from dealing in Country Bonds & Mortgages, he came to deal in Stocks. He was successful, & amassed a fortune of $300.000. In 1844 he made his will, & gave the Bulk of his property to various Charities. He died, in Decr. '45. The will is contested on one single ground, viz, that *Theophilus Parsons Phelps*, one of the witnesses, was not a competent witness, being, as was alledged, at that time an *insane person.*

We were, of course, to give the primary proof, & to call the three subscribing witnesses, all being living, & in the County.

First, we called *Charles Phelps*, the father, a Gentleman of 60 years; one of the witnesses. He answered the common questions, about signature &c, was not cross ex[amine]d, & withdrew.

Next we called his son, Charles P. Phelps, another witness, who answered the common questions, & was then cross examined, for 4 hours, relative to the state of mind of his brother, Theophilus Parsons Phelps, the alledged insane witness. This being thro., we called, of course, Theophilus himself; a shy, silent, down looking young man. He answered the common questions, all right. Then, shall we give him up to X examination? It was thought we must—I said, *no.* The other side has so far opened their case, as to show that they rely on proving the insanity of this witness. We may meet that case, now, & go on *& examine him, himself, on that point.* This was somewhat of a surprise; but it was important. It gave us the first *dealing*, with this alledged insane witness; & the Judge decided we had a right to go on, & examine him, at large. It was a delicate matter. The will was attested by him, in July '44. It was clear, that in Aug. '43, he was out of his right mind, & had been to the Hospital. Could we venture to take *his own* account, of these successive states of his own mind?—the other side contending, that his insanity, of 1843, continues to the present moment? Resting a good deal on his father's judgment, *I ventured*, agt. the opinion of others; & he has been on the stand three hours, & has so gone thro. the examination, as that this will be a remarkable case. He said, he is now of sound mind, tho not of good bodily health, & greatly troubled with headache, & dispepsia; that he has been thus more or less sick, since 1840; that in 1843, an accident to his father brought on an excitement, which caused a delusion, & loss of sanity. That he knew it then, but could not control it. That he threw himself into the River, in Aug. '43—he can hardly tell why; but got out again, of his own accord, that this delusion, or insanity, lasted till the winter of '44, when it went off. That in March 44, he wrote a little Treatise, "a History of the 5 Books of Moses"; which was published by the Tract Society, & was produced. That when he attested the will, he was perfectly free from delusion, & insanity &c. &c. Now, it is rather a new case, I think to bring a man to testify to his own sanity, when it is impeached. I feared the result, he was so shy, & timid & shrinking. I think I went thro. with him, pretty well. If I have any skill, I exerted it, in encouraging him, & leading him along, & persuading him to talk of himself, freely, on such a subject, & before a most crowded audience. He went thro. nobly, carrying every body's sympathy; & then I handed him to opposite Counsel,[12] for X examination. Here, he was still more successful; no shrewdness could entrap him, or bring him into inconsistency; nothing could make him ashamed to tell the whole truth about himself, altho' some things must have been exceedingly painful; nor could any multitude of questions, or ingenuity of interrogation, confuse him. He saw every thing, as clear as light, & answered accordingly. His examination closed at sunset, & the Court adjourned. I think he has sealed the whole matter. We shall see. He has at least done a good days work, & I have not done a bad. I am quite rejoiced, on his fathers account, who is a very good man, & an old friend of mine. The young man is grandson of Ch. Jus. Parsons.

My Dear Sir;

I am not reporter, to any Court—but thought I would give you this acct. of our first days work. Mr Choate is on the other side, full of intellect & activity, knowledge & illustration.

Tomorrow, they go on their main evidence, *by the Doctors*, to prove insanity. We shall see what they will do. If it comes fairly in my way, I shall say what I think of this modern idea of making so many persons *insane*. If we leave it to the Drs they will make one fifth of mankind madmen, & exempt them from responsibility. I have a book now before me, in which the writer speaks of "the rights & privileges of the Insane";[13] as if they were a class, enjoying peculiar exemptions & benefits. But you will be glad, that I am tired. Yrs D. W.

ALS. NhD. Possibly written to John Plummer Healy.

DOCUMENT 21. REPORTED ARGUMENT TO JURY

[July 8, 1847]

Now what is a competent witness under the law? Must he be an expert? If so, he must be a doctor. Must he be a skilful? Every one knows it is common for a man to call in his cook, or his chamber maid, or his stable boy, to witness an instrument. I differ from Lord Camden[14] as to the

12. According to the report of the case, Reuben Atwater Chapman conducted the cross-examination.

13. The reference is probably to Isaac Ray's *Treatise*, note 16, below.

14. Charles Pratt (1714–1794), lord chancellor, chief justice, English court of common pleas (1762–1766).

necessity of a witness being capable of '*inspecting*' the testator's mind. We know of no such practice, except so far as this, that a witness would wish to know whether the testator was of sound mind and memory. When a respectable old man rides over, on a morning, from Hatfield to Hadley, in a chaise, and promises to execute a Will; reads it, and calls in young men to witness it; such an idea as the young men inspecting and catechising that old man, would be new in Massachusetts. The idea of 'inspecting' the testator's mind arose in this way. In former times, there were no witnesses to Wills. A notorious case of fraud occurred in the time of the English Commonwealth. A testator went to one Baynam, a lawyer, to make his Will. Lawyers are not always as honest as they should be. Baynam made the Will, and Baynam was the only witness, and Baynam was the principal legatee to the whole estate. This Will was sustained, and by Lord Camden. This led to a reformation of the law and the statutes, from which we have borrowed.[15] The law intended that witnesses should be disinterested—competent. I know of no law that places the competency of a witness to a Will on any other or different ground, than a witness in any other case. Any competent witness in a court of law is a competent witness to a will. He must have intelligence and not be infamous. A witness competent to testify in a case of assault and battery, is competent to witness a Will. This had been decided to be the doctrine of this court. All that is required is disinterestedness and freedom from infamy. Chief Justice Parsons says, 'witnesses are credible (competent) whom the law will trust to testify at the trial.' They must have understanding to know the nature of an oath. All competent witnesses are sufficient inspectors and guardians. If in July 15th, 1844, Theophilus Parsons Phelps was a person who could be sworn in an assault and battery case, he was competent to witness this Will. The great thing to be guarded against is incompetency on account of interest.

Mr. Webster then spoke of the burden of proof, which was contended by opposing counsel to rest on them. He said we will prove anything the case requires. Presumption is in favor of sanity. They who deny sanity, must prove insanity. We must go on the facts in each case. If a man's mind is capable at the time, of doing what he undertakes to do, he is competent. The insanity must appear to be incurable, like a malady from a blow on the head. If insanity is temporary, or coming and going, no such inference arises.

It is not every degree of insanity, that incapacitates a man for business. A witness must have power and intellect enough to apply his mind to the subject before him. Incipient madness could not incapacitate a man for business. Look at the practical results of the theories set up

15. DW refers to s. 5 of the Statute of Frauds, 29 Car. 2, c. 3 (1677), amended by 25 Geo. 2, c. 6 (1752). See *Amory* v. *Fellowes*, 5 Mass. 219 (1809).

here. A man is competent to do anything he undertakes to do; and yet the doctors prove a lurking insanity, which unfits him for business, and exempts him from crime.

The precise test in this case is this. If Theophilus Parsons Phelps had been brought into court, as a witness, on the 15th of July, 1844, he could not have been rejected as a witness. The other side resort to theory. Call in the Dr.—'Canst thou not minister to a case diseased?' There was no witness to show insanity on the 15th of July, 1844. Witnesses are false, or else the witness was competent. The other side were brought into the unenviable position of defeating their own cause. They have knocked away their own platform. They made no objection to the witness on the stand. The counsel spoke of him as mentally dead—dead—dead! Can a dead man testify?

Mr. Webster then recapitulated the history of the young man, after some further remarks in reply to the opposing counsel, proceeding to say that the magnitude of the case justified the course pursued by the heirs. Experts had been called to give their opinions agreeably to modern progress in the diagnostics of insanity.[16] I am content with Locke and Reid.[17] The theory of Dr. Woodward is, that if ill health continued, derangement continued. But he says that the state of mind, at the time of the transaction, is the true test to be regarded. He thinks the mind could not have been clear. Other evidence is that it was.

Mr. Webster then summed up the points of the argument, and closed by reminding the jury of the sad effects of a verdict declaring the young man insane, and of the satisfaction which a different verdict would give to him and his friends.

Extract. James W. Boyden, pp. 34–35.

3. JURY ARGUMENT: THE ASTOR LAND CASES

In the late 1820s Webster lent his assistance to New York State in a

16. Besides Woodward, doctors Isaac Ray and Luther Vose Bell testified to Phelps's sanity. Ray (1807–1881; M.D. Bowdoin 1827), author of *A Treatise on the Medical Jurisprudence of Insanity* (Boston, 1838), superintendent, Maine Insane Hospital (1841–1845), superintendent, Butler Hospital, Providence, Rhode Island (1845–1866); Bell (1806–1862; Bowdoin 1823, M.D. Dartmouth 1826), physician, and politician; as state legislator (1835–1836) he promoted New Hampshire's first insane asylum, superintendent, McLean Hospital for the Insane at Charlestown, Massachusetts (1836–1856), author of *On a Form of Disease Resembling Some Advanced Stages of Mania and Fever* (1848) (thereafter called "Bell's Mania").

17. DW probably meant a reference to the theory of personal identity treated in John Locke, *An Essay Concerning Human Understanding* (London, 1690) and Thomas Reid, *Essays on the Intellectual Powers of Man* (Edinburgh, 1785).

series of cases designed to test the validity of John Jacob Astor's claim to a large part of Putnam and Dutchess counties.[1] The lands in question had been granted by William III to Adolph Philipse in 1697. When Adolph died in 1749, the land passed to Frederick Philipse, his nephew and sole heir. Frederick made out a will shortly before his death in 1751 in which he devised the land to his children in fee tail. In 1752 his survivors docked the entail, and, two years later, partitioned the land. Mary Philipse, one of Frederick's daughters, received about 50,000 acres. When Mary announced her intention of marrying Roger Morris, an English naval officer, her siblings became afraid that Morris might squander Mary's portion. To preclude this, they prepared a marriage settlement in which Mary released to her siblings her title to the land. They in turn agreed to transfer to Roger and Mary, upon solemnization of their marriage, a life estate in the land, with the remainder to Mary's children. In the event that Mary left no living children, her will would control the descent of the estate.

The parties signed the document in 1758, but instead of recording it, they left it in the hands of Mary's brother-in-law. When the American Revolution began, the loyalist Morrises left New York for England. In 1779 New York took the Morris land under a bill of attainder authorizing confiscation of loyalist land. The commissioners of forfeiture did not know that Roger and Mary had only a life estate. Thus, when the state sold the lots in fee simple in 1784 to the former Morris tenants, it was unaware that it could not pass complete title. In 1787 the holder of the marriage settlement finally recorded it in New York. He apparently believed he had acted in the best interests of Mary's children, then living in England, by concealing his knowledge of the state of the title while the confiscation process progressed. In 1786 the English commission for compensating holders of American claims had awarded Roger and Mary compensation for their lost life estate; the peace treaty (the 1782 Treaty of Paris), the commission ruled, protected the children's remainder interest. In 1794 Roger died, survived by Mary and four children.

In London, sometime around 1809, someone discovered the marriage settlement and realized that the Morris children had a potential claim to the land sold by New York.[2] When Astor learned of it, he decided to

1. This rendition of the Astor claim relies on Kenneth Wiggins Porter, *John Jacob Astor* (2 vols., New York, 1931), 2: 876–892; *Statement and Exposition of the Title of John Jacob Astor to the Lands Purchased by him from the Surviving Children of Roger Morris and Mary his Wife* (New York, 1827); and Edward V. Sparhawk, *Report of the Trial . . . in the case of James Jackson, ex dem. Theodosius Fowler and others, vs. James Carver* (New York, 1827).

2. Another of Astor's biographers believes that Aaron Burr uncovered it; see Arthur D. Howden Smith, *John Jacob Astor* (Philadelphia, 1929), p. 263.

gamble that if he purchased the interest of the Morris heirs he could force New York to buy his claim. In December 1809 the three surviving children of Mary Morris sold their claims to Astor for $100,000. Their remainders would remain inchoate until Mary's death terminated her life estate. In 1810 Astor publicized his claim hoping to settle it quickly before resorting to litigation. In 1813 he offered to settle for $300,000; in 1819, he raised his bid to $415,000. Although a state committee investigated the claim and concluded that it had merit, no action took place. Astor meanwhile sold a small part of his claim to other speculators. After Mary died in 1825 real negotiations began. It soon appeared likely that New York's unwillingness to settle would force Astor to establish his claim in court. The state approached Webster to become one of its counsel. He agreed, and in 1826 the state retained him and three other prominent New York attorneys. Webster's role would be to argue the state's case to the jury. As the letter from Samuel A. Talcott, printed below, reveals, the state had also hired Webster as a showpiece to demonstrate to the worried farmers that the state would not neglect their interest.

Early in 1827 Astor again offered to settle the claim without litigation. In April New York made a counter offer of $450,000 in New York State stock, with the promise of an additional $250,000 if the United States Supreme Court eventually decided Astor had a valid claim to the improvements as well as the land. The offer, however, was contingent upon Astor's winning three out of five test cases. The statute gave Astor until October to accept the offer. Meanwhile Astor's attorneys had begun the first ejectment action in U.S. circuit court in May.[3] In a procedural skirmish won by them, Justice Smith Thompson ruled that they could use the names of the Morris heirs in their declaration without the heirs' permission. Webster and his co-counsel had hoped that a ruling in their favor would break Astor's chain of title and enable them to defend the occupant's claim on grounds of title by adverse possession.

When Astor allowed the state's deadline to pass, the case moved to trial in November. Beginning on November 7, 1827, Astor's attorneys presented their evidence dealing with the circumstances surrounding the Morris marriage settlement. Astor's case had few weaknesses. On Saturday morning, November 10, 1827, Martin Van Buren summed up the state's case. He was followed by Webster (Document 22). With the facts against him, Webster tried to win the jury's sympathy to his side by portraying the suit as one between hard working farmers, on the one hand, and speculators, on the other. If the jury responded positively, he might then persuade them that sufficient doubt existed in the plaintiff's

3. *Kelley ads. Jackson ex. dem. Fowler et al.*, 2 Paine 440 (1827) and 14 Federal Cases 244 (1827).

proof to justify a verdict for the defendant. When Webster finished, David Bayard Ogden argued Astor's case.

On the following Monday Astor's chief counsel, Thomas Addis Emmett, closed for the plaintiff. He sought to defuse Webster's *ad hominem* against Astor and to convince the jury that they should decide the case strictly on its merits:

> The great and powerful State of New York, he observed, had stepped forward to oppose the claim set up by the plaintiff. Arrayed on the side of the State, were counsel famed for their talents and eloquence; and so warmly did the State enter into this controversy, that even the aid of the Goliath of the North [i. e., Webster] had been called in to her assistance. . . . The gentlemen have argued that one thousand families are to be turned out of their homes, to want and misery—that it is an obsolete claim, so old indeed that it is scarce worth while to inquire whether or not it be a just one. . . . I cannot excite your sympathies for Mr. Astor; he does not need them. . . . Nevertheless, he is entitled to justice.[4]

Following Emmett's summation, Justice Thompson commented on the evidence and instructed the jury that Astor would be entitled to a verdict if they believed that the marriage settlement of 1758 had been properly executed. The jury retired and then returned a verdict for Astor.

FROM DEWITT CLINTON

Sir Albany 2 November 1826

I am desirous of retaining you as Counsel for the State of New York to assist in the defence of certain suits brought by John Jacob Astor[5] Esquire and his associates against Grantees under the State for lands in Putnam & Dutchess Counties and on your signifying your assent to act I shall remit to you a retaining fee of 500 dollars.[6] I am very respectfully Your most obedt servt DeWitt Clinton

ALS. NhHi. Mistakenly recorded as a letter from "Daniel Clark" in *Correspondence*, 2, Calendar: 469 and mDW 5696. DeWitt Clinton (1769–1868; Columbia 1786), New York lawyer and politician, admitted in 1790, state legislator, U.S. senator (1802–1803), mayor, New York City, lieutenant governor, New York (1811–1813), governor, New York (1817–1821, 1825–1828).

4. Sparhawk, pp. 39–40, 57.

5. John Jacob Astor (1763–1848), New York fur trader, capitalist, and real estate investor.

6. DW agreed to the retainer. On December 20, 1826, Governor Clinton informed DW that he had directed the payment of his fee and suggested discussion of the case with Martin Van Buren, of counsel to the state, who had participated in the state investigation several years earlier (mDW 5775). See also William Learned Marcy to DW, December 28, 1826, mDW 5788.

FROM SAMUEL A. TALCOTT

Sir New York May 14 1827

I received your favour of the 2 Instant, which was forwarded to me from Albany, a few days ago,—and should have answered it immediately, but it was then doubtful whether the Counsel for Mr Astor would not conclude to postpone the trial of the causes.[7]

After several consultations, however, they informed me that they could not say definitively that the causes should not be tried at the next term, and of course we must proceed as if the trials would be brought on.

In this view of the case I must repeat my request for your personal attendance at the time unless you hear further from me upon the subject. And let me assure you that notwithstanding the modesty with which you speak of your own services and the complimentary manner in which you allude to other counsel who will represent the interests of the State,[8] we feel, here, that your professional assistance can not but be highly valuable; & I am convinced that if from any circumstance the causes should be lost, in your absence, it would be impossible to satisfy the minds of the tenants upon the lands, and perhaps of others whose opinions might be of quite as much importance that they would not have been better managed had you been present.

With great respect, Sir your Obedt Servant Saml. A. Talcott

ALS. DLC. Samuel A. Talcott, New York attorney general (1821–1829), one of the state's counsel.

7. Letter not found. Astor was represented by Thomas Jackson Oakley (1783–1857; Yale 1801), New York lawyer, admitted in 1804, U.S. representative (1813–1817, 1827–1828), New York attorney general (1814–1821), judge, New York City superior court (1828–1857); Thomas Addis Emmett, Irish physician and lawyer, emigrated to the U.S. (c. 1800), New York attorney general (1812); Jonas Platt (1769–1834), state legislator, U.S. representative (1799), judge, New York supreme court (1814–1821); Josiah Ogden Hoffman (1766–1837), New York lawyer, state legislator, New York attorney general (1798–1801), recorder, City of New York (1808–1815), judge, New York superior court (1828–1837); David Bayard Ogden (1775–1849), New York attorney.

8. DW's co-counsel were Talcott, Ogden Hoffman, Martin Van Buren, and Henry Booth Cowles. Hoffman (1793–1856; Columbia 1812), studied with his father, Josiah Ogden Hoffman, admitted in 1818, district attorney, Orange County (1823–1826), moved to New York City in 1826, district attorney, New York County (1829–1835), U.S. representative (1837–1841), U.S. district attorney, New York (1841–1845), New York attorney general (1853–1855). Cowles (1798–1873; Union College 1816), practiced at this time in Putnam County, state legislator (1826–1828), U.S. representative (1829–1831), moved to New York City in 1834.

DOCUMENT 22. ARGUMENT TO JURY

Gentlemen, [November 10, 1827]

For adding any thing to the topics urged by my associate,[9] I must find an apology in the magnitude of the subject and in the state of the discussion now before you: if my learned friend has not convinced you, I can have little hope of doing so. I trust, however, gentlemen, that in a case of such importance, not arising from its magnitude alone—and which is the first of a series of cases, all involving the same consequences, it will not be unpardonable to reiterate the points of law and fact on which the defendants rely. With no desire to do any thing but establish the law as the people have declared it to be, and to impress upon you again the great importance and unknown consequences of the verdict you are about to give, I shall in the course of the remarks which I shall address to you, necessarily revert to the facts and arguments which have already been treated of by my learned colleague.—The claim under litigation is one of far greater amount than is often submitted for decision in a court of justice. It is a claim for lands—not in their wild and forest state, but for lands the intrinsic value of which is mingled with the human labor that has been expended upon them. It is no every-day purchase: for it extends over towns and counties, and even almost takes in degrees of latitude. It is a stupendous speculation. The individual who now claims it has not succeeded to it by inheritance—he has not attained it as he did that vast wealth, than which no one envies him less than I do—not by fair and honest exertions in commercial enterprise, but by speculation; by purchasing up the forlorn hope of the heirs of a family driven from this country by a bill of attainder. The deed by which this claim was transferred to him declares, that he gave 20,000 pounds in consideration of the claim. This may, or may not be so. He might have given 20 shillings, or he might have given nothing. We are not to know, and cannot know the fact. The instrument is a plain release, securing the purchaser from all liabilities, forfeitures, and attainders. It is a claim under the law, and what it is good for let it stand for. It is not, however, to be passed by lightly. Every bearing which it presents to the jury must be scrutinized; for it is necessary in order to arrive at the truth, to subject it to the most rigorous investigation, and, I may say, to torture from it a just and equitable decision. The lands to be affected by the verdict in this cause were held as a patrimony by the defendants. They had purchased them of the original patentee—they had labored for years to improve them. The rugged hills had grown green under their cultivation, before a question was raised as to the integrity of their titles. They have grown with the lands around them—and they have a right to retain them, until a legal claimant comes, to turn them out of their possession.

9. Martin Van Buren had just finished his summation.

And unless the testimony upon which that individual founds his claim is as clear as possible, it is your duty to reject his title, and retain the lands in the hands in which they now are.

Let us see, then, how the question stands. Let us examine the testimony which has been brought before you—for we at the bar are more likely to have papers and dates in our minds than you are. First, the lands in question were granted to Adolph Philipse, who was succeeded by his heir at law, Frederic Philipse. He made his will, leaving the property to his children, Margaret Philipse, Susannah, afterwards Mrs. Robinson, and Mary, afterwards Mrs. Morris,[10] in tail. Margaret died, and left her part to the others. Subsequently the heirs suffered an act of recovery, and the property was vested in them in fee simple. In 1754 they divided their interests in it and the title became several. You have thus arrived at the most important fact. It is that, in 1754, Mary Philipse, afterwards Mrs. Morris, became seised in fee simple with the estate. All dates and circumstances to this time are, to the decision of the case, unimportant—and now comes the disputed point. Having established that Mary Philipse became seised in fee simple, let us, before proceeding regularly with the subsequent testimony, notice in advance a few things of equal importance. In 1779, twenty-five years afterwards, the legislature of this state passed a bill of attainder, by which the property of Roger Morris and Mary his wife was confiscated, and thereafter vested in the state. Now, if she still held in fee simple, if the title had not changed since 1754, so as to vest it out of her, then the case is clearly with the defendant. If then the plaintiff cannot show that in 1779 there was *not* a real substantial title vesting in Mary Philipse, and that it had been carried out of her previous to that date, and subsequent to 1754, the case is clearly against him. This is for the plaintiff to establish; and if he leaves a particle of doubt, his case must fall. What then, is he to show? Why that the estate did not vest in Mary Morris in 1779, and in that point we are prepared to meet him. He has offered to show it, and we accept his offer. Let us see then, what proof he has adduced that there was in 1779, a title to the estate out of Mrs. Morris. It is, that as far back as previous to the marriage, there was a marriage settlement, by which Roger and Mary Morris were to have only a life estate out of the property. This instrument is said to have been dated in 1758, and conveyed the title out of Mrs. Morris, and that title remained out of her until 1779. This they attempt to do; but it appears to me that in bringing your minds to this result, they have a heavy task upon their hands. For the proof to sustain this position, the plaintiff has produced a parchment, dated the 7th of January, 1758, signed by Roger Morris and Mary Philipse, on one part, and by Joanna Philipse and Beverly Robinson on the

10. See genealogical chart, printed below.

other, and purporting to have been proved before Judge ———.[11] There is such a paper:—it is here, and we do not deny it. But does this paper prove a legal conveyance of property twenty years afterwards? We say it does not, and we aver with confidence, that it proves no such thing. I shall state the reason for this conclusion at large. The ground we go upon will lead us to consider solely the weight of evidence in relation to this instrument. Taking for granted that the formal proof was complete; taking for granted that it was signed on the day of its date,—still I maintain that there is enough internal evidence to show that it never was duly executed. One of my opponents remarked the other day that almost any thing might be presumed. On this very ground, I am about to state the facts, which I think will make it almost impossible for you to presume otherwise than that this deed is not valid. I said before, that the paper was dated in 1758. The marriage did not take place until long after; and during that interval of time it was not unnatural that the parties should have changed their minds—that other considerations should have presented themselves, to induce them to give up the proposed marriage settlement. To arrive at such an effect, it required no deed or instrument of cancellation. It was only necessary to give up the six papers, to which the parties had set their hands, and of which each of them held two, and to throw them into the old family chest to remain without virtue or validity, among other lumber, equally unimportant. It is a fair presumption that this was done, for such a presumption is powerfully borne out by subsequent facts. It therefore does not lie in the plaintiff to call on us to show any deed giving up the proposed marriage settlement, or any formal relinquishment whatever, if that presumption is sustained by facts perfectly relevant and consistent with it. The mere agreeing by the parties that it should go for nothing, makes it go for nothing. It is not an act of the parties—it is not a law, which we are called upon to consider; but a piece of parchment, which the mere consent of the parties could revoke, as well as any instrument that could be framed. I say, gentlemen, that there is abundant evidence, to which you cannot shut your eyes or be blinded, that at some time subsequent to its date the intended marriage settlement was given up, leaving the title of the property still remaining in fee, in Mary Philipse. It would otherwise require some proof of a conveyance of property to Roger Morris, but the circumstances induce a conviction that it did vest in his wife. Another important circumstance is, that the instrument purporting to have been dated in 1758 was neither proved or recorded until 1787, 29 years afterwards. Where, then, does this instrument come from? We are told that six copies were executed in '58;—and the argument with us is, that the inten-

11. The settlement agreement was proved in 1787 before John Sloss Hobart, a judge of the New York supreme court.

tion was to destroy or set them aside: the argument on the other side is, that it was intended to retain them. If they are right, where are the other five?

The gentlemen say they have been lost by time and accident. But it is not probable, we say, that this paper alone should have been preserved; and it seems cogent evidence, that the parties intended to give them up. We say that one has been preserved by accident, and they, that five have been lost by accident. Which is the most reasonable presumption? And here the mystery thickens—it does not appear who preserved the sixth paper—We should like to know. A hand is stretched forth, but we do not see the body that impels it; and all around is dark as midnight. Who dictated at a late day, many years after the assumed date of the marriage settlement, its proof and enregisterment? Why was not this instrument recorded and proved at the time? I say, if there was not some change of purpose, by which the marriage settlement was thrown aside, the failure to register it was a most unpardonable neglect on the part of the individuals concerned. In some cases it might not be so essential to place a deed on record. But this was the very case for recording, because the change of the title did not change the possession. Such are the very transactions in which recording is indispensable—for if a man takes a mortgage, he will record it, because prudence dictates that, the title being changed and the possession not changed, the record of the alteration of the title is necessary. And how much more natural would it have been in this case, when the deed was framed to protect the rights of unborn children.—And what imaginable motive could there have been for neglecting to do all that was requisite for the protection of those who could not protect their own interests? And why did not Colonel [Beverly] Robinson, to whom the interest of those children was intrusted, take the proper steps for making that instrument effectual? Did he not know that unless all the formalities were complied with, the children could never come to their rights? It must have been self-evident to him that as a trustee for the children, it was his duty to do all in relation to this transaction which their interest required, and hence that he was bound to register the deed. I say, therefore, that if it had not been decided to give up this marriage settlement, such a neglect would never have taken place. The trustees would otherwise have registered the deed, so that, if he should have died before the children came to their property, their interests might, nevertheless, have been protected.

Against all these presumptions the counsel for the plaintiff have brought a single paper—one link in a chain of documents. And yet, gentlemen, I can assure you that every thing that could have been done, has been done. There is no danger that they have neglected any available testimony that would have been in any way useful to them. If they could have given a reason for the absence of the papers, they would have done it. But we are told that the antiquity of the case must account for these discrepancies. Yet, gentlemen, there is not a title in the state more clearly made out than that of the estate in question. Previous to this marriage settlement, all the deeds have been produced entire. Transactions more antique than this deed of settlement, are proved without difficulty—they start up fresh before us; and even the leases of that period have been preserved with care, in the family chest. Yet we are told that this marriage settlement, on the score of its *antiquity*, is to enjoy a great many presumptions in its favor.

This marriage settlement dated in 1758, embraced in its purview, an estate of great magnitude, which was in progress of settlement. New tenants were coming in every day, and sales and leases were continually occurring. And what has been shown? The fact cannot be contradicted that from 1758 to the date of the attainder, Roger Morris, making conveyances every day, and living among three hundred tenants—not one of them ever heard of the marriage settlement in question. They sold and gave titles—and those titles are totally different from those they would have given under the marriage settlement. I say, that having the whole testimony in relation to the family from the time of the marriage, down, through all its ramifications—with the single exception of the recollection of Col. Barclay,[12] there is no proof that the marriage settlement was ever heard of, thought of, or known until the year 1779. I allow, that in the treaty of '82 there was a clause in favor of marriage settlements,[13] and yet, the very next year, the first was ever publicly heard of this marriage settlement. I repeat, that from '58 to '79 this deed was suffered to sleep in oblivion, with the exception of Mr. Barclay's having heard of it. He, it appears, did hear of it; but, on the other hand, we have brought a great number of persons living on the land, interested in knowing the title under which they were continually taking out and renewing their leases, not one of whom ever heard of it until after the purchase by Mr. Astor had become known. Is is not reasonable, is it not legal, to suppose that if there was a marriage settlement, it would have been named in the deeds? This is not only true; but it is also true that several conveyances have been brought before you, containing clauses that make them totally inconsistent with the supposition that a marriage settlement was in existence. Before we examine this part of the subject, let me advert to another point of equal importance. The fifty years embraced in the period during which the transactions alluded to

12. Thomas H. Barclay, a key witness for the plaintiff, testified that he had heard of the marriage settlement prior to 1770.

13. The preliminary and definitive peace treaties declared that all persons "who have any interest in confiscated lands, either by debts, marriage settlements or otherwise, shall meet with no lawful impediment in the prosecution of their just rights." Miller, 2: 99 and 154.

occurred, comprised some most interesting periods. First, they were years of peace, and then came years of war, in which individuals were called upon to hazard their property and their lives. Roger Morris and his wife adhered to the side of the enemy; and they lost their lands in consequence. Now what was the evident duty of the trustees of this property under the marriage settlement, when the state was about to confiscate the possessions of these children? It appears to me, that nothing could have induced them to refrain from making known their rights, and bringing forward the deed of settlement, to sustain them.

Let us now advert to the testimony of Judge Benson,[14] who was intimate with Col. Robinson. Judge Benson was called upon as a member of the Legislature, to insert the name of his friend Col. Robinson in the general bill of attainder: and is it at all probable that Col. R. could not have made interest for the protection of the innocent children, who could not have been implicated in their parents' offences? But the argument seems to be, that the Legislature knew of the marriage settlement, and that the children not being competent parties, could not have been considered to have taken part with their parents. This would have been a good argument if the facts carried it out. But had this been the case, Col. Robinson would not have concluded upon concealing the marriage settlement. On the other hand, he knew enough to be aware that, had he shewn the deed to the venerable witness, he would have told him that it was, if not a contingent remainder, so nearly assimilated to one, that it would have been destroyed by the destruction of the life estate. It appears very strange, that if burdened with so important a trust, in times so perilous, Col. Robinson did not ask the advice of Judge Benson. It appears also, that Col. Robinson remained here six months or a year after the peace, while Col. Morris and his wife were absent. Would not Col. Robinson then, have considered himself bound in honour and conscience to protect the interest of the children of the marriage of Roger and Mary Morris? Would he not have sent to England for proof, where the claim of the heirs might have been proved? But was the proof ever in England? We have nothing to show us that the heirs ever knew they had such a claim until the purchase by Mr. Astor. They have not been brought forward in this litigation, nor are they made to play any part in the establishment of the claim. In a matter of so much importance, involving so large an amount of property, is it not a subject of surprise, that the heirs of the estate should sell out a title without ever having examined into its worth or validity? It has been shewn in evidence that they were never in this country since the peace; consequently, they could

14. Egbert Benson (1746–1833), New York attorney general (1777–1787), judge, New York supreme court. The legislature enacted the bill of attainder October 22, 1779, convicting the Morrises, among others, by name and declaring their property forfeit.

know little or nothing of the estate which they conveyed to Mr. Astor. They seem to have been passive instruments in the matter. They appear on the stage, sign a simple deed of release, and then disappear. Why was it that Beverly Robinson did not act in this affair previous to his return to England? There is not a particle of proof that he ever intimated that he was the depositary of such a claim. So much for Col. Robinson, and the engagement he had entered into, to preserve the rights of the children of Roger and Mary Morris.

Let us now revert to the evidence in relation to Mr. and Mrs. Morris. We find no proof that they ever did any thing in accordance with the marriage settlement; but we find abundant proof that they acted in direct contradiction to its stipulations. We find them treating the estate in every respect as if it were theirs, or hers, or his, without the slightest mention of any other title. And here you must excuse me if I endeavour to turn your attention particularly to the marriage settlement, dated in 1758, while I detail some subsequent circumstances having a bearing upon it.

We have proved before you, a conveyance from Roger Morris and Mary his wife, to William Hill,[15] dated September, 1765, of land therein mentioned. And how did they convey it? They did not act under the marriage settlement; but, on the other hand, they acted clearly against it. And I say that when seven years after the date of the marriage settlement, they conveyed this property, if that marriage settlement had ever been duly executed, they might have been sued in a court of law, for this conveyance. I wish you to examine this part of the case particularly, and I call on my learned friends to shew you, without mystification, how this conveyance could have been made, had a marriage settlement been in existence. By referring to this instrument which has been submitted to your examination, you will perceive that a power is reserved to Roger and Mary Morris, to sell a certain portion of the estate, not to exceed £3000 in value. And had this lease been made under this clause, it would have been so stated: as in every conveyance, the authority to convey, is legally required to be recited. I maintain that in this case, there would be very great ground of doubt, if the deed did not recite the authority on which the parties sold the property. In this and every other deed produced, a recital is contained of the grounds on which the parties convey. But is it under the marriage settlement? No. The deed recites the title as that of Mary Philipse, as devisee of her father, Frederick Philipse, and goes on to detail the title of land granted to Adolph Philipse, devised by him to Frederick Philipse, and by him to Mary Philipse: and then followed up by a covenant, that Roger and Mary Morris are seized

15. Not identified; evidently a farmer.

with a good and clear estate in fee of the land. Now, if there was a marriage settlement, I say, that Roger and Mary Morris might have been sued for making an unlawful conveyance of this description: for here is a positive declaration of seisin of the land. There are also other conveyances, one in 1758, another in 1761, in which it is set forth, that Roger Morris is seized with the land in absolute fee simple. I think it is impossible to convince the jury that there existed a *sleeping* title. Either the marriage settlement existed, and these deeds were void, or the deeds were valid, and the marriage settlement void. On this head, I look upon the facts as clear and decisive. It is to be considered whether the marriage settlement was referred to at all; for if there did exist a marriage settlement, which, as far as Mr. Barclay recollects, was considered a mark of prudence in the mother of Mrs. Morris, then it is to be supposed, that the object for which it was framed, would be followed up. The grand object of the prudence of Mrs. Philipse was, that the husband should not convey away the property. It is clear then, that no purpose was attained that was contemplated by this settlement, supposing it to have existed: because, here you find this very prudent woman allowing, without remonstrance, the husband of her daughter to sell and convey the property which the marriage settlement had contemplated preserving for the children of the marriage. Thus, it appears self-evident, that the contemplated marriage settlement was given up. On this ground, I wish you to fix your attention. I know who is to follow me.[16] I know how easy it is to obliterate, by the power of eloquence, what has been said by us. But I pray you to hold on upon the facts which are presented to you. No one can deprive you of your consciences, and to them I wish you to address, in relation to this part of the subject, a few questions. Ask yourselves why, if there did exist a marriage settlement, it was not proved and recorded? Why, if an honest man was trustee to the deed, he neglected his duty and betrayed his trust? Ask, also, why it was never known; and what motive there was for its concealment? Why, whenever Roger and Mary Morris saw fit to convey property, they did convey it in the teeth, in very derision, of the marriage settlement? and why, when the war came on, nothing was ever said of this instrument? I wish you to use your judgment as plain, honest men. I wish, that, if you find the claim unsound, you may restore tranquillity to the inhabitants of Putnam county. And I conjure you to adhere to the point to which I have just turned your attention, and it will lay the axe to the root of the tree of bitterness, and lead you to a decision against the plaintiff. I beg of you to retain your own convictions, unaltered by the gloss that may be given to the case, and to exercise your own judgment as to the facts. This course will lead

16. A reference to David Bayard Ogden.

you to decide that no such marriage settlement as that to which your attention has been drawn, was ever entered into.

Another ground of argument has been alluded to in the list of authorities with which we have been supplied by the opposing counsel.[17] The gentlemen have cited authority to show that the denying of the release, and not the lease, is an estoppel to us. We shall contend that the sovereign of a country, the people, are not subject to an *estoppel.* An *estoppel* I take to be entirely a matter of law; and from the application I have been able to make to books, there appears to me nothing to warrant an *estoppel* before a jury, because if the case is *estopped*, there is nothing further for a jury to act upon. I may be allowed to explain to you how this question becomes important. The conveyance is said to have been made by lease and release. A lease is first given, and the party is suffered to enter on the property: and then the party granting, gives a deed of release. If there was no lease, and certainly here has been no lease proved to exist, the transaction operates as a bargain and sale, and the effect would be, in this case, to vest the estate in Beverly Robinson, into whose hands, as trustee for the children, the property was conveyed. Now this is an important question; and it is submitted to you, whether you are, or are not to presume the existence and execution of that lease. The presumption we think is carried rather too far. But the plaintiff on this point cannot go but one inch before we stop him with his own presumption. He wishes you to presume the execution of the absent lease. If you find that there was one, the case is doubtless with him. But is it produced? certainly not. It is neither produced nor accounted for, and yet you are to presume its existence. Now I deny that there is any legal presumption that such a lease was ever executed. There has no one thing ever been done which required the existence of such a lease, while every thing that was done, was as consistent with the non-existence, as with the existence of it. We have authority to shew that a grant of land is the same as a grant of fisheries. They may be presumed; but the presumption of a grant cannot exist, where all the circumstances of the case are consistent with the non-existence of the grant. Now, how is the existence of this lease to be presumed? Every thing in relation to it, being consistent with its non-existence? They have not conveyed under it; they have not recorded it, and they have not acknowledged it. The main argument to support its existence has been the antiquity of the transaction; and they say that there is no record of the lease, because the record of the release is sufficient, and confers the property, making the lease unimportant. If the conveyance had been from A. to B. there would have been no need of preserving the lease, because possession would immediately have been taken, and all doubt as to the change of title would

17. No list has been found.

have been avoided. But in such a case as this, it is exactly the reverse. Without a lease, the estate would have gone to the lessee to uses, and stopped there. The counsel on the other side say there is no necessity for the lease; but I maintain that, as the property was only transferred to Beverly Robinson in trust, the lease should have been preserved; and that, because it was not requisite in ordinary cases to preserve leases, was no reason why it should not have been done in this, which was an extraordinary case. But there was an absolute reason for preserving it, if such a claim as this was ever to be set up. The *release* recites the lease: but does not prove it, and the court will inform you that you are to treat it as a matter of fact, and judge accordingly. If you can fairly presume that there was no lease, you have sufficient ground to go upon.

As to an *estoppel*, where a matter was to go to a jury, the party could not be *estopped*. I say that all the defence is erroneous, and that the conveyances are evidence against the existence of the marriage settlement. As to the supposition that the lease has been lost, I would ask why leases of far less importance, and bearing date much farther back, have been so carefully preserved? Every tenant has preserved his lease with care; and you are entitled to some more substantial evidence than mere presumption, that the lease was ever executed; and also some good reason why the documents are not here. For you are called upon to make one kind of conveyance account for another kind of conveyance, and then to presume the existence of the lease merely from the recital of the release.

Again, let us look to the antiquity of the transaction. Why gentlemen you are called upon for a presumption of the existence of a paper in favour of the person who would rationally have it in his possession. Is not such a demand from you as weak as water, from one who ought to have it, or account for its non-production? If a man is to be allowed to look to a jury for presumptions on grounds so loose, it is a dangerous rule, and ought to be set aside. Who will not keep back an imperfect deed, or a deed containing clauses which would destroy it, when he can make a jury presume a deed in his favour? When every thing has been shewn contrary to the existence of the lease, and inconsistent with the execution of the conveyance, they wish to produce a presumption in the teeth of circumstances. I say that such an attempt stands unparalleled in a court of law. It is so well established that a release does not go to shew the title, that an act of Parliament was formerly passed to establish, that, when possession had been given for 20 years, in confirmation of a conveyance, the recital in the release is sufficient. So it appears that, even after a possession of 20 years, the recital in the release did not convey a title without an act of Parliament. This was in cases of common recovery.

The State does not claim under the marriage settlement, neither does

PHILIPSE FAMILY

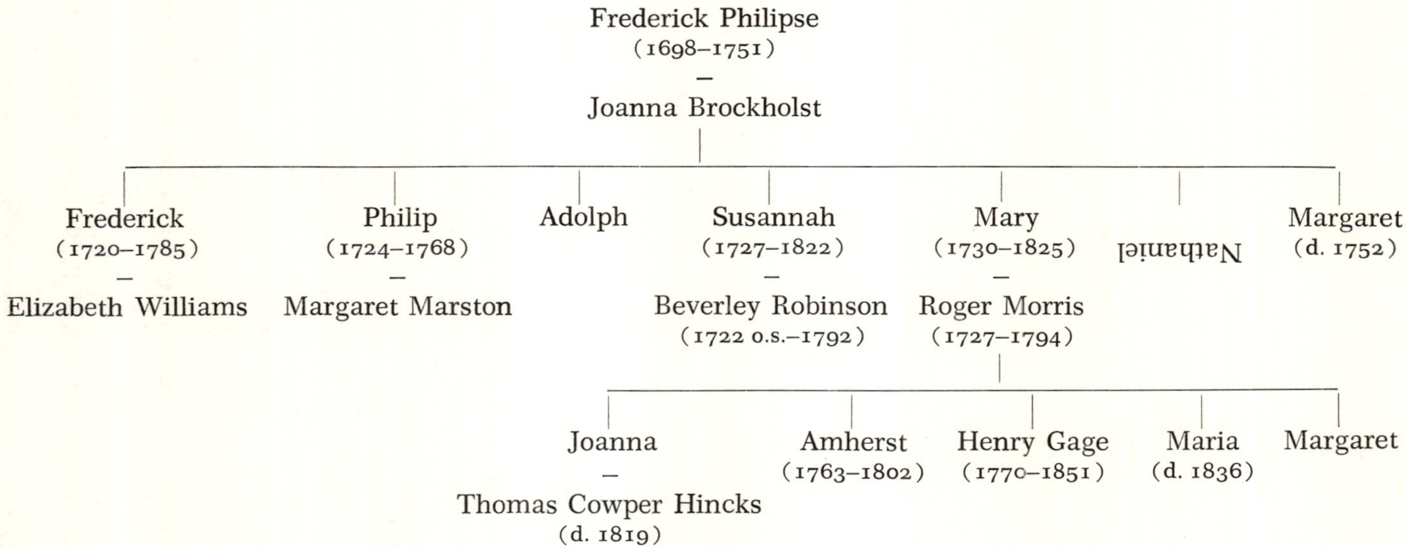

Note. This chart is based on information given in Robert Bolton, *The History . . . of the County of Westchester* (2 vols., New York, 1881), 1: 514, 519–524, 2: 633–637, 695–696, and John Burke, *A Genealogical and Heraldic History of the Commoners of Great Britain and Ireland* (4 vols., London, 1835), 4: 488–492.

Mr. Carver.[18] If it were a case in which the claim had been *estopped*, you would not have been called upon to consider the marriage settlement at all. But as it is, I say under the present circumstances, there is no presumption for the existence of that paper; and I do say to you, and to the court, and to all reasonable men, that there is much stronger presumption to make out the non-existence than the existence of it. In relation to the doctrine of presumptions, it is your duty to draw your own conclusions; and I believe it will be stated to you by the court, that, in presuming any state of things, not positively proved, you are responsible to your consciences alone. To them we leave you, and confide our cause. In conclusion, I shall merely revert to the influences [inferences?] we have drawn from the evidence which has been presented. We say that there are several substantial grounds for presuming a revocation of the marriage settlement. We say that every subsequent act of the parties goes contrary to the conveyance presumed, that the absence of the lease is fatal to the title; and that the whole claim can only be sustained by the most hazardous and most improbable presumptions.

Extract. Edward V. Sparhawk, *Report of the Trial . . . in the Case of James Jackson, ex dem. Theodosius Fowler and others, vs. James Carver* (New York, 1827), pp. 18–32.

FROM HENRY BOOTH COWLES

Dear Sir. New York Nov 16th. 1827

You have doubtless seen by the public prints that a verdict was rendered for the plaintiff in the Astor cause in the trial of which you was engaged. I am requested by the Attorney General to inform you that the remaining causes will in all probability be brought to trial at the present term of the Court & that from the state of the calender one of them will be reached on Monday. Indeed they have gone over till Monday by consent, since there is no prospect of trying them before that day & perhaps not then. I have reason to believe that your arrival here on Monday Evening will be in due season to take a part in the trial.[19] I am instructed to add that your presence is solicited by the Attorney General who will expect your aid on the trials. Your Obdt Servant Henry B. Cowles

ALS. DLC. Inscribed by DW "Ansd. the 18—I wd. come as soon as I could."

The legislature, having lost the case, now confronted the prospect of its liability to the landowners who faced ejectment. Since those potential

18. James Carver, the current occupant of the land.

19. On November 20, 1827, Judge Thompson postponed the next case. He stated to the attorneys that since it did not offer the prospect of raising any new points, he preferred to wait until the defendant appealed to the USSC.

damage suits exceeded Astor's demand, it became incumbent on the state to reach a settlement. In March and April 1828 a legislative committee proposed a new offer based on the law of April 1827. Late in April the bill passed. Besides giving Astor thirty days to agree to its terms, the law provided that the Morris claim would be extinguished and that the November 1827 trial would not count as one of the three victories needed by Astor. He agreed to its terms, and his attorneys soon filed five new actions. In November 1829 the federal circuit court heard the new ejectment suit against James Carver, and again Webster's side lost. They quickly appealed to the Supreme Court. After a lengthy argument, in which Webster participated, the court ruled in favor of Astor. Astor's lawyers soon won two more actions in the lower court. The state again appealed to the Supreme Court. In 1831 Webster and Ogden Hoffman argued a procedural question and lost.[20] By April of 1832 Astor had won his third case, and the state began to pay the settlement.

TO [MARTIN VAN BUREN?]

My Dear Sir — Boston Sep. 27. [18]28

I recd your's this morning,[21] & my first inclination was that I would meet you & Mr Cowles at New York, on the 4th Oct. according to your suggestion. I find, however, on reflection, that I have engagements, which would render *that day*, rather an inconvenient one, for such an appointment. Engagements are on me, for the latter end of next week, which it is not easy to shake off. I am disposed, however, to conform to your suggestion, in its general object, & varied only as to *time*. At the same time, it may be worth considering, whether it be not practicable to accomplish the object by one journey, instead of two. In other words, whether it would not be as useful, in regard to the main object, & less inconvenient to ourselves, to be in N York four or five days before the sitting of the Court. Upon reflection, this rather appears to me to be, under all circumstances, the preferable course. Still, I do not feel positive about it; & if it be, in your mind, matter of doubt, the previous conference is the safer mode, & ought to be adopted. What has led to this impression, on my mind is, that we have no testimony, that I am aware

20. The first case was *Carver* v. *Jackson*, 4 Peters 1 (1830). The next two cases came up together as *Ex parte Crane and another in the matter of Jackson, ex dem. Astor et al.* v. *Crane* and *Jackson, ex dem. Astor et al.* v. *Kelly*, 5 Peters 190 (1831). After the loss, the state's attorneys reformulated their bill of exceptions and appealed once more. In 1832 the case was argued on the merits (6 Peters 598) and affirmed for Astor. DW did not take part. Astor still held nine tenths of the claim. He eventually received over $500,000, a profit of 350% (Porter, 2: 887). A fuller treatment of the subject of land-title disputes will appear in Volume 3 of this series.

21. Letter not found.

of, farther off than Putnam County; that our chief labor will be, to consider how best to use what materials we have; & that coming together, four days before the Court, each having, in the meantime, turned his attention to all known questions in the cause, there will be time enough to settle the course of the defense, & summon witnesses on any new point; if such should occur to us. It would be somewhat disagreeable to me thus to extend the time of my stay in N. York, at the time of the trial; but on the whole I should prefer this, to another journey.

Nevertheless, My Dear Sir, I am disposed to follow your lead, because you have a better view of the whole ground, as well as for other reasons. Therefore I will meet you and Mr Cowles at N York, any time after hearing from you, but so as that I can be home again by the 15 or 16 October. You will probably receive this the morning of the *first*. If you answer by return of Post, I shall hear from you by the 5th—& can meet you in N York, the 8th—9th—10th—11th or 12th, if you should so conclude.

Allowing me three days after the proper time for the arrival of your letter, you may expect my attendance, on any day you may mention, within the above mentioned period. So much for "the weightier matters of the law."

As to the rest, My D. Sir, I do not hear that the "political health of my friends," in the great State needs, at present, either prescription or nursing. If not decidedly *good*, we are assured it is very satisfactorily *convalescent*. That State, we learn, is likely to enjoy soon what is said to comprize the whole substance of mortal bliss—"*sana mens*, in corpore sano."

Adieu! I would give you the Spanish benediction, ("God preserve your *Excellency* a thousand years!") but that I have not yet heard from *Herkimer*, and you have not informed me what *orders you sent up*.[22] But *masters* must be sometimes *servants*; do you not find it so? Yrs truly

D. Webster

ALS. MHi. Published in *Correspondence*, 2: 365–366.

FROM GREENE CURRIER BRONSON

Albany April 13. 1829

I have this day received assurances from Judge Platt, for the plff, that five of the Astor Suits, in which you are of Counsel for the people of this State, will be brought to trial at the next circuit [court] in New York—May 25th.

Having learned from Mr. [Ogden] Hoffman that you had not seen the

22. At the Herkimer convention in late September, New York Democrats nominated Van Buren as their candidate for governor.

last act of our Legislature upon the subject, I have enclosed a copy, together with a copy of the act to which it is an amendment.[23]

I hope that nothing will prevent your attendance; and I desire to hear from you as soon as your convenience will permit on that subject.

I am with great respect your obedient Hum. servant

Greene C. Bronson Atty Genl.

ALS. DLC. Greene Currier Bronson (1789–1863), Utica, New York lawyer, New York attorney general (1829–1836), chief justice, New York supreme court (1845–1847), judge, New York court of appeals (1847–1851).

FROM GREENE CURRIER BRONSON

Sir

Albany April 29. 1829

I have just received information that the Astor Suits will not be brought on until Monday June 1st.—one week later than the day appointed for the commencement of the Circuit. I do not mention this to induce a delay in the time of your arriving at New York, but to enable you to make such arrangements as will permit you to remain with us to a later period than you mentioned in your letter to Mr. Hoffman.[24] There is no probability that the five suits will be disposed of in one week, and I cannot think of going on without your aid; and absence of counsel is not a sufficient excuse for putting off the trials.

I shall still expect to meet you in N.Y. at the close of the week previous to the appointed day for the circuit, or by monday or tuesday the 25th. May—and desire the earliest day that will suit your convenience. Please let me hear from you upon these matters. Your Obt. Hum. Servant

Greene C. Bronson

ALS. DLC.

TO GREENE CURRIER BRONSON

Dear Sir,

Boston Novr. 12 [18]29

It is quite obvious that somebody is making an attempt to produce an impression on the public mind that the Astor causes are decided. Thus we see one paragraph headed "The Astor Causes settled"—And in another one learn, "The Legislature, it is supposed, will dispense with further trials"—And all the reports, in the Newspapers, which I have seen, of the late trials, keep entirely out of view the real questions. I suggest these things to you, merely that you may consider whether some measures should not be taken to counteract this course of proceeding, should it be persisted in.

Yrs with very true regard Danl. Webster

ALS. NhD.

23. Enclosures not found.

24. Letter not found.

TO GREENE CURRIER BRONSON

Dear Sir Boston Nov. 16, [18]29

We did not converse much, after the trial, upon the matter of moving that the Plff should signify his election, as to which demise[25] he would take his Verdict on; I presume, however, that the subject has not escaped your attention. I am, Dr Sir, with much regard, Yrs D. Webster

ALS. NhD.

4. APPELLATE ARGUMENT: *George Welsh* v. *Charles Barrett*

In *Welsh* v. *Barrett*[1] Webster defended Charles Barrett, a Boston merchant, in a suit by an endorsee to collect an unpaid promissory note endorsed by Barrett. Under the law of promissory notes the endorsee could hold the endorser liable only if he, the endorsee, proved that he had demanded payment from the maker, that the maker had failed to pay, and that notice of that fact had been given to the endorser. The note in question had been placed for collection at the State Bank in Boston. The bank's messenger, who had given notice to Barrett, had died. At the trial in 1818, over Webster's objection, the court admitted the messenger's record book as evidence of notice. When the jury returned a verdict for Welsh, Webster moved to set the verdict aside on the ground that the record book was inadmissible. The parties agreed to argue this evidentiary question at the next law term on the understanding that if Webster's objections prevailed, the plaintiff would be nonsuited.

Webster's adversaries rested their case on two points. First, they argued that the messenger had kept his records in accordance with the bank's by-laws making it a quasi-official document, and that no motive could be shown for him to have made a false entry. In support of this argument they cited two English cases. Secondly, they argued that a rejection of this sort of evidence would have adverse consequences for commerce where "so great a portion of the business of collecting bills of exchange and promissory notes devolves on the banks."[2]

In his argument Webster addressed both the legal and the policy arguments (Document 23). The principal difficulty he faced in answering the plaintiff came from the fact that the rules of evidence in Massachusetts had become more liberal than those of England in admitting written evidence. Although he found English precedents supporting his narrower interpretation, the plaintiff's attorneys, too, had found decisions that recognized analogous exceptions to the stricter rules. Webster

25. Technically, a lease; DW is using the term as synonymous with conveyance.

1. 15 Mass. 379 (1819).
2. Ibid., p. 380.

moved against his opponents by attacking each element of their analogies. He tried to destroy their precedents while laying a foundation for his own. At the end of his argument, he addressed the policy issue, warning the court that a decision favorable to Welsh would make all sorts of *ex parte* written evidence admissible.

Webster's argument did not prevail. Indeed, Judge Isaac Parker expressed surprise that the case had been argued so strenuously. It was clear to him that it came within the best evidence rule. It seemed common sense that "what a man has actually done and committed to writing, when under obligation to do the act, it being in the course of the business he has undertaken, and he being dead, there seems to be no danger in submitting [it] to the consideration of the jury."[3] That the case went as far as it did may be attributable to Webster's research and forceful presentation.

DOCUMENT 23. NOTES FOR ORAL ARGUMENT

Welsh v Barrett

mot[ion] for a new trial—

The Defdt contends that the Book in question ought not to have been recd in evidence

It is not *a corporation Book*; because it is neither kept by the certifying Officer of the Corporation; nor does it purport to record corporate proceedings.[4]

It can make no difference, that this Book was kept in pursuance of a Bye Law. The Bank cannot make a Bye Law which shall affect third persons with new rules of evidence. There is no room to put this on the ground sometimes assumed, that those who deal with Banks must be presumed to submit to their rules. This note was not made to the Bank, nor with a view to be discounted there.

This *memorial*, or *entry*, can bind third persons no farther, than if it had been made by a *merchant's clerk*, instead of the messenger of a Bank.[5]

A merchant has as much right to put his clerk under oath, as this corporation had to put this messenger under oath.

3. Ibid., p. 385.

4. Generally, the books of a corporation were evidence of the acts of the corporate body when kept by the proper officer. Joseph Kinnicutt Angell and Samuel Ames, *Treatise on the Law of Private Corporations Aggregate* (Boston, 1832), p. 406.

5. DW wanted to counteract the plaintiff's argument that the court should consider the messenger in the same light as a public officer. If DW persuaded the court to treat the messenger as analogous to a merchant's clerk, he stood a chance of bringing the case under his strongest precedent: *Cooper* v. *Marsden*, see note 7, below.

If this evidence be admissible, it would be equally admissible, if the Bank had been Plf.

Therefore, the true question is this; the person employed by the holder of a promissory note to give notice to the indorser being dead, & having left behind him a memorandum that he gave notice, is that memorandum evidence agt. the Indorser?

No case, in support of the admission of this evidence has as yet been cited; except such as are supposed to bear upon it by analogy.[6]

Against its admission are two rules of Law; *one*, requiring parol testimony to be delivered under oath; *the other* requiring it to be given *with notice*
1 Espinasse Reps 1. *Cooper v. Mar*[s]*den*—supposed to be directly in point[7]

5. Durnford & East 121. Outram vs Morewood[8]

I take it to be clear, that the *oath* which the authorities speak of must be a *judicial oath*. The cases, in which private Books & Memorials are admissible are collected in the Editor's note to *Greenville v Warren*, 2nd Strange 1129.

This case falls within *neither* of the four classes.[9]

The great objection to such evidence is, it is *ex parte*; & being given *on*

6. The plaintiff's attorneys cited *Pitman* v. *Maddox*, 2 Salkeld 690 (1699), where the court received a shop-book as evidence of the dead clerk's handwriting, and *Price* v. *The Earl of Torrington*, 1 Salkeld 285 (1704), in which the court accepted the entries in an account book of a dead deliveryman.

7. This 1793 case held that book entries by merchants and bank clerks could only be proved by the testimony of the clerk who made the entry. In this case the clerk, though still alive, no longer resided in England. The *Cooper* case implied criticism of the more permissive holdings of the two cases mentioned in note 6 above. Judge Parker seized on the fact that the clerk in *Cooper* still lived to distinguish *Cooper* from the instant case.

8. A 1793 case in which the court rejected the offer of a book of rent entries made by a third person, deceased, to prove the identity of a parcel of land. The judges stressed the necessity for an oath to prove a particular fact. Clearly DW wanted the court to consider the lack of an oath in the *Welsh* case.

9. The reporter in the 1739 *Greenville* case elaborated four classes where the private records of a deceased could be used: 1) where the party charged himself with receipt of money; 2) where hearsay evidence of the declaration would have been allowed; 3) in the case of ecclesiastical dues; 4) in the case of shopkeepers' books (the cases discussed in note 6). Clearly this fourth category, by strong analogy, supported DW's opponents. His main task, then, was to undermine it.

oath is not sufficient—vid. 2nd East 54—*Rex v. Inhaba. of Fe*[*rry*]*frystone*[10]

1 Salkeld 285 The case of *Price v Torrington* was cited on the other side. The answer to this, is

1. That was the case of *shop keepers Books*, & the proof was of *the delivery of the articles*; & that is one of the excepted cases.
2. The authority of this case is *doubtful*. It has been questioned, & does not seem to have re[ceive]d the approbation of subsequent judges, & of the Profession. 2nd Pothier 190.[11] It is conformable to our American practice; but it is not certain, that it wd. now be acted upon by the English Courts. It certainly would *not be extended by analogy*.

☞ A decisive answer to all the arguments *ab inconvenienti*[12] on the other side is this; the law has provided a regular mode of proving notice, & perpetuating the proof by notarial certificates. Most, or at least some, of the Banks follow this course. If others do not, they must abide by the misfortune of the loss of evidence.

If this evidence be admitted, where will the rule stop?
not with Banks; for Banks have no more right to use the Memoranda of deceased agents in evidence than other people.

Not with proof of notice, on notes & bills; because there is as much reason why other facts, payments, for example, should be proved in the same way.

It must come to this; that if a person puts his agent under oath to perform his duty, the memoranda of that agent of acts done by him shall, after his death, be evidence to bind third persons.

This would be, it is conceived, a vast innovation upon the existing law of evidence. *It would be evidence ex parte; & it would be parol evidence not delivd. under the sanction of a judicial oath.*

AD(DW). NhD. Dudley Atkins Tyng used these notes in publishing DW's argument: 15 Mass. 379, 380–383 (1819).

10. 2 East 53 (1801) held that neither the hearsay evidence of a dead pauper nor *ex parte* evidence in writing on oath was admissible on the question of residence under the poor law.

11. Robert Joseph Pothier, *A Treatise on Obligations, Considered in a Moral and Legal View* (2 vols., Newburn, N.C., 1802), 2: 190, argued for the civil law position that a merchant's journal, kept in accordance with usual business practices, was complete evidence of a debt only when coupled with his testimony on oath; furthermore, Pothier argued that the books of small shopkeepers ought not to be introduced in evidence. Shopbooks and journals, however, could always be used against the merchant.

12. *From inconvenience or hardship*, an argument based on the difficulties to which a certain decision could lead. DW then offered his own version of the adverse consequences of a judgment for the plaintiff.

CHAPTER 3. Attorney Fees

In our own "Bank Note World," on this side the Atlantic, and in an age when the greatest poets or novelists are willing to confess that they toil "for gain, not glory," it is ridiculous to attempt to perpetuate a monstrous legal fiction, by which the hard working lawyers of our day, toiling till midnight in their offices are to be regarded in the eye of the law in the light of the patrician jurisconsults of ancient Rome.[1]

Webster correctly anticipated that his move to Boston would enable him to increase his income. This was of immediate importance, since he had left New Hampshire indebted to several merchants as a result of an unsuccessful land speculation. In November 1816 he wrote to one of these creditors:

> I have found better encouragement here than I expected, & I feel at length, as if I could see thro my embarrassments notwithstanding the loss of property in the fall of my Country lands. . . . If I have ordinarily good fortune at Washington, my earnings, this winter will be respectable.[2]

In his Massachusetts practice, he not only earned statutory attorney fees, but charged his clients the higher Boston rates for legal services. Since 1796 the Boston bar had followed a schedule of minimum fees.[3] This eliminated cost competition between lawyers and placed a floor under their incomes. A Boston practice also held out other advantages. Boston clients gave attorneys retainers, both on an annual and individual case basis, to employ their services. The larger volume of commercial litigation found in the Boston area enabled Webster to cultivate clients in need of a lawyer's skills in the specialized world of commercial law. When manufacturing began in the 1820s, Webster's expertise in the law of business organization and patents brought him many new clients. Unlike the country lawyer who earned a modest living handling many different minor matters, the commercial specialist of the city serviced

1. Senator Gulian Crommelin Verplanck in *Adams* v. *Stevens & Cagger*, 26 Wendell (N.Y.) 451, 466 (1841).

2. DW to Nathaniel Appleton Haven, November 9, 1816, *Correspondence*, 1: 203–204.

3. For a MassCCP case an attorney received $1.50; for a MassSJC onc, $2.50; and for attendance, 33 cents a day: *Suffolk County Bar Book, 1770–1805* (Cambridge, Mass., 1882), pp. 29–30.

the business world. The greater sums at stake prompted the litigants to pay more for legal services.

The changing nature of the legal profession also had an important impact on Webster's professional income. In New Hampshire statute and custom had hedged an attorney's compensation. The legislature limited the amounts given in the bill of costs; custom and a notion of just price determined what an attorney charged his client. This dual set of restrictions reflected both public suspicion of lawyers and the earlier ideal of the lawyer as gentleman. In the seventeenth and eighteenth centuries, communities most heavily influenced by the English view of the legal profession thought of it as something different from other "callings."[4] In this idealized conception an attorney's compensation was considered as a gift from the client rather than a debt. As such, an attorney could not sue for the value of his services. In the latter part of the eighteenth century, the gentleman ideal became eroded by a newer entrepreneurial ethic that conceived of the practice of law as a money-making enterprise. The lawyers who had looked to the gentleman ideal to legitimate their profession now realized that it had an adverse effect on their incomes. When a Pennsylvania lawyer tested the gentleman ideal in 1819 in a suit for the value of his services, the defendant's attorney argued that the "character and honour of the profession, as well as the ties of confidence between its members and their clients" would best be furthered by a denial of the action.[5] The court agreed. The intrusion of entrepreneurship would undermine the standards and standing of the bar. This rearguard action, however, proved fruitless. While lawyers easily circumvented the restriction on suits for fees by taking promissory notes from their clients (a practice begun before the decision), pressure began to build to force the courts to recognize lawyering as a business. In 1830 the Pennsylvania supreme court implicitly overruled its earlier decision. An 1835 case made this recognition explicit. Lawyering, the court said, is a "profession which is now as purely a calling as any mechanical art."[6]

Although the Massachusetts courts had not followed the earlier Pennsylvania position on lawyers suing for fees, lawyers, themselves, considered it dishonorable to do so. Massachusetts, however, did respond to the intrusion of entrepreneurialism into the profession. In 1823 the SJC decided that contingent fee agreements (long employed by the Boston

4. In England the courts did not permit barristers and physicians to sue for fees; solicitors and surgeons operated under no such handicap. See *Newman* v. *Washington*, 8 Tenn. 79 (1827), for a rejection of the English rule.

5. *Mooney* v. *Lloyd*, 5 Sergeant and Rawle (Pa.) 412, 413 (1819).

6. *Gray* v. *Brackenridge*, 2 Pa. 75 (1830); *Foster* v. *Jack*, 4 Watts (Pa.) 334 (1835). This interpretation draws on a conversation with Morton J. Horwitz.

bar) were illegal.[7] But such a decision could do little to stem the overthrow of the earlier ideal. By the 1840s it was commonly accepted that a lawyer's "service is worth just what it will buy; what the communities are willing to pay. It has its market value, like all other services."[8] Although this view freed the lawyers from the older tradition of gratuitous service, it posed a danger to the earning of large fees. If lawyering amounted to a business within a market structure in which competition determined rates of compensation, how could one lawyer demand a greater fee for the same service? Although in the realm of fees lawyers found the gentleman conception constraining, they did not want their compensation regulated solely by the law of supply and demand. They solved this predicament by renominating themselves a profession. This again separated them from the other "callings" and enabled them to claim greater compensation for their "intellectual" activity. Moreover, between individual lawyers, compensation could vary because of different levels of experience.

> Skill, and faculty of using professional knowledge, make differences, even where there is the same diligence and fidelity. These qualities will command higher rates of remuneration; and because they will command more, they are worth more.[9]

FROM SAMUEL BELL

Sir, Chester Jan 12. 1818.

I send you two hundred dollars towards fees in the defence of Bullard's action,[10] and will pay you such additional sum as will be considered a liberal compensation.

Mr French[11] has placed in my hands a written obligation to pay you one thousand dollars in the event of your success in obtaining a decision, that the Courts of the United States have not Jurisdiction, that the action of Debt cannot be sustained, or on the Statute of limitations.

I have requested Judge [Jeremiah] Smith and Mr. [Jeremiah] Mason

7. *Thurston* v. *Percival*, 1 Pickering (Mass.) 415 (1823). See DW to Robert Elwell, June 7, 1825, pp. 139–140, below.

8. *Curtis* v. *Nye*, a MassCCP,S decision reported in 6 Pennsylvania Law Journal 475, 477 (1847).

9. Id. at 478.

10. Silas Bullard, a Boston merchant and holder of bearer notes from the defunct Hillsborough Bank (New Hampshire), sued Bell, a stockholder of the bank, to force Bell to pay for dishonored bank bills. The statute incorporating the bank made the stockholders ultimately responsible for outstanding bank bills. *Bullard* v. *Bell*, 1 Mason 243 (1817) (DW did not appear). In 1819 the USSC heard the appeal; DW argued for Bell. The court reached no decision and in February 1820 ordered new arguments in 1821. See note, 5 Wheaton vii (1820).

11. Frederic French, another bank stockholder. See p. 125, below.

to forward you the papers mentioned in my last which they will do seasonably.[12]

After you have been at Washington long enough to ascertain from the state of the docket the prospect of being oblidged to go to trial at the first term, you will be so good as to write me on the subject.

If there should be a certainty or even a considerable probability of a trial, I will set out for Washington on the receipt of your letter, as I wish to be present when the question is decided.

Should you desire it, I will engage other Counsel to aid you, but should prefer delaying it until I am at Washington unless you should advise otherwise. Your humble servant Samuel Bell

ALS. NhD.

Webster kept a book of receipts in which he recorded the sums paid him by his clients. Of this record four fragments remain. Three of these are reproduced in this chapter.[13] They are only an approximation of his income since he did not record the statutory fees earned in preparing cases. From these records his yearly income, on a fiscal year basis beginning in September, was:

1816–1817	$ 4,621[14]
1817–1818	7,767
1818–1819	15,181
1819–1820	8,393
1820–1821	10,240
1821–1822	12,805
1822–1823	5,095[15]
1823–1824	7,019
1824–1825	7,285
1825–1826	13,238 (1800)[16]

12. Bell's USCC counsel, Mason and Smith, had lost each of these points: the lower court ruled that debt was the proper form of action; that a bearer note did not fall under the eleventh section of the Judiciary Act of 1789 requiring a holder to establish the diverse citizenship of his assignor; and that the New Hampshire statute of limitations did not bar an action of debt for a bank bill. Papers not found. See also DW to Jeremiah Mason, February 4, 1819, mDW 2631; DW to Bell, February 11, 1819, mDW 2639; DW to Mason, February 23, 1819, mDW 2650; DW to Bell, March 1, 1819, mDW 2668.

13. The fourth was for the Spanish claims, presented in Chapter 4, pp. 266–275, below.

14. The first three sets of figures are taken from the receipt books, printed below; those for 1819–1820 through 1831–1832 are from *W & S*, 17: 545.

15. His income for 1822–1825 appears lower because he did not include the Spanish claims compensation.

16. The figures in the parentheses represent his congressional salary, which he counted among his receipts.

1826–1827	16,936 (1120)
1827–1828	16,000 (2000)
1828–1829	10,840 (2000)
1829–1830	12,690 (2000)
1830–1831	14,774 (2000)
1831–1832	15,700 (2000)
1832–1833	8,212 (2000)[17]
1833–1834	13,140 (2000)
1834–1835	15,184 (2000)
1835–1836	21,793 (2000)
1836–April 1837	15,600 (2000)
On a fiscal year basis beginning in June:	
1843–1844	12,900
1844–1845	11,075 (620)
1845–1846	17,050
1846–March 1847	7,900

The first set of fee records (1816–1819), printed below, indicates the level of Webster's customary charges at the beginning of his Boston practice. In this short span of time his charges for advice go from $10 to $30, his retainers from $20 to between $30 and $50, and his fees for arguing Supreme Court cases often double.

DOCUMENT 24. BOOK OF RECEIPTS

[August 14, 1816–August 14, 1818]

1816.		
	came to B[oston] Aug. 14—1816	
	Recd	
Sep.	of Mr Beyerman	100
	vid R[etainer?]	
	of Mr Gray—vid R	50
Oct.	1. of Mr Colburn for advice	10
	relative to M[anufacturers] & M[echaniks] Bank	
Oct	5 of Mr [Richard] Crowningshield in action	20.
	Sturgis—vs him	
	of Mr Beyerman, further fees, in action	
	Cremer & al v Higginson	200
	of Mr Wood, for fees in case of Margaretta[18]	500.
		880.

17. The figures for this year and those following are taken from the receipt books, printed below.

18. In the fee documents in this chapter, case citations are given only for lawsuits we have identified. Hugo Beyerman, Rotterdam lawyer and agent for Adrian Cremer (a

	Brot over	880.
Oct.	30. of W[arren] Lovejoy, in behalf of Jas. Wilson, retainer in case v T. Lyman	20
	of C. & J. H Hayward, retainer in case of goods at Hampden	125.
	of —— by note, fee in case of Ariadne[19] at W[ashington]	500.
	of Smedes, by bill, in case of George	500
	of W. N. Boylston, Retainer	30
	of Lt Legge, retainer in Bevins case	60
	of Coats, in action Wightman v him by Geo S[ullivan] Esq[20]	20
		$2135

	Brot over	2135
Feb.	of T. Merrill jr, in case U. S. v Barque Argo in S. C. of U. S.	130
	of C. Coolidge, in case Inglee v Coolidge	100
April	of O. C. Wyman, retainer in Inglee v W[yman] & St[one]	20.00
	of T. Melvill, in action Jarvis v Melvill, retainer	30.00
	of G. H. Apthorpe, in action Boardman & Pope v him	50.00
	of W. Lovejoy for advice[21]	10.
		2475

Dutch merchant); John Gray, Boston merchant; possibly James S. Colburn, Boston merchant; *Sturges* v. *Crowninshield*, USCC,DMass, May 1819; *Cremer et al.* v. *Higginson and Perkins*, USCC,DMass, October 1817, 1 Mason 323 (1817); John Wood of Boston, captain of the *Margaretta*; *The Margaretta* (two cases), USSC, unreported, 1816, File Nos. 802–803.

19. Warren Lovejoy, a merchant, had recently moved to Boston from New Hampshire; James Wilson (1766–1859; Harvard 1787), New Hampshire lawyer and legislator; *U.S.* v. *T. Lyman*, USCC,DMass, October 1818, 1 Mason 482 (1818); Charles and Joseph H. Hayward, Boston merchants; *The Ariadne*, 2 Wheaton 143 (1817).

20. Alexander and George W. Smedes, New York merchants; *The George*, 2 Wheaton 278 (1817); Ward Nicholas Boylston, Boston merchant. Legge has not been identified. *U.S.* v. *Bevans*, 3 Wheaton 336 (1818), DW probably refers to the unreported USCC,DMass case; Joshua Coates, English cabinet maker; *Wightman* v. *Coates*, MassSJC,S, March 1818, 15 Mass. 1 (1818); George Sullivan (1783–1866), Massachusetts lawyer, studied with his father, James, admitted in 1804, state senator.

21. Thomas Merrill, Jr., Portland, Maine distiller; *The Argo*, 2 Wheaton 287 (1817); *Inglee* v. *C. Coolidge*, 2 Wheaton 363 (1817), and 15 Mass. 66 (1818); Oliver C. Wyman, Boston insurance broker; Thomas Melville (d. 1832), surveyor, port of Boston, and sheriff, Suffolk County; George H. Apthorp, Boston merchant.

			2475
		of A. Peabody Esq, last fall, advice &c	10.00
April			
	12	of Munroe & Grosvenor for advice, in Winslow's case	10 00
	14.	of H. Rice, retainer &c respecting bonds	200.00
	30	of Messrs Tappan & Searle on acct of the Brutus[22]	250.00
May		of F. French, in Bullard's action v him	50.
		of S. Bell in Bullard's action v him	50
			3045
			3045
		of Blunt & Wright, on Wheeler & Farley's Comp[lain]t	20
		of Upton & Adams, last Decr. at W.	100
May		of Mr. Chadwicke, in case of Bedford v Baker	50
		of Mr Blunt, on his Indict	25.
		of N Bryant, retainer in cases v him respecting Schooner Ocean	50
		of Winslow Lewis, retainer in Lowell v Lewis[23]	50
		Brot over	3340
	19	of Upton & Adams	100.
May	30.	of U.S. for retainer in action v. Theo. Lyman	250
	31	of Winslow Lewis & Co. fee for arguing Lowell v Lewis	200

22. Edmund Munroe and Lemuel P. Grosvenor, Boston merchants; Henry Rice, Boston merchant; Lewis Tappan (1788–1873), Boston merchant, moved to New York in 1828, where he became well known not only for his mercantile activities but also as a leading abolitionist; George Searle was Tappan's partner in Boston at this time.

23. John Blunt and Chandler Wright, Moses Wheeler and Ebenezer Farley, Boston mercantile partnerships; Samuel Upton (1791–1842), merchant, moved from Salem to Castine, Maine (1816), subsequently lived in Bangor, Boston, and Washington, D.C.; Adams, not identified, was his partner in Castine; Chadwicke has not been identified; *Bedford* v. *Baker*, USCC,DMass, May 1818, one of a series of patent infringement cases filed by John Bedford; Nathaniel Bryant, Boston merchant; Winslow Lewis (1770–1850), Boston inventor, manufacturer, and lighthouse builder, state legislator (1828–1833); *F. C. Lowell* v. *W. Lewis*, 1 Mason 182 (1817).

June		
2nd	of Messrs B. & K. for comm[ission]s on M. S. 344. M. S.	251.
June 5.	of M. Park, fee for arguing Park v Bell in C.C.P.	40
6.	of [?] Jarvis, retainer in Jarvis v Rogers[24]	20
		4201
	Brot up	4201
July		
	of A. Lovejoy	10
16	of Jno. Morland	20
22	of A Lovejoy	20
26	of Mr Dyett, for opinion on policy	10
	of W. Lovejoy	530
	of A Lovejoy	30
		4821
deduct for credited more than recd of N. Goddard by G. S[ullivan] in case of Ariadne.[25]		200
		$4621

Aug. 14. 1817—DW

1817	Aug. 14—	
	of Mr Holker, retainer in case vs Stackpole & others	20.00
	of Russell Freeman Esq, in action abt. Church in Sandwich	20.00
	of Abel Harris, retainer in case v Underwriters on Volant	20.00
	of D R Rogers, in case relative to Dr Cutter's Will	20.00
	of Wm Vinal, Wiscasset, in case Perkins v him, retainer	20.00
30th.	of Robt. D. Lawton, retainer in case Harvey v Richds, & vid ag[reemen]t on file[26]	100.00
		200.00

24. B., K., Park, and Jarvis have not been identified.

25. Andrew Lovejoy, Warren's partner. Neither Morland nor Dyett has been identified. Nathaniel Goddard, Boston merchant.

26. John Holker and his wife, residents of Springbury, Virginia, sued the heirs of William Stackpole of Boston, *Holker et ux.* v. *MacKay et al.*, USCC,DMass, October 1822; Freeman (d. 1842), collector of the port of New Bedford, state representative; Abel Harris, Portsmouth mer-

	Brot up		200.
Sep. 3.	of S. Tuttle		12.
	of Jno Holker, in case aforesd.		50.
8	of Lewis Tappan, in case Searle v Wms & Wood		25.
9	of Jos. Adams		5.
	of C. Sawtell[?], note for tuition		50.
	at Exeter of Fr. Brown	30.	
	" Jon. Peirce	36	
	" of R. Harris	10.	76
	of Pearson, retainer in Pearson v Goodrich[27]		30
			448

	Brot over	448
	of Ch J. Stuart at Exeter	25
	of A. Lovejoy, N. York, by bill in favor Eastburn	30
30	of Mr. Freeman, Sandwich, in case Nye & al v Tilden	55
	of R. Hoxie, Sandwich,	20
Oct 4.	of Mr Kimball, for one years tuition	166
	of Mr Marston, cash & note, fees in case Ind[ictmen]t v Kenniston	65
	of W Sullivan, in case Ramdo Colder[?] v Shapley[28]	40
		849

chant; *Harris* v. *Elwell*, USCC,DMass, May 1819, one of a series of cases involving the *Volant* (see pp. 418–438, below); Daniel R. Rogers of Portsmouth, New Hampshire was an executor of the will of his brother-in-law, Dr. William Cutter, also of Portsmouth, who signed his will on May 16, 1817, only six days before his death; William Vinal of Wiscasset, Maine; *J. Perkins* v. *W. Vinal*, MassSJC,S, March 1819. Lawton has not been further identified. *Harvey* v. *Richards*, USCC,DMass, May 1819, 1 Mason 381 (1818), see pp. 584 629, below. The agreement has not been found.

27. Tuttle has not been identified. *G. Searle* v. *E. Williams et al.*, MassSJC,S, November 1818, Sawtell has not been identified. Francis Brown (1784–1820; Dartmouth 1805), minister (1810–1815), overseer and trustee, Bowdoin College (1810–1815); in August 1815 the trustees of Dartmouth College removed the president and offered the position to Brown, thereby precipitating the *Dartmouth College* case; Pierce was a Portsmouth merchant; probably Robert Harris, Portsmouth merchant, brother and partner of Abel Harris; Ebenezer Pearson brought suit for malicious prosecution, Fuess, 1: 212.

28. Charles Jesse Stuart (1788–1837; Dartmouth 1809), New Hampshire lawyer, admitted in 1813. Neither Eastburn nor Hoxie has been identified. Edmund Kimball (1793–1873; Harvard 1814), Boston lawyer, admitted in 1817, was one of DW's law students; possibly, Ste-

	Brot up	849
Oct 6.	of H. Gosset & Co. retainer in case Pray v them	30.
	of Laurason & Fowle, retainer in suit v Nickerson	100
7.	of N. C. Betton for one years tuition	166.
	For two small services	10
15	of Thadeus Mayhew, thro P. O. Thacher	50
	of R. Crowningshield, in Sturgis v Crowningshield[29]	50
		1255

	Brot over	1255
Oct. 25.		
	of Mr Hoyt, in action Whitimore v Danvers Factory	30
	of Otis Saul, for advice	10.
Nov. 3	of Mr Beyerman, in Cremer v Higginson	200
	of Mr B	300
	of Otis Saul	10.
12	of T. W. Thompson	20.
	of J. C. Bartlett	10.
	of Mr Greenleaf, for Mr T. Wiggin	30.
	of Mr Jas Penniman, in case Weston [v] him C[ircuit] C[ourt].[30]	60
		1925

	Brot up	1925
Nov		
14.	of Calvin Fillmore for advice	20
22	of Saml Dilloway, in actions Emery &a v him	20
26.	of Mss Steamboat Co. vs Dodge	40
	of G. H. Apthorpe	100

phen W. Marston, Essex County lawyer. DW had successfully defended the Kenniston brothers against a charge of armed robbery, Fuess, 1: 210–212.

29. H. Gosset & Company has not been identified; Laurason & Fowle, a Washington, D.C. mercantile partnership; *Laurason & Fowle* v. *Nickerson et al.*, MassSJC,S, November 1819, see pp. 345–356, below; Ninian C. Betton (1787–1856; Dartmouth 1814), read law with DW (September 1816–October 1817); Thaddeus Mayhew, New Orleans merchant.

30. Joseph Hoyt, agent of the Danvers Cotton Factory Company; *Whittemore et al.* v. *Danvers Cotton Factory Company*, MassSJC,M, October 1818; Saul has not been identified; James Penniman, Boston merchant; John C. Bartlett, Boston merchant; Samuel Greenleaf and Timothy Wiggin, Boston merchants, partners in Wiggins, Greenleaf & Hale; *Weston* v. *Penniman*, USCC,DMass, October 1817, 1 Mason 306 (1817).

Decr	of Mr Holker, in MacKay's case	30
	of Wm Ladd, in Bank v Ladd	40
23	of Wm Welsh, in Fisk v Welsh & genl retainer	50
30	of Gilmore & Aiken, in action Bean v them[31]	30
		2255

	Brot over	2255
1818		
Jan. 10.	of Mr Stoughton, in Divina Pastora	250
	of F. Brown, in [Dartmouth] College cause,	1000
13	of Thos. Agry, in case of pet in legislature	50
	of Francis Bachelder, in case v S. Wiley	75
	of Israel Thorndike, fee in case Gray v him & als (pd. on note)[32]	1000
14	of Saml Bell Esqr. in case Bullard v him, Washington	200
		$ 4830

Brot up	4830
Jan. 20	
of Arowsick Petitioners	25
of Bridgwater Petitioners	50
of J. Coates fee Wightman v Coates	100
of Thos. Mellville, balance fees in action v Brown & two real actions to this term	90
of Jno Hopkins, for advice	20
of Jno L Sullivan	50
of S. Brown, fee in C. Ct. Gilman v. him & als	70
of same, towards fee in Sup. Court	350
of Chs Rivers, in case v Dana[33]	50
	5635.

31. Fillmore, Dilloway, Ladd, and Welsh have not been identified. Josiah Gilmore and John Aiken, Boston merchants; *Bean* v. *Gilmore et al.*, MassSJC,S, November 1819.

32. Don Juan Stoughton, Spanish consul, Boston; *The Divina Pastora*, 4 Wheaton 52 (1819); Thomas Agry of Hallowell, Maine, shipbuilder; Bachelder has not been identified. Israel Thorndike (1755–1832), Essex County shipowner and later Boston real estate investor, one of the wealthiest men in Boston. *W. Gray* v. *J. Gray and Thorndike*, unreported MassSJC,S (1817) grew out of the cases involving the ship *Volant*. See pp. 418–438, below.

33. *Melville* v. *H. C. Brown*, 15 Mass. 82 (1818); John Hopkins, Boston merchant; John Langdon Sullivan (1777–1865; M.A. Harvard 1807), engineer, inventor, and physician; Samuel Brown, Boston merchant and one of the directors of the New England Mississippi Land Company; *Gilman* v. *S. Brown et al.*, USCC,DMass, October 1817, 1 Mason

	Brot up	5635
1818		
Feb.	of Thos Merrill jr, at Washington in case of Argo	50
	of Mr Suckley, in case of Experiment	150
	of Wm Prout in case v Lewis Deblois	20
March.	of Dedham Bank, in case King v Bank	10
	of Jno Blunt jr, for advice	30
	of Geo Odiorne for advice	20
	of Mr. Henry, to retain in case Jenkins v him	10
Ap. 6	of [Winslow?] Lewis, on Wyman's Indi[c]t[ment]	50
	of Wm R Lee[34]	20
	Brot up	5995
Ap. 15.	of A. Peabody, in Park v Bell	50
	of Joshua Jackman in Com[monweal]th v him	150
	of D Sewall, retainer	20
	of Mr Bridge	10
	of [Oliver C.] Wyman & Stone, & O. C. Wyman balance acct.—say—	70
	of Mr Robinson, Essex[35]	20
	of T. Mayhew, by P. O. T[hacher] Esq	50
	of Jno Blunt jr, balance of fees	20
	of Upton & Adams	100
		6485
	Brot over	6485.
May 24.	of Staunton, Fiske & al in claim v Fales' Estate	50
27th.	of Caleb Eaton, retainer in Eaton v Hartshorn	20
June 1.	of H. Rice, in case U. S. v him	350
3.	of Jno. Morland, balance of fees, in Exeter	

191 (1818), and 4 Wheaton 255 (1819). Rivers has not been further identified. *Rivers* v. *Dana*, MassSJC,S, November 1818 (no papers found).

34. Suckley has not been identified. *The Experiment*, unreported USCC,DMass case affirming a USDC,DMe decision, 4 Wheaton 84 (1819) and 8 Wheaton 261 (1823). Neither Prout nor Deblois has been identified. *King* v. *Dedham Bank*, MassSJC,S, March 1819, 15 Mass. 447 (1819), see pp. 528–530, below; George Odiorne, treasurer of the Boston Exchange Office. Henry and Wyman have not been identified. William Raymond Lee (1745–1824), Marblehead, Massachusetts merchant, selectman and state representative, collector of customs, Salem (1802–1824).

35. Jackman, Sewall, Bridge, and Robinson have not been identified. Jonas E. Stone, Wyman's partner in brokerage firm.

	Factory case	50
11.	of Mr Chickering, for Dedham Bank, in King's Pet.	20
	of Messrs J. S. & E. Dwight, fee in case Sherwin v Baldwin	30.
	of Mr Bullard, in Barrett v Lewis[36]	25

Brot over	7030
of Mr Reed, opinion in Rice & Reed	20
of J. W. Tilford, in Tilford v Sweat & others	20
of Mrs Holker, in H. v Mackay	150
of Jno. W Tilford, by Mr Welby	100
of Mess[rs] Thorne & Haukherd by bill, say	50
of Mr Shaw, bal fees in case Russell v Perkins	25
of Jno. Amory, in case v U.S.	50
of Mr Barker, in Corliss[?] v Barker, retainer[37]	30

	Brot over	7475
	of Mr Thacher, in LeRoy v Blanchard	25.
	of Mr Sohier for Mr Colburn, on his indem[nit]y to Baldwin, & retainer in any action v Baldwin on that acct.	80
Aug 12	of U. S. Bank, in dispute with Maryland, retainer	100
13.	of Mr Dearborn, in Lottery case retainer	20
	of Mr. Apthorpe, in his case with B & P & others by receipt to S. Green[38]	117
		$7.767

Aug. 14. 1818 D. Webster

ADS. MHi.

36. Francis Stanton, Horatio H. Fisk, and Thaddeus Nichols, Boston mercantile partnership. Eaton has not been identified. *U.S.* v. *H. Rice*, USCC,DMass, May 1818, and 4 Wheaton 246 (1819); Jabez Chickering, cashier of the Dedham Bank. The Dwights have not been identified. Sampson Bullard, Boston trader; *Barrett* v. *W. Lewis*, MassSJC,S, March 1824.

37. John T. Reed and Henry G. Rice, Boston merchants. Tilford has not been identified. Nancy Holker, see n. 26, above. Welby, Thorne, and Haukherd have not been identified. John Amory, Boston merchant; Barker has not been identified.

38. William Davies Sohier (1787–1868; Harvard 1805), Boston lawyer, studied with Christopher Gore. Baldwin has not been identified. *McCulloch* v. *Maryland*, 4 Wheaton 316 (1819). Neither Dearborn nor Green has been identified.

DOCUMENT 25. BOOK OF RECEIPTS

Receipts 1818 to 1819.—August 14.

1818		
Aug. 15.	Of Mr. Odiorne, in his patent cause	$ 80 00
" 20.	Of Salem Bank, in cause *v.* Gloucester Bank	30 00
	Of Messrs. Torrey, Warner, and Co., for advice respecting guarantee	15 00
" 24.	Of Messrs. Munson and Barnard, for opening in case of Acct.	25 00
" 28.	Of Arthur Gilman	20 00
" 29.	Of Mr. Dearborn in lottery case	150 00
Sept. 3.	Of Mr. R. Crowninshield, in case Sturgis *v.* Crowninshield	150 00
" 4.	Of Mr. B. Smith, for advice, on will of Abiel Smith	20 00
	Of Mr. Noyes, in Robinson's business	25 00
" 6.	Of S. T. T., fee in case T *v.* Skinner	30 00
" 9.	Of Samuel Wait in dispute with Mill corporation, retainer	50 00
	Of Wm. Tucker, retainer in action *v.* Weld[39]	40 00
		$635 00

1818.	Brought over	$635 00
Sept. 11.	Of Cline and others, indicted for riot	20 00
Oct. 15.	Of Mr. Barnard, fee in Penniman *v.* Barnard	25 00
	Of B. Eaton, Jr., in Simpson *v.* Eaton	20 00
Oct. 15.	Of United States in action *v.* Lyman	250 00
	Of S. Hubbard, retained in Richardson causes	50 00
" 25.	Of Jas. Otis	50 00
" 28.	Of H. G. Otis, Jr., in case respecting bridge	30 00
	Of Capt. Tracy, in case respecting Galen	20 00
Nov. 2.	Of Mr. Gray, advice about Bond *v.* Essex Bank	25 00
	Of Mr. Marsh, fee in Harmon *v.* March, C. P.	40 00
	Of Silas Bullard	100 00
" 3.	Of Mr. Foster's Ex'rs at Salem	70 00
	Of John Paine, in Page *v.* Paine, in Essex	50 00
	Of Caleb Smith, in tobacco cause, Cir. Court	25 00

39. *Odiorne* v. *Amesbury Nail Factory*, 2 Mason 28 (1819) (DW was not attorney of record); *Salem Bank* v. *Gloucester Bank*, MassCCP, E, September 1817, MassSJC,E, October 1820, 17 Mass. 1, 33 (1820), see pp. 533–537, below. Torrey, Warner & Company has not been identified. Israel Munson and Charles Barnard, Boston mercantile partnership. Gilman, the Smiths, Noyes, Wait, and Tucker have not been identified. *Weld* v. *Tucker*, MassSJC, S, March 1819 (no papers found).

"	9.	Of Bryant and Sturgis, in Paul Jones	100 00
		For opinions about Spanish dollars	20 00
"	10.	Of Exr's of George Crowninshield, for case on will, and retainer in "Bonds"	150 00
"	13.	Of defendant, in case Stanwood *v.* Stanwood Essex	50 00
		Of Salem Bank *v.* Gloucester Bank	70 00
		Of Col. Little, in Little *v.* Bradstreet	20 00
		Of Dr. Thomas Sewall	100 00
		Of Mr. McIntyre, in Poole *v.* McIntyre	30 00
		Of J. J. Jackson, retainer in N. Hamp. case	40 00
"	14.	Of Mr. Barker, in Calis [Corliss?] *v.* Barker[40]	30 00
			$2,020, 00

1818.		Brought over	$2,020 00
Nov.	17.	Of Mr. McIntyre, for the fees, in Poole against him	20 00
"	19.	Of Mr. Webb, retainer in causes *v.* Capen	20 00
"	24.	Of Dr. J. S. Stoughton, retainer in The Industrier	100 00
"	24.	Of James Rundlet, in factory cause *v.* Winkley	180 00
"	26.	Of Mr. Dillaway, in Boardman *v.* him	40 00
		Of Isaac Danforth, in Lovejoy *v.* Lyman	30 00
"	27.	Of W. Taggart, in Taggart *v.* Lewis	20 00
Dec.	2.	Of Mr. [William?] Tucker, retainer Armstrong *v.* Gray	50 00
		In case of Neal and Walton	100 00
		Of Mr. Baxter, retainer in E. V. Baxter's case	20 00

40. Possibly Anthony Cline, Boston laborer. Benjamin Eaton, Jr., has not been further identified. Samuel Hubbard (1785–1847; Yale 1802), Boston lawyer, judge, MassSJC (1842–1847); probably *Packard* v. *J. Richardson et al.*, MassSJC,S, March 1821, 17 Mass. 122 (1821); James Otis, Boston carpenter, DW represented him in *Commonwealth scire facias* v. *Otis*, MassSJC,M, March 1820, 16 Mass. 198 (1819), see pp. 629–643, below; Harrison Gray Otis, Jr. (1792–1827; Harvard 1811), Massachusetts lawyer, studied with his father, admitted in 1814. Tracy, Gray, Marsh, Paine, and Smith have not been identified. George Crowninshield (1734–1815), Salem shipowner; John Bryant and William Sturgis, Boston merchants; *Sarah Stanwood* v. *Joseph Stanwood*, MassCCP,E, June 1818, MassSJC,E, October 1820, 17 Mass. 57 (1820); Thomas Sewall (1786–1845; Harvard Medical School 1812), practiced a few years in Essex County, then moved to Washington, D.C. Little, McIntyre, and Jackson have not been identified.

"	11.	Of Mr. Henry, in Jenkins *v.* Henry	45 00
		Of Mr. Malagamba, in the case from R. [I].	200 00
		Of Mr. Touro, sometime since, in Goddard's case	20 00
		Of Mr. Barker, in Curtiss [Corliss?] *v.* Barker	100 00
		Of Mr. Chesley, in Mill Corporation *v.* Chesley	20 00
		Of Mr. Bryant, in the causes *v.* him	50 00
		Of Mr. Brackett, in Niles *v.* Brackett	20 00
"	15.	Of Natha'l Russell and Company, in the Herring causes[41]	30 00
			$3,085 00

1819.			
Jan.	2.	Of Mr. [Ebenezer] Pearson, in case *v.* Goodrich	110 00
		Of Mr. [Harrison Gray] Otis, Jr., retainer in Pet. abt. Bridge	100 00
		Of Mr. Laurence, Fees in Searle *v.* Williams	70 00
		Of *Casus extraordinarius*	400 00
"	14.	Of Mr. [George] Blake, for fees in Hughes case[42]	500 00
		Of William Sullivan, for Dr. Stoughton	250 00
			$4,515 00

1819.		Brought over	$4,515 00
Jan.	14.	Of Mr. Hamilton, retainer in Amory *v.* him	20 00
		Of Coolidge and Deblois, retainer	40 00
		Of Mr. Prince, in The London Packet cause, at Washington	200 00
		Of Mr. [Richard] Crowninshield, in Sturgis *v.* Crowninshield	100 00
		Of S. Brown, in Yazoo case	150 00

41. Webb and Stoughton have not been identified. James Rundlett, Portsmouth merchant; probably Samuel Dilloway; William Taggard, Boston merchant; *Lewis* v. *Taggard*, MassSJC,S, March 1819 (no papers found); Edward Vose Baxter (d. 1820), second teller of the State Bank (1817–1818), see pp. 537–549, below. Danforth, Neal, Walton, Henry, and Malagamba[?] have not been identified. Abraham Touro (1782–1822), Boston merchant and insurance broker; Joseph Chesley, 3rd, formerly of Durham, New Hampshire, stonemason; *Boston and Roxbury Mill Corporation* v. *Chesley*, MassSJC,S, March 1821. Neither Brackett nor Russell has been identified.

42. Probably William Lawrence, Boston merchant, a trustee of the principal debtors, *Searle* v. *Williams*, MassSJC,S, November 1818; *Hughes* v. *Blake*, USCC,DMass, October 1818, 1 Mason 515 (1818), and 6 Wheaton 453 (1821).

		Of R. D. Lawler [Lawton], in Harvey *v.* Richards	550 00
		Of Mr. Bulfinch, in case about Whitcomb's will	20 00
		Of Mr. [Augustus?] Peabody, in Osgood *v.* Breed	50 00
		Of Mr. Hubbard, in the Richardson causes	100 00
		Of Mr. Warner	50 00
		Of Mr. Tucker, balance fees in Armstrong *v.* Gray	30 00
"	25.	At New York, of Mr. Prince	50 00
"	28.	At Baltimore, of Mr. McCullough, in the Bank cause	500 00
Feb.	12.	Of Mr. [Samuel?] Bell's son, at Washington	200 00
Mar.	13.	Of Dr. Haywood's [Hayward's?] son, for his father	30 00
"	21.	Of Mr. Munson, for proprietors of Rowe's wharf	20 00
"	25.	Of Mr. [Reuben?] Whitney	166 00
		Of Mr. Holker	100 00
		Of Mr. Waddington, N. Y. retainer	100 00
		Of John S. [L.] Sullivan, retainer in Patent causes	150 00
		Of Mr. Mitchell of Bridgewater, retainer	50 00
		Of Mr. S. Dilloway, paid Mr. Bliss	35 00
April	7.	Of Bank of United States, Balance of fees	1,500 00
		Of Mr. L. Tappan, in Barrell *v.* Gilman	50 00
		Of George Sullivan, Esq. in James *v.* Rogers[43]	160 00
			$8,936 00

1819.		Brought over	$8,936 00
April	8.	Of Nathan Hale, Esq. in Guild *v.* Hale Executors	70 00
"	9.	Of R. Crowninshield, Esq. retainer	100 00
"	10.	Of Messrs. A. and A. by Mr. Peters, acceptance	2,000 00
		Of Mr. Farley	20 00
		Of Mr. Potter, in N. E. Bank *v.* him	50 00

43. James Hamilton, former Halifax merchant; *J. Amory* v. *J. Hamilton*, MassSJC,S, March 1821, 17 Mass. 103 (1821); Prince has not been identified; *The London Packet*, 5 Wheaton 132 (1820); perhaps George Storer Bulfinch (1799–1853; Harvard 1817), Boston lawyer, admitted in 1825, for some time librarian of the Boston Public Library. James William McCulloch (McCulloh) (c. 1792–1861), banker, state legislator, cashier of the BUS, Baltimore branch (1816–1819), U.S. comptroller (1842–1849), defendant in *McCulloch* v. *Maryland*; probably Lemuel Hayward (1749–1821; Harvard 1768), eminent Boston physician. Warner, Waddington, and Mitchell have not been identified.

" 13.	Of Mr. Parkman, by Mr. Gallison	50 00
" 14.	Of Dedham Bank, balance of account	100 00
	Of Theodore Ely, retainer by R. D. Tucker	50 00
	Of Mr. Hooper	250 00
" 19.	Of Mr. Gardiner, advice about marriage articles	20 00
	Of Mr. T. L. Winthrop and Mr. R. Sullivan, Trustees under Mr. Bowdoin's will	100 00
	Of W. Mitchell, Jr., in Allen and Mitchell's causes	50 00
	Of Mr. Lovering, Jr., retainer in Herrick *v.* Gilman, &c.	50 00
" 26.	Of Benjamin Eaton, Jr., in settlement of Halliburton cause	40 00
" 29.	Of Mr. Tucker, through Mr. Hubbard, balance in Weed suits	100 00
May 1.	Of Jas. Holmes, retainer in New Orleans cause, C. C. New Hampshire	50 00
" 6.	Of State bank, by J. T. A[ustin], in case v. Baxter and Boardman	50 00
" 7.	Of F[ire] & M[arine] Insurance office, account	150 00
	Of John Jacob Astor, retainer	50 00
" 17.	Of Mr. [Joseph] Balch, retainer for owners of The Prometheus	50 00
" 18.	Of Mr. Welch, in Dr. Shattuck's action	25 00
" 22.	Of Mr. Hooper	1,000 00
	John Richards, in Maury's [Tillinghast Mowry's] case	540 00
June 1.	Of Mr. Vaughan, in Hallowell Bank case[44]	30 00
		$13,931 00

44. Peters was a Boston merchant. Potter has not been identified. Samuel Parkman, Boston merchant; John Gallison (1788–1820; Harvard 1807), Massachusetts lawyer, admitted to the Essex bar in 1810, practiced chiefly in Boston, published two volumes of reports of the first circuit, USCC (1812–1815). Ely, Hooper, Gardiner, and Sullivan have not been identified. Richard D. Tucker, Boston merchant; Thomas Lindall Winthrop (1760–1841; Harvard 1780), a director of the New England Mississippi Land Company, lieutenant governor of Massachusetts (1826–1833), his son, Robert Charles Winthrop read law in DW's office; James Bowdoin (1752–1811), Boston merchant and diplomat. Mitchell, Jr., Lovering, and Holmes have not been identified. James Trecothick Austin (1784–1870; Harvard 1802), Massachusetts lawyer, studied with William Sullivan, admitted in 1805, state's attorney, Suffolk County (1807–1832), state senator (1825–1826, 1831), Massachusetts attorney general (1832–1843); Dr. George Cheyne Shattuck (1783–1854; Dartmouth 1803, Pennsylvania, M.D. 1807), prominent Boston physician. Neither Welch nor Hooper has been identified. John Richards, Boston mer-

1819.		Brought over	$13,931 00
June	1.	Of Messrs. R. and S., advice in slander case	20 00
"	3.	Of Mr. Gilchrist, retainer	20 00
"	4.	Of Mr. Eaton, in the Bradley cause	50 00
"	5.	Of the Charlestown committee	200 00
		Of R. D. Tucker and Company, retainer, in United States Bank *v.* Brown	50 00
		Of Benjamin Hale, for writ against Manning	20 00
		Of Munson and Barnard, in M. and B. *v.* Amory	20 00
July	2.	Of C. J. Catlett, retainer	100 00
"	3.	Mr. Wait	40 00
"	5.	In Holker's cause with Mackay	100 00
		Of Mr. Maury [Tillinghast Mowry], deducting error in first credit	210 00
		Of Mr. Russell, in New York, say in his account in Ledger	50 00
June[45]	11.	Of Mr. Bradbury, on settlement of Mr. Astor's case	90 00
"	22.	Of Executors of John Brooks	40 00
		Of Messrs. Gurney and Putnam, retainer paid Mr. Bliss	50 00
		Of R. D. T[ucker], as fee, for advice in their business and concerns one year from this time	50 00
		Of Mr. Brigham, retainer for Samuel Williams	50 00
		Of R. Freeman, in behalf of Sandwich	20 00
Aug.	11.	Of Mr. Clarke, balance of fees in Capen causes	50 00
"	12.	Of Mr. Briggs, Esq., by H. Hace [Rice], Esq.[46]	20 00
			$15,181 00

I have omitted several small affairs and sums under ten dollars.

D. W.

Text from *W&S*, 17: 291–296. Original not found.

Beginning in 1821 Webster entered a period in which he spent much of his professional time preparing and arguing the Spanish claims cases.

chant, administrator of the estate of John Mowry; probably a reference to *Harvey* v. *Richards*, n. 26, above.

45. This should read "July."

46. Gilchrist, Hale, and Catlett have not been identified. Charles Bradbury, Boston insurance broker; *Astor* v. *Soule*, MassSJC,S, March 1819. Brooks, Gurney, Putnam, Brigham, Williams, Clarke, and Briggs have not been identified.

His agreements with the claimants usually specified a 5 percent commission on the amount recovered, with a maximum of $20,000.[47] Prior to 1823 the Massachusetts courts enforced such contingent fee arrangements. In fact, the Boston bar in its 1819 fee schedule specified a 2.5 percent commission for collection of debts less than $1000. But in that year the MassSJC voided a compensation agreement in which the attorney agreed to collect a debt for 10 percent of the sum recovered.[48] The court decided that the arrangement was champertous. Judge Isaac Parker recognized that his decision might prevent meritorious claims from being pursued but felt constrained by the English precedents. In a letter to Robert Elwell, printed below, Webster indicated that he abided by the rule, at least in Massachusetts. In his Supreme Court practice, however, he did make contingent fee arrangements.[49]

TO EBENEZER CLOUGH

Dear Sir, Washington April 10. 1824

I am honored with yours of the third instant,[50] enclosing a fifty dollar Bank note, and desiring me to be retained for You, in case any law suit should arise, relative to the will of William Clough.[51] It will give me pleasure to render you any professional services in my power; & I shall, of course, be retained for You. You are aware, however, that I cannot promise to be at home, at the time a trial may come on. Perhaps that consideration may lead you to think that your retaining fee could be better bestowed, in some other quarter. Nevertheless, I am quite willing to be retained, if such be your wish, under the circumstances. Your friend & obt. servt Danl. Webster

Dear Sir, Boston April 16th 1824

I have this moment recd Yours of the 10th Instant, and have only time to say, that I am happy in recognizing Your honor my Attorney for the Will. Respectfully Sir Your Ebenr Clough

Excuse shortn[e]s[s].

ALS. NhD. Ebenezer Clough, Boston resident.

TO RICHARD WARD GREENE

Dear Sir Boston Nov. 2. 1824

I have made a pretty thorough investigation of cases & principles, in

47. See pp. 202–204, below.

48. *Thurston* v. *Percival*, 1 Pickering (Mass.) 415 (1823).

49. See, for example, DW's memorandum on his fee in *Colin Mitchel* v. *U.S.*, note 78, below.

50. Letter not found.

51. Not further identified.

regard to Mr. Arnolds case;[52] & am willing to give a written opinion, or aid in drawing the necessary Bills.

In a case of this importance, however, I would not wish to be engaged, unless the party expected considerable attention, & to make it an object to me to give it. I should not be desirous of being retained, unless he esteemed it of such importance as to be willing to send me 200 Dlls. I practice out of the State, at some sacrifice; & in a case of this magnitude, he had better have none of my attention, than to have only a little of it; for he might, in that case, place a reliance which would fail him.

If required, I will give two days, out of the first four of next week, to framing the outline of a Bill—or Bills—if you could come over. This I mention, as I go South week after next, & I should suppose it would be desirable to have the Bills filed soon—& a rule to answer obtained.[53]

I address this to you, as I suppose Mr Arnold has left Providence. Yrs

D. Webster

ALS. MWA.

FROM ISRAEL THORNDIKE

Dear Sir May 9th 1825

A question of some importance has arrisen between Mr. David Sears & myself respecting the lease of the Commercial Coffee house tavern,[54] princapally respecting the rebuilding those stores which was destroyed by the late fire. I wish you to consider yourself retained by me upon this question, & also upon all other questions which I may have in the Courts of Massachusetts or else where. I am with respect your friend & obt Servt Israel Thorndike

ALS. NhD.

TO ROBERT ELWELL

Dear Sir, [Boston, June 7, 1825]

I shall have great pleasure in being engaged for my old friends Mr Shaw & Mr Bell[55]—but we find it necessary to have a rule on these subjects, which prohibits us from being *contingently* engaged.

52. Probably Isaac Arnold of Providence, Rhode Island.

53. A *bill in equity* is a formal written complaint to the court; a *rule to answer* required the defendant to respond to the bill or face a judgment by default.

54. At this time Thorndike leased the tavern from Sears. See John Douglas Forbes, *Israel Thorndike, Federalist Financier* (New York, 1953), p. 147.

55. Abraham Shaw (1776?–1828) and Andrew Bell (former ship captain), Portsmouth, New Hampshire merchants, incorporators in 1824 of the Portsmouth Distillery and Central Wharf Company.

My usual retainer in Ins. Causes is $50.—if you wish me to be *engaged*, that must be paid, or considered as charged. Otherwise I could not, with propriety, if called on by the other side, say I was *engaged*. Yrs very respectfully Danl. Webster

ALS. NhD. Robert Elwell, Boston merchant.

TO ALEXANDER BLISS

My Dear Sir Washington Feb. 18. [18]26

An acceptance of mine, due Feb. 27th, or thereabouts, for 1,000—must be provided for. I have written to Mr. Paige, on the subject, & when it appears you must get his aid, to take it up. Several persons have written me to be concerned in their causes, whom I have referred to you, telling them that *I am retained when I am retained*. I do not learn whether any of them have deposited the needful.

I should be glad to hear from you, to know how the Court gets on; what the news is, & so forth. For the ensuing month, I shall be a good deal busy with the Court. Mr. Stocktons case[56] is now on trial. Yrs

D Webster

ALS. DLC. Published in *Correspondence*, 2: 88–89.

FROM RUFUS CHOATE

Sir Salem Oct. 6. 1829.

I take the liberty at the urgent request of my client to inquire, whether you have been retained for the Defendants in the action William Hook vs B. Merril & al—to be entered at the Nov. Term of the S.J.C. in this County. If not, Mr. Hook is extremely sollicitous to obtain your aid for him. The action originates in a failure of one Hersey[57] of this town, and is brought for the purpose of avoiding a note of $4000 given as Mr. Hook supposes—by Hersey, in favor of his creditors. If it be possible for you to suffer yourself to be engaged, I will call on you any day this or the next week which you will appoint for your advice upon such evidence as we have procured already. I am Sir Your obedient servant

Rufus Choate

ALS. MHi.

56. Robert Field Stockton (1795–1866), U.S. naval officer (1811–1850), U.S. senator (1851–1853), president, Delaware & Raritan Canal Company (1853–1866). As captain of the *Alligator* he captured the slave trader, *Marianna Flora*, the subject of a USSC case, in which DW appeared for Stockton. 11 Wheaton 1 (1826).

57. Probably Benjamin Morrill, Salem cabinetmaker. Hook and Hersey have not been identified.

In Webster's only appearance as prosecutor in a criminal case, his right to accept a fee was challenged by the defense. The case arose out of the brutal murder on April 7, 1830, of 82-year old Joseph White of Salem, a wealthy retired sea captain. Captain White's will left the bulk of his estate, estimated at $200,000, to his nephew, Stephen White, a prominent Salem merchant, member of the state legislature, and brother-in-law of Supreme Court Justice Joseph Story. A niece, Mrs. Mary Beckford, was the old captain's housekeeper, but had been virtually disinherited because her daughter had married Joseph Knapp in defiance of Captain White's wishes. The authorities, spurred on by a vigilance committee, arrested four men: Joseph Knapp and his younger brother John Francis, and George and Richard Crowninshield, shiftless members of a prominent Salem family. According to a confession extracted from Joseph under some pressure from a local minister, the Knapps were under the impression that if Captain White died intestate, the estate would divide equally between Stephen White and Joseph's mother-in-law, Mrs. Beckford. The murder was therefore to be accompanied by the destruction of the will. A will was indeed destroyed, but only an earlier document, which by then had been superseded. According to this confession, the actual killing was done by the Crowninshields, who were hired by the Knapps for that purpose, and it was Richard who wielded the bludgeon, thus becoming the principal in the trial.

Richard learned from his defense attorney, Franklin Dexter, that under Massachusetts law an accessory before the fact could not be tried for a felony unless a principal were first convicted. Richard reasoned that his brother George could not be tried if he himself were not convicted, and moved to insure that outcome by committing suicide. The grand jury, instructed by Chief Justice Parker as to the distinction between "principal" and "accessory," then indicted Francis Knapp as principal, and Joseph Knapp and George Crowninshield as accessories. The case was in progress before the MassSJC when Chief Justice Parker died of apoplexy on July 25, forcing an adjournment until August 3.

At this point Webster, at the instigation of Judge Story and Stephen White, was invited by the attorney general, Perez Morton, to assist the prosecution, for which White, and not the commonwealth of Massachusetts, paid a fee of $1000. Webster's role in the trial of John Francis Knapp was conspicuous and probably decisive. He succeeded in convincing the jury that Frank Knapp, although he had been no closer than outside the house while the crime was being committed, was indeed a "principal" rather than an accessory. Knapp was convicted on August 20 of first degree murder, and the following day was sentenced to death. Webster's presence at this trial was not questioned, nor was his right to be paid for his services. At the subsequent trial of Joseph Knapp in November, however, his presence was questioned and the legality of his fee challenged (Document 26). He responded that he was receiving no fee in the case before the court—truthfully enough, for the $1000 he had been paid by White was for the trial of Francis Knapp. He aided the prosecution of Joseph Knapp, technically without compensation.[58]

DOCUMENT 26. EXTRACT FROM TRIAL RECORD, COMMONWEALTH V. JOSEPH JENKINS KNAPP

The prisoner's counsel referred to *St.* 1807, *c.* 18, which requires county-attorneys to act in behalf of the commonwealth, "provided, that the attorney-general, when present, and, in his absence, the solicitor-general, if present, shall, in any court, have the direction and control of prosecutions and suits in behalf of the commonwealth." The second section provides, "that no attorney-general, solicitor-general or county-attorney shall receive any fee or reward from or in behalf of any prosecutor, [for services in any prosecution] to which it shall be his official duty to attend."

Dexter and *Gardiner* objected, that as both the attorney-general and the solicitor-general were present, and neither of them disabled to conduct the prosecution, Mr. *Webster* ought not to be permitted to act in behalf of the commonwealth. They had understood that he was to receive a compensation for his services from a private prosecutor, and they questioned the right of a private individual to retain counsel to aid the law officers of the government in effecting a conviction for a crime punishable with death.

Morton (Attorney-General) remarked that it was not a novel practice for the prosecuting officers to call in the aid of other counsel.

Davis (Solicitor-General) said the counsel for the government would be greatly embarrassed, if Mr. *Webster* were not permitted to act in the case, as the preparation for the trial had been made under the expectation of his assistance.

Webster stated that he appeared solely at the request of the attorney-general, and without any pecuniary inducement.

The next day the opinion of the Court on this question was delivered by

PUTNAM J.[59] The Court have considered the application of the attor-

58. "Aug. 14. 1830 Recd of Hon S. White One thousand Dollars, in full of fees for all services rendered or to be rendered, in the prosecution vs Jno. F. Knapp. Danl Webster" (mDW 39732). The trials are fully reported in John D. Lawson, ed., *American State Trials* (17 vols., St. Louis, Mo., 1914–1936), 7: 395–670; and in Howard A. Bradley and James A. Winans, *Daniel Webster and the Salem Murder* (Columbia, Mo., 1956). An account of the case is in Harriet Martineau, *Retrospect of Western Travel* (3 vols., London, 1838), 1: 167–168. See also Joseph Story to DW, April 17, 1830, DW to Joseph Story, August 6, 1830, and Stephen White to DW, December 17, 1830, *Correspondence*, 3: 56–57, 83–84, 90–91.

59. Franklin Dexter (1793–1857;

ney-general for the admission of Mr. *Webster* to assist him in the management of this cause.

The counsel in behalf of the prisoner object, and contend that the statute of 1807, *c.* 18 (revived by *St.* 1811, *c.* 10,) respecting the offices and duties of the attorney-general, solicitor-general, and county-attorney, makes it their duty exclusively to conduct the prosecutions on the part of the commonwealth.

We have examined that statute and are of opinion that it was not intended to prohibit the appointment of the counsellors of this Court in aid of the law officers, whenever the circumstances of the case should require the Court, in the exercise of a sound discretion, to make such appointments. It is one of the incidental powers of the Court, and has heretofore been exercised in cases within our own recollection.

In cases where civil rights are in controversy and the form of proceeding is by indictment or information, the Court do not perceive any objection against permitting the party in interest to employ counsel in aid of the law officers. The same reasons would not apply to cases involving public considerations only. In such cases the statute supposes that the prosecution will be conducted by the law officers, for their salaries, and without any other compensation whatever.

In the present case Mr. *Webster* avows that he is induced to aid the attorney-general merely at his request, and without any other consideration: so that this case presents the question, whether a counsellor may, at the request of the attorney-general, be admitted to aid him in the prosecution, without any pecuniary consideration being paid to him, or any other consideration which may be supposed to influence him, excepting a disinterested regard for the public good. And we all think that under these circumstances the application should be granted.

It is to be recollected, that at the trial of John Francis Knapp, Mr. *Webster* was, at the request of the law officers, appointed to aid them, and that there was no objection then made by the prisoner or his counsel. And although that appointment strictly was for the then pending trial, yet if the other trials had followed immediately, the counsel for the government would have had reason to suppose that they were to receive

Harvard 1812), Boston lawyer, studied with Samuel Hubbard, admitted in 1815, associated respectively with Charles G. Loring, William Prescott (his father-in-law), William H. Gardiner, and George Phillips, state legislator. Perez Morton (1751–1831; Harvard 1771), Massachusetts lawyer, admitted in 1779, Massachusetts attorney general (1810–1832); Daniel Davis (1762–1835), Massachusetts lawyer, studied with Shearjashub Bourne, admitted in 1782, state legislator, U.S. attorney, Maine district (1796–1801), Massachusetts solicitor general (1801–1832); Samuel Putnam (1768–1853; Harvard 1787), Massachusetts lawyer and judge, practiced in Salem, state senator, judge, MassSJC (1814–1842).

his assistance in those trials, unless good objections should have been made. It is said by the law officers, that the preparations for this trial have been made under a similar expectation on their part, and no objection was made to this measure until the jury were empannelled.

It is to be understood that the solicitor-general concurs in this application on the part of the attorney-general, and that two gentlemen only are to address the jury in the case, in behalf of the commonwealth. It is further to be understood, that the "direction and control of the prosecution is to be with the attorney-general"; who acts under oath and upon his official responsibility.

We give no opinion upon any application of this nature under any other circumstances than such as are found in the case now before us.

Extract. *Commonwealth* v. *Knapp*, 10 Pickering (Mass.) 477, 480–482 (1830).

As Webster's political activities began to take a greater toll on his time, he found it expedient to accept annual retainers from the numerous Boston insurance offices. In a letter to Henry Willis Kinsman, printed below, he indicated that he intended to raise his fee to $100.

TO HENRY WILLIS KINSMAN

Dear Sir, Washington Jan. 29. 1831

I hope you recd sundry blank notes, checks &c in season to meet their object.

I know of but 2 things falling due this month, viz, an acceptance of Wm Taggard & Co's draft, $750—due feb. 8/11—A note to Mr. Breck, $1000, due feby. 23/26.—

I suppose you may be already in funds for the first. I shall remit in season for the 2nd.

You may say to Mr Wells,[60] of the Atlas Office, that I receive an Annual Retainer from several Offices in Boston. A majority of them give me 100 Dollars each a year, as a retainer, & for any advice & opinions they may need or require. The others give 50 each; but I find I lose the chance of so many good fees from Pltfs, that I do not contemplate renewing my engagements with any office, under 100 Dollars a year.

Indeed it would be greatly for my pecuniary interest to discontinue them, altogether; but, nevertheless, I like, for several reasons, to be on the side of the offices, provided I am reasonably compensated. You may say, therefore, to Mr Wells, that I will place my relation with his Office, if he so pleases, on the same footing as I stand with Mr. Perkins, Mr

60. Breck has not been identified. Samuel Adams Wells, president of the Atlas Insurance Company.

Balch, & Mr Snelling, that is to say, a retainer of $100 a year; & that I shall not, hereafter, renew Engagements with the other Offices, on <any> other terms. (perhaps you will do well to copy the foregoing paragraph fairly, & send it to Mr Wells)
Please make my remembrances to Mrs K. I hope you are all well

D. W.

ALS. Dr. Gurdon S. Pulford, Palo Alto, California.

TO [EDWARD?] LIVINGSTON

Dear Sir Boston Nov. 5. 1832

I have recd your favor of the 30th. Octr.[61] For some years I have acted on a settled rule, not to take part in causes, for compensations altogether *contingent*. Living entirely by my profession, I have found it quite indispensable to bestow my labor on objects, which should render a *certain*, tho' it might be a *moderate*, remuneration.

I use the occasion to express to you, My Dear Sir, my personal good will & esteem Danl Webster

ALS. N. Addressed on the back, in another hand, to "His Exc. Don Mariana Ricaforte President Governor & Capt Gen of the Island of Cuba."

FROM JOHN RENSHAW THOMSON

D Sir: Princeton N J July 12. 1833

Enclosed I take leave to hand you a note of the Trenton Banking Company for One hundred Dollars,[62] which I beg you will receive as a retaining fee from the "Delaware & Raritan Canal & Camden & Amboy Rail Road & Transportation Companies"

There are no suits at present against the companies of any importance, but we desire in case any thing serious should occur, to have the benefit of your services. With gr respect I have the honor to be yr ob St

Jno R Thomson
Secty D & R C. C.

ALS. NhHi. John Renshaw Thomson (1800–1862, attended Princeton), merchant in China from 1817, U.S. consul, Canton (1823–1825), settled in New Jersey, director and secretary, Delaware & Raritan Canal Company, U.S. senator (1853–1862).

TO JOHN RENSHAW THOMSON

My Dear Sir Boston Aug. 6. 1833

On my arrival in Boston, a few days after I had the pleasure of exchanging a word with you on the Rail Road, I found your letter of the

61. Letter not found.

62. DW returned the enclosure to Thomson, see following letter.

12th. of July, enclosing a bank note of 100 Dlls, as a Retainer from the "Delaware & Raritan Canal & Camden & Amboy Rail Road."[63] My family being at Marshfield, I proceeded immediately to that place, & have there been staying ten or twelve days, to recruit from the fatigue of a long journey.

On coming to town, & recurring to your letter, it occurs to me that there may be some difficulty in accepting this Retainer, especially as it is a *general* one, & for all causes. I have understood that some other Rail Road was in contemplation, thro N. Jersey, which may possibly come in competition with this. So I was informed, while in N. York on my way home, & so I have since learned also. And it so happens, that in this new projected road, family friends & connexions of mine are interested, I believe, to some considerable extent. I have not been retained, by those concerned in this new road, but on account of the connexion of Mr LeRoy,[64] & other members of his family in it, I feel unwilling to be retained for any opposing interest. If I am in any error, as to the controversies which your Company anticipates, or there be any other question, respecting which they would desire my professional advice or aid, I shall very gladly render both.

Under all the circumstances, it has seemed to me to be the proper cause to return the Retainer, & leave the matter for the further consideration of your Company, in this view.

I pray the most respectful remembrance to Mrs Thompson, & the members of her family, & am, with regard, Your ob. Servt.

AL draft. NhHi. Published in *Correspondence*, 3: 261–262.

DOCUMENT 27. BOOK OF RECEIPTS

[October 8, 1832–September 9, 1833]

1832.			
Oct.	8.	Of Merchant Ins. Co., for retainer for two years to come	$200 00
		Of Suffolk office, retainer up to Dec. 1, 1833	100 00
		Of Mr. Dewolfe, in Dodge *et als. v.* Dewolfe	200 00
		Retainer for Dr. Nott, patent causes, through Mr. Codman	100 00
"	23.	In case of Bradbury Cilley's will	100 00

63. See preceding letter.

64. Herman Le Roy, DW's father-in-law. In 1834 DW endorsed an opinion of James Kent supporting the right of the Philadelphia & Trenton Railroad to build a line to compete with the Camden & Amboy Railroad. Stanley I. Kutler, *Privilege and Creative Destruction: The Charles River Bridge Case* (New York, 1978), pp. 69–70.

Nov. 12.	Of P[eters,] P[ond] and Co., retainer	100 00
	Of D. Sears, Esq., for Jackson Co.	100 00
	Of N. E. Ins. Co. and Boston Ins. Co., fee in The Dover	400 00
	Of Washington Ins. Co., annual retainer	100 00
	Of N.E. Ins. Co., annual retainer	100 00
	Of Boston Ins. Co., annual retainer	100 00
" 20.	Of Messrs. Baring, Brothers and Co., annual retainer through Mr. Ward	100 00
Dec. 4.	Of Wm. Savage, Esq., balance fee due	100 00
	Of Rob. Fuller, Esq., retainer	50 00
" 7.	Received of John A. Lowell, $100, as an additional retainer for Locks and Canals, which is to serve as a retainer in all cases	100 00
" 12.	Of W. Phillips $30, retainer in Revere *v.* Copper Co.	30 00
" 18.	Of Messrs. Black and Co, Smyrna, retainer against suit of Mr. McTier	50 00
	Of S. A. Welles, retainer	100 00
" 21.	Of John R. Willis, in behalf of Orthodox Quakers	250 00
1833.		
Jan'y 1.	Of Thos. P. E. of Arkansas, for opinion	100 00
Feb'y	Of Mr. Avery of North Carolina, through Mr. Badger	200 00
	Of Col. White	250 00
	Of Mr. Tomlinson, for Mr. Davenport[65]	100 00
		$3,030 00

65. Dewolfe has not been identified. Eliphalet Nott (1773–1860; Rhode Island College, A.M. 1795), Albany, New York clergyman, president, Union College, inventor of various methods for the application of heat to steam boilers and generators; probably John Codman, Boston merchant; Bradbury Cilley (1760–1831), wealthy resident of Nottingham, New Hampshire, U.S. representative (1813–1817); John Peters and Sabin Pond, Boston merchants; Baring Brothers & Company, English banking house; Thomas Wren Ward (1786–1858), Boston merchant, became resident American agent for Baring Brothers & Company (1830–1853). Neither Savage nor Fuller has been identified. John Amory Lowell (1798–1881), Boston merchant. In 1825 the Merrimack Company, one of the developers of the industrial town of Lowell, undertook a corporate reorganization. The company transferred its water-power rights with adjacent lands to the Proprietors of the Locks and Canals, a company first created in 1792 and subsequently owned by Merrimack. The managers created two companies, one for manufacturing, the other for development of water power and factory sites. Willard Phillips (1784–1873; Harvard 1810), Boston lawyer, admitted in 1818, state representative (1825–

1833.		Brought over	$3,030 00
Mar.	3.	Congress pay	992 00
		Of Mr. Johnson, balance fee	50 00
"	25.	Of Mr. Blount, fee in Danish claim	190 00
		Of Mr. Payne and Mr. Donelson, fee for Mr. Wheaton, in his cause *v.* Mr. Peters	500 00
"	27.	Of Mr. Griswold, retainer	100 00
		Of same, on account French claims	500 00
"	29.	Of J. H. Clarke, in controversy with Field	50 00
April	5.	Of Dr. Van Rensselaer, retainer	500 00
		Of T. W. Ward, for divers professional services	500 00
		Of Mr. Gifford	100 00
		Of Mr. [William J.] Lawrence at Worcester	200 00
		Of Mr. Sergeant, through Mr. Snelling	100 00
May	9.	Of Isaac D., retainer, in behalf of his patent baker	100 00
		Of Mr. Loring, for Mill Corporation *v.* Railroad	100 00
Aug.	3.	Of Mr. Curtis, in Daggett *v.* Barney, *finale*	150 00
		Of Mr. Jones, on Corporation *v.* him	50 00
"	7.	Of Edward Curtis, *de bene esse*	250 00
		Of Stephen White, general retainer for three years	300 00
		Of Newark people, in May	200 00
Sept.	5.	Of Mr. Chever, through Mr. Choate, in Stone *v.* Chever[66]	50 00

1826), judge of probate, Suffolk County (1839–1847), president, New England Mutual Life Insurance Company (1847–1873); *Revere* v. *Boston Copper Company*, MassSJC,S, November 1835, 15 Pickering (Mass.) 351 (1834), see p. 345, below. Black and McTier have not been identified. Possibly John R. Willis, New York City official; Thomas P. Eskridge, Arkansas politician and superior court judge, see his letter to DW, November 12, 1832, mDW 10346; possibly Isaac Thomas Avery, Burke County, North Carolina planter and cashier of Morganton Bank; George Edmund Badger (1795–1866), North Carolina lawyer, judge, North Carolina superior court (1820–1825), secretary of the navy (1841), U.S. senator (1846–1855) appointed to the USSC (1855) but confirmation denied; see *Lattimer* v. *Poteet*, 14 Peters 4 (1840); Stephen White (1787–1841), Salem and Boston merchant; Thomas Ash Tomlinson (1802–1872), Keeseville, New York lawyer, began practice in 1823, millowner and dealer in lands, state assembly (1835–1836), U.S. representative (1841–1843); probably George Davenport (1783–1845), soldier, postmaster, Rock Island, Illinois (1825), trader with American Fur Company (1826), a founder of Davenport, Iowa.

66. Joseph Johnson (1785–1877), Virginia farmer and politician, U.S. representative at various times from

	Of B. and L., retainer	100 00
" 9.	Of Mr. G. and Mrs. [Charles] T[horndike]	100 00
		$8,212 00

Sept. 9, 1833.—Thus done and concluded, Sept. 9.—A very poor year's work. Nullification kept me out of the supreme court all last winter.

D. Webster.

Text from *W & S*, 17: 297–298. Original not found. We believe the printed text contains several misreadings.

DOCUMENT 28. BOOK OF RECEIPTS

[September 1833–April 22, 1837]

Receipts

1833.

Sep. of Mr Healey, Retainer in Dykes vs Healey, N. H. Circuit Ct. 50

1823 to 1847, governor of Virginia (1851–1856); in May 1832 he wrote asking DW to state the balance due on his fee for arguing *U.S.* v. *Saline Bank of Virginia*, 1 Peters 100 (1828). See J[oseph] Johnson to DW, May 31, 1832, mDW 10077. Blount has not been identified. Henry Wheaton (1785–1848; Brown 1802), lawyer, diplomat, and author, briefly practiced in Providence, judge, marine court, New York City (1815–1819), reporter, USSC (1816–1827), member, New York Commission of Law Revision (1825–1827), chargé d'affaires, Berlin (1835–1837), minister to Prussia (1837–1846); Wheaton's law partner Elijah Paine ("Payne") served with DW as Wheaton's attorney in *Wheaton* v. *Peters*, 8 Peters 591 (1834); "Donelson," Robert Donaldson, publisher of *Wheaton's Reports*, joined Wheaton as plaintiff in the suit; Richard Peters (1779–1848) succeeded Wheaton as USSC reporter, and published 16 volumes (1828–1842) in addition to other legal works; either George Griswold (c. 1778–1859), director of the Columbia Insurance Company and the Bank of America, or his partner Nathaniel L. Griswold, New York merchants; probably John Hopkins Clarke (1789–1870; Brown 1809), Rhode Island lawyer and cotton manufacturer, admitted in 1812, state representative (1836–1842, 1845–1847), U.S. representative (1847–1853). Field has not been identified. Jeremiah van Rennselaer, New York City physician. Gifford and Isaac D. have not been identified. Possibly Ignatius Sargent, Boston merchant; possibly Charles Greely Loring (1794–1867; Harvard 1812), Boston lawyer, studied at Litchfield Law School and with Charles Jackson, admitted in 1815, formed partnership with Franklin Dexter (1816–1819), practiced extensively until 1854, actuary, Massachusetts Hospital Life Insurance Company; *Boston Water Power Co.* v. *Boston & Worcester Railroad Corp.*, 16 Pickering (Mass.) 512 (1835). Jones has not been identified. Probably Charles Pelham Curtis (1792–1864; Harvard 1811), Boston lawyer, studied with William Sullivan, admitted in 1814, member, Boston common council (1823–1826), state representative (1842); George Barrell Cheever (1807–1890; Bowdoin 1825,

of G[eorge] P. Richardson Esqr, thro. Mr Beals		20
25. of J. G. King Esq, thro. T. W. Ward, for opinion abt. Bank of N. America		50
Octr. 9.		
of J. L. Cilley, fee in cause for trial of Col [Bradbury] Cilley's will		800
12. of Mr Walcutt, of Pawtucket, Retainer & advice, in question between Mill owners at P[rovidence] & Blackstone Canal[67]		100
		1020

Oct: 15	Brot up	1.020
of Elihu Swain, of Nantucket, in U.S. vs Pavedo[?]		50
of R. D. Tucker & als. thro. Mr Morey, in case vs Mrs Andrews, Essex Co.		50
24. of Amos Binney Esqr fees, in various cases		400
of C. G. Loring, for Mrs Charles Thorndike		500
29. of Wm. K. Smith, N. Y. thro H. Maxwell Esqr Retainer[68]		250
		2.270

Brot up	2.270
29.	
of Isaac Jackson, retainer, in suits, on notes	

Andover Seminary 1830), installed as pastor of Howard Street Congregational Church in Salem in 1833, was sued for libel by Deacon Stone, fined $1,000, and imprisoned for one month. See Rufus Choate to DW, September 6, 1833, mDW 11114.

67. Possibly Joseph Healy (1776–1861), New Hampshire hotel keeper and agriculturalist, U.S. representative (1825–1829), New Hampshire executive council. Beals and Richardson have not been identified. James Gore King (1791–1853; Harvard 1810), New York banker, studied law with Peter van Schaack and at Litchfield Law School, after practicing briefly turned to commercial affairs; Joseph Longfellow Cilley (1803–1868), Exeter, New Hampshire farmer. Edward Walcott, not further identified.

68. Elihu Swain (1784–1863), merchant; George Morey (1789–1866; Harvard 1811), Massachusetts lawyer, studied with Luther Lawrence, admitted in 1818, state legislator; Amos Binney (1803–1847; Brown 1821, M.D. Harvard 1826), of Boston, zoologist, was at this time active in the business ventures of his father, Colonel Amos Binney, who died on January 10, 1833; Maria Martha Thorndike, née Purnell (1805–1881), widow of Charles Thorndike (1795–1833), a son of Israel Thorndike. Smith has not been identified. Hugh Maxwell (1787–1873; Columbia 1808), New York lawyer, district attorney, New York County (1817–1829), collector, port of New York (1849–1853).

said to be forged	50
30th. of J. B. Brown retainer	50
Nov. 1. of M[assachusetts] F[ire] & M[arine] Ins Co.	
Annual, 1 yr in advance	100
" Occan Office, fees to this time, & Retainer, 1 yr	
in advance	200
Novr. 6. of Jno. Ames, Retainer, Patent, abt.	
paper-making[69]	100
of Suffolk Inse. Co. Annual Retainer,	
to Decr. 1. 1834	100
	2.870

Brot up	2.870
Nov. 6.	
of Franklin Ins Co. Annl Retainer, to Decr. 1 '34	100
of N. E. In Co. Annual Retainer, to Decr 1. '34	100
of Boston office, Annual Retainer for 1 yr,	
viz to Decr. 1. 1834	100
Nov. 7	
of Capt. Geo: P. Richardson	100
7. of Gardiner & Swift (by dr[a]ft on them) Retainer	
in case with Phenix Bk[70]	100
9 of Jno. Ames, Retainer, plf, Patent Cause,	
vs Howard & Lathrop	300
	3.670

Brot up	3.670
of H. Hall Esqr. Retainer in suit, Boston v Nichols,	
(for Nichols) in Sup. U. S.	100.
11. of Washington Ins Co. Retainer for 1 yr,	
viz to Decr. 1834	100
13. of T. W. Ward Esqr. for Messrs Barings	
Bros & Co Retainer, for 2 yrs to come	200
14. of Christopher Colt, Retainer, vs Ware	
Manu. Co.	50

69. Isaac Jackson, Boston merchant; Jonas Bond Brown, Boston merchant and manufacturer; John Ames of Springfield, Massachusetts, whose announcement in 1832 of his intention to apply to Congress for renewal of his patent rights triggered protests from competitors. See memorials of citizens of Massachusetts, mDW 45111, 45115. His patent was upheld in *Ames* v. *Howard*, 1 Sumner (Mass.) 482 (1833) (DW did not argue the case).

70. Neither Gardiner nor Swift has been identified.

of F. J. Oliver—fee, for *trial by jury,*	
Alsop vs Coml. Ins Co.[71]	500
	4.620
Brot up	4.620
Nov. 16.	
of Jenkins & Mann	200
of Thos. Leland	300
Novr. 22 of Boston Marine Ins Co. Retainer,	
for one yr, Jany to Decr 1834	100
of Mr. Oliver, bal. of fees in Alsop v Com.	
Ins Co.	300
28. of N. Rutgers Esqr. for N. York offices	500
Decr. 5 of Mr Greene, N. Bedford thro Col	
Adams, Retainer, in Riders v Greene, Admr	50
1834 Jan: 7. of Stanton Parker jr, for Birckhead	
& Co., Genl. Retainer[72]	200
	6.270
Brot up	6.270
Jan: of the Treasurer of Mass: in R. Is. vs Mass:	500
of Wm King, in the Sallwaks[?] case	250
Feb. of Bk U. S. States, in causes in Sup.	
Court, last [t]erm & this—enumerated in receipt	500

71. Hall, Nichols, and Colt have not been identified. Francis J. Oliver, Boston insurance broker; *Alsop* v. *Commercial Insurance Company*, USCC,DMass, October 1833, 1 Sumner 451 (1833).

72. William Jenkins and Samuel Mann, Pawtucket, Rhode Island, manufacturers; Thomas Leland (1784–1849; Middlebury 1809), Claremont, New Hampshire lawyer, studied with Jonathan Hatch Hubbard, practiced in Windsor, Vermont (1812–1834), and then in Claremont, New Hampshire (1834–1849); *Leland et al.* v. *Wilkinson*, 2 Peters 627 (1829), 6 Peters 317 (1832), remanded to the USCC,DRI for trial at the June Term, 1833, upon division of opinion between the judges, the case was returned to the USSC, 10 Peters 294 (1836) (DW did not appear at this last hearing). See DW to William Thomas Carroll, June 22, [1830], mDWs; DW to John Whipple, December 10, 1834, mDW 12001; Jonathan Hatch Hubbard to DW, February 10, 1835, mDW 12311; DW to Richard W. Greene, February 2, 1836, mDW 12943. Rutgers and this Greene have not been identified. Stanton Parker, Jr., originally from Boston, was associated in mercantile business in Brazil with James Birckhead, brother of Hugh Birckhead (1788–1853), a Baltimore merchant engaged in the South American trade. See Jules von Wallenstein to DW, October 3, 1833, mDW 11157.

Mar: of Merchnts Office in case of Gen Carrington		500
of N. E In Co.—case of Dawn		500
May. [Mr. Avery] of N. Carolina, thro. Mr Badger,[73]		1.000
		9.520
	Brot up	9.520
May		
of Mr. of Baltimore, respecting Patent		100
July 14		
of Jared Coffin, Esqr retainer, in all cases whatever, & to be renewd when called for[74]		100
June 30. Amt. Congress pay		2.000
July 24 of Mr Barker, retainer		50
of Jno. Welsh, Retainer		100
Brot up		11.870
Aug 1.		
of Merchts office, Retainer for 2 yrs from Oct		200
25. of Mr Hogan		70
Sep. of Mr Asa Arnold, retainer abt. Patent[75]		500.00
20. of Jno. Welch Esq. fee on Indictment		500
		$13.140

Thus done & concluded,
Sep. 22, 1834
Danl Webster

1834	
Sept. of Mr D. Leavitt, in case of lead statues[76]	250
of Mr Healy, in Dykes case	200

73. *Rhode Island* v. *Massachusetts*, 12 Peters 657 (1838), 13 Peters 23 (1839), 14 Peters 210 (1840), 15 Peters 233 (1841), 4 Howard 591 (1846); probably William King (1768–1852), Maine merchant, shipbuilder, and banker, state representative, leader in the movement to separate Maine from Massachusetts, Maine's first governor (1819–1821), commissioner, Spanish Claims Commission (1821–1824), collector of customs, Bath, Maine (1830–1834); *Carrington et al.* v. *Merchants' Insurance Company*, USCC,DMass, October 1837, and 8 Peters 495 (1834).

74. Jared Coffin (1784–1860), Nantucket merchant, state legislator.

75. Hogan has not been identified. Aza Arnold (1788–1865), of Pawtucket, Rhode Island, holder of an 1823 patent for a roving machine used in cotton spinning; he instituted a series of patent infringement suits when textile machine manufacturers failed to pay him royalties.

76. David Leavitt, New York merchant; *U.S.* v. *David Levitt et al.*,

Octr. 29. of the the following [insurance] Offices, on annual Retainer, to Decr. 1835.	
viz. Franklin office	100
Washington "	100
Ocean "	100
New England	100
Boston Marine	100
	950
Brot up	950
of Mr Grimes, in N. Orleans case,	500
Oct. 31.	
of Suffolk office, Retainer, 1 yr, to Decr. 1835.	100
of Boston office, for same purpose, (Mr Pope)	100
of Mr Rogerson (four days ago) genl. Retainer	100
Nov	
of Tremont[?] Co.	100
of Elisha Parks,	300
26 of Paul Revere jr[77]	200
28 of T. W. Ward, annl Retainer &c	500
	2.850
Brot up.	2.850
Decr.	
of Mr Greene of N. Bedford	300
of Mr Tobey, of N. Bedford thro Mr Baylies	20
Feb. of Ford & Chapman, by note	500
Mar. 7. of Peter Mitchell, in Colin Mitchells case,[78] by note	2.000
24. of U.S. Bank, as pr bill recd.	2.250
April 3rd. of Ocean Office, in cases of Telegraph & Silver Grey	500

USDC,DMass, December 1834, 26 Federal Cases 919 (1842).

77. John Randolph Grymes (1786–1854), Louisiana lawyer, state legislator, U.S. district attorney, Louisiana attorney general; possibly *City of New Orleans* v. *De Armas and Cucullu*, 9 Peters 224 (1835); Lemuel Pope, president of Boston Insurance Company; probably Robert Rogerson, Boston merchant; Elisha Parks, Boston merchant; Paul Revere, Jr., Plymouth manufacturer.

78. Jonathan Tobey, Tiverton, Rhode Island farmer; William Baylies (1776–1865; Brown 1795), Massachusetts lawyer, studied with Seth Padelford, admitted in 1807, state and federal representative; Ford & Chapman, of Clyde, Wayne County, New York, otherwise not identified, see mDW 9225 and 9895; Colin Mitchell, a partner in John Forbes & Company, Florida traders, and operator of a large trading business in Havana, was thought to have bribed

Brot up	8.420
Amt of Congress pay, including service in Vacation	1.586.40
at N. Y. of N. Goddard, in Goddard v Pratt, thro Mr [Jeremiah] Mason	100
April. of Oakly & Co., Retainer, vs Protection office	50
April. 21. of Neptune office, in case of the Good hope	50
22. of Soule & Scholfield,[79] retainer vs [illegible]	300
29. of Atlas Ins. Office, retainer, up to Feb. 1836.	200
	10.706.40

Apl. 30 Brot up	10.706.40
of the Protection office, Annual Retainer	100.00
May 7. of Purrington & others, in the Bangor case, thro. Mr McGaw	500.
My half of the Comm[ission]s in the Neapolitan claims	1.237.34
May 11. of Locks & Canals thro. Mr Dutton[80]	500
19. of Mr Tobey,	85
June 15. to 21. at Newport of Jenkins & Mann	200
In Jenks v Coleman	100
	13,428.74

Spanish functionaries to forge and alter records to assist him in his suit before the USSC. See Alfred J. Hanna, "Diplomatic Missions of the United States to Cuba to Secure the Spanish Archives of Florida," in A. Curtis Wilgus, ed., *Hispanic American Essays* (Chapel Hill, N.C., 1942). In his memorandum the same date (mDW 12394), DW noted he had received Peter Mitchell's note "in payment of the money part" of his contingent fee in the case, and that there remained "400 acres of land to be selected in Little River." *Colin Mitchel* v. *U.S.*, 9 Peters 711 (1835), and 15 Peters 52 (1841).

79. Oakly has not been identified. Protection Insurance Company, Boston; Richard Soule and Isaac Scholfield, Jr., Boston merchants, partners in John Brown & Company.

80. James Purrington, of Orono, Maine; *Veazie* v. *Wadleigh*, USCC,DMe–W, May 1837, and 11 Peters 55 (1837); DW handled Neapolitan claims in the mid-1830s; Warren Dutton (1774–1857; Yale 1797), Massachusetts lawyer and editor, studied with John Lowell, admitted in 1803.

Brot up	13,428.74
of Capt. Mathewson, in Clark v him	200
of Geo. Howland, for advice, respecting his factory business	50
of Mr Vernon, retainer, in Adams v him	25.
of Mr Taft, retained, in Coverly Co vs him	100
of Isaac Arnold, Retainer, in Arnold vs Clifford	300
of Crawford Allen, for advice respecting ship Genet[81]	30
of Mr. Walcot, in the behalf of the Mill owners	100
	14.233.74

Brot up	14.233.74
June 22. of Capt Miller, (on his note),	
thro' Mr. Hathaway, Retainer, in case of charge abt. trading slaves	150.
bal. of fees, in Arnold vs Clifford	200
July	
1. of Mr Whipple, for opinion relative to the assignment of Saml. Shore	50
10	
of Sprague & Gray, in behalf of Mr Cross[82]	50
	14.783.74

Brot up	14.783.74
July 13. of Mr Tedior[?] in dispute with Mr Mann	100.
Of N. E. Ins Co. in the case of the Sarah Ann[83]	150
of Mr Leavitt, thro' Mr Kinsman	150.
	$15.183.74

Sepr. 1. 1835.

81. Henry Mathewson of Providence, Rhode Island; *Clarke* v. *Mathewson*, USCC,DRI-Pr, November 1842, 2 Sumner 262 (1835), 12 Peters 164 (1838), and 6 Howard 122 (1848); possibly George Howland, New Bedford, Massachusetts merchant; William Vernon of Boston; *Lawrence and Adams* v. *Vernon*, 3 Sumner 20 (1837) (DW did not appear). Taft has not been identified. *Arnold* v. *Clifford*, 2 Sumner 238 (1835); Crawford Allen, Providence, Rhode Island merchant.

82. Miller has not been identified. Probably Thomas S. Hathaway, New Bedford merchant; *U.S.* v. *Battiste*, USCC,DMass, October 1835, 2 Sumner 240 (1835). Whipple, Shore, Sprague, Gray, and Cross have not been identified.

83. Tedior and Mann have not been identified. *The Brig Sarah Ann*, 2 Sumner 206 (1835) (DW did not appear), and 13 Peters 387 (1839).

1835		
Sep.		
	of Wadleigh & Purrington, to go to Wiscasset	1000
	of same at Bangor	200
Oct. 3.		
	of same at Wiscasset, Genl. retainer	1000
	of Col Perkins, thro W. H. Gardner Esq. case with U. S. Ship Mentor	50
	of Mr Ketcham, retainer in Patent suit	100.
	of Mr Burger of N York, opinion abt. a will[84]	50
		2.400
	Brot up	2,400.
Oct. 22.		
	of Theodore Parker, Retainer in Geo. Weld & Co v him	100.
	of Mercht's office, in case of Brig Katharine	50
Nov. 5		
	of Mr Vernon, in Adams vs him	50
	of Mr Jona. Tobey	100
Nov. 7.		
	of Messrs Ellis & Mayo retainer, vs Rob Beale thro Mr Morey	50
	of Mr Tobey, in full[85]	200
		$2.950
	Brought up	2.950
	Of the following offices, for Retainers up to Decr. '36	
	Franklin	100
	Boston Marine	100
	Washington	100
	Ocean	100
	New England	100
	Boston	100
	Mass. F. & M.	100
	Suffolk	100

84. Ira Wadleigh, of Orono, Maine; possibly Hiram Ketchum, New York lawyer; probably Timothy P. Burger, New York lawyer.

85. Possibly Theodore D. Parker and George M. Weld, Boston merchants; Charles Ellis and John M. Mayo, Boston merchants. Beale has not been identified.

Nov. 14	
of Mr Greene, N. Bedford	200
Decr. 1. of Mr Brooks, on acct of Chs	
R. Bridge, on new agreement[86]	1.000
	4.950
Brot up	4.950
of Messrs Frazer & Thos, Duxbury, retainer	50
Decr. 2. of Mr Dorr, retainer, in favor	
Chaffees India Rubber Pat	100
Decr. 7. of Mr [illegible], bal. of fees in	
Florida land case, instead of land	3.000
14. of Jno. Baptiste, thro Mr [Charles Pelham]	
Curtis bal. of fee	125
Decr.	
of E. Curtis Esq, in N[ew] B[runswick] Turnpike case[87]	100
1836.	
Jan. 8. of Jenkins & Mann, bal. of fees	200
	12.355
Brot up	12.355
Jan. 10th.	
of B[ank] U[nited] S[tates] "refresher"	500
Jan 15.	
of Jno. Randell jr in his Dispute with	
Ches. & Del. Canal	1.500
18. of Jos. Grafton Esq	250
Feb. 12. of Mr Leonard, of R. I. thro R. W.	
Greene, in suit v U. M. Co.	50
Feb. 25.	
of G. W. Pickering by dr[a]ft on S. D. Peters as	
Retainer in Land causes[88]	100
	14.755

86. *Charles River Bridge* v. *Warren Bridge*, 11 Peters 420 (1837).

87. Frazer & Thos, Duxbury merchants; Samuel Adams Dorr (1775–1855; Harvard 1795), Boston lawyer and businessman, studied with James Sullivan, admitted in 1798; John Battiste, New Bedford sailor charged with slave trading; *J. Tobey* v. *Inhabitants of Bristol*, USCC,DMass, October 1835, and 3 Story 800 (1845); *J. Tobey* v. *Claflin et al.*, USCC,DMass, October 1838, 3 Sumner 379 (1838).

88. *Crowell* v. *Randell*, 10 Peters 368 (1836). Randell, a shipmaster, otherwise not identified. Grafton, Leonard, Pickering, and Peters have not been identified.

Brot up	14.755
feb.	
20. by authority to draw on Dudley & Stuyvesant, N. York, by J. W. M. retainer &c, in Allagon case	2.000
Mar. 29. of Storer Rines, thro Messrs Sprague & Gray, retainer in case in Worcester Co.	100
April 6. of D. R. Greene, bal. fees in Ryder's case vs Shepherd[89]	100.00
of Mr Loring, Retainer for B[oston] & P[rovidence] Railroad Co	500
May 3 of Mr Leonard, thro. R. W. Greene	50
	17.505

Brot up	17.505
May 21. of Danl. Whitney, Retainer about lands in Cossulla & Navarino, by cash & acceptance	500
25. of Joseph Grafton, by note	250
June.	
Congress pay, in full for the session	2088
21. of David Stone, for opinion respecting claim on British Gov[90]	50
	20.393

Brot up	20.393
Aug. of Messrs Wm. H. Gardiner & Peleg Sprague	200
11. of J. Temple Bowdoin	200
of S. H. Mann & J. R. Adams[91]	1.000
	21.793

21.793.

Septr. 1836

Danl Webster

89. DW probably meant Joseph M. White (1781–1839), Florida lawyer, admitted in 1821, appointed to an 1821 commission to settle land claims within the Florida territory, U.S. representative (1825–1837). In the mid-1830s DW, White, and Edward Livingston prepared legal opinions on the claim of the Spanish Duke of Alagon to a portion of the Florida territory. *Legal Opinions . . . in Relation to the Title of the Duke of Alagon* (New York, 1837). DW's opinion is dated March 4, 1836. See also *W & S*, 15: 122–125. Neither Rines nor Ryder has been identified.

90. Daniel Whitney (1795–1862), a native of Gilsum, New Hampshire, settled in Green Bay, Wisconsin in 1819, speculator and businessman. Stone has not been identified.

91. Peleg Sprague (1793–1880; Harvard 1812), Massachusetts and Maine lawyer, studied at Litchfield Law School and with Levi Lincoln and Samuel Hubbard, admitted in

1836.	
Sep.	
of Merchts office, retainer for two years, from Oct. 1.	200
of Providence & N. Y. transportation Co., thro Mr Pratt[92]	300
Oct. 29. of J. Tobey	100.
Nov. 2. of Wm. Vernon	200
of Fulton[?] Bank respecting lost money	100
Nov. 15. of the following offices for retainers to Decr. 1837.	
viz. Boston Marine In Co.	100
	1.000
Brot up	1.000
Boston Ins Co	100
Franklin "	100
Ocean "	100
N. England "	100
Suffolk "	100
Globe "	100
Nov. 23rd. of Mass. F. & M.	100
24. of Baring Bros & Co., thro Mr Ward, general retainer for one year	100
	1.800
Brot up,	1.800
Feb.	
In U. S. v Lefler	200
In New Orleans case,	7.500
April. of Capt Cobb.	50
of Mr Wadleigh, by accept[ance]	1000
April 22 of C. N. LeRoy	50
of Jno. L. Bogardus, fee, in suits vs Trinity Church[93]	5.000

ADS. MWalB.

1815, state representative, U.S. representative (1825–1829), U.S. senator (1829–1835), judge, USDC,Mass (1841–1865); James Temple Bowdoin (1776–1842; Columbia 1795), nephew of Boston merchant James Bowdoin; see DW's opinion of August 11, 1836 (mDW 13505) supporting Bowdoin's title to various Massachusetts properties. John R. Adams has not been further identified. *Wood, Jr.* v. *Mann et al.*, 1 Sumner 506, 578 (1834), 2 Sumner 316 (1836) (DW did not appear) and 3 Sumner 318 (1838) (DW did not appear).

92. Pratt has not been identified.

93. *U.S.* v. *Leffler*, 11 Peters 86

It does not appear from Webster's correspondence that he had many problems collecting fees from the prominent clients he represented. In one instance, however, presented below, he found he had to take positive measures. Webster had been retained by a defendant's brother in a criminal case. When Healy sought payment from the brother, he refused to pay on the ground that he had only acted as the defendant's agent. Healy notified Webster of the problem; Webster told him to consult another lawyer about a suit. But, Webster noted, he preferred to settle for a lesser amount than go through the process of a law suit.

TO JOHN PLUMMER HEALY

Dr Sir Jan: 13. 1840

I think it high time that Mr Samuel Adams[94] should see my fee paid, in the case of the Commonwealth agt his brother, in which Mr Saml. Adams retained.

I sacrificed other important Engagements, in order to be here to attend the trial.

Mr. J D Adams'[95] friends & sureties had the benefit of those services; & you will please therefore to request Mr Saml. Adams to send you for me Three hundred Dollars, without further delay.[96] Yrs D Webster

ALS. MHi.

FROM JOHN PLUMMER HEALY

Dear Sir, Boston February 11, 1840.

The acceptance Mr. [Henry?] Wheaton holds against you, amounts, principal & interest, to a few cents more than $348. It was originally $421.43—$100. was paid—leaving $321.43 & interest from Oct. 3 '38 now due.

(1837); probably *New Orleans* v. *U.S.*, 10 Peters 622 (1836). Cobb and LeRoy have not been identified. John Bogardus claimed a one-fifth interest in land owned by Trinity Church in New York City. Bogardus traced his claim to his seventeenth-century ancestors. In December 1830 he filed a bill in chancery seeking recovery of his interest. The Church filed its answer in October 1831; Bogardus challenged the sufficiency of the defense. Bogardus died in March 1833. In August the vice-chancellor ruled in favor of the Church and ordered the bill dismissed unless a replication was filed, 4 Paige (N.Y.) 178 (1833). In October 1834 Bogardus's heir Nathaniel revived the suit and appealed it to the court of errors. That court affirmed the vice-chancellor's decision, 15 Wendell (N.Y.) 111 (1835). Nathaniel Bogardus then filed his replication but evidence was not presented until 1845. In 1847 the court of chancery dismissed the bill on the ground that lapse of time precluded any inquiry into the Church's title, 4 Sandford (N.Y.) 633 (1847). A similar case begun by another claimant met a like fate, *Humbert* v. *Trinity Church*, 7 Paige (N.Y.) 195 (1838), aff'd. 24 Wendell (N.Y.) 587 (1840).

94. Not identified.

95. Not identified.

96. On January 31, 1840, DW

Mr. [Samuel] Adams has not paid, & does not intend to pay. He denies all obligation on account of your services rendered to his brother, & says that he did not employ you, only as the agent of his brother, & that the money he paid as a retaining fee was recd. from his brother. Having already been subjected to expense, to the amt. of about $2,000, on account of that prosecution, he does not feel disposed to pay any more bills, unless in a case of necessity, or clear equity. This is his story. When he came here to retain you, his brother was in gaol. He said nothing about any agency, & was careful, if I remember rightly, to have the receipt I gave him, express that the money was recd. of him. Any directions you may give, in regard to the matter, will of course be followed.

The list of payables for March are as follows.

6/9 Messrs. Geo. & Edwd. Curtis[97] acceptance of your draft $800—payable in New York

13/16 Note to Hingham Bank, payable at sd Bk.—$750.

23/26 Note to Merchants' Bank Boston $1,800.

We have done nothing in the Legislature as yet, except the 15 gall. Act.[98] That work is done. The bill respecting that act recd. the signature of the Governor today.

There is a paragraph going through nearly all the Van Buren papers, & by many of them it is often reiterated, that you said in 1835 in reference to Gen. Harrison, that you would not aid in electing a man to the Presidency who was an object of scorn & contempt to his enemies, & of pity to his friends. Perhaps you have observed it. My object in mentioning it, is, if you have not seen it, that you may think whether it is worth while to contradict it, considering its wide circulation. Very respectfully & truly yours, J. P. Healy.

ALS. MHi.

TO JOHN PLUMMER HEALY

Dr Sir Washington feb. 15 [18]40

I have yrs of the 11th.[99] I shall try to send you some cash, or a draft, this week coming. As to Mr [Samuel] Adams, I wish you to tell the story

wrote to Healy, mDW 16286: "*Mr. Adams must pay* & if on receipt of this he shall not have done the needful, please inform me, & I will give you specific directions."

97. George Curtis (1779–1884; Union College 1822), New York lawyer, brother and law partner of Edward Curtis.

98. In 1838 Massachusetts enacted a piece of temperance legislation that forbade the retail sale of liquor in quantities less than fifteen gallons, Laws, Mass. (1838): 442–443. Two years later the legislature repealed it, Acts and Resolves, Mass. (1840): 180. Healy was a Boston representative to that session.

99. See preceding letter.

to Brother [Augustus] Peabody, & if he thinks an action can be maintained, on your evidence, ask him to sue him at once—for $300—although, if he would pay, I would rather take two than to be obliged to sue for fees. As I understand you, he said nothing about any agency, his brother was in gaol, & he was his bondsman. I think if he is sued at once, he will settle.

The three little things you write about, viz. Curtis, Hingham Bank & Merchants Bank, you must manage as well as you can. Be careful to be in season, in your operations for renewal, let me know how much money you must have, & when, & I will find it, & forward it. Probably you will have to write to Chs H. Thomas[100], Duxbury, abt. Hingham Bank. I do not know how that matter is. Ray Thomas[101] is here, & will remain here a week or 10 days longer.

A ferocious loco foco spirit is breaking out in the Senate of the U. S. Benton, & Allen of Ohio,[102] are not a whit behind the movers of the French Revolution. They carry on a daily War, against all the securities of property, under pretense of denouncing Corporations, monopolies, &c. They are generally answered, but the answers will never be seen by those who read their outrageous Speeches. What is to be the end of all this? Yrs always truly D. Webster

N.B. Cotton is selling in some parts of Georgia at 4 cents per lb.

ALS. MHi.

When Webster left the Tyler administration in 1843 and returned to the practice of law, he needed to earn large fees to pay debts incurred from his speculative losses. In the agreement with Charles Sibbald, printed below, he took a case for a one percent commission. In the second document he lent his name for $1000 to aid the marketing of Chesapeake and Ohio Canal Company bonds. If the sale succeeded, the company would pay him an additional $4000.

DOCUMENT 29. FEE AGREEMENT

Washington
May 15. 1843.

Whereas, Chas. F. Sibbald[103] of Philadelphia, has a large claim upon

100. Charles Henry Thomas (1807–1894) managed DW's Marshfield farm.

101. Nathaniel Ray Thomas, brother of Charles Henry Thomas.

102. The Locofocos were the radical wing of the Democratic party embracing the egalitarianism of the Equal Rights and Workingmen's parties. Thomas Hart Benton (1782–1858), Missouri lawyer and politician, U.S. senator (1820–1850), had been a leading foe of the BUS; William Allen (1803–1879), Ohio lawyer, admitted in 1829, U.S. representative (1833–1835), U.S. senator (1837–1849), Ohio governor (1874–1876).

103. Charles Fraser Sibbald, a Philadelphia merchant whose name

the government of the United States, growing out of the illegal seizure & dispossession of his property in Florida. And whereas, by an Act of Congress,[104] for the relief of said Chas. F. Sibbald, the Third Auditor of the Treasury Department, under the direction of the Attorney General, is instructed to audit said claim; and the Secretary of the Treasury is directed to pay whatever amount may be found due to said Sibbald. And whereas said Sibbald is desirous of obtaining the legal advice and professional aid of Daniel Webster, in supporting his just claims upon the government. Now this agreement witnesseth, that the said Danl. Webster hereby agrees to prepare a legal argument, or to give his legal opinion in support of the other Counsel in this case (if he should concur with them) in maintaining the rights of the said Chs. F. Sibbald. And the said Daniel Webster further agrees to return to Washington to give any further professional aid and advice, in support of said claim, whenever such advice may be deemed necessary.[105]

In consideration of these services, the said Charles F. Sibbald, hereby agrees to allow & pay to the said Daniel Webster, one per centum out of whatever sum may be awarded & paid to him, as an indemnity, under the provision of said Act of Congress for his relief

John Connell
on behalf of
Chs F. Sibbald

Danl Webster

ADS(DWp). NhHi. John Connell (1783–1860), a Philadelphia merchant.

---

appears in the city directories from 1825–1850.

104. 6 U.S. Statutes at Large 864 (1842), 9 U.S. Statutes at Large 682 (1846).

105. Sibbald had sued the U.S. for damages arising from delayed confirmation of title to a pre-cession grant of timber rights to 16,000 acres in Florida. Although he won his case in 1836 (10 Peters 313) and received further aid from the USSC in 1838 (12 Peters 488), apparently he was unable to get the land surveyed. In March 1844 the USSC dismissed his last petition (2 Howard 455). There is no indication that DW participated in this phase of the proceedings. He did, however, pursue Sibbald's claim against the government in Washington. See references to a printed argument (Philadelphia, 1845) by DW and John MacPherson Berrien, addressed to attorney general John Nelson, in *Executive Documents*, 32d Cong., 2d sess., serial 684, No. 68, pp. 76–77; opinion by Berrien and DW, dated March 22, 1849, in *Committee Reports*, 31st Cong., 2d sess., serial 606, No. 38, pp. 43–44. See also DW, George Mifflin Dallas, and John MacPherson Berrien to Robert James Walker, March 23, 1847, mDW 27739; same to Secretary of the Treasury (Walker), March 29, 1847, mDW 27768, both published in *Correspondence*, 6.

DOCUMENT 30. FEE AGREEMENT

July 15. 1845.

This certifies, that having paid to D. Webster, Esq One thousand Dollars, for his advice & assistance relative to the negotiation of the Bonds of the Chesapeake & Ohio Canal Co., to be issued for the purpose of finishing the said Canal, I am bound, in behalf of Mr. W. B. Thompson,[106] & others, his associates, to pay Mr Webster the sum of four thousand Dollars more, in case such negotiation should prove successful.

Walter Cunningham

ADS. (DW). NhHi. Published in *Correspondence*, 6. Walter Cunningham was a contractor for the canal from September 1845 to November 1847, together with Walter Gwynn, William Beverhout Thompson, and James Hunter.

DOCUMENT 31. BOOK OF RECEIPTS

1843. [May 1843–March 1847]

Receipts, since May 8.

May		
	From merchts in N. Y. retainer, respecting certain N. Y. laws	500
	of Mr [George] Griswold	500
	of W. Wyman, at various times	2.000
	of Merchants Bank, general retainer	500
Oct.		
	of Merchants Inse. Office, retainer, for 2 yrs	200
	of Mr Belknap, Concord retainer in suit with R. Road	100
	of Messrs Thompson & Prentiss, in Mexican matters[107]	2000
		5.800
	Brot up	5.800

106. William Beverhout Thompson (1805–1867; United States Military Academy 1824), chief engineer, Chesapeake & Ohio Canal (1844–1848).

107. William Wyman, president of the Phoenix Bank, Charlestown, Massachusetts, see pp. 549–564, below; Andrew E. Belknap (1779–1858), writer and commercial agent; Gilbert L. Thompson, as a colonel in the United States Army, served as a special messenger to Santa Anna in 1844, bearing news of the Texas treaty of annexation, later moved to Washington and was active in the Union Land Company; James Prentiss (d. 1857), New York speculator in western lands.

	of Hollis Street Church, in dispute with Mr Pierrepont	100
	of Messrs Baring Brothers, retainer	100
	of Horace Gray Esq. retainer in Patent cause	100
	of A. G. Benson, retainer	200
	of Mr Dehon, in Clamorgan case	1.000
Nov. 14	of Locks & Canals Co. retainer	200
Nov.	of the City of Boston retainer in dispute with Providence R. R.[108]	200
		7.700

	Brot up	$7.700
Oct:	of Mr Cummings of Portland, abt. Canada lands	100
Nov. 15.	of Mr. Willard Phillips, in behalf of his clients, in cases relative to East. Lands	100
20.	of Mr Thurlow, thro Mr Cho[a]te, retainer, license case	100
24.	of W. Wyman	100
28.	of Mr Winthrop, in full of fees in Mr Bowdoins case	200
Decr. 2.	of Messrs Fitz, Wesson & Gary, retainer[109]	150
		8.450

	Brot up	8.450
Decr		
4.	of Lispenard Stewart, retainer in case of the will of Alice Stewart	500
9.	of Calvin Emmons, retainer in suits respecting this Emmons' Patent for cylindrical planing machine	100
12.	of Manufacturers Ins Office, for retainer for one year.	100

108. Rev. John Pierpont, minister of Boston's Hollis Street Church; Horace Gray (1799–1873; Harvard 1819), Boston merchant, iron manufacturer; Alfred G. Benson, commission merchant in New York, partner of Charles March. Dehon has not been identified. *Providence Railroad Company* v. *Boston*, argued April 3, 1844, *W & S*, 11: 185–216.

109. Nathan Cummings has not been further identified. Samuel Thurlow, Georgetown, Massachusetts, trader; *Thurlow* v. *Massachusetts*, 5 Howard 504 (1847), one of the *License* cases; James Temple Bowdoin, Jr. (b. 1815), became involved in a dispute with Bowdoin College over title to land willed to him by his father (see n. 91, above); the parties settled in 1843. Fitz, Wesson, & Gary, Charlestown, Massachusetts merchants.

23. of Mr Carlisle, retainer in the case of Birckhead v Brown[110]	250
	9.300
Brot up	9.300
23. of T. W. Ward, in case of Barings v Exchange Co	250
28. of Mr Coles, retainer, in case Harlaam Bridge v. Harlaam R. R.	100
29. of Mr Proctor,[111] in his claim, on Govt	250
Jan: of Mr. Emmons	50
of I.[?] Co.	250
Mar: of T[homas] H[andasyd] P[erkins]	200
	$10.400
Brot up	10.400
Mar: at N. Y. of Mr Ketchum	50
of Messrs Adrean & Mott	125
April. of Mr Healey, in the case of Bulfinch Ch: &c	200
of Mr Morey, Retainer for Worcester R. R.	250
of C. G. Loring, for Lowell R. R.	250
of Mr [John] Pickering, for the City of Boston	500
In the case of Windsor Bank v. *Suffolk* Bank[112]	100
	11.875
Brot up	11.875
Add for error in adding up on 4th. page	100
Add Ringue's[?] note	1000
	12.975
Deduct for loss, on Proctor's Bill, say	125
	12.850
add Mr Wilder's retainer[113]	50
	$12.900

May 8. 1844

110. Stewart, a New York merchant; Emmons, a New York engineer; probably James Mandeville Carlisle (1814–1877), Washington lawyer. *Birckhead* v. *Brown*, 2 Denio (N.Y.) 375 (1845).

111. Coles has not been identified. Amos Proctor, of New York, in a claim arising from a customs case during the War of 1812. See *House Reports*, 28th Cong., 1st sess., serial 446, Rep. No. 474.

112. Adrean has not been identified. Richard Mott, New York lawyer; *Mussey* v. *Bulfinch Street Society*, 1 Cushing (Mass.) 148 (1848); *Windsor Bank* v. *Suffolk Bank*, USCC,DMass, May 1845.

113. Ringue and Wilder have not been identified. DW made the error in the 9.300 total, p. 166, above.

May 1844.	
18. of Geo. Morey, in behalf of Worcester R. R. Co.	400
20. of Mr Adrean in Striker v Kelley	125.
31. of Mr Goodyear, retainer, in relation to metalic rubber[114]	100
of T. W. W[ard]	200
of A F	2.000
of Mr [Franklin?] Haven	500
of Windsor Bank	400
of Suffolk Bk	500
	4.205
Brot up	4.205
of Locks & Canals	500
of Lowell R. R. retainer	250
of Horace Gray	100
of J. & J. Chamberlin	200
of Eben Smith	500
of Merchts Bank in Steam Boat case	500
<Lowell R. R.	250>
Jan. 16. of E. Smith	500
18. of Eastern R.R.	500
of R. M N. Smyth, Genl Retainer[115]	150
	$7.405
Brot up	7.405
Jan:	
21. L[owell] R. R. in full for services before Comee.	500
Jan. 27 of Mr Lawrence, Van Wagenon in N. Y. in Lawrence v City of N. York	250.
Feb. of Mr Thurlow	200
of Mr Wilbur	100
April of Mr Windsor[116]	50
	8.505

114. Charles Goodyear (1800–1860), inventor of the rubber vulcanization process; *Striker* v. *Kelley*, 7 Hill (N.Y.) 9 (1844). DW did not argue the appeal, 2 Denio (N.Y.) 323 (1845).

115. J. & J. Chamberlin, New York importers; possibly Boston merchant Ebenezer Smith; *New Jersey Steam Navigation Company* v. *Merchants' Bank of Boston*, 6 Howard 344 (1848) (known as *The Lexington*); *Same* v. *Felt*, unreported USSC case, File No. 2733, decided January 2, 1849; Smyth, a Boston real estate broker.

116. DW appeared before the state railroad committee on January 20, 1845, on behalf of the Boston & Lowell Railroad to argue against the chartering of two proposed new lines (mDW 26080, *W & S*, 15: 373–401).

Brot up	8.505
April.	
of Dry Dock, Co. N. Y.	500
of City of Boston, thro. Mr [John] Pickering	300
May 3. of Genl Veazie, for agreement at Portland, with previous retainer thro. Mr Rogers	600
Omitted, in Striker v Kelly, last summer	250
of D. P. Hall,[117] in Storey's case	300
	10.455

Brot over.	10.455
Add Congress pay, Special Session of the Senate	620
Personal earnings	$11.075

I believe I may have omitted some small fees; but not of much aggregate amt.

May 8. 1845.

This finally added up, N. Y. May 16. [18]45

June. of Mr. Van Wagenon, thro. Mr Blatchford	250
10. of Ezekl. Hale jr. thro. Mr Choate, Retainer	100

Abbott Lawrence (1792–1855), leading Boston merchant and textile manufacturer, U.S. representative (1835–1837, 1839–1840), minister to Great Britain (1849–1852), founder of the factory city of Lawrence, Massachusetts. In 1844 DW argued Lawrence's appeal from the New York supreme court in *Lawrence et al.* v. *Mayor of the City of New York* before the court of errors. Lawrence and other merchants had sued to recover the value of merchandise blown up by the city in an attempt to stop the disastrous fire of December 1835. Judge Bronson's supreme court opinion is reported in the body of the opinion in *Russell* v. *Mayor of the City of New York*, 2 Denio (N.Y.) 461, at 464–465 (1845). The court of errors was unable to reach a decision in *Lawrence* and allowed the case to be reargued in the summer of 1845. At the December 1845 term the court affirmed a decision in favor of the city in both the *Lawrence* and *Russell* cases. The opinions of the judges in *Russell* disposed of the issues raised in the *Lawrence* case. The court ruled that the merchants could not recover for losses sustained as a result of actions taken under the police power. Either Gerrit Gerritse Van Wagenen (d. 1858; Columbia 1821), or William Wheeler Van Wagenen (d. 1880; Columbia A.M. 1834), both New York lawyers. A fragment of DW's notes may be found in mDW 26404–26409. Neither Wilbur nor Windsor has been identified.

117. Samuel Veazie, of Bangor, Maine, shipbuilder, lumber mill owner; Jonathan Palmer Rogers (1802–1846), Maine and Massachusetts lawyer, studied with Ruel Williams, admitted in 1826, practiced in Bangor until 1840, and then in Boston, attorney general, Maine (1832), state senator (1834). *Veazie* v. *Williams*, USCC,DMe–Pl, May 1845, 3 Story 611 (1845); David Priestly Hall (1798–1868; Harvard 1820), New York lawyer, admitted in 1824.

in N. Y. of J. Horseley Palmer thro Mr Blatchford	500
of J. G. Wilson	1000
of H. Gray	100
of Mr Draper, in Patent cause, for Mr	100
July of Jona. Tobey	100
of Mr. Wilson, N. Y. retainer abt. Patents[118]	1.000
	3.150
Brot up	3.150
of Mr [William] Wyman	750
of Mr Duncan, in N[ew] O[rleans] Steamboat cases,	100
In the dispute about water rights, Blackstone River	250
of Mr Emerson of Bangor, retainer, case in Sup. Ct. U. S.	250
of Col. Hallett, retainer in case in Supreme Ct.[119]	250
	$4.750
Brot up	4.750
of Genl. Cunningham, in behalf of Grogan & Co.	1.000
Oct. of same, for check	600
of Mr. Rowley, retainer, agt. Steam Boat	250
At Albany, of Mr. Russell, retainer[120]	100
Oct: 25. of Mr Birckhead by dr[a]f[t] in Birckhead vs Brown	500
Nov. 18.	
of Locks & Canals	2.500
	9.750

118. John Horsley Palmer (1779–1858), governor of the Bank of England (1830–1832), and thereafter its senior director, appointed to the royal commission on bankruptcy and insolvency (1839); James G. Wilson, New York inventor, owner of a patent on a planing machine. *Wilson* v. *Rousseau et al.*, 4 Howard 646 (1846) (DW argued); *Simpson et al.* v. *Wilson*, 4 Howard 709 (1846); *Wilson* v. *Turner et al.*, 4 Howard 712 (1846) (DW argued); *Woodworth et al.* v. *Wilson*, 4 Howard 713 (1846); *Wilson* v. *Simpson et al.*, 9 Howard 109 (1850) (DW argued). Hale and Draper have not been identified.

119. Greer B. Duncan, a New Orleans lawyer; *Waring et al* v. *Clarke*, 5 Howard 440 (1847); although DW did not argue this case, he probably consulted on the issue of jurisdiction. Emerson has not been identified. *Veazie* v. *Williams*, 8 Howard 134 (1850). Russell Hallet, Boston piano manufacturer.

120. Walter Cunningham, U.S. agent for the Mineral Lands of the Upper Mississippi. See *Senate Documents*, 28th Cong., 2d sess., Serial 456, Doc. No. 98. Rowley has not been identified. David Abel Russell (1780–1861), district attorney for the northern judicial district of New York (1813), state representative, U.S. representative (1835–1841).

Brot up	9.750
Nov. 19.	
of Saml. Thurlow	300
of Locks & Canals, additional	500
28. of D. Russell	3.000
of Jno. Whipple Esq, in the R. I. cases, viz cash $500, & his personal engagement for $500—in all	1000
Decr. 6. of the Treasurer of the State, in Mss v R. I.	500
	14.050

Brot up	14.050
Decr. 7	
of Abrahm Colby, in Colby v Ledden, S. C. U. S.	200
of Genl Cunningham, in Texas Case	500
of Mr Storrow, in N. Y. thro. Mr. B[latchford] in Mississippi case	100
Mar: of Hon. T. G. Carey, in Wells River Bridge Case	250
Ap. 1. of Messrs Lowber & LeRoy, N. Y. retainer, in Paten[t] case[121]	200
	15.300

Brot up	15.300
April 3.	
of Mass: thro Mr Healey in full for fees in R. I. vs Mass:	1.500
	16.800
add: recd May 4. of C. G. Loring, for his client, DeFoe v Vermont Bank	250
	$17.050

1846	
June 3rd. of Hon. W. C. Johnson, fee for opinion in respect to Houmas lands, in note & cash	500

121. *Abraham Colby* v. *J. Ledden*, unreported USSC case, File No. 2521, decided February 5, 1849. See also 7 Howard 626 (1849). Storrow has not been identified. *Planters' Bank of Mississippi* v. *Sharp*, 6 Howard 301 (1848); Thomas Greaves Cary (1791–1859; Harvard 1811), studied with Peter Oxenbridge Thacher, admitted in 1814, practiced in Boston, afterward in Brattleboro, Vermont, moved to New York City (1821), where he engaged in the China trade, returned to Boston (c. 1830), state legislator; possibly DW meant West River Bridge. *West River Bridge Company* v. *Dix*, 6 Howard 507 (1848); Robert W. Lowber and Thomas Otis Le Roy & Company, New York manufacturers of lead pipe. See Lowber & Le Roy to DW, March 23, 1846, mDW 26796.

June	
23. of Jas. Wilson, paid to D. A. Hall, fee in Patent causes	3.000
since June	
of Col Mather, in case abt. Dubuque Bank	200
of Hartford Comee. about Bridge at Middletown[122]	300
	4.000
Brot up	4.000
Nov. of Mr Francis, in causes respecting flats	500
of Mr Curtis Do	300
20. of Locks & Canals, case at Washington	500
Decr. 25. of Dr Moreton, retainer in Patent case[123]	200
26. of Michigan R. R. for drawing Charter	500
of Horace Gray Esq; in full, for water power case, & Retainer in other cases	500
	6.500
Brot up	6.500
of the Hancock Bank, thro. P. Harvey Esq	500
1847	
Jan: 4. of Merchants Inse. Co. retainer	200
<In Decr>	
<of Hancock Bank thro. Mr Harvey>	<500>
1847	
Jany. of Jacob LeRoy Esq.	200
Mar: of Geo. Griswold, in Curtis v Inerarity[124]	500

AD. MHi.

122. William Cost Johnson (1806–1860), Maryland lawyer, state representative (1831–1832), U.S. representative (1833–1835, 1836–1843). The Houmas lands were in Ascension Parish, Louisiana. *J. McDonough* v. *L. Millaudon et al.*, 3 Howard 693 (1845). See *Senate Documents*, 28th Cong., 2d sess., Serial 450, Doc. No. 45. Possibly Thomas Mather (1796–18–), of Springfield, Illinois, president, Illinois State Bank, state representative. *Miners' Bank* v. *The United States*, 5 Howard 213 (1847); the proposed bridge at Middletown was for a straight railroad line from New York to Boston, see DW to Edward Curtis, undated, mDW 38314.

123. Ebenezer Francis, Boston merchant; John Curtis, otherwise not identified. *T. Drake* v. *J. Curtis*, MassSJC,S, November 1848, 55 Mass. 395 (1848), see pp. 570–581, below; *Reed* v. *Proprietors of Locks and Canals*, 8 Howard 274 (1850); William Thomas Green Morton (1819–1868), dentist and pioneer in the use of ether as an anesthetic, whose patent was issued in 1846. He later asked DW to reaffirm the opinion he had given on the validity of the patent. See Morton to DW, December 17, 1851, and DW's reply, December 20, 1851 (both mDWs).

124. Peter Harvey, a close friend of DW's; *Jacob Le Roy* v. *Baldwin*,

In his last case, Webster argued in favor of Charles Goodyear's rubber patent. Goodyear enticed Webster to take the case by offering him a fee of ten thousand dollars with a bonus of five thousand more if successful. Though ill and occupied with government affairs, Webster's financial situation did not allow him to decline the offer. Shortly before Webster argued the case in March 1852, George Griswold of New York promised him an additional one thousand dollars if he won, see letter printed below. A few months later the court upheld Goodyear's patent. Webster wrote Griswold a note, printed below, gently reminding him of his promise.[125] In slightly more than two weeks, Webster would be dead.

FROM GEORGE GRISWOLD

Confidential New York
Dear Sir, March 18th, 1852.

A number of my friends are deeply interested in the result of a suit, now pending in the U.S. Circuit Court, in New Jersey, to be held in a few days at Trenton.[126]

You will find inclosed a statement of amount of property invested in India Rubber Factories, under Goodyear's patent. I understand that parties interested have engaged your professional services to argue the cause and have made a satisfactory agreement with you for fees.

Particular object of this letter is to say that in the event of the suit being decided in favor of Goodyears Patent, and against Days claim,[127] I will remit you One Thousand Dolls. in addition to what may have been promised you by the parties who made the agreement with you to argue the cause.

It is a cause of great interest to the parties and they rely on your exertions for success believing as they do that Day is entirely wrong in his pretended claims. With Great Respect, Yr. Obt. Svt. Geo. Griswold

LS. NhHi. Published in *W & S*, 16: 665.

TO GEORGE GRISWOLD

Confidential
My Dear Sir, Marshfield, Oct. 8th 1852

I trust you have been satisfied, as well as the rest of us, with the De-

---

unreported USSC case, File No. 2582, decided February 19, 1850; *Same* v. *Nichols*, unreported USSC case, File No. 2584, decided February 19, 1850; *Curtis* v. *Innerarity*, 6 Howard 146 (1848).

125. DW's argument is printed in *W & S*, 15: 436–472; see also Fuess, 2: 319–321.

126. *Goodyear* v. *Day*, 2 Wallace Jr. 283, 10 Federal Cases 678 (1852).

127. Horace H. Day (1813–1878) New Jersey manufacturer of rubber fabrics, lost the famous patent infringement case to Charles Goodyear.

cree, which has been entered up by the Court in the India Rubber cause at Trenton; & I hope My Dear Sir, that you will not think me obtrusive, if, in connection with this subject, I call your attention to your very kind and confidential letter to me of the 18th of March last.[128] Always most truly & cordially yours D. W.

Copy. NhHi. Published in *W & S*, 16: 665.

128. See preceding letter.

CHAPTER 4. The Spanish Claims Commission

I. INTRODUCTION

a. A brief history of the Adams-Onis Treaty of 1819.[1]

On February 22, 1819, the Adams-Onis Treaty between the United States and Spain was signed.[2] The treaty was the culmination of several years of negotiation between the American Secretary of State, John Quincy Adams, and Luis de Onis, the Spanish minister to the United States. It is best known as the agreement that ceded the Floridas to the United States, but a number of additional diplomatic matters had been the subject of dispute and negotiation between the two nations for almost twenty years. Prominent among them were claims against Spain for losses to American shipping suffered at her hands between 1796 and the end of the Napoleonic wars.

These claims were a legacy of America's complex relationship with Europe throughout the period. They fell into three basic categories. First were those purely Spanish in origin, comprising primarily American vessels seized and embargoed between 1796 and 1802 as a result of Spanish blockade policy. Under the Convention of 1802[3] a commission had been

1. The following account has relied heavily on Moore, *Arbitrations*, 5: 4487–4507, and Dexter Perkins, "John Quincy Adams," in Samuel Flagg Bemis, ed., *The American Secretaries of State and their Diplomacy* (10 vols., New York, 1927–1929), 4: 7–35. Also consulted were Henry Adams, *History of the United States during the Administrations of Jefferson and Madison* (9 vols., New York, 1889–1891), 2: 249–251, 259–260, 276–280; Philip C. Brooks, *Diplomacy and the Borderlands, the Adams-Onis Treaty of 1819* (Berkeley, Cal. 1939); French E. Chadwick, *The Relations of the United States and Spain* (New York, 1909); and Charles C. Griffin, *The United States and the Disruption of the Spanish Empire, 1810–1822* (New York, 1937). These sources provide a fuller discussion of the complex negotiations which led to the treaty.

2. Treaty of Amity, Settlement, and Limits, February 22, 1819; for the full text see Miller, 3: 3–18. The treaty was unanimously ratified by the U.S. Senate on February 24, 1819, but Spain delayed ratification for a considerable time, ostensibly because of the pending disposition of certain Spanish land grants in Florida. At issue also was U.S. conduct toward the revolutions in Spain's American colonies. Ratifications were finally exchanged on February 22, 1821—two years to the day from the original signing.

3. Convention for Indemnification, signed at Madrid, August 11, 1802. See Miller, 2: 492–497.

established to dispose of these claims, but the convention was still unratified in 1818 when negotiation of the new treaty superseded it.

The second category of claims against Spain concerned those arising after 1802. Though purely Spanish in origin, many of the claims in this category hinged on the relationship between the United States and Spain's American colonies, many of them already in revolt by 1818. At times Spain, seeking to protect her colonial interests, had interdicted commerce to those ports no longer "in her control."[4] American ships occasionally had been seized, and claims subsequently lodged. The issue was exacerbated by Spanish suspicions of America's real sympathies in the revolutionary colonial struggles.

Finally there were particularly complicated claims arising from French activity directed against American vessels and cargoes but carried out within Spanish territory and jurisdiction. Was France or Spain to be responsible for these acts? Spain, of course, disclaimed responsibility for French acts even within her borders. The United States, while attempting separately to pursue these claims against France, also sought redress from Spain for French acts committed under some form of Spanish authority. Spain claimed she was faultless with regard to the French; the United States thought otherwise, both in fact and in international law. The issue of French interference in American foreign commerce and Spain's accountability for it had been raised first during discussions over the Convention of 1802. The issue, which had been set aside then, was revived in the new treaty negotiations. It was no less troublesome now. The Treaty of 1819 sought to resolve at least these three outstanding claims issues.

b. A brief explanation of the treaty provisions settling the claims

The nations, through Articles IX and XI of the treaty, sought to put to rest the various claims. To that end they reciprocally renounced "all claims for damages or injuries which they, themselves, as well as their respective citizens and subjects, may have suffered until the time of signing this treaty."[5]

The United States then specifically renounced the following categories of claims: first, "all injuries mentioned in the convention of the 11th of August, 1802"; second, "all claims on account of prizes made by French privateers, and condemned by French Consuls, within the territory and jurisdiction of Spain"; third, "all claims of indemnities on account of the

4. Moore, *Arbitrations*, 5: 4494.

5. This passage and the renunciations by the United States that follow are taken from Article 9 of the treaty. Spain's renunciations are also listed but will not be discussed, since they bear no relationship to the operation of the Spanish Claims Commission established in Article 11.

suspension of the right of deposit at New Orleans in 1802"; fourth, "all claims of citizens of the United States upon the Government of Spain, arising from the unlawful seizures at sea, and in the ports and territories of Spain, or the Spanish colonies"; and finally, "all claims of citizens of the United States upon the Spanish Government, statements of which, soliciting the interposition of the Government of the United States, have been presented to the Department of State, or to the Minister of the United States in Spain, since the date of the convention of 1802, and until the signature of this treaty." Renunciations one, two, and four comprised the heart of American claims and complaints against Spain. Now they were officially to be concluded.

The vehicle for resolving the claims was created in Article XI of the treaty. By that article the United States began the process of "exonerating Spain from all demands in future, on account of the claims of their citizens to which the renunciations herein contained extend, and considering them entirely cancelled, undertake to make satisfaction for the same. . . ." The device for "ascertaining" the claims was a three-member commission, composed of U.S. citizens appointed by the President with the advice and consent of the Senate. The Commission, sitting at Washington, was authorized to "receive, examine, and decide upon the amount and validity of all the claims. . . ." The work was to be completed within three years, and the "satisfaction" was not to exceed five million dollars.

2. THE COMMISSION UNDER THE TREATY

a. Formal Structure and Personnel

Congress lost no time in establishing the Commission. An "act for carrying into execution the treaty" was approved on March 3, 1821.[1] Section four, which established the commission, also authorized the appointment of a secretary "well versed" in French and Spanish, and a clerk. Four weeks later President Monroe sent the Senate three names for confirmation as commissioners—John W. Green of Virginia, William King of Maine, and Hugh Lawson White of Tennessee.[2]

Webster's reaction to the appointments was immediate and negative. Preparing to represent the Boston merchant claimants, he found the choices inexplicable.

> It is seldom worth one's while to attempt that, in which he knows he must fail. This consideration restrains me from undertaking to express my surprise at the appointment of these Commissioners. Can you tell me who *Judge White* is or who his associate, *Judge*

1. 3 U.S. Statutes at Large, 637–39 (1821).

2. Moore, *Arbitrations*, 5: 4500. In addition, Tobias Watkins was appointed as secretary, and Joseph Forrest as clerk.

> *Green*, is? I confess I was wholly unprepared for such a result, notwithstanding I thought the long delay, & the half apology by way of anticipation which appeared some weeks ago in the Intelligencer, augured ill. As it is, my desire to have much to do before the Board is a good deal *cooled*. I know not how I may finally act, but my present feeling is not to make any effort for business before the Board. I am curious to know what sort of *influence* brought these nominations about. For, even after it was decided that no fit person should be appointed, which, I presume, must have been made a preliminary, still I do not understand how, among the unfit, this trio should have been fallen upon.[3]

Why did Webster react so harshly? A number of possible reasons may be offered. First, he was acquainted only with King; White and Green were unknown to him. Green quickly declined to serve, and Monroe instead nominated Littleton Waller Tazewell, a Virginia lawyer with whom Webster probably had some acquaintance at the Supreme Court bar.[4] He knew King from a variety of sources. At the time, King was serving as Maine's first governor, having led its recently concluded successful battle to become separate from Massachusetts. And King was also the half-brother of the well-known Rufus King. Apparently Webster did not think any of them qualified, although his test for qualifications is not clear. White does not seem to have had much experience in matters of commerce and trade, which would occupy so much of the Commission's time. But he had been a judge of Tennessee's highest court and was also a bank president. Tazewell's lengthy practice had familiarized him with many issues of international law, and King had been a successful merchant, shipowner and banker before actively pursuing a political career.[5] All therefore had some background and training that might prove valuable in deciding the claims.

Webster's criteria probably ran a little deeper. Monroe's appointments fell outside the commercial axis most likely to gain from the claims adjustments. Though the nominations were geographically distributed, they

3. DW to Joseph Hopkinson, April 13, 1821, *Correspondence*, 1: 283.

4. Tazewell was never entirely happy with his function as a commissioner. Troubled by self-doubt, he thought of resigning on more than one occasion. (See Tobias Watkins to Tazewell, November 5, 1821, and William Wirt to Tazewell, August 25, 1823, Vi, Tazewell Papers.) This particular propensity of Tazewell's plagued him throughout his career. He resigned both from the U.S. Senate and the governorship of Virginia.

5. All of the preceding sketches have been based on the *Dictionary of American Biography* essays on the individuals, and on additional material available in Hugh Blair Grigsby, *Discourse on the Life and Character of the Hon. Litttleton Waller Tazewell* (Norfolk, Va., 1860), and Nancy N. Scott, ed., *A Memoir of Hugh Lawson White* (Philadelphia, 1856). Both Tazewell and White went on to become members of the Senate, where they served with Webster.

were not distributed according to Webster's desires. Maine, Virginia, and Tennessee (that is, northern New England, the upper South, and the West) were not Boston, New York, Philadelphia, or Baltimore.[6] Monroe seems to have intended this, perhaps hoping to forestall animosities over what clearly was going to amount to a windfall for merchants and insurance underwriters.[7] By appearing to draw elsewhere than from the mercantile community for his commissioners, Monroe probably sought to diminish any adverse impact from the large claims awards. He found the nominees doubly qualified; first, because the merchant, the lawyer, and the judge had exhibited some of the talents necessary for this technical, quasi-judicial work, and secondly, because they were untainted by sectional or economic relationships.

The claims perhaps also threatened to revive previous political categories. Many of the claims would be presented by old Federalist merchants, whose losses were suffered during Jefferson's tenure in office or as a result of American difficulties with Spain and France before Jefferson became President. The animosities were mostly gone now, and Monroe almost certainly wished to insure that they remained buried. But they were not entirely forgotten, as the maneuvering to secure appointments attests. Within a month after the treaty was signed in 1819 (and two years before the commissioners were appointed), the jockeying began. Joseph Hopkinson reported to Webster that he had been approached about his interest in appointment as a commissioner. "It was stated that there is a multitude of applications, strongly supported. The offer therefore is the greater compliment for a *federalist*."[8] Monroe's selections ignored the old political labels and evinced a commitment to the middle, nonvolatile path. The President had one version of safety and security in all of this; Webster, with different interests, defined safety otherwise.

b. Workload, Flow of Business, and Procedural Rules

During the three-year life of the Commission, 1,859 claims were considered. Webster filed about 125 of these claims on behalf of clients and also participated in approximately 100 cases on behalf of the Philadelphia insurance groups.[9] The workload was strenuous to the attorneys and

6. For further observations on the importance of sectional and commercial interests in the claims settlement, see pp. 227–228, below. See also DW to [Peter Chardon Brooks?], February 24, 1819, on "Persons Interested in the North," p. 202, below.

7. For instance, the Philadelphia-based Insurance Company of North America was to find its "wealth" increased by "about 50 per cent" as a result of these claim dispositions. See Marquis James, *Biography of a Business, 1792–1942: Insurance Company of North America* (Indianapolis and New York, 1942), p. 117.

8. Joseph Hopkinson to DW, March 11, 1819, *Correspondence*, 1: 250.

9. These figures are derived from the Commission's records, on deposit in RG 76, Records of the Boundary

agents as well as to the commissioners, and they often complained.[10] At various points, the Commission attempted to facilitate the process by adopting procedural rules to govern the time and manner in which claims were to be presented. The various stages of this process are illustrated and explained more fully as they arise in the section on Webster and the Commission, below. A chronology of Board meetings and events interspersed with general descriptions of important procedural rules is presented here as a brief introduction and orientation to the Board's life span.

Chronology[11]

June 9, 1821	Commission organized.
June 14, 1821	Commission issued first order soliciting claims, with guidelines governing the filing of memorials to present those claims; adjourned until September 10, 1821.
September 10–26, 1821	Commission considered 302 memorials filed to that date, and issued a second order requiring the submission of claims before the next session in January 1822. Two important rules were also promulgated. The first required that all memorials formally received should be set down for examination six months from their reception. There were, however, two exceptions: a memorial could be set down sooner if the claimant wished; or could be postponed beyond six months if the claimant could show that further time was needed to obtain proofs. This second exception became a liberally-used delaying tactic. The second rule permitted submission of written arguments in support of claims.

---

and Claims Commissions and Arbitrations, National Archives. Samuel Jaudon was agent of record for the majority of the Philadelphia claims submitted by the Insurance Company of North America. DW and Jaudon worked closely together, and DW was in fact employed and played a major role in these claims. See in particular pp. 216–218, and 229–235, below.

10. See, for instance, Hugh Lawson White to John Overton, February 11, 1822 ("We are engaged so constantly I do not even find time to write my wife and children as often as I could wish"), Claybrooke Collection, John Overton Papers, Tennessee Historical Society, State Library and Archives, Nashville, and also Tazewell's recollection that "the duties of this Commission proved to be very burdensome," reprinted in Scott, *Memoir of Hugh Lawson White*, p. 34.

11. The chronology and rules are summarized from the Final Report of the Board reprinted in Moore, *Arbitrations*, 5: 4507–4518.

January 7–March 11, 1822	Commission considered 768 new memorials, together with others suspended from the previous meeting. A third order required that all claims be submitted by June 1822, when the next meeting would be held, and stipulated that no memorial would be received after that date without satisfactory reason for the delay. A rule of January 29, 1822, established that after a memorial had been set down for examination, no document or other evidence could be added to those already filed without special permission.
June 11–July 2, 1822	Commission considered 534 new memorials, including 20 filed after the deadline but allowed because the good cause requirement was satisfied. The Commission continued its third order of January 1822, agreeing to accept new memorials through May of 1823.
October 15–November 22, 1822	Commission set down for examination all memorials received six months before, except where an exception was clearly justified.
February 18–April 18, 1823	Commission followed its October 1822 format and issued an order carrying the same policy over to the next session. It was further ordered that proofs must thereafter accompany all new memorials filed, and that such memorials would be set down for examination at once.
July 15–August 5, 1823	Commission continued the same format and announced that it would no longer postpone examination of cases.
November 12, 1823–January 25, 1824	Commission concluded the "process of examining memorials and pronouncing upon their validity, according to the nature of the proofs offered to sustain them." On December 31, 1823, a new rule allowed claimants to petition for reexamination of rejected claims, to be accompanied by new proof. Petitions might be presented only until January 17, 1824, but in fact the deadline was later extended.
January 25–June 8, 1824	Commission met, until its final adjournment date, only for the purpose "of adjusting and *ascertaining the amount* of the claims which had been received, examined and allowed as valid."

c. *Guiding Legal Principles*

Two distinct sets of principles were used by the Commission to decide key issues. First, the Commission addressed the problem of claim reception and validation. In order to be received, a claim had to fall within one of the renunciations of Article IX of the treaty. Some cases were clearly within the treaty, but others were less so. In the less concrete cases, the Commission had to employ a level of analysis other than merely matching the claim to the renunciation. The determination hinged rather on how the Commission interpreted Spain's responsibility for her acts. This interpretation was guided by two sources—the law of nations, and Spain's obligations to the United States under the Treaty of 1795.[12] In other words, would Spain have been accountable for the alleged acts if the present treaty of 1819 had not been concluded? Principles of international law were employed to answer that question.[13]

The second crucial set of principles involved the problem of "adjusting the amount of the claims allowed." After a claim was received and validated, a proper measure of damage had to be adopted to set the final claim award.[14] The rules of damages, drafted to indemnify for actual loss and not to compensate for lost profits, were derived from standard commercial and maritime practice. General rules were formed for both total and partial loss. From a very early date, the merchants and underwriters played a role in educating the Commission in this regard.[15] Webster, a lawyer skilled in these matters, was thus a logical choice to represent the commercial interests.

An important subcategory of this problem related to identifiable groups of claimants entitled to apply for the awards. Among Webster's clients were a substantial number of insurance underwriters. Were they allowed to seek compensation under the treaty? The Commission decided they were covered under the treaty, but not as claimants in their own right. Only as assignees of parties with valid claims could the underwriters seek their derivative claims. The result was good enough for both the insurers and Webster.[16]

The Commission's rules, then, operated at two levels. First, the process of treaty construction itself was buttressed by the law of nations, and sec-

12. Treaty of Friendship, Limits, and Navigation, October 27, 1795 (Miller, 2: 318–345).

13. For a full explanation of the principles used in determining the reception and validity of claims, see the final report of the Commission, reprinted in Moore, *Arbitrations*, 5: 4512–4516.

14. For a full explanation of the preceding principles, see Moore, *Arbitrations*, 5: 4516–4517.

15. For example, see Peter Chardon Brooks to William King, December 26, 1821, pp. 188–192, below.

16. For an example of the Commission's internal debate on this issue, see Tobias Watkins to Littleton W. Tazewell, October 17, 1821, pp. 196–198, below.

ond, private commercial practice and law operated to fill the interstices of the treaty. Webster's practice before the Commission provided examples of both modes of legal argument.[17]

d. Informal Realities

i. External Communications. The letters printed below deal with both direct and indirect attempts to communicate with the commissioners. The Peter Chardon Brooks letters indicate a variety of problems facing the Commission. On one level, there was a real concern with what the guidelines should be as the Commission drew up its rules for deciding the claim amounts. (This process, of course, occurred after a decision had been made on whether to receive the claims—a process that had its own set of criteria. The Rufus King letter of January 15, 1822, printed below, is an example of opinions received by the Commission on the original admissibility of certain categories of claims.) The commissioners, who for the most part were not as skilled in commercial affairs as they would have liked, apparently solicited and received counsel from the merchant community as to the customs that governed their transactions.[18] As the Brooks letters show, the advice was freely offered, and in the process, Brooks provides an interesting insight both into commercial practice and the commercial mentality.

Brooks himself was a claimant before the Commission and had a real stake in its deliberations. He was also Webster's most prominent Commission client. The letters, however, do not reveal any attempt directly to influence the results of particular claims. Rather they seem to be good faith efforts to guide the commissioners in areas where they were unlikely to have much experience. Brooks probably would have been horrified at any suggestion that his conduct was anything less than entirely above reproach, and as the letters indicate, King apparently encouraged Brooks to write. The commissioners were looking for guidance. As a fluid relationship developed between claimants and commissioners, other occasional requests would surface, as in the letter of August 3, 1821, printed below.[19]

17. See pp. 224–227, below.

18. The rule finally adopted by the Commission for "adjusting the amount of the claims" was substantially similar to the one suggested by Brooks to King in his letter of December 26, 1821. See the final report of the Commission as reprinted in Moore, *Arbitrations*, 5: 4516–17.

19. For evidence of additional contacts between claims agents and the commissioners on matters formally before the Commission, see Samuel Jaudon to Robert Stephens, November 9, 1822, PPINA ("I have had a talk with Mr. Tazewell with respect to these two cases"), and Samuel Jaudon to John Inskeep, April 7, 1823, PPINA ("I took occasion on Saturday evening, in reference to the principle adopted in the case of the Peggy, to ask Judge White. . . ."; the letter includes a report of Judge White's reply).

Webster's own letters introducing Alexander Bliss to various people in Washington (including Commission personnel) indicate a peculiarly Websterian trait and also a pattern of conduct before the Commission. First, it is apparent that, as in his Boston law practice, Webster relied on Bliss to do a lot of the heavy preparation and careful detail work. The merchants apparently employed Webster because of his growing reputation and Washington connections. Since Webster was occupied elsewhere with a variety of lawyering and political interests, he preferred to let Bliss do most of the work (for which Bliss received compensation). Webster was, however, to take an active role in the actual argument and superintendence of the cases. Secondly, close contact and a comfortable working relationship were important to success before the Commission. Bliss had to be made known to the Claims Commission community, and Webster arranged for that.

Another group of letters, printed below, includes the troubling ones from Wall Street broker John E. Hyde to commissioner King. The letters, written toward the end of the Commission's life, are a direct attempt to influence King to capitalize on whatever "inside" information he acquired about the resolution of the claims, for the financial profit of either Hyde alone or of both Hyde and King. The claims, long dormant, would result in a substantial increase in working capital for the insurance companies, who had a generation ago paid and written off the claims. The companies that would now profit from the Commission's favorable rulings would soon have higher stock values. Hyde saw an opportunity; King's response was not recorded, but as the letter of May 27, 1823, printed below, indicates, at the very least the two met and discussed the prospect. Apparently the private discussion was serious enough to have led Hyde beyond his initial New York insurance stock inquiries and into an investigation of insurance company stock prices in Baltimore. Whether a joint endeavor resulted is speculative, but the letter does indicate that many people saw the Spanish Claims Commission as an opportunity to capitalize.

PETER CHARDON BROOKS TO WILLIAM KING

Dear Sir Boston June. 4. 1821

I ought to apologize for not having waited upon you on Friday morning as you politely proposed. My family is out of town, and it rained so very fast that I felt myself forced to stay at home.

You will have, Sir, a most difficult and delicate duty to perform in deciding on the various claims which will come before you under the Florida treaty; and I am very glad that a Gentleman of your discriminating & independent mind has the assignment of that duty. The other Gentlemen I have not the honor of knowing any thing about.

After the lapse of so many years, and on the subject of claims which had been almost given up, as of no value,—it must be that the documents will, in many cases, be wanting; and it is to be hoped that the Commissioners will feel themselves authorized to become so much a Court of Equity as to admit an account which shall appear to them a just one—tho' not attended with all the usual vouchers. In addition to the want of proof caused necessarily by length of time—other things will be found to increase the difficulty. In Madrid American papers were destroyed, with the Spanish archives, when Joseph Bonaparte became master of that kingdom,—and as our captains usually sent their papers and claims to our public agents on the spot, and at the time of capture, it will prove, I imagine, that many documents were there destroyed, relating to losses in Europe, which cannot now be replaced. When Washington was burnt by the British the same thing occurred there. I have lately received a letter from Moses Young Esq,[20]—a gentleman who was long in public life in Spain,—a very accurate man—now in the department of State,—informing me that much loss of papers must have arisen in both of those ways. To all this may be added, as you perfectly well know, the extreme difficulty there always is, in cases of depredation, of getting even the common & most ordinary vouchers. Our captains & supercargoes were not unfrequently sent home without being able to make a protest. Under these circumstances the gentlemen Commissioners will no doubt adopt such a course as the nature of each case may seem to require. And here I would beg leave to suggest whether our government might not, without much trouble or expense, serve claimants essentially by instructing our public agents abroad to have extracted and sent to your Board any evidence which the Commissioners may state to be wanting as to vouchers and documents. A direction of this kind from the government would be promptly attended to—but you know Sir how hard an individual finds it, generally, to obtain information of this nature. There is no way of getting papers from Public Records abroad so easy and effectual as by the agency of our public officers, under the direction of the government. How difficult would it prove for an individual to get papers from such places as Porto-rico, St. Domingo, Cuba generally, ports in the Gulph of Mexico &c, where our vessels were carried, and where the doings of Prize Courts were the most irregular and the most difficult to obtain? The same may be said, in some measure, of papers and records in Europe & in Spanish Colonies such as Teneriffe &c. I mention this Sir in the hope that, should the Gentlemen see fit to suggest it, our government will afford all reasonable aid in this regard.

At their first meeting will the Commissioners prescribe rules for the evidence of claimants in making out their acco[unt]s and in directing

20. Departmental clerk, former U.S. consul, Madrid (appointed in 1798).

where they shall be sent and within what time it would be most convenient to the Comrs to receive them? Many no doubt have delayed making out & sending on their claims in expectation of directions from the Commrs so definite as to leave them at no loss how to proceed, not only as regards the manner of making them out, but as to the kinds of claims likely to be allowed. Will it be proper for instance, to trouble your Board with cases of siezure for illicit trade, or is it probable that any claims will be allowed which could not have been sustained in regular Spanish Courts conformably to the laws of Spain? Should the judgment of the Board in this regard, be signified, it might save much trouble all round. A very great portion of our losses by the Spaniards, especially in South America & the Colonies generally have, as I apprehend, arisen under attempts to violate their laws of trade, & as no demand of restitution would be countenanced in such cases, in the Spanish Courts, it has been presumed that all such would be precluded by the Board. Then as to the mode of making out accounts—will claimants be informed when to charge the original cost, and when the prices abroad? How as to freight—interest—damages? The Gentlemen will probably have before them the doings of the Commn. under the British treaty—to follow or not as they may deem proper.

I have thus hastily thrown out the few remarks which have occurred to my mind. I hope you will pardon me for the trouble I am giving you. Should you deem it possible that I can serve you, in any of your inquiries, I shall feel honored in your commands. And as my own claims are not yet made out—if it be not asking too much I shall be much obliged by a word of advice as to the time of sending them on, and such other hints as may occur to your mind. Such intimations may prove of general use in this quarter. I have the honor to be, Sir, very respectfully yr. obed. servt

P.C. Brooks

ALS. MeHi.

PETER CHARDON BROOKS TO WILLIAM KING

Sir — Boston Aug. 3 1821

Will you permit me to trouble you again? Did I recollect any gentleman at Bath to whom I could write I certainly would not take this liberty, and now Sir I beg not give yourself any care about it, but merely if agreeable favor me with short reply stating what may be within your recollection.

In the year 1797 Messrs. James Davidson & Co of Bath insured the brig Venus, John Pearcy[21] master, for a voyage to the West Indies, and

21. Neither has been identified.

she was captured on her return and sent into the City of St. Domingo, a Spanish port, and condemned before a French tribunal established there. What I wish to enquire is who were the partners making this firm of James Davidson & Co? Mr. Davidson I know is dead, but have thought his partners might be living, or some of his heirs, and that you might recollect who they were. If any such persons are alive and at Bath you would do me & them a kindness by sending them this letter & requesting them to furnish me with all the papers they can find relating to that capture. Do you know Capt. Pearcy Sir? He also lived at Bath. Should he be living he could perhaps furnish some information.

I am preparing memorials for Washington agreeably to what I understand to be required. I deem it my duty to state, as minutely as possible, all the facts in each case. The documents I do not propose to transmit at this time. In this notion I hope I am right. I am Sir very truly your obliged & humb servt. P.C. Brooks

ALS. MeHi.

TO [WILLIAM KING]

Sir Sep. 3. [1821]

May I beg permission to make you acquainted with Mr. Bliss. He goes on, with such cases as have been committed to me. He is a young man of excellent character, & very respectable professional standing.

I have the honor to be, with great regard, Yrs D Webster

ALS. DLC.

TO WILLIAM WIRT

Sir, Boston Sep. 4. 1821

May I beg permission to introduce Mr Bliss, to You, a Young Gentleman of our Profession, who goes to Washington, as Representing certain claims before the Commrs under the Florida Treaty.

Perhaps you may find it convenient to make him known to Mr Tazewell;[22] which would be a favor. We are *all* sorry that you came no nearer to us than the Springs. With true regard, Yrs D. Webster

ALS. DLC. William Wirt (1772–1834), Virginia and Maryland lawyer, studied with William P. Hunt, U.S. attorney general (1817–1829), Anti-Masonic presidential candidate (1832).

22. Littleton Waller Tazewell (1774–1860; William and Mary 1791), Virginia lawyer, studied with John Wickham of Richmond, admitted in 1796, U.S. representative (1800–1801), state legislator, commissioner, Spanish Claims Commission (1821–1824), U.S. senator (1824–1832), Virginia governor (1834–1836).

PETER CHARDON BROOKS TO WILLIAM KING

Dear Sir Boston Dec. 26. 1821.

You have kindly requested me to write to you freely on the subject of Spanish claims, and particularly as to the manner in which the amount payable to each claimant should, in my opinion, be ascertained. As a practical man,—one who has for more than thirty years been somewhat conversant with mercantile affairs, and especially those relating to insurance, it is barely possible that I may suggest some things which may be of use to you in the important commission in which you are engaged. Should this be the case I shall be highly gratified indeed.

Much has been said as to the rule to be adopted in ascertaining the amount of each claim. It has appeared to me that the Honorable commissioners will deem it proper to assume one of two modes of coming at this. One is that of allowing the claimant what his adventure really cost, at the port of lading, or what it would have produced at the port to which it was bound. If the first mode be adopted, as I presume it will, the way seems plain. To the actual cost of the ship & cargo should be added the premium of insurance to cover them; and to this amount should be added two thirds of a reasonable sum for the freight of said cargo for the passage in which she was captured—to be covered by insurance in like manner. Less than this would not indemnify the adventurer for his outset, and even then he will get nothing for the gain which every merchant contemplates when he undertakes a voyage. Some doubts may arise, in the minds of gentlemen who have not been engaged in commerce, as to the allowance of insurance, but all such doubts must I think be removed on a due consideration of the subject. Insurance constitutes a part of the cost of every adventure as much, and as necessarily, as wharfage, or truckage, or the commission paid for purchasing a cargo. No man sets out an adventure without calculating the charge of insurance. If he makes a full or partial insurance he actually pays out the money for it as much as he does for the articles of merchandize which he sends;—and if he takes the risk wholly or partly on himself,—as many merchants in our country are in the habit of doing,—he becomes his own insurer, and runs the risk, instead of the insurer, which amounts to the same thing.—And you know Sir that no merchant, who deserves the name, ever undertakes a voyage without the expectation of profit to himself, after paying the cost of his adventure with all the charges—including the premium that was required to secure it against loss. Otherwise he had much better keep his money at home and put it out at interest, because he not only gains no interest by sending it abroad, but incurs the risk of loss of capital by bad markets and bad agents.—We mean therefore, when we speak of *covering* an adventure by insurance, that a merchant has a right to take out a policy for as much more than the first cost as will leave him that cost after paying the premium. If a man makes a shipment which costs him ten thousand dollars, and has to pay three thousand more to have it insured, to the port to which it is bound, he has a right to take out a policy for thirteen thousand,—as otherwise he will not be indemnified in case of loss. Perhaps I cannot render this more clear than—should the amount to be allowed a claimant for a cargo,—be not the cost but what it would have produced in Europe, or the port to which it was bound, the sum would be of course *the net proceeds*, only, because this includes not only the Freight, insurance, & charges of shipment, but also whatever profit would have been made on the adventure—if it had arrived safely. I have not dwelt on this mode of making up claims because I have presumed it would not be adopted by the Hon. Commissioners—owing to the difficulty of coming at the truth, and the danger of imposition. But it may be asked, is there no difficulty in coming at the actual cost of a ship and cargo, and in finding a fair value for the freight? As between owners and underwriters difficulties have rarely arisen in this regard. The cost of a ship, is, like other things, the sum paid for her, including such repairs as may have been put upon her to fit her for the voyage; or if she is on her second or third voyage &c, the sum she may be worth in the market at the time. A just value is generally agreed upon and inserted in the policy, in case of insurance, and perhaps this valuation will afford a safe guide,—because the fair owner wishes to put it at about the real value, and the insurer does not readily consent to its being put at more. It will be necessary to inquire, however, whether such valuation is meant to include the premium or not,—as insurances in different places, are made both ways. Our custom has been—generally—to value *ex*clusive of premium. Where no value is fixed in the policy—it may be well to notice that the provisions and advance wages and port charges, of a voyage, are not considered as making a part of the cost or value of a ship, because those charges are viewed as belonging to the freight, and this is one reason, among others, why an owner has always been allowed to insure upon freight. He has no other way of securing his whole outset against loss.

In coming at the cost of a cargo our rule has been the real cost by purchase whether at home or abroad, or if a merchant has the goods by him, the sum at which they were selling at the time; and to this is added the necessary charges of loading, and a commission of 2½ prcent on the amount, for the trouble of purchasing. It will be recollected, however, that in exporting articles which have been imported,—we do not allow them to be invoiced at the long price, because the debenture or drawback is received from the Custom house, and therefore forms no part of the sum at risk.

The sum to be allowed for Freight will be in many cases, more difficult to find than in the cases of ships and cargoes. If a ship be on *Freight* the bills of lading will show the value, and here it will be clear enough, but if loaded on Owners' account, which is a very common thing,—it must be estimated at so much a piece. That is pr hogshead, barrel, bale, package, quintal—&c,—or by the ton or the tonnage of the ship, or by the ton of merchandize by measurement,—or an outright sum for the run of the ship, or so much a ton a month on the tonnage of the ship. Found in either of these ways *two thirds* only are to be allowed, as before hinted. I beg leave here to give the reason why only two thirds of the freight should be allowed, instead of the whole, as in the case of ship & cargo. If a ship is to have $6000, by bills of lading, for taking a cargo to Cadiz, for instance, we do not consider that the owner has a right, strictly, to insure more than $4000 or two thirds,—because if he did, he would, in case of loss, be better off, than he would if she arrived safely,—for in case of safe arrival, it is always supposed that one third part of the freight money will be taken to pay off the seamen, and port charges abroad,—charges which would not arise in case of loss. In adjustments of general average, therefore, in this country & Great Britain, the rule is to make the ship and cargo contribute on the full value, while the Freight does it on only two thirds of its *nominal* amount.

I hope you will pardon me, Sir, for troubling you to read so much on subjects with which I trust you are already pretty well acquainted.

In some of the claims it will be found that insurances were made on Freight *out and home*—& valued accordingly,—while others—and probably far the greater part—will be the Freight for a single passage. In such cases will your allowances for freight vary, in conformity, or shall there be one rule in this respect, applicable to all alike? Again.—Some insurances on ships and cargoes will be *out and home*—and some only, *out* or *home*, and here the same question arises. In England it is not usual to insure more than one passage, at one time, and this by their writers is called a voyage: but in this country nothing is more common than to insure out and home in one policy, and this *we* call a *voyage*, while *out* or *home* only—*we* call a *passage*.

In making out my Memorials, Sir, I did not have this duly in mind. I covered the adventure by the premium named in the policy, whether the policy was out and home or not,—and probably put down the Freight as valued in the policy—whether it was the freight for a passage or out and home. But on more reflection I am well satisfied that, on these points, I was wrong, in not noticing the difference. I now think that the only course which the Hon. Commissioners can take, to do that equal justice at which they aim, will be, in all cases alike, to allow a proper premium for the *passage* on which the ship was captured, and a reasonable freight—for one passage—in the same way,—so as to put the double voyage, in both cases, out of the question. It frequently happens that we include not two only, but three or four passages, in one policy, and take a premium for the whole, and I can see at once that if the Hon Commissioners do not confine their allowance for insurance and freight to one passage,—without regarding the rates named in the policy, they will hardly know where to stop. Should a rule of this kind be adopted it will affect both owners and underwriters, but the latter much more than the former; and you will perceive Sir in a moment that in many of my memorials it will bring the sum to be allowed considerably below the face of the policy. Still I am satisfied it will be right, and only wonder that it did not occur to me before. You first presented it to my mind. Permit me to add Sir that when a premo [premium] is charged for a voyage out and home, in any of the claims, it may not be quite right to *halve* it, because when they are blended a smaller premium is demanded. in proportion, as the long premium is deducted in case of loss in either passage. Thus while two passages together would be done at 5,—a single one would be 3—and this proportion would hold very nearly in all cases.

One thing more occurs on the subject of insurance. By our policies in Massachusetts it is agreed that only 99 pct. should be paid in case of a total loss. In New York and Philadelphia it is I believe but 98. This deduction was intended originally to compensate the broker for collecting the loss from the insurers, but since business has been done by corporations, it goes to the credit, or is for the benefit, of the Company. This abatement the owner is also allowed to cover by insurance—as otherwise he would, in case of loss, fall short of that indemnity which the law allows him to secure by insurance. Altho' the rule to cover by premium must have been familiar to yourself long ago,—yet it may not be amiss to repeat it on this occasion,*—lest you should have forgotten it. I am Dear Sir, very truly, Your respectful servt P. C. Brooks

Should you wish to make inquiries, which you think I can satisfy I pray you to command me.

*To cover by insurance take the rate of premium, and the one or two prct. deduction in case of loss, from the $100.. and divide it by the remainder.

—Suppose the sum to be covered 100
at a prem. of 9.
— Deduction — 1.
10
111.11 90 / 100 / 111.11.. would be

at 10— 11.11 / 100 - - - - - the sum covered.

90 / 100 the sum of the policy to cover
90 / 100
90 / 100
90 / 10

ALS. MeHi.

RUFUS KING TO WILLIAM KING

January 15. 1822.

I have endeavoured to revise the subject of our conversation of this morning, but have not been able so to recollect the course of facts concerning the Revolution of Spain, as to be sure that I may not have mistaken their Dates; but if this has been the case, I am not aware that the Mistake is of importance in the application of the Principles by which the St. Sebastian Cases[23] ought to be decided.

The reciprocal Independence of Nations, precludes the people of one, from taking part in, or interfering with, the internal controversies of another. By this Principle, the U.S. have constantly, & without Exception been governed during the eventful Period of the late Struggles in Europe.

We have seen Revolution in Holland, France, Spain, & Italy, and have still pursued our commercial Intercourse with them all. At the period when the american ships & cargoes were prized at St. Sebastian, Spain was not free from Agitation, in consequence of the Revolution which had recently occurred: King Ferdinand the 7th, with the dethroned King his father, had been carried into France, where they were detained in confinement, and Joseph Bonaparte occupied the Throne of Spain; the whole country except Cadiz was under his control, and Cadiz, where the Junta sought Refuge, was besieged by the Army of King Joseph.

France, Austria, & Russia, acknowledged Joseph as King of Spain and sent ambassadors to, & received them, from him. Events that subsequently occurred in Spain, and which extended to France, & afterwards to Italy, overturned the Power, not only of King Joseph, but of the Emperor Napoleon, and of Murat the King of Naples—in consequence of this new Revolution the actual Kings of the House of Bourbon, have been restored to their several Kingdoms. In the Settlements which have since

23. These were cases involving American vessels taken as prize to the Spanish port of San Sebastian at a time when Spain was under the control of France.

been made by Treaties, with France & Naples, the Identity of these nations is recognized, notwithstanding the convulsions, called the Usurpations, which they had suffered; and compensations, and indemnities, have been made to England, Prussia, Austria, and other States, for injuries sustained by their respective subjects during the convulsions of France and Italy, and similar compensations, & Indemnities, are demanded from each of these Nations, as they have been demanded from Spain for injuries committed on american Citizens.

Those Demands are still depending, and the subject of Negotiation, with France, & Naples—in like manner as they have been with Spain—each of those Nations were held responsible to us for Injuries done before the Restoration of their actual sovereigns; and they were, & still are rightfully held answerable to the U.S. as they have been made responsible for like Injuries done to the People of other Nations—we know that Nations are liable to, & often experience, changes and Revolutions in their forms of Government—but the nation still endures. The Rights and Duties of the members of such nation may be and frequently are materially affected, and altered: but the national Identity continues the same; the french & Spanish Nations were still the french & spanish Nations whether under Napoleon & Joseph, or Lewis & Ferdinand; and their Relations and compacts with other nations, as well as their respective Duties to make compensation to others for Injuries received from them have suffered no change.

If this were not the case, nothing would be more easy than by an alteration of its Form of Government, for one Nation to release itself from the Performance of an inconvenient obligation to another. But the Law of Nations gives no countenance to a fraud of this sort. While Strangers respect the existing Government of a nation, they are under no obligation to inquire into its legitimacy—this may be an important Question among themselves: but Foreigners are not supposed to understand, & not permitted to take a Part in its Decision.

It is upon this Principle of public Law, that England in particular, with Prussia and other German Powers, has required & received Indemnities of France, for injuries sustained, at different stages of the french Revolution, by the English and German Subjects—like injuries sustained by american Citizens from France, Spain, & Naples, have produced similar Claims on these Nations respectively for indemnities; and it cannot be supposed that in the late treaty with Spain, which provides a Fund for these indemnities, that a case so indubitably within the class of claims for which the actual Government of Spain is responsable, can be excluded from any share of the Fund—in being restored to the throne of Spain, Ferdinand has repossessed it, subject to all its Duties, as well as intitled to all its Rights—to decide otherwise, would be a Decision, that will strengthen the Disinclination of the actual Government of

France, to make reparation to american Citizens for injuries to a very great amount sustained from france under the Rule of Napoleon.

It would moreover be contradictory to the Course pursued by the Govt. of the U S in persisting in their Demand of Indemnities from France & Naples, and formerly from Spain. faithfully yrs Rufus King

ALS. MeHi. Rufus King (1755–1827; Harvard 1777), lawyer and politician, studied with Theophilus Parsons, admitted in 1780, member, Continental Congress (1784–1787), delegate, U.S. Constitutional Convention (1787), moved to New York City (1788), U.S. senator (1789–1796, 1813–1825), U.S. minister to Great Britain (1796–1803, 1825–1826).

TO JOSEPH HOPKINSON

My Dear Sir, Boston June 8. 1821 [1822].

Allow me to give you this, as a line of introduction for my friend Mr. Bliss.

Mr. Bliss is concerned with me in these Spanish cases. He is now going to Washington, to see what is to be done this Session.

I am *afraid* it will be my fate to be obliged to follow him, to the same place, next month. Yours always D. Webster

ALS. DLC. Joseph Hopkinson (1770–1842; University of Pennsylvania 1786), Philadelphia lawyer, admitted in 1791, U.S. representative (1814–1820), judge, USDC, eastern district of Pennsylvania (1828–1842).

JOHN E. HYDE TO WILLIAM KING

Sir New York 11th. April 1823

I have taken the liberty to inclose you a line from our mutual friend Col. Henry Orne[24] of Boston; and a list of the *present value*, of the various stocks in this City.[25]

I presume the claims of the *Marine Insurance Companies*, are passed as far as they will be allowed under the *Spanish Treaty*; and the principles probably settled, although not made publick.

Your official situation as Commissioner under that Treaty, will give you an opportunity of judging as to the increased value, of any of them, and should you think it an object, I should be willing to purchase, and divide any advantages that may accrue therefrom. If there is anything to warrant a procedure of the kind, we do not see, why you may not fairly and honestly profit by it.

I will with pleasure communicate to you any information I possess, or can obtain, relative to their state, & what constitutes their present Capital. Yours Respty Jno E. Hyde

ALS. MeHi. John E. Hyde (1781–1844), New York stock and exchange broker.

24. Enclosure not found. Henry Orne (1792–1853), lawyer, judge, Boston Police Court.

25. List found but not printed.

JOHN E. HYDE TO WILLIAM KING

Dear Sir New York 27th. May 1823

Since I had the pleasure of seeing you, I have seen Mr. Colt[26] of Baltimore. I have not given him the most distant intimation of my object, but he has communicated the following, in the course of our conversation upon the subject. Maryland passd 100,000—yet depending 200,000. Baltimore passed 120,000—200,000 depending. Marine 30,000 passed —depending 50,000. Chesapeake 200,000 depending, Union 500,000 depending. He thinks the stocks have risen fully in proportion to what has been passed; & that they are fully informed on the subject. Some of the N. York which I had purchased for a person on speculation prior to our conversation upon the subject, has been sold since at 7½ / 8 pr. ct prem[ium] 15 is asked in the United for what will be recovered on the Spanish claims, and 11.50 offered, on the share of 50 Dolls. nominal. At this moment, I see nothing to justify a purchase for those having claims are higher in proportion than others. Should they be depressed I will immediately write. Yours Respty J. E. Hyde

ALS. MeHi.

JOHN E. HYDE TO WILLIAM KING

Dear Sir New York 23rd. Jan. 1824

From what I have seen in the papers of the proceedings in Congress, I have drawn the conclusion that something definitive will be done soon, relative to the claims under the Spanish Treaty. I have taken the liberty to enclose you a list of prices of the stocks this day.

The out door claims are not offering; neither are there any of the *United* in the market, but of the New York Insurance some may be bought if the price is not too high. I think from 500 to 1000 shares might be bought in 3 or 4 weeks, by prudent management; at from 20 to 25 per cent premium; but my opinion is that it would not be an object, unless there was a certainty of 30 pr. ct. at least on their capital— which is 500,000 Dolls. Their shares are 50 Dolls each. What effect will it have here; in the rejection of the St. Domingo losses.

The state of the money market is such now, that I would buy to any amount at which the stock would be an object, or at which it could be obtain'd.

Should the state of those claims in *your opinion* justify any purchases;

26. Roswell Lyman Colt (1779–1856), a son of Peter Colt of Hartford, Connecticut, was at this time a merchant in Baltimore and also governor of the Society for the Establishment of Useful Manufactures, which founded the town of Paterson, New Jersey, in 1831. He changed his residence from Baltimore to Paterson in 1835.

I again renew my pledge to you, that I will make no use of the information, unless it be for mutual benefit.

Possibly some of the United would be brot. into the [market?] if 15 to 18 Dolls pr. share of 50 was offer'd. Yours Respty Jno E Hyde

ALS. MeHi.

ii. Internal Communications. The Board, as an internal working body, was also concerned with many of the same questions that troubled the merchants whose claims were being considered, and as the letters below between Commission secretary Watkins and commissioner Tazewell illustrate, the debate was conducted openly within the deliberations of the Commission.

TOBIAS WATKINS TO LITTLETON WALLER TAZEWELL

Dear Sir, Washington 17th. Octr. 1821.

The perusal of the very interesting dialogue with which you were good enough to favour me a short time before the adjournment of the Board, suggested to me, as I mentioned to you, several additional questions, which I should be highly gratified to see treated in the same free, perspicuous manner observed in your dialogue. If you should have leisure to attend to them, may I hope that you will not regard me as improperly intruding on your confidence, if I ask for your views of the subject presented in the following queries? It is hardly necessary for me I hope, to add that I have no other object than to gratify that natural desire which every man feels to be well informed upon matters connected with his official station, and that your communications shall be confined to myself. Until lately, I have been under the constant impression, that *insurance* was a species of *gambling*, in which the parties had no right to look beyond *each other*, for compensation in cases of loss arising from their respective speculations. But a fuller examination of the law of insurance and of commercial usage, has induced a different opinion, and I am very solicitous to know whether my reasoning upon the subject has been legal and logical, or fallacious.

1. Is an Act of incorporation by a State Legislature, sufficient to give an American character to an Insurance Co.?

2. Is it sufficient, that *the company*, be shown to possess an American character, without reference to *the individual* character of its members?

3. In cases of Insurance, where a total loss is sustained, and the assured call upon the underwriters for payment, which is duly made, have the former (even where no assignment has been made) *any further right* in the thing so insured, and for which payment is so made?

4. If this question be answered in the negative, *in whom* then is the right vested?

5. If the underwriters, by payment of the amount of insurance, *ipso facto*, acquire a right to the thing insured, is a formal act of assignment by the assured, necessary to strengthen that right?

6. May not the *demand* upon the underwriters for payment, be regarded *in itself* as an abandonment by the assured of his right to the thing for which payment is demanded?

7th. If the assured abandon by the very act of demanding payment, may not the *receipt* for satisfaction of that demand be considered equivalent to an assignment?

8. May not underwriters, then, *by showing that they have made payment*, claim *as such*, without an assignment?

9. Are all claims, which would have been valid against Spain, equally valid, under the restrictions of the Treaty, against the U. States?

10. Under the fair and general interpretation of international law and commercial usage, would the claims of Underwriters, *consideratis considerandis*, have been good against Spain?

11. Can the amount of *premium* received by the Underwriter, in any manner affect his claim to the full amount of *insurance*?

12. Let us suppose one of the strongest cases of this nature which may occur—*A* has a vessel and cargo valued at $10,000, to which amount he calls on *B* for insurance. B demands a premium of 75 pr. cent, which A, under the supposition that if he makes a safe voyage his profits will justify it, agrees to the demand of B, and the vessel proceeds on her destination. C, contrary to the good faith reposed in him by A & B, and in violation of an existing compact, intercepts the vessel on voyage, illegally detains her, and perhaps converts the property to his own use. In this event, A calls on B, abandons all chance of recovery, assigns to him his right, and demands the $10,000 according to the policy of insurance, which B immediately pays. C, in the mean time acknowledges the illegality and injustice of his interference, and promises to make restitution. B, comes forward legally authorised to receive this restitution—has C a right to inquire into the *terms* of the agreement between A & B, and to regulate his restitution according to the *amount actually paid* by B to A?

13. It is clear, in the case just stated, that though A has received the full amount of his legal demand for the loss sustained, he has nevertheless recovered but *one fourth* of the actual value of the thing lost—having, however, assigned his right to B, he has no further claim in law or equity. B.

on the contrary, though he has fulfilled his agreement with A. and *nominally* paid him $10,000, is *actually* a gainer by the transaction, to the amount of 5,000, even before restitution is made by C. But, if C is permitted to regulate his restitution according to the *amount actually paid* by B to A, there will be *no restitution* at all; for, B. so far from having *in fact* paid any thing, has made a clear profit of $5,000, and the whole amount of vessel & cargo, to wit, $10,000 will remain unrestored in the hands of C. But, as neither A. nor C. has either legal or equitable title, to whom does the property, thus illegally seized and detained by C. belong?

In the same manner, supposing the premium to have been only 25 per cent, and that B actually pays, and is out of pocket by the transaction, $7.500—if he can receive *this sum only*, though standing in the place of A, there will remain an *unrestored surplus* in the hands of C. of $2,500.

I beg you to pardon the intrusion, and to believe me to be Dear Sir, with very high respect Yr. Ob. Svt. T. Watkins

P.S. Memorials are still coming in, though more slowly than heretofore. The number of my docket now amounts to 592.

ALS. Vi. Tobias Watkins (1780–1855), secretary to the commissioners. An attorney, he also represented some claimants before the Commission.

TOBIAS WATKINS TO LITTLETON WALLER TAZEWELL

My dear Sir, Washington 15th. Decemb. 1821

The short interval that will elapse before I may expect the pleasure of seeing you again in Washington, would probably have determined me not to trouble you with another letter, had it not been for the purpose of transmitting to you the enclosed,[27] which came to me yesterday from the Post Office. I seize the occasion to thank you for your favour of the 9th. instant, and to express the very great satisfaction it has given me to find that you will not in all probability be compelled to abandon us.

I received a long letter a few days ago from Mr. White, whose recollections and conjectures with regard to the Memorial 234. correspond exactly with yours.[28] But I have again examined the Memorial with critical attention, and unless I am deceived by some ignorance of legal technicalitie, I am confirmed in the opinion that there must be a mistake in the Order, as entered. The averments of ownership, citizenship and domiciliation are full and complete with regard to [Jonathan] Amory, so

27. Not found.

28. Hugh Lawson White (1773–1840), Tennessee lawyer and politician, admitted in 1796, judge, Tennessee supreme court (1801–1807, 1809–1815), state senator (1807–1809, 1817–1825), U.S. district attorney (1808), member, Spanish Claims Commission (1821–1824), U.S. senator (1825–1840). Watkins is referring to a question he had about claim no. 234. See Watkins to Tazewell, November 5, 1821, Vi, Tazewell Papers.

that it was not necessary to invoke any other Memorial on *his* account; and they are equally full with respect to all the *associates* of Amory. With regard to the two other memorials embraced under the same number, no difficulty occurs: the question arises upon them, as you have correctly stated, whether underwriters can claim *as such* without assignment.

Mr. White, like yourself, complains that the recess of the Board, is no time of repose to him. He has been almost constantly from home attending the Courts of his State, with a view to put his business into such a train as will enable him to leave home, so as to arrive here on the 6th. Jany.

I met with your Landlady this morning in Market, who begged me to ascertain whether you intended to take up your quarters again with her. She says she will require some little previous notice, that she may otherwise provide for the present occupants of the rooms. You hinted, the last evening I saw you, that you would probably take a furnished house, and bring on your family. If this is still your intention, and you will make me your agent in the business I will look out for suitable accomodations for you. A very neat house, next door to the Bank of Washington, is offered for rent *during the Session of Congress*; but it is not furnished, nor is there I believe one in Washington to be so rented. I am, Dear Sir, with very sincere esteem Your obedient servant T. Watkins

P.S. You will probably have a long Session, as the number of Memorials to be examined already exceeds four hundred, and will actually [?] be more than five hundred, before the 1st. January. My Docket stands at present at 717. No *arguments* have yet been filed; but I shall no doubt be overwhelmed with them *on* the 7th. January.

ALS. Vi.

3. WEBSTER AND THE COMMISSION

a. The Gathering of Clients

Webster's work before the Commission was devoted to representing two major groups of clients: New England merchants and insurance companies. Of the latter he favored those based in Boston and in Philadelphia, foremost among them the Insurance Company of North America. As early as 1819, Webster began thinking about a possible arrangement with the Boston groups in the hope that "pecuniary profit" would result (See DW to [?], February 24, 1819, printed below). They were, in a sense, a natural clientele. His reputation as a commercial and corporate lawyer had made him a logical choice—sound, cautious, politically safe, and well known. In addition his exposure in commercial practice to the particular concerns of merchants no doubt made him sympathetic to their plight and conversant with their customs. His understanding of those customs would be translated, it was hoped, into effective advocacy before the Commission as it sought to adopt rules governing damage awards made on accepted claims. The agreement between Webster and the claimants gave him broad discretion in handling the claims and paid him 5 percent of the proceeds of the claims until he earned $20,000. This last provision with the maximum fee stipulation was later amended by the consent of at least one client.[1] Clearly the claimants reposed absolute confidence in Webster—a confidence that shortly was to be rewarded.

The Philadelphia connection was not made until after the Commission had commenced work in the fall of 1821. Webster had limited contacts there, but through the intervention of a friend, Joseph Hopkinson, he was able to conclude fairly rapidly an agreement with some Philadelphia underwriters. In October of 1821, Hopkinson wrote to Webster both inquiring and offering:

> what are you going to do respecting the Spanish claims? I have heard you have made an arrangement with some of the Boston claimants, who have made it worth your attention. If this is the case and you expect to attend the sittings of the Commissioners regularly, I may be able to add something to your business there; which tho' not of itself a sufficient inducement to go, will do well enough as an additional service to a better employment. I have altogether declined it, partly on account of my establishment here; and partly (inter nos) because I perceived in our Claimants a disposition to economize in their allowance of compensation, produced by the *low offers* from men of the South. Walter Jones & Geo Hays are candidates. I do not know the terms of the latter but Jones seems to be willing to take any thing, provided he can get $1000 in hand.[2]

Two weeks later Webster replied that he would "probably attend the whole sittings of the Board. I shall be glad to do any thing, for any friends of yours, which they may wish." And shortly thereafter Webster acknowledged to Hopkinson that he was "sensible that I owe to *your* kindness the circumstance of being asked for Professional assistance by the Ins: Co: of N. America."[3]

Any lingering doubts in the INA office were soon resolved. As their agent shortly reported:

> I strongly suspect . . . that those who have employed Mr. Webster will have no reason to regret that they did not employ in preference Mr. [Walter] Jones; nor do I think, that even Genl. [John] Mason's influence would much contribute to the success of any of their

1. See Peter Chardon Brooks to DW, October 10, 1823, mDW 3609.
2. Joseph Hopkinson to DW, October 14, 1821, *Correspondence*, 1: 293–294.
3. DW to Joseph Hopkinson, October 28 and November 24, 1821, *Correspondence*, 1: 294–295, 297.

> cases. Mr. Webster's talents and judgement evidently stand as high in the estimation of the Commissioners as Mr. Jones's and *influence*, I will venture to say will not help a *bad* case; and a good one does not require it.[4]

With all of this out of the way, Webster now set forth to accomplish his task before the Commission.

TO [PETER CHARDON BROOKS?]

Dr Sir Washington feb. 24. 1819

The Spanish Treaty will be ratified, by the Senate either today or tomorrow. I understand it provides for the creation of a board of Commissioners with power to make compensation for Captures &c, not exceeding, in the whole five millions of Dlls. The Insurance Offices in Boston must, of course, have heavy claims of this character. The Commissioners will sit, probably, in this City. I have ventured to think, that those Offices might, usefully to themselves & me, make me their agent, in those claims. A general agency, for all or most of the Offices, would make it worth my attention, & justify me in appropriating as much time to the subject as the nature of it required. If this suggestion should meet your approbation, I hope you will communicate it to the Gentlemen at the Suffolk Office, & also to Mr. Cabot.[5] If, however, any, the least, doubt, difficulty, or impropriety occurs, to you or to them, I beg you at once to forbear pursuing the suggestion. I have asked Mr [Jonathan] Mason to write to Genl. Welles' Office[6] on the same subject. I do not remember that I ever before sought any employment with a view to pecuniary profit. No doubt I may make an awkward figure at it, now. Perhaps, too, I misjudge the importance & amount of these claims. But if it be a case in which I might render service, & receive equivalent compensation, it would suit my objects entirely to be employed in it.

I suppose Comm[issione]rs will not be appointed until the Treaty shall be ratified by Spain.

4. Samuel Jaudon to John Inskeep, January 29, 1822, PPINA.

5. Suffolk Insurance Company; not the Cabot identified in *Correspondence*, 1, but probably George Cabot (1752–1823), Boston merchant and politician, U.S. senator (1791–1796), president of the Boston Marine Insurance Company.

6. Jonathan Mason (1756–1831; Princeton 1774), Boston lawyer and real estate developer, studied with John Adams and Josiah Quincy, admitted in 1777, state legislator, U.S. senator (1800–1803), U.S. representative (1817–1820); Arnold Welles (1761–1827; Harvard 1780), president of the Massachusetts Fire and Marine Insurance Company, general in the Massachusetts militia, first president of the Washington Benevolent Society (1812), with his brother John Welles signed a power of attorney to DW on February 1, 1824. Mason and Welles both misidentified in *Correspondence*, 1.

It has been suggested to me, from a pretty high source, that the persons interested in the North might have some influence, in regard to the nomination of one or more of the Comm[issione]rs. It will be in season to think of this hereafter. In the mean time I think no partial recommendation should be forwarded, if it can be avoided.

I suppose our Western boundary is fixed as follows— Beginning at the mouth of the Sabine River, following the western boundary of Louisiana to the Red River; up the Red River to the 100th deg. of W. Longitude;—thence due north to the Arkansaw; up the Arkansaw to the 42nd deg. of N. Latitude, & thence West to the Pacific—giving us about 7 Degs of Latitude on the Pacific—& the mouth of Columbia River. We also get the Floridas, in cons[ideratio]n of the 5 millions paid to our own citizens.

I am, Dr Sir, very truly Yours Danl. Webster

ALS. NhD. Published in *Correspondence*, 1: 247–248.

DOCUMENT 32. AGREEMENT NAMING WEBSTER AGENT FOR CLAIMANTS UNDER SPANISH TREATY

[July 27, 1821]

At a meeting of Claimants under the Spanish Treaty, in the Hall of the Massachusetts Bank, July 27th 1821, convened for the purpose of taking such measures as may be necessary in the appointment of an agent to present and manage their claims before the Commissioners under that Treaty, it was Voted

That a Committee be raised to consider what measures may be expedient under existing circumstances for promoting the purposes of the meeting.

A committee was accordingly appointed, and now Report,

That having met together they deemed it proper, in the first place, to wait upon the Hon. Mr. Webster whom it was proposed to employ as counsel. They learned from him that he would accede to the following terms; to wit, that he will give his particular attention to claims of persons whose names may be subscribed to the proposed agreement, and who reside in Massachusetts N Hampshire or Maine, provided he shall represent a sufficiently large proportion of the claims owned in those States:—that he will undertake for none whose losses happened from smuggling, illicit trade, the Slave trade, the occlusion of New Orleans, or any offence against the law of Nations, and, generally, for none whose claim is, in his judgment, inadmissible under the Treaty; but, if permitted, will oppose all such claims:—that he will act as agent & counsel for the Claimants; will inspect memorials drawn by others, or draw them himself, if desired; and, after gentlemen have put into his hands their documents & accounts stated, he will do, or cause to be done, all necessary subordinate business.

For his compensation—he will charge a commission of five per cent upon the amount paid to the claimants under the awards of the Commissioners, provided that said commission shall not exceed twenty thousand dollars. His expenses while at Washington, & in going & coming, he expects will be advanced to him from time to time, & shall be deducted from said compensation at the final settlement. Should nothing be recovered, however, on the claims to be urged by Mr Webster, he is not to refund the money so advanced to him for expenses.

The Committee further report that they deem it highly expedient that Mr. Webster should be agreed with and engaged upon these terms. They further report that a committee be appointed to make final arrangements with Mr. Webster and advance him from time to time the sums for his expenses. They further report that no gentlemen should be considered as coming within the terms and advantage of this arrangement, whose names are not subscribed to the following agreement; to wit,

We the undersigned, claimants under the late Spanish Treaty, do agree and engage to employ the Hon. Mr. Webster, as our counsel and agent, to present our claims before the Commissioners under that Treaty, and manage the business arising therefrom. And we agree to pay him, as compensation for his services proportionately to our several awards, agreeably to the terms herein by him proposed.

P[eter] C[hardon] Brooks
Gorham Parsons
Fitz William Sargent of Gloucester—
by Theophilus Parsons.
John Welles for himself and the late
Firm of John & Saml. Welles
Benja[min] Joy
For the Massa. Fire & Marine Insurance
Company—John Welles pr order.
Stephen Higginson
William Parsons
Nathan Bridge Executor
to the late Matthew Bridge
William Davis, of Plymo[uth] Massa.
Barnabas Hedge—by William Davis
Thomas Dennie
J[ohn] Brown
Josiah Knapp
Timo[thy] Williams
Henry Hatch administrator of the Estate
of Crowell Hatch (dec[eased])
James & Tho[mas] H[andasyd] Perkins

Nath[aniel] Fellowes
Benja[min] Rich
John C. Jones
Caleb Loring for the late firm of
Loring & Curtis
Tho[mas] K Jones
John Pedrick 3d
David Eckley Administrator of the
Estate of Nathaniel Fellowes

DS. NhHi. In the same repository there is another copy of the document, drawn up with minor variations. On it Webster wrote: "This agreement is signed, in Boston, by [the above list down through Nathan Bridge.] There are several others, ready to sign when presented." The following original signatures are on this copy: Nath[aniel] West, John Barr, James King, Willard Peele, Nathan Robinson, Jonathan Carnes, Joseph Waters, Saml Orne Exor by Jona. Hodges his Atty.

TO ALEXANDER BLISS

Portsmouth [July 30, 1821]
Monday afternoon

Dear Bliss,

I am this moment arrived from our ride into the interior. The weather has been so hot, that our journey has been a day longer than I expected. I shall leave here Tomorrow morning, & go home as fast as possible. I will be happy to meet the Comee. of the Claimants, at 10 oclock, on Wednesday morning, at my Office. On receipt of this, I wish you would send word to as many as you can, to prevent their taking the trouble to call tomorrow morning. You can send to Mr [Gorham] Parsons, & he can see Mr. Brooks, & others. Nothing probably will prevent my being ready to meet them Wednesday morning at 10 o'clock.

I hear that one of our children has been sick. Send word by Mr. [George] Blake when we may be expected.

In haste Yrs D. Webster

ALS. DLC.

b. The Memorial Stage

The first of a number of crucial procedural steps before the Commission was the memorial stage—the first formal presentation of a claim under the treaty. The Commission had by order of June 14, 1821, established the procedure for filing memorials of claims, and had declared with some detail what information was expected in the memorials.[7] Among the requirements were that the memorial "must set forth minutely and particu-

7. The order is reprinted in Moore, *Arbitrations*, 5: 4501.

larly the various facts and circumstances whence the right to prefer such claim is derived, and must be verified by the *affidavit* of the claimant."[8] In addition, the memorial had to "declare . . . for and in behalf of whom the . . . claim is preferred," the citizenship, original and current domicile of the claimant, and any previous compensation received for the injuries now claimed. A memorial that failed to pass muster here effectively doomed acceptance of the claim. William Boyd's memorial, prepared by Webster, printed below, is an example of the standard form of memorial.

The Bliss-Webster correspondence for this period (primarily from September 1821, when the Commission first met to examine memorials filed after the publication of the June 14 order) illustrates their working relationship. Webster and Bliss established a pipeline between Boston and Washington. Webster remained in Boston supervising the preparation of the memorials. He was responsible for contacts with the merchant and insurer claimants, and for getting them to tell their stories so that he could translate them into the appropriate memorial form. He also had to begin gathering proofs at this time, so that he might have some sense of the relative strengths of the claims. When he had reduced the claims to the necessary form, he forwarded the completed memorial to Bliss, stationed in Washington. Bliss duly filed the claim and was on hand to answer any questions about the memorials, or report back to Boston additional requests for information or proof. He and Webster remained in constant correspondence with each other as they both monitored the different ends of the crucial memorial stage.

There was some initial confusion over the import of the June 14 order. Webster wondered what it really meant:

> The published order says that the Board will at that time proceed to *decide* whether any memorials which may have been filed with the Secretary shall be recd. for examination. Now, as the Memorial is to set forth the facts of the case particularly and minutely, and therefore cannot be varied, are the Commissioners . . . to *decide* at the September meeting, what cases do, & what do not, come within the Treaty? This . . . may depend on construction, & interpretation, and no doubt much discussion must be had before the points can all be settled. If these questions or any of them are to be *settled*, at the ensuing meeting, I must attend it, in behalf of certain claimants.[9]

Webster did not travel to Washington, since the Commission did not at this time call for examination or argument on any of the claims. But as the above comment indicates, when that stage arrived he clearly considered it his responsibility to make the arguments.

8. Ibid.

9. DW to Joseph Hopkinson, August 6, 1821, *Correspondence*, 1: 289–290.

Editorial Note. In the documents and correspondence that follow throughout the rest of this chapter, numerous references are made to individual claims either by name (usually of both ship and captain) and/or by docket number before the Commission. We have not identified every claim. To avoid a plethora of footnotes and interruption of the narrative flow, we have supplied the information only when it appeared useful and important in its particular context. For those interested in a particular claim, two sources are available, one manuscript and one printed. The manuscript source is on deposit in the National Archives, RG 76, Records of the Boundary and Claims Commissions and Arbitrations. The documents of the Spanish Claims Commission available there include its Journal, Register of claims received, Claims adjudged, Claims adjudged: awards and decisions, Claims admitted, and the Report of the Commissioners, with a list of awards. There is also an incomplete alphabetical listing of claimants' names. The printed source may be found in *Executive Documents of the Senate of the United States, for the First Session of the Forty-Ninth Congress, 1885–1886* (Washington, 1886), 5: 22–30, 186–202. The documents included contain all awards arranged alphabetically by vessel and by claimant, and payments are also listed by Treasury warrant number and payee (names are not always correctly or consistently spelled). No rejected claims are noted.

TO ALEXANDER BLISS

Dear Bliss, Boston Sep. 11. 1821

You will find on the Secretary's files the memorial of Stephen Codman, Thomas Amory, & Jona. Amory jr. as Adm[inistrato]r of T. C. Amory—claims for the Betsey, Halliburton. The same Vessel as Mr Brooks claims, No 7. Please put this memorial on our List, as No. 92—& indorse my name on it, as usual.

I send you several others also enclosed. I have not yet heard from you, but am now looking for letters. If the Commssrs take up your list, please inform me, from day, of the course of proceedings.

[Have] you such *minutes* as that you can make any inquiry at Baltimore, for papers in Mr Hudson's & Thomas case?

We have little news here—attention to these cases keeps me much occupied. Yrs. D.W.

ALS. DLC.

TO ALEXANDER BLISS

Dear Bliss Boston Sep. 13. [1821]

I send you another memorial. Before I have occasion to send more I shall probably hear from you, & learn the length of your stay, in W. By a letter from Genl. Winder, I learn that he and Mr Ogden[10] intend proposing some time in *January*, as the fittest opportunity to discuss some questions arising under the Treaty. That time will suit me well, & the *later* in January, the better. I hope not before the 15th. Yrs D. Webster

ALS. DLC.

TO ALEXANDER BLISS

Dear Bliss Boston Sep. 19. 1821

You will find on file the Memorial in the case of the Schooner "Spring-Bird," Tucker, Master, George Barker, Admr.-Clt.—please enter this on your list, as No. 98, indorse it, & take care of it.

I have several other Memorials, but as I suppose they would not, if sent, be cons[idere]d at this time, I shall forbear sending them, until I hear from you further. I have no letter today, but shall hope for one tomorrow. I am exceedingly glad you went on, as it seems necessary somebody should be there.

We have little local news. I miss you very much, & have to work hard. But hope you will not come home while there is any thing undone at W. Yrs. D. Webster

Tomorrow Messrs Perkins & Curson[11] will write you in order to enable you to obtain, if you can, those *Spanish* Papers, which you speak of, relative to the Genl Washington, in yr letter to Mr Curson.

ALS. DLC.

TO ALEXANDER BLISS

Dear Bliss Boston Sep. 20. 1821

I saw yr letter recd by Mr Gray yesterday. Today I have none from you, but look for one Tomorrow. In 89, on our List, The "Eleanor", Williams & als Clts, a letter has been recd.—from Mr. Williams, now at N. Orleans, stating some material facts, not known here when the Memorial was drawn up. It will be best to ask the Commrs. to pass this case, stating to them the reason, & reading the letter of Mr Williams, if necessary,

10. William Henry Winder (1775–1824) and David Bayard Ogden represented several claimants.

11. Samuel Curson, or Curzon (1781–1877) was a nephew of William Burling of Baltimore, who gave him his name and took him as a child to the West Indies, where Burling was associated with the Thomas H. Perkins firm. Samuel Burling, as he was then known, was later sent to Boston, where the Perkins family educated him and took him into their business. He was for many years thereafter the Boston firm's commercial agent in South America. By 1817 he had established himself as a merchant in Havana, in the firm Marilla & Company; in 1834 he moved to New York.

which I now enclose—& which you will be careful to preserve. In due season we will prepare & file a supplemental memorial.

The following Salem Gentlemen have signed my contract—Willard Peele—Nathl. West—John Barr—James King—Nathan Robinson—Jona. Carnes—Joseph Waters—Saml. Orne, Exr by Jona. Hodges, his Atty. Wherever you find one or more of these names on a memorial—please indorse that Memorial—take the No. of it—& take care of it.

We have nothing but what the newspapers contain, in the way of news. Yrs always—D. Webster

ALS. DLC.

TO ALEXANDER BLISS

Dear Bliss, Washington Jan. 13. 1822

One of the greatest inconveniences I suffer at present arises from the want of copies of Memorials. In all future cases, as far as possible, I wish copies might be furnished. I wish also you would send me the copy of the Memorial of Perez Morton & others;—please divide it, into proper parcels, & enclose them to me, under cover to Mr. Gorham;—I can readily reunite them—& if you have copies in any other cases, where I have not, please forward them in like manner. I wish also you would send me your paper about St. Domingo, & tell me all you know about. I shall be obliged to draw up a full historical account of that City, during the years in which these claims arose. If Mr Brooks could readily lay his hands on some of the Protests, entered before Mr Blake, as late as '98, '99, they, or copies of them might be of great use. I shall look at the papers you mentioned, in the Office of the Clerk of the Sup. Court.

The Commrs. are proceeding to dispose of cases:—They have recd. the case from Portsmo[uth] of the *Sterling*; & rejected that of the *Helen*, in which the N. E. Office was claimant. I have written Mr Hall on the subject. None of the suspended cases are decided yet.

Dr. [Eliakim] Morse must execute & send on his supplemental memorial. The Commissioners are not at all pleased to find that he left off so short, in his former *Memorial*. It has hurt his claim, somewhat;—but we must make the best of it. His supplemental Memorial must state the facts, as Mackay states them, & he must make oath to their truth, according to his best knowledge & belief—please give him notice of this; as the sooner it is done the better. Let him give the best reason he can, if he can give any, for not stating the whole story at first.

Shall be glad to hear from you often. Yrs D. Webster

You will do well to complete Mr Coolidges case at once; so that the supplemental Memorial be recd & filed before the Commissrs. reach that [which] is already filed.

ALS. DLC.

TO ALEXANDER BLISS

Dear Bliss— Boston June 10. 1822.

I send you sundry Memorials from Portsmouth; two of them being those which were mislaid, on their way.

I have also recd. the proofs in the case of the Sterling, which I shall forward, if I find an opportunity. Yrs D. Webster

ALS. DLC.

DOCUMENT 33. MEMORIAL OF WILLIAM BOYD FOR SPANISH TREATY DISALLOWED CLAIM (NO. 1129)

[June 27, 1822]

To the Honorable the Commissioners appointed under the eleventh article of the Florida Treaty to receive and liquidate all such claims upon the Spanish Government as are provided for, or referred to, in said treaty.

The memorial of William Boyd of New Orleans in the State of Louisiana, Merchant, by Daniel Webster of Boston in the Commonwealth of Massachusetts, his agent in this behalf, respectfully represents that the said William Boyd is a native citizen of the United States and domiciled within the same; that on the 27th. day of September in the year of our Lord 1796, the said William Boyd then residing at Portsmouth in the State of New Hampshire and having his domicil there, subscribed a policy of assurance in the office kept by John Goddard in said Portsmouth, by which he assured unto Edward Cutts, a native citizen of the United States, and domiciled within the same, the sum of five hundred dollars on the Brig Resolution and cargo, on a voyage at and from Demarara to her port of discharge in the United States, at a premium of 3½ per cent; that in consequence of the capture of said vessel during said voyage, and of her being carried into the island of Porto Rico, as is particularly set forth in the memorial of said Edward Cutts, to which your memorialist respectfully begs leave to refer, the said vessel and cargo became totally lost to the assured; and abandonment thereof was duly made to the several underwriters thereon so far as they had assured the same; by reason of which said loss and abandonment, the said William Boyd became liable to pay, and actually did pay to said Edward Cutts said sum of five hundred dollars.

And the said William Boyd avers that the said foregoing claim is made for his own sole benefit and behoof; that at the time when it arose, it did wholly belong solely and absolutely to him the said William Boyd; and that if allowed, it will now and every part of it belong solely and absolutely to him and that no other person hath any interest therein.

Wherefore your memorialist respectfully prays that his claim for said sum of five hundred dollars and interest, may be allowed.

William Boyd, by his Atty Danl Webster

DS. DNA. Misdated June 22 in *Correspondence*, 1, Calendar: 444. William Boyd (1759–1826) was inheritor of the Portsmouth property of his wealthy father, Colonel George Boyd.

c. Examination of Proof

The Commission established in September of 1821 a basic rule to "set down" all memorials which had been received "for examination of the proofs which might be offered thereafter."[12] When the Commission "received" a memorial, it was simply notifying the parties that, at least on its face, the allegations in the memorials were sufficient to establish a claim within the specific provisions of the treaty. The "examination" phase meant that the claimant had now to prove by appropriate evidence that the claim was valid.

Webster spent a good deal of his time gathering and organizing the "proofs." The problem of finding and presenting evidence was obviously exacerbated by the fact that many of the events alleged to have taken place had occurred in foreign countries from twenty to twenty-five years before. Careful underwriters often kept careful records, but if these were not available, difficulties arose. Oral testimony had to be obtained from survivors, or documents had to be procured from foreign countries.[13] The letters and documents below show the often elaborate nature of the proof required to establish that the alleged events had actually transpired and that the resulting loss was within the purview of the treaty.

DOCUMENT 34. INDEX OF PAPERS IN THE CASE OF THE NAUTILUS

[June 19?, 1822]

Index of papers in the case of the Nautilus.

These papers are filed under the hope that an authentic copy of the whole proceedings in Spain may yet be received in season to be considered together with these proofs. What pains have been taken to obtain that Record will hereafter be stated.

12. See Moore, *Arbitrations*, 5: 4508.

13. For another aspect of this problem, see pp. 214–216, below, on strategies. Obviously delay become a key strategy in order to find time to produce evidence.

Papers now presented.

No. 1. Proofs of interest, authorities &c, acct. Sales at Trieste & *acct. Sales at Cadiz.*

2. Original letters of Richd. Hughes, Supercargo, from 25 Jany. 1802 to March 1805, containing a full account of all the transactions.

3. The *Moratorio*[14] in favour of Torres & Co. certified by Isnardi, Am[erican] consul, & transl[ato]r.

4. Order of the Gov. of Cadiz, 18 March 1803, to stop all proceedings against Ballesteros & Co.
This order is at present no otherwise certified than by Mr. R. Hughes, whose original signature is at the bottom of the paper. It is in Spanish & English, precisely as recd. from Mr. Hughes. It is spoken of in all the correspondence, & there can be no reason to doubt its authenticity, altho' one of Mr. Welles' objects in sending to Spain for the Records was to obtain an authenticated copy of this order. The translation is in the writing of *Mr. Isnardi.*

5. Memorial of Mr. Hughes to Ch. Pinckney Esq., 8 Aug. 1803. Copy of Mr. Pinckney's letter to Mr. Cevallos. Mr. Hughes' letter to Mr. Madison enclosing same. These papers were recd. from Mr. Hughes at the time, & are authenticated by his signature.

6- Mr. Cevallos' letter to Mr. Pinckney, Sep. 7. 1803. This appears to be a copy only. The original sent to Spain several years ago by Mr. [George] Sullivan.

7- Mr. Hughes to Mr. Pinckney, Nov. 1803, & his letter to Mr. Cevallos. These were forwarded by Mr. Hughes at the time, and are authenticated by his original signature.

8- Copy of Mr. Cevallos' letter, March 8. 1804. This was recd. from Mr. Hughes. His signature is not to the paper, but its correspondence with the other papers will sufficiently authenticate it.

9- Letter of R. Hughes to Mr. Pinckney, Oct. 2. 1804, with his original signature.

10.- Protest of Mr. Hughes, Apr. 8. 1805, giving a full account of the transactions from the commencement to that time. This protest was before the Am: Vice Consul. It does not appear whether this is the original or a copy, but it has Mr. Hughes' original signature to it.

11- Copy of the Order of the Gov. of Cadiz, Dec. 11. 1805; certified by R[ichard] W. Meade.

12. Power to R. W. Meade, & Geo. Sullivan to prosecute the claim after Mr. Hughes left Spain. Sep. 1805.

14. The Spanish word *moratória*, meaning a letter of license granted to a debtor, or moratorium.

13. Original correspondence between Mr. Meade & Geo. W. Irving Esq.
14- Deposition of R.W. Meade, giving a full acct. of the transaction.
15- letters of J. & S. Welles, & Mr. Madison's letters to Mr. Pinckney —recd. from the Department of State.
16. Deposition of two Spanish Lawyers stating the Spanish law in reference to this case.
17- Application for the Autos.[15]

I think it will appear from the examination of these papers that all the facts in the Memorial are well proved, even without the help of the expected papers from Spain. Mr. Welles however has made unceasing efforts to obtain those papers as will appear from his affidavit, & the correspondence attached to it. There is added also the correspondence that has taken place since the date of that affidavit.

Mr. Welles now produces the evidence of the Spanish Lawyers to shew the illegality of these proceedings. The Laws themselves are referred to and are also produced for the examination of the Commissioners. If by any chance the papers should yet arrive from Spain, other opinions of other eminent jurists will probably also be found in them as directions were given to that effect. It is hoped however, that the testimony of Mr. Meade & the two Spanish lawyers, and a reference to the laws themselves will prove fully satisfactory to the Board. D. Webster

ADS(DW). DNA.

TO ALEXANDER BLISS

Dear Bliss, Washington Feb. 23. 1823

I believe all your packages, & communications respecting Spanish claims came safe. I have bestowed all my leisure on them, & done the needful, as far as I could. Those that appeared to be ready, I have set down for examination, & mean to enclose a list of them, in this. The Mercury, Ayres, Phenix, Two Marias, & Three Brothers, I have not yet presented. The Mercury Pearson I think I shall present tomorrow. Please state to Mr. [George] Sullivan, or Mr [Jonathan] Amory, that I have not recd a copy of instructions. I do not know that I shall wait for it.

I do not know, nor can I find, that I have any paper or letter, respecting the Reindeer. I have mentioned the subject to the Commrs, & there will be no difficulty in obtaining delay; & probably none, in getting their application, to Spanish Govt., but I have not the means of *specifying* what we want.

I wish Mr. [Benjamin] Rich to send me an affidavit stating as particularly as he can what papers he wants, & what reason he has to suppose

15. *Aútos*, the pleadings and proceedings in a law suit.

that they are in the custody of Spanish Authorities; and also his unsuccessful attempt to obtain them or why he thinks a private attempt wd. be unsuccessful. You seem to think I have <Mr. Forsythe's[16] letter> the necessary data. I shall look again before I close this, but I think I have not anything. The sooner I get the affidavit the better, as it is time to send out.

I think you sent on more cases than could have reasonably been expected. You must have used all yr usual industry. There are several more which I hope to hear of. Pray, assist Mr [James] Pope to get up the *Topaz.* I have sent you, (thro Jaudon) a list of vouchers, in the case of the Sally[,] Stephenson, filed by him. Supposing those to make out a complete case for Mr [Samuel] Cobb & als, I have filed their case. Is that right? Three of my cases have been decided—*Success*, Hill Clt, *allowed.* Hannah, Dighton, not allowed. Commrs. being of opinion, on the evidence, that she was cond[emne]d at Gauadaloupe. I have written the owners.

The *Alert*, & the *Echo* will be decided tomorrow morning. I wrote Mr [Peter Chardon] Brooks, yesterday, abt. his cases, & took occasion to state the present predicament of Mr [Richard W.] Meade's case.[17] Yours mo. truly D. Webster

P.S. I have written to a client to send you in some *cash*, supposing it may be necessary to meet exigencies. I shall also write you, in three or four days, including some money. If you see Mr. [Silas] *Bullard* tell him he will hear from me *in season.*

I hardly know how I did leave my pecuniary affairs. I left them in charge with Mr [William Townsend] Hadduck, who seems in a very unaccountable manner, to have abandoned our concern. If Mrs. W. has returned from her sleigh ride, let her know that I am well at this present writing.

ALS. DLC.

TO ALEXANDER BLISS

Dear Bliss, Washington July 14. 1823

I wish to call your attention to the case of the Iris, Conway.

This vessel & cargo were owned by *Henry Gray*;

His interest insured by *William Gray.*

16. John Forsyth (1780–1841), former Georgia congressman, was at this time U.S. minister to Spain.

17. See n. 50, p. 21, above. After the commissioners rejected Meade's claim, he commenced legal action that dragged on, in one form or another, until 1900. See also John Bassett Moore, ed., *A Digest of International Law* (8 vols., *Washington*, 1906), 6: 1012–1014.

These interests are represented by Francis C. Gray.[18]

John Conway, the Master, had an adventure, amt. to $1566.93 cts—consisting of 23 Boxes Hav[ana] Seegars, & 2 H[ogshea]ds rum—

On this adventure he carried an insurance to be made, for 1.000 by *Samuel Gray*: —who paid the loss—

P. C. Brooks Esq & Wm Ward Esq are Exrs of the Will of the said Samuel Gray.

They have presented a Memorial for the 1000 paid by him on his subscription—

John Conway has presented a Memorial for the uninsured residue of his adventure—viz 566.95.

These two Memorials are presented by me.

The general proofs have been collected by Mr. F. C. Gray, so far as relates to the voyage & loss; & also the interest of Henry Gray, & insurance by Wm. Gray. But our part of the case is deficient. We want the following things

1. A Probate certificate that P. C. B. & W. W. are Exrs of Samuel Gray.
2. Proof of amount of John Conway's invoice &c—I have no doubt Mr Ward or Mr Brooks has the invoice, as the Memorial states it particularly.
3. The policy, & common proof of payment of loss.

Will you have the goodness to forward these without delay, as the want of them keeps the case open. Please direct your answer contingently to me or F. C. Gray; & let it come *quick*.[19]

I arrived yesterday, exactly 5 days to an hour after leaving home, including one day spent in N. York. Last week & yesterday the weather was very oppressive. Today the fires of heaven burn with less fervor.

Judge [Bushrod] W[ashington] is here, Mrs. S[tory] expected Tomorrow. Yrs always D. Webster

ALS. DLC.

d. Strategies

Strategies for presenting claims before the Commission developed in response to two basic problems. One was the availability of evidence to establish the admissibility of a claim. Since documents often had to be obtained from foreign governments (including Spain) or testimony had to be procured from ship captains out of port, the strategy was to seek delay as legitimately as possible in order to postpone rejection of the

18. Francis Calley Gray (1790–1856; Harvard 1809), philanthropist and writer, secretary, U.S. legation, Russia (1809), returned to Boston in 1813, was admitted to the bar in 1814, but did not practice; state legislator.

19. Brooks and Ward, Claim no. 518, were awarded $1,000; Conway, Claim no. 519, received $381.27.

claim for lack of evidence. It was clearly wiser to wait and risk nonproduction of evidence than it was to force a weakly documented claim on the Commission and see it rejected.[20] Jaudon reported, for instance, that "Webster & myself spent some time in examining . . . cases, and concluded to withdraw all but six of them, as in their present state, they would undoubtedly be otherwise rejected."[21] Likewise, it was better to wait and try to give affirmative proof of the appropriateness of admitting a claim under the treaty than to watch it accepted by the Commission under questionable proof, thereby opening up the floodgates for allowing other dubious claims. (At the crucial moment, however, when doubtful claims were finally presented, it was clear, as indicated in John Inskeep's letter, printed below, that as effective a campaign as possible would be waged—including urging one's paid and prestigious counsel to appear.) A combination of the Commission's heavy workload and its predilection for immediately considering newly formed rules as precedent induced a certain deference for decided claims and their principles. As one observer noted, "The old principles are acquiring more stability by being frequently acted upon, and as at the last session, the decisions [of] the Board are pretty generally acquiesced in without hesitation by those who are present & attentive enough to understand [them?]."[22]

The fear of losing their claims was only one cause for the caution of the claimants. There was another factor—a second basic problem—that determined the claimants' strategies, and that was anxiety about cutting up the five-million-dollar pie. Bad claims poorly proved but received might lead to further bad claims accepted, and slowly the pie would be cut thinner and thinner. So a two-front war developed: first, proving as strongly as possible that one's claims were appropriate, and secondly, guarding against the introduction of other species of claims or weak claims that would ultimately diminish the total award under the treaty dollar limitation. The lesson was not lost on anybody. Evaluating one's position in the total scheme of things was crucial. "It is said," Rufus King noted, "that the question of the St. Sebastian cases in wh. the insurance offices are so deeply concerned, is under consideration and that the admission of their claims is doubtful. I speak from rumour; should these claims be excluded it will be of great importance to others whose claims shall be allowed, since the Fr. claims (i.e. those of St. Sebastian) are supposed to amount to 15 Mil. Dollars."[23] Or as a somewhat sheepish

20. Motions for postponement were specifically provided for in the rules of the Commission; see Final Report of the Commissioners, Moore, *Arbitrations*, 5: 4508.

21. Samuel Jaudon to John Inskeep, February 6, 1821, PPINA.

22. Samuel Jaudon to Robert Stephens, March 18, 1821, PPINA.

23. Rufus King to Charles King, January 15, 1822, in Charles R. King, ed., *The Life and Correspondence of Rufus King* (6 vols., New York, 1894–1900), 6: 452. See also Rufus King to William King, January 15, 1822, printed above, pp. 192–194.

William Pinkney is reported as saying, "you know in these cases we are all Ishmaelites—every man's hand is against his neighbor."[24]

TO ALEXANDER BLISS

Dear Bliss Boston Sep. 7 [1821]

I now send you several more Memorials, together with a copy of the *List*. Whatever I send hereafter I shall enter on my list here, & you must enter in like manner on yours. I presume you will stay several days, at least, in the City, & I shall therefore continue to send such as are forwarded to me for some days to come.

I hope you remember that the great object is, <to prevent the> that the Commrs. may not hastily decide for or against, any claims that are doubtful; and also to get thro with such of ours as admit no doubt. But this object is not so important as the former. I would rather they would at this time decide *nothing*—not even the clearest case—rather than that they should decide doubtful cases *either way*. Perhaps there is quite as much to be feared from the admission of improper claims, as the rejection of those which are proper.

We have no news Yrs D Webster

ALS. DLC.

TO ALEXANDER BLISS

Dear Bliss Boston Sep. <20.> 18. [1821]

Your several letters to the 13th instant, have been recd. They give great satisfaction to the concerned, & are very honorable proofs of your attention & intelligence. The more detail you give us of all the proceedings of the Board the better. You are very right to stay to see our cases thro. Whatever *formal* difficulties exist may be easily removed by supplemental Statements. I am glad, on the whole, that for the present they receive none which are not clearly within the Treaty.

I have not time to say more today but intend writing you again tomorrow. In haste Yrs D. Webster

ALS. DLC. Published in *Correspondence*, 1: 292.

TO JOHN INSKEEP

Dear Sir, Boston Nov. 13. 1822

I have seldom regretted any thing more than the circumstances which have detained me from Washington. As I wrote Mr. Jaudon, I intended to have left home the 29th of last month. I waited, for a few days, in con-

24. James A. Hamilton, *Reminiscences . . . during Three Quarters of a Century* (New York, 1869), p. 57.

sequence of the Report in the papers, that the Commissioners were to adjourn. When the reports failed to be confirmed, I had prepared to set out, when on the 28th, I was taken violently ill, and have been confined to my House almost ever since. Yesterday was the first day in which I have attempted to attend to any business, & I then found myself unable to do any thing, & now do not expect to go out again till the end of the week. In the mean time Mr. Gray has had the charge of my concerns at Washington, & I hear from him today, that all cases, in which I am concerned, except such as being quite ready, & embracing no question of difficulty, I am willing should be examined, are postponed.

My own opinion is, that the Commissioners will not finally settle any important question at this term. I may be mistaken, but such is my opinion. None of the New York or R. Island cases are yet before them. Most of those entrusted to Genl. [John] Mason I understand are postponed. Under these circumstances, I do not think it all probable that they will suppose themselves possessed of all the grounds, necessary to form final judgments. Indeed it seems to me very important, for many reasons, that the Commissioners should *not* now settle any important principles. The longer their judgment is delayed, the greater is the probability of a favorable result. On the question of *interest*, & some others in which you are interested, we have here great hopes of a favorable result, if the decision be not hastened.

I have nothing to prevent my setting out for Washington, at any time, but the state of my health. I think I might expect to be able to go in a week, If, on the receipt of this, the state of your information from Washington is such as leads you to think my presence there would be any way useful, I will set out the day after receiving a communication from you to that effect. I shall send a copy of this, by this mail to Mr Jaudon. I shall also write Mr. Gray, with a view of obtaining a postponement of interesting general questions.

One embarrasment is, that so many cases have been put over, it is uncertain whether I should find the Board in session.

Will you please answer this, as soon as may be, & believe me to be, With great regard, Yours, Danl. Webster

ALS. DLC. Published in *W & S*, 16: 70–71. Inadvertently inscribed to "Joseph" Inskeep, it was enclosed by DW in his letter to Joseph Hopkinson, November 13, 1822, *Correspondence*, 1: 317–318.

FROM JOHN INSKEEP

In[suranc]e Office N. America
Phild. Novr. 16. 1822.

Dr. Sir,

Your letter of 13. Inst. is just recd.[25] & in reply have to observe that,

25. DW to John Inskeep, November 13, 1822, preceding.

your absence from Washington cannot be more regretted by you than it is by us. Indisposition however, is a sufficient reason to justify such absence; but could this unfortunate event have been foreseen by us, official duty would have urged the necessity of employing some other professional gentleman to stand by our agent, faithful & competent as he is, during this momentous session. Several questions (unnecessary to detail at present) which deeply involve our interest, have already come before the Commissioners & no doubt others of equal, if not greater importance will; consequently your absence has occasioned us great anxiety, being under daily apprehension that the Interest of the Co. might suffer thereby. Some of our cases have been taken up & decided upon Viz; Ship Commerce, Ship Genl. Butler, Brig Fame, Brig Mary, Sloop Port Packet, Brig Sally, Schooner Industry, & Brig Liberty, all which have been allowed to say about 90,000 as valid Claims. The Schooners Jenny & Twin[?] Sisters have been rejected, amounting to about $13,000, hence we have much to be thankful for, & but little to complain of at least for the present. One of the rejected cases however, we entertain some hope may be saved, by a suitable argument. Some of Mr. Mifflin's[26] cases have also been reached & favourably decided; but he has also manifested great anxiety in consequence of your absence.

The state of our information from Washington is such as to induce a belief that the Session will not continue beyond the present mo[nth]; if so we could not ask you (especially in your present delicate state of health) to undertake such a journey, which might prove altogether fruitless.[27] But as your information will be at least as good as ours on this subject, you can judge whether it will be necessary for you to set out for Washington on the rect. of this, as you propose, or not. Should the Commissioners however, determine to continue the session longer, or if it appears probable they will, we do in such case most ardently desire that you will proceed to Washington as soon as practicable. With much respect &c, Jno. Inskeep Prest. In[suranc]e Co. N. America.

P.S. Your argument in the case of the ship New Jersey[28] has been looked for at Washington for some time. J. I.

ALS copy. PPINA. John Inskeep (1757–1834), Philadelphia merchant, mayor, Philadelphia (1800, 1804–1805), president, Insurance Company of North America (1805–1831).

26. Samuel Mifflin, Philadelphia attorney practicing before the Claims Commission.

27. On November 9, 1822, Jaudon had written to Robert Stephens at INA that, "I do not know that Mr. Webster could be of much use to us here—perhaps however, he might have been of service in the case which was rejected yesterday, as it seems to be very similar to one which was allowed a few days since" (PPINA).

28. The case of the *New Jersey* was also brought up by Inskeep in his letter to Webster of February 23, 1822, printed below, pp. 234–236. On Janu-

DOCUMENT 35. APPLICATION TO POSTPONE CASES

[July 21, 1823]

Washington. Comm[issio]n of claims under the Spanish Treaty, July 1823.

Daniel Webster, counsel & agent for the several Claimants in the following cases, now prays that the examination of said cases may be postponed to the next meeting of the Board: viz:

No. 50. Brig Neptune, Jno. Barr & als Cl[aiman]ts

81. Schooner Swallow, [Joseph] Waters & als Clts

849. Schooner George, Wise & Emerson Clts

261.1277. 185. The Betsey[,] Clarke, P.C. Brooks & als Clts

190. The Crisis, Cook, same

208. The Nancy, Athearn, same

1282. The Priscilla, Knapp, Clt

62. The Patty, [Nathaniel] West & al Clt

1347. 424.- The Mary, Appleton, Smith Clt

1337. The Mary, Schott, [Gideon] Snow & als Clts

<1346>

These are West Indies cases, in which further evidence is wanted & expected. In some of them agents are employed, at considerable expense to obtain it

1139. The Catharine [Joseph] Coolidge [claimant]. This case has been delayed by the unexpected absence of Mr. [Samuel] Curson, whose evidence is needed. He has returned from N. Orleans, & arrived in this City the 19th. The papers being at Boston, the case cannot be now prepared.

1285. The Nautilus, Jno Welles & als Clts.
Papers expected from Spain. Recent letters assure the claimants they shall be forwarded.

229. The Rein Deer, Rich & als Clt. Application sent out by Mr Nelson

85. The Levant, [Stephen] Codman Clt.
Papers sent for & expected from Spain

1335.1349. 520. Minerva, Parsons, N[athaniel] A. & J[ohn] Haven Clts.
Proofs ready, except the Depo[sition] of one witness now at sea, & expected home in six weeks.

ary 1, 1823, Webster wrote to Jaudon that he was afraid nothing could be done for this claim (*Correspondence*, 1: 319–320). It was disallowed by the Commission on March 21, 1823.

848.1277. 203. Louisa Joanna, Grewham
Proofs & papers expected from Spain.

No. 212 The Phoenix, Roberts

1539 Information wanted from Spain.

518. 519. The Iris [John] Conway; proofs ready, except as to Capts adventure. It was supposed his invoice was with his underwriter, but it cannot be found. Capt Conway is now at sea—expected home in a month or two—& can probably then furnish proof of interest.
Mr. [William] Gray's two memorials, on same case, must probably be contd. also.

838. Henry Ladd's Memorial

843. N[athaniel] A. & J[ohn] Haven's Do.

844. Same

859. Pèrez Mortons, Do

1140. The Jane, N. Hamp. F[ire] & M[arine] In[surance] Off. Clt.

<1335> Wm Gardiner's Memorial

1610 Jno Haven, Adm[inistrato]r, Memorial

1611. Joshua Havens Memorial

1664 1609 Wm. Boyds Memorials

1606 Elijah Halls Memorial.

1650 Benj: Brierly, Exrs, Memorial

1284 <1246.> The Superb, Barnard

1137 The Mercury, Ayers

819. The Alert, Thorndike & Leach Clts

216. The Tyre, Brown, P.C. Brooks & als Clts

1138. The Hiland, Loring & als Clts

1342. The Mehetable

These cases were continued last term, for causes which still subsist. Most of them are claims by underwriters, waiting for the principal cases; and the residue are delayed for evidence.

Daniel Webster

Sworn to before me
this 21st July 1823
Joseph Forrest J. P.

[Endorsed by DW]
D. Webster's Application to postpone cases . . . July 1823
Note: If I have omitted any cases, represented by me, not otherwise disposed of, it has been by mistake; & I wish them to be postponed with the rest. I believe there are none omitted.

ADS(DW). DNA.

TO ALEXANDER BLISS

Dear Bliss. Washington Dec. 30. 1822 [1823].

I have made up the case of the Mary, Appleton, & shall present it tomorrow. The Copy will answer all the purposes of the original; there is no difficulty on that ground; but I fear much for the general merits of the case. We have had a general blow up, on the subject of these W. India cases. I cannot now give you particulars, but the effects are *fearful*. Many cases, hoping to get in, are *barred out*—& many, *actually in, will be turned out* neck & heels. The *Swift Packet—The Sea Flower*, I fear are not worth six pence.

It is now late in the Evening, & I have just finished an argument for Mr [Stephen] Codman. I shall put in his case, in a day or two. I am fully persuaded—I am quite *sure*—his case is a good one. I do regret, most deeply the lurch which the Board seems to have taken, on the subject of these Spanish Captures. Whether they will ever change their view, I do not know.

I believe I shall put in the Phenix, this week.

I hardly know what to say about the Mercury Ayers. It is particularly circumstanced—more hereafter.

Mrs W's love—& Ned's—& Julias—& mine. D.W.

ALS. DLC.

TO ALEXANDER BLISS

Dear Bliss Jany. 4. 1824

There are two more cases, to which I must entreat your attention

1. The Louisa Joanna. I learn from Col Perkins that the expected papers have not yet arrived. When the Board reassembles, on the 17th, they will be urgent, if not peremptory, on the subject of the continued cases. My own opinion is, that the papers should be made up, & the case strengthened as much as may be, & sent on to me. I will keep off the hearing as long as possible, waiting for the expected papers—but when they will allow us to wait no longer, we will rather try the case on what proofs we have, than abandon it. It may be well to let Col P's deposition state very fully what has been done to get further information. You know the point that *labors*, in this case; & if the papers do not come you must strengthen it as well as you can.

2. Capt. [Benjamin] Rich's prize case, the Rein Deer. Here, you know the Commrs have applied to Spain. As yet, they have no answer to any of these applications; and from the present state of things in Spain, it is very doubtful whether they ever get any. We must be prepared, therefore, to make out as good a case as we can, without the Spanish papers. Has Capt Rich recd. the proofs from England? If not, why not? & when will

they come? Capt. Rich should remember that his is not among the *favored* cases—that it will receive little indulgence—& that if he does not bestir himself actively, he may lose it. The case ought to be prepared, in regard to every thing but the Spanish Documents, immediately, and in the most perfect manner; and provision must be made to supply the want of the Spanish Papers, as well as possible, in case they should not come. Please say to Capt. Rich, that on this subject, like the French Assembly, we must "decree urgency."

You might whisper half a word—of doubtful success—rather possible than probable—into Mr Lambe's[29] ear, respecting Mercury Ayres—no more D.W.

ALS. DLC.

TO ALEXANDER BLISS

Dear Bliss Jan. 10. 1824

I have recd yours of the 5, & am glad the papers for Capt Rich's case have arrived from England. I hope you will have sent them by Mr [George] Blake. Please to let me have the benefit of your remarks on them, as to the letters &c which you think may as well not be presented.

If you shall not have sent it by Mr Blake and no other private conveyance offers, you must send it by mail—together or a part—perhaps Judge Story would find room for it.

As to the little remnant of the case of the John, certainly it cannot be tried over again. There was no dispute about facts. They must be taken as the evidence shews them. As to any further trial of facts, it is all out of the question.

There is note at U.S. Bank—due—as I wrote you 15 & 18—for 600—I send you a check therefor enclosed. Yrs D. Webster

ALS. DLC.

e. Written Arguments

"I understand," reported Rufus King, "that the Commissioners on the Spanish claims are hard at work: they require written arguments, which the Gentlemen of the Law dislike."[30] During the September 1821 session, the Commission did issue an order pertaining to written arguments. The Commission noted that "every Claimant might be permitted to support

29. Probably Thomas Lamb, Boston merchant, who became president of the Washington Fire and Marine Insurance Company, incorporated February 7, 1824.

30. Rufus King to Charles King, January 15, 1822, Charles R. King, ed., *The Life and Correspondence of Rufus King*, 6: 452.

his Claim by arguments of counsel, provided all such arguments were committed to writing and filed with the Secretary."[31] Oral argument does not seem to have been permitted, probably in the interest of saving valuable time needed to examine the often voluminous proofs. The request for arguments in support of claims apparently came from the memorialists, and the Commission acquiesced partially to help it in its consideration of "the important, novel and difficult questions . . . presented."[32]

The arguments were conceived of by the claimants and their attorneys as opportunities first to present their own particular constructions and interpretations of the treaty provisions (and not merely offer up their claims in memorial form), and secondly to guide the Commission in its deliberations on the proper measure of damages in allowed cases. Webster's successful argument in the case of the *Minerva*, printed below, is an example of the first category.[33]

Webster was seeking recognition of the claim under the first renunciation of Article 9 of the treaty. It stipulated that the United States renounced all injuries mentioned in the convention of 1802 between Spain and the United States, which now was declared annulled. The Convention of 1802 had only recently been ratified (in December 1818) after a long and stormy history. It was originally designed to cover appropriately decided claims by American citizens against Spain that arose between 1796 and 1802. The claims totalled at the time between five and eight million dollars and involved approximately one hundred twenty-five ships. The convention was ratified by the Senate in early 1804 (after first being rejected), but died when Spain finally refused to exchange ratifications. The Treaty of 1819 was now designed in part to cover those claims that should have been disposed under the long abated Convention of 1802.[34] Webster argued that this claim was clearly one arising under the provision of the Convention of 1802 covering "excesses committed" contrary to the law of nations or the Treaty of 1795 between

31. Moore, *Arbitrations*, 5: 4508.

32. There were a handful of elaborate written arguments actually printed and placed before the Commission. Two of them involved the particularly complex problem of claims arising under the second renunciation of Article 9 of the treaty (commonly called the "no. 2 cases"), relating to responsibility for the activities of French privateers and consuls within the jurisdiction of Spain. See William Pinkney, *Remarks . . . on case number two, before the Board of Commissioners. . . .* (Washington, 1822), and William Wirt, *An Argument on the cases designated as No. II. and on the Brigand Cases* [Washington, 1822].

33. For a description of a Webster argument falling in the second category, see Samuel Jaudon to John Inskeep, January 29, 1822, PPINA.

34. The account in the preceding paragraph is based on Moore, *Arbitrations*, 5: 4487–4493, and Charles E. Hill, "James Madison," in Bemis, ed., *The American Secretaries of State and Their Diplomacy*, 3: 48–51.

Spain and the United States. Webster then went on to present his notions of how the "excesses," now incorporated into the new treaty under which the Commission sat, finally were to be defined.

DOCUMENT 36. ARGUMENT IN THE CASE OF THE MINERVA[35]

Washington July 15. [18]23

The Convention of August 11. 1802, provides for the adjustment of claims of the following description; "claims which have arisen from excesses committed during the late war by individuals of either nation contrary to the laws of nations or the treaty existing between the two <nations> countries."

In the Title of the convention the persons, having a right to indemnification, are thus described; "those who have sustained losses, damages, or injuries in *consequence* of the excesses of individuals &c."

In the third section the Commissioners are required to receive "all claims which, in consequence of this convention, may be made &c by the citizens of the United States who may have a right to demand compensation for the losses &c."

By the sixth section "claims originating from the excesses of *foreign cruisers*, agents, consuls, or tribunals, in Spanish Territories, which might be imputable to the Government" are reserved to future negociation.

There can be no doubt from the foregoing clauses that excesses committed by *Spanish cruisers* upon American property, contrary to the Treaty or the laws of nations, & resulting in loss or damage to American citizens, were meant to be embraced in the convention. 1. Because the positive provisions point to the excesses of *individuals*; & 2. because the exception of *Foreign cruizers* was inserted to narrow the application of the general description; which, if it were not thus comprehensive, it would not have been supposed necessary to restrain. What descriptions of acts, then, are intended by "excesses" of "cruizers", that are contrary to the Treaty or the laws of Nations?

It is clear, I apprehend, that such acts were intended to be embraced as would render the individuals liable to damages in a civil action; and that the contracting Governments meant to assume the payment of such damages in like manner as, in the fourth renunciation of Article ninth,

35. Claim no. 205. DW represented Peter Chardon Brooks in this claim. The claim award for Brooks totalled $3,000 ($500 of which was for an uninsured interest in the vessel). DW also successfully handled another claimant's interest in this ship (no. 859, for Perez Morton and others, $2,000). Though DW signed this argument, he apparently credited it to Bliss (see DW to Bliss, July 18, 1823, printed below, pp. 239–240.

Spain engaged to compensate for unlawful seizures by the Government itself. The whole inquiry would seem, therefore, to result in this: first; whether the capture complained of were unlawful, so as to be a just ground of action for damages against the captors? and, secondly; whether a decree awarding damages against the captors, *which is unsatisfied*, extinguishes or bars the claim against the Government?

And the first question may be very shortly, & satisfactorily, disposed of, since the tribunals of Spain have adjudged the case between the parties, adversely contending before the Court, upon a view of all the evidence produced by either of them, & under circumstances the most favorable for giving weight to all that could be urged by way of excuse or justification to the captors.

By decreeing restitution of the property and awarding damages, the Court decides, not only that the property is not subject to condemnation, but also that the capture itself was without probable cause.

But without resorting to the opinion of the Spanish Tribunal, the unlawfulness of the capture is obvious from the circumstances under which it was made. Spain was a belligerent. The United States was a neutral power. The vessels of American citizens had a right, under the Treaty with Spain,[36] Article fifteenth, to carry the goods of an ennemy of Spain. And the privateers of Spain had no right to inquire into the ownership of the cargo. The American character of the vessel being once ascertained, the authority of the cruizers ceased, & the right of further search terminated. (See Pizarro, 2.Wheaton Rep. 227)[37] The capture of the merchant vessel in such case was a violation of the faith of Treaty. The circumstance that Spain had bound herself by Treaty to permit American vessels to carry the goods of her ennemy, free of search & inquiry, was the occasion of the vessel being placed in that situation. Altho' by the general laws of nations a Belligerent has a right to seize the goods of her ennemy wheresoever they may be found, yet, it is competent to her to give up that right by contract, &, when she has done so, she becomes, by exercising the right, a wrong doer and responsible for the injury she may thereby commit.

Nor, on the second point, can it well be doubted that it was the intention of the contracting parties to include losses arising from the excesses of cruisers, whether the injured party had recovered a judgment against the wrong doer or not: *unless that judgment had been satisfied.* An unpaid judgment is no compensation. The language of the Treaty is sufficiently general to comprehend such cases, & there are no words of exclusion or exception applicable to them. If the Treaty was meant to embrace all such cases, as were fit to be embraced as subjects of indem-

36. Treaty of 1795 (Miller, 2: 318–337).

37. Case of the Spanish ship *Pizarro*, 2 Wheaton 227 (1817).

nity, these ought to be taken to be included; because there were no cases in which the wrong, committed by the captors, was more clear; none, in which the losses & damage of the captured was better ascertained, or the hopelessness of the redress from the immediate trespassers more apparent. A judgment against the trespasser, without the hope of getting satisfaction, is the best evidence of a good claim. It establishes the original wrong & shews there has been no redress. These cases were not out of the view of the negociators. On the contrary, they were pressed upon both Governments, & had been for sometime the subject of complaints, petitions & importunity.

It is no answer to these claims to say that Spain had done all which, as a nation she was bound to do; all which she could have done, if the suit had been between her own subjects; or that, as the nation was faultless, it could not be intended to make her liable.

A nation which lets loose an armed force upon the high seas, empowered to make war in its name, is responsible for the damage they may do its friends. Without its commission the injury would not be committed. It furnishes them with the means of doing harm; and if, in furnishing the means, it omits to take proper security for their good conduct, the omission is a fault. A Sovereign is bound, says Vattel (B.2.c.6.§76)[38] to compel his subjects to do justice to his friends. This duty is not performed by simply condemning them in the Tribunal, in a case where the ability to make restitution was not provided for, when the power to do the injury was conferred. The case of inability to render satisfaction, as it must always be foreseen, should, in all reason, be guarded against; and the want of such precaution is a wrong, for all the consequences of which Spain was liable in equity & justice. It is well proved that privateers are obliged, in most countries, to furnish adequate security, upon receiving their commissions, to answer for the injuries & compensate the damage they may do, in the ex[ercise of] their power. Where the security proves insufficient, the nation, & not the injured party, surely, ought to bear the loss.

But if this liability were even doubtful, Spain undertook, by the Treaty, to make compensation to the sufferers, &, by the ninth article, expressly provides for a release to her own subjects. The claimants, it is apprehended, could not now enforce their judgments against the individual wrong doers; and doubtless, Spain must be considered as having assumed all that the United States release to her subjects.

Therefore, if Spain *were* faultless in regard to these cases, she might assume a responsibility which her subjects have incurred; and she has chosen to assume it.

38. Emmerich de Vattel, *The Law of Nations* (London, 1797), bk. 2, chap. 6, sec. 76.

The Treaty affords another case in which her liability was only collateral & secondary; namely, that of French captures followed by a condemnation in her ports by French consuls; in most, if not all, of which cases the French captors were the original wrong-doers; & wrong-doers in a most agravated manner. Yet, in as much as Spain has stipulated to make compensation for those cases,[39] her obligation to do so is not diminished by the fact, that other parties may be, or are, also liable.

There is a wide difference between this case, & the case of a French Capture. In the latter, if the cause be brought before a Spanish Tribunal, & that Tribunal do all that is in its power to afford the injured party redress against the captors, Spain is in no fault. She has done all that can be required of her. Not being responsible for the original wrong, she owes no duty but to right that wrong, & to do justice between the parties, when they come into her tribunals. But in this case, the original captors were Spanish subjects. The capture itself was wrong, & without excuse, & has so been adjudged by the Courts of Spain itself. It is, therefore, I apprehend a clear case of *excess* committed by a Spanish subject; & so is within the provisions of this Treaty.

Danl. Webster

AD(DWp). DNA. Endorsed by DW: "No. 205, Argument, Minerva, Riddle. Claimants submit that this the case of an 'Excess,' committed by Spanish subjects; & so within the 1. Renunciation."

f. Results

Through the various Commission sessions in 1822 and 1823, Webster acted as a central reporting agency for the claimants. He communicated actual results and evaluated possible outcomes. Keeping his clients informed became a primary concern. In his role as a reporter, though, he rarely indicated the substantive basis for decision. The Commission seems to have issued opinions in only broad classes of cases or on controversial issues. If a case fell into a particular category, the decision on its allowance followed from its placement within the generic grouping. Occasionally Webster would comment on the larger grouping of cases, but he generally focused on decisions in the individual claims. And he sent the kind of news that most claimants were interested in: whether their own claims were accepted or rejected. The hectic pace of the sessions left him little time to digest and reflect on the principles involved in the decisions. Merely keeping his reports up to date was difficult enough.

Though the discernible legal pattern in the decisions obviously interested him and helped dictate his strategies, he was concerned with another developing series that the unfolding decisions indicated: who was winning? whose interests were being protected? The answer had sec-

39. "No. 2 cases," see n. 32, above.

tional and commercial overtones. Webster knew where his responsibilities lay. Relatively early in the proceedings, he commented that "The Comm[issione]rs begin to see, I think, now, the *real commercial* losses, which occasioned the Treaty."[40] Soon he observed that "The general course is favorable to the North, & the real mercantile losses."[41] The implications were clear. "I do not see that your friends and mine have, in general, much to complain of, as to the decisions of the Commissioners. In some cases they have disappointed us, it is true, but in those or similar cases they have also disappointed others, who made claims on the fund to a large amount."[42]

That people were counting the distribution of outcomes was evident. When the business was concluded, one observer reported:

> We cannot tell exactly what is the allowance to each section of the country but we suppose about $1,250,000 to Philada.

to all New England—		1,750,000—	
to New York	—	1,000,000	
to Baltimore	6 or	700,000	
to the South of the Potomac		300,000	$5,000,000

> Probably New York has not as much as a million, and New England more than $1,750,000.[43]

Webster was clearly more than simply a legal representative.

TO ALEXANDER BLISS

Dear Bliss — Washington Jan. 19. 1822

For the benefit of all concerned, I now give you a note of the most important decisions which the Commissioners have as yet made.

1. Claims founded on contracts, entered into with the Spanish Government, voluntarily, and alledged to be violated or not fulfilled by that Government, are not within the Treaty.

2. Seizures made in the north of Spain, by the French Military, in the time of Joseph Buonaparte, are not within the Treaty.

3. It is not absolutely necessary for underwriters, claiming for a total loss, to shew a cession, or formal assignment of the property; it is enough if they shew themselves entitled to such assignment.

4. No claims will be recd. from underwriters, for losses on *foreign* property, insured by them.

5. In cases of capture by Spanish Vessels, brought into Spanish ports, proceeded against in Spanish tribunals, & the case settled by compro-

40. DW to Joseph Hopkinson, February 1, 1822, *Correspondence*, 1: 305.

41. DW to Jeremiah Mason, March 23, 1822, *Correspondence*, 1: 312.

42. DW to [Samuel Jaudon], January 1, 1823, *Correspondence*, 1: 319. For a further discussion of DW's closing point, see pp. 214–217, above.

43. Samuel Jaudon to Robert Stephens, June 22, 1824, PPINA.

mise before final judgment, no compensation will be allowed under the Treaty: otherwise, in cases of compromise after condemnation by French Consuls, in Spanish Ports, & pending appeals.

6. In cases of condemnation, by French tribunals, sitting in French Ports, of vessels carried into Spanish ports, each claim must depend on its particular circumstances. In a mere naked case of this kind, there would be no compensation allowed; but in very many cases other considerations arise, & form exceptions, favorable to the cases, too numerous and complicated to be here stated.

In regard to those cases, which have been called cases of *consequential* damage, the Commrs. will probably be governed by the ordinary rules of law; and hold the wrong-doer responsible in each case for such damages as necessarily or probably followed from his wrongful act.

I have as yet set down no case for hearing. The Commissioners have told us, that when our evidence is in, & our case set down for hearing, they shall proceed to hear and decide it, upon the *evidence then in.* A trial is to go for a trial; nor will they allow a new trial, or the introduction of new evidence except in cases in which a rehearing would be allowed in judicial proceedings. At least so I understand them. Yrs with much esteem D. W.

ALS. DLC.

FROM JOHN INSKEEP

Ins. Office N. America
Phild. Jany 24, 1822

D. Sir,

Your esteemed favour of 19 Inst.[44] came duly to hand, stating several important decisions which had then been made by the Commissioners & which in the main we view as not unfavourable to the interest of this Co. Indeed some of them are the reverse, being altogether satisfactory. I am pleased to know that you have not been disappointed in your expectations as to the result of these very important questions.

I have written to Mr. Jaudon & advised him, provided it meets your approbation, to withdraw any of our Memorials that are manifestly excluded by the decisions of the commissioners; I must therefore beg that you will in all such cases judge of the expediency & advise him accordingly. I am with great respect &c. J. I - Prest. &c

ALS draft. PPINA.

TO JOHN INSKEEP

Dear Sir, Washington Jan. 30. 1822.

In the progress of the Commissioners on the docket they arrived this

44. Not found.

morning at the first of the claims of your Office, & proceeded to dispose of *seven* of them; viz Schooner *Commerce*, Ship *Genl. Butler*, Snow[45] *Polly*, Ship *Swansborough*, Ship *Commerce*; *all of which were received*; —Brig *Maria* & Brig *Molly*, which are left open, *for further consideration.* I am inclined to think there will be no great difficulty about the *Maria*;— but the *Molly* is more doubtfull.

The Commissioners will proceed with the rest Tomorrow, & we shall have of course another set of decisions to communicate next mail.

We have been much occupied lately with arguments and discussions on the questions of *freight* and *premium*; subjects which have occasioned some doubts and difficulties. I am, Sir, with great regard Your Ob. servt Danl. Webster

ALS. PPINA.

TO JOHN INSKEEP

My dear Sir Washington Feb. 2. 1822

The Commrs. have this morning disposed of the following cases, presented by your Company. The *Two Cousins*, Duval; *Welcome Return*, Vanneman; *Francis Lewis*, Evans; *Gover Brooke*, Whelan; all these are *received*; The *Aurora*, Vincent, suspended *as No.* 2. In the case of the Francis Lewis, the Memorial was not recd. for the *policy* on *profits*; the commrs. being of opinion that insurances on mere *profits* are not within the Treaty. It will be some days before we reach the residue of your claims. With great regard, Yr's D Webster

ALS. PPINA.

TO ALEXANDER BLISS

Dear Bliss Washington Feb. 4. 1822

I have generally informed those immediately interested, of any decisions made of their cases here. On the opposite page you have, I believe a pretty full view of the decisions yet made.

The Commrs are now at No. 700. The Memorials which are sent on by Mr Gray begin at about 800; we shall reach them probably in four days; & it will probably take a week to go thro them. It is not likely that those filed since the commencement of the term will be taken up at this Term.

Capt. Rich's Prize case, & Mr Lloyd's case are not yet decided. Several others of ours are suspended as *No.* 2.

No case has as yet been heard, *in proof*; nor do I mean to set down any

45. *Snow*, a small sailing-vessel resembling a brig, formerly employed as a warship.

case for proof at this term. I think I begin to understand how the proof must be made out, & we have a summer's work before us.

All Mr. Touro's Memorials were, of course, rejected. I have recd. Mr Coolidge's supplement, & also the Copy of the argt. by Thos. Coolidge, who, with Judge S[tory] arrived safely last night. I have recd. also sundry copies, enclosed to Mr Gorham, & also Dr. Moore's Supplement.

As to your Administrator-Mortgagor-Mortgagee case, my first impression is, that such a discharge must be considered *fraudulent*. Its only effect could be to throw the debt off the *land*, on to his sureties. If the Admr de bonis non was to call on him to pay the debt, I do not see how he could say it was paid—it was in fact *not* paid;—no money was carried by him to the credit or uses of the estate—& his discharge was a mere *fraud* on the Estate which he represented. So I think at present.

I am almost tired to death; I have come nearer giving up in despair, than ever before. I have written some *cords* of arguments, such as they are;—& have fortunately got thro far the greater part of this sort of labor, before the [Supreme] Court came. Their honors assembled this morning. Mr Wirt, Atty Genl. was taken suddenly *ill* on Saturday—a sort of fit—this will occasion some derangement of the business of the Court. He is a little better today. Yrs as always D. Webster

Gov. Carver, Parsons & Davis, Clts; *Received*
The Molly, Mass. F[ire] & M[arine] & Bost[on] M[arine] In[surance] Co's —Clts; *Received*
The Martin, Thos. Parsons Clt *Received*
Do [Nathaniel] Williams *Received*
Atalanta, [Daniel] Sargent claimant, *Received*
Genl. Washington, Higginson & Parsons Clts, *Received*
Perseverance, Jona. Amory & others Clts, *Received*
Sally, N. Appleton & als Clts—*Rejected*:—French seizure
Sterling, [Daniel I.] Huntress [and others] Claimants; *Received*
Helen, New En[gland] Ins. Co. Clt—*Rejected*
Martin, Ignatius Sargent, Clt—*Received*
Do [Nathaniel] Williams *Received*
Enterprize, L[ynde] Walter, Clt—*Received*
Eleanor, Thos Williams & als clts—*Rejected*—French seizure
Joseph, John Pedrick, Clt—*Rejected*—as above
Iris, P[eter] C[hardon] B[rooks] & W. Ward, Clt—*Received*
Iris, [John] Conway Clt *Received*
Nancy, Benja. Smith Clt *Received*
Ship Salem, Townsend & als, Clts, *Rejected*—French seizure
Echo, Sumner—Clt—will be recd.—being now put right.
Polly, Titus Wells Admr. Clt. *Received* (last term, I believe)

ALS. DLC.

FROM JOHN INSKEEP

Ins. Office N. America
Phild. Feb: 4. 1822

Dr Sir,

Your very interesting letters of 30. Jany, 1st. & 2d. Feb: came duly to hand;[46] conveying intelligence in relation to the fate of our claims before the Comm[issioner]s. The result we must confess, far exceeds our most sanguine expectations; there being only 4 or 5 suspended & 3 rejected cases out of 40 odd.

With respect to the two Commerce[?] cases, we did not expect success; but we certainly did consider the Isabella as a good case, & indeed if the Com[missioner]s had not done so well for us in the main, we perhaps should be so uncharitable as to blame them for rejecting it. We are pleased however, to hear that you do not mean to give it up without a struggle; & also that you entertain hopes of bringing in some of the suspended cases.

Those cases recd. for proof, we find amt. to upwards of $400,000 & altho' we do not entertain a remote hope of realizing any such sum out of them, we consider it a promising beginning. In compliance with your request, Mr. Smith[47] & Mr. [Samuel] Mifflin have had the perusal of your letters & they are likewise well pleas'd. Please to present my respects to Mr. Jaudon & tell him that his letter of 29 ult. was duly recd. am with much respect &c. J. I. Prest. &c.

ALS draft. PPINA.

TO ALEXANDER BLISS

[February 19, 1822]

968. Paschal P. Pope & others		Recd. Feb. 14
Ship Topaz		
973 Jos. Coolidge & others		
Ship Belle Sauvage		Recd. do.
Ship Iris—Brooks & Ward		Recd.
Do —Conway Clt.—		do
Brig Nancy—Benj. Smith—		do.
Sch. Esther—Israel Thorndike—		Rejected as 18[48]
—Alert	Thorndike & Leach	Recd.
Sch. Atlantic.	Wm. Cottle	Recd.

46. DW's letters of January 30 and February 2 are printed above, pp. 229–230. His letter of February 1 has not been found.

47. Probably Daniel Smith, president of the Insurance Company of Pennsylvania, as identified in DW to Samuel Jaudon, January 1, 1823, *Correspondence*, 1: 319–320.

48. "18" is the correct reading, rather than "IS" as rendered in *Correspondence*, 1, the reference being to claim no. 18, Henry Prince Meserve, rejected January 18, 1822.

S[uper] C[argo]	Josiah Knapp	do.
	Hugh McKullock	Rejected as 18
Ship Galen	Caleb Eddy	Recd
Brig Betsey	Abiel Winship	Recd. in part.
	W. H. Boardman &c.	Recd as to Fame Susp[ende]d as to George Rejd. as to Olive.
Ship Mercury	David Hinkley	Recd.
Ship Galen	Jas. Mackay—	Do.
Atlantic	Sam. Taylor &c.—	Do.
Sch. Sally—	Lynde Walter—	Rejected as 18
Louisa Johanna	—C.W. Greene—	Recd.
Seaflower—	Hudson & others—	Recd.
Mercury—	[William] Dall	Recd.
America	Godfrey & others	Recd.
Endeavour	Woodbury—	Do.
S[uper] C[argo]	Griffin—	Do.
Franklin—	Titus Wells &c.	Rejected as 18
	Perez Morton—	Recd. as to sundries.
	P.C. Brooks—	Recd.

Dear Bliss Washington Feb. 19. 1822

Above is a hasty sketch of the decisions in our cases, since I last wrote you. Many are suspended, as *No.* 2, & we expect the general doctrine in that case to be decided tomorrow or next day. I am now much occupied in the Court—having tried three causes in succession.[49] Mr. [William] Pinkney was taken dangerously ill, the day after he finished a *nine hours* speech for your friend Mr [Thomas] Williams. He is better today, but not yet entirely out of danger—cause not yet decided. Bullard & Bell will be continued, I presume, in consequence of his sickness.[50] So will two other causes in which I am concerned,[51] in consequence of the illness of Mr [William] Wirt, who has not been in Court this term. There are two more causes which I must argue, or help to argue—one an important one from Virginia.[52] I hope to bring my concerns in Court to a close about the

49. *Ricard* v. *Williams et al.*, 7 Wheaton 59 (1822), argued February 13, 1822; *Society for the Propagation of the Gospel in Foreign Parts* v. *New Haven*, 8 Wheaton 464 (1823), argued February 15, 1822; *Brown* v. *Jackson*, 7 Wheaton 218 (1822), argued February 19, 1822.

50. William Pinkney suffered a heart attack while arguing the case of *Ricard* v. *Williams* and died February 25, 1822. Thomas Williams (1764–1823), a Roxbury, Massachusetts lawyer. *Bullard* v. *Bell*, see pp. 121–122, above.

51. *Gibbons* v. *Ogden*, 9 Wheaton 1 (1824); *Kirk* v. *Smith*, 9 Wheaton 241 (1824).

52. *Blunt's Lessee* v. *Smith*, 7 Wheaton 248 (1822); *The Santissima Trinidad and the St. Andre*, 7 Wheaton 283 (1822).

same time as before the Commrs., & to wind up all next week. Let Mrs. W. know that I am well at this present writing. Yrs D.W.

ALS. DLC. Published in *Correspondence*, 1: 306–307.

TO ALEXANDER BLISS

My Dear Sir— Washington Feb. 20. 1822.

The Commissioners have formally announced their decision, respecting the cases classed as No. 2, *favorable* to those cases.[53]

By this decision it is settled, that in cases of American Vessels, captured by French Privateers, carried into Spanish ports, & the property there distributed, *without any condemnation made any where*, the Spanish Govt. is liable; & the Clt. has a claim on this fund; at least, if it appear that he has presented his case, previously, to the Govt. so as to bring it within the requisitions in the *fifth* Renunciation;—*perhaps*, without this, it might be brought in, under the fourth renunciation.

It will not, however, be enough for Claimants to say that they do not know whether there was, or was not, a Condemnation. They must furnish such ground to convince the Commrs that there *was not*, as may be expected in regard to such a negative proposition.

Please communicate this to Mr Brooks, & others concerned. You will see it affects many of my cases. Yrs truly D. Webster

ALS. DLC. Published in *Correspondence*, 1: 307–308.

FROM JOHN INSKEEP

Ins. Office N. America
Dr Sir, Phild. Feb: 23d. 1822

Your favour of 20. Inst. came duly to hand, advising that those of our suspended cases were that day recd. in consequence of a decision that American vessels, captured by the French, carried into Spanish ports & the property there distributed without condemnation, furnish claims within the Treaty; provided the facts should be supported by such reasonable evidence as the nature of the case may admit. With this decision, as well as others generally in which our interest has been concern'd we have abundant reason to be satisfied; 39 Cases out of 45 having been recd., amounting to nearly half a million of dollars & only 6 rejected; some of the latter we hope may hereafter be revived, as also part of those which you deemed it expedient to withdraw.

53. For a fuller description of the results in this class of claims, see the Final Report reprinted in Moore, *Arbitrations*, 5: 4512–14; Samuel Jaudon to Robert Stephens, December 31, 1823, PPINA. Citations to printed arguments in the no. 2 cases may be found in note 32, p. 223, above.

As we have a heavy interest depending upon the question whether the City of Santo Domingo was French or Spanish during certain feudatory times, we hope that question will not be finally settled during the present Session; unless indeed there should be sufficient proof at hand, to satisfy the Commissioners that the Spanish authority prevailed, which we have no doubt of being able to prove, if time and opportunity is allow'd.[54] To accomplish which we shall if necessary send out an agent for the special purpose; and in which event, we shall stand in need of your advice, as to the manner we shall proceed, as well as the form & character of the proofs that may be deemed necessary to procure. We still hope, however, that satisfactory proof can be obtained, here without the necessity of sending abroad for it.

There is a Gentleman residing in this City Mr. John Gibson, who was super cargo of the ship New Jersey (one of our recd. Cases) when she was captured & carried into Porto Rico in Feb: 1798 from which place he went to the City of Santo Domingo to attend the Trial, where he remained until Decemr. 1798 nearly 11 mo. during which time Mr. Gibson petitioned the Spanish governor & frequently called upon him in person & claimed his protection against the proceedings of the French Tribunal. During all which time the civil police was Spanish, & the City garrisoned with two Regiments of Spanish troops. Mr. G— passed the Spanish Centinals daily. Not a vestige of French authority existed there, except the Commissary, Pierre Detremat[?] & the privateers in the Harbour. All which & much more Mr. Gibson will depose too if required. Mr. G— however, has a small interest in the case of the New Jersey, which perhaps might invalidate his testimony; but as he expects to leave this, on an India voyage in all next mo. he will if possible, sell out his interest <in the New Jersey> before he goes; in which case he would become a disinterested witness. Would you advise us to take his deposition under these circumstances, whether he divests himself of interest or not? It is quite certain we think & trust we can prove that altho' the Spanish port of St. Domingo might have been ceded to France by Treaty in 1795, possession was not given, until the year 1801 or 2. With much respect &c.

J. I.

54. The Commission eventually received the "Santo Domingo claims"; see the Final Report, Moore, *Arbitrations*, 5: 4513–14. Inskeep's letter is in response to the previous month's action of the Commission regarding these claims. As DW reported, it was now "less necessary to investigate the history of St. Domingo immediately, since the Comm[issione]rs incline to receive Cases, in which it is stated that St. Domingo was Spanish, & leave it to be made out on proof" (DW to Alexander Bliss, January 16, 1822, *Correspondence*, 1: 304). The problem arose because, though a treaty between France and Spain had ceded the Spanish half of Hispaniola to the French, the Spanish continued to occupy their former half until 1801.

P.S. Please to present my respects to Mr. Jaudon & inform him that his letter of 22d. is recd.

ALS draft. PPINA.

TO ALEXANDER BLISS

Dear Bliss, Washington Feb. 26 [1823]

The following is the result of the examination of sundry of our proofs.

Giles Lodge & al—*United States*—not allowed; the Commrs. not being able to see any thing which was done by the Spanish Govt. which it might not lawfully do; and nothing omitted by it which it was bound to do.

S. Higginson—Pattern; allowed, for vessel, freight & cargo

E. White, & als—*Alert*; not allowed. I have written to Mr. [Benjamin] Pickman, stating the reasons, & think the case can yet be saved.

Cabot & Snelling—*Molly*—*allowed.*

P.C. Brooks—*Fame*—Jordan—*allowed.*

I do not at present remember any other cases as yet decided, in addition to those I mentioned before—unless it be the *Echo*, which is *allowed.*

I have recd your communications, thro Mr Nelson,[55] transmitting papers in the *Ocean*, & other cases.

In the Mary, Appleton, we must wait, & try to get proof [of] an actual sale in Porto Rico before condemnation in Guadaloupe. Nothing else will save the case. Where is the *Topaz*?—pray to speak to Mr Pope to forward on his proofs.

The "Two Marias" is quite hopeless;—and I am sorry for it.

Some of the other reserved cases I have not yet examined.

The Commrs are very laborious. They meet at 10, & sit till dark. I hope to get thro most of our cases, before I go home.

I had at home, somewhere among my Spanish, or Washington Papers, a little file, tied up with a string, put into my hands by my Brother, to get a *pension* for a Mr. Little.[56] I will thank you to look for it, & if you can find it, send it to me.

I sent Mr Bullard a drft, yesterday—please ask him if he recd it. Yours very truly D. Webster

ALS. DLC.

TO ALEXANDER BLISS

Dear Bliss, Washington March 20. 1823

I begin to be tired of staying here, & feel as if I must beg of you to

55. Jeremiah Nelson, attorney and claims agent.

56. Joseph Little (1761–1843). See DW to Ezekiel Webster, February 10, 1823, *Correspondence*, 1: 321–322.

come, by & by, to my relief. Most of my cases will be decided, in the course of a fortnight, I think, but all will not, & I fear there will be complaints, if some body be not here so long as the Commissioners stay. I left my affairs in such state as to make it necessary to go home some time next month, even if I should be obliged to return. My present opinion is, that the Commissioners will sit till June; & if that should look probable, a fortnight hence, I must try to persuade you to come, & *spell* me. You shall name your own compensation, & I will try to take care of your affairs at home. In the mean time I shall endeavor to dispose of the *responsibl[e]* cases; such as the Washington, Phenix, Diana, &c. There will not be much to do; but there will be a number of little cases, requiring attention. It is *possible*, indeed, that I may continue them; but I do not think it probable.

I shall, of course write you farther on this topic; but will beg you to be thinking about Washington, in the mean time.

I write, this post or the next to Mr E[dward] Brooks, which contains the principal intelligence about cases decided. In three or four of Mr Brooks' cases—some of them large ones—I have not quite the success I expect. The *Swift Packet* is allowed.

I have filed *another argument*, in Mr [James] Lloyd's case, & also Pet[ition] for rehearing in Mr Coolidge's.

I find great difficulty in getting in the Memorial for the Union Insurance Office. At present, it is *rejected*. I have *petitioned*, again, an affidavit, &c. What do you think about the Mercury, Ayers? Wd. you present it now, or not?

I have not heard a word about an acceptance of 500 dollars, about which I wrote you sometime days ago. Supposing the drft might be returned to N. York, I wrote there to have it taken up, but have heard nothing. I now enclose a drft for 350; & shall send the rest, next mail, if I do not hear that the Bill is sent back to N. York. In which last case, please deposite this to my order in U. S. Bank. Yrs D. Webster

Let Mrs W. know that I am quite well.

We have had a great contest here, between Col. Cuthbert, M.C. & Mr Jaudon, for Miss Margaret.[57] In the end, Mr J. has beaten the Col off the field, & will secure the prize.

ALS. DLC.

TO ALEXANDER BLISS

Dr Bliss, Washington Mar: 25. [1823]

Since I wrote you last, things have assumed such a face, as to afford a

57. Margaret was the stepdaughter of Judge Hugh Lawson White, one of the claims commissioners. She opted to marry Jaudon instead of Cuthbert.

hope that I may get thro my affairs here, partly by continuance, & partly by decision, so as not to make it necessary for you to regale yourself on Washington strawberries this year. I imagine the Commissioners will not sit longer than the first of May, & that I may be able to leave them safely about the 15 of April. At least, such is my present hope.

Mr. Yard's cases, which are closely connected with the Diana, are not yet due—& will probably not come on this term; & not, neither will the Diana. Mr. Coolidge's, being a *rehearing*, I fear will not be taken up till the *hearings* are thro; & if it should be so decided, I shall put that case off to the next term. Mr Lloyd's case will probably be decided in ten or twelve days. The Phoenix may as well stand over as not; & so may the Topaz. In this last case some translation is necessary. The Mercury, Pearson, the Betsey, Halliburton, & the Minerva, Riddle will probably be decided soon; and one or two cases of Mr Brooks'. These arrangements will nearly clear my docket, of the cases set down—& I do not mean to set down any more, unless I should hear from you that it is best to try the Mercury Ayers, now; abt. which I am doubtful. The Ocean, Wadlin, & the Sally, Stephenson, also, will be decided before I leave.

I have two or three *arguments* to stitch together before I go. I have raised one new point, likely to save the *Nora*, I hope, & some other cases of that sort—especially the *Louisa Joanna*, not yet set down—of this hereafter.

Pray let me hear what is going in Court.

I hear from Mrs Webster that you kindly officiate as her Beau, in my absence. I hope you will not be led into a course of dissipation.

Let her know that I am, at this present, right well, & have just recd. hers, saying that you are refreshed with a new fall of snow, so as to have the comfort of a little sleighing. It is wet, & cold here, but not quite so bad as six inches snow. The weeping willows are quite green; other trees are showing their buds, & the grass, where it has a bed to grow in, is beginning to wear a comely appearance. Yrs always D. Webster

ALS. DLC.

TO ALEXANDER BLISS

Dear Bliss, Washington April 3. 1823.

I have recd yrs respecting the 589. note, which I had forgotten. If your drft comes, I shall accept & pay it; if it does not appear, in a day or two, I will remit the money. In the mean time send the enclosed order to Mr [Samuel Sumner] Wilde, & ask him to give you cash for it.

Three notes of mine will fall due at the U. S. Bank. one, 800 Dlls, with Mr Blake's indorsement, April 14—one for $1000, secured by stock, April 14—also—& one for 1000, with Mr. Blakes indorsement, April 21. These days may not be precise, but I believe they are the exact times of renewal. I now send you enclosed, the notes, which you will please to fill up, & take the necessary care of.

So much for Notes & Banks. This morning the Commrs. awarded *favorably*, on the case of the Betsey, Halliburton; & the Mary-Ann, Anthony —both as to Mr Touro's Claim, & Mr Tudors.[58] Tomorrow the Sally Stephenson will be decided.

Nothing said about the Mercury Pearson, but my hope has not failed. Not that the case is certain, at all; but I think it *probable* that it will get along. The business before the Board begins to assume the appearance of winding up. Four or five of our cases, set down, are yet to be decided. All not set down are con[tinue]d, on motion; and two or three that were set down, were, under peculiar circumstances, con[tinue]d also. My opinion is the Commrs will get thro by the 15th, & that they will probably adjourn to meet again in October. Many cases have been rejected, this session, but I believe *we* have fared as well as our neighbors. Yrs

D. Webster

ALS. DLC. Published in *Correspondence*, 1: 324–325.

TO ALEXANDER BLISS

Dear Bliss July 18. 1823

The *Minerva*, Riddle; not allowed, notwithstanding your good argument. The Commrs, I humbly think, are *wrong*, in regard to this class of cases; and I intend making one more effort.[59]—I have written Mr Brooks.

The *Three Brothers*, Giles; not allowed; the Commissioners think this is a suspicious case, & that probably there was an intent to break the laws of Spain. They did not seem to like the general complexion of the case—please inform Mr Rantoul.

The *Genl. Washington*, Perkins & Lloyd; *allowed*. I have written Mr Ll[oyd]. Topaz, *allowed*: I have written Mr Pope.

Atlantic, allowed. I have written Mr. Brooks.

The *Mermaid*, allowed. I have written Mr B[rooks].

The Success, (Union Ins Office) allowed. I shall [write] Mr. Perkins.

The above are all my cases which have been decided. I think I shall

58. Touro is misspelled "Abram Tours" and "Abrain" Touro in connection with this case in *Executive Documents*, 49th Cong., 1st sess., Serial 2337, pp. 191 and 202. Frederick Tudor (1783–1864), Boston businessman, developer of a method of shipping ice from Boston to tropical markets.

59. See argument in this claim, printed above, pp. 224–227. For the ultimate fate of this claim and claims similarly situated, see p. 249, below, where DW did make one more effort, and succeeded in getting a reversal of the Commission's previous decision.

bring on no others this term, unless Mr. De Forest, who is now here should incline to bring on the Phoenix.

The Commissioners proceeded immediately to hearing causes, Tuesday Morning, & will get thro all the business which is ready for them I should think in a week or ten days more. They have some little things to do, not requiring the presence of parties—so that on the whole they may find employment for a month.

I believe Mr Sullivan has left the City, not being very well. The business of the claim will of course be suspended. Yrs D. Webster

I hope to sett off by the 22. or 23.

ALS. DLC.

TO ALEXANDER BLISS

Dear Bliss Dec. 2. [1823]

We have lost the *George*, in spite of all our pains & labor. The difficulty is, that we cannot shew what ultimately became of the property. The u[n]loading it, which is the most we have proved, the Commers do not deem sufficient proof of *spoliation*, in as much as it might have been for safe keeping—& afterwards reshipped. Please inform the concerned. Yrs. D. Webster

½ past 1 ocl. We have been waiting an hour & a half for the message[60]—it was *due* at 12 oclock.

ALS. DLC.

TO ALEXANDER BLISS

Dear Bliss, Decr. 3. 1823

I am getting up the papers in the Mary, Schott, & believe I shall make out a case. Capt. Schott has come here, from beyond the Allegheny, to att[end] to it. On cargo in this case, was insured in Thomas' Office—viz—

By Jno. P. Schott—	350—W Smith—underwriter
By Wm Dinsmoor	800—Jno C. Jones
Henry Messinger	530 E. S. Livermore, 300, & Jno. C. Howard 230—
Nathan Webb	350—Wm Smith
Thos Godfrey—	450 W. Stackpole

60. DW had just returned to Congress, this time as representative from Boston. The message referred to was President Monroe's 7th Annual Message on the State of the Union, in which the Monroe Doctrine was proclaimed.

by Schott, on freight— 800—I[saiah] Doane 400—&
J[ames] Prince—400—
Do on outfits 350—I. Doane
On Comm[ission]s— 700—Isaac Rand

This is the statement in Touro's Memorial. We now want the Policies—and also the Invoices, Bills of Lading, or other proofs of property. The general facts are likely to be made out, so that there will be a recovery. Pray hasten this matter—as the Commrs are very impatient.

There is no memorial for cargo, except by Schott & the Underwriters.

Let me hear from you. Yrs D.W.

Henry Messinger & Nathan Webb I suppose are now both in Boston—but if their Invoices are in Touro's papers, it will be all we need.

ALS. DLC.

TO ALEXANDER BLISS

Decr. 4. 1823.

In the Mary, Schott, it is stated in the Memorial of Olive Grow, Ex[ecutri]x of Timo. Grow, that Timo. the owner, for his own acct, & acct of Moody, the other owner, recd. 450, for insurance in Touro's Office. This is not mentioned in Touro's memorial. Touro's memorial is signed—by *Touro*—who says he is entitled to Rand's & Jones' subscription—by Geo. B. Doane, as Admr. of Isaiah Doane—and by Touro, as Atty to Hepz[ibah] C. Howard, Adx of Jno. C. Howard—& by same as Atty to Agnes Prince, Exx of Jas. Prince—neither Francis Welch—nor E. S. Livermore appear to have signed at all. There is not, here, any *powers* to Touro—or assign[men]ts.

What has become of the papers in the Mercury, Ayers? I thought I had brought them, but I have them not—please send them on. Yrs

D.W.

ALS. DLC.

Dr Bliss Dec. 16. 1823

I can find nothing of the lost paper, in the case of the *Mary, Appleton.* Where it can be, I am wholly *at a loss* to conjecture. It occurs to me as being possible that I may have filed it away as, [or in], a letter from you. I kept every letter I recd. from you, and they are all now either in my Spanish claim drawers, or Spanish claim trunk. As I recd. it about the 26th of Feby you can easily look at the files, & see whether it is there.

We have *lost* the Mary, Schott. The Commrs say the lights they have recd respecting W. In[dies] cases happening since 1803 have been such as will even make it necessary to review some cases which have been allowed. They admit, that the Mary is a very good case, of that class; & if they eventually receive any they will receive that case.

Tomorrow I shall try the Mercury Ayres, but with no great hopes of success. The Commrs will be exceedingly apt to think the seizure, in that case, was for illegal trade. Nor do I expect to make out much better with the Phenix.

I shall write you tomorrow, with some *cash*. Yrs D.W.

ALS. DLC.

TO ALEXANDER BLISS

Dear Sir, Washington Dec. 17th 1823

I send this for your use, as you are indebted to Mr Paige &c. The Commrs drive us along, pretty fast, & the present time before the Board is like the last days of Court—nonsuits & defaults are the order of the day.

I have put in the two cases of the Betsey, Clarke, and the Mercury, Ayres, today—& expect a *non allocatur*, as to each of them, tomorrow morning.

We are likely to lose the Mary, Schott. On all that class of cases—viz carry[ing] in to Spanish Ports since 1803, the Commrs think they have obtained a new & better view of facts Yrs D.W.

ALS. DLC.

g. Rehearings

Nearing the end of its three-year term, the Commission issued an order (on December 31, 1823) allowing claimants who wished to have their rejected claims reexamined "to file a petition for that purpose." The Commission adopted the rehearing rule because of its concern that claims might have been set down for examination "at a time when [there] had not been obtained any proof to sustain them; and . . . consequently there were some rejected merely for the want of proof." Accordingly the Commission required that the petitions for reexamination be "accompanied by any new proof . . . procured after the first decision."[61]

61. Moore, *Arbitrations*, 5: 4510. The order also required that the petitions be filed by January 17, 1824, a scant eighteen days away. As Webster's petition indicates in the case of the *Nancy*, printed below, he barely met the deadline. However, as his petition shows in the case of the *Alert*, printed below, there were occasions when the petitions were filed well after the deadline, but still accepted. The Commission commented that "so soon as it was seen that" their duties "might be accomplished without a strict adherence to either the letter or intent of the rule, but

The correspondence and petitions, printed below, illustrate exactly what the search for the "new proof" required. Actually, in most cases the search was more a continuation of the quest for the original proof. Something additional was required, and if it could be produced by his claimant-correspondent, Webster quickly incorporated it into the petition. In addition to presenting the new facts, he also skillfully appended legal argument explaining the full significance of the "new proof." Oddly enough, in one of the cases for which he won a reversal or rehearing he had conceded he had "no new evidence" (that of the *Nora*, printed below). He simply and briefly asked the Commission to reconsider their rule in a class of cases, and referred them to his earlier argument. They apparently changed their minds on fuller examination of his prior effort. The result stands in contrast to the cases in which he and the claimants seemed to scramble for new evidence as the life of the Commission was expiring. The Commission was apparently unimpressed by what was produced under those circumstances.

FROM EDWARD BROOKS

Dear Sir, Boston Dec. 11. 1823

By all means keep back the Nancy[,] Athearn for the present. It appears that Mr. Watmough[62] sold the vessel to a Mr. Stephen Dutilh[63] of Philadelphia. This gentleman wrote to Messrs. S. Higginson & Co.[64] of this place that Mr. Watmough had deposited the Decree of Condemnation &c in the Custom House of Philadelphia. Upon this letter the underwriters for the sum of $200 relinquished the vessel. With this information I shall probably set out forthwith for Philadelphia. The discovery of these letters was accidental and the fact that Mr. Dutilh had any thing to do with the vessel was never known to us until this morning. Yours sincerely E. Brooks

ALS. DNA. Edward Brooks (1793–1878; Harvard 1812), eldest son of Peter Chardon Brooks, Boston lawyer, studied with Benjamin Gorham, admitted in 1815, state representative.

little regard was paid to it by the board. Applications for the re-examination of every kind of claim have been received, altho' not offered until after the time limited. New evidence has been suffered to be introduced up to the last moment possible" (Id: 4510).

62. Perhaps James H. Watmough, a merchant whose name appears in James Robinson's *Philadelphia Directory* from 1797 through 1807.

63. Dutilh, a merchant, listed at 164 South Second Street in the *Philadelphia Directory* for the years 1805 through 1809.

64. Stephen Higginson (1743–1828) was a prominent merchant who had moved from Salem to Boston in 1778.

FROM EDWARD BROOKS

Dear Sir, Philadelphia Dec. 29 [1823]

Your favor of the 19th was duly recd. I have been three days fully occupied in this place in search of the paper we want—I am sorry to say without success. I have ransacked the Custom House throughout as well as the papers of Messrs Watmough and Dutilh. I have no doubt that the decree of Condemnation of the Nancy was lodged at the Custom House as stated in Mr. Dutilhs letter and that either in the removal of the papers from the old Custom House to the new or some other way it has been lost. As I have met with every facility in all quarters I think every thing possible has been done and am satisfied that unless by a mere accident it will not be found. With regard to the Crisis as she is a No 2 case and none of the Crew can be found I have never had much confidence in her. She was taken into a very obscure port where she [there] was no court of any kind and probably no condemnation ever took place. But of all this you are much better able to judge than I am. If I know of any particular service I could render by going to Washington I would gladly do it, but I am not aware that I could suggest anything that would be useful. I shall return tomorrow and shall be ready at all times to do any thing that may help the business, with sentiments of respect. Your ob st E. Brooks

ALS. DNA.

DOCUMENT 37. PETITION FOR REHEARING

Washington Jany. 17. 1824.

In the case of the Nancy, Athearn M[aste]r

To the Hon. the Commissioners, &c &c

The Petition of Daniel Webster, Agent of P. C. Brooks & others, claimants in the case of the Nancy, Athearn.

This case was disallowed *by consent*, some weeks ago. It is a case of French capture, in 1800, the prize carried into Porto Rico, & a condemnation rendered *somewhere*. The difficulty has been to shew where the Condemnation was had. Many circumstances conspire to shew that it was rendered in Sto. Domingo by the French Consular Court there. Some of these circumstances have come to light since the disallowance of the case. It seems that Mr. John H. Watmough being then in Porto Rico, purchased this vessel after her Condemnation as appears by his letter to the Owners which is already on file. His application to the Owners was for their conveyance to them of the vessel, for the purpose of procuring a new Register. Since the disallowance of the Claim, another letter has been found, which is herewith presented from Stephen Dutilh Esq. to Stephen Higginson & Co. Nov. 1801, Mr. Dutilh either having purchased the vessel from Mr. Watmough, or writing as his friend & agent, and from this letter it appears that this Vessel was actually condemned, & the Condemnation lodged in the Custom House at Philadelphia. Upon the discovery of this letter, Mr. Edward Brooks, in behalf of the Claimants immediately proceeded to Philada. & had a search made in the Custom House but without success, as appears by his deposition herewith exhibited. Thinking that a second search might possibly turn out more fortunate, this Petitioner wrote to Mr. John H. Barnes, of Philada. a person whom he believes to be very competent to such business & directed him to have a further search made at the Custom House without regard to time or expense. Mr. Barnes' success was no greater than Mr. Brooks' had been as appears by his deposition also herewith exhibited. In the mean time this Petitioner having understood that Mrs. Blake, widow of Mr. [James] Blake, formerly U. States Consul at Sto. Domingo lived at Chester Town on the Eastern Shore of Maryland, employed a gentleman to go thither, & search among Mr. Blakes papers for any document that might refer to the case of the Nancy. That gentleman John E. Frost Esq. has returned, on this 17th Jany. after an absence of ten days & reports that altho' he found Protests, abstracts of condemnations and other papers relating to transactions of the year 1798 he could find nothing relating to the year 1800 or the case of the Nancy. That Mrs. Blake informed him that there were two other trunks of papers belonging to her husband one of which she represented to be in the possession of Mr. Stewart in Baltimore & the other in the possession of Mr. Dominick Blake her husbands brother in New York. That he thereupon returned to Baltimore, but there learned that the trunk of papers which had been in Baltimore, had also been sent to Mr. D. Blake in New York. Mr. Frost having brought an order from Mrs. Blake in favour of the Petitioner on Mr. Dominick Blake for any papers which may be in his possession, he has taken measures to procure from New York any papers relating to this case & hopes to receive them before it comes on, in order to be decided. But if that search should prove unsuccessful the Petitioner humbly trusts that the circumstances proved afford satisfactory evidence that there was a Condemnation at Sto. Domingo. There certainly was a Condemnation *somewhere*—the question is, where? Now to settle this question we must in the absence of other proof look to the time of capture & the place of carrying in. The time of capture was say Septr. 1800. The place of carrying in, Porto Rico. Now the Claimants suppose, that an examination of the cases allowed before this Board will shew that the practice was universal of obtaining Condemnations for vessels sent into Porto Rico, at Sto. Domingo, if any where. She was not condemned by any Spanish Tribunal because the temporary register taken out at Philada. & here produced speaks of her as condemned by the French—and if the fact regarding condemnations be as these claimants suppose, it would seem to raise a violent presumption that this vessel was condemned at Sto. Domingo. Mr. Watmough is dead, & there is nobody who can give a full account of the transaction. The Captain, it will be perceived, was compelled by mere want, to leave Porto Rico before the result of the trial was known. He therefore brought home no sentence of Condemnation, & the Underwriters paid the loss without the production of any such paper. He too, is dead. Under all these circumstances, the Petitioner trusts that the Board will not think it unreasonable to conclude that this vessel shared the fate of others, & was condemned by the French Tribunal at Sto. Domingo.

DS. DNA. Endorsed "134. Nancy, Athearn Petition for Rehearing. P. C. Brooks & others, Claimants."

FROM DUDLEY L. PICKMAN

Dear Sir, Salem April 26. 1824

I have recd yours of 19th. inst, which has been communicated to the parties concerned. We are all surprized & disappointed at the result.

We believe & have always so understood, that the capturing vessel was not a public ship, but a Privateer—originally a public vessel, but then in private employment. She had been commissioned & her Commission had expired—this appears from the documents. Public ships have no Commissions. In the papers, she is termed "fragata" which has been translated frigate. Neuman's Spanish Dictionary, (Phila 1823 Edition) gives —"Fragata—ship—vessel—*Fragata de guerra*, Frigate. *Fragata de aviso*, Packet boat—*Fragata ligera*, a light, fast sailing vessel." It would seem therefore that the Spanish word "Fragata", is only the general term for vessel. We know of only two persons now living, who were of the original Crew. The mate, William Fairfield is now Master of a Ship—he may be home in a month or two, but this is quite uncertain. The other, Christopher Kilby is now here. We have seen him, & I enclose you memorandum of his account, to which he is ready to attest. From this alone, I should think no doubt could be entertained the capturing ship was private not publick—she certainly was not a Frigate & every appearance indicates a privateer only. We have no doubt this was the fact, & should be willing to give our deposition we always so understood & believed. It is difficult after so long a period to get evidence, very direct to this point.

We understood after the former hearing, that the distinction between a public & private ship was given up—otherwise we should have endeavoured to procure evidence from France of the character of the vessel. It would now, after this second decision, be difficult or impossible to change the opinion of the Commissioners on this point—strange as it seems to us & to learned men with whom we have conversed—but we hope evidence will still be admitted & a reconsideration be had, as to the fact on which the case seems to rest—whether the ship was public or private. We are very unwilling to give up so just a claim as this appears to us. Will you see what can yet be done. If the evidence can be got before the Comrs. please inform us as particularly as you can, what we shall offer—give any form you prefer to the enclosed. Kilby is here & will testify very fully as to his understanding & belief from all he saw. If Fairfield arrives in season, we have no doubt he will do the same. If any thing can be done by us, please suggest it, & we will endeavor that every thing possible shall be accomplished.

If there has been in all cases of capture by public ships, a Consular Condemnation, there being none here would seem to shew this a private vessel. The case as against the Spanish Govt, I should think stronger, from the property being disposed of in her ports, without any form of trial—especially after the subject had been regularly brought before the Govt. of the Country, as in this case. We still hope by your influence & exertions, we may obtain a just decision. When does the Commission close? Yours truly, Dudley L. Pickman

After writing the within, we determined to take the deposition of Kilby, & shall send it to you as soon as it can be prepared.

ALS. DNA. Dudley L. Pickman (1779–1846), Salem merchant.

DOCUMENT 38. PETITION FOR REHEARING

[c. May 1824]

To the Commissioners appointed under the eleventh Article of the Treaty of 1819 between the United States & Spain

Daniel Webster, as Agent for, & in behalf of the several Memorialists in the case of the Brig Alert, Gray, No. 1107. heretofore presented, & on the 24th of February last disallowed; respectfully prays for a rehearing & reconsideration of the aforesaid claim.

The Memorialists have understood that the said claim was rejected on the ground that the capturing vessel was a publick national Ship of France, & not a private armed vessel.

Supposing the fact to be so, the Memorialists would, with great respect, presume to ask for a reconsideration of the question, & to suggest a doubt whether, for the purposes of this & similar cases, there can be any difference between acts which Spain allows public Ships of France to commit in her ports, & the same acts when committed by private armed vessels, cruising under French Commissions. Private cruisers sail & make war under the sovereign authority of the State; they are a part of its Marine force; & the sovereign is as much accountable for their conduct towards neutrals, as for that of public ships. In consequence of this responsibility, it is usual to take security of them, that they shall not violate the neutral relations of the State, nor do any illegal act.

It would follow, therefore, as the Memorialists apprehend, that if Spain were bound to protect American property, in her ports, against the lawless acts of French cruisers, she was equally bound to protect it against similar acts of French public ships; since both cruise & make war under the same sovereign authority; the only difference being, that one, being equipped at public expense, makes war on public account; the other, being equipped at private expense, makes war on private account.

But the Memorialists believe that a reexamination of the papers will shew that the capturing vessel was not a public ship, in public service.

The Memorialists have themselves, as they believe, been led into a mistake, on the point, & in turn have misled the Commissioners. The Spanish Document, on file, No. 17. seems to prove sufficiently that the Captor was a Privateer. She is called "Corsario", several times in that document; the expressions are "Fragata corsaria", and in the Protest Captain Gray speaks of her *Commission*—& of her *Commission having expired*—& of her being consequently a Pirate &c—none of which expressions could be properly applied to public vessels.

The Protest, document No. 18, it is true calls her a *frigate*—but this Protest was entered in Spanish, & fragata, in Spanish means nothing more than a large ship—or perhaps a ship with three masts. Neuman's Spanish Dictionary gives the following definition—"Fragata—Ship—Vessel—Fragata de guerra Frigate." The mistranslation of this word from the original Spanish document has occassioned the mistake. The words Corsaria Fragata occur together, in the original document—where they must mean a private cruising ship—or Privateer—for if Fragata meant Frigate, the two words would mean a Privateer frigate. Neuman defines Corsario thus,—"Corsario—Corsaria—cruising; applied to a Privateer, or a letter of Marque, authorised to cruise against the enemy."

The Memorialists will only add that Fairfield the Mate, whose Deposition is in the case, & who, in that Deposition follows the former mode of expression & calls the capturing vessel a *frigate*, went to sea soon after the giving of that deposition, on an In[dian?] voyage, & is not expected back before next Winter [or] Spring: so that the Memorialists cannot now call on him to explain how he came to use that expression.

Danl Webster
in behalf of the Memorialists

DS. DNA.

DOCUMENT 39. PETITION FOR REHEARING

In the case of the Nora, Grinberg, Master.[65] [c. May 1824]

To the Honourable the Commissioners under the 11th Article of the Treaty between the United States of America and Spain, concluded at Washington, Feb. 22nd 1819.

The Petition of Daniel Webster, Agent of P.C. Brooks & others, Claimants in the case of the Nora, Grinberg, for a Rehearing of their claim

Respectfully represents:

That your Petitioner has no new evidence or new fact to adduce as the ground of his petition; but makes this application for a Rehearing in the hope that your Honourable Board may see fit to change the rule of decision respecting the construction of the Convention of 1802, and that so the case of the Nora may be in a situation to reap the benefit of such change. The Argument is on file in the case of the Minerva, Riddle,[66] to which your Petitioner respectfully refers, And will ever pray &c &c

Danl. Webster

DS. DNA. Listed as [c. April 22], 1824 in *Correspondence*, 1, Calendar: 466.

DOCUMENT 40. PETITION FOR REHEARING

In the case of the Brig Betsey, Snow Master [c. May 1824]

To the Honourable the Commissioners under the 11th article of the Treaty between the United States of America & Spain, concluded at Washington, Feb. 22nd, 1819.

The Petition of Daniel Webster, Agent of P.C. Brooks & others, claimants in the case of the Brig Betsey, Snow M[aste]r for a Rehearing.[67]

Respectfully represents:

That the claim of the said P.C. Brooks for the Brig Betsey & Cargo having been disallowed on the 10th. March 1823, on the ground that it did not satisfactorily appear that there was a final loss of the property, there being an intimation that the proceeds were secured upon landed property in Malaga measures were taken to procure from Spain *further proof* on this point, and others connected with this claim, which further proof is herewith presented.

The documents before filed prove, it is believed, that the Betsey was captured, in May 1797, by the French within the limits of Spanish jurisdiction, and carried back to Malaga whence she had just sailed—That

65. Claim no. 209. Webster won a reversal of the previous rejection of the claim. He filed precisely the same petition for a rehearing in the case of the schooner *Lucy* (claim no. 850), but it was rejected again.

66. See the argument in *Minerva*, Riddle, pp. 224–227, above.

67. Claim no. 182. The claim was finally allowed.

the Captain General of the place decreed the restitution of the property, on the ground of the violation of Spanish territory, which decree was confirmed by the Council of War at Madrid, in January 1798—That the *Captors* appealed from this decision of the Council of War and that, tho' every exertion was made by the Owners, aided by the American Minister, & the American Consul General in Spain, no decision on the appeal could be obtained.

The proofs recently procured, [and] herewith filed shew that the vessel perished [in] port and so was totally lost—That the Cargo was sold at a great loss, and the proceeds, less exp[enses] amounting to 110958.18 Reals Walloon, or $5547.9 deposited with Messrs. Martinez & Co. of Malaga, [secured?] by a Mortgage on their dwelling house;—said depos[it] payable on six months' notice "to whomever it may belong.["]

This deposite to the amount of it, might possibly have been realized by the claimants if the Spanish Government had proceeded to decide upon the Captors' appeal, or had compelled the captors to abandon their appeal. But this the Spanish Government could never be prevailed on to do. What the Claimants complain of is, that the Spanish Government would not do them justice, or decide the cause. It is now five & twenty years since the seizure; and the Claimants persued the law suit and pressed for a decision thro' many years, and at great expense, until all hopes of obtaining a decision were given up. The Claimants beg leave most respectfully to submit that they could do no more than they have done for the recovery of their property. They have spared neither time nor expense; and the reason that they have not recovered their property, as they humbly think, is the fault of the Spanish Government. The reason perhaps why the Spanish Govt. did not do the Claimants justice in this case may be found in the history of the times. It is known, and in fact provisions of this treaty proceed upon the fact that during those years the Spanish Government surrendered its own authority within its own territory to French authority. In this case there was a clear and admitted violation of Spanish territory. The Spanish Government is certainly answerable for this to the Claimants, unless the Claimants have failed to use due diligence to obtain redress by the ordinary means. They humbly contend that they have used such diligence and that they have failed thro no fault of their own but thro' the fault of the Spanish Government.

But should the Board be even of the opinion that this deposite should be deducted from the claim for the cargo of the Betsey, there will still remain a loss on the cost of the *cargo* of $12389 13/100 besides a total loss of the Vessel, Freight, and the Captain's, and Supercargo's adventures; and your Petitioner hopes that at all events these claims may be allowed. And will ever pray &c.—

Danl. Webster

DS. DNA. Misdated February 28, 1822, in *Correspondence*, 1, Calendar: 443.

h. The Appropriation Bill

As the Commission's term drew to a close, a major concern of Webster's was to secure a congressional appropriation for the awarded claims. By the treaty, the United States had merely agreed to assume the claims. Now it had to provide for payment of them after they had been decided in the appropriate forum.

A considerable amount of congressional maneuvering occurred over what appeared to be both a relatively straightforward obligation and an innocuous proposal. The bill was complicated from the beginning by two factors: early presidential politics in the 1824 season (the election that was to raise John Quincy Adams to the presidency), and the self-interest of some of its proponents.

There were several strong personalities at the forefront of the skirmish over the bill, each seeking some temporary advantage over the others. Dominating the scene politically were three of the presidential aspirants: Adams who, as secretary of state, had negotiated the treaty; William H. Crawford, secretary of the treasury, who would be called upon to disburse any money appropriated; and Henry Clay, speaker of the House of Representatives, which would have to pass upon any appropriation made to carry out the treaty. The combination was momentarily volatile and caused some alarm among the interested:

> We have all been for some days electioneering for our 5 million bill. We have heard that Mr. Clay is opposed to the bill reported by the Committee of Ways & Means, and intends proposing to give us a six pr. Cent stock principal and interest both payable from the proceeds of sales of Florida lands. He says that the Treaty will bear this construction; and we suppose because we can see no other object that he wants to attack Mr. Adams thro the medium of the Treaty. There are so many persons here both in and out of the House, who are interested in this business, that tho' we see the necessity of exertion yet we hope to defeat Mr. Clay by a large majority. Mr. Adams & friends must support the Treaty, and Mr. Crawford's friends must support the treasury recommendations. The Bill will not come up until some time next week. This gives us time to act; and every member who can be induced to read with fair intentions of the provision of the Treaty relating to the mode of payment, must be on our side.[68]

More than a fair reading was used to marshal support for the bill. Webster was very explicit. "*My* great business of the Session remains yet undone; that is, to get thro the law for paying the Spanish claims."[69]

68. Samuel Jaudon to John Inskeep, April 26, 1824, PPINA.

69. DW to Jeremiah Mason, April 19, 1824, *Correspondence*, 1: 357.

Webster's interest was twofold: to see that his clients were paid their claims, and, contingent on the first interest, to see that his fees were paid. His 5 percent commissions would not be forthcoming unless the claimants he represented received their awards. As a member of Congress, Webster was particularly well situated and suited to see that his private interests were protected by a piece of national legislation implementing a treaty provision. His proprietary interest in shepherding the bill through the House was clear—it was "our bill." The interests were arrayed; it does not seem to have occurred to him or anyone else that he was doing anything unethical. Rather, he was protecting his constituents, who, after all, were receiving their compensation by agreement of two nations. The bill passed both houses[70] and so set in motion the final stage of the process that yielded Webster a considerable amount of money.[71]

TO ALEXANDER BLISS

Dear Bliss. Washington April 24. 1824

I am of opinion that Congress will rise on Monday, May 17th—unless some unexpected occurence prevent.

Whether I shall then go home, may depend perhaps, on another question—or two others.

1. Whether any thing remains to be done, in the way of *proof*—in any of our cases—if not, then

2. Whether, in the mean time, Congress shall have passed any, &, if any, what, Bill for the payment of the awards.

The Bill now pending proposes to pay the awards in *cash*. For this purpose it authorizes the creation of Stock bearing an interest not exceeding 5 pr ct, & redeemable after 1832. If this Bill should pass, & the money be immediately raised, the Treasury will be ready to pay us, as soon as the award is made; viz June 10. Now if Congress should sit till May 17—& my Spanish money be ready by June 10—it may be very uncertain whether I shall go home—before I get it. If I do, it must be but for a short visit. This renders it convenient to be collecting the *powers*.[72]

I have written to several Gentlemen (this being, I think, about the 12th letter—of this *sitting*) to forward powers—& I now enclose a *list*

70. 4 U.S. Statutes at Large 33–34 (1824). DW is recorded as speaking only once in Congress on the bill. On May 6, 1824 he spoke in opposition to a motion to postpone consideration of the bill until the following December 1—obviously an event that would have been intolerable to him. The motion was defeated 105 to 53; see *Annals of Congress*, 18th Cong., 1st sess., p. 2555. For further consideration of Congressional ethics, see pp. 306–307, below.

71. For exactly how much money, see pp. 265–266, below, on his fees resulting from the Spanish claims.

72. See the explanation of the problem of the "powers," in the following section.

of such as I wish you to obtain. If, in any cases, it is not full enough, as to the names of the claimants, & you have not the means of ascertaining the names, you must write me, & I will consult the papers here. Of course, one power is enough for one person, however many cases he may have.

I have written to the Offices—& to many individuals. I wish you would send down a bundle of blank powers to N.A. Haven Jr., Esqr. Portsmouth—& ask him to get them filled & signed by our friends there, & forwarded to me. You can send them for 25 cts by the Eastern Stage Driver, Anne Street.

Let me hear from you soon as convenient. Yrs D. Webster

ALS. DLC.

TO ALEXANDER BLISS

Dear Bliss [May 1824]

I return these powers, for the reasons already suggested. You must have patience—"like a grain of mustard seed".

Our *Bill* encounters various difficulties—but I believe it will *go*—please *expedite* the execution of the *regular* powers.

Yours, in fatigue D.W.

ALS. DLC.

i. The Power of Attorney Problem

Webster and other attorneys and agents superintending clients' claims in Washington were faced with a practical problem as the time for award payments approached. Since few if any of the claimants were physically present in Washington, how was payment to be arranged? Technically payment issuing from the Treasury of the United States was to be made directly to the claimants. The solution to the problem was rather obvious: a simple power of attorney would suffice, authorizing the named attorney or agent to collect the awards in place of the claimants.

For Webster, however, the simple answer became complicated for two reasons. First, he had so many clients that it became difficult to notify all of them and insure that the powers would be drafted, signed, and sent in time to be used. (An incidental hindrance was that the Commission did not finally decide a handful of cases until the last minute.) But Webster wisely anticipated the mechanics of payment well in advance.[73]

73. For an example of an attorney who apparently did not initially perceive the problem, see W. Sargent to Theophilus Parsons, Jr., May 6, 1824 (The Papers of Theophilus Parsons, Jr., Boston Public Library). Sargent told Parsons that he observed Webster busily gathering powers of attorney in Boston, and wondered out loud to Parsons whether it was time that they executed a similar plan for Sargent's claim.

In order to canvass his clients effectively, he began the process of procuring powers of attorney early. The first letters mentioning his concern surface in February of 1824—fully five months before final payment.

The second complicating factor was concern about the appropriate technical form for the powers of attorney. Webster feared that unless the powers were impeccable, the Treasury would not recognize their binding effect and would refuse to issue payment. That would mean delay in dispersing funds, which would in turn have a number of side effects—one of which would surely be unhappy clients. Webster also was anxious to leave Washington before much of the summer was gone and even more anxious to begin receiving his fees. So he badgered Bliss in Boston with suggestions and revisions as to the proper form in which to draft the powers. Finally, as May began to disappear into June, a somewhat exasperated and exhausted Webster, realizing that not all forms would be perfect, conceded the futility of his insistence on totally satisfactory technical detail. Reluctantly he began to accept less than "perfect" powers of attorney, and hoped the Treasury would look the other way.[74]

TO ALEXANDER BLISS

Dear Bliss — Washington feb. 22nd. 1824

I am not unmindful of the $673.—acceptance—or note—due, ni fallor, about the 3/6 of March. I shall send you the means. If it should not arrive at the day, Mr Page [James William Paige] must let you have the cash—but probably I shall send it in season.

I am aware it is a work of time to get up the necessary powers. I shall make out & send you, shortly, a list of persons, whose powers I shall need. The Bill to provide the fund has not yet been acted on. If it pass, the money, perhaps, may be paid in June or July. We are all well, & busy. D. Webster

You know I have not the Louisa Joanna Papers. I believe you had better

74. A sample power of attorney read as follows:

———have made & appointed, & do by these presents, make & appoint Daniel Webster of Boston, in the County of Suffolk, & Commonwealth of Massachusetts, Counsellor at Law, *my* attorney & agent for *me* & in *my* behalf to claim & receive from the Commissioners, appointed under the Eleventh Article of the Treaty of Amity, Settlement & Limits, between the United States of America, & his Catholic Majesty, concluded at Washington, on the 22nd day of February, in the year of our Lord 1819, the compensation, whether in money or certificates, which may be awarded to *me* or to him in *my* behalf on *my* claim(*s*) under said Treaty; & also to do & perform all things necessary or proper in relation to the prosecution & recovery of said claim(*s*) with power to substitute any person or persons to act under him in the premises. (Miscellaneous Documents, Records of the Spanish Claims Commission, RG 76, DNA).

send them on, at once. I doubt whether the Commrs will be willing to wait longer.

ALS. DLC.

TO ALEXANDER BLISS

Dear Bliss, Washington Feb. 24. 1824.

I find it will be necessary for all the persons claiming in the Preze [Perez] Morton's Memorial, to furnish *me* a power of Atty, to receive the payment. The Commrs will make up their report, in that case, to me, as agent of the Claimants; & not to each man separately, which would be a difficult labor for them, & mistakes might also be made, if they were to undertake it. A short general power will be sufficient. I want it *soon*, as I believe that part of the Commrs Report will probably be soon drawn up. Those persons living in Boston can sign the same power. Those living out of town, like Mr Gilman, can easily be sent to. I think there is, in my trunk, now, a certificate that Nathl. Gilman Esq is Exr of Nicholas Gilman.

There will also be a necessity for many other powers, about which I shall write you soon. Perhaps the best way is to have some short powers printed. I will give you the names, necessary to be applied for in the several cases, shortly. Yrs D. Webster

ALS. DLC.

TO ALEXANDER BLISS

Dear Bliss, March 27. [1824]

I am glad you have adjusted the 1020 Dec note. You must look out, also, for the notes in Bank, renewed by you, since my coming away, with Mr Blakes indorsment. I know not when you have made them payable. Write me, if you need new notes. Mr Blake is yet here, but will leave on or abt. the 1st. & be home probably the 15. or 20th April—or perhaps a little sooner. I now send check for 4080—being the amt. of the three things which I mentioned to you, in my letter some days ago, as falling due abt. the 7. 9. & 10 of April.—viz.—2081.50 Ap. 9. 1500 Ap. 7. 500. Ap. 10—or abt. those days respectively. If no unexpected accident shall have happened, you will find the cash in Bank at the time. You can inquire; if there be a deficiency, Mr Paige must help you make it up for a few days; but I think there will be none.

As to the time of my coming home, I cannot speak with any certainty. I shall of course stay out of the session; & I imagine that will not close before the 10th of May. Then, whether I can go immediately home, will depend on the state of my other business, I expect, however, to go immediately, & to return, perhaps, in July, for a week. But this depends on the provisions *yet to be made* for the payment of the claims. I should be glad to receive the *powers*, & every thing else remaining on the subject of the Claims. The Commrs will re-assemble shortly, & wind up the concern. There will be many powers to be obtained, hereafter, beside those for which I have written. But that business can be attended to after I go home, probably. If not, I shall write you in season.

I believe you may tell our clients that I hope to be at the Circuit Court —but not at home earlier. Indeed, if I can live without it, I do not mean to engage in much professional work for the Spring & Summer. I am as thin as a hatchet, & must contrive to recruit; & you & the rest must have both the labor & the profit of the law.

Mrs W. is quite well, & desires her regards to you. Yrs D.W.

ALS. DLC.

TO ALEXANDER BLISS

[May 1824]

The Commrs. will make an *award*—setting forth that they have allowed to A. & B. &c—so much. This will be paid, rateably, at *the Treasury*. But your power is to receive from the Commrs.—who pay nothing.

Please send this to Mr [Dudley L.] *Pickman*—with a form for a better [power]. The words "or from the Treasury of U. S"—after the word *nineteen*—wd. have made it complete. How should you, who are the prince of all *accuratists*, fall into such an error.

Pray set about correcting it. I have returned one recd from Ropes & Ward—& one from Judah Hays—with directions how to correct it. Yrs, in haste D.W.

In the Perez Morton Memorial I shall send over to get the award made *in my name*—so that you need not, for the present, get new powers there.

ALS. DLC.

TO ALEXANDER BLISS

My Dear Bliss— [May 1824]

I am afraid your *Powers* are all wrong—it should be, to receive the compensation, &c from the *Treasury of U. S.* The Commrs pay nothing.

I have just recd two or three in the former mode—& I am afraid they will not answer. Yrs. D. Webster

ALS. DLC.

TO ALEXANDER BLISS

Dear Bliss, Washington May 10. [1824]

I should be very glad to give our clients any information in my power, as to the present state of the claims, *amounts allowed* &c. But you know the Commrs do not state *amounts*, nor do they intend to do so, until they make public their final award. *Please explain* this. I have attended, in every case, & endeavored to suggest the grounds on which I thought damages ought to be calculated. The Commrs have weighed these things, & the result, for the present they do not disclose. The rehearings, such as Mr Codmans, we have yet no information from. We have been engaged in getting the Bill along. It will doubtless pass.

I note what you say in Mr Whitney's case. It corresponds with what I wrote you yesterday.

I hope to get along, without new powers in the Perez Morton Memorial. In all other cases, powers must be had, in a corrected form, as I wrote yesterday.

Wm. H. Boardman & als, were memorialists in 3 cases
viz: Fame, Jordan
Olive, Smith
George, Grant

The first only is allowed, & of the underwriters in that case, I find only that we have the following Perez Morton, Benja. Humphrey, Exr. of Leml. Gardner, Jona. Merry, & John T. Apthorpe. Exr. of Wm Foster. Yrs, D. Webster

I shall bring home a certified copy of the award, in each case, for the benefit of the concern.

ALS. DLC.

TO ALEXANDER BLISS

Dear Bliss. May 19: [1824]

I have recd Mr Brooks' power; & also his & Mr. Wards, as Exrs. of Saml. Gray. The first is in your manuscript, & may perhaps be sufficient, under the *general* clause. The last is not sufficient; &, indeed, I should prefer new ones, in both cases. To save you trouble of looking up the names again, I have filled a Blank—for the Iris, Conway—& have also made our work-loving friend, Jaudon, write off a new power for Mr Brooks. Yrs D. W.

Please return them soon—unless you have already sent others.

ALS. DLC.

TO ALEXANDER BLISS

[May 1824]

I have recd Mrs Cobbs scrip—also Mr Pope's power. I have written him, enclosing a proper blank.

I will examine the *list*—& write [you] again tomorrow.

I shall not send back any more powers—&, on reflection, regret that I have sent any back. If, in any Case you cannot get new powers return the old ones—possibly they might pass, in a particular instance tho' I think they wd. *not*. Yrs DW.

ALS. DLC.

TO ALEXANDER BLISS

Dear Bliss, June 7. [1824]

I find a great deficiency of *Powers*, yet, & this day's mail has brought me none. In the cases in Touro's Office, I hardly find any powers. Titus Welles, as Administrator, or Exr, sent on a power in the old form, but not in the new. Mr Jaudon is now hunting over the papers to see what is missing, & we shall try to write you again this Evening. If you have not got new powers, pray send back the old. If I stay here long enough for an answer to this, *it will be the last moment*. I shall melt here, if I stay longer than 8 or 9 days—but I hope the *Powers* are already on the Road. Yrs D. Webster

I fancy the rate will be 91, and two thirds pr ct.[75]

ALS. DLC.

TO ALEXANDER BLISS

Dear Bliss, Washington June 15. 1824

Powers must be forwarded—in the form I mentioned yesterday, to me *or* Mr Jaudon, from Jona Amory, Ass[ign]ee of Payson & Holbrook.
from Same as Admr of Thos. C. Amory (abt. which I believe I wrote yesterday)
Titus Welles, Admr. of A. Touro—
J. Thomas (in Mercury Pearson)
Henry Davidson, in same—
Moses Pearson & als—in same—
Isaac Winslow & B. P. Tilden in same case—
Saml. B. Harris—& Hall & Parker same case—

75. Webster is referring here to the fact that the aggregate of awards under the treaty exceeded the $5 million treaty limitation. As a result, each award had to be proportionately reduced in order to bring the total awarded in all the claims within the treaty limitation figure.

All these persons are included in one general award to Titus Welles & others. I am afraid we shall have difficulty in separating & assigning to each his own—but at present we want *powers.*
Thomas Dennie—
I shall write you again tomorrow Yrs. D.W.

ALS. DLC.

TO ALEXANDER BLISS

[June 18, 1824]

List of Powers, which seem to be wanting, in order to receive claims; except so far as Mr Bliss may have forwarded them, within the last ten days—or since my return from Philadelphia—

	Jona. Amory, Admr. of Thomas C. Amory— Thomas Amory }	*Betsey* Halliburton
Marblehead	Bessom (or Bescome) Phillip, & { Caleb Loring, & Thomas Curtis }	*Hannah*, Griste
	Dall, William Davidson, Henry }	*Mercury*, Pearson
	Dennie Thomas—	#P. S.
	Green H. F. Admr.#	I believe I have this—
Weymouth	Harding, James—	*Hannah*, Harding
E[benezer] Francis	Lee Joseph Jun	*Betsey*, Snow
	{ New England Ins Co Hathaway & Clap }	*Helen*
	Pickard, Mark, **died**	Jane, Knight,
	Plumer, Catharine M.—	
	Shaw, Leml. Admr of J Gray	
	Snow, Gideon— Brig Betsey —	*Orleans. Cape Cod—*
	Tudor, Frederic—power to Minot	
	<Watson Benja M.>	
	Wells Titus, & others—that is: of Wells as Admr of Stocker	
done	<Winslow Isaac>	

Jos. Tilden

	Wm Shattuck Elisha Bangs Wm Woods	These persons were, inter alios, underwriters on the *Fame*, Jordan, with Morton, Merry, Gardiner, & Foster—whose
Doct Cheever	Jona. Williams	power you sent. If you can get any of
Sanger recd word	Joseph Fosdick	these remaining powers please forward them—but I take **it** they are all dead —& have empowered nobody.—& per-

haps you may as well let this rest till I come home.

J. Thomas. He is a debtor to Govt—& we shall not get any thing.
Saml. B. Harris— (only 183 Dls)
Moses Pearson—
Isaac Winslow
B. P. Tilden
Sarah Tilden Admx
Hall & Parker— (188.97)

Dear Bliss

I send you a list of powers wanted. How soon you can get them, or whether you can get all of them at all, is more than I know. However, we must do as well as we can. I am in hopes to get away the first of the week. Mr Jaudon will remain here. The parties may either make out their powers to me, or him—or to him—or wait till I come home, & make them to me with power of substitution. In the Mercury case, however, they should lose no time, as the money cannot be distributed till it is all I recd—& I have only recd part of it. Yrs always D.W.

We have got through a little award of abt. 8.000 Dlls in the Helen.

ALS. DLC. Scattered words by Bliss are rendered in boldface type. The deletions seem also to be his.

j. Final Payment

The Commission finally adjourned on June 8, 1824.[76] Shortly thereafter the Treasury began issuing payment, and Webster, using the powers of attorney, began collecting the money for his clients. His very first instinct seems to have been to get rid of the money as soon as possible. Of course, quick delivery would please his clients, but Webster also wanted to avoid any entanglements that might develop between his clients and their creditors, or possible competing interests on any given claim. To this end, he began forwarding the Treasury drafts at once either to the clients or to Bliss. Above all, he did not wish to become involved in litigation through the Massachusetts trustee process.[77] Bringing clients' assets with him into Massachusetts could possibly subject him to that process, and even if it meant buying up a claim (as in DW to Bliss, June 25, 1824, printed below), Webster was willing to go to that length in order to put everything to rest at once.

76. Moore, *Arbitrations*, 5: 4507.

77. Massachusetts trustee process, also called foreign attachment, was authorized by statutes which allowed creditors to reach debtors' assets held by other persons. Laws, Mass., c. 65 (1794) and c. 5 (1798).

TO ALEXANDER BLISS

Dear Bliss Washington June 14. 1824

The Commrs made their Report, as you know, on Tuesday last. By very great exertions, it was put into such a shape, as that the Treasury could pay the awards, without further calculation. I have observed some errors, both in names & sums; but nothing as yet very material. On Saturday I recd. a draft for part of our money, & immediately remitted it to the respective owners; as perhaps you may have heard, if you have been in State Street, within the last twenty four hours. Tomorrow I shall probably receive more which I shall dispose of in like manner, as quick as possible. The Treasury gives me drfts on the Bank at Philadelphia, & no where else. Mr Lloyd & Col Perkins, Mr Ropes, Mr Codman, &c took theirs in the same way. We can get drfts on Boston. This you must state fully to our friends. It is possible that if I were to go to Philadelphia I might make some arrangement with the Bank to transfer a part of the fund—but it could only be a very small part—to Boston. But this would require time—& the money would, in the interim, be standing in my name, which I do not wish. The Claimants will in general be able to do better for themselves than I can do for them—& I therefore draw my checks on the Bank at Philadelphia and transmit them at once.

In some cases, we have found trouble, & shall experience disappointment. The law, you are aware, provides that no person indebted to Govt. can be paid an award, until the debt to Govt. is first discharged. I am called on therefore to state, & prove, the name &c of every person *interested* in the award. There will be some claims of ours affected by this. "*Rice & Savage*" appears to be one of these. Mr [Henry] Rice, as it would seem, is a debtor to Govt. on bonds. His part, therefore, will be withheld, or, if paid to me, it will be done on my obligation to hold the money, & repay it to the Treasury, unless it be made shortly to appear that it is some other *Rice*, or that the Bonds are paid. Jona. Merry appears to be in the same condition—so does E. H. Robbins, & so do several others. These things must be treated delicately. Perhaps you had better say nothing about them at present, to any body; except that I wish you would speak confidentially on the subject to Mr Savage, & write me, (at Philadelphia or New York) what he says. I take it for granted Mr Savage is entitled to one half and Mr Rice or his creditors to the other—if wrong in this, Mr Savage can put me right. I wd. speak to no one else.

Then, again, there is another subject. *Trustee processes* may be <out> brought agt me, if I carry any money home. I wish you to mention to me if there be any danger of such an occurrence, in any case known to you. I wish, as far as is right & proper, & no farther, to avoid all such troubles. The claims in Taylors office, being generally, in small sums, I should perhaps omit to pay, in general, until I get home—unless there were some advantage in paying them before.

I wish you would write me on this head; and also state to me, if, as far as you know, there are any cases in which any thing should be retained except the Commns. There may have been expenses for papers &c. I have a sort of Spanish claims acct, some where in my ledger, which you can turn to.

As far as you can answer this letter the day you receive it, I wish you would do so, & direct your answer to Philadelphia—& perhaps one day later, a letter may come there also. After that, for two or three days, address to New York.

I shall probably send to you Mr Davis' & Mr. Hedge's drafts—as those Gentlemen, or one of them, may probably be in Boston when they will arrive.

Among the lost cases are:

The Prize case   Mary Appleton
The Louisa Johana
The Bell Savage
The Nautilus
Mr. Whitney's claim

I have no time to say more. Yrs.   D.W.

ALS. DLC.

TO ALEXANDER BLISS

June 19 [1824]
Saturday Evening

Dear Bliss

I wrote you yesterday. For two days I have no letters, which seems to indicate that I am not expected to stay longer here. At present, I intend to be *off* on Monday, or Tuesday. You will please to attend—all in due season—to the list of *needed* powers which I sent yesterday—except Shattuck—Woods—Fosdick—&c whom it is useless to regard. The powers furnished will enable me to get the award for all who joined in the Memorial.

I shall send you, tomorrow, a great many letters, enclosing the accts to the persons entitled to receive money as underwriters in Taylor's[78] Office. I am so anxious to get rid of the money in my hands, that, by Mr Jaudon's assistance, I have made out these accounts; & shall forward them to you, with my drft for the balances. These will go, in letters unsealed, enveloped in covers addressed to You, unsealed. You will please

78. Perhaps Charles Taylor of Boston, whose power of attorney to Webster was signed on February 28, 1824. He was executor of the will of the deceased Boston merchant Joseph Taylor.

look at them, and if they appear to you to be right, seal them, handsomely, & deposite them in the Post Office. I chose to send them to you, for your inspection, thinking there might be reason, known to you, in some cases, to shew that the account was not rightly stated—or that the amount ought not now to be paid to the Claimant. If, for these reasons, or any other, you should see cause to retain the payment, till I come home, you will be careful to do so. You will observe that I have deducted, in the principal cases, 10. 20. 30. or 40 Dlls—to pay Secy's fees, & for translations. This will do something towards discharging that account—& the rest must go to profit & loss. Still, if the[r]e are charges, in any one case, fit to be b[orne] by that one case, exceeding this amount considerably, you will please retain the payment. I would rather lose a hundred or two dollars, than be obliged to retain the money till a particular & exact account could be made. I am solicitous to get rid of the money—& settle the accounts—so that when I get home I may have repose. Yrs.

D. Webster

ALS. DLC.

TO ALEXANDER BLISS

Washington
June 20. [1824]

Dear Bliss

According to my intimation yesterday, I forward by this mail sundry accts & letters enclosed to you. You will run your eye over the accts, & see if they appear right. If so, then consider whether there be any reason, in any case, to forbear or delay the payment. If you know of none, then seal the letters & send them. Otherwise retain them.

I shall get away on Tuesday—at Philadelphia I shall probably hear from you. Mr Jaudon will remain here & any thing you wish to say to him he will attend to. Yrs D.W.

I find we have *Sarah Tilden's* power—but I believe not B. P. [Tilden]'s

ALS. DLC.

TO ALEXANDER BLISS

Washington
June 20 [1824]

Dear Bliss,

By tomorrow evening I shall have remitted a great portion of the money to the Claimants. There are some cases, however, which it is convenient to adjust here. The Mercury Pearson cannot be settled till the powers come. The Mercury Ayres cannot well be settled here—nor the mixed up cases of the Ocean and Enterprize. Mr [Joseph] Coolidges Catharine I shall also leave till I get home—& some other smaller ones.

In general, as the check is drawn to order, & purports to be for Spanish Claims, the check itself I suppose will be a proper & sufficient receipt. Some writers in Taylor's Office I have remitted to directly, without troubling you. Such as Mr Gilman, Mr Sheafe & Mr Ladd.

Yrs D. Webster

ALS. DLC.

TO ALEXANDER BLISS

Philadelphia June 24. 1824
Thursday morning

Dear Bliss,

I arrived here last eveg. & found yours of the 20. We can do little or nothing abt. the Mercury till I get home. I have all the minutes to explain the matter, so far as it can be explained.

In my zeal to get rid of my money, I have done two things too soon; perhaps more than two.

1. in sending Mr. Davis his Williams, Holbrook, money, before it was subjected to some little expenses in Mr. Brook's Office. You may drop a hint, to Mr Davis, in convenient season, on this head.

2. I have remitted the *Topaz* money to Mr. Pope; deducting 60 Dlls, for translations & postages. If this be not enough, please send my compliments to Mr. Pope, with a note of the proper amt. I paid, I think, 7 Dlls—or 7.50 postage on the papers to Washington.

I have paid Mr Ignatius Sargent, & he will settle with the concern. The checks, remitted thro yr hands, you will retain in all necessary cases, as before requested.

I left Jaudon at Washington. He will stay there some time yet.

Am glad to hear Mrs W. is safe at home. Yrs D. Webster

If I keep July 4th with you, I shall do well

ALS. DLC.

TO ALEXANDER BLISS

Dear Bliss, Philadelphia June 25. [1824]

After writing you yesterday, I recd yours, with three or four powers, et cetera. As to poor Mr Rice, I am inclined to make an effort, & run some risk for him. I shall write to Washington today. Is there no danger of his creditors, *trusteeing*, me, if the money should get into my hands? This you must look to. If there is no danger of this, let every thing rest as it is, till I get home. If there be danger, *buy him out*, & get an order on me. If he owns *half*, it wd. come perhaps, Comm[issio]n et cetera off, to 1800 Dlls—possibly a little more. Or you may *pay* him, & take his receipt in full—for payment, give him your negotiable note, at 10 days. I think I can manage it, with the Govt. I have recd the money, in fact, but under an agreement to pay it back, in case &c. I think it possible, however, I can negotiate for the relinquishment of this agreement, or part of it, if, in the meantime, there are not private creditors, to *trustee* me, as soon as I get home. You look out for this & I will look out for the rest. Take care to learn, if you make any payment, whether Mr. Rice owns *half*. I hope you will get along without making payment, as I may succeed for part, perhaps, & not for the whole. Do as well as you can—but by all means keep off all trustee processes if possible. Yrs D. Webster

ALS. DLC.

k. Fees

"Mr Stephens paid me, yesterday, the compensation due me from your Office, under the agreement; & beg leave to express my thanks for the kindness & courtesy of the Gentlemen with whom I have had intercourse, on this occasion."[79]

Webster wasted no time in beginning to collect his fees after the Commission permanently adjourned on June 8, 1824. Within a fortnight, he had collected close to $50,000, and within a month approximately $60,000 of what turned out to be a total of around $70,000. His clients in the aggregate seem to have collected about $1,850,000 of the $5,000,000 awarded under the treaty.[80]

Webster's list of commissions received for the Spanish claims, printed below, is a who's who of the early nineteenth-century commercial elite of New England, and particularly of Boston. Merchants, insurance underwriters, and shipping interests are generously represented. In addition,

79. DW to John Inskeep, June 25, 1824, PPINA. Webster is, of course, referring to his fees earned from representing the Insurance Company of North America. Philadelphia was his first stop on his journey back to Boston, and his welcome was prearranged. "Mr. Webster left us this morning, and I have been very busily engaged for some days past in preparing him for his departure. He will stop a day in Philada. and give you a call. As he does not very well know the gentlemen of the Pennsa. & the Philada. Offices, he would be glad that you would accompany him in his visit to them." (Samuel Jaudon to Robert Stephens, June 22, 1824, PPINA.)

80. Webster's fees, in this and other matters, have been the subject of some speculation in the past. Marquis James, in his book on the Insurance Company of North America, estimated that DW's " 'commission' . . . appears to have been about $20,000" (*Biography of a Business*, p. 117 and p. 399, n. 8); James's estimate is based upon his reading of the INA Directors' Minutes. Webster, however, reported his fee from INA at $3,329.93 (exactly one percent of the INA award). Both James and DW reported the total INA award of $332,993 accurately. There does not seem to be any reason for DW to have hidden his total fee in his private account book. For more on DW's fees from his general law practice, see chapter 3, pp. 119–174, above.

Webster's reward for his work on behalf of the Philadelphia insurance companies is listed.

It is probably from this relatively obscure event, the disposition of the Spanish claims, that one can trace, at least in part, Webster's growing identification as a lawyer and spokesman for the eastern commercial world. Webster's devotion was well rewarded, at this time and in the future, for the merchants had discovered a reliable and willing ally.

Most of the fees were five percent of the amount awarded—the standard commission he and many of the prominent Boston claimants arrived at in 1821.[81] A number of the commissions were 10 percent, however, and occasionally, as in the case of some of the large awards garnered by the Philadelphia insurance offices (including INA), the figure settled on was one percent. The claims business had been as lucrative for Webster as it had been for insurance companies and merchants who had absorbed their original losses a generation ago. His fondest hope of "pecuniary profit," voiced some five years before, had been realized.

DOCUMENT 41. WEBSTER'S COMMISSIONS FROM SPANISH CLAIMS

Receipts of Commissions, on acct. of Spanish Claims.

1824

June 9.	of James Lloyd, by check on U. S. Bank—5 pr ct on 36.251.41—being one third of award in the case of the Genl. Washington.		
			1.812.57
deposited June 12.	of Th. Perkins, (by due bill) 5 pr ct on ½ Betsey[,] Clarke & Diana—	22.638.72	
	2/3 Genl. W.	72.502.84	
		95.141.56	
			4,757.07
			6.569.64
		Brot up	6.569.64
June 12.	of Messrs Ropes & Ward on 76.777.80		3.838.89

81. See pp. 202–204, above.

"	of P. C. Brooks,	
	on 172.817.29	8.640.86
"	of Joseph Head,	
	on 24.338.66	
	Pomona	1.216.93
"	of N. G. Snelling, Prest.	
	on 61.890.64—3094.53	3094.53
	$500 of this recd. in advance.	
"	of Danl. Sargeant, Prest.	
	on 60.160.53	3008.02
	Recd. in advance $500.	
"	of Jonathan Amory	
	on 5188.63 (Kavanaugh)	259.43
		26.628.30
	Brot up	26.628.30
June 12		
	of Gorham Parsons	
	on 42.125.06	2,106.25
"	Stephen Higginson	
	on $26,708.47 (Pattern)	1,335.42
"	James King Admr. (Polly)	
	on $21,546.12	1.077.30
"	West & Ropes (Patty)	
	on $13.383.93	669.19
"	Willard Peele & others	
	on $11.069.82	553.49
15.	Henry Hatch, Admr.	
	Julia & Nora	
	on $16.479.83	823.99
"	Jesse Sumner	
	on $9342.67	467.13
	Danl Sargeant—Atalanta	
	on $7698.97	384.94
	over	$34.046.01
	Brot over	$34.046.01
1824		
June 15—	John Barr	
	$10.372.44	518.62
	Extra on the Neptune $500	
" 16	Benj. Pickman—Katy	
	on $4194.13	209.71

Date	Name	Memo	Amount
" "	Paschal P. Pope		
	on $10.083.33		504.17
	Mem: Extra for transl[atin]g.	$60—	
" "	Philip Chase		
	on $5.908.44		295.42
"	Wm. Pickman		
	on $1398.04		69.90
"	Winthrop Sargent Ex[ecu]tr. Benj. K. Hough & Elias Davis		
	on $4.686.88		234.34
"	Ignatius Sargent		
	on $4580.24		229.01
			36.107.18
		Brot up	36.107.18
1824			
June 16	Thos. Parsons self & as Agent		
	on $2596.36		129.82
"	Capt. Nat. Williams		
	on $438.33		21.92
"	Hugh Hill		
	on $3.428.34		171.42
"	Nabby[,] Lefavour, atty		
	on $140.11		7.00
"	Higginson & Parsons		
	on $13.436.78		671.84
17	Thos. Atwood		
	on $313.59		15.67
"	Gideon Holbrook		
	on $612.57		30.63
"	Union Ins[uran]ce Co.		
	on $3.466.67		183.33
			37.338.81
		Brot over	37.338.81
1824			
June 17.	Wm. Davis & B[arnabas] Hedge		
	on $5.989.16		299.46
" "	Wm. Davis, surv[ivin]g Partner		
	on $13.916.27		695.81
" "	B. Hedge & M. Whitten		
	on $9.093.98		454.69
" "	Josiah Knapp		
	on $2.646.08		132.30

"	"	Saml. Taylor & others		
		on $388.73		19.43
"	"	Danl. Sargent		
		on $1057.12 (Touro)		52.85
"	"	D. Sargent, Admr.		
		on $2053.22 (Taylor)		102.66
"	"	Samuel Mifflin		
		on 187.224.88		1872.24
				40.968.25
1824			Brot up	40.968.25
June	17	N. A. & J. Haven		
		on $10.394.79		519.74
"	19	John C. Jones		
		on $4840.11		242.—
		Exp[ense]s $40		
"	"	Jacob Sheafe		
		on $2504.6		125.20
		Exps $12		
"	"	David Eckley		
		on $2115.40		105.77
		Exps $25		
"	"	Saml. W. Pomeroy		
		$2543.10		127.15
		Exps $20		
"	"	John Hancock		
		on $2435.56		121.77
		Exps $20		
"	"	Danl. D. Rogers		
		on $1308.61		65.43
		Exps $10		
				42.275.31
1824			Brot up	42.275.31
June	19			
"	"	Rufus G. Amory		
		on $2881.29		144.06
		Exps. $20		
	"	Agnes Prince		
		on $1605.45		80.27
		Exps. $10		
	"	John T. Apthorpe		
		on $1575.29		78.76
		Exps. $10		

"	Nathl. Gilman Extr		
	on $4298.75		214.93
	Exps. $30		
"	Isaac P. Davis		
	on $1330.7		66.50
"	Arnold Welles		
	on $1826		91.30
	Exps. $10		
"	John Welles		
	$1406.44		70.32
	Exps. $10		
			43,021.45

1824		Brot up	43.021.45
June 19	Arnold & J[ohn] Welles		
	on $1375		68.75
	Exps. $10		
"	Henry Ladd Extr		
	on $1925		96.25
	Exps. $10		
"	John Brazer		
	on $5350.68		267.53
	Exps. $40		
"	Wm. H. Bo[a]rdman		
	on $2403.30		120.16
	Exps. $25		
"	Joshua Haven		
	on 687.50		34.37
	Henry Hatch, Ad[ministrato]r		
	on $1.696.29		84.81
24.	of N[orth] A[merican] Ins: Co. on		
	$332,993 @ 1 pr ct		3.329.93
			47.023.25

June		Brot up	47.023.25
24.			
	of Penna. Ins: Co.		
	on 103,539 . @ 1 pr ct		1035.39
	of Philadelphia Ins Co.		
	on $36.254 @ 1 pr ct . . .		362.54
	Mr [Henry S?] Waddel, per agt. on Molly $100 . . .		
26.	of Jno. Cruft, on 726.39		36.31
28.	of Judah Hays, on $2995.67		149.78

	of Wm McIntire, 3 pr ct on 2277	62.62
		48.669.89
	Brot up	48.669.89
July 3.		
	of Jona. Mason & Thos Perkins, Exrs, on 1483.70 (20 Extra)	74.18
	of Thos Perkins, on 871.74	43.59
	of Jona. Merry, on 733.33 (10 Extra)	36.66
	of Benja. Smith, on 8.682.96	434.14
		49.258.46
	Brot over	49.258.46
July 6		
	of Wm Mackay on 733.33	36.66
	of Jno. Mackay, on	
July 6.	of N[athan] Bridge on 1333.29	66.66
"	of B. M. Watson, on 2911.04 (10 extra)	145.55
July 6		
"	of the owners of Mercury, Ayres, on 22.158.82 @ 10 pr ct	2.215.88
"	of Caleb Hopkins Admr on 1116.95	55.84
	of S. H. & S. G. Perkins, on 22.638.72	1.131.93
		52.910.98
	Brot up	52,910.98
	of Andrew Ritchie, Admr. on 3075.55	153.77
	<of Henry Hatch, Admr. on 1830>	<84.81>
	of Jona. Amory on 6.883.74	344.18
	of J. & F. Amory, Exrs of Jno McLean, on 1.766.94	88.34
	of Francis Welch Admr. on 850.28	42.50
	of Jos: Coolidge & others, in Catharine, on 19.167.48	958.37
		54.498.14
	Brot up	54.498.14

July 7	of Thos Cushing	
	on 183.33	9.16
	(paid 76.17)	
	of Eph: Locke on 664.17	22.90
	of Agnes Prince, ad[ministratri]x on 1605.45	80.27
	of R. G. Amory, on 2881.29	144.06
	of John Hancock, on 2435.56	121.77
		54,876.30
	Brot up	54.876.30
	of D. D. Rogers, on 1308.61	65.43
	of Rice & Savage on 1283.32	64.16
	of S[amuel] W. Pomeroy, on 3276.45	163.82
	of R. Dexter Adm[inistratri]x on 326.51	16.32
	of Benj: Bussey, on 871.29	43.56
	of Saml. Cobb. Admr, on 741.85	37.09
		55.266.68
	Brot up.	55.266.68
	of Sam. Cobb & others on 1974.50	98.71
	of Hep[zibah] Howard on 221.06	11.05
	of Geo. B. Doane Admr, on 265.26	13.26
	of H. Sigourney, Admr, on 850.28	42.50
	of C. Cushing, Admr on 442.13	22.10
	of Jos: Foster, Admr on 765.30	38.26
		55.492.58
	Brot up	55.492.58
	of E. S. Livermore, on 307.55	14.09
	of C. W. Greene, on 2790.08	139.50
	of [David] Little, Sugden[?] & Wadlin, on 8.507.86	425.35
	of M. Wise, on 754.98	37.74
	of Tobias Lord, on 458.33	22.90
	of H. McCullough, on 458.33	22.90
	of Clark & Wacker, Admrs on 1375.	68.75
		56.223.81
	Brot up	56.223.81
	of B. P. Tilden, on 136.67	6.80
	of W. Dall on 3025.	151.25
	of T. Wells, Admr, on 1067	53.35
	of Same, on 46.13	2.30

of E. Gay, assee. of English, on 366.67	18.33
of David Hinkley, on 930.91	46.50
of C. Brown Exr, on 458.33	22.91
of Leml. Shaw, Admr on 2464.15.	123.20
of N. E. Ins. Co. on 4592.50	229.62
of Hathaway & Clapp, on 2755.50	137.77
	57.015.84
Brot up	57.015.84
of Thos. D Cutts, on 1022.35.	51.11
of W. Shaw, & als, Exrs of D. Huntress, on 2755.50	137.77
of D. Sargent, Admr, on 470.25	23.51
of M. Wheeler, on 281.92. & 261	27.14
of S. Codman, on 17.595.72 & on 709.28	915.22
of Thos. Dennie, on 459.41	22.91
of Thos. Lewis, on 630.45.	31.52
of Jona. Mason, on 1375	68.75
	58.292.97
Brot up	58.292.97
of C[aleb] Loring, surviving part[ne]r on 2499.79. & 1615.21	205.74
of L[ynde] Walter, on 2108.	105.44
of P. Bessom, 833.26	41.66
of Eliza. Amory, Adx, on 3385.67	169.28
of Edw. Cruft, on 107.59	5.37
of Peter Coffin on 137.50	6.87
of B. Brierly & als Exrs on 91.67	4.58
of J[ames] Shapley & als, on 146.61.	7.33
of Jno Haven, Admr, 91.61	4.58
	58.843.82
Brot up	58.843.82
of Wm Gardiner, on 36.67	1.83
of Perez Morton, on 3475.97.	173.79
of B. Humphrey, on 366.66.	18.33
of N. Whiting, Admr, on 939.41.	46.97
of N[ehemiah] Parsons, Assee, on 265.26.	13.26
of S. Gorham, 618.97	30.94
of Thos. Williams on 229.17	11.45
of B[enjamin] P. Homer, on 2701.21.	135.06

of H[annah] Smith, Adx, on 10.987.48	549.37
of M. L. Pickard, on 1680.69	84.00
of S. Bean, Admr, on 2980.12	149.00
	60.057.82
Brot up	60.057.82
of Titus Welles, Exr of Touro, on, 3180.	159.00
of J. C. Jones, on 2073.04	103.67
of E. Hall, & als, on 1054.16	52.70
of C. M. Plumer, 1143.68.	57.16
of E[benezer] Gay, Assee of [Samuel] Soley on 248.69 @ 2 pr ct	42.96
of R. Newcomb, on 1283.33	64.16
of J. Thomas, on 220.74	11.00
of Jas. Harding on 1638.45.	81.92
of Mr [William] Gray, 1 pr ct, on 110.000	1.100.00
	61.730.39
Brot up	61.730.39
of Jas. Thompson, on 8.878.71 @ 3 pr ct	266.35
of Jas Sheafe, on 4.738.16	236.90
of Jos. Cutts & also on [6691.68][82]	[334.58]
of [Gideon] Tucker & [Edward] Norris [on 62.26]	3.11
Deductions from Comms.	
— refunded J. Sumner	233.56
paid to J. Nourse, on R. Shapley's claim	125.76
Comns. on checks Nos 58.39.45.47, 44.43.46 retained, & cancelled amt to 16.414.92	820.64
Extras	
Neptune	500
Topaz	60
Various little charges, for translating, & in Mercury	1004.
Waddel[l]	100
Cutts	50
Mercury, Pearson	4500
Dickerson	1000
Boyd	1000
Robbins	
Fame	1.500
Newcomb	200
Ocean	500

82. Bracketed figures are supplied from the printed list.

M[ercury] Ayres	1000
<Mr. Waddell of Philadelphia	100>
<of Cutts	50>

AD. MWalB.

CHAPTER 5. A Lawyer in Congress

Webster's eight years in the House and nineteen in the Senate presented him with opportunities to use his legal experience to further legislation favored by his political allies. His position in Congress also allowed him to promote laws that directly benefited both his current and his future clients. His attention to bills authorizing the payment of foreign claims, for example, dovetailed with his expected employment by the potential claimants. There is no evidence, however, that his manipulation of the legislative process in the interests of private parties involved bribery or the theft of public funds. Although he strove to keep these machinations secret, he did not consider them unethical. Rather, he feared the political repercussions from their disclosure. Webster operated in a gray area. In the acrimonious political atmosphere of Jacksonian Washington, the nation's representatives rewrote the rules of the political game. The moral rhetoric of public duty that characterized the early years of the nation gave way to partisanship and the open politicization of federal office holding. While at times Webster lamented these changes, he fully understood their potential for personal financial gain. In the three sections that follow, we present material illustrative of Webster's participation in the legislative process. The first examines Webster's life-long concern with federal bankruptcy legislation and the treatment of insolvent debtors. The others explore the ethical dimension of Webster's legislative career through an examination of his relationships with the Bank of the United States and the businessmen who held claims against Denmark, France, and the Kingdom of the Two Sicilies.

I. LEGISLATION: FEDERAL BANKRUPTCY LAW

During his first two terms in the House (1813–1817), Webster took no significant part in the legislative process. In the 1820s, however, when he returned to the House and took the chairmanship of the Judiciary Committee, he became the focal point for the promotion of several pieces of legislation designed to strengthen the national government. These included a national bankruptcy law, the restructuring of the federal judicial system, and a new federal criminal code.[1] In the formulation of this

1. Reform of the federal judicial system and federal criminal code will be covered in *Legal Papers*, 3.

legislation Webster drew on the assistance of his friends, especially Joseph Story and Jeremiah Mason. Sectional rivalry between the North, on the one hand, and the South and West, on the other, and the clash of agricultural and commercial interests, permitted enactment of only the last of these projects during this decade.

Upon moving to the Senate in 1827, he became chairman of its Judiciary Committee and, in 1832, of the Finance Committee. As an opposition senator he took less of a lead in drafting new legislation, choosing instead to sit on special committees that dealt with the tariff, the rechartering of the Bank of the United States, and congressional reapportionment. When the onset of hard times in the late 1830s brought renewed calls for federal relief, he resuscitated one of his earlier pet projects, a national bankruptcy system.

In 1800 the Federalist majority in Congress enacted a bankruptcy law patterned after the existing English system.[2] Although this law gave only large-scale creditors a remedy against merchant debtors, its sponsors believed it would preempt the field and counteract the fraudulent practices that occurred under state insolvency laws. A national system, moreover, would cure defects in the common law which favored local creditors over distant ones. Under the common law, the first creditor to attach a debtor's property received a priority over later attachments. Under the bankruptcy system, all the creditors shared in the debtor's property on a *pro rata* basis.

The statute gave any creditor claiming a debt greater than $1000 the authority to institute proceedings against a commercial debtor if the creditor feared the debtor had committed an "act of bankruptcy" (i.e., fraudulent concealment or conveyance of goods, or an intention to flee the jurisdiction). In return for the surrender of the debtor's property, and with the concurrence of two thirds of the creditors, a U.S. district court judge could discharge the debtor from all his debts. Creditors who held debts less than $1000 would continue to rely on common law collection procedures; noncommercial debtors retained the benefit of state insolvency laws.

The Federalists did not intend this bankruptcy statute as a general system of relief. It did not give small creditors, shopkeepers, or artisans power over small debtors, nor did it envision a system of voluntary bank-

2. 2 U. S. Statutes at Large 19 (1800). Bankruptcy laws provided a procedure for discharging the debts of bankrupt merchants; insolvency legislation began as a means of freeing any debtor imprisoned for debt. By the early nineteenth century commercially oriented states began to incorporate into their insolvency laws provisions for discharging debts. It was this latter feature which raised constitutional questions for the Supreme Court. Most lawyers and judges at the time did not draw a clear distinction between bankruptcy and insolvency.

ruptcy in which a debtor, on his own initiative, surrendered his property in exchange for a discharge of his debts. It reflected, instead, an eighteenth-century view of the economy—that men who engaged in commerce formed a separate segment of an ordered society for whose benefit the legislature might enact specific legislation. The Jeffersonians, who rejected both this traditional view and the centralist tenets of the Federalist program, worked to end the bankruptcy system as quickly as possible. After three years of controversial operation, they finally repealed it.[3] In the absence of federal bankruptcy, the states broadened their insolvency statutes, setting the stage for the adjudication of their constitutional status.

When Webster came to Washington in 1813, he involved himself in working for the reenactment of the Federalist bankruptcy system. In December 1816 he wrote to Justice Story seeking his advice on possible alterations to a bill then in committee. Webster was sensitive to the necessity of changing the scope of the bill in order to gain enough support for its passage.

> The Committee will report a Bankruptcy Bill, in a few days, & some of us are determined to bring the House to act upon it, one way or the other.
>
> If the Bill should pass at all, I fancy it will not pass before the first of February; but I should nevertheless thank you to forward me any suggestions that may occur to you, for altering any part of the Bill as reported last year. My own notion is, to limit as far as may be, the description of persons liable to the Act, so as to shut out shoemakers, tailors, & other artificers, & to confine the Bill to such as are really & substantially merchants & traders. If, however, the Bill should find more friends, by being more general, I wd. not object to giving it that shape.[4]

Though Webster left his seat at the close of the session, his Supreme Court engagements brought him to Washington for each new Congress. At each session he observed the attempts by representatives from the commercial cities to enact a new bankruptcy law. In 1818 the bill again lost when representatives from rural New England joined the southern and western opposition.[5]

In 1819 the Supreme Court heard the first of the constitutional cases dealing with the validity of state insolvency laws, *Sturges* v. *Crownin-*

3. 2 U. S. Statutes at Large 248 (1803).

4. DW to Joseph Story, December 9, 1816, mDW 2007; *W & S*, 16: 36–37. On February 24, 1817, the House postponed action on the bill indefinitely.

5. "The Bankrupt bill is lost—it might have been carried, if all N. E. had been in favor of it" (DW to William Sullivan, February 27, 1818, mDW 2184; *Correspondence*, 1: 219).

shield.[6] Although Webster had participated for the defense in the lower court case, he did not argue the appeal. Crowninshield's attorneys asserted that a discharge under the New York insolvency law provided a good defense to Sturges's suit to collect a debt. In an opinion that reflected division among the justices, Chief Justice Marshall ruled that states might enact insolvency legislation in the absence of federal legislation, but that such statutes could not operate retroactively in violation of the contract clause of the Constitution.

Following the *Sturges* decision, Congressional proponents of bankruptcy made new attempts to enact legislation in the belief that only Congress had the power to sanction the discharge of debts contracted prior to the passage of a bankruptcy law. The depression of 1819 fed these efforts. In 1820–1821 bankruptcy supporters proposed legislation in the Senate which for the first time offered a form of voluntary bankruptcy, in which any person imprisoned for a debt might file a petition in bankruptcy to gain both freedom and a discharge. In broadening the scope of the bill, its supporters reflected the opinion that a debtor's obligation to repay his creditors should no longer be considered a sacred moral duty. Rather it was a feature of a market economy that utilized commercial credit. The duty to repay did not exist outside the law, but was a function of the law itself.

Webster, too, had begun to see the danger in a system that failed to free the debtor to begin anew. Only widespread property ownership, he believed, guaranteed a stable society. In 1820 he wrote a response to an article that had appeared in the English *Quarterly Review* (Document 42). The article pictured New York as a debtor's paradise where the insolvency law provided debtors with a quick release from both prison and obligation. After asserting that American practices did not favor debtors, Webster set forth his formulation of the role of property ownership in a republican society.

When Webster became chairman of the Judiciary Committee on his return to Congress in the fall of 1823, his first task was to seek the support of the House to bring a bankruptcy bill to the floor. When his own committee opposed the legislation, he tried to maneuver around its recommendation (Document 43). The following April he asked Story for his suggestions: "As to the bankrupt law, pray give me your ideas of an

6. 4 Wheaton 122 (1819). DW's pleadings are in *Sturges* v. *Crowninshield*, USCC, DMass, May 1819. On February 15, 1819 DW wrote to Jeremiah Mason: "Nothing has been as yet done with the Bankruptcy—and it seems too late to say any thing. The question is before the C[our]t whether the state Bankruptcy Laws are valid. The General Opinion is, that the six Judges now here will be equally divided on the point. I confess however I have a strong suspicion, there will be an opinion, and that that Opinion will be *against* the state laws." mDW 2643.

outline, as I must bring forward some resolutions on that subject before the end of the session."[7]

Webster offered a resolution but the House took no action on it. At the fall session of Congress Webster pressed Story to send him a draft bill.

> I regret not to have seen you, altho. I have nothing very particular to communicate. I should feel greatly obliged to you, if in the multitude of your concerns, you could find time to make a drft of a Bankrupt Law. I am pledged to do something on that subject; & mean to bring it forward early in the Session. The fewer the *words* in which the bill can be drawn the better. As far as convenient, please place *references*, in margin.[8]

At the same time South Carolina Senator Robert Y. Hayne presented a long bill of ninety-four sections based on both an earlier Senate bill and the revised British Bankruptcy Law of 1825.[9] This bill incorporated a semivoluntary provision which allowed any debtor petitioned into bankruptcy to receive a discharge by consenting to the proceedings. Webster's House committee was also hard at work. In December 1825 Webster sent Story a draft resolution in which he proposed voluntary bankruptcy for noncommercial interests.

> By direction of our committee I brought in today a resolution for a bankrupt law. I think there is some chance for it if we get a good bill. I must call it up on Monday, the 16th instant, by which time I hope to hear from you. What say you to the following:—
>
> "Resolved, that all merchants, &c. (using the common terms,) committing an act of bankruptcy, shall be liable to a commission, at suit of creditors, &c.; and that other persons, not merchants and traders, who shall file a voluntary declaration of insolvency, shall be subject to the law," &c.
>
> Unless we make some provision for the non-traders, we cannot possibly carry along the bill.[10]

A few days later he received a letter from a friend, printed below, with information on the new English law. On January 3, 1826, Webster reported a simple resolution (Document 44) in favor of a bankruptcy system. In the Senate, Hayne prepared to introduce his bankruptcy bill. Webster informed his brother of its progress:

> The Bankrupt Bill will be introduced, & has a fair chance of being past. I hope it will be first brought in to the Senate, but if it does not

7. April 10, 1824, *Correspondence*, 1: 356. On January 4, 1824, Story had written to DW: "What hope of a Bankruptcy Act, why will you not ask me to put one into the shape of a code of articles. I want to try my hand at codifying a Bankrupt ordinance." W. Story, 1: 437.

8. November 19, 1825, mDW 5142; *W & S*, 16: 116–117.

9. 6 Geo. 4, c. 16, s. 133–134 (1825).

10. December 31, 1825, *PC*, 1: 400–401.

> soon make its appearance there, I shall begin the business in the House. The late revision of the English system has greatly facilitated our Labours.[11]

The Senate, however, did not act.

At the 1826–1827 session Webster took Hayne's bill, and after altering it, offered it as House Bill 332. In his version, Webster approached a fully voluntary system by permitting the discharge of any nontrader who declared his insolvency with one creditor consenting.

> *Sec. 94 And be it further enacted, That whenever any person resident within the United States, not being a merchant or person actually using the trade of merchandise by buying and selling in gross or by retail, not dealing in exchange, nor as a banker, broker, factor, underwriter, or marine insurer*, shall file in the office of the clerk of the District Court of the Judicial District in which he or she may reside, a declaration in writing, signed by such person, acknowled[ging] before the sd. clerk, or before any Judge of any court of record in the U. States, that he is insolvent or unable to pay his debts, and any one creditor of such person, or a greater number being Partners, whose single debt shall amount to <five> 300 dollars, or any two or more creditors, whose debts shall amount to one thousand dollars, shall petition in writing against such person that he may be made a Bankrupt, such declaration and petition shall then be published in some Newspaper, and such publication thereof, shall be deemed and taken to be conclusive proof, of an act of bankruptcy and such person <that> shall thereupon be declared a bankrupt and shall be subject to all the provisions of this act.[12]

The House never acted on Webster's proposal, and in January 1827 the Senate defeated Hayne's bill. Story summed up the fate of such legislation:

> The bankrupt bill has been lost, and under circumstances which will forbid any attempt to revive it for many years. It has had much of the best talent, eloquence, and influence of the Senate to support it; but it has failed from causes not likely to be overcome in future times. It interferes with State policy, pride, and prejudice; with the interests of some, with the political expectations of others; with the anti-federalism of others; and, above all, with that mass of public opinion, which in different States of the Union floats in opposite directions, even when apparently impelled by the same common cause. I have always had some confidence that a bankrupt law would be passed, but I now begin to believe that the power will, in the National Government, forever remain a dead letter.[13]

11. DW to Ezekiel Webster, January 29, 1826, mDW 5274; PC, 1: 402.

12. The amending language is in DW's hand. *Bill to establish a uniform system of bankruptcy*, January 2, 1827, mDW 41427, 41516–41519.

13. Joseph Story to Reverend Bra-

Later, in February, the Supreme Court announced its long awaited decision in *Ogden* v. *Saunders*.[14] The case dealt with the question left undecided in the *Sturges* case: the validity of a state insolvency law which discharged debts incurred after the enactment of the law. In a split decision, the court held such laws to be constitutional. In a separate opinion, however, the court decided that a discharge of indebtedness would be effective only in the state where it had been obtained. Webster, who had argued for the creditor Saunders against the validity of the New York law, had won the battle for his client but lost the war over the constitutional question. By sustaining the New York statute, the court made it less likely that future bankruptcy legislation would come forth from Congress. Moreover, the passage of state stay-and-appraisal laws and the easing of the rigors of imprisonment for debt weakened the pressure on Congress for national legislation. Not until the panic of 1837 would pressure again build for federal legislation.

During this intervening period Webster occasionally expressed his views on the subject of insolvency. In April 1830 the founder of the Boston Prison Discipline Society solicited Webster's opinion on the subject of imprisonment for debt. Webster's response, printed below, reveals the position of a moderate who favored banning imprisonment for small debts. In the Senate, Webster also worked in favor of an insolvents' relief law for federal debtors.[15] In 1834 he applauded the efforts of a Massachusetts legislator who had fought to abolish the practice of secret attachment of debtor property (DW to Samuel B. Walcott, February 28, 1834, printed below), and reflected back on his own experiences as a young attorney.

The onset of hard times in the late 1830s renewed the call for federal bankruptcy relief. On April 1, 1840, Webster introduced a bill that featured both voluntary bankruptcy for any debtor and involuntary bankruptcy for merchants.[16] For two months the Senate debated the merits of the voluntary and involuntary aspects of bankruptcy and its application to corporations. During the course of the debate a New Jersey resident forwarded his comments to Webster on several questions about the law

---

zer, February 4, 1827, W. Story, 1: 514.

14. 12 Wheaton 213 (1827). DW argued for Saunders, the plaintiff below. He had also argued the case in 1824 but the court had not been able to reach a decision.

15. 4 U. S. Statutes at Large 467 (1831); DW to James Buchanan, September 24, 1831, mDW 9586.

16. Joseph Story's son claimed that his father drafted this bill (W. Story, 2: 407). There is no evidence in the second volume of the Story correspondence to substantiate this assertion. In fact, Story's letter of May 10, 1840, printed below, indicates that Story did *not* draft the bankruptcy bill. In 1837 Van Buren had proposed a bankruptcy bill applicable only to banks. The Whigs defeated it.

raised in a letter by "An Old Merchant" published in the *Newark Daily Advertiser*, printed below. The problem of the applicability of the proposed law to corporations under the involuntary provisions also troubled Justice Story. On May 10, 1840, he wrote Webster a letter, printed below, indicating the damaging consequences to New England manufacturing if corporations became subject to an involuntary petition of bankruptcy. As the focal point in the agitation for a bankruptcy law, Webster received many letters from the law's potential beneficiaries. One of these, printed below, drew a parallel between indebtedness and Southern slavery.

On May 18, 1840, Webster delivered a major address on the legislation (Document 45). Arguing in favor of both forms of bankruptcy, he stressed the inclusion of voluntary bankruptcy as a relief measure. Bankruptcy, he said, meant no more than failure, "an occurrence in the life and fortunes of an individual."[17] In June he spoke again. This time he sought to assure creditors that even a purely voluntary system of bankruptcy protected their interests by ending the system of preferences.[18] On June 25, 1840, the Senate approved Webster's basic voluntary-involuntary system. The House did not act on it, however, and the session ended. With the presidential campaign in full swing, the Whigs made passage of the bankruptcy bill part of their party program. In June 1841 at a special session of Congress, the Whigs reenacted the Webster bill in the Senate. When the House seemed about to defeat it, Clay packaged the bankruptcy bill with two other pieces of legislation. Together they gathered sufficient support to win passage. The law went into effect in February 1842, but encountered so much hostility that in 1843 it met the same fate as its Federalist predecessor. Though the Whigs offered to sacrifice the voluntary provision in order to save the involuntary part, opposition to all forms of federal bankruptcy was too strong to save it.[19]

DOCUMENT 42. WEBSTER ON RIGHTS OF CREDITOR AND DEBTOR

Examination of some Remarks in the Quarterly Review on the Laws of Creditor and Debtor in the United States.

* * * * * * * * * * * *

We have space at present to take notice of one only of the topics, dis-

17. *W & S*, 9: 6.
18. *W & S*, 9: 26–39.
19. DW had become Harrison's secretary of state, and was therefore not in the Senate when the bill passed: 5 U. S. Statutes at Large 440 (1841); 614 (1843) (repeal); Charles Warren, *Bankruptcy in United States History* (Cambridge, Mass., 1935), pp. 60–86. Warren overstates the Whigs' support for voluntary bankruptcy. They saw it principally as a short-term relief measure which they would have had no qualms about abandoning.

cussed in these articles. It relates to the American law of *creditor and debtor*; about which the reviewer has published extracts from Mr. Bristed's book,[20] with comments. Mr. Bristed is an Englishman, by birth and education. He has lived, as it appears, for some time in the city of New York, and has published a book upon the resources of this country. Some observations were made on that work in a former number of this journal.[21] Referring to these observations, we have now only to say of Mr. Bristed's general character, as an authority, that he is beyond ordinary measure destitute of all accuracy and precision. There are, of course, many important facts collected in his book, and a mass of extracts from public documents, in some degree useful, perhaps, to those who do not possess the same matter in a better form; but his own opinions, and inferences, and observations upon manners, are not to be received but with great allowance. Mr. Bristed never speaks with any qualification. He has little general, and no intimate knowledge of the state of things in this country, and he speaks only from what lies within his own immediate and confined observation. With him all peculiarities are general truths, and all exceptions become rules. We have hardly patience with a man, who could write such a paragraph, as the first, quoted from his book, in the article in the Quarterly Review,[22] which we beg leave to transcribe again, and to proceed to make some remarks upon it.

'The laws of this country generally favour the *debtor* at the expense of the creditor, and so far encourage dishonesty. The number of insolvents in every state is prodigious, and continually increasing. They very seldom pay any part of their debts, but get discharged by the state insolvent acts with great facility, secrete what property they please for their own use, without the creditor's being able to touch a single stiver. There is no bankrupt law in the United States, and no appeal, in these matters, to the Federal courts; whence in every State the insolvent acts operate as a general jail delivery of all debtors, and a permanent scheme, by which creditors are defrauded of their property. The British merchants and manufacturers, who have trusted our [*our*?] people, doubtless understand this.'

He adds, 'that in a single city, New York, more than six thousand of its inhabitants were declared insolvent in one year.'

Now in the first place, almost every matter of *fact*, asserted in this paragraph, is stated incorrectly and untruly. It is *not true*, that in every state the insolvent laws operate as a general jail delivery of all debtors; there being, in a majority of the states, no insolvent laws at all.

It is *not true*, that there is no appeal in these matters, to the Federal courts; on the contrary, there is an appeal, in all cases, from decisions in

20. John Bristed (1778–1855), author of *The Resources of the United States of America* (New York, 1818).

21. *North American Review*, 7 (September 1818): 401–427, signed by John Gallison.

22. *Quarterly Review*, 21 (January 1819): 1–25.

the state courts, on the insolvent laws of the state, to the supreme court of the United States; an appeal, which exists not only theoretically, but practically, and has been resorted to often, and with effect.

It is *not true*, that the number of insolvents, meaning such as have been discharged under statute provisions, is prodigious in every state, and increasing. In most of the states, as we have observed, there are no such laws, and of course no 'prodigious numbers,' who have been, or who can be, discharged under such laws.

Having now shown how destitute of all correctness and all *truth* is the foregoing paragraph from Mr. Bristed's book, we proceed to describe the real state of the case.

At the formation of the present government in 1787, it was provided by the national constitution, that Congress should have power to establish uniform rules on the subject of Bankruptcy throughout the United States. This power was not exercised until 1778 [1798], when a uniform system of Bankruptcy was established by act of Congress. It met with great opposition, arising in a great variety of motives, and was repealed four or five years afterwards. It is, no doubt, to be lamented that a fair experiment was not given to this law. It is a subject on which it seems necessary that there should be some legislative provision; and notwithstanding the frauds which will be, and are committed under Bankrupt laws, even well administered, and which have led such men as Lord Eldon, and Sir Samuel Romilly[23] to express doubts of their general utility, yet we know not any other mode of providing for the cases continually arising in commercial societies, and which call loudly for some provision. After the repeal of the law, however, individual states, acting upon the supposition that as Congress had not exercised the power, or had discontinued its exercise, of establishing a general law, for the whole country, they had a right to provide insolvent laws, as a part of their own local legislation, enacted such laws, and gave them operation. Among others, the state of New York passed an insolvent law, in the year 1811,[24] and, as was to be expected, in the first year of its operation, many discharges were obtained under it. It was found that this law not only gave too great facilities in obtaining discharges, but that it led also to fraudulent applications from debtors, coming from other states. The law was repealed, we believe, within a year after its enactment; and it was, we suppose, during the period of this very short and extraordinary act, that Mr. Bristed finds his six thousand discharged in one year. Here then is a single act, from which a general law, and a general practice, is unhesitatingly inferred. 'The British merchants and manufacturers who have trusted our people

23. John Scott (1751–1838), Earl of Eldon, Lord Chancellor (1801–1806, 1807–1827); Samuel Romilly (1757–1818), English lawyer and law reformer, sponsored an amendment to the English bankruptcy act in 1806 (46 Geo. 3, c. 135).

24. Laws, N.Y., c. 123 (1811).

doubtless understand this.' Does Mr. Bristed mean that the credit of American merchants is not good, in England? It would be new to us, indeed, to hear such a remark. Surely never was, not only all due credit, but all undue credit more easily obtained, than by the American merchants, for British manufactures.

The flippant and off-hand remark, that the laws of this country generally favour the debtor, at the expense of the creditor, is grossly incorrect, and can hardly be pardoned. There may be, among the state legislatures, an occasional relaxation, but to say that the general scope of the laws of this country is to favour the debtor at the expense of the creditor, is absolutely untrue, and calumnious. We still hold in almost, if not in every state, to the imprisonment of the person for debt; we still hold every man, to be in law capable of paying to the uttermost farthing; and therefore we apply the old principle, *solvat per corpus, qui non possit crumena.*[25] We discourage marriage settlements, and family settlements, to an extent, in the opinion of some, far too great; even lawgivers and tribunals all look with jealousy on trusts and entailments, and all the various modes of tying up estates, and rendering them unalienable; and all this simply from respect to the rights of creditors.

In most of the states also, the fee simple of the debtor's estate may be taken, to satisfy the creditor; and lastly, we hold, that whatever laws the individual states may pass respecting insolvents, such laws, if they in any manner impair the validity of contracts, are absolutely null and void. We have from the first introduced and maintained this great and salutary, and protecting principle in the fundamental articles of the national government; and yet Mr. Bristed can say, and the Reviewers in England can believe, that in this country the laws are generally made to favour debtors at the expense of the creditors! Every well informed man knows the difficulty of legislating on the subject of insolvents; and none better than the eminent living judicial characters in England. We now speak of the *insolvent laws*, as distinguished from the bankrupt laws; since the insolvent laws which individual states have sometimes enacted in this country, resemble the *cessio bonorum*[26] of the civil law, and the insolvent laws of England, much more than the bankrupt system of that country.

* * * * * *

We have thus alluded to the experience of England on the subject of insolvent debtors, not by way of an idle retort, but to expose the intrinsic difficulty of the subject, and to shut up the mouths of half-

25. He who does not have a purse, pays with his body.

26. Cession of goods, the assignment by a debtor of all his property for the benefit of creditors.

informed, superficial and self-sufficient scribblers and rebukers, on both sides the Atlantic. Would it not be wrong from the facts which we have stated to infer a plausible case of enormous fraud and corruption against English justice? If we were to try our hand at such a paragraph as Mr. Bristed has written and the Quarterly Review has cited against us, might we not say, 'England is not a country for a man to recover his debts. All her merchants, who are debtors, are provided for, by what she calls her system of Bankruptcy, a stupendous system, which many of her most eminent lawyers have been honest enough to confess was productive of unmeasured fraud and injustice; and as to all the rest of her subjects who may owe any thing, there is the insolvent debtors' court, where any body may be discharged; and of this court it is enough to say, that during all its existence, although no man can be discharged without surrendering all his property, which the law says shall go to his creditors, yet in truth no creditor ever gets any thing. How much the officers of the court get, we do not know; and what becomes of that part which they do not get, we do not know, but we do know that the creditor gets nothing.' We forbear. It is hardly fit to write such paragraphs, even for the mere purpose of shewing how easily they may be written. It is a dangerous curiosity to commit sins, only to learn or to show with what facility sins may be committed.

An act of the last session of Parliament was intended, we believe, to have continued the insolvent debtors' law to the present session.[27] Owing to mistake, however, the purpose was not effected, and the law is supposed to have expired, and proceedings under it are for the present discontinued. The subject, however, is before Parliament, and it will give us unmixed pleasure if the English Government shall be able to adopt such legislation on this equally important and difficult subject, or shall satisfy the necessities of its own case, and afford light to the lawgivers of other countries. In the mean time let it not be understood that the law of creditor and debtor is in a worse state for the creditor in this country than in others. As before observed, some of the states may have occasionally departed, and may still occasionally depart from the dictates of enlightened wisdom on this subject, from a disposition to relieve hardship, and from a vain and illusory hope of finding, in mere remedial legislation, a relief against the pressure of the times, and the stagnation of trade. But the general scope and tendency of our laws is to give creditors full and ample remedies, and to render property of all sorts convenient for debts. We may say, indeed, that there is no country in the world, in which a regard for the rights of property is more likely to prevail; for in no country was property ever so equally diffused, or

27. Debtors Relief Act, 2 Geo. 2, c. 22 (1729); 59 Geo. 3, c. 129 (1819).

was so great a portion of the numerical population interested directly in the laws which protect it. We look upon this so equal distribution of property, and to the regard paid to the rights of property in this country, as the great safeguards and security of the Commonwealth. Almost every man among us is interested in preserving the state of things as it is; because almost every man possesses property, and while he cannot see what he might gain, he sees clearly what he might lose, by change. We think we may perceive here a fair ground of belief in the preservation of our republican forms of government. It is not less the language of reason than of experience, that property should have influence in the state, whenever such a state of things exists, as that military fame is not supreme. If the tendency of the laws and institutions of society be such, as that property accumulates in few hands, a real aristocracy, in effect, exists in the land. This is not a merely artificial, but a natural aristocracy; a concentration of political power and influence in few hands, in consequence of large masses of property having accumulated in such hands. There is not a more dangerous experiment than to place property in the hands of one class, and political power in those of another. Indeed such a state of things could not long exist. We have seen something like it in the ancient noblesse of France, in relation to whom the attempt seemed to be to make up, in positive power, or artificial distinction, what was wanting in the natural influence of property and character. The generality of these personages with all their pretensions to rank, and all their blazoning of heraldry, were infinitely inferior in respectability, and in just influence in the state, to hundreds of the untitled but independent landholders of Great Britain. It will be disastrous, indeed, for this latter country, whenever a separation shall take place between the influence, the indirect, but the natural and salutary influence of property, and political influence, or political power. They would not, and as we have already observed, in the absence of direct military despotism, cannot be long separated. If one changes hands, so will the other. If the property cannot retain the political power, the political power will draw after it the property. If orator Hunt and his fellow labourers should, by any means, obtain more political influence in the counties, towns, and boroughs of England, than the Marquis of Buckingham, Lord Stafford, Lord Fitzwilliam, and the other noblemen and gentlemen of great landed estates, these estates would inevitably change hands. At least so it seems to us; and therefore when Sir Francis Burdett, the Marquis of Tavistock,[28] and other individuals of rank and fortune, propose to

28. Henry Hunt (1773–1835), English radical politician; Richard Temple-Nugent-Brydges-Chandos-Grenville (1776–1839), Marquis of Buckingham; George Granville Leveson-Gower (1758–1833), Marquis of Stafford; William Wentworth Fitzwilliam (1748–1833); Francis

introduce into the government annual parliaments, and universal suffrage, we can hardly forbear inquiring whether they are ready to agree that property should be as equally divided as political power; and if not, how they expect to sever things, which to us appear to be intimately connected.

These speculations, however, are beside our present purpose. We mean only to say, that, in the present state of the world, wherever the people are not subject to military rule, the government must in a great measure be under the guidance of that aggregate of indirect but salutary influences, of which *property* is an essential ingredient; along with other ingredients, doubtless, of intelligence, public spirit, and high and fair character. And that as in this country almost the whole people partake of the blessings of property, so must they also partake in the desire to protect property, and of course in the laws which furnish that protection. The evils and difficulties which exist among us, in regard to insolvency, belong to the subject itself, and are not confined to our community. The highly commercial state of the world has elevated two subjects of legislation, in our day, to a very great degree of importance. One respects the prevention and punishment of those crimes which are committed on property, such as theft, forgery, &c. which have increased, in late times, far more than the more violent offences, such as murder, and assault, and the other crimes which spring from passion, revenge, or cruelty. The other respects the provisions necessary to be made relative to insolvents, and the proper degree in which there may be a mitigation, in certain cases, of the ancient rigour of imprisonment for debt. These important subjects are full of inherent difficulties. None of the ancient codes furnish examples which can be safely followed, because such a state of society as exists now existed in none of the ancient states. The systems adopted among the modern nations are not yet satisfactory to themselves. In France, we know that these subjects have lately attracted much consideration. In Holland, a revision of the whole system is before a commission appointed for that purpose. In England, one of these subjects, the reformation of the criminal code, is before a committee of the House of Commons, at the head of which is Sir James Mackintosh.[29] The bankrupt laws are, or lately have been, under investigation before another committee, and the Insolvent Debtor Act is receiving great attention from some of the principal men in either House of Parliament. In our own country, we know that Congress has for two sessions discussed a proposed system of bankruptcy, and that several of the state legislatures are desirous, as far as their power extends, to make just and

Burdett (1770–1844), politician and popular reformer; Francis Russell (1788–1861), Marquis of Tavistock.

29. James Mackintosh (1765–1832), English lawyer and scholar.

wise provisions on the subject of insolvency, in case the power of Congress to establish a bankrupt system shall not be exercised.

Extract. *North American Review*, 11 (July 1820): 197–208.

DOCUMENT 43. REPORT ON A SYSTEM OF BANKRUPTCY

[December 30, 1823]

Mr Webster, from the Committee on the Judiciary who were instructed to inquire into the expediency of establishing an Uniform System of Bankruptcy, reported that it is not expedient to establish such system.[30] Mr Webster observed that the Committee had thought it proper to make an early communication of their opinion on this important subject to the House. In this opinion a great majority of the Committee concurred; indeed, he believed, he was the only member who had the misfortune to differ from that opinion. The whole Committee, however, were desirous of giving a fair opportunity to those Gentlemen, who, like himself were in favor of the system, to bring the question before the House. Such an opportunity would now be afforded, as any member might move to amend the Report, by altering it from a negative to an affirmative character. It seemed to him to be proper, on several accounts, that the opinion of the House, on the general question of the expediency of a Bankrupt law should be taken, before a Bill should be brought. In such a Bill there must necessarily be much of prolixity, & detail; and very much discussion might be expected to arise on particular provisions, which would seem to be misplaced, until there should be some reason to think that the general measure, itself, was acceptable to a majority of the House. Until there was reason to believe that, such a discussion upon details would have no effect but to consume time.

If the House should now reverse this Report, the Committee would cheerfully prepare & bring in a Bill. He would take the liberty to suggest, however, whether the best way would not be to proceed by Resolution.[31] In this way, perhaps, not only the general question might be settled, but, if settled in favor of the measure, subsequent Resolutions might proceed to settle some of the general outlines of the system; such, for example, as what classes of persons the system should extend to,—whether only to Traders, technically or legally so called, or to all persons,

30. For the report, see mDW 41045.

31. DW is suggesting that instead of considering a statute at this time, the House merely express its opinion on the various issues raised by the proposed bankruptcy legislation. This would keep the subject before the House but not present the members with a decision on whether or not to enact it.

(by proper description,) who have, ordinarily, occasion to use extensive credits;—and whether it shall be a temporary, or permanent system, &c &c. He made these suggestions, only for the consideration of those, who, like himself, were in favor of the system;—and to the end that they might have an option, to proceed by way of Resolution, or by motion to amend the present Report, he would move that the Report lie upon the Table.

AD(DW). NN. Published in *Annals of Congress*, 18th Cong., 1st sess., pp. 895–896.

FROM CLEMENT CORNELL BIDDLE

Dear Sir, Philadelphia 31 December 1825

Thinking that a copy of the English bankrupt act, 6 Geo. IV. Cap. 16. sent me by a friend in England, might at this time, as chairman of the committee on the Judiciary, be highly useful to you, in framing the provisions of whatever bill you may deem it expedient to report to the House on this important subject, I have taken the liberty to forward it to you. I exceedingly regret that it is not in my power, at the same time, to place in your hands, (as but a single copy was received by the last packet,[32]) a *treatise* on the bankrupt law, *as amended by this new act*, which was published in London on the 1st of September, the day the act in question went into effect.[33] Its author, the Hon. Robert Henley Eden, one of the commissioners of bankrupt, was, it appears, entrusted by the Lord Chancellor[34] to prepare the Statute; a task for which he proves himself to have been well qualified. Should you, however, be very anxious to obtain a sight of Mr Eden's work, and cannot procure it from New York or Boston, I have but little doubt, that its owner here, can be prevailed upon by me, to lend it to you.

In looking over the treatise, I was so forcibly struck with its great excellence, and the value and importance of such a copious and well digested commentary upon the law embraced in the present act, to any committee that might be instructed to prepare and report a bill on the same subject, that I have ventured to present you an abstract of the author's account of the *alterations* in the present Statute. Until you receive the work itself, this may serve to direct your attention to a comparison between the provisions of the old and new enactments, and thus

32. A transatlantic passenger and freight ship.

33. Robert Henley Eden (1789–1841), English barrister, commissioner of bankrupts, master in chancery (1826–1840), wrote *A Practical Treatise on the new Act of 6 George IV* (London, 1825), from which the excerpts related by Biddle are drawn.

34. John Scott, Lord Eldon.

enable you to test their relative merits; and, at all events, will at once, very distinctly bring under your eye all these alterations. Without then any further apology, I will proceed with this abstract.

The description of traders is collected and *extended*. Several *new acts of bankruptcy* are introduced. An insolvent trader may now *declare* it, and take steps to secure a distribution of his estate. The *proof* of various debts, not *before* proveable is now permitted; such as, contingent debts, costs, interest on promissory notes, and sureties for annuities. Peculiar indulgencies are allowed to clerks, servants, and apprentices. The *commissioners* have the power of *expunging proofs*. *All* payments, either *by* or *to* the bankrupt, without notice of bankruptcy, are protected down to the date of commission. Besides these alterations, all the old provisions, when re-enacted, were examined along with the decisions upon them, and a great number of alterations, minute in size, but important in effect, have been introduced in order to embrace or exclude cases which the old law had improperly omitted or excluded. Important alterations are made in the following points:—The expenses of witnesses; the warrant of commitment; proceedings on habeas corpus, or actions for false imprisonment; proof under joint or separate commissions; the choice, the duties and the liabilities of assignees; in liens for rent or under execution; in the mode of taking the account in set-off; in the audit and proceedings upon dividends; in the enlargement and adjournment of bankrupt examination; as to his maintenance and allowance; as to the legal objection to the certificate; and, as to requiring a new promise to pay a debt barred by the certificate, to be in writing. All debts are allowed to carry interest in the event of surplus, according to certain priorities; and finally, "an important provision has been adopted from the Scotch Sequestration Act,[35] termed the *Composition Contract*, by which, if a composition, or security for a composition, is offered, which is approved by two meetings of creditors, and by a majority of nine tenths in value of the creditors at each of such meetings, the Lord Chancellor is directed to supersede the Commission."

Such are the alterations effected in the bankrupt law of England by this new act. But, as the two closing paragraphs of Mr Eden's introduction have an important bearing upon the *system itself*, and in one of them, he touches upon the debated question, as to the *primary administration* of these laws, I will venture to transcribe them both entire.

"The above, says Mr. Eden, is a short sketch of the amendments introduced by this act. They are not only most beneficial in themselves, but they may be hailed as a prelude to a change which will alone be

35. 12 Geo. 3, c. 72 (1772) and 33 Geo. 3, c. 74 (1793), established a process for attaching the personal estate (later the entire estate) of the debtor for distribution to the creditors under civil law principles.

worth them all, and without which their value cannot be adequately appreciated; for unless a complete alteration be made in the *Tribunal* by which Bankrupt Law is *primarily* administered, it will be in vain to expect that the reproach that has attached to the system, will be removed. But as it seems certain that this subject will be brought under the consideration of Parliament in the ensuing sessions, and as the country has every prospect of receiving a vigorous, able and efficient tribunal, *in the room of the present system of commissioners*, it becomes unnecessary to enlarge, at present upon this point. It is sufficient to observe, that the present act cannot be properly objected to as premature, because it has preceded the intended alteration in the tribunal. The subject matter of each species of provision is distinct; the one relates to the *system* of law, the other to the *persons* who are to administer that law. When both are complete, we may be assured that we shall possess, if not the cheapest, at least the best and most efficient code of Bankrupt Law in Europe."

"To those who look only to the present size of the Act, without reflecting upon the extent of collateral learning which it embraces and effects; who overlook the multitude and intricacy of those decisions which it was necessary to bear in mind, not only for the purpose of amending where amendment was necessary, but of preserving, at the same time, that which incautious alteration might have disturbed; who forget the thought and circumspection necessary for accurate consideration [condensation], and the difficulty of reconciling conflicting prejudices and opinions; to such persons it may appear that little has been done. But those who look deeper, will find that this Act has been produced by no ordinary degree of attention and labour; and instead of cavilling at trifling objections, or severely criticising any errors which may be found to have been too little guarded against, they will, it is to be hoped, look to the general effect of it, and regard it as the result of an honourable and meritorious exertion to obtain a great, public, End."

I have now finished this long communication, and am, my dear sir, with sentiments of the highest respect and consideration, your most faithful and obedient servant Clement C. Biddle

ALS. DLC. Clement Cornell Biddle (1784–1855), soldier, economist, translator of Jean Baptiste Say's *Political Economy*, director and president, Philadelphia Fire Insurance Company, founder and president, Philadelphia Savings Fund Society.

DOCUMENT 44. JUDICIARY COMMITTEE REPORT

[January 3, 1826]

The Committee on the Judiciary, to whom was referred so much of the

Presidents Message as respects a uniform system of Bankruptcy.[36] Reported the following Resolution—
Resolved, That it is expedient to establish, by law, a uniform system of Bankruptcy throughout the United States.

AD(DW). DNA.

FROM AN ANONYMOUS CONSTITUENT

Sir Boston Feby 20 1826

As one of your constituents, I take the freedom to make a few remarks, on the contemplated Bankrupt Law, which hope you will excuse, promising howcver, that, fortunately I am not a subject for the operation of that act, should it pass. I am decidedly of the opinion, that no commercial state, should ever be without a uniform National Bankrupt Law. Under the last Bankrupt Law,[37] I lost money, but never complained because I probably should have lost it, had there been no such Law. It was a subject of complaint, under that Law, that the dividends were small, sometimes nothing; & that the expenses were too great, & swallowed up the greatest part of what some had to surrender. It is true that dividends frequently were small; & this is easily accounted for. There had been no *previous* Law of the kind, at that time, & many, very many, who had been unfortunate, had to work like the mole, & under every disadvantage, to get bread for their families; had been compelled to feed on the remnant left from the rapacity of creditors, besides being a constant tax on the purses & sympathy of their friends, untill both were nearly exhausted, and still the Law afforded them no relief, & the just, & unjust, were swept down the current together. When relief did come after years of suffering, they had little or nothing to surrender. Such will probably be the case in some degree should the Law now pass, & go into operation. But hereafter, when men come under that Law, as fast as they fail in business, it will be otherwise. If the expenses of that Law, were too great, I hope in this, they will be diminished. Allow me to say (& this is my principle motive for addressing you) that if my memory serves me rightly, under the late act, when a man had surrendered all his property, still he had to obtain the signature of 3/4 of all his creditors in number & amount before he could obtain a full discharge.[38] I think this shoud not be—the old saying will hold good, "that it is a poor rule, that will not work both ways." It should not be left with creditors who generally feel some irratation & also some jealousy & suspicion that the surrender is not fair to withhold, or prevent a debtor from getting a

36. In his message of December 6, 1825, President Adams urged the passage of a bankruptcy law.

37. 2 U. S. Statutes at Large 19 (1800).

38. Ibid., section 36.

discharge. When he has been *lawfully* & *sufficiently* examined, & the *competent legal authority in the case* is satisfied that the surrender is fair, or rather if it cannot be shewn by the creditors or others to be unfair; the duty of the commissioners or judge should be *imperious*—they should discharge him, & not let the *suspicion* of fraud, keep him in "durance vile"[39] perhaps as long as he lives—he is imperiously called on to surrender & should be imperiously discharged if his surrender is fair. Let the Law be *severe*, no *matter how much so*, but let him who is compelled to fall under its operation, pass *quickly* through it, & be discharged at once, *if all is fair otherwise hang*. There are Sir at this moment, thousands of worthy, but unfortunate men in these United States who if their future gains coud be protected, & their friends assist them without hazard, woud immediately emerge from the shade of despondency, resume their active occupations in society & be an acquisition to their country & friends—possibly their latter end might be like Job's of old—and their honest creditors at some future day receive their money. In fine Let the *Law be severe*—Let the *expenses attending* it, be *small* as possible—Let i[t]s operations be *short*—& let the *Law*, discharge those who are worthy of it. *Leave it not* to *the option of creditors*.

Having retired from the busy scenes of life, [and] having seen something more than half a century, I now feel no immediate interest in this business, but would offer my mite, to correct an error which I think existed in the late law, and which ought to be corrected in this, perhaps it has not escaped your notice. The subject is in good hands, & I ask pardon for the liberty I have taken. With great respect & esteem I am Sir very truly your friend, & a friend to humanity, as well as, Justice.

AL. NhHi.

FROM LOUIS DWIGHT, WITH RESPONSES BY WEBSTER

MY DEAR SIR, *Boston, April 19, 1830.*

Will you have the goodness to express your opinions on the following subjects:

1 *What do you think of imprisonment for debt for sums less than one dollar?*

2 *What do you think of imprisonment for more than one, and less than five dollars?*

3 *What do you think of imprisonment for more than five, and less than ten dollars?*

4 *What do you think of imprisonment for more than ten, and less than twenty dollars?*

39. Ten days imprisonment; here the author means imprisonment of indefinite duration.

5 *What do you think of imprisonment for more than twenty, and less than one hundred dollars?* agt it; at least to 50 Dollars; perhaps to a 100.

6 *What do you think of imprisonment for debt in any case in which there is no evidence of fraud?*

7 *What do you think of imprisonment for thirty days in cases in which the poor debtor's oath is to be taken?* useless—

8 *Can Christian imprison Christian for debt, in any case in which there is no evidence of fraud, with a good conscience?* Every Christian must judge for himself, if the law allows it. I should imprison nobody, for a debt due me, without evidence of fraud.

9 *Can Christian imprison infidel for debt, in similar circumstances, with a good conscience?*

10 *Is the penalty of imprisonment for debt well proportioned to the aggravation of the offence, in cases where there is no evidence of fraud?* I think not.

11 *What* EVILS *would result from abolishing imprisonment for debt?* frauds might, w[ithou]t very good guards.

12 *What* BENEFIT *would result from abolishing imprisonment for debt?* This wd. depend on the modifications, & the substitute.

13 *Have you ever found it necessary to imprison a man for debt due to you personally?* I never did it.

Please to communicate any facts or remarks, on other points, not embraced in these questions, but touching the general subject, which you may deem important.

By answering the above questions, in such manner as you may think proper, in order to express your opinion on the general subject of imprisonment for debt, and returning the answer to me, you will greatly oblige

Your sincere friend and obedient servant, LOUIS DWIGHT

6. question. It seems to me that when one does not pay his debts, for example, to his butcher, & baker, & Tailor, *he ought to show that he is unable, & that his inability is not fraudulent.* That is to say, he ought to show a full & fair excuse, for not paying. It does not appear to me to be enough merely for him to *say* that he cannot pay, & then to call on his creditors to *show* that his inability is merely pretended, or is fraudulent. The debtor ought to show *why* he cannot fulfil his promise—& that he has not acted fraudulently. When he has showed this, his person ought no longer to be held. He ought to be called on, first, for his own oath, & secondly, for any reasonable explanation of suspicious circumstances, if such exist. Having done this, his person ought to be discharged.

The great remedy for evils of this kind is obvious. Nineteen twentieths of the whole of it woud be relieved, if imprisonment for small debts were abolished. Small credits are often given on the confidence of being able to collect, by the terrors of the jail; great ones never.

In my humble judgment, two simple provisions would accomplish all that is absolutely required, in Massachusetts.

1. No imprisonment to be allowed, where the debt, exclusive of all costs, does not exceed 50, 75, or 100 Dlls.

2. Do away the necessity of the imprisonment for 30 days, in order to take the poor debtors oath; & to give to the magistrate, taking the oath such further powers as may be necessary to a full investigation of the fairness or fraud of the debtor's conduct. The Insolvent Laws (not Bankrupt Acts) of England might well be looked to for useful hints on this subject.

These, My Dear Sir, are very hasty thoughts. They are intended *for your use only, & you must not make them public*. If you wish for any opinions of mine, on these questions, *to be made public*, you must send this sheet back, & let me prepare what I have to say with more deliberation, & express it more fully, & with more care[40]—Yrs with regard

D.W.

Printed circular with MS notes and ANS by DW. NhHi. Published in Van Tyne, pp. 155–156. Louis Dwight (1793–1854; Yale 1813; Andover Theological Seminary 1819), founder and secretary of the Prison Discipline Society of Boston. This letter was part of a nationwide solicitation. See *Reports of the Prison Discipline Society of Boston, 1826–1835* (Boston, 1855), 1: 376–395.

TO SAMUEL BAKER WALCOTT

My Dr Sir Washington Feb. 28. 1834

I have noticed your efforts in the Legislature to abolish the practice of secret attachment of real estate,[41] & cannot omit to give you my thanks for attempting to wipe out that foul blot from the jurisprudence of Massachusetts.

Nothing but habit can enable any just mind to contemplate such a provision in our code, without abhorrence. I suppose originally no *secrecy* was intended; it was probably thought that the return, being in the Sherriff's office would be likely to afford notice; but then it came to be the case often, that the Plf would *direct* the Sherriff to keep the attachment secret. Now, it has always been my opinion, and is now, & I should so decide if I were a Judge (as I never shall be) that every attachment, made under such *direction*, is void, as being a direct fraud against creditors & subsequent purchasers. The object of such attachment can only be to secure the p[ro]p[ert]y agt. creditors & purchasers, & if in executing this purpose, pains be taken to keep the proceeding

40. DW prepared a formal reply. DW to Dwight, May 2, 1830, *Correspondence*, 3: 65–67.

41. Laws, Mass., c. 28 (1784).

secret, it is in my judgment one of the clearest cases of fraud which can be stated. I remember to have conversed with Chief Justice [Isaac] Parker on this subject, & to have told him that I should make that question, before the Court, if any reason arose in my practice.

But the true course is to abolish the whole practice, altogether. I now look back with real astonishment, at the directions, so often given to sheriffs by myself, when young in the profession, at the request of Plfs; the object of which was to attain a secret lien, & leave unsuspecting creditors & purchasers to go on blindfold to loss & harm. It pretty soon occurred to me, however, that there was something morally wrong in this, & that therefore there ought to be something legally wrong in it; & reflection brought me at last to the opinion which I have above expressed. I hope you will persevere, My Dear Sir, & I trust that all our professional brethren will look at this question, free from the influence of association & habit, & they will then I think all see it in the same light.

Nothing of interest has occurred here for some days. The President manifests little disposition to retrace his steps. It is said however that some consultations have recently been had, to see whether nothing could be done. Friends at home press the Administration, exceedingly, *to do something*, as from considerations of party, as those of Country.

The Bank Directors, nominated by the President, have been negatived.[42] Yrs very truly Danl Webster

ALS. MHi. Samuel Baker Wolcott (1795–1854; Harvard 1819), Massachusetts lawyer, studied with DW, admitted in 1824, state legislator.

FROM ROBERT LEE

Rahway New Jersey
April 13, 1840

For the Newark Daily Advertiser.

Individuals frequently, and sometimes whole communities, under any extra ordinary suffering, resort to expedients of relief, from a momentary impulse; expedients which a little sober reflection would condemn as affording no suitable and adequate remedy for the evil sought to be removed. The writer of this fears that amidst that intense suffering, and almost universal bankruptcy brought upon the nation, by the ill advised measures of the Jackson and Van Buren administrations, some ill-judged and ill-advised measures will be resorted to, which, far from remedying the evil, will increase it.

Very few, if any examples can be drawn from the practice of any part of Europe adopted to the U. States. We are a people peculiar in many and important respects, differing in the original organization of our governments, and in our manners, customs and pursuits from every other

42. On February 27, 1834, the Senate rejected Jackson's nominees to the board of directors of the BUS.

people. I name three distinctive features, and which will require a different organization of the principles of a bankrupt law to adapt it to our wants. These are, first; our state governments extending over and regulating a vast proportion of the intercourse and business of our citizens, in all the common concerns of life. Second; innumerable incorporations, such as States, Counties, Townships, Cities, Banks, Insurance, Manufacturing, Railroad, Bridge and Ferry Companies; thousands of Religious, Literary, Charitable and Benevolent institutions, immensely exceeding in number, and in the interests over which they spread influence, that of any other people. And thirdly; our character of a new people, rapidly increasing in number and as rapidly expanding over new territory, and from these circumstances requiring an extent of credit, according to the actual amount of business done, far beyond that of any of the older nations.

In relation to a NATIONAL *Bankrupt Law I submit a few questions.*

Shall it extend to incorporations, as well as to individual persons,—and if so, to all incorporations?—By the Constitution of the United States a Bankrupt law, if passed, must be uniform. No—To individual persons only; The uniformity required, is, uniform as in the several States.

Will it extend to past transactions, as well as to the future? Yes. But as answered to the 5th enquiry.

Will it extend to the Agricultural class of citizens, as well as to the Mercantile and Manufacturing classes? In other words will it extend to all debtors? Yes. [But as answered to the 5th enquiry.]

Who will appoint the Commissioners of Bankruptcy? Will that tremendous power, with its keen searching and far extending influence, be added to the already overwhelming patronage of the general government? If so, it is one step more towards the establishment of a perfect despotism. The Creditors, on due notice to convene them, either by the debtor or a part of the Creditors.

Will the system intended to be established, leave it optional with the debtor to be declared a Bankrupt? Will it vest the power in creditors, of declaring the debtor bankrupt?—or will it vest that power in some fixed board of Commissioners of Bankruptcy? Optional with the Creditors when 2/3ds in amount desire it, and with the debtor in all cases, when he desires it.

And lastly, will not a National Bankrupt Law, especially if extending to incorporations as well as to all classes of individual debtors, add immensely, FOR THE PRESENT, *to the general embarrassment of the country, by compelling all solvent Banks, and individuals, to restrict within the smallest possible limits, their business operations, until experience has tested the effects and operation of the new Bankrupt system?* It will.

AN OLD MERCHANT

The Commissioners of Bankruptcy, when chosen by the Creditors, as in answer to question 4, to be authorized to act by some *state* Court, either Chancery, or Common Pleas, or orphans Court—and to account for their proceedings, before such Court, on due citation, by any person interested.

I shall be pleased if your time will permit you to acknowledge the receipt of this, and favor me with a copy of any such Bankrupt Law as may be reported. I am (tho' a stranger) very respectfully and sincerely your friend Robt. Lee.

ANS. NhHi. Robert Lee (1786–1842), a prominent citizen of Rahway, New Jersey. Lee sent Webster the newspaper clipping reproduced above, adding his own answers to the questions posed.

FROM JOSEPH STORY

My Dear Sir: Cambridge, May 10th, 1840.

I am just returned from my Eastern Circuit, a good deal exhausted by it, and have time only to say a few words. I do not know, that there are any absolutely insuperable objections to bringing corporations within the reach of a Bankrupt Law; but there are some practical difficulties. The same machinery which would be complete as to individuals, would require many complex provisions in cases of corporations. What would you do as to Railroads, Turnpike, and Bridge Corporations? Should Banks be also entirely subject to the same summary proceedings, as common trading and manufacturing corporations, considering the sudden changes in circulation and markets, which may compel them sometimes to suspend for a short time? What would be the effect of requiring all debtors to a Bank, suddenly to pay all their notes and liabilities? How would you manage with Insurance Companies, when there are many policies of insurance outstanding on long voyages? Here again, you must reach the assets of corporations, not only by examining the officers thereof on oath, but also the stockholders on oath; otherwise, in many cases, the remedy would be ineffectual. Consider what difficulties would arise in cases of numerous stockholders residing in different States; some infants, some married women, some trustees. I see much practical embarrassment in bringing them compulsorily within a Bankrupt Act. But if they are brought within such an act, I think the stockholders should have the benefit of a discharge, upon surrendering all their stock and the corporation assets, exactly as individuals. Their sacrifices, otherwise, would be enormous, and the future creation of corporations would be greatly discouraged.

But one main difficulty with me, is, that if corporations, now existing, should be brought within a Bankrupt Law, without such a discharge, it would at once shake all confidence in corporation stock, and depreciate it excessively. The corporation capital in New England would at once lose a large part of its present value, and be scarcely marketable. This would be a sad consummation of all our public calamities, and depress us still more.

I confess, too, I have some doubts, as to the constitutionality of a Bankrupt Law, which should put corporations upon a different footing from individuals, giving the latter a discharge, and not the former; and providing different rules of bankruptcy in the one case from the other. The act would not be a "uniform act on the subject of bankruptcy," in the sense of the Constitution.

No Bankrupt Law in England, or, indeed, in any other country, as far as I know, ever has reached corporations. Is not this a strong, practical objection? Is it quite certain, that State Rights, as to the creation and dissolution of corporations, are not thus virtually infringed? I confess, that I feel no small doubt, whether Congress can regulate State Corporations by any other laws than the State laws. A State Corporation is entitled to just such rights and powers, as the charter gives it, and I do not well see where Congress can get the power to alter or control them, or to suspend or extinguish them.

These are first, hasty thoughts. Pray consider them. I have not time to think more, but merely sketch these sentences as they arise in my mind, without any attempt at arrangement.

Send me a printed copy of your Bankrupt bill. Do not suffer any bill to be limited to less than five years. This is the shortest time to see its fair operation. It will otherwise be run down before its just effects are seen, exactly as the old Bankrupt Act. . . .

Yours, most truly and affectionately, Joseph Story

Text from W. Story, 2: 330–332. Original not found.

FROM EBENEZER JESUP, JR., ET AL.

Dr Sir New York May 11th. 1840.

We are among the hundreds of thousands of your fellow citizens who are praying for the passage of a Bankrupt Law. We look to you as the great statesman and philanthropist who will be anxious and willing to use the great energies of your comprehensive mind, to relieve the country from its present prostrate state and release us from a bondage more insupportable than the inherited servitude of the Southern slave. We have been freemen. Once character talent and experience was valuable to us and of service to the Country. Once industry and integrity brought its reward now it is our bane our curse. Because the creditor hopes to secure his claim by it while he release the idler and drunkard.

It is in your power to raise us from this depth of despair and pain. You can devise means by which this can be accomplished *now.* We shall consider *postponement death.* We have before witnessed this course of proceeding, and therefore we shall cease to hope if Congress adjourn without passing a Law.

We beg of you to allow no minor obstacles to induce you to oppose any measure of relief. Give us freedom and we shall feel that to you we are indebted for it. We know that your efforts can overcome all difficulties, and we hope to be able to prove to you that we can remember with gratitude our benefactor. With great respect we remain your most obt serts:

Ebenr Jesup Jr
S. I. Joseph
John J. Swift
John Deane
Saml R. Childs
E. L. Reynolds
J. B. Hyde
Jas. M. Duffield
H. C. Morgan
E. W. Horgan
L. R. Shaw

ALS. NhHi. Ebenezer Jesup, Jr. (1805–1861; Yale 1824), lawyer, studied with Judge Gould, Litchfield, Connecticut, lived in Ohio, moved to New York in 1835 and a few years thereafter to Southport, Connecticut where he took up farming; probably Solomon I. Joseph, James M. Duffield, Latimer R. Shaw, New York merchants and Samuel Russell Childs, New York physician. The other signers have not been identified.

DOCUMENT 45. SPEECH

[May 18, 1840]

Shall the bankruptcy act, in its application to individuals, be voluntary only, or both voluntary and compulsory? It is well known that I prefer that it should be both. I think all insolvent and failing persons should have power to come in under its provisions, and be voluntary bankrupts; and I think, too, that, as to those who are strictly merchants and traders, creditors ought to have a right to proceed against them, on the commission of the usual acts of bankruptcy, and subject them to the provisions of the act. But the committee think otherwise. They find many objections to this from many parts of the country, and especially from the West. In a country so extensive, with a people so various, with such different ideas and habits in regard to punctuality in commercial dealings, great opposition is anticipated to any measure so strict and so penal as a coercive bankruptcy. I content myself, therefore, with what I can get. I content myself with the voluntary bankruptcy. I am free to confess my leading object to be, to relieve those who are at present bankrupts, hopeless bankrupts, and who cannot be discharged or set free but by a bankrupt act passed by Congress. I confess that their case forms the great motive of my conduct. It is their case which has created the general cry for the measure. Not that their interest is opposed to the interest of creditors; still less that it is opposed to the general good of the country. On the contrary, I believe that the interest of creditors would be greatly benefited even by a system of voluntary bankruptcy alone, and I am quite confident that the public good would be eminently promoted. In my judgment, all interests concur; and it is the duty of providing for these unfortunate insolvents, in a manner thus favorable to all interests, which I feel urging me forward on this occasion.

* * * * * *

The States, then, cannot pass effectual bankrupt laws; that is, effectual for the discharge of the debtor. There is no doubt that most, if not all, the States would now pass such laws, if they had the power; although their legislation would be various, interfering, and full of all the evils which the Constitution of the United States intended to provide against. But they have not the power; Congress, which has the power, does not exercise it. This is the peculiarity of our condition. The States would pass bankrupt laws, but they cannot; we can, but we will not. And between this want of power in the States and want of will in Congress, unfortunate insolvents are left to hopeless bondage. There are probably one or two hundred thousand debtors, honest, sober, and industrious, who drag out lives useless to themselves, useless to their families, and useless to their country, for no reason but that they cannot be legally discharged from debts in which misfortunes have involved them, and which there is no possibility of their ever paying. I repeat, again, that these cases have now been accumulating for a whole generation.

It is true they are not imprisoned; but there may be, and there are, restraint and bondage outside the walls of the jail, as well as in. Their power of earning is, in truth, taken away; their faculty of useful employment is paralyzed, and hope itself become extinguished. Creditors, generally, are not inhuman or unkind; but there will be found some who hold on, and the more a debtor struggles to free himself, the more they feel encouraged to hold on. The mode of reasoning is, that, the more honest the debtor may be, the more industrious, the more disposed to struggle and bear up against his misfortunes, the greater the chance is, that, in the end, especially if the humanity of others shall have led them to release him, their own debts may be finally recovered.

Now, in this state of our constitutional powers and duties, in this state of our laws, and with this actually existing condition of so many insolvents before us, it is not too serious to ask every member of the Senate to put it to his own conscience to say, whether we are not bound to exercise our constitutional duty. Can we abstain from exercising it? The States give to their own laws all the effect they can. This shows that they desire the power to be exercised. Several States have, in the most solemn manner, made known their earnest wishes to Congress. If we still refuse, what is to be done? Many of these insolvent persons are young men with young families. Like other men, they have capacities both for action and enjoyment. Are we to stifle all these for ever? Are we to suffer all these persons, many of them meritorious and respectable, to be pressed to the earth for ever, by a load of hopeless debt? The existing diversities and contradictions of State laws on the subject admirably illustrate the objects of this part of the Constitution, as stated by Mr. Madison;[43] and they form that precise case for which the clause was inserted. The very evil intended to be provided against is before us, and around us, and pressing us on all sides. How can we, how dare we, make a perfect dead letter of this part of the Constitution, which we have sworn to support? The insolvent persons have not the power of locomotion. They cannot travel from State to State. They are prisoners. To my certain knowledge, there are many who cannot even come here to the seat of government, to present their petitions to Congress, so great is their fear that some creditor will dog their heels, and arrest them in some intervening State, or in this District, in the hope that friends will appear to save them, by payment of the debt, from imprisonment. These are truths; not creditable to the country, but they are truths. I am sorry for their existence. Sir, there is one crime, quite too common, which the laws of man do not punish, but which cannot escape the justice of God; and that is, the arrest and confinement of a debtor by his creditor, with no motive on earth but the hope that some friend, or some relative, perhaps almost as poor as himself, his mother it may be, or his sisters, or his daughters, will give up all their own little pittance, and make beggars of themselves, to save him from the horrors of a loathsome jail. Human retribution cannot reach this guilt; human feeling may not penetrate the flinty heart that perpetrates it; but an hour is surely coming, with more than human retribution on its wings, when that flint shall be melted, either by the power of penitence and grace, or in the fires of remorse.

Sir, I verily believe that the power of perpetuating debts against debtors, for no substantial good to the creditor himself, and the power of imprisonment for debt, at least as it existed in this country ten years ago, have imposed more restraint on personal liberty than the law of

43. *The Federalist, on the New Constitution, written in the Year 1788 by Mr. Hamilton, Mr. Madison, and Mr. Jay* (Washington, 1818), p. 268. Madison's remarks are in No. 42.

debtor and creditor imposes in any other Christian and commercial country. If any public good were attained, any high political object answered, by such laws, there might be some reason for counselling submission and sufferance to individuals. But the result is bad, every way. It is bad to the public and to the country, which loses the efforts and the industry of so many useful and capable citizens. It is bad to creditors, because there is no security against preferences, no principle of equality, and no encouragement for honest, fair, and seasonable assignments of effects. As to the debtor, however good his intentions or earnest his endeavors, it subdues his spirit, and degrades him in his own esteem; and if he attempts any thing for the purpose of obtaining food and clothing for his family, he is driven to unworthy shifts and disguises, to the use of other persons' names, to the adoption of the character of agent, and various other contrivances, to keep the little earnings of the day from the reach of his creditors. Fathers act in the name of their sons, sons act in the name of their fathers; all constantly exposed to the greatest temptation to misrepresent facts and to evade the law, if creditors should strike. All this is evil, unmixed evil. And what is it all for? Of what benefit to any body? Who likes it? Who wishes it? What class of creditors desire it? What consideration of public good demands it?

Sir, we talk much, and talk warmly, of political liberty; and well we may, for it is among the chief of public blessings. But who can enjoy political liberty if he is deprived, permanently, of personal liberty, and the exercise of his own industry and his own faculties? To those unfortunate individuals, doomed to the everlasting bondage of debt, what is it that we have free institutions of government? What is it that we have public and popular assemblies? What is even this Constitution itself to them, in its actual operation, and as we now administer it? What is its aspect to them, but an aspect of stern, implacable severity? an aspect of refusal, denial, and frowning rebuke? nay, more than that, an aspect not only of austerity and rebuke, but, as they must think it, of plain injustice also, since it will not relieve them, nor suffer others to give them relief? What love can they feel towards the Constitution of their country, which has taken the power of striking off their bonds from their own paternal State governments, and yet, inexorable to all the cries of justice and of mercy, holds it unexercised in its own fast and unrelenting grasp? They find themselves bondsmen, because we will not execute the commands of the Constitution; bondsmen to debts they cannot pay, and which all know they cannot pay, and which take away the power of supporting themselves. Other slaves have masters, charged with the duty of support and protection; but their masters neither clothe, nor feed, nor shelter; they only bind.

But, Sir, the fault is not in the Constitution. The Constitution is beneficient as well as wise in all its provisions on this subject. The fault, I must be allowed to say, is in us, who have suffered ourselves quite too long to neglect the duty incumbent upon us. The time will come, Sir, when we shall look back and wonder at the long delay of this just and salutary measure.

Extract. *W & S*, 9: 1–39. A Uniform System of Bankruptcy, delivered in the Senate May 18, 1840. Published in *Speeches*, 2.

2. CONGRESSIONAL ETHICS

It is difficult for the twentieth-century student to come to grips with the nature of congressional ethics in the early nineteenth century. To our heightened sensitivity many of the practices of this period seem questionable. In theory at least, we have developed a clearer conception of the difference between public and private obligations. We have realized how the latter can subvert the former. We demand that our representatives disclose their financial affairs and divest themselves of potential conflicts of interest. In Webster's day this was not the case. A lawyer came to Congress both as representative of his constituents and guardian of the interests of his clients.[1] As part of his responsibility to his clients, he might sponsor legislation in their behalf. No questions of ethics arose. If, after helping to pass favorable legislation, the congressman billed his client somewhat more than usual, no one was the wiser. But if he stole public funds or accepted a bribe, he crossed over into forbidden territory.

In the eighteenth-century scheme of things, officeholders held "property" in their positions. The appointment of men of the upper classes to major offices, it was believed, guaranteed the ethical performance of their duties.[2] Following the Revolution, however, this aristocratic conception of public office and character came into conflict with republican ideology. In a society where civic virtue counted for more than noble birth, the idea that an official had a property interest in his office seemed abhorrent. The people expected the officeholder to serve the people, not to make a profit from them. Thus in the nineteenth century the venality and corruption engaged in by those in public positions became hidden from view. On the one hand, republican ideology offered an inspired view of governmental service; on the other, the behavior of those in office often demonstrated human frailty. Webster, too, could succumb to the temptation to use his position to help himself professionally.

In 1834 he set forth his view of the ideal in government service.

1. Congressional salaries were low. Webster, who was accustomed to a professional income that averaged over $10,000 during his years in Congress, watched for opportunities to use his position for profit.

2. William E. Nelson, "Office Holding and Power Wielding in Nineteenth Century America," *Law and Society Review*, 10 (1976): 18.

> These principles [of 1776] teach us that Government is a trust, that those who administer it, are but agents and servants; that offices are created, not for the benefit of the holders, but for the good of the People; and that public office is grossly abused, and its uses corrupted, when it seeks, mainly, not the benefit of the community, but its own emolument and perpetuation, and that the whole essential character of representative Government is dangerously perverted, and its true manner of operation reversed, when the opinions, which the people are expected to receive, are prescribed to them by those whom they have appointed to places of power, instead of being the spontaneous result of their own intelligence and their own patriotism.[3]

In the following two sections the reader may judge how well Webster conformed to this standard.

a. Webster and the Bank of the United States[1]

i. Creation of the Relationship. The second Bank of the United States (BUS), chartered by Congress for a term of twenty years, opened its doors in January 1817, but came very near closing them again in less than two years. A combination of poor management, political pressure, and outright dishonesty in the Baltimore branch, and perhaps other branches, brought the institution to the verge of collapse by 1819 and precipitated a nationwide depression. Langdon Cheves, South Carolina lawyer, merchant, and former speaker of the House of Representatives, became president of the bank at that time. He succeeded in restoring solvency by rigorous contraction, but the cure, to the average debtor, was worse than the disease, and the hostility of the state banks was palpable. His mission accomplished, Cheves resigned in 1822 and was succeeded by Nicholas Biddle, who made the BUS over the next ten years into both an effective administrative tool of the government and an early version of a central bank.

From BUS headquarters in Philadelphia, Biddle used the bank's network of branch offices to bring the issuance of bank notes by southern and western state banks under BUS control. By issuing BUS notes and quickly sending all other bank notes it received back to the issuer for redemption, the BUS soon produced a national currency.[2]

3. DW to Benjamin G. Welles, April 15, 1834, *Correspondence*, 3: 339–340.

1. In Volume 3 of this Legal Series, we intend to treat the law of banking as delineated in the federal courts. We shall pay particular attention to the relationship of banking law and the development of a national economy. The correspondence and documents presented here are used to illustrate a different point.

2. Bray Hammond, *Banks and Politics in America from the Revolution to the Civil War* (Princeton, N.J., 1957), pp. 251–325; Peter Temin, *The Jacksonian Economy* (New York, 1969), pp. 50–53.

Although the BUS retained Webster to argue two major constitutional cases in 1819 and 1824,[3] his formal connection with the bank did not begin until 1826. In that year President Adams named the bank's usual counsel, John Sergeant, to attend a diplomatic meeting in Panama. In Sergeant's expected absence, bank president Nicholas Biddle hired Webster to handle a series of BUS cases docketed for the 1826 Supreme Court term. With the Spanish claims complete, Webster probably welcomed the work. Biddle also knew that hiring the chairman of the House Judiciary Committee would not jeopardize bank interests in that quarter.

FROM NICHOLAS BIDDLE

Bank of the U. States
Feby 4. 1826

My dear Sir,

The delay in deciding on the Panama Mission induces me to request at the instance of Mr Sergeant that you will at once engage Mr Wirt to act with you in the case of the Bank against Dandridge.[4] Mr Sergeant will forward to you the record, I hope by this mail.

You will oblige me also by looking at the Docket of the Court, and giving me a memorandum of any causes in which the Bank is concerned, stating the degree of forwardness in which they are & the names of Counsel who are engaged to attend to them, as it is possible that some cases may hence come up with regard to which some provision is necessary. With great respect & regard Yrs N. Biddle Prest.

ALS. DLC. Published in *Correspondence*, 2: 83–84.

TO NICHOLAS BIDDLE

Dear Sir Washington Feb. 7. [18]26

I recd yesterday the record in the Va. case,[5] from Mr Sergeant; & have spoken to Mr Wirt, who readily promises his assistance in the cause.

Enclosed you have a list of what causes I find on the docket,[6] in which the Bank is party, with the names of the *States*, where they origi-

3. The cases were *McCulloch* v. *Maryland*, 4 Wheaton 316 (1819), and *Osborn* v. *BUS*, 9 Wheaton 738 (1824).

4. John Sergeant (1779–1852; College of New Jersey 1795), Philadelphia lawyer and chief counsel for the BUS, studied with Jared Ingersoll, state legislator, U.S. representative (1815–1823, 1827–1829, 1837–1841). The case referred to is *BUS* v. *Dandridge*, 12 Wheaton 64 (1827), not argued until the next session.

5. *BUS* v. *Dandridge*, n. 4, above.

6. Enclosure not found. See DW to Biddle, February 10, 1826, following.

nated, & of the Counsel who appeared entered on the docket for the parties. I am, Dr. Sir, very truly, Yours Danl. Webster

ALS. PU.

FROM NICHOLAS BIDDLE

Bank of the United States
Feby 10, 1826

Dear Sir

Your favor of the 7th inst was received last evening.[7]

I am instructed by the Board to request that you will take charge of the following causes in which the Bank is interested, now pending in the Supreme Court of the U. S. viz:

No. 37. James Finley vs The Bank of the U. S. from Kentucky
38. William Coleman vs The Bank of the U. S. Do
52. Micajah T. Williams vs The Bank of the U. S. Ohio
89. Peter Mills vs The Bank of the U. S.[8] Do

In the three first of these cases the Bank has hitherto been represented by Mr Clay. At his retirement from the Bar,[9] they would naturally have devolved on Mr Sergeant the Standing Counsel of the Bank, but as he will not be able to attend the Court, it is the desire of the Board, that they should be committed to your charge. You will have the goodness therefore to confer with Mr Clay, who will no doubt readily give you every assistance & information necessary to render you master of the questions to be argued.

In regard to the last case No. 89, we are not informed of the nature of the case, tho' Mr Clay will probably be able to afford the requisite information. The case of Magill & others vs the Bank[10] is so low on the list that it probably will not be reached this term & no provision need be made for it. I have written today to Connecticut for a copy of the record and have only to add, that in case any inconvenience or injury may be sustained by the want of Counsel, or the interest of the Bank may be promoted by any movement at the present session of the Court, you will in that case represent the Bank. Our object would be to defeat as soon as possible the appeal which we consider groundless, & avail ourselves of the verdict below in our favor.

I shall be obliged to you for any communication as to the progress &

7. See preceding letter.

8. *Finley* v. *BUS*, 11 Wheaton 304 (1826); *Williams* v. *BUS*, 11 Wheaton 414 (1826); *Mills* v. *BUS*, 11 Wheaton 431 (1826); Coleman's unreported case was dismissed on motion, see n. 11 below.

9. Clay "retired" more than once.

10. *M'Gill* v. *BUS*, 12 Wheaton 511 (1827), argued the next term, grew out of the suspension of the cashier of the Middletown, Connecticut, office for breach of trust.

prospects of these suits whenever your leisure will permit, & remain meanwhile Yrs very resp[ectfull]y N Biddle Prest.

ALS. DLC.

TO NICHOLAS BIDDLE

Dear Sir Washington Mar. 1. 1826.

In compliance with your request, I have paid the necessary attention to the several actions in which the Bank is interested.

Coleman vs Bk U. S.

Findley v Bk U.S.[11] These cases are two appeals, from the same Decree, rend. by the Circuit Court in Kentucky. One of them has been dismissed, on motion, as irregularly claimed & allowed; the other has been argued, & I have reason to think the Decree below will be affirmed. But that is not entirely certain.

Williams v Bk U. S.

Mills v B U. S.[12] These are cases from Ohio. The suits were against *indorsers*, & the grounds of defense are, improper joining of parties, *want of regular notice to indorsers, &c &c* Some of these objections seem to have weight in them. The proceedings below do not appear to have been remarkably regular. The amounts are small.

We approach Dandridge's case,[13] & shall be ready, on the part of the Bank, to try it as soon as it is reached. I am, Sir, with very true regard, Yours Danl. Webster

ALS. PU. Published in *W & S*, 16: 121–122.

The BUS's charter required its president and cashier to sign all circulat-

11. *Finley* involved the question whether the court should set aside the USCC decree confirming the foreclosure sale by the BUS of Finley's property. Coleman, who held another Finley mortgage prior in time to the BUS mortgage, had not been made a party to the sale. The Supreme Court held that since the USCC had no knowledge of Coleman's mortgage, it would not set aside a completely executed decree. The Supreme Court left Coleman to pursue his remedies in the state court. See also DW to Biddle, March 3, 1826, mDW 5345.

12. The Supreme Court dismissed the writ of error in the *Williams* case for failure to join all three defendants. In *Mills* the USCC held in favor of the BUS that parties to a promissory note are bound by the local customs of a bank. In this case it was Chillicothe, Ohio custom for payees to demand payment on the day after the last day of grace. On a sixty-day note a payee generally had three days of grace to present the note; Chillicothe gave one extra day for presentment. Justice Story, extending the rule of an earlier case, held that the BUS did not have to prove that Mills had personal knowledge of the Ohio custom.

13. Wirt had agreed to associate with DW on this case.

ing bank notes. As the bank grew in importance and established branch offices all over the nation, this task became more burdensome. In fact, the signature provision soon made it impossible for the bank to issue large numbers of small denomination notes. Appeals to Congress had brought no alteration in the charter to allow the appointment of additional signers. In February 1826 Biddle enlisted Webster's aid.[14] In the letter of March 1, 1826, printed below, Webster outlined a course of action in Congress. When Congress failed to act, the bank took an alternative measure and began to issue branch drafts, signed by the president and cashier of each branch. Biddle based his decision to use this subterfuge on an opinion signed by Webster, Wirt, and Philadelphia lawyer Horace Binney.[15]

TO NICHOLAS BIDDLE

Private

My Dear Sir, Washington Mar. 1. [18]26

My engagements in the Court, and elsewhere, have been such as to prevent an earlier answer to your letter of the 16. Feb. on the subject of a proposed alteration in the Charter of the Bank, as to the officers who sign Bills & Notes.[16]

The reasonableness of what you wish, is too plain to be doubted, & I think the public, as well as the Bank, are interested in accomplishing the object. It is, indeed, impossible to be *sure*, before hand, that the subject might not bring on *debate*; as almost every subject does, or may. Still, the matter is of so much importance, I think it advisable to bring it forward. Your suggestion, as to the mode of proceeding, meets my approbation. Let the old Memorial be called up, & referred to a Com[mitt]ee. This should be done by Mr. Hemphill, as the City member. It may be referred, either to the Ways & Means, or Judiciary. Either of these Comees will doubtlessly report a Bill.[17] It may, possibly, be thought expedient *to originate the measure in the Senate*; although I think, at present, it may as well begin with us.

14. Nicholas Biddle to DW, February 16, 1826, *Correspondence*, 2: 86–88.

15. For a fuller treatment of this problem, see Hammond, pp. 397–404. Binney drafted the opinion, and Webster simply appended his concurrence. 22nd Cong., 1st Sess. HD 460.

16. See *Correspondence*, 2: 86–89.

17. The bill was referred to the Committee of Ways and Means, headed by Louis McLane. He told DW that the committee would make an unfavorable report. See Ralph C. H. Catterall, *The Second Bank of the United States* (Chicago, 1903), p. 117; DW to Biddle, December 28, 1826, *Correspondence*, 2: 144. Joseph Hemphill was chairman of the House select committee handling memorials from South Carolina banks, insurance companies, and the BUS.

Probably you will think it most prudent to write to Mr. Hemphill, on the subject, desiring his attention to it, & saying that you have, or shall, ask *my* cooperation with him. Let *him* bring forward the matter. I, in the mean time, will consult with some other members. I feel confident the thing *can be done*; & altho. we may be disappointed, I think it proper the attempt should be made, & shall feel disposed to give it an earnest support. We can but relinquish it, at last, if we should find it likely to bring on a war of words of great duration. Yours, very truly, Danl. Webster

ALS. PU. Published in *Correspondence*, 2: 93–94.

TO NICHOLAS BIDDLE

Dear Sir Washington Mar. 13th. [18]26

The two cases of Williams vs the Bank, and Mills vs the Bank are argued. It is doubtful what may be the result. The question in the Circuit Court was on the sufficiency and regularity of the notice *to indorsers*. I incline to think the *merits* of the question, in both cases, are with the Bank; but the suits were conducted in a strange & novel manner, joining promissors & indorsers *together*, according to some Ohio Law; & I fear there may be danger that on this account the judgments will be reversed. Your Office there might, perhaps, be usefully advised to avoid such embarrassments for the future. We shall know the results of these appeals, I suppose, in a day or two.

It is doubtful whether Dandridge's case will be argued. It is about as far on the docket as the Court will be able to get, if not a little farther. I am, Sir, with true regard, Yours Danl. Webster

ALS. PU. Published in *W & S*, 16: 122–123.

TO NICHOLAS BIDDLE

Dr. Sir, Washington Mar. 15. 1826.

We have had better success in the Ohio causes than my last may have led you to anticipate.[18] In the principal one, (Wms, abt 12.000 or 13.000 Dlls) the judgt is affirmed, & in the other (Mills) we succeeded in a motion to dismiss the writ of error. I shall take care to see the proper *mandates* issued &c. Yrs very truly Danl. Webster.

I fear Dandridge's case will not be reached.

ALS. PU. Published in *W & S*, 16: 123.

As the chairman of a committee that originated legislation of interest to the BUS, Webster used his position to show his value to the bank. In

18. See preceding letter.

a letter of February 4, 1827, printed below, he informed Biddle that he had amended a piece of criminal legislation to aid the prosecution of banking crimes. Webster continued to mix the public and private aspects of his relationship to the bank when he gave an opinion (Document 46) upholding the bank's authority to develop real estate. Upon John Sergeant's return in 1827, Webster wrote to Biddle (February 24, 1827, printed below), coyly suggesting that he would like his relationship with the bank continued. He repeated this mild form of arm twisting several years later.

TO NICHOLAS BIDDLE

Dear Sir, feb. 4. [1827]

I am about reporting a bill,[19] supplementary to the several acts for the punishment of crimes, & have prepared a section for removing, in future cases, all such doubts as Mr. Swann has here suggested.[20] I shall report the section, unless Mr. Swann shoud be of opinion that such a proceeding, at the present moment, would lessen his chance of obtaining a conviction under the existing law. Yrs D. Webster

ALS. PU.

TO NICHOLAS BIDDLE

Dear Sir, Washington, Feb. 24. 1827

In the case of Conelly's heirs vs Lytle, & als in regard to which you forwarded me an extract from Mr Shippen's letter,[21] (at Louisville), I have to say, that, not finding that the Appellants prosecuted their appeal, by entering the action here & filing the record, I wrote to Kentucky for a certificate of the Clerk that the Appeal *had been claimed*; & having recd the Certificate today moved the Court, according to the practice in such cases, *to dismiss the Appeal* which was accordingly so ordered. Mr Shippen speaks of this case as one "in which it is all important to the Bank that no reversal of the judgment below should take place" It may be well to inform Mr Shippen, that the appeal being thus disposed of, the judgment below, in all things, *stands*.

There are two or three more causes, in which the Bank is party, yet on the docket, but I believe they will not be tried at this term. They appear to be of less importance than those which have been discussed. The *mandates* &c, proper to be sent to the respective Courts below, I shall

19. Report of the Committee on the Judiciary on a bill for the punishment of crimes, February 6, 1827, mDW 41973.

20. Thomas Swann was the Washington, D.C., district attorney.

21. No additional information has been found on this case; Shippen has not been identified.

see obtained from the Clerk, & forwarded to you, in due season, to be sent to their several destinations.

When Mr. Sargeant went away, and I was left in charge of the concerns of the Bank here, he told me that the Bank had, at that time, *not lost any cause in the Supreme Court.* If he should return, at the next Term, I shall have the happiness, I trust, to tell him, that *it has lost none since.* Dandridge's cause is not yet decided, but I have confidence the judgment below will be reversed; so that that will form no exception to our good fortune.

I shall forward a little statement of my *fees*, & Mr Wirts receipt, tomorrow. In Dandridge's case, I shall take the liberty of charging somewhat *liberally.* I never gave more attention, either to the preparation, or the discussion of a cause; & am vain* enough to think that my labours were not without some influence on the result.

I have considered myself as having been intrusted with these cases in consequence of Mr Sargeants absence, & that my *stewardship* will naturally terminate on his return, which probably may be before the next term. But one does not like to part with an old client, any more than an old friend, provided there be no good cause of separation. If therefore it should be your good pleasure to have it understood hereafter, that in suits here, in which Mr Sargeant may chuse to have assistance, he may put my poor services in requisition, unless he sees reason to do otherwise, I should not object to such an understanding; & should not consider myself at liberty to accept retainers against the Bank hereafter. This however is not important either to me or the Bank & may [be] decided either way, (like many of our Congress questions) without harm. So much for secular affairs.

Our session is nearly through & is likely to terminate in the impunity of having done nothing. The Senate has a return of that talking sickness, with which it was so much afflicted, about this time last year. The Colonial trade bill will be discussed, at large in that body, partly on its own account, & partly to keep off the woolen Bill.[22] The fate of this last is very doubtful. Its present prospect is rather melancholy, if we may judge from the mournful pastorals of those who are in the sheep interest.

The loan Bill[23] will probably become a law; & that, I suppose, is the only measure of the session, in which you men of finance take much

22. The trade bill represented an attempt to resolve the dispute in which the U.S. had closed American ports to British vessels in retaliation for the British closing of the West Indies to Americans. DW supported the woolen bill.

23. This bill authorized the secretary of the treasury to exchange 5 percent government stock for 6 percent stock and to make up the deficiency by a loan. It passed the House on February 14, but failed in the Senate. *House Journal*, 19th Cong., 2d sess., 1826–27 (Serial 147), p. 299.

interest. The various appropriation bills are thro. our house, so that, if the Senate happen to think to pass them, the Govt. will go another year. The Ex chairman of the W[ay]s & M[ean]s took occasion, on the passage of one of these bills, to expound those views of his, in which he differed from the Committee. Yrs very truly Danl. Webster

*This vanity is a very comfortable thing.

ALS. PU.

DOCUMENT 46. LEGAL OPINION

March 23. 1827

The provisions of the Charter which have, or may be supposed to have more or less bearing on this question, are the 7th & 12th Sections, & the 7th fundamental Rule.[24]

By the 7th Sec. the Corporation is made capable of purchasing, having, enjoying, & retaining, lands, tenements, and hereditaments, to an amount not exceeding 55 millions of Dollars, including the Capital.

But this power to purchase & hold lands, which would thus be general, (within the limited amount) were there no further provision in the Charter, is qualified, or restrained, by the 7th fundamental Rule, which confines the exercise of the power to the holding of such lands & tenements only as shall be requisite for immediate accomodation of the Bank, in relation to the convenient transaction of its business, *and such as shall have been BONA FIDE mortgaged to it, by way of security, or conveyed to it, in satisfaction of debts previously contracted, in the course of its dealings, or purchased at sales upon judgments which shall have been obtained for such debts.*

In the case now under consideration, the lands are sta[ted] to be such as fall within the latter clause of the sectio[n;] and the question is, *whether the Bank may improve the lands and tenements, which have thus fallen into its possession, by repairing & enlarging the buildings, or by constructing new buildings, on the premises.*

I see nothing, in this section, to prevent its doing so. The Sec. imposes no limitation on the *use* of the property. It looks only to the *origin* & *cause* of the title or conveyance, under which the corporation holds.

It was not intended to allow the Bank to become a great landed proprietor; but it was foreseen, first, that it must own Banking Houses; and second, that, in a country where land is almost universally subject to be taken for debts, it must, like other creditors, occasionally, take lands, for that purpose, as well as receive it, for security, by way of

24. 3 U. S. Statutes at Large 266 (1816); Section 11 contained the rules.

mortgage. The Bank is, therefore, authorized to hold lands & tenements, the title to which is, *bona fide*, derived in either of these ways; & being thus authorized to *hold*, it is wholly unrestrained in the *manner* of holding, and in the use & improvement of the property. It may erect new fixtures, or destroy old ones; construct houses, or demolish houses already constructed. Keeping always within the general limit, as to amount of property (55 millions) & possessing no lands not *bona fide* coming to its possession as security, or in payment, it has as free & full a discretion in the use of what it does thus hold, as an individual proprietor would have.

The 12 Sect restrains the Corporation from trading in buying *or* (probably means *and*) selling, goods wares and merchandize. The Bank is not permitted to become a *trader*. But the purchase of building materials, no more makes it a trader, or brings it within the prohibition of this sect., than similar purchases by an individual would make him a trader, within the Statutes of Bankruptcy.

On the whole, I entertain no doubt, that the Bank may improve this property by enlarging and repairing existing buildings, or constructing new ones as its own sense of interest and convenience may prescribe.

Danl. Webster

ADS(DW). PU. *House Reports*, 22d Cong., 1st sess., Doc. No. 460 (Serial 227), pp. 496–497. Published in *W & S*, 15: 288–289.

ii. "Our little bill." Probably Webster's most suspect act on the bank's behalf came in 1831 when he sponsored legislation to give the bank authority to sue in states that had no federal circuit courts.[25] Webster had discovered the problem when the Supreme Court dismissed one of his bank cases for lack of jurisdiction.

> I find there is a defect, probably, in our Judicial System, in relation to the District Courts, in states in which there are no Circuit Courts. In most of these States, (*Mo., Alabama, Louisiana, Mississippi*, &c &c)—the Bank *cannot sue* in U. S. Courts. I sat up last night, quite too late, in hunting up the various Acts, establishing these Courts; —& have, today, drawn a Bill to cure the evils—I shall try to get the Jud[iciary] Com to sanction it & if so, will report it tomorrow, & try to get it thro.[26]

25. Webster, of course, supported efforts to renew the bank's charter. It is clear he believed that the national interest required a national financial institution.

26. DW to Nicholas Biddle, February 2, 1831, *Correspondence*, 3: 100; Senate Bill 142, "Respecting the jurisdiction of certain district courts," mDW 42494. See also DW to Biddle, February 4, 1831, *Correspondence*, 3: 100–101. At this time DW served on the Senate judiciary committee.

Webster drafted the bill in general terms; if President Jackson knew it aided the bank he would surely veto it. The bill passed: "Our success has been marvellous. The little *Bill* has actually passed both Houses! In this House—perhaps in the other—the very name of the Bank was not uttered."[27] The unsuspecting Jackson signed it. In a letter of March 7, 1831, printed below, Webster sent Biddle his bill for past legal services. For the case which had prompted his preparation of the jurisdiction bill he charged $500 and made it clear to Biddle that the payment applied to his services in the Senate and not in court.

TO NICHOLAS BIDDLE

My Dear Sir Washington Feb. 8. 1831

I recd yours yesterday.[28] The Bank question, as stirred here, has gone off well. On the *jurisdiction*, I have got a bill to its third reading in the Senate, which will give the Courts jurisdiction *hereafter*. Causes now pending must be abandoned, & may be brought again, if the Act passes. It *will* pass the Senate; & Mr. Buchanan[29] says it will also pass the H. of R. He seems friendly. I put the Bill on *general* grounds; not exclusively as a convenience to the Bank.

I thank you for your kind sayings; but truly, I am tired of staying here, encumbered, as I am, with professional labors, at the same time.

But of this hereafter Yrs D. Webster

ALS. DLC.

TO NICHOLAS BIDDLE

Dear Sir feb. 9. 1831

Our little *bill* has had excellent luck so far. It was read a second time this morning, in H. of R. & stands for a third reading tomorrow. I hope it will be a law in a week—but it may not—something may defeat it. If it gets thro', it will be of *immense* importance to the Bank, especially if it should be obliged to wind up its concerns.[30] Yrs D. Webster

ALS. DLC.

27. DW to Biddle, February 10, 1831, *Correspondence*, 3: 101–102.

28. Letter not found.

29. James Buchanan (1791–1868; Dickinson College 1807), Pennsylvania lawyer and politician, state representative, U.S. representative (1820–1830), minister to Russia (1831–1833), U.S. senator (1834–1839), U.S. secretary of state (1845–1849), President of the United States (1857–1861).

30. The bill passed the next day.

TO NICHOLAS BIDDLE

Saturday Eve
Dr Sir [February 26, 1831]

Binney & Winship vs Bank U. S.[31] is decided; judgt below *affirmed*—so all is well, as to this. Yrs D. Webster

The bill respecting the Jurisdiction of the District Courts was presented to the President *Feb. 19th.* As yet, we have not heard from him. I am a little suspicious he thinks there is meching malicho[32] in it.

ALS. DLC. *Correspondence*, 3: 103–104.

TO NICHOLAS BIDDLE

Private & confidential

My Dear Sir Washington Mar. 7. 1831

I enclose you a small acct. for fees &c, in regard to which I wish to say a few private words to you.[33]

The Winship, a Binney, cause, was one of importance & difficulty. We just steered it thro., with a divided court.[34] The sum is near 12,000 Dlls.

In that the fee charged is quite modest. The case vs Martin, the Alabama case, is one in which little was said in Court.[35] It was quite clear, both to Mr Sergeant & myself, that we could do nothing with it. Owing to a defect in the Statute, the Alabama Court had no jurisdiction. I therefore went to work, in another quarter, to remedy the law—& was successful. The amending law is passed, without its being suspected, any where, that it was especially useful to the Bank. It opens the Courts of the U. S. to the Bk in 4 states, where there are, or are to be, Offices, viz, Missouri, Louisiana, Alabama, Miss:—this is of great importance, in any event; & of very great, if the Charter is not to be renewed.

I bestowed good attention on this measure; which makes me willing to charge a *fee* in the cause itself—Indeed I had half a mind to write 1000, instead of 500—but am well satisfied as it is—

If you see nothing out of rule, in the acct., please present it. If otherwise, lay it aside, till I see you.

31. *Winship et al.* v. *BUS*, 5 Peters 529 (1831).

32. "Skulking mischief" is from *Hamlet*, act 3, scene 2, line 131. Jackson signed the bill that day: 4 U. S. Statutes at Large 444 (1831).

33. Enclosure not found.

34. The *Winship* case involved the liability of two inactive partners for the debts incurred by the active partner. DW participated in the lower court case, *BUS* v. *Binney et al.*, 5 Mason 196 (1828). The Supreme Court affirmed the judgment in the bank's favor.

35. *BUS* v. *Martin*, 5 Peters 478 (1831). When DW admitted in court that the lower court lacked jurisdiction, the Supreme Court dismissed the appeal.

I shall give you notice of the day I expect to be in Philadelphia. Yrs truly D Webster

ALS. DLC.

iii. Toward Disengagement As the attack by the Jacksonians on the BUS grew more heated, Webster became aware of his political vulnerability should the extent of his financial dealings with the bank become known. For many years he had been accustomed to writing notes on his account at the bank's Boston branch. As an accommodation to him, the BUS had paid them, even when his account held insufficient funds. To the suspicious these debits looked like loans that the bank did not intend to collect. At the moment when the bill to recharter the bank passed the House, Webster wrote Biddle of his desire to paper over his indebtedness to the bank:

> before there shall be another discussion of the Bank question, a new Com[mitt]ee, or another examination of lists &c, the little notes of mine, at the B[oston] Branch, may be diminished, or extinguished, if I remain in Congress.[36]

Webster wanted Biddle to arrange a loan for him with a Philadelphia businessman. He would use these funds to pay off his BUS debts.

On July 10, 1832, Jackson vetoed the recharter bill. During the next year and a half Webster sought a political accommodation with the Jacksonians on the issue of nullification. When this failed and the Jacksonians persisted in their hostility to the BUS, Webster returned to the Clay-Calhoun faction. Webster used his position as a leading supporter of the bank to press Biddle to keep him on the BUS payroll. In the letter of December 21, 1833, printed below, Webster threatened to take cases against the bank if the bank did not pay his annual retainer. He enclosed with his letter to Biddle another letter for presentation to the bank's directors. Webster has traditionally been criticized by historians for the December 21st letter.[37] Most critics have simply reported the enclosure—i.e., "refresh my retainer"—without either knowing or mentioning the covering explanatory letter. The cover letter, though, is somewhat exculpatory. It explains in part the motivation for the enclosure. Webster apparently had no intention of abandoning the bank. He did understand, however, the delicate positions that both he and Biddle occupied. He therefore suggested that, if necessary, Biddle use the enclosure before the bank's somewhat hostile board to secure payment of Webster's fees. He was saying that he trusted Biddle's discretion and appraisal of the politics of the matter, while reassuring Biddle that

36. About July 4, 1832, *Correspondence*, 3: 185.

37. For example, see Irving H. Bartlett, *Daniel Webster* (New York, 1978), pp. 142–143.

he would "not undertake, professionally, agt. the Bank, whether you answer this, or not." The threat was simply a strategy to secure future fee payments. As the previous section indicates, Webster's conduct with the bank was not beyond question, nor was he shy about fees. In presenting these materials we have not attempted to defend his beleaguered reputation. In the matter of the December 21st letter, however, historians may have overdrawn the case.

TO NICHOLAS BIDDLE

Private

Dear Sir, [December 21, 1833]

I have thought it proper to write the enclosed letter; to which, however, you need give no attention, if you think it more *prudent* to wait a while. I shall not undertake, professionally, agt. the Bank, whether you answer this, or not. If such things have to go before the *Board*, I should prefer the subject should be *postponed.* Will you tell me whether you apprehend any danger, from my writing to you, on account of infidelity in the P. Office—& tell me, also, if you are careful to burn *all* letters. Yrs D.W.

ENCLOSURE: TO NICHOLAS BIDDLE

Sir Washington Decr 21 1833

Since I arrived here, I have had an application to be concerned, professionally, against the Bank, which I have declined, of course, although I believe my retainer has not been renewed, or *refreshed*, as usual. If it be wished that my relation to the Bank should be continued, it may be well to send me the usual retainer. Yours with regard, Danl Webster

ALS, with ALS enclosure. DLC. Published in *Correspondence*, 3: 288.

FROM NICHOLAS BIDDLE

My dear Sir Philada. Dec. 25th 1834 [1833]

I of course do not wish to see you engaged against the Bank in any case, and should therefore send the refreshment in question at once. But as you leave it to my discretion, I think it better to delay it for a short time—& for a reason which furnishes perhaps the best illustration of the necessity of abating the nuisance which now annoys us. The simple fact—so simple as to be a matter of course, of retaining counsel in a suit would be instantly perverted. If it were done by the Board it would be in the hands of the Editor of the Globe in forty eight hours—if by the Officers of the institution, it would not be there for a week—and the fact would be either immediately announced, or it would be treasured up to be used on the first occasion, when any vote of yours gave displeasure to that gang. The people who would do this are the same people who watch your account and the account of every political antagonist—who paraded in the Globe your visit to my house in the country and the discount to Mr [John] Connell at that time—who take no share in the affairs of the Bank, except to report & misrepresent every transaction of every individual opposed to them. Depend upon it these people should be expelled now that you have the power. Whilst they are here, I think it would be better to delay the matter in question for a short time.

Every body says that the Post Office in Washn. is faithless—but I know nothing—yet I generally have my letters addressed by other hands.

I always and scrupulously burn what I am requested to burn—otherwise not: so that you must dictate your wishes. With great regard Yrs

N. B.

LC. DLC. Published in *Correspondence*, 3: 292.

During the winter of 1833–1834, Biddle used the remaining power of the bank to contract credit in the major cities. The ensuing economic depression, he believed, would force the administration to accept the rechartering of the bank. The strategy backfired. It was the bank that came to be seen as the villain. The friends of the bank would no longer support it. By February 1834 the Democrats in the House controlled the bank's fate. They passed four resolutions opposing the rechartering and supporting the removal of government deposits. The fourth resolution authorized a seven-member committee to study the bank's affairs. Webster's friend Edward Everett of Massachusetts was one of only two Whigs named to it. When Biddle refused to permit the committee access to the bank's records, he sealed the bank's fate. The committee's report, on May 22, 1834, condemned the bank for the financial crisis of the previous winter. Conscious of the drift of public opinion, Webster began to maneuver to disengage himself from the bank.

TO EDWARD EVERETT

Dear Sir Washington April 26. '34

I am obliged to you for your letter of the 23rd.[38] All things with your name on them shall be taken care of, so as that you shall find no trouble, in that regard.

If, in the course of your investigation, the Com[mitt]ee should incline

38. Letter not found.

to notice my name, I wish you to state, as on my authority;—That I never had any particular or unusual accomodation from the Bank, to the amt. of a single dollar;—
That since I went to Boston, in 1817, I have kept my account, & done my necessary banking business at the Boston Office; & notes, bills of Exchange &c, &c, with my name on them have been collected, & discounted, &c as often as occasion required, precisely as would have been done in the case of any other person, & not otherwise. I have reports of mortgages, standing loans, &c &c between the Bank & myself, in all which there is not a single word of truth. I never gave the Bank any mortgage, & never had any standing loan, or any other accomodation, except in the way of discount of bills and notes, as at other Banks.

As to Mr Connell's notes &c., they arise in a strictly professional transaction. He obtained the agency of the claims of our Boston Merchants & Insurance Offices, under the French Treaty.[39] They made it a condition of the bargain, that he should secure my professional services, in all cases; & having the agency of a vast amount of other claims, Mr Connell engaged my professional aid in the whole, as matter of contract, & the notes were given in pursuance of this contract. That is the whole matter. You may make any use of these facts, public or private, which you deem proper.

I recd yr former letter,[40] at Boston. All things look exceedingly well in N York. They can hardly fail to go right, in their further progress. I am glad you propose writing to Col Perkins. He is now here, & will probably remain a few days longer. If the suggestion is put to me, I shall make something like what you suggest *a condition*, to any effort on my part. We now consider Va. as gone decidedly & strongly agt. the President. The Protest[41] has finished the work. Did you ever see any thing better than the Baltimore Resolutions?[42]

It will oblige me *much*, if you will keep me advised of yr proceedings, & let me know the general temper manifested by the Com[mit]tee. We think something of making a like Committee from the Senate.[43] Yrs truly ever D. Webster

ALS. MHi. Published in *Correspondence*, 3: 342–343. Edward Everett (1794–1865; Harvard 1811), clergyman, teacher, and public official, editor, *North*

39. See pp. 325–326, below.

40. Letter not found.

41. On April 17, 1834, President Jackson sent to the Senate a "protest" against the resolution passed by that body censuring his conduct in the removal of federal deposits from the BUS. See *Register of Debates*, 23d Cong., 1st sess., pp. 1317–1336.

42. On April 23, 1834, a Whig meeting in Baltimore condemned Jackson's protest. See *Niles' Register*, 46 (May 3, 1834): 165–166.

43. The Senate established a committee on June 30, 1834, but it was too weak and too late to shift public opinion in the bank's favor.

American Review, U.S. representative (1825–1835), Massachusetts governor (1836–1839), U.S. ambassador to England (1841–1845), U.S. secretary of state (1852–1853).

TO SAMUEL JAUDON

My Dear Sir, Boston July 25, 1834

I enclose you a letter from Mr. Connell. In reply,[44] I have written him that he must let the drfts be renewed till fall, & have added that I suggested to you, while in Philadelphia, a mode of arranging the matter, if we could accomplish it, without stating particulars. It is of great importance to get these matters out of the Bk of the U. S. I feel very anxious, on this matter, & fear I shall find a necessity even of going to Philadelphia, which I should be most desirous to avoid, for a thousand reasons.

As to the small drft, falling due the 24./27 current, please pay it if it go on, & draw on me for the amt, at 10 d[ay]s—and send an acceptance for same sum to Mr. Frothingham.[45] It gives me great pain to trouble you with these affairs. But here they are, & we must manage them as well as we can, till times turn a little better. I have means ultimately, to pay them; & that is one comfort.

Mr. Connell ought to make no difficulty in renewing the two small drfts, (5.000 each) as I indorse the renewals of the note, (10.000) which is his. If they cannot be arranged else where, they must be renewed in the Bank for a short time, say 60 or 90 ds; & in the mean time I must go to Philadelphia, if necessary; though such a journey, without some known object would attract a great deal of attention. Yrs truly

D. Webster

I must depend on your kindness to write me early, on these subjects, as I shall have no *quiet* till I see they are likely to be satisfactorily disposed of. I enclose a draft for 268.17[46]—

ALS. NHi. Published in *Correspondence*, 3: 357–358.

TO [SAMUEL JAUDON]

Dear Sir, Boston Aug. 2. 1834

I am obliged to you for your letter of July 30th.[47] It is my wish & intention to have my name out of the Bank, & all its branches, in the course of the Summer. I think this desirable on all accounts, & I believe it can easily be accomplished.

44. Neither letter has been found. Two months earlier DW had written to Jaudon on this matter, May 5, 1834, *Correspondence*, 3: 344–345.

45. Samuel Frothingham, cashier of the Boston branch, BUS.

46. Enclosure not found.

47. Letter not found.

1. Mr Connells two drafts. His acceptances of my drafts, guaranteed by you, (on a separate paper) could be discounted here, & with the proceeds the outstanding acceptances paid.
2. Mr. Connells note for $10,000 indorsed by me. By a little pains, & with the assistance of friends this cd. probably be discounted at some other Bank in Phila. either in one note or two.
3. Two or three small matters of mine in the Branch here will be paid off.

These things being done, I can take an early occasion, next Session to say, that I neither owe the Bank a dollar, nor am on any paper discounted at the Bank, for any body, to the amt. of a dollar.

In these times of the prevalence of slander & falsehood, it seems important to be able to make this declaration, on some fit occasion, in my place.

The only difficulty will be, if there be any, in regard to Mr Connell's note;—but I should think that might be easily arranged.

In a day or two, I will send you the papers, for yr consideration, for carrying this plan into effect.[48] Yrs. D Webster

ALS. NHi. Published in *Correspondence*, 3: 358–359.

TO HENRY HUBBARD

My Dear Sir, Boston, November 18, 1834.

I have received your two letters.[49] The note accompanying the last I have indorsed, and sent to the bank, where it will be doubtless discounted, according to your wishes.

Will you allow me to say, my dear sir, that I had one objection, though a trifling one, to indorsing your note. You know what stories have been circulated (and nowhere more diligently than in New Hampshire) of my pecuniary obligations to the Bank of the United States, heavy mortgages, etc., etc. Now, the truth is, that the bank never discounted or advanced to me a cent in the world, except in the ordinary way as they have done for others; and, at this moment, the indorsement of your note, and one other signed by another gentleman, constitutes nearly, if not entirely, my whole liability to the bank; and, to put an end to such slanders, and to have been enabled myself to say that the bank did not hold my name for a dollar, I should perhaps, if you had lived here, have suggested to you the obtaining of some other name instead of my own. But, as you

48. See DW to Samuel Jaudon, August 6, 1834, *Correspondence* 3: 360, in which DW sent Connell's drafts.

49. Hubbard to DW, November 2, 1834, mDW 11949; other not found. Hubbard sought DW's endorsement to obtain a loan from the BUS-Boston.

lived in the country, it might have been inconvenient to you; and, after all, I suppose there would be just as much libellous matter published, let the facts be one way or the other. Mr. Frothingham will probably write you. I hope you will find the rogue that took such liberties with your name.[50] Yours with regard, Danl Webster.

Text from Curtis, 1: 498–499. Original not found. Published in *Correspondence*, 3: 372–373. Henry Hubbard (1784–1857; Dartmouth 1803), lawyer, U.S. representative (1829–1835), U.S. senator (1835–1841), governor of New Hampshire (1841–1843).

b. Foreign Claims

Besides the claims settled under the 1819 treaty with Spain, other Americans pressed demands for compensation for injury to ships and cargo. Most of these claims arose from captures during the Napoleonic Wars. In each case negotiations with a particular nation resulted in a compromise that left the U.S. with a sum of money (always less than the total amount of damages claimed) to disperse among the claimants. Webster followed these negotiations closely. When the treaties came to the Senate for ratification, he sought to represent the New England claimants.

In 1827 Webster's friend Henry Wheaton began negotiations with Denmark. These resulted in the treaty of March 1830 in which Denmark gave the U.S. $650,000 for distribution among the claimants. When the agreement came to the Senate for ratification at the end of May, Webster wrote to Kinsman:

> There is a Treaty with *Denmark*—it will be well for you to go immediately to Mr Snelling & get him to go with you to the other [insurance] offices, & secure the agency of their claims.[1]

Boston insurance companies who had paid for losses held many of the claims. Although the Senate quickly ratified the treaty, it was not until 1831 that Congress established the commission that adjudicated the claims.[2] That body met from April 1831 to March 1833.

Concurrently the U.S. government concluded two more treaties. The first and more important was signed with France on July 4, 1831. Although the French government agreed to a set sum for distribution by the U.S., the French chamber of deputies balked at appropriating the money. France did not make the funds available until early in 1835.

50. In October 1834 DW received a letter, purportedly from Hubbard, asking him for two $500 bank notes for use in a counterfeiting case. DW correctly suspected a hoax and sent back the letter. (DW to Hubbard, October 27, 1834, mDW 11923.)

1. May 28 [1830], mDW 9470, and Van Tyne, p. 158.

2. 4 U. S. Statutes at Large 446 (1831).

Webster did not obtain the agency for these French claims. Instead he had to settle for service as legal counsel to the claimants. He thus lost the opportunity to earn the sizable commission an agency brought.

The other settlement, signed October 14, 1832, was with the Kingdom of the Two Sicilies (Naples). In this case as well, Webster acted on receipt of the treaty by the Senate. In December 1832 he wrote to Thomas Wren Ward, agent for the Baring Brothers:

> I believe you are interested, in your own right or as trustee for others, in claims under the treaty with Naples. I take the liberty of saying, that I shall be glad to take charge of any such claim, if agreeable to you to place it in my hands.[3]

On March 2, 1833, Congress enacted legislation establishing a claims commission.[4]

One other claims matter occupied Webster's attention. In 1800 the U.S. signed a convention with France which released France from responsibility for all claims by U.S. citizens for injuries that had occurred prior to 1800. When the claimants applied to Congress for relief in 1802, they were rebuffed. In the mid-1820s these claims surfaced again. Known as "French spoliations prior to 1800," they represented a sizable amount of money. If Congress ever passed a bill favorable to the claimants, an agent for a group of them could earn a large commission. As chairman of the Senate finance committee, Webster stood to gain if he could engineer passage of claims legislation while at the same time arranging to become the representative of the New England claimants. The letters that follow illustrate Webster's activities involving the claims commissions and the phantom French spoliations.

FROM HENRY WILLIS KINSMAN

Dr Sir　　　　Boston Jany. 6. 1831 [1832]

I commence to day the sending of documents in relation to the Danish claims.

The course which has been taken is this, the memorials of the several claimants have been sent on to the Commissioners, most of them drawn by themselves, in consequence of their living at such a distance as rendered it impossible for me to confer with them personally. The evidence also, that is, the depositions which we have been able to procure <of living witnesses> (only two I believe), has also been sent directly to the Commissioners. I have furnished for you in each case an

3. December 8, 1832, mDW 10363.

4. 4 U. S. Statutes at Large 666 (1833). The French claims commission met from August 1832 to December 1835. 4 U. S. Statutes at Large 574 (1832), 679 (1834), 778 (1835).

abstract or copy of the memorial together with such papers & documents, being accounts of the parties, vouchers for expenditures, &c as could be procured, & a statement of the nature of the claim, & of the evidence by which it is supported. This of course varies according to the care of parties interested, in keeping, & attention in procuring evidence. In one or two cases the principal evidence is that of the party himself under oath as stated in his memorial.

I have urged upon all of them the importance of procuring the necessary testimony & have pointed out to them what I thought important. If they fall short, they must take the consequence. However, if any thing should be required that can be obtained, no doubt the Commissioners would allow a reasonable time to procure it.

In some instances I have referred, as you will perceive to documents which are supposed to have been sent to Washington. It is probable too, that the records of the proceedings of the Court of Denmark in condemning vessels, may be on file there also. Many Protests & other documents in relation to the losses are *known to have been filed at the time* the loss occurred, in the depart. of State, although the parties from lapse of time & other circumstances, have lost their recollection, as to what precisely was done in their respective cases.

I send documents respecting Mrs. Lewis's claim[5] today.

Moreover in relation to this very matter I observe, that the Commissioners in their first advertisement, state, that measures have been taken by our Govt. to procure from the Danish Govt. the records of such proceedings of its Courts, as affected the seizure & condemnation of Am[erican] vessels. If these measures have been successful, by reference to such documents as have been procured, you will probably find all that may be wanting to complete the proof of the loss of the Jane of Portland, & the Commerce of Boston.

AL draft. NhHi.

TO JAMES STRONG

Dr Sir Washington April 3. [18]32

I cannot say much about the probability of passing the French Spoliation Bill.[6] It will, I think, go thro the Senate, unless it should lose its chance, by the pressure of other matters, but how it will be recd in H. R. I cannot say. Yrs truly, D. Webster

We need you here

ALS. NhPoS. James Strong (1783–1847; University of Vermont 1806), U.S. representative from New York (1819–1821; 1823–1831).

5. This claimant has not been identified; enclosure not found.

6. The Senate did not act on the bill. The House generally opposed the claims legislation.

TO PETER CHARDON BROOKS

My Dr Sir Philadelphia Decr. 27. 1832

You will have observed, that steps have already been taken in Congress to bring forward the Bill for indemnifying persons who have claims on France, for spoliations previous to 1800. I wish to take an early opportunity to say to my friends in Boston, that should the Bill be passed, & should it be their pleasure that I should be concerned in the Agency of their claims, it will be agreeable to me, *provided I am to be concerned, as under the Spanish Treaty.* On the other hand, if they have made, or shall make, such arrangements, as to need my services only as *Counsel*, as under the *French* Treaty, I must beg to decline the engagement.

Will you have the goodness to show this, to such friends as you may think fit, & as soon as convenient inform me whether the principal holders of claims are already committed, as to the agency of them.[7] Information on this point may be important to me, as it may enable me to answer inquiries from other quarters. Yrs always very truly

Danl. Webster

ALS. NhD.

TO HENRY WILLIS KINSMAN

Dr Sir, Jan. 4. 1833

I have recd yrs. of the 1, with Mr Fettyplace's Memorial, in case of the *Reward*.[8]

I note also that you have paid Mr. Farnham's note.[9]

I send you a minute, furnished today, of the Danish Cases.[10] Having copied it, perhaps you may as well send it back. Is there any other case, before that Board?

I would mention now, while it occurs to me, that in addition to the Invoices & Bills of Lading, it will be well, in collecting proofs under the French Treaty, it will be well to add the *Manifest*—that being a sort of official Paper. And even where the loss was on the homeward passage, I

7. See Brooks's reply of January 6, 1833, below.
Brooks had been a principal client of DW's during the life of the Spanish Claims Commission. See Chapter 4, above.

8. William Fettyplace, Salem merchant and one of the French claimants. In this case DW acted as counsel. See Henry Willis Kinsman to DW, January 1, 1833, mDW 7477. When the Commission rejected the claim in 1835, DW resubmitted it. *Memorial of William Fettyplace*, Sen. Doc. 272, 24th Cong., 1st sess., March 24, 1836.

9. Not identified.

10. Enclosure not found.

would yet, where I could, add the Manifest of the outward Cargo, by way of shewing the continuity of interests. Yrs truly D.W.

Please send me a printed list of the members of the Genl. Court, so soon as there is one.

ALS. Dr. Gurdon S. Pulford, Palo Alto, California.

FROM PETER CHARDON BROOKS

My Dear Sir Boston Jan 6. 1833.

I have delayed a reply to your letter of Dec. 27 from Philadelphia,[11]—for the purpose of making inquiries. I have seen Mr. Sargent of the Marine Office, Mr. Titus Welles, who represents the late Mr. Touro,—and some private writers.[12] They are uniformly of opinion that you should be requested to take the agency of the claims on our government for French captures prior to Sep. 30. 1800. They have, some of them, requested to know the terms on which you would be pleased to do it. The amount, they suppose, will be large. I need hardly say, my dear Sir, that I heartily unite in the wish to have your agency. You know I do.

In this concern you will stand alone. In July 1823 . . there was an agreement made here with Mr. Causten,[13] and I know of no other. The substance of that agreement,—which is informal,—will be found in the following extract. It was dated July 3. 1823.—"should a law for our relief, or reference to a tribunal, be had, *within four years* from the commencement of the next Session of Congress,—*in either of which cases your agency will terminate*, we promise to allow and pay you, out of the proceeds thereof, or otherwise, at the rate of two & a half pcent on whatever sum or sums may be awarded to us; and we do now advance in cash for your use, the sum of fifty dollars each, which is eventually to be deducted from said 2 1/2 pcent. And it is well understood that Mr. C is not authorised to call on us for any further advance or reimbursement of expenses." This was signed by a number in the form of a letter. Mr. Causten had never any agency but to endeavor to get a law passed.

Should a law pass granting any considerable sum,—you know already pretty well the amount that will be attended to by me. It will be several

11. See DW to Brooks, December 27, 1833, printed above.

12. Insurance underwriters not affiliated with insurance companies. Daniel Sargent, president of the Marine Insurance Company; Welles was a Boston merchant.

13. James H. Causten, founder and Washington representative of the Agency of French Spoliation Claims. DW appears to have worked to displace Causten. The latter believed himself to hold the agency for all the claimants. See pp. 339–343, below.

hundred thousand dollars—nominally. How many of the claims will be good for any thing is another thing. I notice that previously to your arrival the bill in the Senate was laid *on the table*. I hope this is not tantamount to laying *under it*. It will be unnecessary for me to inform you how much we all rely on you, as being a friend of the claim, to get it sustained. It will be letting the government off very easily to pay five millions only. The common opinion has been, but without any certain date,—that the claims amount to three times that—to say nothing of 32 years interest.[14]

* * * * * *

I am my dear Sir with the utmost respect your obedt. servt

P. C. Brooks

Extract from ALS. H. Bartholomew Cox, Oxon Hill, Maryland.

TO HENRY WILLIS KINSMAN

Dear Sir Washington Jan. 25. [18]33

I have examined the Memorials,[15] recd up to this time, & today present all of them, except *two*, which I doubt about and retain, & *nine*, which appear to me defective, and which I return to you. You will find a paper accompanying them, pointing out the necessary alterations. The necessity of these alterations, at least of some of them, could not have been foreseen, until the decisions of the Comm[issioner]s in other cases had been known.

For the future, it will be better, that all memorials be acknowledged before *Notaries*, & under *seal*. The Commrs do not know *justices*, & it gives us a great deal of trouble, sometimes to prove the *fact* that they *are* Justices.

In several memorials, it is not stated whether the Petitioners are *native* or *naturalized* citizens. The rule *expressly* requires this to be stated. This omission I have endeavored to cure, thus far, by my own statement. In regard to *agents*, the Commrs have not, as yet, recd any memorial by an *agent*; & I have no expectation they will receive any, unless in cases where the principal is *abroad*. Even that point is not yet decided; & therefore I hold back the Memorial, for the present, in which Mr Fettyplace appears as agent to his brother; viz, Reward, Goss[16]

These observations, with the notes on the accompanying papers, will shew you, I believe all the necessary amendments. Let these be returned, as fast as they shall be put right. Yrs truly Danl Webster

ALS. NhHi.

14. The rest of this letter concerns the *Charles River Bridge* case. It will be published in *Legal Papers*, 3.

15. French claims.

16. William Goss, captain of the *Reward*.

TO HENRY WILLIS KINSMAN

My Dear [Sir] Washington Feb. 5th. 1833

Among the Danish Claims, that of the Brig Commerce, Otis, is very badly prepared, & will certainly be rejected, if strict and immediate attention be not paid to it. The minute I sent you, from the Secretary, was incorrect. It was another *Commerce*.

In this case, are two memorials, one of Otis Little, Ellsworth, Maine, drawn by himself, very badly; & one by Daniel W. Rogers, of Gloucester, Adm[inistrato]r of Timo. Rogers, drawn by you.[17] Each of these parties claims, I think, 1/3 of 1/2. The residue of vessel & cargo is not claimed.

1. Defect. There is no proof of property in the vessel. No copy of the Reg[i]s[te]r, & no bill of sale. Otis states, that the vessel was built in Plymouth, Mass; & was purchased in Lisbon, in the Spring of 1809, by himself and David Sawyer,[18] (both vessel & cargo) on acct. of themselves, and of Jno. & Saml. Welles, Patrick Grant,[19] & Timo. Rogers. But there is no copy of Register—no bill of sale—nor any other proof of p[ro]p[ert]y in vessel. This is *indispensable*. She was captured, June 1809. An Invoice, purporting to be original, & also bill of Lading, are in the case; *but nobody swears to them*. There is also what purports to be a copy of the Acct of Gould Brothers & Co., Lisbon; but it is not sworn to. All this must be attended to, *without delay*; as no paper can be recd. after Mar. 1.—Get copy of Reg[i]s[te]r—& proof of purchase of vessel. Get Little's affidavit—let him swear to purchase, &c, & produce bill of sale, if he has it. Let him swear that the Bill of Lading & Invoice, forwarded by him, are the true & original Bill of Lading & Invoice. Write to D. W. Rogers, Gloucester, immediately, & set him to work.

If you doubt about having time to hear from Ellsworth, see what papers Mr Rogers has—perhaps Mr Jno. Welles can give you information. I suppose he, & his brother, & Mr Grant, & Mr Sawyer[19] were insured in England, & on that acct. do not claim.

This case is urgent. I see no *proof* of the value of the vessel. Has Mr Rogers sent on proof that he is Admr. of Timo. Rogers—I do not recollect whether I saw that paper in the files. Yrs D. Webster

ALS. NhHi. Published in *W & S*, 16: 226–227.

FROM HENRY WILLIS KINSMAN

My Dear Sir Boston Feby. 11. 1833.

Your letter respecting the Commerce was this morning received &

17. Otis Little, Daniel W. and Timothy Rogers have not been identified.

18. Not identified.

19. Patrick Grant, Boston merchant.

shall be immediately attended to. As to the bad *preparation of the case* I do not feel responsible for it; inasmuch as I was aware of the defective character of the evidence to support the claim, & have written frequently, to Mr. Otis upon the subject, desiring him to furnish you or me with the necessary proof. Mr. [Daniel W.] Rogers has informed me that he had no papers of any kind, but relied on Mr. Otis entirely. I believe I stated all the above to you in a letter which I wrote in January 1831.[20] I have once sent on proof that Mr. Rogers was Administrator, but will write to him to procure another certificate from the Judge of Probate. I shall get all the information from Mr. Welles that can be obtained. I enclose a Power of Atty. from Saml. Sanford of Boston for you to appear for him, in the case of the Joseph, a Danish claim. Mr. S. is my landlord, Mr Walter[21] prepared the Memorial, but the claimant feels a little anxious & doubtful & is desirous to have it attended to, for which he is willing to pay the usual commission. The amount claimed is $7000. Will you please take charge of it, & if any thing is wanting which can now be procured it shall be immediately attended to. He only spoke to me this morning on the subject. I am yours &c Henry W. Kinsman

ALS. NhHi.

FROM HENRY WILLIS KINSMAN

Dear Sir Boston Feby. 20. 1836 [1833]

I have, by much exertion procured a deposition from Mr Welles, which I hope will so far corroborate Otis's Memorial as to satisfy the Commissioners. When I first went to Mr. Welles, he recollected little or nothing about the business, but after talking with him several times, & getting him to look over his books, I have at length put his testimony into such a shape as to prove I think 1st. that Otis & Sawyer purchased the Commerce at Lisbon for account of S. & J Welles, Rogers, Grant & Otis 2d. That the vessel cost $6000. (& this with outfits may reasonably make her value $7000. as claimed)—3d. That the Welles's were insured in Europe & therefore do not now claim. 4th. That the cargo was fruit & wine & was paid for through Bainbridge & Brown & belonged to the above named parties, as to the value of the cargo we could find no further account <nor any invoice>, than what may be inferred from the amount stated to have been insured by the Welles in Europe for their half. Nor could <we> ascertain from Mr. Welles what portion of vessel & cargo was owned by Rogers, Otis, & Grant, but his testimony seemed to show they were equally interested in one half.

20. See Kinsman to DW, January 6, 1832, printed above.

21. Sanford has not been further identified; possibly Arthur M. Walter, Boston lawyer, studied with Harrison Gray Otis, admitted in 1802.

I have written to Otis for Bill of Sale but do not much expect to hear from him, or that he cannot furnish any evidence whatever, because I have before written to him without effect, if I get any thing I shall of course forward it, but also not like to detain the Deposition any longer. I have also sent to Plymouth & obtained a Register, which was all that could be found at the Custom House. The sale of the Brig having taken place in Europe & she having been soon after captured probably the reason that no change was ever made at the Custom House. I have requested Mr Dexter, who took Mr. W's deposition, to send it directly to Mr. Fulton[22] the Secretary & now send you a copy of the Regr. Mr. Rogers has already forwarded proof of his being administrator which you have before this time, probably received. Be good enough to advise me of the receipt of the above papers.

AL draft. NhHi.

TO HENRY WILLIS KINSMAN

Dr Sir Washington feb. 26 [1833]

I have recd this morning yr. letter, with Copy of Regi[ster], in case of Commerce, & copy of Mr Welles' Depo[sition],[23] I fancy we shall be able to get along with the case. Yrs D. Webster

ALS. Dr. Gurdon S. Pulford, Palo Alto, California.

TO [HENRY WILLIS KINSMAN]

Dear Sir N. York Mar. 24. [18]33

I have just recd news that the Commerce, Otis, *is allowed*. So, if you [have] not sent on already, you need send nothing. Any thing sent *now* might possibly do hurt.

Please draw a power of Atty, from Capt. Otis to me, with power of substitution, "to receive from the proper Officer or Officers of the Treasury Department of U. S. any sum or sums of money awarded to him by the Commissioners under the Treaty of the (insert date) between the U. S. & His Majesty the King of Denmark"—&c—& get a like power from Mr. [Daniel W.] Rogers.

I write today to Mr Frothingham, who will enable you to meet any thing which it may be necessary to pay, till I get home. I do not know of any thing, not already mentioned.

I hope to be home before the month is out. Yrs truly D. Webster

ALS. NhHi. Published in *W & S*, 16: 227.

22. Dexter has not been identified; Robert Fulton, secretary of the Danish Claims Commission.

23. See preceding letter.

TO SAMUEL JAUDON

My Dear Sir, Boston April 12, 1833

I mentioned to you, in Philadelphia, that I might have occasion to ask of you the repetition of a kindness, & that when I reached home, I would write you on the subject.

During our connexion as agents for claims under the Spanish Treaty, & afterwards, before your removal to New Orleans, you occasionally accepted my drafts, when I had occasion for money, as you remember. I am now in such a situation as that a similar friendly accomodation would be useful. In a year & a half, or two years, I hope to be receiving considerable sums, as comm[issio]ns on claims under the French & Neapolitan Treaties, to which claims I am now giving much attention. In the meantime, certain private matters render it convenient that I should anticipate these receipts. If you have no objection, therefore, I should be glad of permission to draw on you. Proper care will of course be taken, in all cases, to see the necessary provision made for your indemnity, & you may be assured that even in the event of accident happening to me, your liability, whatever it might be, would be provided for, out of the fund, now already, in great part *earned*, arising from the commns on the claims.

I pray you to remember me to Mrs Jaudon. We look forward, with much hope & some confidence, to your promised visit, a few months hence. In the meantime, if I can get rid of sundry private & professional engagements, I intend a trip as far as to the Bank of the Ohio. Yours always with cordial regard, Danl Webster

P.S.

If instead of drawing myself, I should authorize any other person to draw, I shall of course give you due notice. Formerly, you accepted drafts of mine for as large amts as $5.000. I do not propose now to draw any bill for a larger amt.

ALS. NHi. Published in *Correspondence*, 3: 242–243.

During the second session of Congress in the fall of 1833, Webster secured the appointment of a Senate committee to report on the French spoliations question. As the time approached for the committee to act, he moved to make his desire for the agency known to his Boston contacts (see letters of January and February 1834, printed below). The committee, however, took no action until early in the next winter. On December 10, 1834, Webster's special committee reported a bill favorable to the claimants authorizing the distribution of five million dollars. Shortly thereafter, a newspaper article appeared accusing Webster of having accepted in 1832 a $20,000 fee from the claimants. Webster first asked James H. Causten, the claimants' lobbyist, to write a rebuttal, and then Webster himself prepared a response which Causten signed. Causten's view of Webster's action appears below (Documents 47 and 48). Webster had not accepted the alleged fee. But as his correspondence reveals, he was maneuvering to represent the New England claimants. Out of the 956 claimants, 262 came from Massachusetts.[24] So in fact he obviously stood to gain financially if his congressional efforts in favor of the bill were successful.

Causten did not appreciate Webster's activities, although Causten knew that Webster's support for the legislation was critical. In January 1835 Webster spoke in favor of the bill. After first disclaiming any financial interest in its passage, he proceeded to stress the equitable nature of the claims (Document 49). The bill passed the Senate but died in the House. Periodically thereafter new bills appeared but never became law.[25] The issue of the French spoliations continued to occupy congressional attention until the early twentieth century.

TO [HENRY WILLIS KINSMAN]

Private & Confidential

My Dear Sir, Washington Jan. 11. 1834

I wish to write you a letter, in confidence, for your own eyes & Mr [Peter Chardon] Brooks'.

The subject, is the French claims, before 1800. I moved on that subject, early in the session, had a Committee appointed, myself at the head of it, & we have reported a Bill. By proper pains, this Bill *will assuredly pass the Senate.* Two members of the Com[mitt]ee (Mr Grundy & Mr Preston)[26] told me they shd. be glad to vote against it, if they could, but

24. House Report No. 445, 25th Cong., 2nd. sess., January 20, 1838, p. 171. See also James H. Causten, *A Sketch of the Claims of Sundry American Citizens on the Government of the United States for Indemnity* (Washington, D.C., 1871); George A. King, *The French Spoliation Claims* (Washington, D.C., 1916).

25. "Beyond all expectation, the Bill for the old French claims will probably pass the House today—(I believe it has passed)—Give notice, immediately, that you propose to act as agent for claimants, before the Board. Set all yr. friends immediately at work." DW to Daniel Fletcher Webster, August 4 [1846], mDW 27370.

26. Felix Grundy (1777–1840), Kentucky and Tennessee lawyer, Kentucky state representative (1800–1805), judge, Kentucky supreme court (1806–1807), U.S. representative from Tennessee (1811–1814), Tennessee state representative (1815–1819), U.S. senator (1829–1838; 1839–1840), U.S. attorney general (1838–1839); William Campbell Preston (1794–1860; South Carolina College 1812), South Carolina lawyer, state representative (1828–1834), U.S. senator (1833–1842), president, South Carolina College (1845–1851).

that they could not answer the argument in its favor. I have proposed Wednesday, the 5th. of Feb., for taking it up.

It is time, therefore, I think to move in the matter of the Agency. If the Gentlemen in interest, in our quarter, desire my aid I wish them to settle that point, before a host of other persons apply. Will you, therefore, show this letter to Mr Brooks, &, if necessary, to Mr Edward Brooks; —it need go no farther. If Mr Brooks thinks proper, let him draw up an agreement, substantially like that in the case of the Spanish Treaty; let him sign it himself, & ask others to sign it. If this can be done, to such an extent as to make it an object, you may say to Mr Brooks that it is my intention very much to relinquish other, professional employment, & give my strictest personal attention to this business. It will [be] an object to do so, provided I can obtain the Agency of the greater part of the interest, in our region.

If such an agreement shall be signed by Mr Brooks & others, Mr S White would take pains to get signers. Indeed if Mr Brooks enters into the object, you may afterwards show this letter to Mr White. I do not wish to be connected with any other persons, in the Agency, whatever. For what assistance you render, I shall of course compensate you, as we may agree; but I wish to take the whole responsibility on myself, with nothing to do with any other agents.

It would oblige me if you could attend to this soon, & let me know the result. Tell Mr Brooks, there is nobody here, out of doors, that can do any good. Yrs D. Webster

ALS. NhHi. Published in Van Tyne, pp. 720–721.

TO [HENRY WILLIS KINSMAN]

Dear Sir Washington Jan. 13. 1834

I have recd the enclosed, this morning.[27] It wd. be a good thing, I think, for Mr Brooks to write to Mr Bartlett, or Mr Nelson,[28] on the subject of my letter of yesterday. It may be very probable that all the Newburyport Gentlemen are already engaged to Mr Cushing;[29] if so, it

27. Enclosure not found.

28. William Bartlett of Newburyport, otherwise not identified; Jeremiah Nelson (1769–1838; Dartmouth 1790), Newburyport merchant, state representative (1803–1804), U.S. representative (1805–1807; 1815–1825; 1831–1833), president, Newburyport Mutual Fire Insurance Company (1829). DW probably meant the letter of January 11, 1834, above.

29. Caleb Cushing (1800–1879; Harvard 1817), Massachusetts lawyer and scholar, studied with Ebenezer Moseley and at the Harvard Law School (1820), practiced in Essex County, state legislator, U.S. representative (1835–1843), minister to China (1843–1845), brigadier general, Massachusetts volunteers in war with Mexico, justice, MassSJC (1852–1853), U.S. attorney general (1853–1857), member, Mexican

is well. But if unengaged, very probably they wd. sign my paper. Of course, Mr. Brooks will not mention any thing of this letter.

Mr. Charles Russell,[30] of New Bedford, has a claim, I believe a large one. You might write to him, saying you are connected with me, & that we should be willing to take the Agency of his claim on the same terms as that of others. Yrs D. Webster

Mr Russell has written me, like many others, to press the indemnity.

ALS. NhHi. Published in *Correspondence*, 3: 310–311.

FROM HENRY WILLIS KINSMAN

Dear Sir Boston Jany. 17. 1834

Anticipating the probability of the appropriation for the old Fr. claims, & knowing how the agencies of the Neapolitan & other claims had been scattered about, I had just prepared the draught of a letter to you of inquiry, as to the best mode of securing the management of the old claims, when yours dated the 11th. but post marked the 13th, arrived.[31] According to your request I have this day seen Mr. Brooks, Edward; It seems that his father had proposed to him to take the management of their claims himself, but to this he observed, that he felt himself unequal, for various reasons, one of which in particular, was that the great number of the cases, & the variety of the papers, documents & books from which the proofs were to be made up, would render it necessary for him to be here all or most of the time, & of course make it impossible for him to be at Washington. He therefore was perfectly willing to acquiesce in the arrangement, & upon consulting his father, he also was perfectly satisfied & promised to write to Mr. Nelson today. I ventured to say to Mr. E. Brooks, on your part, that I thought you would have no objection to making such discount from the usual commission, as might appear to be reasonable, in consideration of the services which he must render in preparing the Memorials & cases; I mentioned this to him, because he several times remarked, that this part of the business must necessarily be done by him & by nobody else, inasmuch as the papers & books through which these transactions run, were such that it would not be agreeable to him to have them go into the hands of strangers, and also because he alone could be able perfectly to understand them. I hope I did not go too far in this, but it appeared to me very important to secure the agency of Mr. Brooks' cases to begin with. I further mentioned to him that I did not think you would be disposed to attend to the busi-

Claims Commission, member, commission to codify laws of the U.S. (1866–1870), nominated to USSC, but not confirmed (1874), minister to Spain (1874–1877).

30. Not identified.

31. See the two preceding letters.

ness at all, unless you could have enough of it to make it an object, in which case, you proposed to make it your principal business during the existence of any Commission which might be appointed for the examination of the claims.

We are daily expecting our new Governor,[32] until the arrival of whom nothing important will probably be done by the Legislature. With much respect I am Yrs &c H. W. Kinsman

ALS. NhHi.

FROM HENRY WILLIS KINSMAN

Dear Sir Boston Feby. 3d. 1834

I this morning had a conversation with Mr. P. C. Brooks about old French claims. He has not yet found the agreement, & seems to doubt the expediency of preparing any agreement at present, because, as he says, it might have an unfavorable effect to call a meeting of the claimants at this time. I told him, that I did not suppose it to be necessary to have any public meeting to accomplish the object; but, that it would answer every purpose to have a paper drawn up & presented to persons interested for their signature, without the formality of any notice to call them together, & I named to him what I thought were reasons for such a course. That, in the three recent Conventions,[33] you had all the nice questions to give opinions upon, & many of them to argue, questions upon which large classes of claims had been decided, & that other persons had obtained the benefit of your labours. I told him moreover, that you did not wish to divide the responsibility with any other persons, but wished the whole charge, & would employ, under your immediate direction, such assistance as might be found necessary in preparing papers & memorials, & that in order to make it an object to do this to the neglect of other business, it was important, that you should have the management of all, or nearly all of the claims, from the North, & that therefore it would be well immediately to commence obtaining agencies before any other person should anticipate you, & that it would be convenient for the parties themselves, if solicited by other persons, to be able to say that they had already employed you. I had previously had the same conversation with Mr. Edward Brooks about a fortnight ago. They are both very willing to take any course you may see fit to recommend to secure you the business, & I understood Mr. P. C. B., that he had written you, & should be governed by your answer.

One thing more, Mr. Brooks mentioned, that he had heretofore suggested to Edward, that *he* might take charge of these claims himself, but

32. John Davis (1787–1854).

33. The treaties settling the French, Danish, and Neapolitan claims.

he observed, that he had given up the idea, because it seemed to him, that the attention of one person would be required *here* all the time; in order to prepare the documents & papers, & furnish such proofs as might, from time to time, be called for—and, that from the character of the books and papers to be consulted, being rather of a confidential nature, no one could so well do this, as Edward, & consequently, that he could not be present at Washington, at the meetings of the Commissioners. As it appeared, from this Statement, that they had at one time entertained the idea of getting up the claims themselves, & that, at any rate, a considerable part of the labour of preparation was to be undertaken by E. Brooks, I thought myself justified in saying for you, that you would recompense him for his services out of your commissions, or make such a deduction from the commissions on his father's claims, as might be thought reasonable under the circumstances. I hope in this I did right.

I do not mean, by repeating what I have said to the Messers. Brooks, to intimate that there was any unwillingness on their part, to assent to your proposition, on the contrary, they were both very well satisfied to employ you, & appear to be desirous to do every thing to forward your views. Mr. Brooks has had a favorable answer from Mr. [William] Bartlett, also from Mr. [Henry] Hatch & Mr. Parsons.[34] I am Yrs:

H. W. Kinsman

ALS. NhHi. Published in *Correspondence*, 3: 315–317.

DOCUMENT 47. JAMES H. CAUSTEN'S DIARY ENTRY

Dec 16, 1834

Mr. Webster sent a note, from his seat in the Senate, requesting to see me. I forthwith visited him in the Senate. He submitted to my perusal the slip from the "Evening Post," hereto attached,[35] and said, "it must be answered and ought to be answered by you", to which I replied that I would instantly write an article for Gales & Seaton's paper denying said statement about $10,000—as paid to him by me; and left him for the purpose of preparing it.

I had scarcely reached my office when a Senate Messenger from Mr. Webster presented to me the draft, hereto annexed,[36] of the form of publication he desired; to which I subscribed my name (without any hesitation) and it was on the next morning published in said paper.

34. William Parsons (1755–1837), Boston shipowner and merchant.

35. The *New York Evening Post* of December 13, 1834, reprinted parts of an article that appeared in the *Albany Argus* on December 10, 1834. The article accused DW of having received in 1832 a fee of $20,000 from an "agent for French claims prior to 1800," obviously Causten.

36. See the next letter.

The proper explanation is as follows: An opponent of this class of claims (1800) and a vindictive enemy of Mr. Webster—believed to be Mr Benton—wantonly perverted intentionally a fact, for this twofold purpose.

Mr. John Connell, who was the agent of several Insurance Companies & individuals, who had claims under the Convention with France of July 4. 1831, then fully ratified and exchanged and a Board to audit the claims appointed, made an engagement with Mr W as counsel to advocate said claims before said Board, for a fee in hand of $10000. The engagement therefore had no reference direct or indirect to the claims then before Congress, those prior to 1800, all of which were in my agency. The turpitude of the writer of said article is manifest.

J H Causten

ADS. H. Bartholomew Cox, Oxon Hill, Maryland. Excerpt published in *Correspondence*, 3: 378, n. 1.

TO JOSEPH GALES & WILLIAM WINSTON SEATON FROM JAMES H. CAUSTEN (IN WEBSTER'S HAND)

Genl. Washington Decr. 16. 1834

A friend has pointed out to my notice an article in the New York Evening Post, copied from the Albany Argus, which article asserts that the Agent for the claimants for indemnity for French Spoliations before 1800, had entered into a pecuniary arrangement with Mr Webster, by which he was to act as Counsel for these claimants. I am, & long have been, agent for those claimants, & I know of no other Agent, & no such arrangement, nor any other arrangement, has been made between Mr Webster & myself. The whole statement is entirely false. Mr Webster has no personal connexion with the claims, whatsoever. He has been induced to take a part in bringing them forward, by my request, in behalf of many claimants, & after expressing an earnest desire that some other Gentleman would take the lead in the business.

I feel it a duty, not only to Mr W. & myself, but to the claimants also, thus to declare the falsehood of the statement in the Albany and N York Papers.

AL draft (DW). NhD. Published in *Correspondence* 3: 377–378. The letter appeared in the *National Intelligencer* of December 18, 1834, signed by Causten.

DOCUMENT 48. JAMES H. CAUSTEN'S DIARY ENTRY

[January 1, 1835]

Note. It was again and again hinted on the floor of the Senate (and probably well founded) that Mr. Webster had himself made speculations in these claims, and in consequence thereof he requested of me a letter to counteract such report. I wrote the letter to him of Jany 1. 1835 (copy enclosed herein) which he returned with this letter, in which he enclosed the draft (A) of a modified letter for me to copy and sign—as I did, and forwarded it to him.[37]

The draft A is in his hand writing.

It will be seen that my letter of Jany 1/35 had a twofold object, to shield Mr Webster and to shield myself—but his draft A is made to shield himself only, leaving myself and the cause without notice. It was a selfish and heartless act on his part—and I take no credit to myself for yielding to the modification. It was not my judgment, but sound policy that thus yielded.

JHC

ADS. H. Bartholomew Cox, Oxon Hill, Maryland. Published in *Correspondence*, 4: 7, n. 2.

FROM JAMES H. CAUSTEN

Dr Sir. Washington Jany 1. 1835

In the recent discussions, in the Senate, on the Bill for the relief of the sufferers by French spoliations prior to Sep 30. 1800, some opposition has been manifested on the supposed ground that the parties interested have employed an Agent for a "moiety" to prosecute the claims, and that they are in the hands of speculators but set forth in the names of Widows and Orphans, in order to profit by the sympathy of Congress &c.

Being the sole agent of the claimants for the last twelve years, it is impossible that I should be insensible to these unfounded charges, or unfaithful to my duty by not offering a prompt and distinct denial of them. In proferring this denial to you, as chairman of the Committee having the Bill in Charge, I have sought for the proper channel, but in any event I rely on your kind indulgence.

For your information I take the occasion to say, that my sole commission is only one half the usual compensation for the most plain and ordinary prompt claims—it is two and a half percent, and that contingent.

In some three or four instances, I was applied to by obscure and impoverished individuals to find purchasers for small claims, which were derivitive as heirs, and whose wants pressed heavily. My answer was uniform—"I know of no purchasers, and would not point them out if I knew such—do not sell your claims, because it would yield little for your

37. Causten's letter is printed below, followed by DW's communication.

relief, and because Congress will eventually do you justice—but I cannot aid you in that shape, as such an act would (justly or otherwise) materially impair the inducement which happily exists to indemnify the claimants."

Subsequently, a remark in the House of Representatives gave rise to an impression that the claimants, or some of them, were such on speculation. I forthwith addressed a circular letter to the claimants in all parts of the United States, setting forth that impression, and requiring the fact: by the answers, extending to some hundreds, I found not a single case of sale or purchase, but some assignments in Bankrupt and other analagous cases.

Perhaps there has been few subjects before Congress in which Widows and Orphans are so generally the complainants; the mere lapse of time and course of nature has placed them in the situation they are now found without any act or effort of their own. But such persons do not make themselves conspicuous; nor in this case have they been put forward, either properly or improperly, since few of them are seen upon the Memorials; and all the petitions and arguments offered, refer to the naked justice of the claim: And, for the truth of this assertion, I can safely appeal to the files of the Senate and to the recollection of every Senator with whom I have had intercourse.

I give you this information on the responsibility of my name, to be used in any manner you may deem proper.

I may be permitted to add, that no Counsel, auxiliary, or aid of any kind has been employed or contemplated—the claimants have selected for their Agent a plain and unpretending Citizen (not even a Lawyer), with the only qualification of patiently enduring protracted labor. His high respect for the body with whom his duty calls him to act, added to self respect, has marked the exercise of his functions with all the studied delicacy of which he is capable. I am, dear Sir, with great respect, Your Obedient Servant James H. Causten

ALS copy (by Causten). H. Bartholomew Cox, Oxon Hill, Maryland. Published in *Correspondence*, 4: 6–7.

TO JAMES H. CAUSTEN

Dr Sir [c. January 1, 1835]

Your letter is much too long—we want something like the enclosed—

ENCLOSURE: DRAFT OF A MODIFIED LETTER TO BE ADDRESSED TO WEBSTER BY CAUSTEN

I see, with much regret, that an objection is made to the claims for French Spoliation before 1800, on the supposition that a <great> large portion of those claims have been purchased up, & are holden by Speculators. This is certainly a great mistake. My means of information are such, that I think I cannot be misled on this subject; & I assure you I am fully convinced that the idea of extensive speculation in these claims is founded in error. I have known no transfers, except in the ordinary settlement of estates, or by merchants, to pay or secure debts; & am perfectly sure that a vast majority of the whole still remains in the hands of the original holders, their heirs & representatives.

If you think it would be useful, you may communicate this to the members of the Comee or others. Yrs &c

AN and AL draft (in DW's hand). NhD. Published in *Correspondence*, 4: 8.

DOCUMENT 49. SPEECH

[January 12, 1835]

The assertion[38] . . . was wholly and entirely false and malicious. I have not the slightest interest in these claims, or any one of them. I have never been conferred with or retained by any one, or spoken to as counsel, for any of them, in the course of my life. No member of the Senate is more entirely free from any personal connection with the claims than I am. It has been the pleasure of the Senate, on several occasions, to place me on a committee to which these petitions have been referred. I have on those occasions examined the subject with a desire to acquit myself conscientiously of my duty, by exercising my best judgment upon the claims, as questions of mere right and justice.

Extract. *W & S*, 7: 152–178. French Spoliations Prior to 1800, delivered in the Senate, January 12, 1835.

38. A reference to the rumors that DW had a financial interest in the legislation.

CHAPTER 6. Substantive Aspects of Webster's Boston Practice

Webster practiced law in New Hampshire for eleven years. During that time he handled a broad range of cases that included commercial litigation for the leading merchants of the state. This experience with basic business law enabled him to build a Boston practice that leaned heavily on commercial matters. In Boston he discovered that the large volume of commercial litigation had spawned a rudimentary specialization among the local practitioners. Webster became a master of such nascent specialties as marine insurance, corporate, and patent law, while retaining his expertise in general mercantile and property law. The materials in the six sections that follow illustrate some of the legal disputes in which Webster played a significant role. These selections from the extensive body of documents that remain available to the historian show Webster at different moments of time in his Boston practice.[1]

At the time Webster moved to Boston, business practices in the leading commercial states were in the process of change. As a national market economy emerged, long-range transactions between businessmen became increasingly formal and impersonal. Nineteenth-century judges began making their decisions with an eye toward the creation of the clear and certain rules which they believed these new entrepreneurs desired. The colonial practice of extrajudicial merchant arbitration atrophied in the wake of judicial rulings that strengthened the hands of the judges in commercial disputes. Judicial activism also resulted in the narrowing of the jury's role in commercial disputes. Relegated to the narrow confines of a fact-finding function, the jury no longer presented a threat to the enforcement of the bargain made between the parties.[2]

The principal change in the law affecting commerce was the acceptance of the will theory as the paradigm for contractual relations. When Webster practiced in New Hampshire, his understanding of contract law reflected the eighteenth century notion that the exchange of equiva-

1. Much of DW's early Boston practice resembled the commercial case load of the Portsmouth period. For illustrative material on this phase of his career, see *Legal Papers*, 1, ch. 12. We have not included material on corporations and patent law in this volume. We will treat these subjects in Volume 3 in the context of DW's federal practice.

2. For a discussion of arbitration and the jury's interventionist role see *Legal Papers*, 1: 322–332, and Horwitz, pp. 141–144, 149–155.

lents was the basis for enforceable bargains.[3] Juries were expected to examine the bargain to see if it was fair. Businessmen who wanted to avoid such jury intervention had to use sealed bonds. By the 1830s, however, the adoption of the will theory had made the bargain sacrosanct. Evidence of the intent of the parties in the words of the contract foreclosed further court inquiry. This view was clearly expressed by Judge Lemuel Shaw in an 1834 case in which Webster participated on the plaintiff's side.[4] The dispute grew out of an employment contract signed by two metal workers, on the one side, and a metal fabrication corporation on the other. In exchange for a promise to work only for the company, the company promised to pay the artisans $1500 a year for as long as the employment relation continued. After four years of losses, the stockholders dissolved the corporation. One of the artisans then sued for two years' wages. In the argument before the MassSJC, attorneys for the defunct corporation argued that the written contract was unequal and unreasonable. Shaw refused to examine the nature of the exchange.

> The first and fundamental rule in the construction of a contract, is to ascertain the meaning and intent of the parties; and the second is, to look at every clause and word of the instrument in which they have imbodied their contract, to ascertain that meaning. . . . [I]f the terms of the contract are plain and perspicuous, it is not enough to say, that the parties could not have intended what their language has plainly expressed. The bargain may have been hasty or improvident, or one of which we cannot see the reasons or ground. Still, if such was the contract, and entered into fairly, it is not for a court of law to vary or alter it, or change its legal effect, upon vague notions of improvidence or inequality, or on account of its being founded upon expectations which have not been realized.[5]

In this world in transition lawyers found a fertile field for their services. Businessmen, who were advised to put their dealings in writing to "avoid the imprudence of trusting to understandings,"[6] were certainly aware of the costs and uncertainties of litigation. Although they may not have welcomed the intervention of lawyers into their affairs, they had little choice.

I. COMMERCIAL LAW

a. *Thomas Laurason et al.* v. *Ebenezer Nickerson, principal et al.*[1]

During the fall of 1817, an Alexandria, Virginia, mercantile firm, Laura-

3. See *Legal Papers*, 1: 296–307.

4. The basic documents are in *Revere* v. *Boston Copper Company*, MassSJC,S, March 1834.

5. 15 Pickering (Mass.) 351, 361–362 (1834).

6. Benjamin L. Oliver, *The Law Summary* (Boston, 1831), p. viii.

1. MassSJC,S, November 1819.

son & Fowle, hired Webster to collect a debt from Ebenezer Nickerson, an insolvent Boston businessman. An investigation of Nickerson's dealings revealed a suspicious transfer of seventy shares of stock in a Massachusetts manufacturing company to his brother Nathan. This forced Webster and Bliss to take two steps to ensure the merchants' recovery. First, Bliss filed a trustee action against Ebenezer and Nathan Nickerson and four other men.[2] Second, Webster and Bliss brought a separate action against Ebenezer on the debt and ordered the sheriff to seize the shares of stock in Nathan's possession. In preparation for the trial of the trustee suit Webster drew up a set of interrogatories in which he questioned Nathan Nickerson about the stock transaction and his brother's financial affairs (Document 50). If Webster could prove fraud, the court would treat the shares as Ebenezer's property, and Laurason & Fowle would recover the proceeds of the sheriff's sale.

The defendants' attorney demurred the October trustee action to the March 1818 term of the MassSJC.[3] The court then continued the case to November. At that time Bliss received court permission to question Nathan Nickerson again. Bliss filed the new interrogatories and Nathan's answers in December (Documents 51 and 52). The court continued the action to March 1819. In the meantime, in January 1819 Webster and Bliss moved on the other action against Ebenezer. After the CCP gave judgment for Laurason & Fowle, the sheriff holding the shares made plans to sell them. At this point the parties must have worked out a settlement, for at the November 1819 SJC term neither side appeared. The legal phase of this controversy had ended.[4]

DOCUMENT 50. PLAINTIFF'S INTERROGATORIES AND TRUSTEE'S ANSWERS

Suffolk ss. Boston Court of Comm. Pleas, Octobr. 1817

Thomas Laurason & al vs Ebenezer Nickerson Pr[incipal] & William Mackay[5] & al Trustees—

2. This process allowed a creditor to reach those assets of his debtor which were being held by a third party: Laws, Mass., 2: 441 (1818). For the mechanics of this process in New Hampshire, see *Legal Papers*, 1: 85, 98–99.

3. Called a *sham demurrer*, this procedure allowed the parties to move a case from the CCP to the SJC for a trial. For the New Hampshire experience with this device, see *Legal Papers*, 1: 64.

4. In January 1818 DW and Bliss filed two more trustee actions in the CCP. These were demurred to the SJC, where the lawyers agreed to let the judgment in the first action decide the other two. Bliss appears to have handled most of the courtroom aspects of this case. DW was in Boston in the fall of 1817 and 1818 and for part of January 1819. Bliss would have appeared at the March terms, and probably handled the final settlement of the matter.

5. The 1817 writ named as trustees William Mackay, John Miller, and

Answer of Nathan Nickerson, summoned as trustee. And now the said Nathan appears & saith, that at the time of the service of the writ upon him in this case, he had not in his hands or possession any goods, effects or credits of the said Ebenezer Nickerson, & he submits himself to be examined, on oath, in the premises & prays to be discharged and allowed his reasonable costs.
Boston Octo. 7th. 1817 Nathan Nickerson

Interrogatory [on] behalf of plffs.

Has Ebenr. Nickerson given you an order on William Mackay, & others, for money, or for any balance in their hands—if so, when, & for what sums, & for what consideration, & has it been paid, in whole or in part, & where is it now?
Answer. The said Ebenezer Nickerson hath not delivered to me such order. Nor do I know where it is.

2. Was the said Ebenr. Nickerson indebted to you, on the 30th day of August last, or about that time, in any sum of money. If yea, in what sum, and on what account. If for balance of account, state the account. If on bond, note, or other obligation, describe it.

Answer to the 2d. Interrogatory. On the thirtieth of August last, there was an open account existing between the said Ebenezer Nickerson & this Respondent, which was afterwards, viz on the eighth of September following settled. A copy of the account current, signed by the said Ebenezer Nickerson, is hereunto annexed.[6] The said account reversed was signed by this Respondent, both were signed & mutually delivered on the said 8th. September.

3. When did you first hear of any such order as is mentioned in the first interrogatory—have you ever seen such order—is there any understanding or agreement between you & Ebenr. Nickerson that any such order or writing shall be given to you—or have you any expectation of receiving such order, from any body, at any time hereafter; If yea, on what account & for what consideration—please state particularly the whole matter.

To the 3d Interrogatory this Respondents says, that there is no understanding or agreement between him & the said Ebenezer Nickerson respecting the said order nor hath this Respondent any knowledge of the same.

4. Have you at any time purchased of Ebenr. Nickerson any shares in the Athol Manufacturing Company, or any other Corporation. If yea, when was this purchase made—who was knowing to it—how many

Joseph Howe, Boston merchants, Nathan Nickerson of Phillipstown, and Nathan Nickerson, Jr., of Athol.

6. Not found.

shares did you buy—what were their numbers, & how did you pay for them.

To the 4th. Interrogatory, this Respondent saith, that upon the ninth day of September last, he purchased of the said Ebenezer Nickerson seventy shares in the Athol Manufacturing Company, for which he gave to said Ebenezer his negotiable note of hand of that date, for the sum of Ten Thousand five hundred dollars, payable in one year from the date thereof. The said shares had been standing in this Respondents name from the month of January in the year 1815 & until the sale of the same.

Int. 5. Was the aforesaid note of ten thousand five hundred dollars negotiable, or was it not? Was it given on any condition, or was it not? Was any other writing executed at the same time, & if any what?

Answer. the said note was a negotiable one, and was made payable to the said Ebenezer Nickerson, or his order, absolutely & not upon any condition.

Upon the same ninth day of September the following agreement was made & executed between the said Ebenezer Nickerson & this Respondent: viz. [the note was copied into the answer at this point] The said Respondent saith, that two instruments of the like tenour to the above were executed on the said ninth of September & that each of the parties to the same kept one; and that the said purchase hath not been rescinded, but remains in full force. He further saith, that the price of the said seventy shares was the true value of the same; that he was at the time & still is Treasurer & Agent to the said Athol Manufacturing Company and well acquainted with the affairs of the same.

Interrogatory 6.

Were the said shares yours, in truth, & reality, at any time before the said ninth day of September.

Answer to the 6th. Interrogatory.

The said shares were the property of Respondent in truth & reality before the said ninth day of September. Sixty of the said shares were conveyed to him on the first of January 1815 & were transferred on the books of the Corporation on the third day of the same month, by Henry Chapman. In payment of the same respondent gave to said Chapman his negotiable note of hand with the name of Aaron Brigham[7] as surety thereon for the sum of five Hundred dollars payable to said Chapman, or order, with interest in twelve months, & grace. Five of the said sixty shares were sold by Respondent in the month of March following. On the thirty first of January 1815, Respondent entered into an agreement with said Ebenezer Nickerson that he would transfer to him the said

7. Neither Chapman nor Brigham has been identified.

sixty shares, provided he would pay said note to said Chapman and all other payments & expenses disbursed thereon. About the ninth of May following, Ammi Cutter[8] transferred to respondent fifteen shares more in said Company, which he held likewise under an agreement of like nature with said Ebenezer Nickerson. The said note to Chapman was taken up & paid by the said Ebenezer Nickerson in the course of the year 1815 but Respondent continued to hold the remaining shares & to pay the assessments on same till the ninth September—1817—at which time, being desirous of a full & complete settlement of this concern, and of all other accounts with said Ebenezer, Respondent came to Boston for the purpose of settling the account and of transferring to said Ebenezer the said shares or of purchasing the same as could be agreed. A full & final settlement was then made and the shares purchased & paid for as is stated in a former answer.

Interrogatory. 7.

Did you not know, on the said ninth day of September, that Ebenr. Nickerson had failed or stopped payment?

To the 7th Interrogatory Respondent says, he did know on the said ninth of September, that said Ebenezer Nickerson had failed or stopped payment.

Interrogatory 8. Was it not understood, between you & the said Ebenr. Nickerson, that he should not negotiate or sell your note, or put it out of his hands?

To the 8th. interrogatory he saith, it was not understood between said Ebenezer & this Respondent, that said Ebenezer should not negotiate or sell said note, or put it out of his hands. On the contrary, Respondent knew at the time, that said Ebenezer had right so to do, if he pleased, & Respondent relied solely for his protection & security on the covenants of said Ebenezer, which are contained in the foregoing agreement.

Interrogatory 9. What was the reason which led you to purchase these shares at that time?

To the 9th. interrogatory, Respondent says, that the reason is assigned in the answer to the sixth interrogatory:—he was desirous of a final settlement with said Ebenezer, and was ready to convey or to purchase the shares, as could be agreed.

Interrogatory 10.

What persons were knowing to the sale & purchase of these shares? Did Mr. Porter,[9] one of the subscribing witnesses to the agreement, know the contents of the Instrument?

To the 10th. Interrogatory Respondent says, the said sale & purchase

8. Not identified.

9. Not identified.

were made in the presence of Nathan Nickerson Junr. and William L Porter & were known to them. The instrument was read in their presence, and they were requested to subscribe their names as witnesses to the signatures of the parties which were made in their presence. Respondent hath no doubt, that the contents of said instrument were known at the time to said Porter.

Int. 11. When you purchased these shares in Septr. last, did you know that Ebenr. Nickerson was indebted to the plfs—did he mention their debt—or did you know that he was indebted, generally—or did he tell you he was.
To the 11th. Interrogatory, Respondent saith, that on the said ninth September he did not know that Ebenezer Nickerson was indebted to Plts in particular, nor did he know who were the creditors of said Ebenezer in general, nor the amount of his debts, nor whether he was able to pay in whole or in part. Respondent doth not recollect that said Ebenezer had, prior to the said ninth of September, given to him any particular information of the state of his affairs.

Int. 12. Why was the note made negotiable, if either party was to be at liberty to revoke the sale & purchase?
To the 12th. Interrogatory, Respondent saith, that said Ebenezer was not willing to take a note which was not negotiable.

Int. 13. Did you, or did you not, at the time you purchased the shares know that Ebenr Nickerson was indebted? Did you then believe him to have property to pay all his debts? or did you not? Did he at that time tell you, or give you to understand, that he could not pay his debts?
To the 13th interrogatory, Respondent saith, that said Ebenezer was indebted to him. For a reply to the residue of the question, he refers to his former answers.

Int. 14. Why was Ebenr. Nickerson not willing to take a note not negotiable?—did he give any reasons? if so, state all the reasons he gave.
To the 14th. interrogatory, Respondent saith, said Ebenezer did not assign to him his reasons.

Int. 15. You say you purchased these shares in order to settle your business with Eben Nickerson. Was this your only inducement to the purchase? What business was settled by this purchase? Would not your concerns have been as well closed by your transferring to him the title to these shares? Why was not that done?
To the 15th interrogatory. To such part of this question as is pertinent Respondent refers to his former answers.

Interrogatory 16.

Did you, at the time of purchasing these shares, know or believe that Ebenr. Nickerson was indebted to other persons beside yourself.

To the 16th. Interrogatory the Respondent saith, he did not know the state of said Ebenezer's affairs. He believed at the time said Ebenezer was indebted, because he understood the said Ebenezer had stopped payment. But whether said Ebenezer could pay in whole or in part Respondent saith, as he hath declared in a former answer, he did not know.

17. Did you believe, at that time, that he was not able to pay his debts? To the 17th. Interrogatory Respondent saith, that he had not at that time formed an opinion on the subject.

18. Was the object of this transaction to put the property beyond the reach of his creditors.
To the 18th. Interrogatory Respondent saith, the object of said transaction on his part was to have the property of the shares. What were the secret motives of said Ebenezer he doth not know. Respondent doth not know, that it was the object of the transaction, to put the property beyond the reach of said Ebenezer's creditors.

19. Was any thing said, by him, in your hearing, relative to the matter of putting this property where it could not be reached, by attachment or Trustee process? State particularly, what conversation, & all the conversation he had with you, or with others in your hearing, on this subject. To the 19th. Interrogatory Respondent saith, that nothing was said at the time by said Ebenezer of this nature in his presence & hearing.

20. What was your ability, at that time, to pay so large a sum as Ten thousand five hundred dollars? Were you worth so much money? Are you now worth so much money. In what does your property consist? At the time you <purchased these shares> gave this note, did you expect ever to pay it without raising the money from the shares themselves? To the 20th. Interrogatory, Respondent saith he owned at the time & doth now a real estate in Phillipston, worth eight thousand Dollars, free from incumbrances. His personal property upon the farm in Phillipston, he would not sell at that time nor now for fifteen hundred dollars. He looked into his affairs after his return to Phillipston & after the said purchase, & found himself to possess in other property, not including the said real & personal estates & likewise not including the shares purchased of said Ebenezer or the note given for the same, at least two thousand dollars more than all the debts which he owed at the time, Respondent believes, that he was then & still continues to be in good credit. Whether the said note would be paid by a sale of the shares in whole or in part, or in any other way, Respondent had not then, nor hath he now, formed a determination.

21. How happened you to be in Boston, on the said ninth of September? At whose request did you come down? Did your brother send for you?

Had you heard of his failure, or did you know of his embarrassments before you left home?

To the 21st. Interrogatory, Respondent saith, that for a year preceding the said ninth of September, he had been desirous of a final settlement with said Ebenezer, & had frequently by letter & verbally, requested said Ebenezer to come to Phillipston for the purpose, it being inconvenient for Respondent, on account of the sickness of his family, to visit Boston. Having heard of said Ebenezer's difficulties, Respondent was still more desirous of a settlement. The said Ebenezer had not sent for him nor had he requested Respondent to come to Boston.

The said Nathan Nickerson having answered all interrogatories, which he understands the Plffs intend to put to him at this time, doth inform the Court, that upon the Eleventh day of October current, Alexander Bliss Esqr. Attorney for the Plffs, delivered to him a written notification, of which the following is a copy: —viz.

"To Nathan Nickerson, Sir, You will please to take notice that on the 9th. instant all the shares in the Athol Manufacturing Company which you pretend to have purchased in September last of Ebenezer Nickerson, were attached as the property of the said Ebenezer at the suit of Messr. Laurason & Fowle, and that they will be sold to satisfy any judgment recovered in said suit, which shall not be otherwise satisfied; & that thereupon you will be called upon to execute all such transfers assignments & conveyances of the same shares as law and equity may require.

Alexander Bliss

Boston, Octor. 11th. 1817—Atty to Laurason & Fowle."

The said Nathan saith as before he had not at the time of the service of the Plffs writ upon him—any goods effects or credits, in his hands or possession, unless it should be otherwise determined by the Court upon the answer to the foregoing interrogatories & he prays the advice of the Court thereon, & that he may be discharged & allowed his reasonable costs, having travelled from Phillipston his place of residence which is seventy miles from Boston & having been detained in Boston upon expence from the seventh day of October Current.

Nathan Nickerson

ADS(DWp). *Laurason et al.* v. *E. Nickerson, principal,* MassSJC, November 1819. The questions are in DW's hand.

DOCUMENT 51. INTERROGATORIES

[November 1818]

1. Were not said sixty shares owned by Eben Nickerson before said Chapman transferred the same to you?
2. Were not said 60 Shares transferred by Eben Nickerson to said Chap-

man as Security for a debt due to him from said Ebenr or in Trust to pay his creditors or some of them?
3. Did you never hear Eben Nickerson say that he transferred said Shares to said Chapman as security for a debt due him, or in trust to pay his Nickerson's Creditors or some of them?
4. How long had Eben Nickerson held these shares before he conveyed them to Chapman?
5. Who bargained with Ammi Cutter for said fifteen shares and who paid him for the same?
6 Was it not a part of the original agreement between you & your Brother Ebenr. for the sale & purchase of said Shares, that your note should be cancelled and the shares transferred back to him, if either of you required it within a year after the Sale?
7 Did you not propose that the parties or one of them should have this power of rescinding the Contract for sale & purchase of said Shares, and would you have given your note for $10 500 for said Shares if you had not had yr power of avoiding the sale within the year?
8 Was it not said by Ebenr Nickerson in your hearing in a conversation respecting your giving said Note, that you would run no risk or would be exposed to no danger in giving the note or words to that effect, because it would be in your power to annul or rescind the bargain, if you chose, at any time within the year, or that you would not have to pay the note unless you inclined, or words of that import?
9 Had you any means by which you expected to raise the money to pay this note without making sale of said Shares, and if you had what were they?
10 Did you ever hear your Brother Ebenr. say to yourself or others in your presence that he wished to make a sale of the shares to you to prevent their being attached or that they might not be attached by his creditors, or to prevent expense or words to that effect?
11 Did you ever propose to your Brother Ebenr to take so many of the Shares as would pay the balance of your account & to assign the rest to him.
12 Did you ever at any time hear your said Brother say or know him do any thing, from which you understood or suspected that a motive or inducement for his making the abovementioned bargain with you respecting said shares was to put them out of the way or reach of his creditors?
13 Did you ever hear your Brother Ebenr. or his clerk or Attorney or any person in his presence say that it was necessary or best to make your note payable to order to prevent your being liable as his Trustee?
14 Has not the note which you indorsed for said Ebenezer as stated in your answer to the fifth additional Interrogatory been paid by him?

AD. *Laurason et al.* v. *E. Nickerson, principal,* MassSJC,S, November 1819.

DOCUMENT 52. ANSWERS TO INTERROGATORIES

Suff[olk] & Nan[tucket] ss. Sup. Jud. Ct. Novr. T. 1818.
Thomas Laurason & al v Ebenr. Nickerson Pr & Nathan Nickerson Tr.

To the first interrogatory filed by Pltfs at this term, the said Nathan Nickerson saith, that the said sixty shares were once owned by said Ebenezer Nickerson and were by him transferred to said Chapman before they were by him transferred to me.

To the second & third interrogatories said Nathan saith, I had understood that the said sixty shares were transferred to said Chapman by said Ebenezer in payment or as a security for a debt due to him, but the particular transaction between said Chapman & said Ebenezer I do not know.

To the fourth, he saith, that by the books of the corporation it appears, that said Ebenezer was one of the original proprietors, & that no transfer had been made by him prior to the one to said Chapman.

To the fifth, he saith, that the bargain with Ammi Cutter was made by said Ebenezer. The said fifteen shares were transferred to me with the consent of said Ebenezer, on the following account; viz. the said Aaron Brigham was desirous to be released from his endorsement on the note for five thousand Dollars, which said Chapman held, & said Chapman was willing to give up said note, provided it might be replaced with a note signed by said Ebenezer Nickerson & endorsed by me. As I had paid assessments on said sixty shares,[10] and said Ebenezer was indebted to me at that time, on another account, in a further sum of about two thousand dollars, I refused to endorse a new note for said Ebenezer without further security. He agreed that the fifteen shares should be transferred to me also & thereupon said Brigham's endorsement was taken up & replaced by a note signed by said Ebenezer & endorsed by me.

To the sixth, I have already in my answers to former interrogatories[11] set forth the whole agreement, which was made between said Ebenezer & myself relative to the purchase of the said shares. There was no agreement, express or implied, between us other than what hath been by me before declared.

To the seventh, the property in the said shares was at the time in me, subject to said Ebenezer's right of redemption according to the agreement between us. He would not part with his right, nor would I give the note except on the terms disclosed, and which I at the time deemed

10. Installments of the money which the investors promised to pay when they subscribed for the shares of stock.

11. See Document 50, above.

equal & safe. I considered that the shares were at that time worth ten thousand five hundred dollars.

To the eighth. I do not recollect, that there was at the time in my presence & hearing any conversation of that import.

To the ninth, I have in my former answers disclosed all my means.

To the tenth. I have no recollection, that said Ebenezer ever made any such observations in my presence or hearing.

To the eleventh, I do not recollect, that I proposed to said Ebenezer to take as many shares as would pay the balance due to me and to assign the residue to him. But I was always willing to settle with him in that way. Said Ebenezer declared to me at the time, that he expected the shares would rise in value & that he wished to reserve the right of availing himself of the appreciation of the property. At the same time, that I consented to his wishes, I deemed it reasonable to reserve to myself the right of rescinding the purchase, if it should be for my interest so to do.

To the twelfth, he says he did not.

To the thirteenth, I do not recollect any such conversation.

I further declare & say, that upon the said ninth Septr. 1817 & prior to that time, I held the said seventy shares as my property; that they had been justly & truly transferred to me for a good & valuable consideration paid by me as I have already stated & that I held the same bona fide, and without any fraudulent intent to injure said Ebenezer or his creditors: and I conceive that I was at that time justly entitled to hold & retain the same for all advances made or expences incurred by me upon them or by reason of said transfer, and until the same should be paid & refunded to me. The sole management of the said shares was in my hands, conducted according to my own discretion, & I did not consider myself bound in any degree to consult with said Ebenezer respecting the same, nor did he in any one instance undertake to exercise a controul over the said property or over me in respect of the same. And I further say, that in case the Honourable Court should declare, that the said transaction of 9th. Septr. 1817 between said Ebenezer & myself was, for any cause, invalid, I conceive that I have still a good right in law to retain the said shares according to the original contract between said Ebenezer & myself as the same hath been hereinbefore disclosed.—and as before, I submit myself to the judgment of the Hon. Court in the premises.

Nathan Nickerson

Suffolk ss. Dec. 22. 1818
Sworn to before me Jno. Callender clk

To the fourteenth. The note which was endorsed by me for said Ebenezer, as stated in my answer to the fifth additional interrogatory, was I presume, paid by the said Ebenezer. I was never called upon to pay the same.

Nathan Nickerson

Suffolk ss. Dec. 22d. 1818—Sworn before me

Wm. Sullivan Justice of peace

ADS. *Laurason et al.* v. *E. Nickerson, principal,* MassSJC,S, November 1819.

b. Benjamin C. Ward & Co. v. *Peirce & Washburn*

As to my expectations of future business I can only say that last night I dream'd I was commencing business in Boston but I have no reason to expect it will prove true—and I cannot tell what my business will be, with any more certainty, than I can predict the appearance of a Comet or the eruption of a Volcano.[1]

While Massachusetts judges used their increased control over the litigation process to insulate contracts from jury interference, the actual nature and pattern of commercial transactions continued to resemble Webster's New Hampshire experience. Boston merchants, like their Portsmouth counterparts, maintained informal relations with one another while controlling their individual dealings with retailers and traders in the hinterland. The case presented in this section illustrates how legal intervention occurred when the relationship between some Boston merchants moved from the informal context of everyday business practice into a formal arrangement designed to deal with the financial difficulties of a mutual customer.

William Spooner, a young Plymouth retailer, had stocked his new store with goods purchased on credit from a variety of Boston merchants. In the early spring of 1819 some of his small creditors demanded payment of their accounts and then brought suit to secure their debts. Although Spooner paid these accounts, he knew that if rumors regarding his solvency reached Boston, they could trigger a rush to the courts. He therefore traveled to Boston in March to meet with his creditors. His negotiations resulted in an agreement in which most of the merchants granted him six months grace before they would demand payment (Document 53). He returned to Plymouth confident of his future. In May he purchased more goods on credit from one of the principal signers of the agreement, Peirce & Washburn. Shortly thereafter, however, Peirce & Washburn found themselves in need of cash. Almost immediately, Peirce & Washburn began to hear rumors (or so they later

1. Deposition of William Spooner, *Lane et al.* v. *Peirce et al.*, MassSJC,S, March 1822.

claimed) that made it seem that Spooner was draining off the profits of the store and had already lost the confidence of his principal local backers. This would have left no assets when the merchants' agreement expired in September. Instead of consulting with the other Boston merchants, Peirce and Washburn moved unilaterally against Spooner to secure their own debt. Through a local Plymouth attorney they ordered the sheriff in July to shut Spooner's doors. Desperate to prevent events from snowballing, Spooner first wrote to Peirce & Washburn. Their reply of July 22, 1819, printed below, invited him to visit Boston to meet with them. Then according to Spooner:

> Soon after this attachment, I went to Boston and saw Mr. Peirce at the Store of Peirce & Washburn. I used all the arguments in my power to induce him to relinquish his attachment and abide by the agreement, he seemed undecided, and proposed terms similar to those offer'd by his attorney which I at once rejected. I told him the consequence would be a suit against them for breach of contract. In the course of conversation he said that an assurance of my future custom would be an inducement to withdraw the attachment, but after what had been done he presumed they had lost that, I replied that my anxiety to effect an arrangement would not induce me to promise to be their future customer. That I had determined to have no other business with them but to pay their demand.[2]

On August 2, 1819, Peirce & Washburn, their own debt secure, finally advised the other merchants of their action, printed below. Although Peirce & Washburn offered to share whatever they collected, three of the other merchant firms wanted none of the offer; the sale of Spooner's goods would not be enough to cover their debts. Instead, these merchants decided to sue Peirce & Washburn for breach of the March agreement. In September 1819 Benjamin C. Ward & Company filed suit (Document 54).

Less than a year later two more merchant firms entered actions. In all three suits Webster represented the defendants.[3] William Spooner was the principal witness for the plaintiffs. Prior to his attendance at the trial, Webster (through Bliss) filed cross interrogatories for Spooner to answer (Document 55). In his statement Spooner set out the entire chain of events that led to the closing of his store (Document 56). Other statements from Plymouth residents elaborated the final dissolution of Spooner's business (Documents 57, 58,, 59, and 60).[4]

2. Ibid.

3. *Ward* v. *Peirce et al.*, MassSJC,S, November 1822; *Lane et al.*, (n. 1, above); *Cowing* v. *Peirce et al.*, MassSJC,S, March 1822. There may have been suits by the other merchants in which DW was not retained as counsel. There is no record in the Massachusetts Reports of an appeal by Peirce & Washburn.

4. Two of these documents are from the *Lane* case and postdate the

In March 1820 the SJC tried the first case. In his report Judge Charles Jackson related his rendition of the facts and his instructions to the jury (Document 61). He instructed the jury that if they concluded that Spooner would have had a reasonable chance of paying his debts, they could hold Peirce & Washburn liable for the entire Ward debt. When the jury decided in favor of Ward, Webster moved for a new trial, contending that the verdict was against the weight of the evidence and that the damages were excessive.[5] When Jackson denied Webster's motion, Webster decided to delay making an appeal to the full SJC until the resolution of the other two cases. When the juries returned similar verdicts at the March 1822 term, Peirce & Washburn dropped the appeal and agreed to judgment as of the November 1822 term.

DOCUMENT 53. AGREEMENT OF CREDITORS

Boston March 23d 1819

We the undersigned, Creditors of William Spooner[6] of Plymouth feeling sufficient Confidence in the solvency of said Spooner do agree, not to interfere or molest him in his business for the term of six months from this date, and at the expiration of that time nothing shall be done to enforce or secure payment of our demands by any individual, except it be for the mutual benefit of all the undersigned

Benja. C. Ward & Co.
Peirce & Washburn
Lane and Lamson
West & Wild
Hartshorn & Ellis
D. & P. Thatcher
Pickens & Littlehale
Howland Cowing Jr.
Jonathan Cushing by Nathl M Davis[7]

ADS. *Lane et al.* v. *Peirce et al.*, MassSJC,S, March 1822.

PEIRCE & WASHBURN TO WILLIAM SPOONER

No. 1— Boston 22. July 1819

Mr Spooner Sir yours of the 21. is at hand[8] in noticing the same we find

---

Ward trial. They are included for the light they shed on the entire litigation.

5. For a discussion of postverdict practice in New Hampshire, see *Legal Papers*, 1: 286–289.

6. Plymouth trader.

7. All these are Boston merchants, except Nathanial Morton Davis (1785–1848; Harvard 1804), Plymouth lawyer and state legislator.

8. Letter not found.

you are disposed to settle with us on as favourable terms as we could wish for We do not wish you so much harm as to require you to sacrifice one cent more than is necessary for your Interest, it seems to us that your Friend Miller[9] has been rather amusing you than otherwise with the promise of assistance when in fact he did not mean to afford it. Through Mr Cushing we were inform'd as well as by yourself that when you first commenced trade he would grant you a permanent loan of $2500 to $3.000 which if he had done would have renderd your whole Business a pleasure to you and placed you almost beyond the want of money.

If Mr M was sincere in his professions and will now come forward with his money he sometime since promisd you, you need not fear being able to settle with your creditors to your own satisfaction. We think however you had best complete your account stock so as to make an exibit to your creditors and come to Boston as soon as you are ready to make a statement. Yours &c. Peirce & Washburne

Copy. *Lane et al.* v. *Peirce et al.*, MassSJC,S, March 1822.

PEIRCE & WASHBURN TO BENJAMIN C. WARD & COMPANY

Boston August 2d 1819.

Gent[lemen] we think it proper to inform you that having found it necessary from circumstances to commence an action against Wm. Spooner of Plymouth, we are willing and offer to divide among the creditors in Boston parties to the agreement of March 23d 1819,[10] in proportion to their debts all the fruits of our attatchments in said action so far as respects the debts due us at the date of that agreement, this offer however must be understood to be on condition that the creditors aforesaid meet and determine on measures to secure their debts as far as possible for the benefit of the whole, as the court to which the writs are returnable on which said Spooners goods are attatched is to be holden in Plymouth next week. it seems to us necessary that the creditors meet immediately. Yours &c Peirce & Washburn

Copy. *Lane et al.* v. *Peirce et al.*, MassSJC,S, March 1822.

DOCUMENT 54. WRIT OF ATTACHMENT

Suffolk, ss. Commonwealth of Massachusetts.
To the Sheriff of Our County of Suffolk *or his Deputy, Greeting.*

9. Edward Miller agreed to make Spooner an open-ended loan of $2000. At this time he had given him $1400. Peirce & Washburn doubted Miller's generosity. See Document 58, below.

10. See Document 53, above. Spooner defaulted the action against him on August 9, 1819. Peirce & Washburn recovered a judgment for $955.

WE command you to attach the Goods or Estate of Seth Pierce & Abiel Washburn Junior both of Boston in said county merchants & copartners jointly trading under the firm of Pierce & Washburn *to the Value of* two thousand *Dollars, and for Want thereof to take the Bodies of the said* Pierce & Washburn (*if they may be found in your Precinct*) *and* them *safely keep, so that you have* them *before Our Judge of Our Boston Court of Common Pleas, next to be holden at Boston, within and for Our said County of Suffolk, on the first Tuesday of* October *next*: *Then and there, in Our said Court, to answer unto* Benjamin C Ward & Nathan Appleton[11] both of said Boston, merchants & copartners jointly trading under the firm of Benjamin C Ward & Company, in a plea of the case, for that said Pierce & Washburn, at said Boston on the day of the purchase of this writ, being indebted to the Pltffs in the sum of fifteen hundred dollars, for the like sum of money before that time had & received by them to & for the use & benefit of the Pltffs, then & there in consideration thereof promised the Pltffs to pay them that sum on demand yet though requested said Pierce & Washburn have not paid the same and neglect so to do & also for that whereas the Pltffs at said Boston on the twenty third day of March last were creditors of one William Spooner of Plymouth in the County of Plymouth trader, and the said Spooner was then & there [in-]debted to the Pltffs in divers large sums of money, to wit, the sum of twelve hundred & twenty two dollars, & whereas the said Spooner was then & there indebted to them, the said Pierce & Washburn & also divers other persons in divers sums of money, they the said Pierce & Washburn, by their note or memorandum in writing of that date, by them subscribed feeling confidence in the solvency of said Spooner, & in consideration that the Pltffs did then & there by their note or memorandum of that date, subscribed, agree & mutually promise to & with them the said Pierce & Washburn that they the said Pltfs would not interfere with, or molest, the said Spooner in his business for & during the term of six months from that date, and the Pltffs aver that the said Spooner at the time of the execution of the said agreement, was carrying on business as a trader & merchant at said Plymouth to wit, at said Boston, & was then & there receiving great gains & profits therefrom, yet the said Pierce & Washburn there afterwards to wit at said Boston within the said term of six months next following the date of said agreement, to wit, on the twelfth day of July—last regardless of their promise & agreement aforesaid, & contriving & intending to deprive the said Pltffs of the benefit of their said debt due from said Spooner, by a writ of attachment in favour

11. Nathan Appleton (1779–1861), Boston manufacturer and banker, U.S. representative (1830–1832), formed a partnership with Benjamin C. Ward & Co. in 1815. See Frances W. Gregory, *Nathan Appleton, Merchant and Entrepreneur* (Charlottesville, Va., 1975).

of them the said Pierce & Washburn against said Spooner, caused the whole of the goods, merchandize & stock in trade of him said Spooner, being as the Pltffs aver, a large quantity of goods & merchandize, the property of him the said Spooner, and then being in the store or warehouse of him said Spooner, for sale, of great value, to wit, of the value of two thousand dollars, to be attached & taken into custody, in due form of law to satisfy such Judgment as they said Pierce & Washburn might recover against him said Spooner, & then & there by means thereof caused the said goods merchandize & stock to be wholly taken out of the custody & control of him said Spooner & then & there by means of said attachment, did wholly break up, destroy & put an end to the trade & business of him said Spooner & did then & there by means of said attachment interfere with & molest him said Spooner in his said business, contrary to the promise & agreement aforesaid, by means whereof the Pltffs have lost & been deprived of all means of obtaining payment or security for their said debt & been wholly deprived of the benefit thereof
To the Damage of the said Ward & Appleton *(as they say) the Sum of* two thousand *Dollars, which shall then and there be made to appear, with other due Damages. And have you there this Writ, with your Doings therein. Witness, Esquire, at Boston, the* twenty first *Day of* September *in the Year of our Lord One Thousand eight hundred and* nin[eteen.]

Jno. Tucker[12] Cl[erk]

Copy. *Ward et al.* v. *Peirce et al.*, MassSJC,S, November 1822.

DOCUMENT 55. CROSS INTERROGATORIES

Cross Interrogatories to be put to William Spooner or any witnesses proposed on the part of Mess Peirce & Washburn

1. Do you expect to gain or lose by the decision which may be had in this action?
2. Who were your creditors at the time the agreement, mentioned in Plffs interrogatories was entered into? Please to give the names of all of them, and the sum due to each respectively, and the times when due
3. At the time said Peirce and Washburn made said agreement, did you, or others in your behalf, represent, or intimate to said Peirce and Washburn, that all your creditors would execute the same agreement, and if not *all*, what number or description did you represent or intimate would execute the same? and were the same representa-

12. Possibly John Tucker (d. 1825; Harvard 1774).

tions made to all your creditors who were applied to for the same purpose? and particularly to said Ward & Co.

4. Were not Mess Peirce & Washburn, at the time they signed said agreement, secured by attachment on your goods &c. for the whole debt then due them from you, & were Mess Ward & Co. &c secured?
5. Had you, to induce Mess Cushing & Jackson[13] or Mr. Cushing to execute said agreement, delivered them in notes or a note the value of about five or six hundred dollars, did they upon delivery of said note or notes, and not before, sign said agreement—and did you or not advise Mess Peirce & Washburn of that circumstance? Did you offer such or other inducement to other creditors, if so, to whom?
6. After the execution of said agreement & before the attachment of Mess Peirce & Washburn, did you apply to Mess Ward & Co to purchase goods on credit, and did they sell you any—and did they effect to sell you any on condition of securing to them the payment by another name?
7. Were you, as you conceive, more injured in your property reputation or credit, by the attachment of Mess. Peirce and Washburn, than you would have been by the attachment of any creditor or creditors, not parties to the said agreement?
8. Who attached your property after Mess Peirce & Washburn, what was the amount of his or their debts, and what sum was paid thereon, arising from the sale under their executions. Did these attachments include all your property, and did it produce its full value, if not what proportion of its value?

9 Have you any property now, if any, what—& of what amount in value, and what is the amount of your debts, have you paid any debts or liability since said attachment, if [so] to whom, and of what amount?

10. When the aforesaid agreement was presented to your creditor[s] and particularly to Mess Peirce & Washburn, did you not inform them, that your means of raising money were such that you should be able to pay them in about thirty days or at a certain time a moiety or part of your debts—that a brother of yours would advance a certain sum &c., and were not your expe[cta]tions in this particular wholly disappointed, did you pay afterwards any considerable sums toward your debts—if any what, and at what times—and did your brother advance afterwards any such sum of money as you had expected, & do you not know that Mess Peirce & Washburn when they attached your stock &c had reason to suspect your immediate failure in business, and that they expressed such their fears.

11 Do you know any other matter or thing which may be of advantage

13. David B. Jackson.

to Dfts. to be known in this action, if so state the same as if particularly requested & interrogated thereto

Daniel Webster by A Bliss of counsel for Defts

ADS *Ward et al.* v. *Peirce et al.*, MassSJC,S, November 1822.

DOCUMENT 56. ANSWERS TO INTERROGATORIES

[January 10, 1820]

In the Action of Benjamin C. Ward & Al vs Seth Peirce & al, I William Spooner of Plymouth in the County of Plymouth in answer to the first interrogatory of the Plfs Counsel testify & say—Yes

The circumstances which led to the agreement were as follows—On or about the 17th of March last Nathan Hayward,[14] the Sheriff met me in the street & informed [me] that he had a writ against me in favor of Vinton & Cox[15] of Boston. I told him I was ready to discharge it on the spot; he proposed settling it in the evening, as it was inconvenient for him to stop, which was done accordingly, & I paid him the amount of the note one hundred & twenty two Dolls 54/100 & interest & cost eight Dolls 23/100. This note had not fallen due when I had last been in Boston.

The next evening my Clerk informed me, that T. Spooner Deputy Sheriff had called & wished to see me. I went to his house; he had a writ in favor of Charles Winslow,[16] the amount of whose demand against me with interest & cost was one hundred & one 11/100 Dollars. This note was not due when I last left Boston. This I paid. Presuming my other creditors in Boston would hear of these transactions, & apprehensive, they would pursue the same course, I advised with my friends & they recommended my going immediately to Boston. I called on Dr Hayward to ascertain if he had received any other writ or writs against me. He had one in which Smith & Gore[17] were Plfs. I paid the demand, interest, & cost amounting to Forty 37/100 Dolls. This account also was not due when I had last been in Boston. On the 20th March I went to Boston. I met on the road with Mr Jonathan Cushing, one of my Creditors, & informed him what had taken place. He had heard of it, but promised not to make any attachment on my property before leaving Plymouth. The Sheriff had writs in favor of Nathl Spooner[18] & Edward Miller, which were not to be served unless others came. Mr Cushing made an attachment on the goods in my store in favor of himself first & Peirce & Washburn next. The Writs of E. Miller & Nathl. Spooner were first served. About this time a Sch[oo]ner arrived from Carolina, on board of which I

14. Nathan Hayward, sheriff of Plymouth County.

15. Boston merchants.

16. Boston merchant.

17. Boston merchants, successors to Gore, Miller, & Parker.

18. William Spooner's father, also a Plymouth trader.

had property to the amount of seven hundred, & fifty Dollars. On this property Mr Cushing made the first attachment. I was informed of this circumstance, a short time previous to promising him a joint note for five hundred Dollars. I believe however he was ignorant of the attachment last mentioned, when he authorized his Attorney to sign the agr[ee]ment. On Monday the 22d of March, I called on my Creditors & informed them of what had taken place. Most of them were ignorant of the circumstance, and they appeared disposed to do whatever might be thought most proper for the interest of all concerned. On the 23d of March the agr[ee]ment was entered into, & signed by my Creditors on which this action is founded. Mr Cushing said he would relinquish his attachment, & sign the paper, when the others had but after the others had signed, he declined, under the belief, as he stated, that he was secure in his attachment on the goods in the store, and would not sign the agreement without an equivalent. He required a joint note of my Father & myself for five hundred Dollars at six months and my note for the balance. As nothing else would satisfy him, & being unwilling that the agreement should be frustrated, I promised to do as required, if my father would sign the note. Mr Cushing then gave me a letter to his attorney in Plymouth, authorizing him to sign the agreement on my compliance with the condition. The note was signed by my father, and the agreement was signed by Cushing's Attorney in his behalf. I made a full disclosure of my situation according to the best of my knowledge. I stated to my creditors & particularly to Peirce & Washburn the situation of my affairs. All whom I expected to sign the agreement, did sign it. I stated to them, that there were some other debts, but was certain, that I should not be molested in consequence of them. I also stated that in six months, I should be able to pay more, than half my debts, & would then make such an exhibit of my concerns as would in all probability restore me to their full confidence. It was understood, that I should first pay off my small debts, in order to lessen the number of my creditors, that on any future occasion, I might not have so many to consult. My credit at that time was perfectly good, if I may judge from the readiness of those I dealt with to supply me with goods—particularly Messrs Peirce & Washburn, who urged me to take goods to the amount of fifteen hundred Dollars in September previous.

In answer to the second Interrogatory by the Plfs Counsel, I testify & say.

In May following I went to Boston & purchased some more goods, chiefly such articles, as were necessary to keep a good assortment in my store—for some of these I paid cash. I also purchased of Peirce & Washburn goods to the amount of four hundred & forty eight 49/100 Dolls. Nothing was said respecting the terms of credit. Nor did I ever have any conversation with them on that subject, since my first purchase of them, when they assured me that six months was their credit on sales. They appeared as usual willing to sell to me, & urged me to take more. They did not take a note for this purchase, but remained charged in account, as they had done once before. In conversation with them relating to their demand against me, they felt, as they expressed as much security as any demand they had, & would wait my convenience were it not for the scarcity of money. I promised to Do all that I could to perform my part of the agreement.

In answer to the third interrogatory proposed by the Plfs' Counsel I testify & say—Yes.

Sometime in the latter part of June I received a letter from Peirce & Washburn, stating their want of money and calling on me to pay a part of their demand. I wrote in answer that I should soon be in Boston, & would pay them a part of whatever sum I might collect. I was making arrangements for this purpose, when on the 12th July, the Sheriff entered my store, & attached my goods therein at the de[mand] of Peirce & Washburn. I called on their attorney, who said he was instructed to relinquish the attachment on condition of my paying in cash four or five hundred Dolls, & give a note for the Balance with an undoubted endorser. I stated to the Attorney (Mr [Nathaniel] Davis) that a compliance with the condition was impracticable, & shewed him the agreement. The store was closed, & the Sheriff kept the key 'till the goods were sold by Auction in Septr—excepting when I was admitted with a Deputy Sheriff to take account Stock. Soon after the attachment, I went to Boston, & saw Mr Peirce at the store of Peirce & Washburn. I used all the arguments in my power to prevail on him to relinquish his attachment & abide by the agreement,—he seemed undecided, & proposed terms similar to those offered by his Attorney, which I at once rejected. I told him the consequence would be a suit against them for breach of contract on the agreement. In the conversation he said that an assurance of my future custom would be some inducement to withdraw the attachment, but after what had been done, he presumed they had lost that. My reply was, that my anxiety to make an arrangement with them, would not induce me to promise to be their future customer,—that I had determined to have no other business with them, than to pay their demand. He admitted the attachment was made by their orders, and said it was made in consequence of a report, that I was repairing a house at an expense of fifteen hundred or two thousand Dollars,—that I was furnishing it at an expense of one thousand or twelve hundred Dollars,—that Mr Miller was withdrawing the money he had loaned me, and that their property was going in this way. I assured him that this representation was entirely false, he said he was convinced it was not true. I then urged him to discontinue his suit, as he was now convinced he had acted under a false impression. He replied that he had not done it without proper advice, & reflection, and having proceeded so far, he should persist, & abide the consequences. I was in Boston three days, endeavoring to obtain a positive answer, & then returned home on the 25th March

In answer to the 4th Interrogatory proposed by the Plfs Counsel I testify & say—Yes
Immediately after the attachment was made, & before I went to Boston, I wrote to Peirce & Washburn, offering to turn them out goods to the amount of their demand at co[st] or if unwilling to take them at the prices I had given to ha[ve] them appraised by good & disinterested men, which would ha[ve] prevented the sacrifice & loss, resulting from an Auction Sale. This offer they declined. They persisted, as before stated in their attachment, recovered judgement, execution a[nd] levied to the amount of sixteen hundred, & seventy five Dolls & ninety seven cents, & the goods were sold at Auction in due course of law.

In answer to the 5th Interrogatory proposed by the Plfs' Counsel I testify & say.
After the attachment was made I obtained admission into the store for the purpose of taking an account of Stock. The goods at cost amounted to a sum, exceeding four thousand Dolls.

The Amt at Cost I think was	4100
Amt Debts due me by note & Acct	2300
Advance on goods at retail a[t] 15 pr ct	615
Cash on hand, say	550
	$7565

My Debits as follow

Peirce & Washburn	1726.10
B. C. Ward & Co.	1232.—
Lane & Lamson	370.20
West & Wild	175.58
Hartshorn & Ellis	371.93
D & P. Thacher	92.34
Pickens & Littlehale	90.54
Howland Cowing Jr	277.13
Jonathan Cushing	750.
Jonathan Cushing & Co.	38.18
	$5124

I was also indebted to James Vila[19] & Co. in the sum of two hundred & nine 17/100 Dolls, secured before the agreement by a joint note, & paid

19. Boston merchant.

after the attachment by Peirce & Washburn. I was also indebted in the following sums, contracted *after* the agreement.

Thomas Tarbell	85.57
Saml. Davis & Co.	115.38
Mcriam & Brigham	117.79
Saml Cook[20]	27.14

The above is a correct schedule, except the debts to my Father & Edward Miller, the amount of the latter was fourteen hundred Dolls. The former I have not the means of ascertaining, without access to his papers, & he is absent. This debt was not contracted, since I have been in this business, & the payment of it would not have been enforced to the injury of my other creditors, had I not been interrupted by them. The whole amount of Sales by the Sheriffs return was ab[out] twenty six hundred Dolls of which Peirce & Washburn received their debt, & cost, Jona. [Cushing] & Co. received $49.71, and seven hundred, eighty three 97/100 was endorsed on N. Spooner's execution. The probable loss by the sale at Auction could not have been less than two thousand, one hundred & fifteen Dollars. The consequence to me was an entire suspension of business & loss of mercantile credit. I cannot say to what certain amount I was prevented from obtaining the assistance of my friend[s] & can only state, that while Mr Peirce was hesitating whether to persist in, or relinquish his attachment, and on my representing to Mr Miller, that I believe he would give it up. He Mr Miller, advanced me two hundred Dolls, and promised to render further & greater assistance within the six months stipulated in the agreement.

In answer to the 6th Interrogatory I testify & say—Yes. At the time said agreement was entered into, I owed Messrs Ward & Co. twelve hundred & eighty two Dolls, & when the attachment was made, I was indebted to them twelve hundred & thirty two Dollars with interest, which sum is still due.

In answer to the 7th Interrogatory I testify & say. It is entirely out of my power to pay the Plfs any part of their demand.

In answer to the 8th Interrogatory proposed by the Plfs Counsel I testify & say.

That I have already stated that the demand of N. Spooner did not originate while I was engaged in this business, & would not have been enforced to the injury of other creditors—as tending to prove this, I will state, that he has bought goods of me to a considerable amount, and has repeatedly settled, & paid his accounts, without ever mentioning the de-

20. Boston merchants.

mand he had against me, a part of which is of some years standing, and the amount of which I cannot now ascertain.

In answer to the first cross Interrogatory proposed by the Counsel for the Defendants, I testify & say. No

In answer to the second cross Interrogatory proposed by the Counsel for Defendants. I testify & say.
That I refer to my answer to the fifth Interrogatory proposed by the Counsel for the Plfs. The terms of payment I cannot ascertain without considerable difficulty.

In answer to the third cross Interrogatory proposed by the Counsel for Dfts, I testify & say.
That at the time this agreement was entered into I had a list of those of my Creditors, whom I expected would sign the agreement, & all did so sign it. I also mentioned that I was indebted to Saml. Davis & Co. Thomas Tarbell, & James Vila & Co. I presume I disclosed these circumstances to all of my Creditors. I had no intention of keeping it a secret from any one of them.

In answer to the fourth cross Interrogatory proposed by the Counsel for Defendants, I testify & say.
The Writs of Nathl. Spooner, Edward Miller, & Jonathan Cushing were served before that in favor of Peirce & Washburn, & I can say with confidence, that no part of their debt was secure. Messrs. Ward & Co. had no security.

In answer to the fifth cross Interrogatory proposed by the Dfts Counsel I testify & say. Yes.
The circumstances which induced me to this are stated in my answer to the first Interrogatory proposed by Plfs Counsel. I did not offer to any other creditor any such inducement. I do not know, that I informed Messrs Peirce & Washburn respecting the note to Cushing. It was late, when Cushing required it, as a condition to his signing the agreement. I left Town early the next morning without seeing Messrs Peirce & Washburn, or any of my Creditors. I had no intention of keeping it a secret. The note did not fall due, 'till after the six months of the agreement had expired.

In answer to the sixth cross Interrogatory proposed by the Counsel for Defendants, I testify & say—
I went to Boston in May to purchase goods, & called on Messrs Peirce & Washburn, & stated to them that I was in want of a few spring goods, & that I could procure them on a credit notwithstanding the situation of my affairs—if they were not perfectly willing to let me have them, I wished them to say so. They consented, as stated in my answer to the second Interrogatory proposed by the Counsel for the Plfs. I made the

same proposition to Mr Ward, who declined any further supply without security, 'till the six months had expired, stating as a reason that his partner was absent, & he did not like to do it, without consulting him.

In answer to the seventh cross Interrogatory proposed by the Counsel for Defendants, I testify & say—
I do not know, that I was more injured by the attachment of Peirce & Washburn, than I should have been by the attachment of any other Creditor to the same amount.

In answer to the eighth cross Interrogatory proposed by the Counsel for Defendants, I testify & say
The next attachment after Peirce & Washburn was Jonathan Cushing,—his attachment was withdrawn a day or two previous to the sitting of the August Court—next to him was Jona. Cushing & Co., the amount of their debt & Cost was $49.71, which they received—next was Nathl Spooner's, who received $783.97. Edward Miller also attached, but did not receive any thing from the sale of goods. This included all my property—for farther particulars, I must refer to my answer to the 5th Interrogatory proposed by the Plfs Counsel.

In answer to the 9th cross Interrogatory proposed by the Counsel for Dfts, I testify & say
That I have now no property, except the notes & accounts which were due me, when my business was stopped a part of which have not been paid amounting to about thirteen hundred Dolls. The amount of my debts is as follows

B. C. Ward & Co.	1232.—
Lane & Lamson	370.20
West & Wild	175.58
Hartshorn & Ellis	371.93
D & P. Thacher	92.34
Pickens & Littlehale	90.54
H. Cowing	277.13
Jona Cushing	250.—
Thomas Tarbel	85.57
Meriam & Brigham	117.79
Saml. Cook	27.14
Saml. Davis & Co.	115.38
Ed. Miller	1330 —
N. Spooner	

with interest from the time when they were due I believe I have not paid any debts, or liability, since sd attachment, except the debts to James Vila & Co.—the note to Jonathan Cushing for $500—to E. Miller $70. & to N Spooner six hundred Dolls.

In answer to the 10th cross Interrogatory proposed by the Counsel for Defendants, I testify & say.
I never promised Messrs Peirce & Washburn any certain sum at any certain time. I engaged to do all in my power to satisfy them at the expiration of the six months. With a view to this I made all my sales, calculating to receive the payment within that time—and I have no doubt, but that I should have done better, than I had given any reason to expect, had it not been for the unexpected attachment of Messrs Peirce & Washburn. My expectations of assistance were not wholly disappointed, —on the contrary I had perfect confidence in the renewed assurances of assistance from Mr Miller. I know nothing of Messrs Peirce & Washburns reasons for suspecting my immediate failure, when they attached my property, except what I have stated in my answer to the third Interrogatory proposed by the Counsel for the Plf. The money loaned me by Mr Miller was not a temporary accommodation, but was a permanent loan for me to use in business, as long as I should wish to keep it, and he has at all times, & within the last month expressed his willingness for me to retain it, & employ it in business whenever I can do so with safety.

In answer to the 11th cross Interrogatory, proposed by the Counsel for Defendants, I testify & say—No.

Wm. Spooner

ADS. *Ward et al.* v. *Peirce et al.*, MassSJC,S, November 1822.

DOCUMENT 57. ANSWERS TO INTERROGATORIES

I Nathaniel Spooner of Plymouth of lawful age to the aforegoing Interrogatories, proposed by the Counsel for the Plaintiffs in the Action Benjamin C. Ward & al vs. Seth Pierce & al answer in manner following, viz

To the first Interrogatory I testify & say. That I was a creditor of William Spooner to the amount of between eleven & twelve hundred Dollars, a part of which had been due for five years. In March 1819 I was informed that suits had been commenced against him by Vinton & Cox, Charles Winslow, & Smith & Gore, in consequence of which, & under apprehension others might do the same, I delivered to the Sheriff writs against him with directions to serve mine first, should he receive any more. William Spooner was assured of my readiness to meet any terms that would best promote his business. When he made an arrangement with Pierce & Washburn & his other Creditors, I withdrew my attachment. In order to enable him to make the arrangement, I became responsible by signing a note for $500. to Jonathan Cushing, he having made an attachment on considerable property of said William on board a vessel in the Harbour, & declining to relinquish his attachment on any other terms. I paid Cushing the note, and was refunded the same by William Spooner.

In answer to the second Interrogatory I testify & say. That in May following I purchased & paid for him for goods to the amount of about two hundred Dollars.

In answer to the third Interrogatory I testify & say, Yes, I certainly should not have enforced the payment of my demands, while he was doing business; I afterward caused an attachment to be made in consequence of Pierce & Washburn's suit.

In answer to the fourth Interrogatory, I testify & say That I have no knowledge of his having lost any thing, or his being liable to any extraordinary expense. I always had the satisfaction of being pleased with his habits, behavior & con[duct.] His prospects in his business I thought were as good as those of any young man in Plymouth in that line with the same Capital. The attachment of Peirce & Washburn broke him up entirely.

In answer to the Fifth Interrogatory I testify & say, In respect to my own demand, I can state, that it was not my intention to exact it during the term of his extended credit directly or indirectly, nor ever under any circumstances, that would distress or embarrass him in his business. I regularly paid him the bill against me at the store. I sincerely believe had not Pierce & Washburn sued him, he would have now been in good credit, & doing business to advantage.

To the following Interrogatories proposed by the Counsel for Defendants I answer in manner following.

1st After the arrangements your son made with his Creditors in March 1819, did you not continue a writ in the hands of a Deputy Sheriff against your son with directions to serve it first, upon his goods, in case other writs against said William should come into his hands? I testify & say—Yes I did so, with injunction not to serve it, unless others came.

2d When did you give a note to Cushing for your son Wm's debt, when did you pay it, & at what time, did William refund you the amount? I testify & say. The note was given I think at six months from March 1819 & paid as due. Some several times afterwards he refunded the same to me.

3d Did not your son William suffer a great loss by the purchase of Jonathan Cushing's stock in the year 1817? I testify & say—I knew nothing of it, and was not consulted in the purchase.

Nathl Spooner

ADS. *Ward et al.* v. *Peirce et al.*, MassSJC,S, November 1822.

DOCUMENT 58. AFFIDAVIT

March Term AD. 1820

In the year 1817, I entered into an agreement to advance to Wm Spooner of Plymouth $2000.00, and by the 1st of March 1819, had advanced him about, $1400.00

Some time in the same month I heard that one or two actions had been commenced against said Spooner when I proceeded to Plymouth and delivered a writ to an Officer with orders to secure my demands in case he shou'd know of any writ being sent. The Officer the next day hearing of others made an attachment for my benefit. Mr Spooner got an extension of credit for six months from his creditors, and had not his business been interrupted, before the expiration of the six months I was so well satisfied of his solvency that I shoud have advanced the remaining six hundred Dollars. I never entered into any agreement with any of Mr Spooner's creditors that I wou'd not commence a suit against him for the $2000.00 but I always considered it a permanent loan.

Edward Miller

Sworn to in Court by the said Miller

Jno. Tucker

Suffolk. SJC
March T. 1820 Ward & al v Pierce
We agree that the above may be read in evidence in this cause, as the testimony of Edw. Miller Esq.—A Bliss Atty of Dfts.

ADS. *Ward et al.* v. *Peirce et al.*, MassSJC,S, November 1822.

DOCUMENT 59. DEPOSITION

[March 2, 1821]

I Nathan Hayward of Plymouth in the County of Plymouth testify and say, that I am Sheriff of the County of Plymouth and in the year 1819, I received several executions against William Spooner of said Plymouth in favor of Peirce & Washburn, Nathaniel Spooner & others—my orders on each were from the attornies of the Plaintiffs, directing me to sell the property attached on the original writs, without any further instruction that I can recollect and I sold the goods of said William Spooner on the said executions.

Question by Nathl M. Davis Esq Atty for Defts.

On the morning appointed for the sale of said goods was there or was there not any unwillingness or backwardness on the part of those, who attended the auction to bid, if yea please state the reason of such unwillingness or backwardness

Answer by the deponent

At the commencement of the sale, there appeared a reluctance or rather backwardness in those, who attended to bid. I requested them to be more expeditious. William Spooner immediately said, that he presumed no person would bid on the goods or words to that effect. I told him the goods had been regularly attached, advertised & now offered for sale at public vendue & whatever his feelings might be on the occasion I should not permit any observations from him or any other person tending to embarrass or injure the sale on which William Spooner left the store & returned again in two or three minutes and addressed the persons present as near as I can recollect as follows—I wish you to bid, Gentlemen, for the goods & run them up as high as possible—the more they sell for, the better for me & my creditors[;] there was no interruption to the sale after what I have stated & the people bid a fair price for the goods.

Question by the same.

Did you or did you not understand that pains had been taken by Nathl Spooner or William Spooner or both of them to prevent if possible the inhabitants of Plymouth and such as should attend the auction from bidding so that the goods might be purchased in at a small price for the benefit of Nathl Spooner or William Spooner or to the injury of Peirce & Washburn—if yea, state particularly all you know of the means taken for that purpose or of such a tendency, and also if you heard any conversation on this subject, please state the same particularly and by and between whom such conversation was had

Answer by the deponent

I know nothing of the interference of Nathl Spooner in said sale and nothing further of the conduct of William Spooner in relation to said sale, than I have above stated. I have no recollection of any attempt to influence said sale except as above mentioned.

Question by William Thomas[21] Attorney for Pltf

Is not a public sale of dry goods in Plymouth of very rare occurence, has there ever occurred within your recollection a sale to this amount.

Answer by the deponent

Public sales of dry goods rarely happen here, at this moment I recollect but one during my official duty the last seven years and the amount there was very inconsiderable

Question by same

Have you any reason to believe that the prices were affected by any thing William Spooner did or said previous to or during the sale

21. William Thomas, a Plymouth lawyer.

Answer by the deponent

I have no reason to think that they were

Nathan Hayward

ADS. *Lane et al.* v. *Peirce et al.*, MassSJC,S, March 1822.

DOCUMENT 60. ANSWERS TO INTERROGATORIES

Suffolk ss. March 12 1821

Josiah Lane & al vs Seth Peirce & al

Boston C. C. P.

I, William P. Ripley[22] of Plymouth in the County of Plymouth of lawful age depose as follows

To the first & second Interrogatories I say, I am a Retailer in the Town of Plymouth, & attended the public sale of goods of Wm Spooner in 1819. My opinion is the goods brought their value at that time, not at retail price, but at fair wholesale price. Some of the purchasers, after the sale offered to give up the goods they bought for the same money they paid for them. The object of the Traders in Plymouth in attending the sale was to prevent the Inhabitants from being supplied at a cheaper rate than themselves sold. Many goods of course sold at a retail price. The goods were in as good order, as at any retail store. Many of the goods were suitable for the season. I think remnants & cut pieces brought more than whole ones would have done for this reason—the Inhabitants bought the greater part, the traders made them pay well for them by running them up to keep up the price of their own goods, and oftimes got taken in by making others pay a handsome price for them. I know of no other circumstance of use to the Dfts.

To the cross Interrogatory I say, That I know of no circumstance of use to the plfs

William P. Ripley

ADS. *Lane et al.* v. *Peirce et al.*, MassSJC,S, March 1822.

DOCUMENT 61. REPORT OF THE TRIAL JUDGE

Suffolk ss. Supreme Judicial Court. March Term 1820.

Benjamin C. Ward & al

vs.

Seth Peirce & al.

This is an action of Assumpsit founded on an agreement in writing of the following tenor. "We the undersigned creditors of Wm. Spooner of

22. Not otherwise identified.

Plymouth, feeling sufficient confidence in the solvency of said Spooner, do agree not to interfere nor molest him in his business for the term of six months from this date, and at the expiration of that time nothing shall be done to enforce or secure payment of our demands by any individual except it be for the mutual benefit of all the undersigned. March 23d. 1819." This paper was signed by the Plts & the Dfts, and seven other creditors of the said Spooner.

In declaring on this agreement the Plts allege that in consideration they would not interfere nor molest the said Spooner & the Dfts promised the Plts that they would not so interfere &c and then set forth a performance on their part, & a breach of the contract by the Dfts.

When the paper was produced in evidence, the Counsel for the Dfts objected that it did not maintain, nor comport with the declaration; first, because the consideration, if any, for the Dfts' promise was the promises of all the other creditors who had signed the said paper, & not the promise of the Plts alone, as alleged in the declaration; and secondly, because the promise, if any, made by the Dfts, was made to all the other creditors who had signed the said paper, & not to each of the said creditors severally; and therefore, the said Counsel contended, that the action, if maintainable at all, should be brought by the Plts & all the said other creditors jointly & not by the Plts alone.

These objections were overruled and the question reserved for the consideration of the whole Court.

On the trial it appeared that the said William Spooner kept a retail shop in the town of Plymouth; & in March 1819, before the making of said agreement, was indebted to certain persons besides those who signed the agreement; particularly to his father Nathaniel Spooner, & to his brother in law, Edwd Miller. On or before the 20th. of said March two or three actions had been commenced against him, which he settled by paying the debts; & thereupon his said father & brother caused his goods to be attached to secure their demands. He then went to Boston for the purpose of making the said agreement with his creditors there; his father & brother having agreed to relinquish their attachments, if the creditors in Boston would make the said agreement. After this, & before the agreement was written, Jona. Cushing, one of the creditors who signed the agreement, went to Plymouth to make an attachment for his own demand & for that of the Dfts, & procured a writ, or writs, for that purpose; but it was not ascertained at that time whether he had obtained any security for his demand. The said Cushing was not in Boston when the said William Spooner first arrived there, & did not see the agreement until it had been signed by the Plts, the Dfts, & two other of the creditors. He, then declined to state to the said Spooner upon what terms he would join in this arrangement; & after all the others had signed, being again applied to by said Spooner, he refused, unless said Spooner's father would sign or endorse a note for him for 500 Dollars, part of his demand, leaving due thereon nearly 300 Dollars more. This being agreed to, he took the note, & signed the paper, the last of those creditors. He did not communicate to any of the other creditors this agreement between him & said Spooner as to the said security for 500 Dollars; nor did he remember any injunction or request by said Spooner to conceal it from them.

At the time of the said agreement the said Spooner owed to all his said creditors in Boston the sum of 5124 Dollars, to the said Miller about 1400 Dollars, & to his father about 1100 or 1200 Dollars. His mother in law Mrs Nicholson, afterwards brought an action against him for 2000 Dollars, claimed as due to her in March 1819, for board & lodging of himself & his wife. This action was brought on the 12th July 1819, after the attachment hereinafter mentioned made by the Dfts, & she did not get any security for her supposed demand. Spooner was defaulted in that action. There was no other evidence of that demand, excepting that said Spooner & his wife had boarded with her mother for about five months; and there was no evidence whether he had paid her anything on that count. No judgment was made up, & no execution issued, in that action. Between the said 22d March, & 12th. July, the said Spooner had bought other goods of the Dfts & others, & contracted debts to the amount of three hundred & thirty four Dollars. The goods in his shop on the said 12th. July had cost, as he testified 4100 Dollars, & were worth 15 per Cent advance, as he retailed them. He also testified that the debts then due to him amounted to 2300 Dollars, & that he had 550 Dollars in cash. The same goods, when sold on the executions of the Dfts & others in Septr. 1819, produced only about 2600 Dollars. The debt due from said Spooner to the Plts in July 1819, was 1232 Dollars. That due to the Dfts was about 1700. In July, the debt due from said Spooner to his [father] was increased to about 2100 Dollars.

The said Spooner testified that at the time of making said agreement in March, he disclosed the situation of his affairs to the Dfts, & others his creditors in Boston, & then had a list of all his creditors, whom he expected to sign said agreement, & that all whose names were on the list, did sign it. Another witness (Joseph West,[23] one of the subscribing creditors) testified that he was present, before the said agreement was written at the first meeting in March between the said Spooner, the Dft, Peirce, & the Plts, when the said Spooner proposed that all the creditors in Boston should enter into such an agreement. That it was then known to the persons present that the said Miller & Natl Spooner were creditors of said William, & that they had attached his goods as before mentioned; but said William said it was not necessary for them to sign, as they would release their attachments, & would not interrupt him in his business, if

23. Boston hardware merchant.

the Boston creditors would agree to his proposition; & that the said creditors who were present expressed their opinion also that it was not necessary that said Miller & Spooner should sign the agreement.

After the agreement was signed, the said Miller & Natl. Spooner released their said attachments, & the said William went on with his business until the 12 July 1819. But the said Miller & Natl. Spooner placed in the hands of the Dep. Sheriff in Plymouth, writs upon their said demands, with orders to attach the goods of said William in case any other of his creditors should undertake to attach the same. On the said 12th July the Dfts did attach his goods, by a writ served by the high sheriff of the County, & this was effected before the said Dep. Sheriff had any intimation of it. The next attachment was in favor of Jona. Cushing & Co. for a demand of about 70 Dollars, & the third for said Natl. Spooner upon the writ previously proposed as aforesaid. The said Miller attached the same goods afterwards, upon his said writ, but the whole proceeds of the sale on the executions were absorbed by the prior attachments; & the amount received by the said Natl. Spooner therefrom was only $783.97 cents. Between March & July 1819, the said Miller advanced to to Spooner about 200 Dollars, & the said N. Spooner advanced him an equal sum. His business was broken up by the said attachments, & he is now unable to pay anything.

The reason assigned by the Dfts to the said William Spooner for making said attachment was, (as he testified) some stories they had heard of his extravagance in repairing & fitting his house, & in the purchase of furniture. He undertook to satisfy them that these stories were untrue, & urged them to relinquish the attachment; but they said they should proceed, & take the consequences.

On the 2d August 1819,[24] the Dfts wrote a letter to the Plts, stating that they had made this attachment, & offering to divide among all the said subscribing creditors what they should recover, first retaining the amount due to themselves from Spooner for goods sold after the said 22d March.

Upon this evidence I instructed the Jury that if there was no deception nor fraud practiced on the Dfts to induce them to sign the agreement, they were bound by it; & that it was a valid & legal contract on which the Plts might recover for whatever damage they had sustained by the breach of it. That the consideration for the Defts' promise was sufficient in law, although there were other creditors who did not sign the paper, if it was previously known to the Dfts that such other creditors were not to sign it: and that the security so given to the said Jona. Cushing for a part of his debt to induce him to sign, did not of itself avoid the contract as between the Plts & Dfts.

24. See p. 359, above.

As to the damages, I instructed the Jury to ascertain as well as they could from the evidence, what was the amount of debts due from the said Wm. Spooner, & what were his means of paying them, & what reasonable probability there was of his having paid the said debt due to the Plts if his goods had not been attached by the Dfts in manner aforesaid; & that they ought to assess such damages as would indemnify the Plts for all the loss that the Jury should believe they had sustained by the breach of contract (if any) committed by the Dfts. And that if the jury believed that the Plts might, & would have received their whole debt of the said Spooner, if the Dfts had not so attached his goods, they might assess damages to the whole amount of the debt due from the said Spooner to the Plts.

The jury found a verdict for the Plts for [$1232]

The Dfts move for a new trial on account of the several opinions & directions given to the jury as above stated; & also because the damages are, as they allege, excessive; & because the verdict is against the weight of evidence—as more particularly set forth in the grounds of the motion which are written & filed in the case.

Chas. Jackson,[25] Just. SJC.

ADS. *Ward et al.* v. *Peirce et al.*, MassSJC,S, November 1822.

2. CONTRACT AND ARBITRATION: *Thomas Tilden* v. *Israel Thorndike*

Whether [*in*] *consideration* [*of*] *yr relative situations in the world it would not be expedient to meet his wish . . .*

But, if he prefers a trial by jury, it will not be in my power, consistently, to prevent him.[1]

During the first quarter of the nineteenth century, Israel Thorndike was reputed to be one of the wealthiest persons in Boston, if not the wealthiest. His fortune had been obtained in shipping and commerce in the eighteenth century, but by the time of his death in 1832 his empire had been diversified and strengthened by numerous shrewd investments in transportation, insurance, banking, and textile manufacturing.[2] In addition, Thorndike devoted one aspect of his investment policy to real

25. Charles Jackson (1775–1855; Harvard 1793), studied law with Theophilus Parsons, admitted in 1796, moved to Boston from Newburyport in 1803 and practiced with Samuel Hubbard; judge, MassSJC (1813–1824).

1. George Sullivan to Israel Thorndike, February 29, 1820 and December 19, 1820, both printed below.

2. For an account of Thorndike's various enterprises, see J. D. Forbes, *Israel Thorndike, Federalist Financier* (New York, 1953), pp. 134–143.

estate in Boston. His "most important single real-estate undertaking . . . was centered on the property just up the hill from the waterfront on Summer Street and Otis Place."[3] Between 1809, when he originally purchased property in the area for twenty-six thousand dollars, and 1826, when his Summer Street holdings were assessed at $187,800,[4] Thorndike followed a relatively straightforward plan. His "method . . . was to buy the land and build brick houses on it and then rent them out."[5] Occasionally he might sell a house, but generally Thorndike purchased this land in order to develop it as a residential neighborhood. And he succeeded, for Summer Street was remembered by an historian of the city's evolution as "long . . . a pleasant and uncrowded place to live."[6]

But Israel Thorndike's reputation had another side to it. He could be "cold, hard," and "when he considered himself imposed upon, he was terribly passionate; rage could hardly have expressed it."[7] He was also "litigious by nature," and his biographer reported that "the Suffolk County Court of Common Pleas dockets contain Thorndike cases for every year that he lived in Boston." Apparently, and perhaps not inconsistently for such a wealthy Bostonian at this time, "no amount was too large or too small to be the cause of suit if Thorndike felt strongly in a situation." In short, Israel Thorndike "could be a hard man in money matters."[8] In 1818 a number of these factors, as disparate as real estate holdings and the idiosyncrasies of personality, drew together and produced a lawsuit in which Israel Thorndike met his match—if not in terms of acquired wealth, at least in terms of stubbornness and an appreciation of the worth of one's labor. His name was Thomas Tilden, and he was a bricklayer by trade.

Thorndike and Tilden had agreed in 1818 that Tilden would provide the mason work for three new houses that Thorndike wanted to build on Summer Street.[9] Apparently, Tilden had worked fairly regularly for Thorndike on other occasions.[10] As part of the bargain, Thorndike had

3. Ibid., p. 144.

4. Ibid., pp. 144–145.

5. Ibid., p. 145. Perhaps it is best to note here (even though it somewhat anticipates the emergence through the documents of the main characters in the story) that among Thorndike's tenants in the houses of the Summer Street area were at various times DW himself, William Prescott (like DW, one of Thorndike's lawyers in the case), and Bryant P. Tilden, the original referee in the dispute. For DW and Tilden, see Forbes, pp. 145–146; for Prescott, see Harold Kirker, *The Architecture of Charles Bulfinch* (Cambridge, Mass., 1969), p. 377.

6. Walter Muir Whitehill, *Boston, A Topographical History*, 2nd ed. (Cambridge, Mass., 1968), p. 33.

7. Forbes, p. 149 and p. 151 (an excerpt quoted from a Beverly, Massachusetts newspaper article "half a century after his death.")

8. Ibid., p. 153.

9. The following brief account is drawn entirely from the documents and letters printed below.

10. For examples of the other

agreed to pay Tilden in part by giving him a stipulated lot of land. However, the adjustment of the account between the two became subject to dispute. One of the items that irked Tilden was Thorndike's decision to withdraw his offer of the promised lot. The parties agreed to arbitrate the matter and adjust the accounts between them. They selected a merchant, Bryant P. Tilden (no relation to Thomas), who quickly returned an award in Thomas Tilden's favor. But Tilden was not satisfied with the award; even after the referee adjusted it slightly in his favor, Tilden still rejected it and hired an attorney, George Sullivan, to begin negotiating with Thorndike for what Tilden thought was a more appropriate sum. Sullivan, a son of the late Massachusetts governor James Sullivan, was a well-respected lawyer, and apparently acquainted with Thorndike. He pursued a number of contacts with Thorndike, at first amicably, but increasingly he had to face Thorndike's impatience. As the inevitability of a suit to seek what Tilden thought was his due (obviously in excess of what the referee awarded him) became clearer to Thorndike, he made one last tender of the arbitrated sum. Tilden rejected it, and filed suit on a theory of *quantum meruit*, to recover not under the original contract but for the reasonable value of his services and materials. Seeking damages under a theory of implied contract and, in effect, alleging that Thorndike had become unjustly enriched at Tilden's expense, he asked for $2,000—slightly more than twice the amount allowed him by the referee, who had examined the actual accounts between the parties. Appearing for Thorndike, Alexander Bliss and Webster countered eventually by specially pleading the referee's award and the agreement of the parties to abide by it.[11] Thorndike was contending that Tilden had no right to seek a recovery by this lawsuit; his remedy was confined to the referee's award by mutual agreement of the parties, and therefore Tilden was now barred from pursuing an action at law.

The original arbitration in this case took place prior to any judicial proceeding.[12] References by formal rule of court—that is, once the litigation was formally instituted[13]—stood in contrast to informal agree-

work, see the accounts reproduced in the appendix to this section.

11. For a fine analysis of the distinctions between special pleading (as in this case) and a general denial (or the general issue) for Massachusetts, see William E. Nelson, *Americanization of the Common Law: The Impact of Legal Change on Massachusetts Society*, 1760–1830 (Cambridge, Mass., 1975), pp. 21–23, 72–74.

12. For the technical distinction between arbitration and reference, and an historical sketch of the extrajudicial settlement of disputes, see Goebel, 2: 375–389 and *Legal Papers*, 1: 322–333. Massachusetts by an act of July 7, 1786, sanctioned this practice.

13. Undaunted, Thorndike suggested to Sullivan after suit was filed that a new referee be appointed in this way; see Thorndike to Sullivan,

ments to arbitrate between the parties. The movement to stimulate extra-judicial settlement of disputes had drawn encouragement in eighteenth-century America from merchants displeased with what they perceived as an unresponsive, costly and delay-prone system of justice. Preferring to place their disputes both in the hands of people experienced in their customs and in the framework most conducive to their needs, merchants refrained whenever possible from entering the legal system. This pattern slowly changed during the early nineteenth century as commercial law began more closely to reflect commercial reality as viewed by merchants. Judges began to supervise and control reference awards and allowed merchants less discretion to carve out their worlds outside the legal system.[14] Tilden and Thorndike, however, chose to conduct their dispute within a format which was soon to fade from the scene. Their respective situations separated them in several ways from those who would have, in the past, been most likely to employ the device.

First, this dispute was not between merchants, but between a real estate entrepreneur and a mason, someone paid to construct the developer's buildings. There was obviously a substantial disparity in wealth and social status between the parties. To that extent, it was doubtful that both parties shared the same vision of the business world and business relationships, or of this particular transaction. Secondly, they both may have preferred the reference device at the outset for very different reasons. Thorndike hoped perhaps for a favorable disposition from a sophisticated neighbor and merchant; Tilden might have found attractive a vehicle for a low-cost recovery of a debt, and had no reason at first to distrust the circumstances or the arrangement. Slowly, however, the parameters of the case were to be readjusted. Tilden, in effect, started to threaten Thorndike with the specter of a jury that Thorndike might intuitively understand would be less sympathetic to him and more sympathetic to the plight of the poor bricklayer asking merely for his due from an extremely wealthy individual. Tilden also would become less willing to arbitrate once the dispute was formally filed.

As Bliss and Webster's special plea in Thorndike's behalf indicated, they thought that Tilden was legally bound to abide by the referee's award. The original agreement to arbitrate, however, had not been encumbered by any of the usual devices, such as bonds, designed to guarantee that the parties would comply with their promise to abide. All it contained was a simple promise to honor the referee's decision. The legal strategy therefore evolved around the substantive impact and effect

---

December 20, 1820, and Sullivan's reply the same day, both printed below.

14. For an analysis of this development and movement, see Horwitz, chap. 5.

of the informal award. The legal maneuvering around the award began even before Thorndike's plea was entered. During the deposition of the referee, B. T. Tilden (Document 67), Sullivan attempted to undermine the integrity of the award by suggesting that Tilden had not proceeded fairly or finally or with sufficient notice. Bliss had tried, in his questioning of Tilden, to rehabilitate the award. Both were planning future litigation strategy—Sullivan hoping to deflect a potential impediment to his implied contract action, Bliss laying the foundation for Thorndike's defense. The lines would not be clearly drawn until the special plea was filed (Document 68) about nine months after Tilden's deposition was recorded. In addition, as the depositions in Documents 72 and 73 reflect, some time was spent trying to ascertain exactly how to value Tilden's labor and services under the implied contract theory.

The lawsuit was played out on all grounds, some bordering on petty detail. Perhaps Thorndike's "cold, hard" nature was at work in influencing the lawyers. First, Sullivan objected to the timeliness of the special plea, and a number of affidavits were exchanged (see Documents 69, 70, 71). Secondly, Bliss raised the question of the proper taxing of witnesses' costs. He seemed to think the witness fees were inflated and so objected. A weary Chief Justice scrawled a reply hoping to put an end to it all (see George Sullivan to Isaac Parker, February 5, 1822, and Parker's appended note, below). The jury, though, had already accomplished what the Chief Justice longed for. They delivered a verdict for Tilden in the amount of $1,835.28, falling just short of the $2,000 he originally sought. This, of course, meant that the original arbitration award was not a bar to the action. In addition, costs were taxed at the very high figure of $357.13, which probably explains why Bliss was complaining. As all of this was drawing to a close in early 1822, another drama was simultaneously unfolding that related at least peripherally to some of the larger issues in this case of the developer of brick houses and the mason.

> High prices and high interest rates had halted the erection of brick homes in 1822. State laws prohibited the erection of additional wooden dwellings, to the dismay of artisans and mechanics in the building trades and of Bostonians of modest means who wished their own homes. Early in 1822 a town assembly instructed Boston's representatives to the General Court to present and support a bill for the construction of more wooden buildings in the town. Most of the Federalist representatives were wealthy, already owned brick homes, and feared for the town and their insurance premiums if the more combustible buildings were erected. They therefore refused to comply with the instructions.[15]

15. Sydney Nathans, *Daniel Webster and Jacksonian Democracy* (Baltimore, 1973), p. 18, n. 31.

Perhaps the jury was influenced by the sudden emergence as a public issue of brick buildings owned by wealthy Federalists.

DOCUMENT 62. MEMORANDUM OF AGREEMENT

Boston 12th. March 1818

Memo. of Agreement made this day of March 1818— by & between Israel Thorndike Esqr. of Boston on the One part & Thomas Tilden of Boston brick layer on the Other part Witnesseth.—

The said Tilden agrees to do all the masons work of every kind <in a workmanlike manner> appertaining to the houses which the said Thorndike may build on his land in sum[me]r street in said Boston the present year in a good substantial & workmanlike manner on the following terms Viz.—

$1.25./00 One-dollar & one quarter pr. Perch for laying the Celler stones, & ten cents pr. foot for laying the Underpining stones & stone steps to the doors &c paying for the same number of feet as the said stones measure on the face of them.—The whole to be laid in lime mortar & well pin'd up with Slate &c.

$3 1/2 three and an half dollars pr. thousand for laying bricks in the best Manner in lime Mortar, & to make & prepare the Mortar, to find tenders, collect Materials, assort & pile away all the bricks, & take charge of & prevent waste in the sd. Materials, plaster the chimneys, *put up jambs to the fire places, align*[?] *backs*, lay herths, set window & door frames, put on coaping stones, set window Cases & stools, turn Arches, lay edge stones to the side walks put in lead every where, where it may be deemed necessary & in fine, to do every thing appertaining to or Connected with the brick & stone work of sd houses without any additional charge for any extra bill of any kind whatever.—

<To do all the lathing & plastering for the sd houses & find all the Materials therefor, which materials shall be of the best kind, upon the terms following, Viz, for all the Common plastering with a good coat or coats & render the Ceilings and make them perfectly smooth, & white wash the same throughout & find all the Materials therefor & put 5 nails to a lath.—at 27 Cents pr sqhuare yard & wherever one coat of plaster of paris may be put on to add 2 Cents to each square yard, & 15 Cents pr. foot of Common sized stucko Cornises, & smaller Ones in proportion.>

The sd. Thorndike agrees on his part to pay the sd. Tilden, One lot of land <adjoining> in Leveret street near the houses now or lately own'd by Wm Payne Esqr.[16] nearly opposite to the House of Epes Sargent[17]

16. William Payne (1762–1827), broker.

17. Epes Sargent (1748–1822), former president of the Suffolk Insurance Company.

Esqr. at 50 Cents pr foot & to pay the residue in cash as fast as the work shall progress, & to compleat the payment so soon as the work shall be finished.—

We agree to the forgoing & will execute a Contract conformable thereto, except that if the sd. Thorndike should build two large eligant houses, he is to pay three & three quarters dollars pr. thousand for laying the bricks and is to pay for laying the Underpin[in]g stones & stone steps for the same number of feet as he pays the Stone Cutter for & also except the jambstones.

Israel Thorndike
Thomas Tilden

ADS. *Tilden* v. *Thorndike*, MassSJC,S, November 1821. Inscribed in the margin in Thorndike's hand: "Memo of agreement for two houses."

DOCUMENT 63. SUPPLEMENTARY AGREEMENT

Boston 25th. Septr. 1818

I the Subscriber hereby ingage to do all the lathing, plastering & Whitewashing in the three new Houses own'd by Israel Thorndike, now building on Sumr. Street in the *best workmanlike* manner & to skim over or render the whole a second time with a thin Coat, & will collect the *best* of materials therefor at the expence of the sd. Thorndike & will have the mortar made forthwith and will finish & Compleat the whole before the weather shall be so cold as to be injurious to the plastering &c.

(It being understood that the stuckowork plastering is not included in the above) The sd. Thorndike agreeing on his part to pay fifteen Cents pr. yard for the whole plastering &c &c to pay as fast as the work shall progress.

$30 addition for the three houses has been agreed on between Mr. Thorndike & Mr. Tildin.

AD. *Tilden* v. *Thorndike*, MassSJC,S, November 1821. Endorsed: "Mr. Tilden's agt. for Plastering 3 new Houses."

DOCUMENT 64. AGREEMENT TO ARBITRATE, REFEREE'S REPORT, AND AMENDED REPORT

Boston 17th. Decr. 1819

Whereas a difference of Opinion exists in and concerning an Open Account between us the subscribers

We hereby agree to submit Our Accounts[18] & every thing relating

18. The accounts are reproduced in the appendix to this section.

thereto to Bryant P. Tilden Esqr.[19] & to abide by his Opinion which we ingage shall be final.

Israel Thorndike
Thomas Tilden

Mr. Thorndike & Mr. T Tildens compliments to B P Tilden Esqr. & beg the favr. of his attending to this business & will meet him at any time most convent. for Mr. Tilden.
Saturday morng, 17th Decr.

Boston December 22d. 1819 The undersigned having attended to the within named difference between I Thorndike and Thomas Tilden is of opinion that by papers purporting to be contracts between the parties there is now due to Thos. Tilden by I Thorndike a balance as per account herein enclosed of *Seven hundred eighty one dollars and 47/100 in cash.*

B P Tilden

December 23d. 1819. In consequence of my having conversed with respectable Mechanics and in consideration that *three* houses were built and not *two* or *four* as contemplated by the parties I now allow Mr T Tilden the further some [sum] of Ninety One dollars 37 1/2/100 on laying 771 m. bricks, making with the balance of account above mentioned the sum of Eight hundred seventy two dollars .84 1/2/100 to be paid by I Thorndike in cash.

B P Tilden

	$872.84 1/2
Int on 872.84 1/2 frm 23d Decr 1819 to 3d Jany 1821—24 mos 11 ds	106.34
	$979.18 1/2

ADS. *Tilden* v. *Thorndike*, MassSJC,S, November 1821. These documents are placed together according to Tilden's account in his deposition of February 24, 1821; see Document 67, printed below.

FROM GEORGE SULLIVAN TO ISRAEL THORNDIKE

Dr Sir Feby 29 1820

I called to see you respecting Mr [Thomas] Tilden's claim on you for services in building yr houses. He has stated the affair of the reference to Maj [Bryant P.] Tilden but is dissatisfied with his award I have seen Maj T. and believe it can be shewn that Mr. Tilden suffers by this award

19. Bryant Parrott Tilden (b. 1781) was a Boston merchant and a major in the Washington Benevolent Society of Massachusetts.

a loss of several hundred Dollars. & Having assured Mr T that you would do what was just & honorable have called to propose a *recommitment* for further examination—as I have not had the pleasure to see you I beg leave to suggest whether [in] consideration [of] yr relative situations in the world it would not be expedient to meet his wish submit the case to other impartial men associated with Maj T. or otherwise & give Mr Tilden an opportunity of being fully heard.

Respy Geo Sullivan

ALS. *Tilden* v. *Thorndike*, MassSJC,S, November 1821. Endorsed: "From George Sullivan No. 1." A note in an unidentified hand (possibly Thorndike's) placed in the margin of this letter reads "Mr. Thorndike did agree with Mr. Sullivan to recommit the dispute & add Mr. Lancaster & Mr. Malley, but afterwards this was refused."

FROM ISRAEL THORNDIKE TO GEORGE SULLIVAN

Dr Sir March 1st. 1820

I recv'd last ev[enin]g your kind note of yesterday & thank you for the polite attention, & am sorry I was not at home. It appears to me that Mr. Tilden would do well to call & see the Award of Majr. Tilden, & see what it is before he decides as to the propriatey of expressing his dissatisfaction as to its contents. I will do myself the pleasure, some day next week, to call at your office & see you on the subject & would propose an earlier time, but for a pressure of business.

I am very respectfully your Obt servt. Israel Thorndike

ALS. *Tilden* v. *Thorndike*, MassSJC,S, November 1821.

FROM GEORGE SULLIVAN TO ISRAEL THORNDIKE

Dr Sir, 6 June 1820

My client Mr Tilden is as you may well suppose, suitably impressed with your liberality on the occasion of referring his claims on yourself. He thinks however that Majr Tilden has formed an opinion under circumstances which would naturally bias the mind of any man, and to avow all difficulties in the case I have told him I doubted not you would willingly submit the case to persons who knew nothing of the grounds of controversy. Such a course would be perfectly fair for all parties & I have full powers to agree with you upon such referees. Pray you Sir give me opportunity of seeing you five minutes on the subject when you [are] at leisure at yr store or elsewhere that I may conclude at once this little concern & rid you of further trouble about it Respy Geo Sullivan

ALS. *Tilden* v. *Thorndike*, MassSJC,S, November 1821. Endorsed: "From G. Sullivan Esqr No. 2." A note at the foot of this letter (possibly written by

Thorndike) states that "Mr. Thorndike offered to submit the whole dispute to any Referees of Mr. Sullivans Chusing."

FROM ISRAEL THORNDIKE TO GEORGE SULLIVAN

Dear Sir Boston 6th June 1820

Your note of this date is before me & contents noted.

You will please to recollect that you, as Mr. Tildens council, proposed to me in writing to have Mr. B T Tilden togeather, with some other person or persons to be mutually agreed on, associated with him to revise his award, or in other words to take up the subject a new.—I readily agreed to this & *we agreed* on the referees, Viz Mr. B P. Tilden Mr Lancaster & Mr Malley[20] & I think you then told me you were authorised so to do.

I scarcely know the two last nam'd Gentlemen & I assure you I have never spoken to Mr. Tilden upon the subject since the agreement between us. I am well satisfied myself that I am *legally* protected by Mr. B P Tildens award, but as I wish to give Mr. Tilden every reasonable sattisfaction, I am willing to have the subject refered to the Gentelmen we *have* agreed on, unless you should, as Mr. Tildens Attorney, and a Common friend to both parties, advise Mr. Tilden to settle agreeable to the present award.—I have a friend now on his death bed, & am dispatching a Ship, which would make it convenient for me to have the business p[ost]poned to some time next [week?] when I will do myself [the] pleasure of communicating with you. I am very respectfully Your Obt. hum[b]l[e] Servt. Israel Thorndike

ALS. *Tilden* v. *Thorndike*, MassSJC,S, November 1821.

FROM ISRAEL THORNDIKE TO GEORGE SULLIVAN

Dear Sir Boston 13th Novr. 1820

I am fav'd with your Note of ye [date blank] inst, for which I thank you. It may be proper to Observe to you that the Award in the Case between myself & Mr Tilden has never been opened because it was handed to me by the Refferee, with an inscription, "To be Opened in presence of both parties."

If you will be so Obliging as to have Mr. Tilden present at my Counting house or your office or any where else, so that no advantage may be taken as to the man[ne]r of Opening it, I will with pleasure attend to it at any time you may name. I am respectfuly Your obt servant

Israel Thorndike

ALS. *Tilden* v. *Thorndike*, MassSJC,S, November 1821.

20. Lancaster and Malley have not been identified.

FROM GEORGE SULLIVAN TO ISRAEL THORNDIKE

Dr Sir Dec 16th 1820

I have seen Major Tilden possessed myself of his views and communicated them to Mr Tilden, who disagrees to all so entirely that <you> he <will never agree>. He has insisted upon a suit at law, to the very next Court unless you pay the whole amount he demands without any of the deductions made by Major T. He has been advised to this as I have reason to believe [,] indeed he tells me so by persons of considerable standing and it will become my duty to commence such suit on Tuesday next unless before that Day the whole sum claimed by Mr Tilden is paid. Respectfully Geo Sullivan

ALS. *Tilden* v. *Thorndike*, MassSJC,S, November 1821. Endorsed: "No. 4."

DOCUMENT 65. AFFIDAVIT

Boston 19 December 1820. I the Subscriber hereby certify, that I have this day in behalf of Mr. Thorndike called at Mr. Tilden's house between the hours of 8 & 9 o'clock a.m., but not finding him at home, went where I was told I should see him, found him, and then stated to him that I had come to pay him some money; in reply he asked me whom it was from, to which I answered, that I have with me a letter requesting me to pay him some money; but Mr. Tilden said he could not conceive who it was from; I then told him if he would walk into his house I would tell him, and pay to him the money, and when there I laid One thousand dollars upon an open secretary, & telling him I had come to pay him the amount due to him from Mr. Thorndike, & awarded him by B. P. Tilden Esqr.—which he declined receiving, saying that he would not have any thing to do with it, as he had left the business with his attorney for settlement.

I called on him again between the hours of 1 & 2 P.M. of this day, & had the sum due him, counted & laid upon the table, and then asked him if he would receive it in full for his demand against Mr. Thorndike—to which he replied as before.

John G. Gibson

ADS. *Tilden* v. *Thorndike*, MassSJC,S, November 1821. John G. Gibson has not been identified.

DOCUMENT 66. WRIT OF ATTACHMENT

[December 19, 1820]

Suffolk, ss. Commonwealth of Massachusetts.
To the Sheriff of Our County of Suffolk *or his Deputy, Greeting.*
WE command you to attach the Goods or Estate of Israel Thorndike of Boston in our said County, Esquire *to the Value of* two thousand *Dollars*,

and for Want thereof to take the Body of the said Thorndike (*if he may be found in your Precinct) and* him *safely keep, so that you have* him *before Our Judge of Our Boston Court of Common Pleas, next to be holden at* Boston, *within and for Our said County of* Suffolk, *on the first Tuesday of* January *next: Then and there, in Our said Court, to answer unto*

Thomas Tilden of said Boston, Bricklayer and mason in a plea of the case for that said Thorndike at said Boston on the day of the purchase of this writ being indebted to the Plaintiff in the sum of Two thousand dollars for certain work and labour before that time and material found and provided done and performed by said Tilden at the special instance and request of said Thorndike and for his use and benefit and then and there in consideration thereof promised the Plaintiff to pay him said sum on demand—yet though often requested said Thorndike never has paid said sum but refuses

To the Damage of the said Tilden *(as he saith) the Sum of* [two] thousand *Dollars, which shall then and there be made to appear, with other due Damages. And have you there this Writ, with your Doings therein. Witness*, Artemas Ward[21] *Esquire, at Boston, the* Eighteenth *Day of* December *in the Year of our Lord One thousand eight hundred and* twenty

Jno. Callender Clr.

A true Copy Attest Jno Tucker clr

Suffolk ss 19 Dec. 1820 By virtue of this writ I have attached a [illegible] of Israel Thorndike Esquire within named and at seven oclock in the evening I left a summons for him at his dwelling house in Summer Street.
Fees 90 cts.

C. P. Sumner[22] Dep. Sheriff

A true Copy Attest
A true copy Attst Jno. Tucker Clr

Copy. *Tilden* v. *Thorndike*, MassSJC,S, November 1821. Endorsed: "The plff waives his Dem[urre]r & joins to issue by his Atty Geo Sullivan."

FROM ISRAEL THORNDIKE TO GEORGE SULLIVAN

Dear Sir Boston 20th Decr. 1820

I observe the [writ?] served on Mr. Tildens sute was *dated the 18th*.

21. Artemas Ward (1762–1847; Harvard 1783), Massachusetts lawyer, U.S. representative (1813–1817), judge, Boston CCP (1819–1821), chief justice, MassCCP,S (1821–1839).

22. Charles Pinckney Sumner (1776–1839; Harvard 1796), Boston lawyer, studied with George Richards Minot, admitted in 1800, high sheriff of Suffolk County (1825–1839).

It was not served however untill last ev[enin]g a little before 6 oClock. I mention these circumstances because you will recollect that you told me the sute should not be commenced untill *after 5 oClock of yesterday, before* which I had made a tender in American *Coin* to Mr. Tilden agreeable to the *award.* Mr T told the person who tendered him the money that he should do nothing about it that it was left with Mr. Sullivan who would settle it as he thought proper.—Let the merit of this dispute be what it may I want nothing more than strict justice, & as I have always considered you as having the substansial interest of your Client in view, yet I have considered you as friendly disposed so far as that disposition could be manifested without prejudice to the interest of your client.—I now propose to you to leave this whole business to a rule of Court, which will be the most speedy way of settling it.

I am respectfully your Obt humble Servant Israel Thorndike

ALS. *Tilden* v. *Thorndike,* MassSJC,S, November 1821.

FROM GEORGE SULLIVAN TO ISRAEL THORNDIKE

Dear Sir, [December 20, 1820]

The writ was delivered to an officer yesterday with direction not to leave it till after 5 oClock. This direction, I was sure, would be faithfully followed, and this was all I engaged to do. Had you candidly disclosed your object, I should have freely engaged to give you opportunity of making your tender, as an act of common justice; & the writ would have borne date on that day, when you desired service might be made. As it is, I am not aware that its date affects your tender, if this were made before the service. If it does, I shall only regret that you did not frankly disclose your object. Indeed I conjectured after you left me that you had another <objective> view.

Touching your proposal of reference under rule of Court, I shall have no objection, if my client has none; for many reasons. But, if he prefers a trial by jury, it will not be in my power, consistently, to prevent him. I shall communicate your proposal; & will have the honor to return his answer as soon, as may be.

With every disposition to bring this very serious controversy to a happy conclusion, I remain, Dr Sir, Yrs respectfully Geo Sullivan

ALS. *Tilden* v. *Thorndike,* MassSJC,S, November 1821. Endorsed in error: "G. Sullivan No. 6. 19th Decr. 1820." A marginal note (again probably by Thorndike) reads "The writ refered to was served on the 19th Decr. 1820—between 5 & 6 o'Clock in the afternoon."

DOCUMENT 67. DEPOSITION

[February 24, 1821]

I Bryant P Tilden of Boston, in the County of Suffolk, Merchant, of lawful age, do testify & say that some time in December 1819, I was requested in writing by Mr. Israel Thorndike & Mr Thomas Tilden, to act as referee, in settling a disputed account. I soon after saw the parties, & heard them fully upon the several points in dispute, when they both agreed, that two papers then exhibited, purporting to be agreements or contracts between them, which I was requested by them to consider as the ground work to form my opinion upon, so far as they might assist me. One of them I have since seen in Mr Sullivans hands, & also in Mr Thorndike['s] hands, & is the same paper now exhibited to the Justice, & marked No. 10, & a copy of which is hereto annexed.[23] The other paper I also saw in the same hands, it is the same paper now exhibited to the Justice, & marked No. 11. A copy thereof is hereto annexed. The said paper No. 11. is an agreement for masons work, & was so acknowledged by both the said parties, & it was agreed by them, that it should be binding on both of them. I was requested to make up my opinion, as I thought just, & right. Accordingly, I made up & figured an award, which I thought a just & fair award. The original award has now been exhibited to me, & has been marked W M[24] by the Justice. On the same paper, is an agreement of said parties, to submit to my arbitration, what is signed by both of them & was handed to me by said Tilden. The said papers marked No. 10 & No. 11 are in the same state in which they were, when exhibited to me by the parties, at the reference. There are on the back of said agreement, two awards made by me. Said Tilden having been dissatisfied with the first award, dated December 22. 1819. requested me, to revise it & examine my calculation again, which I did, with the consent of Colo. Thorndike & made the second award, dated December 23. 1819. A paper now exhibited to me marked No 12, & identified by the Justice, is an account stated by me, between the parties.

Bryant P. Tilden

Interrogatories by Geo Sullivan Esqr

1. When & where did you first meet the said parties?
Answer At Colo. Thorndikes house sometime between the 17th Decb. & the 23rd day of December 1819.
2. How many times, & in what places, did you meet the said parties?
Answer. I met them once or twice, I cannot recollect which, & at Colo. Thorndikes house.
3. What papers were put into your hands, by the Plff? Was there any account stated by him, in his hand writing? if yea where is said account?

23. None of these "annexed" documents are included here. Tilden was referring to the contracts between the parties. See Documents 62 and 63, printed above.

24. William Minot (1783–1873; Harvard 1802), Massachusetts lawyer and justice of the peace.

Answer. I do not know which of the parties produced the particular papers. They were placed before me by the parties, & I was requested to form my opinion upon them. They both agreed that those were the papers I was to form my opinion upon.

4 Were all the papers, which were laid before you, inclosed with the award, and delivered to Colo. Thorndike?

Answer. Yes they were & were numbered by me

5. At your said first or second meeting did not the Pff & defendt. differ in their statements, so much, that you told them to take back their papers, & that if they could not agree upon their facts, you would not serve as referee?

Answer. That was the case. There was a difference of opinion about a certain lot of land.

6. What was thereupon said by each of the parties, as distinctly as you can recollect, & what was particularly the subject of difference, touching the lot of land?

Answer. All I can now recollect is, that Mr Thorndike gave in to Mr Tildens opinion, rather than have the thing left open, on which, I went on & made up the award.

7. Did the Plff state in your presence, & in presence of Colo. Thorndike, that the description of land mentioned in the paper, purporting to be an agreement between the parties, bearing date 12 March 1818, was different from what had been agreed & that the agreement as it stands, describes a different piece of land, or words to that effect?

Answer. Mr. Tilden did so state, & Colo. Thorndike gave in to his opinion.

8. The agreement appears to have described at first, a piece of land "adjoining the houses lately owned by Wm. Payne esqr., near the house of Epes Sargent Esqr" then to have been altered, so as to describe a lot of land in Leverett Street, near the houses, now or lately owned by Wm Payne Esqr. near the house of Epes Sargent Esqr. The alteration appears in the contract to have been made with different ink from that used in any part of the agreement, & some words are written with a lead pencil. What explanation did the Plff demand or Colo. Thorndike give, of these alterations. Did it not appear, that the land described as the agreement now stands, was on the opposite side of Leverett Street, from the other lot as the agreement first stood & was not the value less than that, & did not the Plff object before you, at your meeting, that he was turned off, with a lot less saleable than the one he expected to receive?

Answer. Mr Tilden did say, that alterations had been made in the contract, respecting the land by interlineations, after the contract was signed. Mr Thorndike made no explanation, that I recollect, as to the interlineations, but rather than not have the business closed, he left it with me, to ascertain the difference, of value, between the lots of land, which I did, & credited the same in account.

9. Was the lot of land which Col. Thorndike proposed to convey to the Plff. of less value than the one originally agreed to be conveyed, & was it, on the opposite side of the Street?

Answer. I cannot recollect whether the lot now described was on the opposite side, or of less value than the other. The Plff did object, that the lot he was to acquire was of less value, than the one Col. Thorndike had contracted to convey to him. He never received the land, but the value of it was credited to him, in account.

10. Did the Plff expresly say, that he was willing to take the value of the difference, between the lots & expresly authorise you, to ascertain the value?

Answer. Mr. Tilden wished it settled in the way I have settled it, in the account of the 22d December 1819; but Colo. Thorndike refused to have it settled in that way, at first; however he afterwards assented to it, by writing me a billet, & I closed the acct.

10.B The paragraph beginning thus, "to do all the lathing &c." appears to be erased crossed & interlined. Did you act upon this as part of the agreement, or consider it no part of the agreement?

Answer. I did not act upon it as a part of paper No 10, but did, as a part of No 11, where the same paragraph is found in substance.

11. At the first meeting after you declined proceeding in the reference, unless the parties would agree about the land, did not the Plff say, he would have no more to do with the business, & walk out of Mr Thorndikes Office? Did not Colo. Thorndike call him back, & propose to him to choose another Referee, Did not the Plff say, he would not then, but would consider of it. And did not you & the Plff go away together, from Col. Thorndikes, without your proceeding any further in the business at that time?

Answer. At the first meeting after I declined proceeding in the reference, unless the parties would agree about the land, the Plff did say, he would have no more to do with the business, & left Colo. Thorndikes Office. I do not recollect Colo. Thorndikes calling Plff back, & requesting him to propose another referee, or that the Plff said he would not, or would consider of it. I left Colo. Thorndikes with Mr Tilden, without proceeding any farther, in the business, at that time. After having been at home some time, in the Eveg, I recd a billet from Mr Thorndike, that I might ascertain the difference of the value of the land, & credit Mr. Tilden for it, in account, that being the only thing unsettled. I accordingly did so.

12 Did you not consider the reference so far at an end, when you & the Plff went away from Colo. Thorndikes, that you would not have done any thing more in the business, if you had not afterwards received a line

from Col. Thorndike desiring you to credit the Plff, with the difference in the land?
Answer. Yes I did
13 Did you not expect that some other person would be associated with you, in the reference, from the conversation between the parties?
Answer. I do not recollect that I did, we parted because the parties could not agree. If they afterwards agreed, one person could settle the business. This was my opinion, but was not agreed so between the parties.
14 Did you ever speak with the Plff after you recd the letter from the Defdt, you have mentioned, & notify him that you should proceed to ascertain the difference in values, between the lots of land, & fix a time & place when you would give him a hearing on the subject?
Answer. No I did not. I made up my opinion that evening, & gave it to Mr Tilden the next morning, who said, he never would agree to it. He took the account to Colo. Thorndike. At the request of Mr. Tilden & by consent of Colo. Thorndike, I requested Mr Lancaster to meet me at my house, where he & I examined the accounts together, thoroughly. Mr Lancaster said he thought them perfectly correct, except that there was not sufficient allowed, for laying 771 M bricks, in consequence of which, I did allow a further sum as may be seen on the back of the award, amounting to $91.37 1/2. When I reported this to Colo. Thorndike, he said he would pay it rather than have any further difficulty, & should always protest against my judgment, in this particular
15 Did you understand this to be a reference of all demands of the Plff. agt the Defdt, in any way, respecting the building of his three houses, opposite Mess. Welles & Gray,[25] in Summer Street? And does your account, stated in connexion with your award, include all the matters upon which you acted?
Answer. I acted upon every thing, that was offered by either party, & received such proof as they offered. Every thing I acted upon, appears in the account & the papers submitted to me, were numbered by me.
16 Was the Plff present with Mr Lancaster, at the time you advised with him, or did you notify the Plff of the time & place of meeting?
Answer. Neither party was present. Mr Tilden wished that I should examine the papers, with Mr Lancaster[;] he knew I was to meet Mr Lancaster, but I do not know that he was acquainted with the precise time of our meeting. Mr Tilden sent Mr Lancaster to me.

25. This is a reference to the house "on the north side of Summer Street at the corner of Otis," built by Thorndike in 1812. It was known as the Welles-Gray house, having been owned at different times by Benjamin Welles (1781–1860; Harvard 1800) and William Gray (1750–1825), and has been attributed to the architect Charles Bulfinch. See Kirker, *The Architecture of Charles Bulfinch*, p. 377.

17 Can you say, that either or both of the parties were before you more than once, at the same time? Did either produce any evidence?
Answer. I cannot say that they were or were not. Both parties produced the evidence in writing which is numbered in my hand writing, & was enclosed in the award.
18 Did you not understand from Colo. Thorndikes conversation, or manner, or both, & did you not then or now believe, that the agreement of the 12th March, had been interlined or altered since it was signed?
18 Answer. The Plff said it was so, but I cannot tell whether it was so or not.
19. Did Colo. Thorndike positively deny, the alterations of the agreement?
Answer. I refer to the answer of the question No. 8, wherein I say that Colo. Thorndike made no explanation.
20 Did Col. Thorndike admit that the Plff had done all the work charged in his bills?
Answer. The bills shewn me, were all that I acted upon & my account Numbered 12 includes them.
21. Will you please to explain the reason, why you give credit to Mr Thorndike for $173, as the difference in the value, between the lots, if Mr Thorndike was to keep both lots? Was it because he was to pay in money, & not in land, or otherwise & how?
Answer. It was because Colo. Thorndike was to pay in money.
22. How did you ascertain the difference in value of these lots?
Answer. By enquiring of Mr Furnace[26] of the Massachusetts Bank & others owning land at that time, in the neighborhood & came to a result such as I thought to be just.

Quest. by A Bliss Esqr. Atty of Defdt Was your first award made & delivered before the breaking off the reference, as before mentioned, or not, & did the parties afterwards agree, that you should proceed with the reference, & was your final award made after such new agreement?
Answer. All points in dispute were settled in my opinion except the lot of land, & as I have before stated, Mr Thorndike having written me a billet, which complied with my ideas of what was right, & what Mr Tilden contended for, I settled the account & handed him the first award. Mr Tilden perfectly well knows that my final award was made, after having consulted Mr Lancaster at his own request. Mr Thorndike told me, that he would agree to any thing I thought proper, & as I consulted Mr Lancaster at the request of Mr Tilden, I did suppose, he would be satisfied after the revision of the account by us both & of all the papers Exhibited to me by Mess. Tilden & Thorndike. Mr Thorndike, as I before stated in

26. Nathaniel H. Furness, first book keeper at the bank.

answer to question No 14, thought it ought not to be allowed, but nevertheless consented to pay the further sum of $91.37 1/2.

B P Tilden

ADS. *Tilden* v. *Thorndike*, MassSJC,S, November 1821.

DOCUMENT 68. DEFENDANT'S PLEA

Suffolk & Nantucket, ss Sup. Jud. Court

Nov. Term 1821 C. A.

Thomas Tilden
vs
Israel Thorndike

And the said Israel Thorndike comes and defends the wrong and injury when &c and says the Plf his action aforesaid thereof against him ought not to have or maintain because he says that after the time when the said several causes of action in the declaration above supposed accrued; & before the commencement of the present action above, to wit, on the seventeenth day of December in the year of our Lord one thousand eight hundred and nineteen, they the said Thomas & Israel agreed together to submit, and did then & there submit, their accounts and differences and every thing else relating thereto to one Bryant P Tilden for his arbitrement and award, and did then and there agree together to abide by the opinion and award thereon of the said Bryant P Tilden, and that his said opinion and award thereon should be final. And there afterwards the said Bryant P Tilden took upon himself the burthen of the said award, & saw the said parties & heard them upon the several points and matters in dispute and received from them the paper or schetches of contracts herein after mentioned which they the said Thomas and Israel admitted and mutually consented should be taken and acted upon by him, in forming his said opinion and award, as the contracts of the parties on which the items of said accounts &c were founded; and there afterwards to wit on the twenty second day of December aforesaid the said Arbitrator came to the opinion & made his award between them the said Thomas and Israel of and concerning the premises so as aforesaid submitted & referred to him in the manner & substance following; that is to say, that by the said papers or contracts between the parties there was then due to the said Thomas by the said Israel a balance as by the account therein referred to of seven hundred and eighty one dollars and forty seven cents in cash—and that in consequence of having conversed with respectable mechanics, and, in consideration that three houses were built, and not two or four, as had been contemplated by the parties he allowed to the said Thomas the further sum of ninety one dollars and thirty seven cents and one half of a cent, on laying 771 m. bricks, making with the balance of account above mentioned the sum of eight hundred and twenty two dollars and eighty four cents and one half of a cent to be paid by the said Thorndike in cash. And the said Arbitrator then and there stated an account between the said parties of and concerning their accounts aforesaid and every thing relating thereto, and made the same a part of his said award & opinion, in which said account the balance aforesaid is stated to be due to the Plf from said Thorndike & no more, and which said account is the same account abovementioned as referred to by said arbitrator. And the said Thorndike further says that no cause of action hath arisen or grown between the said parties from the time of the submission aforesaid to the time of the commencement of the said action, and that no cause of action subsisted between the said parties at the time of the said submission other than such as were contained in said accounts and every thing relating thereto so as aforesaid submitted and referred to the said arbitrator, & balanced and settled by him as aforesaid. And the said Thorndike further says that after the making of said award and opinion, to wit, on the same day, he the said Thorndike offered to pay and tendered to the said Thomas on account of said award & in payment & satisfaction thereof, the said sum of eight hundred and twenty three dollars and eight[y] four cents and one half of a cent, which said sum the Plf of the said Thorndike then & there utterly refused to receive or accept, and this he the said Thorndike is ready to verify; wherefore he prays judgment if the Plf. his action aforesaid thereof against him ought to have or maintain & for his costs.

By his Attorneys D Webster & A Bliss

ADS. *Tilden* v. *Thorndike*, MassSJC,S, November 1821. The endorsement on the back of the plea reads "Objected that it is not filed or offered in season. G. Sullivan Dec. 18 1821."

DOCUMENT 69. AFFIDAVIT

[December 22, 1821]

Supreme Jud Court. Nov. Term 1821
Thomas Tilden
vs *C. A. No. 134*
Israel Thorndike

Alexander Bliss, the attorney of the Dft in the above cause, on oath informs the Court, that sd action came into this Court by appeal from the Boston Court of Common Pleas, that it was entered on the docket of this Court as a new Entry of the Nov. Term 1820, that the Nov Term commenced on the 28th day of that month; that, therefore, the time to plead, or to move for an extension of the time to plead, according to the new rules of this Court, expired within two days from that time i.e. early in December 1820. That, at that time this Deponent could not make such application, because it was not then known to him that said action had an existence, & that he could not know it, because he believes it was not, in fact, then commenced. That the first knowledge this Deponent had of the action was upon the entry thereof in the Common Pleas, where it was a new entry at the January T. 1821. That it continued in the Common Pleas until judgment was rendered therein which was on the 16th of February 1821, from which judgment the Plf appealed, and this Deponent supposed the appeal would be entered at the March Term, now last past, not supposing that by any construction of the Statute regulating appeals, an action could be so disposed as to be pending in both Courts, & subject to two codes of rules, at the same time.

And this deponent further says that seeing that the circumstances of this case were such as to take it out of the general rule, he supposed that a plea furnished at a seasonable time, & according to the old rules of the Court would be receivable, he prepared the plea in question as soon as he was possessed of the merits of the defense, and without any delay, delivered it to Mr Sullivan at his own request, who took it & made no objection on account of the lateness of the time; & gave no notice that he should not abide by it, until he had had it in his hands four or five days.

Alexr. Bliss

ADS. *Tilden* v. *Thorndike*, MassSJC,S, November 1821.

DOCUMENT 70. AFFIDAVIT

Decr 24. 1821

I George Sullivan on oath depose & say that some day this term while the wheel factory case[27] was on trial, I conversed with Mr Bliss, respecting the above entitled cause and he then told me speaking of Mr Webster & himself as counsel for the Defend[an]t that they should give the submission and award in evidence under the general issue that there was no need of pleading it. I further say that said special plea was put into my hands while in court last Friday or Saturday week the 15 inst not at my request: I made none. It would have been absurd to do so—that I separated from Mr Bliss before I read the plea and that as soon as I had time to examine it & had considered of it I gave notice to Mr Bliss in writing that I should not receive the plea—and I think this

27. *White* v. *Union Wheel Factory Company*, MassSJC,S, November 1822. DW was counsel for the defendants.

notice was given on Monday last, but the notice being in writing Mr Bliss can produce it.

Geo Sullivan

ADS. *Tilden* v. *Thorndike*, MassSJC,S, November 1821.

DOCUMENT 71. AFFIDAVIT

I Charles P. Curtis do on oath declare that at the request of Mr. Sullivan I entered an action in favour of Thomas Tilden against Israel Thorndike, at the Boston Court of Common Pleas January Term 1821, and as soon as the practice of that Court would permit, the same was demurred in common form by Mr. Bliss, who appeared as Attorney for the Def't. & myself who acted as agent for Mr. Sullivan—having personally no interest in or control over the said action. After these proceedings were had, I moved the Supreme Court at a late day of the November Term, held by adjournment in February last, for leave to enter the above action & one other, the circumstances of which I explained to the Chief Justice, who was then sitting, and by his directions produced & exhibited to him the Statute by virtue of which I proposed to make the entries. The Ch. Justice after examining the Statute, remarked that the Act was intended to apply to the country counties, but being general in its terms, the Court had no power to limit its Operation—and leave to enter the actions was then granted.

Charles P. Curtis

ADS. *Tilden* v. *Thorndike*, MassSJC,S, November 1821.

TO ALEXANDER BLISS

Dear Bliss New Haven Decr. 30. 1821

That case of Thorndike & Tilden preys upon me a little. I am afraid Mr Thorndike will think himself neglected, & I must *entreat* you to attend the trial, & beg Mr. [William] Prescott to do every thing he can. I hope you will be able to drive the Plf to amend. He has at present no leave so to do. He applied to me for it, & I would not consent to it. If he asks it, you can have a continuance, of course. I shall be particularly obliged to you if you will see Mr Thorndike, in season. Let him know I have written this letter—go with him to Mr. P., & do the best that can be done for his case.

We get on both swiftly & easily. Yrs D. Webster

Please send Mrs. W's letter to the house.

ALS. DLC.

DOCUMENT 72. DEPOSITION

[January 9, 1822]

I William Carroll[28] of Beverly in the County of Essex & Commonwealth of Massachusetts mason of lawful age to give testimony on oath depose & say—that sometime in April at the latter part as I think in the year eighteen hundred & eighteen I was employed by Mr Thomas Tilden to work on the wall of Col. Thorndike's houses in Summer Street, to remove it;—we removed it back some feet from the street, and after finishing it, we began upon the brick work. I worked there until the second floor was laid, when I was obliged to go home; my wages were at the rate of two dollars per day. After the front wall was first put up—it remained some days I should say from one to six, before it was removed; in the mean time I went to work in the house occupied by Col. Thorndike's son Israel Thorndike Jr Esq;[29]—all the hands were kept employed by Mr Tilden,—part were employed in the house last named & part on the other walls of the houses first mentioned, none were discharged;—I recollect that six men during this time were employed in the house occupied by Col. Thorndike's son,—in white washing & plaistering & paving in the cellar; the white washing was done over two or three times.

Question by Geo Sullivan Esq Atty of Plff.
Were there any men employed in other parts of that house while you were there?
Answer. No! I do not recollect any

Questions by dft
1st. How many days work were there in taking down & putting up the wall which was removed, from the time they began to remove it, until it was rebuilt in the same manner as before?
Answer. I cannot tell—I suppose Mr. Tilden kept the account, I kept none myself; I should suppose there might have been from seven to ten hands employed & perhaps more?
2d. What proportion of them were masons & what lumpers or porters?
Answer. I cannot tell—I should suppose there were two <lump> tenders & perhaps more.
3d. Why is it that you cannot tell the number of men at work about this wall—when you so accurately recollect the number employed in the house?

28. Not identified.

29. Israel P. Thorndike, Jr. (1785–1867; entered Phillips Exeter Academy 1800), a merchant and one of the original shareholders in the New England National Bank, established in 1813. The house he occupied was on Summer Street.

Answer. <When there are a great many men employed at work in different places it is difficult to tell what number worked at any> I recollect the names of those employed in the house they were Clap, Madigan, Capt. Dolly, Levi Cook, Ward Litchfield,[30] & myself;—I don't recollect who worked on the wall—but I think Mr Cook & Mr Litchfield did—I won't be positive.
4. Did you hear Mr. Tilden say that he had undertaken to take down & remove the wall by the job or by the day's work?
Answer. I don't recollect hearing him say any thing about it.
5th. How much money did you receive of Mr. Tilden when you were discharged?
Answer. I can't tell, Mr. Tilden has my bill.
6th. Did you receive your money, & sign or deliver that bill at the same time?
Answer. I delivered my bill receipted when I received the balance due—which was sometime in the fall of the year eighteen hundred & eighteen.
7th. At what time did you leave off work on those houses?
Answer. I can't tell exactly the time of the year.
8th. Did you receive any money when you left off work & went away?
Answer. Yes I did.
9. Did you leave any bill with Mr Tilden?
Answer. No!
10. When did you first make out your bill?
Answer. A few days before I came up from Salem in the fall of the year.
11th. Where is that bill now?
Answer. I don't know—I gave it to Mr Tilden in the fall of that year.
12th. Have you ever seen it since?
Answer. No.
13. Have you ever made any additions or alterations in that bill or in any other bill given by you to Mr Tilden for work done by you on those houses?
Answer. No.
14. Were you hired as a first rate or as an ordinary workman?
Answer. He paid me two dollars per day. I don't know what he considered me;—I considered myself a first rate workman as a journeyman, & received the wages of one.
15th. Have you been paid at the rate of two dollars per day for your work there?
Answer. Yes.
16th. Did you see the teams bring the bricks for those houses at any time while you were at work there?

30. Levi Cook is listed as a laborer in the Boston city directory for 1816; a Galen Clap appears as laborer and a James Dolly as mason in 1820, a William Madigan as laborer in 1822. Ward Litchfield not found.

Answer. Yes—I saw some teams bring the faced bricks. I do not recollect any thing about the other bricks.
17th. Did you see Mr Tilden attend to & count every load which you saw delivered?
Answer. No! I did not.
18th. Did you see them discharged from the teams & the teamsters go away without any body's having counted those bricks?
Answer. I could not tell whether they were counted or not, I saw no one count them.

Question by G[eorge Sullivan]
1 How many days have you attended Court as a witness in this case?
Answer. Eighteen days.

Questions by A[lexander Bliss]
1 Who requested you to attend?
Answer Mr George Sullivan
2 Have you been in Court every day?
Answer Yes.
3 Were you requested to come every day?
Answer Yes
4 Were you so requested when first directed to attend Court, or were you requested at different times to attend every day?
Answer I was directed to come the first day—& the cause not coming on—was told to come again—& have been so requested I should say six or eight times; sometimes by Mr Sullivan & sometimes by Mr Tilden; —I was since requested to come verbally.
[5 omitted in manuscript]
6 Have you done any thing else during those eighteen days?
Answer I have been at work on buildings in Union Street whenever the weather would permit, excepting the part of each day I spent in Court as a witness in this cause.
7th. Have you had your usual wages during this time?
Answer No I have had but ten shillings.
8th Were they reduced because of your attending Court?
Answer I don't know.
9th How long at each time have you staid in Court on account of this cause?
Answer Sometimes half an hour, sometimes an hour, & sometimes (I think twice) half a day.
10th Did you stay when you found this cause was not to be tried?
Answer No—I was waiting to see whether this was the next cause.
11th. Can you state what days those were when you staid half of each—
Answer I cannot recollect.

12th. Was it last week or this?
Answer Last week I think.

13. What reason had you to expect this cause on, after those which you were waiting to see ended?
Answer Mr Sullivan said he expected this case on.

14. Did you come into Court on any one of those eighteen days, when you knew this cause was not to come on?
Answer No

15. Did you come in order to see whether it was coming on?
Answer. Not alone—I sometimes came with Mr Sullivan & Mr Tilden to see whether it was coming on.

16. Can a mason who is paid by the thousand afford to lay a wall sixteen inches thick cheaper than one of twelve inches?
Answer. I think it is not worth so much by a thousand to lay the sixteen inch wall as the twelve inch one.

Wm. Carroll

ADS. *Tilden* v. *Thorndike,* MassSJC,S, November 1821.

DOCUMENT 73. DEPOSITION

[January 9, 1822]

I Joseph Jones[31] of Portsmouth in the State of New Hampshire labourer of lawful age to give testimony on oath depose & say that in the month of May and year eighteen hundred & eighteen I was employed by Mr Thomas Tilden to work as a bricklayer upon the houses in Summer Street which he was then building for Mr. Thorndike, and I worked there forty seven days, for which he paid me eleven shillings per day:—it is customary when the master workman employs hands by the day for him to receive more for their work than he pays them; and I believe that at that time it was customary for the master workman to receive fifteen shillings per day for his own services, & from two dollars to two dollars & a quarter for each hand employed by him for the day:—this is the case when the master is working by the day. Mr. Tilden was on the work as early & as late as any one & always busy—& superintending all the workmen.

Questions by A. Bliss Esqr. Counsel of Dft.

1 How many hands were employed in laying bricks while you were there?
Answer I should say from twelve to fifteen constantly employed.

2d. What wages had they?
Answer They had two dollars I believe, but I cant tell, he gave me eleven shillings.

31. Not identified.

3d. Were these twelve or fifteen men all journeymen or were there any apprentices—state their names.

Answer They were all journeymen as I think—viz two by the name of Litchfield, Mr Carrol, Mr Cook, Mr Clap, Mr Daniels, Mr Caldwell, Mr Higgins,[32] & others whom I cannot recollect.

4th. Do you know that they had two dollars each per day?

Answer I don't know—but those were the customary wages.

5 How long have you worked in this town?

Answer Five years; I am now going to Portsmouth.

6 How do you know that it is customary for master workmen to charge fifteen shillings per day?

Answer Only by hearsay,—I have been told so a number of times—I never knew any instance myself of that sum's being paid—but have understood it to be the customary price.

7th. Did Mr Tilden build this house by the job or by day's work?

Answer By the job—I heard him say so.

8th. Did you begin to work on those buildings as soon as any body?

Answer The stonework was done & the first floor laid when I began—& the buildings were ready for the roofs when I left.

Questions by George Sullivan Esqr. of Counsel for plff

1 How long have you been attending Court for this cause?

Answer Eighteen days.

2d. Did you understand that Mr Tilden was to receive a round sum for his services?

Answer No! I understood him that he was to be paid for laying the bricks by the thousand—& this is what I meant when I said he was to be paid by the job.

Questions by Mr Bliss

1 What have you been doing during the eighteen days you say you have been attending Court, have you done nothing else?

Answer I have staid here solely for this purpose & done nothing else.

2d How many bricks can a man lay in one day?

Answer A thousand is called a day's work—where you are carrying up the outside course of a front wall with a flemish bond which requires a great care perhaps not more than three or four hundred are laid by one man in a day,—but taking the average of work, a thousand is considered a fair day's work.

3d In laying a partition wall or other rough work is laying a thousand bricks a day's work?

Answer It is:—in a long day perhaps a man might lay fifteen hundred

32. All unidentified, except as in n. 30, above.

on a partition wall—but a thousand is estimated as an ordinary day's work.

Questions by dft.

1 Do you consider yourself a master <workman entitled> bricklayer & capable of earning as much as any one in your line?

Answer I do not consider myself a master workman because I never undertook jobs;—but I consider myself a bricklayer, and can do my work faithfully and as much at a day as the general run of masons.

2d. Can a mason who is paid by the thousand, better afford to lay a wall of rough work sixteen inches thick than a wall of twelve inches thick?

Answer I do not see how he can afford to lay it any cheaper; it takes the same staging stuff & time to build the stage;—it is true there are more bricks to lay—& more filling in to be done.

Questions by Mr. Bliss—

1 If a man has five thousand bricks to lay, can he not lay them in a wall of sixteen inches thickness, at a cheaper rate, than he could lay them in one of eight inches?

Answer I don't know but that he might, as there is more filling in,—there is no filling in in an eight inch wall.

Joseph Jones

ADS. *Tilden* v. *Thorndike*, MassSJC,S, November 1821.

FROM ALEXANDER BLISS TO GEORGE SULLIVAN

Dr Sir, [February? 1822]

The certificates signed by the witnesses should particularise their days of attendance *by the days of the month*, or in some other manner by which it may be seen that their attendance on those days was proper. Certificates *so general* I can by no means admit to be sufficient especially after seeing the deposition of Carroll[33] to the manner in which he was requested to give, & did give his attendance. Yrs A. B.

ANS. *Tilden* v. *Thorndike*, MassSJC,S, November 1821.

FROM GEORGE SULLIVAN TO ISAAC PARKER

Dear Sir, Feby 5th 1822

In taxing witnesses attendance fees in the case of Tilden & Thorndike their certificates are in the usual general form that they attended a cer-

33. See Document 72, above.

tain number of Days. Some attended 18 to 20 Days. Mr Bliss objects that certificates ought to specify each Days attendance by the Day of the month in order that it may be ascertained whether their attendance respectively was necessary or proper on the Days they did attend, and he desires me to submit the case to your consideration. You will recollect that many Days after the case was in course for trial it was laying over from Day to Day till the admissibility of Defdts plea should be determined & that you directed me to be ready with my replication in case the plea should be held admissible. I was so and the witnesses were required to attend every Day for several Days. The case was then assigned next after the capital cases, and again we were ready But it was again postponed on Mr Websters desire for the case of Imlay & Grant[;][34] again we were in readiness after that cause was finished when Mr Webster particularly requested that the case might lay over to the following Monday & again we were in readiness but the case was not opened till Tuesday, and then after reading the writ & examining one witness it was postponed to the following Monday on the request & for the accommodation of Mr Prescott. The trial occupied three days merely in getting in evidence. I have carefully examined the certificates and am satisfied that in some instances the witnesses have certified to fewer Days than they were actually in court expecting the cause to proceed, and that in no instance except one is the number of Days erroneously stated & that I have corrected because I believe the witness came from Charlestown on other business than to attend Court in this case. But the question submitted by Mr Bliss and all the question is whether the certificates ought to specify each Day's attendance by the Day of the month as aforesaid. Under the circumstances of this case as above stated it is clear the general rule does not apply and it is quite obvious that more particularity is hardly practicable and it would seem in this case quite unnecessary. Mr Prescott does not object as I understand, and as far as I can discern Mr Bliss is only desirous that the costs should be taxed on proper principles

Praying the favor of you to say on this or other paper whether the generality of the certificates in the common form is objectionable—& to return me your answer by the bearer I have the honor to be very respectfully Yr oblig[ed] hble Sert Geo Sullivan

The Certificates are in the usual form; if it is supposed they have certified untruly the objectors may inquire and making it appear then charge will be deducted. I[saac] P[arker]

ALS. *Tilden* v. *Thorndike*, MassSJC,S, November 1821.

34. *William Imlay* v. *Samuel Grant*, MassSJC,S, November 1821. DW appeared for the plaintiff.

APPENDIX

Though this case, in a technical legal sense, falls within a contract and arbitration section, its primary data are important for other than legal reasons. The documents reveal information about the residential construction industry in early nineteenth-century Boston. Social and economic historians will find material ranging from relatively quantifiable data, such as prices of various items, general costs, and wage rates, to the more wide-ranging customs and practices of the building trades. (Impressions along those lines may be found also in the depositions; see Documents 67, 72, 73). In the process, some light is shed on a number of areas, including economic history, labor history, the process of urbanization, and, to a certain extent, architectural history. For some suggestions along the lines of "the cost structure of the residential construction industry in the eighteenth and nineteenth centuries," see Donald R. Adams, Jr., "Residential Construction Industry in the Early Nineteenth Century," *Journal of Economic History*, 35 (December 1975): 794–816. The accounts and bills of particulars printed below, though they overlap to a certain extent, are reproduced here for the information they may yield to scholars in fields other than legal history.

1818. *Israel Thorndike, Esqr. to Thomas Tilden*—Dr.

To Building three Houses in Summer Street in Boston, as follows, Viz.

Mar. 18.	To Laying 407 9/10 Pearch of rough stone	@ 125 Cts,	$509.87 1/2
	" Seting 2492 Feet of Hammered stone	" 10 "	249.20
May 2	" Altering Front wall per agreement		130.—
	" Ditto Front corner on Otis Place the 2nd time		7.—
" 8.	" Takeing down wall at the East end for a Door		3.50
June 18	" Altering Back Entry Windows		6.00
	" Laying 771 Ms of Brick	@ 375 Cts	2891.25
	" Seting—5 Cover stones	" 200 —	10.—
	" Ditto—7 Chimney Caps	" 250 —	17.50
	" Do.—165 Feet of Copeing Stone	" 10 —	16.50
	" Laying 18 Tile Hearths	" 100 —	18.—
	" Lathing & Plastering 4203 Yds.	" 16 —	672.48
Augt. 27.	" 5 1/2 Days work on Dranes	" 225x—	13.62 1/2
Sept. 25.	" 19 1/4 Days work	" Do. —	43.31 1/4
Decr. 29.	" 28 1/4 Days work	" Do. —	63.56 1/4

53

1819.				
Apprl. 7	" 91 1/4 Days work seting fire Places & Rumfords[35]	" Do.	—	205.31 1/4
July 3d.	" Whitewashing 33 Ceilings	" 75	—	24.75
	" Ditto Walls & Ceilings of 12 Rooms	" 125	—	15.—
	" Do. Do. — — 28 Closetts	" 25	—	7.—
	" Do. —Ceilings of 3 Back Entries .	" 150	—	4.50

Thorndike to Tilden
1818–1819

	" Yellow Oaker & Glue for Kitchens	2.25
	" Brushes for Whitewashing Fences & Cellars .	5.—
	" Paveing 39 Yds. with Old Brick at 25 Cts ..	9.75
xx	" 77 3/4 Days work 225	174.93 3/4
Errors Excepted		$5100.30 1/2
	dedt. error x	1.25
		$5099.05

Recd. Payment.

149.87	labour bill piling bricks
5099.05	this Bill
8.62	my house
10.12	House No. 1 Otis st.
150.75	No. 1 Sum[mer] St. imprd. by 972
13.50	– No. 3 Otis St.
17.62	45 India whf
2.25	– 53 C Whf
10.12	House No. 6 Otis St.
16.31	Brig Charles
5478.21	
4080.50	pd. to this 26th. July 1819
$1397.71	bala.

[x]a deduction was agreed upon on this item

35. Rumford, a fireplace stove named after its inventor, Benjamin Thompson, Count Rumford (1753–1814), whose essay "Of Chimney Fireplaces with Proposals for improving them to save Fuel; to render Dwelling-houses more Comfortable and Salubrious, and effectually to prevent Chimnies from Smoking," first appeared in London in 1796, and was included in his *Essays, Political, Economical, and Philosophical* (Boston, 1798).

xxNo extra work was to be allowed by *agreement*, & this must be for Extra work

AD. *Tilden* v. *Thorndike*, MassSJC,S, November 1821.

Dr. Mr. Israel Thorndike in a/c current with Thomas Tilden - - - - - - - Cr.

1819—		
To my Bill, as rendered, for masons work done on three brick houses on Sumr. Street		$5099.05
To my Bill for work No. 6 Sumr Street	$8.62 1/2	
" ditto do. " No. 6 Otis place	10.12	
" ditto do. " counting house	19.87	
" ditto Do. " Otis Place	13.50	
" ditto Do. House Occupd. by Israel Thorndike Jr.	150.75	
" ditto Do. No. 9 Otis Place	10.12	$212.98 1/2
		$5312.03 1/2
" ditto Do. Piling bricks &c.		149.87 1/2
		5461.91
		25 62 1/2

1819—		
By cash at sundry times pr. rects - - - -		$4080.50
By Overcharges as follows - Viz		
On laying 771 m. bricks at 25/100 pr. M.	$192.75	
" Ditto coping stones - - - - - -	16.50	
" Ditto plastering pr. Agreet.	12.03	
" Ditto White washing - - - - - -	24.75	
Do. - - - -	15.00	
Do. - - - -	7.00	51.25
Do. - - - -	4.50	$272.53
By labour charged for piling & taking care of bricks contrary to agreement		349.87
By deduction for days work, in laying edge stones, putting in lead &c &c, which was excluded by the agreement.		30 —
By a lot of land No. 15 on Popular Street containg 1928 feet at 50 cents pr. foot pr. agreement		964.00

AD. *Tilden* v. *Thorndike*, MassSJC,S, November 1821.

Dr	Mr. Israel Thorndike, in a/c with Thomas Tilden		Cr.
1819	To my bill . No. 1 as rendered for mason's work done on three brick houses on Summer Street		5099 5
	To my bill N 2 for work at N 6 S[ummer] street		8 62
	Ditto - N 3 for do. at N 6 Otis Place		10 12
	Ditto - N 4 - - - - - count[in]g house		19 87
	Ditto - N 5 - - - - - Otis Place		13 50
	Ditto - N 6 - for work on house occupied by I. Thorndike Jr.		150 75
	Ditto - N 7 for work at N 9 Otis Place		10 12
	Ditto - N 8 for piling bricks & labour		149 87
	Boston December 22d 1819		
	W[illiam] M[inot] Feb. 21. 1821.		
			$5461 90
1819	By cash recd. at sundry times by rects		4080 50
	By overcharges which on being submitted to B P Tilden who on examing contracts has settled as follows		
	On laying 771 m. brick @ 25/	192.75	
	Ditto coping stones	16.50	
	Ditto Plaistering	12 3	221 28
	By overcharges for whitewashing	51.25	
	Deduct 1/2 allowed by B P T in consequence of 16/. . instead of 15/. . being charged as per contract for plaistering and a further allow[anc]e as on contract of /30	25 63	25 62
	By Bill N 8 for piling bricks & other labor, which by contract it appears to B P Tilden ought not to be charged		149 87
	By Deductions for days' work in laying edge stones putting in lead &c. which by contract B P Tilden now includes pay		30
	By allowance by B P Tilden for difference of value of a lot land N 22 adjoining house of		

W Payne on Poplar Street 913 [x]
1443 feet which Mr Thorndike
now keeps for himself & settles
balance by cash instead of pay[men]t
in land in part by sd. Lot @ 12/100 pr foot — 173 16
By Cash balance — 781 47

$5461.90

AD. *Tilden* v. *Thorndike*, MassSJC,S, November 1821.

Bill of Particulars

	Israel Thorndike Esqr. to Thomas Tilden			Dr.
	For receiving & piling Bricks before house [illegible]			149.87 1/2
	" 407 perch stone: circle, cellar, fence, woodhouse &c.	1.25		508.75
	" 25 do—double face wall	2.50		22.50
a.	" 2320 ft. hammered or hewn stone 172	10 cts		249.20
	" 4376 yards lathing & plastering	16 cts	700.16	
	" Laying 794 1/2 M Bricks	3.75		2979.35
	" Setting 6 Coving Stones	2		12. - -
	" " 7 Chimney Caps	2.50		17.50
	" " 165 Copeing Stones	10 Cts		16.50
a.	" " 18 Tile hearths	$1. - -		18. - -
	" 33 Ceilings whitewashed	70 Cts		24.75
	" 12 Room walls & ceilings in cook loft whitewashed	1.25		15. - -
	" 28 Closets	.25 Cts		7. - -
	" 3 Back Entry ceilings	1.50		4.50
a	" 39 yards paving with old Brick	.20 Cts		9.75
	" altering front wall			130. - -
a	" do. do. corner of Otis place & [illegible]			7. - -
	" taking down wall at East end for Door			3.50
	" Altering back Entry windows			6. - -
	" Laying drains between jobs per day as pr schedule 329 1/4 days			
	" @ 2.25 & jobs per peice		783.36	
	deduct for 14 m brick included		52.50	
	in above @ 3.75			730.86
	" Brushes used in whitewashing cellars & fences			5. - -
No. 7	" setting a fire place at House No. 1 Otis place 2 1/2 d[ay]s whitewashing			10.12 1/2
3	" 4 1/2 days work done at House No. 6 Otis place, seting edgestone & fencing @ 2.25			10.12 1/2

4	" 3 1/2 do do do at No 45 India Wharf @ 2.25	7.87	
	" 1 do do do Central Wharf	2.25	
	" Whitewashing ceiling at do	.75	
	" Raising step at do----4 days at 45 I. Whf.	9	19.87
2	" work done . . . at your dwelling house 3 1/2 days	7.87	
	" cutting hole through wall for a pipe	.75	8.62
	Amt carr[ie]d up.		$ 5665.94

AD. *Tilden* v. *Thorndike*, MassSJC,S, November 1821.

Schedule on Bill of Particulars in case of Tilden vs Thorndike

B.	Removing stone post next to Otis place	2 days at 2.25		4.50
B.	---"--- front fences of all the houses Sumr. St.	5 "		11.25
B	Setting marble tile & Curb stone &c.— 3 houses	8 "		18.--
B	Resetting stone post next to G Parsons land taking up stone wall underpining & digging -------------	4		9.--
B	Altering circular battlement on fence wall	1/2		1.12 1/2
B	Cutting in Lead over porch next to G. Parsons	1		2.25
B	Paving under cellar window next to G.P.	1		2.25
B	Cutting coins for the 2 corners &c elbow house—(This form altering plan of house from square to bevel—East house done by Tilden & others	10		22.50
	Altering end wall in wood house being a battlement from square to slope east house - next to G.P.	1 1/4		2.81
B	Setting soap stone gutter & leading it within	1/2	$2 - 3	3.37 1/2
Cont H	Cutting in lead over three			

	porticos in front	1		2.	2	2.75
Cont H	Cutting out 3 Windows thro' wall for necessaries	1 1/2		2	3	3.37 1/2
Cont H	Whitewashing fences—rough round aperture	4 1/2		2	8	10.12 1/2
H	Oiling houses twice & some three times	20		2	40	15.—
H	Cleaning brick work in upper story between the windows	6		2	12	13.50
H	Cleaning hammered stone twice	2		2	4	4.50
Cont H	Setting 8 heel stones $1	8				18.—
H	Cutting in joist into wood houses	3		2	6	6.75
Cont H	Cutting in lead into wood houses—into main houses	2 1/2				5.62 1/2
	Setting 10 setts of Rumfords - 3 houses	15				33.75
Cont B	Setting fire places—viz—	15				33.75
	16 marble, & soap stone	80-64 days			128	180.—
	large size - 5 ds				16	
	4 small soap stone, &				144	
	marble - 3 ds	12				27.—
	Laying 180 feet of drain - -	9				20.25
B	Levelling Cellar & filling boards under paving	6				13.50
H	Whitewashing 3 Cellars 3 times over - 6ds each	18	x	2	36	40.50
H	Building up sides of 3 Cellar passage ways from Cellar to washhouse	3	x	2	6	6.75
B. H	Plastering round fire places after [illegible]	6				13.50
B. H	Mending plastering bruised by Carpenters in 3 houses	8				18.—
B H	Pointing Windows inside—3 houses	6		2	12	13.50
B H	Cutting down Window jambs in all 3 houses	2		2	4	4.50
B H	Altering 3 back stair case windows setting them					

		lower down	9.	2 18	20.25
		Filling in with bricks round the partitions in parlour Storey	30	(3 days $6)	67.50
B	H	Repairing 2 Vaults & paving in the yard where it had caved in	4 1/2	8	9.—
			2003 3/4		
			Amt carrd up------		654.18 1/2
		amt brot up	290 3/4		654.18 1/2
B	H	Alterations in office setting new fire place, setting up another in place of it - cutting holes into milk Cellar	5 days at 2.25		11.25
B	H	Altering chimney in the East house taking down the inside of it & shifting over the flues & building it up	15	$2	33.75 - 30
	B	To laying large stone over Office Door to found a chimney on as Extra work—per day	2		9.
	H	Setting Cheeks on chimnies —soap stone	6		13.50
	H	Moving wood & fixing cess pools in drains in the East house	4	$2	9.00 8
H	B	Putting Lead on to battlements 300 ft @ 10 Cts a foot 3Cts			30. $9
	B H	Building Curb or coffer round water spout & laying drain to common Sewer in St.	1 1/2		3.37 1/2
	B	Yellow & Glue for Kitchens —3 Kitchens			2.25
	H				
	B	Yellow washing the same	3		6.75
Cont	B	Setting 103 ft of edge stone @ 10 Cts—this is mea-			

sured work to put in Mills bill		10.30
	329 1/4	$783.36

AD. *Tilden* v. *Thorndike*, MassSJC,S, November 1821. Endorsed "Bill Particulars Days work."

Tilden vs Thorndike. The following items of Plfs bill of particulars are agreed to be taken as proved - namely

setting 2492 ft of hammered stone @ 10 cts. - - - - -	$249.20
laying 18 Tile hearths at $1 - - - - - - -	18.00
paving 39 yards wth old brick @ 25 cts - - - -	9.75
Altering the corner of cellar 2d time - - - - -	7.00
Brushes for white washing - - - - -	5.00

The following items are admitted with this qualification that the work was done, but the price charged is not the true price or value —& is therefore to be proved. namely

Laying 407 9/10 perch stone wall for cellar, trenches &c
Altering front wall—by taking down & laying it over
work at No. 1 Otis place, as by bill No. 7.
" at No. 6 Otis Place as by bill No. 3.
" at India & Central wharves, bill No. 4.
" at House in Summer Street of I. T. Junr. as by bill No. 6.
" at No. 6. Summer Street - - - - - - - - - - as by bill No 2

Alexander Bliss Atty of Dft

ADS. *Tilden* v. *Thorndike*, MassSJC,S, November 1821.

3. MARINE INSURANCE

a. Introduction

Marine insurance litigation was one of Webster's specialties. The complexity of insurance doctrine dissuaded many lawyers from tackling such cases. It thus fell to the better trained members of the Massachusetts legal elite to handle the marine insurance business. In the early part of his Massachusetts practice before his attention turned to presidential politics, Webster usually represented the insured. With large sums at stake, he could earn high fees. Juries sympathetic to the insured made his task easier. In lower federal courts from 1818 to 1827, the period of his greatest post-New Hampshire legal activity, he represented insured plaintiffs sixteen times, and only three times did he appear for a defendant insurance company. In the state courts, on the other hand, during the same period, he represented three plaintiffs and eight defendants, seven of whom were insurance companies. In 1831 he wrote to his associate Henry Willis Kinsman that although he preferred to represent plaintiffs, he intended to shift his practice to the companies, to take advantage of the steadier income of their annual retainers.[1] He told Kinsman to double his retainer to $100. From that point on, Webster appeared in only six state or federal insurance cases, in half of which he represented the plaintiffs.[2] Examination of his fee books for the middle 1830s shows he received retainers from five companies in 1832, eight in 1834, and nine in 1835.[3] The companies probably chose to retain him to keep him from appearing in court against them.

The nature of the business of marine insurance underwriting in New England changed during Webster's practice.[4] This metamorphosis had begun in the last decade of the eighteenth century. Prior to the American Revolution, English underwriters handled most American marine insurance. The little local underwriting that occurred represented a form of reciprocal risk-sharing among merchants in which import-export merchants underwrote one another's risks by subscribing to a proportion of the policy. Since most merchants at different times acted as both insured and insurer, their chief interest lay in the indemnification of actual losses. Following the Revolution, the demand grew for more American-written insurance. The absence of British underwriters, the expansion of trade, and the incidence of international conflict made insurance underwriting a profitable if speculative venture. This demand and the consequent need for a larger pool of funds prompted two developments. First, some merchants began to function chiefly as brokers. Acting as agents, they arranged for insurance contracts between the shippers and the group of private underwriting merchants. Second, the states began chartering insurance companies whose stock subscriptions would quickly establish a large pool of capital to meet the demand for insurance. The movement from merchant to corporate underwriting appears to have proceeded most quickly in the middle Atlantic States. In Massachusetts the private underwriters coexisted with the companies well into the 1820s.[5]

1. See pp. 144–145, above.

2. DW also argued eight marine insurance cases before the USSC.

3. See pp. 146–160, above.

4. The general outline of the development of marine insurance presented here follows the stimulating discussion in Horwitz, pp. 226–237. Our disagreement with the details of his presentation will be noted where relevant. See also Edwin Merrick Dodd, *American Business Corporations until 1860* (Cambridge, Mass., 1954), pp. 218–226. For the English experience, see Barry Supple, *The Royal Exchange Assurance* (Cambridge, England, 1970), pp. 186–206.

5. That the Massachusetts merchants still functioned as both insurers and insured in the 1820s weakens Horwitz's argument that conflict between two discrete economic interest groups occasioned the

This differentiation of function in the business of marine insurance underwriting created the setting for conflict between the competing interests of insurer and insured. With risks no longer being shared reciprocally, each side focused on litigation whose outcome might expand or contract the scope of the risk for which the insured might receive indemnification. Furthermore, as the insurance companies came to dominate the field, recognition on the part of some judges of the need to protect a company's resources produced an actuarial approach to the question of risk management.

The law of marine insurance applied in Massachusetts reflected the English bias in favor of the underwriter. Its basic approach recognized the insurer's need to select and control the risk. It did this by requiring the insured to make full disclosure of information affecting the risk and to comply with the express warranties in the insurance contract. Failure to comply with any of these voided the policy. In addition, the English courts had created implied warranties of seaworthiness and against deviation which narrowed the risk. The first required the ship to be seaworthy at the time the voyage began; the second forbade the captain to deviate from the usual course between the ports specified in the policy unless necessary to save the ship and cargo.

These doctrines clashed with the tendency of Massachusetts juries to favor the injured plaintiff whenever a technical rule of insurance law threatened to defeat an insured's claim. The MassSJC judges, on the other hand, took positions that favored the insurance underwriters. They did this by using their power to order a new trial for a verdict contrary to the weight of the evidence, and by narrowly construing the jury's fact-finding function. The approach of the MassSJC also reflected the extent to which it continued to take a pre-actuarial approach to the administration of insurance law. In this pre-actuarial view, the judges saw as the purpose of the insurance policy the indemnification of the insured for his actual loss. They believed that the insured should not profit from an unfinished voyage by collecting the full amount of his insurance if a total loss of ship and cargo had not occurred.[6] But with the growing amount of litigation, the courts of other states began to move away from the indemnity rationale in the interest of clarifying the legal consequences of

---

alteration of eighteenth-century doctrine (Horwitz, p. 228). See *Shepard et al.* v. *Essex Fire and Marine Insurance Company*, below. Horwitz also fails to consider the extent and importance of the brokers during the transition to a corporate organization. Massachusetts chartered most of her marine insurance companies in the first decade of the nineteenth century.

6. This reflected the early problem that the English courts had with insurance contracts. The common law rules did not permit the enforcement of gambling contracts. Since insurance looked like gambling, the courts upholding the policy stressed that an insurance contract was merely an indemnity for an actual loss.

a lost voyage. An actuarial view that focused on the maintenance of the insurance fund began to supplant the concern for the result in the individual case. An early example of this actuarial approach was the creation of a rule of law to deal with situations where a ship had not been totally lost. If a ship had been damaged to greater than 50 percent of its value, the courts considered it a *constructive* (also called *technical*) *total loss* and gave the insured the full amount of the policy.[7] Having adopted this doctrine, the courts of the maritime states were left the task of elaborating rules for determining when a constructive total loss occurred. The MassSJC, while it adopted the 50 percent rule, continued to espouse an approach that was both pre-actuarial and favorable to the insurance underwriters. Thus the court, in the former instance, not only focused on the individual case but admitted post-incident evidence on the question whether the insured had used good judgment. In the latter, the court tried to restrict recovery to actual losses by construing narrowly the scope of the constructive total loss doctrine.

In contradistinction to this approach, the USCC for the first circuit under Justice Story took an actuarial approach. Story did not treat each case as a unique event. Rather, any particular litigation was an aspect of the administration of a risk pool by an insurance company. In this regard, the determination of legal rights and liabilities at the earliest possible moment following an incident was more important than basing a decision on what had actually occurred. Story attempted to elaborate rules to enable the insured to fix his legal rights at the time of the incident on the basis of the probability of loss without giving the jury the benefit of hindsight.[8] The actuarially minded court expanded the concept of constructive loss, since it fixed the parameters of a loss at an early time and allowed the insurance company to work that information into its premium structure. The actuarial court did not worry if the insured made out better than if the ship had completed her voyage.

In New England this basic variation in approaches between state and federal courts presented the lawyers for the plaintiffs with the opportunity to choose between two forums which applied different rules of law. Part of this flexibility, however, depended on the breadth of federal jurisdiction. Story tried unsuccessfully to make his court's jurisdiction as broad as the MassSJC.[9] The cases presented below illustrate both the substantive aspects of marine insurance law and the relationship between the state and federal jurisdictions.

b. Formation of the Insurance Contract and Warranty

i. Nathaniel and John Haven v. *John Holland.* This case illustrates the

7. The English required an actual total loss to occur.

8. On the nature of the certainty of legal rules, see pp. 479–480, below.

9. See pp. 474–482, below.

formation of the marine insurance contract in a noncorporate setting, the insurer's defense of deviation, and the effect of federal and state forums on litigation strategy. Early in 1812 the ship *Volant*, owned by Massachusetts merchants Israel Thorndike and John Gray, sailed from Boston to France. Among the several merchants who shipped goods on the outward voyage were Portsmouth merchants Nathaniel and John Haven and Abel Harris. After the *Volant* unloaded her goods in Bordeaux, she took on a homeward cargo for the merchants. The Havens contacted their agent, Boston insurance broker Charles Bradbury. He obtained the assent of eleven merchant-underwriters to insure the Havens' shipment for $6,000. In the summer of 1812 the *Volant* left Bayonne for New England. As she proceeded across the bar at the mouth of the harbor she ran aground. The captain, Nathaniel Perley, off loaded her cargo and returned her to Bayonne for repair. In order to avoid a repetition of the accident, he directed the carriage of the cargo to Passage in Spain. The *Volant* would then sail to Passage, load the cargo, and continue her journey home.

Before the repairs were completed, however, news of the outbreak of the War of 1812 reached Bayonne. After consulting with local merchants, Perley decided to obtain a letter of marque from the American consul. Although this document gave Perley the right to make reprisals on English ships, he wanted it for defensive purposes only. Under the authority of the letter, he increased the *Volant's* armament from four to fourteen guns and nearly doubled her crew. Early in 1813 Perley received permission to leave Bayonne, and sailed to Passage to load the cargo. The Havens' insurance policy specified a voyage from a French port to America. When Bradbury received word of Perley's intention to load at Passage, he realized that the underwriters might claim that stopping there amounted to a deviation that would void the policy. This, in fact, was the underwriters' position, and Bradbury so informed the Havens (Document 74). The underwriters offered to rewrite the policy from Passage, thereby eliminating any claim for damage arising from the grounding on the bar. The Havens, in a letter of February 22, 1813, printed below, rejected the underwriters' offer, directing William Haven (probably a son) to call on Bradbury to discuss the matter. When William Haven returned to Portsmouth, he told the Havens that the underwriters might have a valid defense. The Havens decided, therefore, to have their policy rewritten and so instructed Bradbury in a letter of February 27, 1813, printed below. As a broker, Bradbury served as agent for both sides. He wrote back that he had obtained the consent of all but one of the original eleven subscribers (Document 75). The reluctant participant reduced his subscription from $1000 to $500.

Even before the Havens and Bradbury began their correspondence, the *Volant* had stopped at Passage, loaded her cargo, and set sail for America. After four days at sea, on February 16, 1813, she spied an unmarked ship that appeared to Perley to be waiting to attack. Perley attempted to evade the stranger but when this appeared unlikely, he prepared to fight. As the ships closed, it became apparent to Perley that his adversary was not a ship of war. The *Volant* fired two shots and the stranger surrendered. She turned out to be the captured American merchant ship the *Criterion*, manned by a British prize crew. Perley decided to take advantage of his good fortune. He put his own prize crew on board with orders to sail the *Criterion* back to France. All this took about six hours (Document 76). The delay, however, proved crucial. On March 25, 1813, just outside Boston, a British cruiser captured the *Volant* and sent her to Halifax as a prize of war.

The shippers and the owners of the *Volant* soon began a series of law suits both against the insurers and between themselves. The cases were first heard in state court and later in federal court. The Massachusetts courts heard the first series of suits between 1813 and 1816 before Webster moved to Boston. They were important because they established several precedents that influenced Webster's choice of forum in the second series of cases. By the time Webster became involved in the litigation, the underwriters had won a significant decision on the question of deviation and seemed safe from suit.

In the law of marine insurance many of the legal rules created by the courts aided the underwriters in controlling the risk. Violation of both express and implied warranties voided the contract. The express warranties appeared in the standard language of the contract. Whenever an adverse ruling created a greater risk of liability, the underwriters responded by engrafting new language onto the standard form contract.[1] Besides the express warranties, the courts recognized implied warranties of seaworthiness, deviation, and illegality. These protected the underwriter who lacked adequate knowledge of a ship's physical condition, who expected a voyage between two ports to follow the usual route, and who did not take the risk that the ship would violate the laws of other nations. The doctrine of implied warranty thus buttressed the policy that required full disclosure by the insured of all facts material to the risk.[2] Although proof that a vessel had not been seaworthy at the time it left port voided the policy, a deviation could be excused if the insured proved that it had been necessary to save the vessel and cargo. The case of the

1. For an example of this, see p. 480, below.

2. Edwin W. Patterson, *Essentials of Insurance Law* (New York, 1957), chaps. 7 and 10. Another aspect of the full disclosure policy was the concealment doctrine. An insurance contract was voidable if the insured did not disclose a fact unknown to the underwriter and the fact was material to the risk. Misrepresentation of a material fact also voided the insurance.

Volant presented a question of deviation since the *Volant* need not have captured the *Criterion*.

In the first case, tried in November 1813, Timothy Wiggin and several other shippers sued one of the underwriters.[3] The trial jury found for Wiggin et al., but on appeal Judge Charles Jackson ordered a new trial. He ruled that any alteration in the usual route or delay changed the risk and therefore constituted a deviation. Capturing another ship, under any circumstances, discharged the contract. Jackson wanted to draw a clear rule of conduct to guide ship captains. Futhermore, his decision would protect the underwriters by enabling them to control the risk closely; they would be protected from adventuresome ship captains. Such a narrowly drawn rule would also reduce the impact of the juries who favored the insured. "If a line is not drawn here," he wrote, "it will be impossible to say, to what extent a ship under such circumstances may depart from the regular course of her voyage: and the underwriter upon a mercantile voyage will be exposed to hazards as great as when he expressly agrees that the ship . . . may make captures."[4]

At the new trial two of the plaintiffs tried again. Jackson's ruling had made the capture a deviation as a matter of law. The plaintiff's attorney, Lemuel Shaw now turned and argued that the capture constituted barratry, one of the perils insured against.[5] Barratry was injury caused by the willful misconduct of the master or crew, an act prejudicial to the interest of the owners of the ship or cargo. At the trial in November 1816, Chief Justice Isaac Parker directed the jury that this deviation did not constitute barratry because Wiggin et al. could not prove that Perley had intended to prejudice the owner's interest.

In Wiggin et al.'s third attempt to collect the insurance, they sued yet another underwriter.[6] This time they had oral evidence that the underwriter had known that Perley had taken out a letter of marque. Did this knowledge raise a presumption that the insurer had assented to the likelihood of a capture? The plaintiffs never found out. The court ruled the parol (word of mouth) evidence inadmissible. The written contract, Parker said, defined the risk. Parker feared that the admission of such evidence in this case would open the door to its use by underwriters in other cases.

By the time the court announced this last opinion in 1817, Webster was in Boston. He became involved in the *Volant* litigation between his

3. *T. Wiggin et al.* v. *Amory*, 13 Mass. 118 (1816).

4. Ibid., pp. 127–128.

5. *J. Wiggin et al.* v. *Amory*, 14 Mass. 1 (1817). Joseph Wiggin must have been a joint plaintiff in the first suit. Horwitz discusses barratry as a matter of defense, pp. 229–230. In the standard Boston policy, it was one of the risks insured against.

6. *J. Wiggin et al.* v. *Boardman*, 14 Mass. 12 (1817).

arrival in 1816 and the delivery of the opinions the following year. Another of the shippers had responded to Justice Parker's suggestion in the second trial of *Wiggin et al.* v. *Amory*, that although Perley's action had not been barratrous, it had involved misconduct. This shipper sued the *Volant's* owners on the theory that they were liable for the misdeeds of their employee, the captain. The owners retained Webster in August 1816, for $50. He successfully defended them in a November 1817 trial and January appeal. For the latter he received a fee of $1000.[7]

Webster was also retained by his New Hampshire friends. On August 14, 1817, he noted in his fee book the receipt of $20 from Abel Harris for the latter's suit against the *Volant's* insurers.[8] Webster must have known that in light of the rulings in the *Wiggins* cases sustaining the deviation defense, a suit in the Massachusetts courts would probably fail. He decided instead on a diversity suit in the USCC. Perhaps he could persuade Justice Story to adopt a different rule of law. Section 34 of the federal Judiciary Act of 1789 stated that the laws of the several states "shall be regarded as rules of decision in trials at common law in the courts of the United States in cases where they apply."[9] This was understood in the first circuit to mean that the federal courts would apply state statutes that affected the rights of persons or property. They would follow decisions of the state courts on the construction of state statutes unless they conflicted with the Constitution or federal law. As far as the application of common law rules was concerned, Story had noted in 1812 that state court decisions were only guides for the federal courts.[10] Since Story had already tried to federalize commercial maritime transactions under the admiralty jurisdiction,[11] it was likely that he would not consider himself bound by the *Wiggins* precedent. Furthermore, the deviation rule set forth by Judge Jackson was not based on a state statute. When Justice Story dealt with state common law rules with which he did not agree, he had little difficulty in finding sufficient factual differences to justify the formulation of a new rule.

In a letter of September 5, 1817, printed below, Webster asked Abel Harris if he wanted his cases sued in federal court. Harris apparently agreed, and Webster filed the two suits in April 1818 for the May term.[12]

7. *W. Gray* v. *Thorndike and J. Gray*, unreported MassSJC,S case (1817); see Willard Phillips, *A Treatise on the Law of Insurance*, 2 vols. (Boston, 1823, 1824) 1:208. For DW's notation of the retainer see *Correspondence*, 1: 204, and for the fee, see p. 129, above.

8. See p. 126, above.

9. 1 U.S. Statutes at Large 92 (1789).

10. *U.S.* v. *Wonson*, 1 Gallison 5 (1812).

11. *DeLovio* v. *Boit et al.*, 2 Gallison 398 (1815). See pp. 474–475, below.

12. *Harris* v. *Elwell* and *Harris* v. *Jones*, USCC, DMass, May 1819.

In a letter of December 23, 1817, printed below, Webster asked Nathaniel Haven to bring the *Volant* correspondence to Boston. In May, Harris's cases were continued to the October term. In December 1818 Webster sent a letter to Jeremiah Mason, printed below, about the conclusion of one of Harris's suits. Webster indicated his readiness to turn his attention to the Havens' claim.

In January 1819 Bliss prepared a diversity action against John Holland, one of the Havens' insurers (Document 77). Webster would use this as a test case. If it succeeded, he would sue or threaten to sue the others. Webster entered the action in May 1819. The parties continued the case for two years, until May 22, 1821, when the trial took place. Webster offered the testimony of William Gill, a passenger on the *Volant* (Document 78), along with his other evidence of capture. He also introduced a memorandum (Document 79) which tended to show that the insurer had known of the letter of marque.

The critical moment in the case came when Story instructed the jury. If he adopted the Massachusetts rule, the Havens had little chance of a recovery. Instead Story instructed the jury that if the *Volant* had captured the *Criterion* out of self-defense, the capture was justified and the deviation excused. This differed from Judge Jackson's ruling. Jackson recognized only the *Volant's* right to defend herself; Story, on the other hand, made the capture and the boarding of a prize crew a logical entailment of the act of self-defense. The jury had to decide only whether the *Volant* acted from reasons of defense or profit. If the former then the fact that she profited was incidental. Story said he wanted to give ship captains a large amount of discretion when confronted by a supposed enemy ship. If the captain chose to stand and fight, he could claim the fruits of victory. "It would be most mischievous to the interests of trade," he said, "to discourage a crew from making a gallant defence by the knowledge that in no event could they reap a reward from the victory."[13] Webster's evidence of the defendant's knowledge of the letter of marque forestalled any defense based on the concealment doctrine.

The jury deliberated and reached a decision in favor of the Havens. Webster reported the good news to Nathaniel Haven, printed below. Holland's lawyers moved for a new trial (Document 80) on the issue of Story's instruction. This would prepare the way for a writ of error if the defendant wanted to carry the case further. Webster anxiously awaited the court's decision. To Jeremiah Mason he wrote on September 3, 1821:

> I send you the policy on the Volant. I have made a little arrange-

13. *Haven et al.* v. *Holland*, 2 Mason 230, 234 (1821); Mason gives the year as 1820. Kent chidingly wrote that Story had carried the captain's discretion "to the very verge of the law" (Kent, 3: 316).

> ment about it. Judge Story will be here tomorrow to give his judgt in the case here. I hope it will be broad eno[ugh] to cover this. I will let you know.[14]

Story denied the motion and the verdict stood. By the middle of October 1821 seven of the subscribers paid their shares (Document 81). Two of the others, however, would not give up without the semblance of a fight. Webster thus brought two more suits, and the defendants defaulted the next May.[15]

DOCUMENT 74. EVIDENTIARY EXTRACT

Extract from a letter of Chas Bradbury to N. A & J. Haven, of the 16 Feb 1813.

"By the last advice from the Volant, it is understood that she was going bound to Passage to complete her lading. As this Port is in Spain, may there not be a deviation on your policy? If so an arrangement ought now to be agreed on."

The same from a letter from same to same of 20 Feby. 1813. "I have conversed with the writers respecting your Policy on the Volant, and find they are pretty strongly impressed with the opinion, that they will not be liable should she load at Passage.[16] They have however offered to make it a new Policy, and take the risk from *Passage*, as it was before from *Bayonne*, meaning to avoid all claim for the accident on *Bayonne* Bar, and the risk from Bayonne to Passage. This seems to be the best & only terms I can get proposed; and I should recommend to have it accepted—the loss at *Bayonne* cannot be much I think.

"You will advise me by return of mail, if this arrangement will be satisfactory, and I will immediately attend to its completion.

14. *Correspondence*, 1: 291. On September 12, 1821 DW wrote to Mason: "Judge Story has given judgment in the Volant case here. On the facts, as presented, he entertains no doubt, that the Volant did no more than she was authorized to do, *with* or *without letter of Marque*." (mDW 3055). DW suggested that Mason bring another *Volant*-related suit in New Hampshire in October.

15. *Haven et al.* v. *Bryant et al.* and *Haven et al.* v. *Valentine*, USCC, DMass, May 1822. DW and Mason also handled a *Volant* suit for Nathan Appleton. There is no record of the litigation other than a letter from DW to Mason, January 10, 1822, *Correspondence*, 1: 301, regarding the disposition of the recovery. DW had agreed to receive a percentage, and expected to earn $500.

16. Among the Massachusetts merchants who underwrote portions of the *Volant's* cargo were John Holland, Benjamin Rich, John Dorr, John Bryant, William Sturgis, John J. Valentine, Jonathan Amory, Robert Elwell, and John Coffin Jones. The insurers considered the trip to Passage an unjustified deviation from the insured voyage.

"The Rambler[17] has a letter of marque, and must have liberty to capture, although we have not the most distant idea of her chasing any thing, as she is too valuable to run any such risque, and the captain is largely interested to come safe."

AD. *Haven et al.* v. *Holland*, USCC,DMass, May 1821.

NATHANIEL AND JOHN HAVEN TO CHARLES BRADBURY

Dear Sir, Portsmouth February 22nd. 1813

You request of us an answer by return of mail, to your favor of the 20th inst.[18] We cannot at present accede to the overtures made by the underwriters, on our policy on the Volant. It is at once abandoning a claim we undoubtedly shall have for a partial loss[19] arising from the accident at Bayonne bar, merely on account of a supposed intended deviation. We have no intimation of the intention of proceeding to *Passage* and our letters are to the 19th. Decr, when our friends say, she would reload with all dispatch and proceed to sea. Should she proceed to Passage we presume it will arise from justifiable necessity in which case the underwriters must be held, and if not justifiable any misconduct of the master would come within the view of the policy.[20] However as our policy cannot we presume be a solitary instance, we should wish to know in what light the case is viewed by others who have had insurance effected and in what manner if any, they have now modified their policies, for this purpose we have written to Mr William Haven[21] (now in Boston) to make inquiry & call on you.

We have no probability of effecting insurance for you on the Rambler as stated in a former letter the rate of premium is not so much objected to as the disinclination to take any risks. Very truly yr friends & obt ser.

N. A & J. Haven

Copy. *Haven et al.* v. *Holland*, USCC,DMass, May 1821. Nathaniel Appleton Haven and John Haven, Portsmouth merchants.

NATHANIEL AND JOHN HAVEN TO CHARLES BRADBURY

Dear Sir Portsmouth February 27th. 1813

We had presumed the sole motive for the Capt of the Volant proceed-

17. A ship in which Bradbury had an interest. He wanted the Havens to insure it but they declined.

18. See Document 74, preceding.

19. Recovery for damage to the Havens' property.

20. A deviation constituted a good defense only if it actually occurred. The Havens believed the master would be found guilty of barratry. This is unlikely, since he had acted in the interest of the owners and shippers.

21. Probably the son of one of the Havens.

ing to Passage was, for the purpose of being in a more favorable situation to proceed to sea, by embracing a wind that would not only be fair for leaving the port, but equally so for quitting the coast; which we understand is not the case at Bayonne. With these impressions we were fully of opinion that such discretionary power is vested in the master as would justify the deviation; no sinister views operating, he would have the right thus to proceed as the more probable means of avoiding an enemy. Since the return of Mr. Wm Haven it has been suggested to us that *another motive* may lead to this deviation viz that of taking in *more* cargo than he could at Bayonne. If such should be the fact the justification of the deviation might perhaps be questionable, and therefore we are desirous that our policy may be so modified as to remove all doubts. The bill of loading which we have received for our goods is dated at Bayonne, the master therein declares bound to Boston. We presume that the Master or Underwriters, or Owners, are answerable for the consequences of this deviation. We understand that policies circumstanced as ours, (say one for Mr [Abel] Harris) has been alter'd without any additional premium, & we think that all that can equitably be required of us, is an additional premium for the sea risk from Bayonne to Passage.—with regard to the general average[22] which has accrued, having no data whereby to ascertain its probable amount, we do not think it proper to wave that claim, preferring the payment of an additional premium; still however we shall leave the matter for you to adjust for us, as the proper person in whom the assured & underwriters should mutually confide

with accustomed regard we are very truly yours. Nath. A & J. Haven

Copy. *Haven et al.* v. *Holland*, USCC,DMass, May 1821.

DOCUMENT 75. EVIDENTIARY EXTRACT

same to same 1 March 1813. "Gent. your favour of the 27th. is received.[23] I have conversed with Mr J Gray, who is an owner of the Volant; he seems to think that there will be no deviation in loading at Passage, on the ground that it is a Province which has been annexed to France.[24] I cannot say what would be the result of an inquiry, nor can I at present give any opinion whether it would be a deviation.

The underwriters will not accede to any other terms than those I

22. "Sea risk" meant a loss due to damage from an accident at sea. It would not include loss by capture or barratry. "General average" (also called "gross average") is the contribution assessed on all the interests for the damage to the ship or cargo incurred for the purpose of saving the rest of the vessel or cargo.

23. See preceding letter.

24. The insurance policy described the voyage from the *Volant*'s "port of lading in France" to the United States. When the insurers redrew the policies they changed the point of origin to the Bay of Biscay.

proposed, and which I should agree to on your behalf, if your letter was not so strongly expressed to the contrary—except the last clause requesting me to adjust it, I should consider the previous observations as a guide for me. I must therefore wait your further orders. The general average expense I do not expect can be more than 3 or 4 p cent, the risque from Bayonne to Passage is worth 3 to 5 p cent.

I cannot now say that the first proposals will be agreed to after this time, as the risque appears to be increasing, and if any thing unfavourable should occur, the writers will not alter the Policy—prefering to take the chance of it as it stands.

If however there should be nothing new occur, I presume the proposals will be agreed to. I wait your answer."[25]

same to same 16 March 1813. "I succeeded in the alteration of your policy on the Volant except for one line, that of B[ryant] & Sturgis[26]—they were unwilling to make the new arrangement, but finally offered to reduce their sum to 500 dollars instead of 1000. and I could not do any thing more with them than that or to leave the original policy. I considered it best to do it, & I hope you will be satisfied. I should have procured another name for the sum, but all the writers are now as much as they wish on a risque, the termination of which is so uncertain. If we knew of her arrival at Passage, I think there would be no difficulty in getting more done on her."

AD. *Haven et al.* v. *Holland*, USCC,DMass, May 1821.

DOCUMENT 76. AFFIDAVIT

Lynn, 11 January 1817

I Benjamin Stacy of Lynn[27] in the County of Essex, Commonwealth of Massachusetts, being of lawful age, do testify & declare, that I sail'd from the Port of Marblehead in said Commonwealth on board the Brig Good Intent sometime in the year 1810 & that I was in France on or about the month of June in the year 1812 where I met with Captain Nathaniel M Perley of the American Ship Volant, & requested him to give me a passage in said Ship to the United States; which he the said Perley agreed to do. I then agreed to ship some Goods on board said Ship on freight, provided John Lewis Brown & Co. of Bordeaux who had charge of said Goods should agree to the same, as I presumed they would do; as they had recommended shipping them in this Ship before. I afterwards corresponded with said Brown & Co. & they agreed to do it; & I

25. On March 2, 1813, the Havens wrote to Bradbury that they wanted him to obtain the new insurance (*Haven et al.* v. *Holland*, USCC, DMass, May 1821).

26. The new policy was dated March 4, 1821.

27. Stacy not further identified.

order'd them to prepare & ship my own goods, & such as I had the direction of. The Goods were sent round to Bayonne, to be shipt in this Vessel; but before the goods were shipped, the news of war between the United States & Great Britain, had reached France, & in consequence of it Captain Perley had concluded to take out a Commission of Lettre de Marque & increase his number of men & add to the armament of the Volant, all which I knew, before the said Goods were shipt, & I think that Messrs. Brown & Co. must have known it also, because it was a thing of general notariety & I thought the goods were safer in consequence of this additional Armament & Commission[.] And I believe that it was the general opinion of every one who knew it at the time, as it was, as I believe the general understanding, that the Volant was not to turn out of her way to take prizes but might Capture such vessels of inferior force as she might fall in with. On or about 12 Feby. 1813, left Passage for America, tack ahead wind about 12 O.C[lock] same night the wind continued westerly for four days, with rain & squals at times, during which time made the best of our way in beating out of the Bay of Biscay. That on 16 by land a/c & 17 by sea a/c we made a Strange Sail ahead while Standing on our starboard tack laying up about S. S W, that we immediately[?] hove about[28] & staid from her under the same sail that was then sett untill a little after three P.M. She came up nearly within gun shot, at which time we could plainly see that She was a merchant Vessel of inferior force. We then hove down on her & hoisted our Colours, gave her two Guns, upon which She lett run her main sail with her Colours at the main peak. Capt Perley hail'd her & found her to be an American Vessel Captur'd by a British frigate—he then sent me on board her as prize master with ten men, & order'd me to Bayonne, & in case there should not be Sufficient Water at the Bar at Bayonne to make a harbour at Passage. That the delay in capturing this Vessel, did not exceed six hours if so much, from the time of the Volants bearing away & firing the first Gun. During which time there did not appear to me that there was any extra risk of the Volant or her Cargo

Capt Stacy declares that this is a relation of facts, after having perused it twice with attention: in presents of Israel Thorndike & John Gray

ADS. *Haven et al.* v. *Holland*, USCC,DMass, May 1821.

TO ABEL HARRIS

Sir Boston Sep. 5. 1817

I think we came to the conclusion, respecting your policy, that it was not expedient to put it in suit at present, if a continuance of the action

28. Hove—to maneuver a ship in a specified direction or manner.

against you could be otherwise obtained. The writ if it be like the summons, is clearly defective, & must be amended. The Court will of course grant the plf leave to amend, but whether on the condition of a continuance, or not, I am not quite certain.[29] In the State Courts in N. Hampshire such amendments never take place without a continuance, if a continuance be desired.

In the [United States] Circuit Court, some amendments are made, without any terms or conditions, & some are only made on condition of continuance, &c. I am a little apprehensive that the Judge would not think this such an amendment as ought to procure a continuance.

Please consult Mr [Jeremiah] Mason on this point, & refer him to the 16th. rule of the Circuit Court.[30]

In case it should be thought expedient to sue the policy at the ensuing term in this District, there is no time to be lost, & I should know it early next week. Yours &c &c D. Webster

ALS. CSmH.

TO NATHANIEL APPLETON HAVEN

Dear Sir, Boston Decr. 23. 1817

As it is a little uncertain on what day my engagements in Court may permit me to be in Portsmouth, I have concluded *to be at home* on Monday next, & hope to have the pleasure of seeing you at that time, in this town.

You will do well to bring the letters which passed between you & the owners, before the Ship sailed.[31] Very truly yours D. Webster

ADS. MBNU.

TO NATHANIEL APPLETON HAVEN

Dear Sir, Boston Jan. 9. 1818

Such is the situation of my family, that I shall write Mr. Morland to-

29. *Harris* v. *Elwell*, USCC,DMass, May 1819. Presumably, Elwell had sued Harris for the unpaid premium. DW must have detected a technical error in the summons.

30. The 16th rule reads: "Amendments in matters of form shall be allowed as of course on motion; but if the defect or want of form be shewn as cause of special demurrer the Court will impose terms on the party amending." *Rules of the Circuit Court of the United States for the First Circuit* (Boston, 1812), p. 12.

31. Presumably, letters between the Havens and Thorndike and Gray. DW had just finished defending the latter in a suit against them by shippers like the Havens. In January DW argued the appeal before the MassSJC. No question of conflict of interest seems to have arisen.

day, that I recommend him to rely on other Counsel.[32] I cannot now undertake to leave home on either of the days you mention.

Stephen Codman Esqr.[33] has bro't an action agt. owners of Volant. He had a small Invoice goods on board, & perhaps had *insurance*.

I do not know yet exactly what his case is. With great respect Yours

D. Webster

ALS. NhD.

TO JEREMIAH MASON

Dear Sir Boston Decr. 12. 1818

The case of Elwell & Harris will probably be *finally finished* today or Monday, & I think it probable all the subscriptions on that policy will be adjusted, in the manner mentioned.

I have not heard yet what could probably be done in regard to the policies in Mr. Bradbury's Office.[34]

I send you minutes of my argt. in Gray v Thorndike. The leading facts you will pick up in the reported cases. For *your* purpose, vid *Max* v *Roberts*, 12 East ___, & a case in Campbell noticed in my minutes.[35] I mentioned to Mr P[rescott] that Messrs. H[aven] intended to sue in Circt. Court. It is time to be *doing*, on that subject. I am disposed to <enter into> agree to your proposition, if things look agreeably.

We are all very well. The weather the day we came was fine, & Julia, after the parting scene was over was, as you may tell Mrs. M. very agreeable.

I hear little from W[ashington] more than appears in the papers. Daggett & Burrill[36] appear to be at work.

32. DW had accepted a retainer from Morland to handle what DW called the *Exeter Factory* case. See pp. 130–131, above.

33. Boston merchant; no other information on this case has been found.

34. A reference to the Havens' cases.

35. 12 East 89 (1810) involved a suit by a shipper of goods against the owner of the vessel. As in *Haven et al.* v. *Holland*, the shipper's insurer had used the deviation defense. Instead of resolving the question whether a shipowner owed a duty to the shipper to deliver the cargo, the court held the plaintiff-shipper's declaration defective. Lord Ellenborough did point out that the shipowner did not make an implied agreement that he would not make intermediate stops. Neither the case in Campbell nor DW's minutes have been found.

36. David Daggett (1764–1851; Yale 1783), Connecticut lawyer, admitted in 1786, state representative (1791–1796, 1805), state councillor (1797, 1809–1813), state's attorney (1811–1813), U. S. senator (1813–1819), judge, Connecticut supreme court (1826–1834), Kent professor of law at Yale (1826–1834); James Burrill, Jr. (1772–1820; Brown 1788), Rhode Island lawyer, admitted in 1791, state attorney general (1797–1814), state representative

I learn that Pinkney means to put our College case on the ground that all the power of *parliament* belongs to the N. H. Legislature.[37] Yrs

D. Webster

ALS. MHi.

DOCUMENT 77. WRIT OF ATTACHMENT

Massachusetts District, ss. } *The President of the United States of America*

To the Marshal of our District of Massachusetts, or his Deputy— Greeting.

WE command you to attach the goods or estate of John Holland of Boston in the State of Massachusetts a citizen of the said State *in our District of Massachusetts,* merchant *to the value of* two thousand *dollars, and for want thereof to take the body of the said* John Holland *(if he may be found in your District) and* him *safely keep, so that you have* him *before our judges of our Circuit Court of said United States for the first circuit next to be holden at Boston, within and for our said District of Massachusetts, on the* fifteenth *day of* May next: *Then and there, in our said court, to answer unto* Nathaniel A Haven and John Haven of [Portsmouth in the State] of New Hampshire, citizens of said State and in the District of New Hampshire merchants and copartners transacting business in the name and Stile of N A & J Haven, in a plea of trespass on the case for that the said Nathaniel A Haven and John Haven on the fourth day of March in the year of our Lord one thousand eight hundred and thirteen at Boston aforesaid in said District, according to the custom and usage of merchants caused to be made a certain policy of insurance purporting thereby and containing therein that the said Nathaniel and John the plaintiffs *do make insurance, and cause to be insured, lost or not lost,*[38] *the sum* of six thousand dollars on merchandize on board the Ship Volant, from her last port of loading in the Bay of Biscay to her port of discharge in the United States as by the said policy of assurance reference being thereto had will fully appear; Of all

---

(1813–1816), chief justice, Rhode Island supreme court (1816), U. S. senator (1817–1820).

37. William Pinkney (1764–1822), Maryland lawyer and diplomat, studied with Samuel Chase, admitted in 1786, state legislator (1788–1792), commissioner to England under the Jay Treaty (1796–1804), attorney general, Maryland (1805), minister to England (1807–1811), U.S. attorney general (1811–1814), U.S. representative (1815–1816), minister to Russia (1816–1818), U.S. senator (1819–1822). See *Legal Papers*, 3 for a discussion of the *Dartmouth College* case.

38. This standard provision made the insurance applicable even if the ship had been wrecked prior to the date of the contract.

which said premises he the said John Holland afterwards to wit on the said fourth day of March aforesaid in the year aforesaid had notice. And thereupon afterwards to wit on the day and year last aforesaid at Boston aforesaid in consideration that the plaintiffs aforesaid at the special instance and request of the said John Holland had then and there paid him a certain sum of money to wit the sum of four hundred dollars as a premium or reward for the insurance of one thousand dollars of and upon the said merchandize in the said ship on the intended voyage in the said policy of insurance mentioned, and had then and there undertaken and faithfully promised the said Holland to do and perform all things in the said policy of insurance contained, on the part of the said plaintiffs to be done and performed[;] he the said Holland undertook and then and there promised the Plaintiffs aforesaid that he the said Holland would become and be an insurer to the said plaintiffs of the said sum of one thousand dollars upon the said merchandize in the ship aforesaid on the said intended voyage and would do and perform all things in the said policy of assurance mentioned on his part to be done and performed, and the said Holland then and there became and was an insurer to the said Plaintiffs, and then and there subscribed the said policy of insurance, as such insurer of the said sum of one thousand dollars upon the said merchandize in the said ship in the voyage aforesaid, and said plaintiffs further say that heretofore to wit, on the twenty fifth day of September in the year of our Lord one thousand eight hundred and twelve certain merchandize of great value to wit of the value of nine thousand dollars were shipped and loaded on board of the said ship Volant, then riding at anchor before Bayonne in the Bay of Biscay aforesaid, to be carried and conveyed therein from Bayonne aforesaid to a port in the United States to wit the port of Boston aforesaid, and the said plaintiffs were then and there and until and at the time of the loss hereinafter mentioned, interested in the said merchandize and owners thereof.[39] And the plaintiffs in fact further say that heretofore to wit on the twelfth day of February in the year of our Lord eighteen hundred and thirteen the said ship with the Plaintiffs' merchandize aforesaid on board thereof, departed and set sail from her port of loading in the Bay of Biscay aforesaid on her said intended voyage towards her port of discharge in the United States. And that afterwards and whilst the said ship was proceeding on her said voyage and before arriving at any port in the United States to wit on the twenty fifth day of March in the year aforesaid, the said ship with the merchandize aforesaid on board thereof as aforesaid, was, on the high seas, to wit, at said Boston, with force and arms and in a hostile manner captured, seized, and taken, by certain ennemies of the United States, and thereby the

39. One of the requirements for an enforceable insurance contract was a demonstration of the plaintiff's financial stake in the subject of the insurance.

said merchandize then and there became and was wholly lost to the Plaintiffs and never did arrive at a port in the United States, of all which the said John Holland afterwards to wit on the first day of January in the year of our Lord eighteen hundred and fourteen at Boston aforesaid had notice and proof and was then and there requested by the plaintiffs to pay them the said sum of one thousand dollars by him insured as aforesaid. And for that the said John Holland at Boston aforesaid on the day of the purchase of this writ being indebted to the said Plaintiffs in the sum of six hundred dollars for so much money theretofore by the said Holland had and received to the use of the Plaintiffs then and there in consideration thereof promised them to pay that sum whenever he should be thereunto afterwards requested.[40] Yet the said John Holland though often requested has never paid said sums or either of them but refuses to pay the same.

To the damage of the said Plaintiffs as they say [*the sum of* two] thousand *dollars, which shall then and there be made to appear* [*with other due damages. And have you there this writ, with*] *your doings therein. Witness the Hon.* John Marshall *Esq.*; *at Boston, the* fifth *day of* January *in the year of our Lord, one thousand eight hundred and* nineteen

Jno W Davis, *Clerk.*

Extract. *Haven et al.* v. *Holland,* USCC,DMass, May 1821.

DOCUMENT 78. INTERROGATORIES AND ANSWERS

[May 4, 1821]

Circuit Court of the United States
Massachusetts District. Oct T. 1820. No. 12
Nathaniel A. Haven & al.
vs.
John Holland

Interrogatories to be administered to William Gill of Philadelphia[41] and such other witnesses as may be produced to the Commissioner, on the part of the Plaintiffs in the above mentioned Cause.

1st. Were you on board the Ship Volant, Nathaniel Perley master, on the seventeenth day of February 1813—and did said Ship, while you were on board, fall in with and take a brig called the Criterion?

40. In this count DW sought return of the premium in case he lost the first count.

41. Gill a passenger on the *Volant,* was a part-owner of the cargo. After this trial DW contacted Jeremiah Mason about conducting a second trial in New Hampshire in October. As to Gill's role DW wrote: "*Mr. Gill,* who is a party, *really or nominally,* in the policy I sent you, was our *best* witness here. I believe we can supply his place pretty well." DW to Mason, September 12, 1821, *W&S,* 16: 64.

1. To the Plaintiffs' first interrogatory, this Deponent answers and says that he was on board the Ship Volant, Nathaniel Perley, master, about the time mentioned in Plaintiffs' said first interrogatory, and that said Ship fell in with and captured a Brig, called the Criterion, while he was on board.
2d. Will you state in detail, so far as you know the same, all the circumstances which attended and preceded and followed the meeting of the said vessels.
2. To the Plaintiffs' second interrogatory, this Deponent answers, that on the fourth or fifth day after said Ship left Passage, bound to Boston, they discovered a strange sail, about noon, nearly ahead of the Volant. Supposing her to be a British cruizer, watching for the Volant, every exertion was made to get clear of her, by making more sails, and altering, in the most favorable manner, the course of the Volant. The strange sail having a fair wind proceeded immediately for the Volant, and when within a short distance, she bore away, as Deponent and others on board supposed, with an intention of coming under the stern of the Volant, and giving her a raking fire. To counteract this, the Volant wore[42] round and then coming near the strange sail, the Volant fired one or two guns, upon which the strange sail immediately struck. Her boat was sent to the Volant, and she proved to be the Brig, Criterion, from New York, prize to a British man of war. A prize master and about sixteen men were taken out of her and transfered to the Vol[ant] and about the same number of men being put on board her from the Volant, said Brig was ordered for France.
3d. What courses were the two vessels steering—and how far distant from each other—and what hour of the day—when the Criterion was first descried?
3. To the Plaintiffs' third interrogatory, Deponent answers, that not being a seaman, and such a length of time having since elapsed, he can not tell the course, by compass, which the said two vessels were steering. But the Volant was close hauled on the wind, making every exertion to proceed on her voyage, and said Brig appeared to be coming down to the Volant with a fair wind. When Deponent first saw said Brig, to the best of his knowledge and belief, she was about eight or nine miles from the Volant, and the time about noon day.
4th. Did the Volant change or alter her course, or sails, before they met—and what were such alterations, and the effects thereof upon her sailing?
4. To the Plaintiffs' fourth interrogatory, Deponent answers, that the Volant did alter her course and make more sail, with a view to escape

42. Presented her stern to the wind.

from said Brig. But the Volant having a head wind, and said Brig a fair one, it was found impossible to avoid her.

5. Did the Criterion alter her course or sails, before they met,—and what were such alterations and the effects thereof upon her sailing?

5. To the Plaintiffs' fifth interrogatory, this Deponent answers, that said Brig appeared to alter her course or sails very little, if any, until she came near the Volant, when she bore away, as Deponent supposed at the time, with an intention of coming across the Volant's stern.

6. How near did they approach before the Volant wore Ship, and what was the position of the Brig, in regard to the Volant, when she began to wear ship—and what after?

6. To the sixth interrogatory of the Plaintiffs', Deponent says, that he cannot answer as to the precise distance between the said two vessels, nor their exact situation; but when said Brig had approached very near the Volant, the former kept away as Deponent believes, for the purpose of raking the Volant. The Volant was then ordered round, upon which she immediately came very near said Brig, and as soon as the guns of the Volant were brought to bear on said Brig, one or two were fired and said Brig immediately struck.

7. What time had elapsed, *after such wearing*, when the colors of the Brig were seen to come down? and what time was taken up in the capture?

7. To the Plaintiffs' seventh interrogatory, the Deponent answers, that it was but a very few minutes after the Volant wore round, before said Brig struck. The time taken up in the capture was altogether about three hours.

8. When the Volant wore ship, did she fire as soon as her guns were brought to bear upon the Criterion—or did she bear down a considerable time, and how long, before she fired

8. To the Plaintiffs' eighth interrogatory, Deponent answers, that the Volant fired as soon as her guns could be brought to bear and that was almost immediately after she wore round.

9. What was, at first, supposed to be the national character, and what the force and appointment of the Brig—and at what stage of the capture or meeting was first ascertained her real character and force?

9. To the Plaintiffs' ninth interrogatory, this Deponent answers, that the strange sail was supposed by himself and others on board the Volant, to be a British cruiser; and when she came near, a tier of ports was discovered, and about the time the Volant wore round, Deponent observed men with British uniforms, on the deck of said Brig, whom he took to be British mariners. Her real character was not ascertained till after she struck. Her force Deponent does not know.

10. What was the force of the Volant in guns and men, and what of the

Criterion—how many men were put into the Criterion, and how many taken from her?

10. To the Plaintiffs tenth interrogatory, Deponent answers, that the force of the Volant to the best of his recollection, was fourteen carronades, small arms, and from eighty to ninety men, [illegible] of which armament was procured in France.

Deponent does not know what was the force of said Brig. She was pierced for a tier of guns. Deponent believes that a prize master and sixteen men were taken out of said Brig and about the same number put on board of her from the Volant.

11. Where, in what sea, and how far distant from any, and what coast, did this meeting take place?

11. To the Plaintiffs' eleventh interrogatory, Deponent answers, that when said vessels met, the Volant was beating out of the Bay of Biscay, and to the best of Deponent's knowledge and belief, not a great distance from the coast of France.

12. Did the Volant, and how soon after the capture, proceed upon her voyage?

[Gill did not answer this interrogatory.]

13. Do you know any other matter of thing which may be of advantage to the Plaintiffs in the above cause, if so please to state the same as fully as if thereto interrogated.

D. Webster & A. Bliss (attorneys) for Plaintiffs

12 [13]. To the Plaintiffs' thirteenth and last interrogatory, Deponent answers, that he recollects nothing in addition, which is material to the cause, except that it was always the intention of the Volant to proceed on her aforesaid voyage, with all care and diligence, and to avoid meeting, or coming in contact with, any vessel whatever.

William Gill

Extract. *Haven et al.* v. *Holland*, USCC,DMass, May 1821. We have juxtaposed the questions DW sent to Philadelphia with Gill's answers.

DOCUMENT 79. MEMORANDUM TO JOSEPH MAY

2nd. Jany. 1813. Insured $1250. @ 40 pr ct on Ship Volant's cargo from Bayonne to U States. Abner Wood for Josiah Bartlet ins[ured].[43] Pol[icy] 4731. p[remiu]m $500.

Jany 22. It being understood that the master of the Volant has armed the Ship & taken a Commission—it is agreed that it shall not be considered a deviation if she shall give chase to or capture any Vessel.

G[eorge] C[abot] presidt.

43. Wood and Bartlet have not been identified.

The Assured are not to abandon in case of capture or restraint until the property is condemned or until it shall be proved to have been ninety days under detention.

10 May 1816.	pd A Wood	1250.–
	less his note	501.–
		749.–
	Interest	103.25
		$ 852.25

AD. *Haven et al.* v. *Holland*, USCC,DMass, May 1821. Joseph May was secretary of the Boston Marine Insurance Company.

TO NATHANIEL APPLETON HAVEN

Dear Sir Boston May 23. 1821

I have to inform you that the action, on the Policy, vs Jno. Holland was tried yesterday, & a verdict rend. for the plfs; the Jury being of opinion, under the direction of the Court, that the Captain of the Volant did no more than a just and liberal notion of self defense would warrant his doing, in relation to the capture of the Criterion.

I do not know whether the other underwriters will pay without further controversy.

I tho't it proper to give you this information. Very respectfully yrs

D Webster

ALS. NhD.

DOCUMENT 80. MOTION FOR NEW TRIAL

[May 25, 1821]

Circuit Court of the United States
Massachusetts. ss.

Haven et al. &. John Holland

And now the sd. Holland moves the Court here, that the Verdict of the Jury be set aside & a new trial granted, because the sd Verdict is against Law, in this, that there was a deviation, which discharged the Underwriters, by the sd Ship Volant's remaining by & manning the Brig Criterion & making prize of her after she had been subdued by & struck her flag to the sd Ship Volant, & after acting in her own defence the Volant had ascertained, that there [was] no further danger to be apprehended from her, as an enemy.

Prescott & Welsh[44] for Deft

ADS. *Haven et al.* v. *Holland*, USCC,DMass, May 1821.

44. Thomas Welsh, Jr. (d. 1831; Harvard 1798), studied law with John Davis, admitted in 1804.

DOCUMENT 81. RECEIPT

Oct. 1. 1821. Recd in full for the subscription of Benjamin Rich, Homes & Bass, Barnabas Hedge, Henry Bigelow, & John Dorr, on this Policy—Danl. Webster Atty to N. A. & J. Haven
& gave a receipt also on the Policy Book

Judgt being rendrd—on Jno. Holland's subscription, that judgment is satisfied, & discharged on the Exeon. D. Webster

Oct. 15. 1821. Recd in full for the subscriptions of Moses Wheeler[45] & William Stackpole— D. Webster Atty to N. A. & J. Haven

ADS(DW). *Haven et al.* v. *Valentine*, USCC,DMass, October 1821.

ii. Corporate Underwriting: Michael Shepard et al. v. *Essex Fire and Marine Insurance Company.* The end of hostilities between the United States and Great Britain in 1814 did not bring a halt to economic warfare between the two nations. The British colonial system remained intact and the British navigation laws still protected the British West Indies from American commercial penetration. Moreover, the failure of New England's re-export trade to revive as it had during the Napoleonic Wars forced ship owners to take more risks in seeking trade. This was especially true for Salem's ship owners. They had given Boston its fiercest competition for the carrying trade before the War of 1812. But the War permanently weakened Salem's position, and she began to slip into Boston's orbit.[46]

In the case presented below, Salem merchants Michael Shepard and John Andrews prepared to send their ship, the *Union*, to Cuba with a cargo of staples. Shortly before the ship was due to sail in January 1819, the following report appeared in a Boston newspaper:

> A Committee of the Legislature of Jamaica have reported that the November storm destroyed the principal articles for the labouring classes in the western parishes, and recommended that the Governor be requested to open the ports of the Island to all Nations for the importation of those articles of provisions required to support the population generally; and in return, to allow payment in produce, or otherwise. But we have not heard that the Duke of Manchester (the Governor) had acted on it.[47]

45. Not identified.

46. Douglas North, *The Economic Growth of the United States, 1790–1860* (New York, 1966), pp. 177–178. By the early 1820s two of Salem's leading lawyers read the handwriting on the wall and left for Boston. See p. 488, below.

47. From the defendant's amended answer, Document 89, below, *Shepard et al.* v. *Essex Fire and Marine Insurance Company*, USCC,DMass, October 1822.

In anticipation that Jamaica would open, Andrews directed the *Union's* captain to sail there. The owners then applied for insurance for the voyage. On January 12, 1819, one of the owners went to the office of the Essex Fire and Marine Insurance Company. He handed the company secretary a memorandum which outlined the proposed trip to Jamaica and asked for $11,000 insurance. After the owner left, the secretary gave the memorandum to the president of the company. He decided to charge a 4 percent premium. When the president informed one of the owners of the proposed premium, the owner decided to confer with his partner. They decided to take only $5000 from the Essex office and to seek the rest elsewhere. That evening Shepard returned to the Essex office and agreed to $5000 at 4 percent. The secretary drew up the policy. He neglected, however, to include the memorandum's phrase "the Union is bound to Kingston (Jamaica) if not allowed to sell there will proceed to Cuba." Instead, the policy merely covered a voyage "to port or ports in the West Indies." The next day Shepard came in and signed the premium note. When the other Salem offices either turned down the owners' application or quoted a ridiculously high premium for a voyage to Jamaica, Andrews traveled to Boston. There the Union Insurance Company agreed to insure the vessel for $6000 at 3½ percent for a West Indies trip. Andrews apparently never mentioned the Jamaica destination in Boston, nor did he or Shepard carefully read the Essex policy. The failure to include "Jamaica" in both policies was to result in future legal problems.

When the *Union* reached the entrance to Kingston harbor, the captain learned that the British had not opened the colony to American trade. Acting on bad advice, he lied to a British patrol that the *Union* was in distress from lack of water. The British examined the ship, concluded that no distress existed, and seized her. In a letter to Shepard and Andrews, printed below, the captain pretended that his entry into Jamaica had been necessary. He must have believed that if the loss of the ship was due to a peril encountered at sea, the owners would be able to collect the insurance. After the matter became the subject of litigation, the captain recounted the true story of the voyage (Document 82).

The ship owners retained Webster and Leverett Saltonstall to sue the Essex company. The lawyers faced a difficult problem. The trip to Jamaica was not specifically mentioned in the policy. Moreover, the British authorities had never opened Jamaica to American shipping. This meant that unless a court agreed to incorporate into the policy the memorandum given to the Essex office, the implied warranty against illegal voyages would void the policy. In Massachusetts insurance practice the risk of capture for illegal trading had to be expressly assumed by the underwriter. Moreover, the limited chancery powers of the MassSJC made it doubtful whether that court had the authority to reform the contract. Although the policy expressly protected the owners from barratry, *Wig-*

gin et al. v. *Amory*[48] made it unlikely that a Massachusetts court would consider the captain's action barratrous. He had tried to protect the owner's interest.

These considerations pushed Webster and Saltonstall to decide on a suit in admiralty for reformation of the policy. Traditionally, an admiralty court could exercise equity powers. Since the parties were all citizens of Massachusetts, the only way into federal court was via the admiralty jurisdiction. Even if the court refused to reform the contract, it might be willing to hold the insurers bound by their knowledge of the Jamaica voyage.

In March 1822 Saltonstall filed the libel (Document 83) in federal district court. The company, represented by William Prescott and Benjamin R. Nichols, contested the jurisdiction of the federal court (Document 84).[49] At a special session in April 1822, the USDC issued a pro forma decree dismissing the libel. Webster and Saltonstall appealed to the USCC's May session. In preparation for the trial, the attorneys for both sides took many depositions from Salem underwriters.[50] The defendant sought to prove that the policy as written defined the scope of the agreement (Document 85), that other Salem companies had turned Shepard down for Jamaica insurance, and that Salem offices never took risks against illegal trade (Document 86). The plaintiffs' witnesses also discussed the business of underwriting. Saltonstall wanted to show that the Essex company followed the practice of making the memorandum the basis of the agreement, that it was common practice for insurance companies to conform the policy to the memorandum, and that underwriters had written insurance for illicit trade in the past (Documents 87 and 88).

On the day set for the hearing, the company filed an elaborate amended answer to the libel (Document 89). Based on a sworn statement from Nathaniel Bowditch, the company president, Essex denied, first, any agreement to insure a Jamaica voyage, second, all liability for the seizure and condemnation, and third, any responsibility for the false statements of the captain. The filing of the amended answer forced the continuation of the case to the fall when the court had scheduled an adjourned term in September. A week after the postponement the company's lawyers obtained a deposition from Thomas Perkins, the president of Boston's Union Insurance Office, the other insurer of the ship (Document 90). In support of the Essex position, he denied having any knowledge of the Jamaica destination prior to the ship's seizure. In August 1822

48. See pp. 421–422, above.

49. See pp. 474–482, below, for a discussion of the question of admiralty jurisdiction.

50. For the plaintiffs, Saltonstall took five; the defendants took three. On May 23, 1822, the lawyers took depositions from Boston underwriters for use at the fall trial.

Webster sent a letter to Saltonstall, printed below. Webster wanted to know whether they should accede to opposition counsel William Prescott's request to argue the case at the regular term in October. Although Webster wrote that he preferred the earlier date, Story and district judge John Davis heard the case in October.

After hearing the evidence and the arguments, Story dismissed the libel.[51] His decision had two aspects. First, he dismissed the case for lack of jurisdiction. Second, he gave an opinion on the case adverse to Webster's clients. On the jurisdictional question Story noted that equity courts had exclusive jurisdiction to reform contracts. Admiralty courts had no general jurisdiction to grant equitable relief. Their equity powers were limited to the subject matter of maritime disputes. Although his court had held that the federal courts had admiralty jurisdiction over marine insurance contracts, those contracts had to be executed. The memorandum that the plaintiffs asked the court to write into the policy was not itself an executed contract. An admiralty court, therefore, had no jurisdiction over it.

On the second point he observed that there must be clear evidence that the parties had made a mistake before an equity court would reform a contract. In this case, the underwriters acted on the belief that Jamaica was open. A court could not, therefore, hold them to have insured an illicit voyage. If trade to Jamaica had been known to be illegal and the underwriters knowingly insured a ship to Jamaica, they would be liable for the loss. Where the risk of illicit trade was not taken by the insurer, a ship that went to an illegal port did so outside the scope of the risks insured. Webster tried to distinguish illegal trading from an illegal arrival. Story rejected it. If the underwriters did not assume the risk of illicit trade, he said, it could be presumed they did not take the risk of illegal arrival. Story put great weight on the clause in the memorandum that said if Jamaica was not free, the ship would go to Cuba. This meant, he argued, that both parties had contemplated the trade as free, therefore the policy covered only ordinary risks. Since no mistake had occurred, an equity court would not reform the contract. Story left the plaintiffs to try their luck in another forum. Considering the position of the MassSJC on this issue, it is most likely that Shepard and Andrews dropped the case.

TO JOHN H. ANDREWS AND MICHAEL B. SHEPARD FROM ALLEN PUTNAM

No 1.

Gent. Kingston February 22d 1819

I arrived here after a very [illegible] without sustaining any damage. You no doubt will be perfectly astonished at hearing from me at this

51. 3 Mason 6 (1822).

place, but I assure you Gentlemen distress & that alone was the reason of my coming into this port. I was in want of water, having but 20 hours water on board.

The following remarks are a sketch of the voyage. Soon after I left Salem I met with winds prevailing from South to S. S W. fearful of falling to Leward, I stood to S. & E until I got into the Long[itude] of 60 W. & Lat[itu]de at that time 28° 30′ N. I then made up my mind to sail through the Ilona passage it being the most convenient route to St *Iago de Cuba*. Having got through the passage I ran down the south coast of Hispaniola until I got cape Tiberon in sight, my course then was N. W. by N for St Iago. Now the wind at this time blew fresh from North to N. N. W. I kept the Brigs head to the westward through the night & next morning at day light saw Morant point (which is the east end of Jamaica) bearing west 20 miles, & soon after spoke a Kingston Pilot Boat. He hailed me and asked me if I wanted a pilot, I answered that I only wanted water; very well said he I will take you into Kingston & you will get plenty of water there, but said I it is a prohibited port—they then all answered to a man (in their lingo, being blacks) that the port was all clear & that one American Schooner had arrived there. I concluded from what these pilots told me that I [mig]ht go into Kingston, without any difficulty, being in distress. [I t]ook one of the Pilots on board. As soon as I had let go my anchor [at P]ort Royal I was boarded by an officer from the Flag Ship [Syb]ille. I reported that I was bound to St Iago, & that I put into this [por]t for water. This report being made to the Admiral the Brig was [si]ezed immediately, & a midshipman & three Marines put on board [to] guard her. I arrived saturday Feb. 13th. Sunday 14 had the broad [R] kings mark put on each bow. I was not allowed to go on Shore or to [mak]e any communications—Monday the 14th—I was ordered on board [the] Flag ship & was there strictly interrogated by the Admiral, to all his [questions] I answered in the most reasonable [way?] that I possibly [could. He] demanded my papers and I delivered them. Tuesday 15th—not permitted to go on shore, nor no communicati[on.] Wednesday D[itt]o—Thursday do Friday do—Saturday sailed to the Custom House Wharf—sunday I was allowed to go on shore for the [illegible] firm of Onffroy & Ohara respectable merchants to act as my agents. I have entered a protest and claim the Brig & Cargo. The Brig will have to stand trial & I have some hope that she will be cleared.

They have discharged part of the deck load[52] & intended to discharge the whole cargo for the good of all concerned, but I remonstrated against such proceedings & have put a stop to it for the present. I never will agree to have the Cargo discharged. I have now given you the outlines of what I have done &c. & I cannot, Gentlemen but anticipate that in the exercise

52. The unlading of a cargo from a vessel.

of my duty, I may be justly chargeable with many imperfections & errors, though not I trust of the heart, or of intention; but amidst these painful anticipations, I have to console myself with the recollection that I have done all that human prudence could forsee, all that my weak talents, judgment &c would admit for your interest.

I shall write you again as soon as I have an opportunity, & remain &c.

(signed) Allen Putnam

Copy. *Shepard et al.* v. *Essex Fire and Marine Insurance Company*, USCC,DMass, October 1822. Allen Putnam, Salem resident and captain of the *Union*. Andrews and Shepard were Salem merchants.

DOCUMENT 82. DEPOSITION

[April 3, 1821]

I, Allen Putnam of Salem in the County of Essex and Commonwealth of Massachusetts mariner, of lawful age depose and say, that I was master of the Brig Union of Salem owned by John H. Andrews & Michael Shepard of said Salem. At Salem we took in a cargo for Cuba, and after she was loaded, the crew shipped, and the vessel cleared out at the Custom House for Cuba, and all ready for sea, the foretopsail was hoisted, and we were all ready to cast off, one of the owners, Mr Andrews, came on to the wharf and beckoned to me, on board the vessel, to come on shore. I came on shore—he observed to me that the voyage was altered, and asked me to walk with him up to his counting room—he there told me that I must go to Jamaica. I then observed to him that I thought it was too great a risk—that I should not like to go the voyage very well. Capt. Andrews then handed me the Palladium, and showed me a paragraph in it, which stated that the ports were open. I still told Capt. Andrews that, in my opinion, it was too great a risk to go the voyage, merely upon that paragraph—that it did not appear to be duly confirmed by authority. Capt. Andrews said "I think [I] have nothing at risk"—or, "I am safe enough," or something to that effect. Then after I had agreed to go, Mr Shepard wrote a new set of instructions directing me to go directly to Kingston in the Island of Jamaica—as soon as he had written them, I took them, with the rest of my papers, and went on board, and sailed from the Union wharf immediately. I made the Island of Jamaica in due time—something like thirty days—and as I closed in with the land, and got up along side of Morant Point, I saw a pilot boat & spoke her. I asked the Captain of her if there was any American vessels in Port, or had been —and if the trade was open for Americans—he said yes, the trade was open, and there had been two Americans in port a few days before. I took a pilot out of the boat for the Port of Kingston, in Jamaica, and arrived—came to an anchor at Port Royal at about four or five o'clock in the afternoon—it was the thirteenth or fourteenth of February in the year eighteen hundred and nineteen. I had the American flag displayed at the main top mast head. I had not more than got to an anchor, before there was a boat came along side from the shore, with a young man on board who came in search of news. He came on board and asked me where I was from. I told him I was from Salem. He said, "you are an American, are you'. I told him yes. Well, said he, "I hope you are in distress"—or, "that you came in, in distress"—or something to that effect. By these observations and from his looks it was easy to perceive that the Port was not open. I thought it for the interest of whom it might concern, and a duty incumbent on me, to say—yes. He then wanted to know whether we had carried away any spars, or what the distress was—I told him I wanted water. He then observed, and advised me to make my distress as great as possible. And also advised me to write to Sir Home Popham[53] the Commander in Chief—and wrote the direction of a letter to him, for me. I wrote to the commander in chief, that I had come in, in distress for want of water, and asked permission to obtain a supply to go to sea again. Then this young man, on being informed that a man of War's boat was coming, left the vessel. In a few minutes the man of war's boat came along side—it was a boat from the Frigate Sybil. A Lieutenant of the Frigate was the Boarding officer, and came on board the Union. He asked me where I was from, I told him from Salem and he asked where I was bound to. I told him St. Jago de Cuba—then he wanted to know how I came there. I told him I came in distress—he asked what the distress was, I told him the want of water. After he had wrote this all down he left the Brig and went on board the Frigate—he was gone about fifteen or twenty minutes and came back again with a midshipman and four marines with muskets. He then demanded all my papers and my Log book. I gave them to him—all my papers relative to the Brig & Cargo (excepting the instructions to go to Jamaica) & the Log book. He took away the papers & Log book, and left on board the midshipman and four marines. The next day the broad R was put on to both bows of the vessel and she was seized. A guard was kept on board, of a midshipman and four marines, with loaded muskets, and the Union was hauled close under the stern of the Frigate. The Brig was afterwards Libelled and proceeded against in the Court of Admiralty, and was condemned with her cargo. I put in a claim in behalf of whom it might concern, and employed Messrs Onfroy and Ohara, merchants there to assist me in the claim. I did not know, at that time, that the vessel was insured,

53. Sir Home Riggs Popham (1762–1820), British naval officer, educated at Westminster School and Cambridge, entered the navy (1778), obtained leave from the admiralty and engaged in the East India and China trade (1787), commander-in-chief on the Jamaica station, with the rank of rear admiral (1817–1820).

but supposed she was. The vessel was afterward sold by order of the Admiralty and I thought it my duty to purchase her, and did so, for the benefit of whom it might concern. I was kept on board the Union all the time, and was not allowed to go on shore, till after she was libelled. The vessel was supplied with water from the Frigate.

Allen Putnam

ADS. *Shepard et al.* v. *Essex Fire and Marine Insurance Company,* USCC,DMass, October 1822.

DOCUMENT 83. LIBEL

[March 22, 1822]

Massachusetts District } United States of America. ss.

To the Honorable John Davis Judge of the District Court of the United States within and for the District of Massachusetts.

The Libel and complaint of Michael Shepard and John H Andrews, both of Salem in the said District of Massachusetts and Citizens of the United States, Merchants, against the President and Directors of the Essex Fire & Marine Insurance Company, a body corporate and politic, established at said Salem by an Act of the Legislature of Massachusetts,[54]

Humbly Shews, That heretofore, to wit, on the twelfth day of January in the year of our Lord one thousand eight hundred and nineteen, at said Salem, the said Shepard and Andrews, being in Treaty with the said Company concerning their, the said Company's assuring them, the said Shepard and Andrews, the sum of three thousand Dollars upon a certain Brig called the "Union" and appurtenances, and the further sum of eight thousand Dollars upon Cargo on board said Brig, for a voyage from said Salem to Port or Ports in the West Indies, one or more times, for the purpose of selling her outward and procuring a return cargo, at and from thence to her Port of discharge in the United States, said Brig being bound to Kingston Jamaica, and if not allowed to trade there, was to go to the Island of Cuba.[55] It was agreed by and between the said Shepard and Andrews on the one part and the said Company on the other part, As Follows, to wit,

54. *Acts and Laws passed by the General Court of Massachusetts, at the session . . . held at Boston . . . January 1803*, pp. 174–178. Some of the smaller insurance companies were virtually one-man operations. The men who ran them continued to engage in general business. This clouds Horwitz's sharply drawn distinction between the insurance and general mercantile interests.

55. This is the libellant's rendition of the argument. The company argued that they never agreed to insure a voyage to Jamaica.

In consideration that they, the said Shepard and Andrews would pay them, the said Company at and after the rate of four per cent on the sum or sums assured, they, the said Company then & there promised the said Shepard and Andrews, that they would cause them to be assured, lost or not lost, one thousand dollars on the said Brig and Appurtenances, also Four thousand dollars on effects on board said Brig for the said voyage, whereof was Master for said voyage or whosoever else should go for Master in the said vessel, or by whatsoever other name or names the said vessel, or Master thereof, was or should be named or called: Beginning the adventure upon the said Brig App[ur]t[enance]s and effects as aforesaid, and to continue and endure during the voyage as aforesaid, and until said vessel should be arrived and moored at anchor twenty-four hours in safety, at her Port of Discharge as aforesaid; And that it should and might be lawful for the said vessel, in her voyage, to proceed and sail to, touch and stay at, any Ports or Places, if thereunto obliged by stress of weather, or other unavoidable accidents, without prejudice to said Assurance. Touching the Adventures and Perils which the said Insurance Company acknowledged themselves contented to bear and take upon themselves in said voyage, they were of the Seas, Men of War, Fire, Enemies, Pirates, Rovers, Assailing Thieves, Jettisons, Letters of Mart and Counter-Mart, Surprisals, Takings at sea, Arrests, Restraints, and Detainments of all Kings, Princes or People, of what nation, condition or quality soever, Barratry of the Master (unless the assured were owner of the vessel), or Mariners, and all other Perils, losses and misfortunes, which had or should come to the hurt, detriment or damage of the Said Brig, Appts, and Effects, or any part thereof.[56] And in case of any misfortune or loss, it was agreed, that it should be lawful to and for the assured, their factors, Servants and Assigns, to sue, labor and travel for in and about, the defence, safeguard and recovery of the said Brig, Appts and Effects, or any part thereof, without prejudice to said Assurance; to the charges whereof, the said Insurance Company would contribute in proportion as the sum assured was to the whole sum at risk.[57] And the Company aforesaid acknowledged themselves contented, and did by their promise aforesaid bind the Capital stock and other common property of the said company, to the Assured, their Executors, Administrators and Assigns, for the true performance of the said promise, confessing themselves paid the considera-

56. Called the "perils clause," it set forth the risks undertaken by the insurers. Note that in this case the insurer did not assume liability for the master's misconduct.

57. The sue and labor clause. It encouraged the insured to make every effort to reduce the underwriters' loss for a peril insured against by compensating the insured for his expenses. It is a promise to pay a sum in addition to the amount of the policy.

tion due unto them for the assurance, by the assured, at and after the rate of four per cent, as aforesaid.

And it was further agreed by & between the said Parties, That if the assured should have made any other assurance upon the Brig, appts and effects aforesaid, prior to the said assurance of the said Company as aforesaid, then the said Company should be answerable only for so much as the amount of such Prior assurance might be deficient towards fully covering the property at risk and that the said Insurance Company should return the premium (excepting half per cent) [illegible] by them assured, as they should be exonerated from such prior Assurance. And in case of any assurance upon the said Brig, Appts, and Effects, subsequent in date to the said Assurance of the said Company, the said Company should nevertheless be answerable, to the full extent of the sum by them assured, without right to claim contribution from such subsequent assurers, and should accordingly be entitled to retain the premium by them received, in the same manner as if no such subsequent assurance had been made. And in case of loss, the assured were to abate one per centum: and such loss to be paid in sixty days after proof and adjustment thereof, the amount of the Note given for the premium, if unpaid, and of all other notes due from the assured to said Company, being first deducted. And it was also agreed between the said Parties that the Assurers were not liable for any partial loss on Sugar, Flax seed, Bread, Tobacco and Rice, unless the loss amount to seven per-cent, nor for any partial loss on other goods or Freight, or on the vessel, unless the loss amount to seven per-cent, but the assured shall recover on a general average.[58]

And it was further agreed between the Parties, that the Assurers were not liable for any partial loss on Salt, Grain, Hemp, Fish, Fruit, Hides, Skins, or other goods that are esteemed perishable in their own nature, but the owners of such goods shall recover on a general average, and on a particular average when the damage happens by stranding; provided such damage amount to seven per-cent. And it was further agreed, that if any dispute should arise relating to a loss on said contract it should be submitted to the judgment and determination of Arbitrators mutually chosen, whose award in writing should be conclusive, and binding on all Parties.

And it was Further Agreed that the said company would cause a Policy of Insurance to be drawn pursuant to said contract and that they would underwrite the same as Assurers for the said sums.

And the said Shepard and Andrews further propound & say that afterwards, to wit on the same day, the said Company caused to be drafted a

58. This clause and the one following was the memorandum clause. It served to limit the insurer's liability for certain goods more easily subject to damage.

Policy of Insurance, and underwrote the same by Nathaniel Bowditch[59] President of said Company; which said Policy was not made pursuant to the said Contract and agreement of the said Parties, in this, to wit, That so much of the description of the said voyage as relates to the said Brig's being bound to Kingston Jamaica, and if not allowed to trade there, to go to the Island of Cuba, was omitted to be inserted in said Policy, by mistake and misapprehension and not other wise.

And now the Proponents further aver that the said Brig in said Policy mentioned, thereafterwards, while proceeding on her said voyage—to wit, in the Port of Kingston, in the Island of Jamaica, was, together with her cargo, seized, captured and carried away by certain subjects of the King of England.

By reason whereof the said Brig and Cargo became and were wholly lost to the Proponents—of all which the said Company on at had due notice and proof and altho the said Shepard and Andrews have done all things on their part by virtue of said contract to be done and performed—Yet the said Company tho' often thereto requested at said [Salem?] have never paid, nor any part thereof, but neglect & refuse so to do.

Wherefore your Proponents pray your Honor, that Admiralty process may issue against the said Company for the said sums so subscribed and assured by them as aforesaid and in duty bound will ever pray.[60]

Danl. Webster Proctor for Libellant

ADS (DWp). *Shepard et al.* v. *Essex Fire and Marine Insurance Company*, USDC,DMass, April 1822.

DOCUMENT 84. PROTEST AND ANSWER

District Court of the United States for the District of Massachusetts. Saturday April 6th. 1822

Michael Shepard & al v The Essex Fire & M. Inse Comp

And now the Said Essex Fire & Marine Insurance Company protesting (against the Court here sustaining jurisdiction in this case because the contract stated in the libel is not an admiralty contract,[61] & reserving to themselves a right to make any other & further answer on the appeal for

59. Nathaniel Bowditch (1773–1838), mathematician, sailed on five trading voyages (1795–1803) and moved to Boston in 1823 to become actuary of the Massachusetts Hospital Life Insurance Company (1823–1833).

60. Bliss also prepared a second count for return of the premium.

61. For a discussion of the question of admiralty jurisdiction, see pp. 474–482, below.

answer now say, that they do not owe the said Insurance Company[62] any thing as stated in their said libel)

by Prescott & Nichols their Proctors

And the said Shepard & Andrews consent to said reservations

D. Webster[63]

ADS. *Shepard et al.* v. *Essex Fire and Marine Insurance Company*, USDC, DMass, April 1822.

DOCUMENT 85. DEPOSITION

[May 3, 1822]

I, Benjamin Pitman, of Salem,[64] in the County of Essex, and Commonwealth of Massachusets, of lawful age, depose, that on the 12th of January 1819 Mr Michael Shepard or Mr John H. Andrews applied to me, as Secretary of the Essex Fire and Marine Insurance Company in Salem, with proposals for insurance on the Brig Union and Effects, in writing, of which the following is a copy

"$3000 on Brig Union and App[urtenance]s } Allen Putnam master
8000 on Effects on board said Brig }

from Salem to port or ports in the West Indies one or more times, for the purpose of selling her outward and procuring a return cargo, and at and from thence to port of discharge in the United States.

& what return if said vessel trades to but one port and arrive safe without loss.

The Union is bound to Kingston (Jamaica) if not allowed to sell there will proceed to Cuba."

The above is a true copy of the original memorandum handed me as above stated. Mr Bowditch, the President of the Company was not present when it was handed me. Upon receiving the memorandum I asked the person who handed it what was the tonnage of the vessel, and her age, and upon receiving the answers I put them down on the memorandum as follows "2 yrs old sheathed last voyage 129 tons". When Mr Bowditch came in I handed the paper to him. Mr Bowditch took a vote of the Directors upon it,[65] and wrote, himself, 4 per cent on the bottom of the proposal the same evening—it was done in about the space of ten or fifteen minutes, and after the applicant had retired. Some time after-

62. An obvious error.

63. Someone else signed DW's name.

64. Pitman not further identified.

65. Insurance companies were organized in the same manner as early nineteenth-century banks. They conducted their business in similar fashion; directors made all the decisions.

ward, in the course of the same evening, Mr Shepard or Andrews called to see what premium was named. Mr Bowditch informed him of the premium, and he hesitated, and said he would go out and consult his partner or enquire at some other office, and would return and let Mr Bowditch know whether they would take it. About eight o'clock the same evening after the President and Directors had retired, Mr Shepard came in and said he would take one thousand on the vessel and four on effects. I then wrote on the memorandum as follows "agreed for 1000 on vessel & 4000 on Effects as above Jan. 12 1819

Mr Shepard then signed the paper in this manner, "Michl Shepard for self & Jno. H Andrews"

Mr Shepard then said, I suppose this binds the office. I replied, yes. Immediately after this I called on Mr Bowditch at his house and told him I had agreed with Mr Shepard for one thousand dollars on the vessel and four thousand on effects. Mr Bowditch said it was not strictly legal for me to make the agreement, yet he would ratify what I had done, and told me to fill a policy, accordingly, the next day. The next day I filled the policy, agreeable to the proposal with general liberty to the West Indies. When Mr Bowditch came to the office the next morning, he signed the policy. I had made it out ready for his signature before he came down. Mr Bowditch immediately upon signing the policy wrote the premium note. Mr Shepard called in the course of the forenoon and took the policy and signed the note—he signed the note for himself & Mr. Andrews as follows "Michl Shepard for self & John H. Andrew"

Afterward Mr Andrews came in to take another policy, on another vessel, and I got him to add the letter "s" to his name on the note, which Mr Shepard had left out.

I do not distinctly recollect whether Mr Shepard took away the policy when he signed the note, as above mentioned, or whether it was left for Mr Andrews to take when he took the other policy. I do not recollect whether the person who took the policy away, examined it or not—but I know it is Mr Bowditchs almost universal practice to read policies to the insured at the time when they are taken away.

Question by Defdts Counsel[66]

1. How long have you been in the office of the Essex Fire & Marine Insurance Company

Ans: I was chosen Secretary I think in 1814 and have been in the office fifteen years.

2. What conversation had you with Mr Andrews or Shepard when the proposal was handed to you

66. Probably Benjamin Ropes Nichols (1786–1848; Harvard 1804), Massachusetts lawyer, practiced in Salem (1807–1824) before moving to Boston.

Ans: No other conversation that I recollect, except the enquiries about the age and tonnage of the vessel.

3. Was any thing said of their being insured against the particular risk of going to Kingston

Ans: Not any thing.

4. Was there not an account, that day, that the ports of Jamaica were about to be opened

Ans: Yes, there was a report to that effect. It was mentioned by the Directors in the course of their conversation on the evening on which the proposal was made, that this would probably be the first vessel there as the general impression was that the ports were open and nobody intimated a doubt of it.

5. Were you present with the Directors during all the time while they were considering the proposals offered for the Union

Ans: Yes.

6. Was any thing said by them of any extra risk on account of the vessels going to Kingston. (objected to)[67]

Ans: Not any thing.

7. What was the usual premium for general liberty[68] to the West Indies and back at that time.

Ans: Four per cent—at our office—we wrote before and after this policy at that rate.

8. What was the regulation of your office respecting the time at which insurance should take effect.

Ans: The following are the standing votes of the office passed the 6th of June 1803,

"The President and Directors consider themselves holden on a marine policy from the time a verbal agreement is made between the President and the person applying for insurance."

"The President in all cases where the person applying for insurance is unable to wait for the completion of his papers will cause a memorandum of the agreement to be made, & signed by the person applying for insurance."

If the person applying for insurance leaves the office without signing a memorandum, the office is not holden.

10. When you wrote upon the memorandum the words "agreed to as above," to what did you refer. (objected to)

Ans: I referred to the terms of the body of the proposal, and to the common form of a West India policy—and I put into the policy the words of the proposal.

67. Presumably Saltonstall attended. His objection here would be to hearsay testimony. Further on, he objects to questions regarding Pitman's opinions or state of mind at the time he made up the policy.

68. Permission to stop at any legal port in the West Indies.

11. What did you consider the other minutes in the memorandum, after the words "United States" (objected to)

Ans: I considered them as an explanation for the direction of the premium—the first—and the next, as to where the vessel was bound.

12. Is it, or is it not common for minutes of various kinds to be inserted in the memorandum, which are not understood as forming a part of the policy.

Ans: Yes, very common.

13. What is the object of having in the memorandum other minutes besides the particular terms which are to be inserted in the policy.

Ans: To guide the Directors in naming the premium.

14. Did you fill up the policy, in this case, agreeable to your understanding of the agreement made the evening previous. (objected to)

Ans: Yes.

15. Did you understand that any other risk was taken than was included in a general liberty to the West Indies & back. (objected to)

Ans. No.

16. During any of the interviews with Mr Andrews or Shepard, before the policy was taken from the office, was any conversation had about any peculiar risk in going to Kingston.

Ans. None, to my knowledge.

17. Were you present when Mr Andrews came to inform Mr Bowditch of the detention of the vessel at Kingston, if so, what conversation took place between them.

Ans: I was present. Mr Bowditch observed to Mr Andrews that he was very sorry for the loss that had happened, but he, Mr Andrews, very well knew that the office was not holden for such a loss. I do not recollect that the point was much contested but appeared rather to be assented to by Mr Andrews than otherwise. I might have gone out of the room, but my impression is to the contrary

18 Did Mr Andews suggest, at that time, that the policy was not correct

Ans: I do not recollect that he did.

19. Did Mr Andrews or Mr Shepard ever pretend, to your knowledge, that it was not the understanding of the parties at the time the insurance was made, that Kingston was a free port.

Ans: They never did.

20. Is it, or is it not the common practice of this and all the other incorporated offices in Salem to refuse taking risks of illicit trade or of violations of the British Navigation Laws.[69] (objected to)

Ans: I think it is. It is so at our office. I know nothing of the other offices

69. 7 and 8 Will. 3, c. 22 (1696). Goods could be imported into British colonies only in British built and owned ships manned by a three-fourths British crew.

except by hearsay, but the general impression is that they refuse them.

21. If an application had been made at your office for insurance against such risks, should you have laid it before the President or Directors; and what answer should you have made to such application. (objected to)

Ans: I should have thought proper to have named to the applicant that such a risk would not be taken according to the custom of our office but if the applicant had insisted upon it, I should, of course have laid it before the President.

22. Did Mr Bowditch give you any particular directions about the manner of filling up this policy.

Ans: He did not give me any directions about it.

Questions by Plffs Counsel.

23. What is your age.

Ans: Twenty eight years.

24. Is it the practice in your office to preserve the memorandums which are signed by persons who apply for insurance.

Ans. Yes.

25. Is it your practice to fill up the policies conformably to the memorandums

Ans: Yes.

26. For what purpose are the memorandums preserved as you have stated.

Ans: For the purpose of reference in cases of dispute.

27. When you filled the policy in this case had you any other paper before you than the memorandum before mentioned

Ans: No other.

28. Was it your intention to fill up the policy for the risk mentioned in the memorandum, or to fill it up for a different risk.

Ans: For the risk mentioned in the memorandum.

29 What time in the evening was it when the application was made for this insurance, & who was present when the party applied.

Ans: No person was present that I recollect but the party applying and myself—it was the first of the evening—probably about six o'clock. I have an impression that the Directors met soon after Mr Bowditch came in—it might be about ten or fifteen minutes after the application

30 For what reason did you ask Mr Shepard to sign the memorandum after you informed him that the risk had been agreed to by the Directors.

Ans: Because there would have been nothing binding except he had signed it—the office would not have been held.

31. Was Mr Andrews or Mr Shepard present when you filled up the policy.

Ans: Neither of them.

32. When you delivered the policy to Mr Andrews or Mr Shepard, was it open or folded up.

Ans: I do not know that I delivered it. I am not certain whether I delivered it or Mr Bowditch.

33. Had you any conversation, before the policy was filled, with either of the plaintiffs, except at the times when the memorandum was handed to you, & when it was signed.

Ans: No.

34. Was there at either of the times mentioned in the last interrogatory, any thing said about any other risk than the one *expressed* in the memorandum.

Ans: No.

35. You have stated that there was a report of Jamaica being open—was there any other information upon that subject, to your knowledge, than the article in the newspaper called the Palladium of that morning

Ans: That is all the information that we had at our office. We take the Palladium, and took it at that time

36. Was an application afterward made by the plaintiffs to have the policy made conformable to the memorandum, by inserting the same, and did or did not the President say they had as lief it would be in as not, and did he or they refuse to insert it.

Ans: There was such an application, and Mr Bowditch said it would be considered a part of the policy with the understanding of the parties, and he should be perfectly willing to have it inserted with that understanding—that is, that Kingston was a free port—that he said at the time. I recollect that Mr Bowditch said that if Kingston, Jamaica, were put into the policy, with the understanding of the parties that Kingston was a free port, it would make no odds, or would have no effect.

37. Did not Mr Andrews observe to the President that you (meaning the Office) took the risk of her going to Jamaica, and it was the intention of the parties at the time that she should have liberty of going there, & ask why it should not be inserted, and did not the President admit that it was an omission.

Ans: I never recollect of hearing Mr. Bowditch say that; but heard Mr Andrews says that Kingston ought to have been in the policy. Mr Bowditch said the policy was filled as the office intended it should be, but said it was the understanding that the vessel was bound to Jamaica. At this or some other conversation Mr Bowditch observed to Mr Andrews that he must know that it was not the custom for offices to take risks against the British Navigation Laws. I do not recollect what reply Mr Andrews made.

38. Did not the President, when he observed that the memorandum being in the policy would not help them (meaning the plaintiffs) refer them to thc policy book of the office, for a policy which the office had written for J. & T. H. Perkins[70] at and from Jamaica to port of discharge in the United States at a premium of two per cent.

Ans: I do not recollect whether he did. I have some recollection that the policy was referred to, on some occasion, but do not recollect that it was on this question.

39. You have stated that it is common for minutes to be made on the memorandum which are not put into the policy. Do you not always insert in the policy such minutes from the memorandum as relate to the risk.

Ans: Not all, particularly, only the general minutes—but the policy is always filled according to the general sense of the memorandum—names of ports are frequently in the memorandum that are not inserted in the policy.

40. Did Mr Andrews the same evening (Jan: 12) offer a memorandum for insurance on the Brig Rebecca.

Ans: Yes—and a policy was written on it, on the thirteenth of January—the number of Mr Andrews's policy is "1183".

41. Was a Letter of abandonment offered, on the Union—and if so, when was it offered, by the insured.

Ans: Yes, there were two Letters offered—one on the twenty third of July 1819—the other on the twenty eighth of the same July—the latter contained a notice that if the office did not accept the vessel in a reasonable time, the insured would proceed to sell her. There was also a written offer by the insured to refer the question between them and the office, and a request that the office would authorize them to prosecute an appeal from the Admiralty Court in Jamaica—both these propositions were declined by the office. Mr Wm. P. Richardson[71] was present when the office gave their answer to Mr Andrews, declining both propositions, and I have understood from Mr Bowditch that he stated, in presence of Mr Richardson, that at the time when the application for this insurance was made, the office considered Kingston a free port.

42. At the time mentioned in the 18th interrogatory, when you state that Mr Andrews did not suggest that the policy was incorrect, do you recollect any conversation at all about the policy.

Ans: I do not recollect distinctly what that conversation was—only it

70. James Perkins (1761–1822) formed a Boston partnership with his younger brother Thomas Handasyd Perkins in 1792.

71. Not identified.

was about that risk. I do not recollect that any thing was said about the correctness of the policy.

43. Has your office written on the Brig Acorn to the Isle of France since you wrote on the Union to Jamaica.

Ans: They have, by policy No. 1331, a copy of which is annexed. They have not written to the Isle of France, to my knowledge, in any other manner than is expressed in that policy—the next night after that policy was written Dudley L. Pickman and Robert Stone,[72] two of the assured called at our [lines missing] for the loss—this was before the vessel sailed. I do not recollect Mr Bowditch requested to have the Isle of France struck out of the policy.

44. Has the case of the Union been frequently a subject of conversation at your office—and have you conversed at different times with the Directors or other persons in the office respecting it, and how long ago, and how lately.

Ans: It has very frequently been a subject of conversation with the Directors. I have not conversed particularly with any of the Directors about it, except that I have talked the subject over with Mr Bowditch and Mr Andrews about the time of the Courts sitting. I have said something on the subject to others when it has been mentioned, but have been cautious of saying much about it, because I knew I was to tell what I knew somewhere else. I have not heard the Directors say any thing about it in particular since the time of the Courts sitting in Salem, last fall. I do not remember to have conversed with them myself since that time.

Questions by Defdts Counsel

45. Do you feel confident that you received the memorandum in this case either from Mr Andrews or Mr Shepard

Ans: Yes.

46. Should you have made the minutes on the memorandum of the age and tonnage of the Union if it had been handed to Mr Bowditch.

Ans: No. Mr Bowditch would naturally have made the minutes himself if he had received it.

47. Are not policies frequently filled up for different sums and with different conditions than are mentioned in the memorandums, by agreement of the parties.

Ans: Yes, very frequently.

48. Is not the object in having the memorandums signed by the assured before the policy is filled, to bind the parties, from the time of signing.

Ans: Yes.

72. Stone not identified.

49. Is it not the duty of the President to require such memorandums to be signed if the applicant goes away before the policy is filled.

Ans: Yes.

50. Is not this the practice at your office, instead of having the premium note signed at the time of the agreement, as is practised at other offices.

Ans: Yes.

51. Did you ever know any memorandum called for by the assured, before this, for any purpose.

Ans: I never did, to settle any dispute about the policy.

52. Do you recollect any conversation between Mr Shepard and the Directors after the news of the detention of the vessel was received.

Ans: I recollect Mr Andrews and Mr Shepard called at the office, some time after the loss. I think it was the 19th of December 1820; but on examining a memorandum, made at the time, I find it was July 21: 1819. The following is a copy of the memorandum—

"Essex F. & M. Ins. Co.

Wednesday evg July 21. 1819

In conversation respecting the capture of the Brig Union with Mich Shepard and J. H. Andrews on the evening of the 21 inst: it was stated by the Directors to them that it was reported that Jamaica was free for trade at the time the Union sailed & this consented to by Shepard and Andrews—Capt John Barr[73] mentioned that he supposed she was bound to Havanna, but Shepard said the plan of the voyage was altered in consequence of the report that Jamaica was open for trade & that she would first touch at Jamaica"

53. Is it not sometimes the case that policies are filled up without any memorandums being signed by the applicants.

Ans: Yes—frequently without any memorandum at all, and frequently a memorandum is made but not signed, the party in such case waiting till the policy is filled.

Questions by Plffs Counsel

54. Have you any recollection of the conversation mentioned in the 52d. interrogatory, except from the copy of the memorandum now produced

Ans: Not any.

55. Is the memorandum of that conversation you have now produced the original one made by you at the time it bears date or is it a copy

Ans: It is a copy.

56. What has become of the original memorandum of that conversation

Ans: I do not know, whether I copied it and destroyed it, or whether it

73. John Barr, one of the Essex directors, otherwise not identified.

is on file in the office. Mr Bowditch has just handed me the original from the office files, which corresponds with that copy.

57. You have stated that policies are sometimes filled up with different sums and other particulars than those mentioned in the memorandum. Had you any other agreement in the present case than the memorandum, or were you directed to fill it up in any other manner than according to that memorandum.

Ans: No.

58. Was Mr John Barr whom you mentioned in the memorandum of conversation, one of the Directors of the Office.

Ans: Yes.

Benj. Pitman

ADS. *Shepard et al.* v. *Essex Fire and Marine Insurance Company*, USCC, DMass, October 1822.

DOCUMENT 86. DEPOSITION

[May 3, 1820]

I, Moses Townsend of Salem in the County of Essex and Commonwealth of Massachusetts of lawful age depose that I am President of the Union Marine Insurance Company in Salem[74] and have sustained that office ever since the institution of the company. We never have taken risks against illicit trade, or a violation of the British Navigation Laws, but in one instance—that was on the Ship Hazard and cargo, in 1805—that risk was against the blockade of Curracoa—this was not an original risk, but was endorsed on the policy. The paper hereto annexed[75] is a copy of the original policy and endorsement in that case. We were incorporated in March 1804. We have never since that taken such a risk, but have frequently refused them—this is the case at our office, but I cannot say that I know it to be so at other offices in town, though I have no doubt it is so. We wrote on general liberty to the West Indies and back, in January 1819, for four per cent, in two cases, viz: the Neutrality and Superior. In March 1819 we wrote on the Washington, the same risk, at the same rate. We did not consider these first rate vessels, but we did not make any difference in the premium on that account.

Questions by Pltffs Counsel.

1. When the ship Hazard was insured, were not premiums much higher than they were in 1819.

Ans: Yes—there was a great difference.

2. Did Mr Shepard, an owner of the Brig Union, hand to your office a

74. Townsend not further identified.

75. Not found.

memorandum for insurance on that vessel, on or about the 12th of January, 1819 with liberty to go to Jamaica

Ans: I think he did. I know a memorandum was handed by one of the owners, with that clause in it, and that clause was the reason why we did not take it—we refused to name a premium at all, on that account.

3. Is it the practice of your office to fill up the policies conformably to the memorandums agreed to.

Ans: It is not our practice to have memorandums signed by the applicant —nothing is binding at our office until the premium note is signed. We have a memorandum book in which the particulars of the insurance wanted are entered, and when this is done and agreed to, or when it is agreed to fill a policy as some other specified policy is filled, we always fill them according to these agreements.

Questions by Defdts Counsel.

4. If any application were made to you for insurance against illicit trade, should you think it worth while to lay it before the other Directors

Ans: No, I should not—unless the applicant particularly requested it— in that case I should lay it before the other Directors but I have no idea they would take it.

5. What additional premium would it have been worth to have insured the Union to Jamaica, expressly taking the risk of the Navigation laws.

Ans: I dont know—it is very difficult to form an opinion about a premium, where the trade is illicit, or where you view it as such.

6. Is it not very common to have a difference of one half of one per cent in different offices upon the same risk.[76]

Ans: I dont know that it is; we generally aim to keep pretty near alike. If we had not a large sum at risk we should not stand so much on the premium as if we had a large sum at risk—there is frequently a difference of from one quarter to one half per cent between Salem and Boston, particularly when premiums are lowering—the premiums generally lower in Boston first—this has been the case particularly since the late war.

7. Is it not sometimes the case that ports and places are named in proposals for insurance which are not inserted in the policy.

Ans: I should say it was—sometimes—not very common—applicants frequently name places to which the vessel is expected to go in the course of the voyage, which are not inserted in the policy.

76. Shepard and Andrews insured the Union in Boston for 3.5 percent. The Essex counsel did not want DW to argue that the higher Essex premium reflected a compensation for a Jamaica risk.

Question by Pltffs Counsel

8. Do you not insert in the policies all the particulars of the memorandum which affect the risk which you agree to take.

Ans: If we have agreed to any particular form we certainly should.

Question by Defdts Counsel

9. Should you on any account insert a clause in a policy that would render you liable for illicit trade.

Ans: I should say not—My opinion is that such a risk would not be agreed to by our Directors.

10. If you wrote on a vessel to a particular port where there was a risk of illicit trade, should you not, as a matter of course, insert a clause exempting your office from a loss on that account.

Ans: We should not agree to it—if they asked for liberty we should not grant it.

Questions by Pltffs Counsel

11. In filling up a policy should you omit any particulars which the office and the insured had agreed to as an essential part of the risk.

Ans: No—we should not.

12. Did your office pay the loss in the case of the Hazard above mentioned.

Ans: We did—and the additional expense of an appeal.

M. Townsend

ADS. *Shepard et al.* v. *Essex Fire and Marine Insurance Company*, USCC,DMass, October 1822.

DOCUMENT 87. DEPOSITION

[May 6, 1822]

I, Stephen Phillips of Salem in the County of Essex and Commonwealth of Massachusetts, of lawful age depose, that I am a Director in the Salem Marine Insurance office,[77] and have been for six or seven years past. I recollect that Mr Michael Shepard applied to our office for insurance on the Brig Union, previous to her voyage to Kingston in Jamaica. We named five per cent as a premium, understanding that Kingston in Jamaica was included in the risk. Her being bound to Kingston was not the objection, nor were the terms of the memorandum, but we had an objection to taking West India risks generally, and wished to get rid of this, and therefore named five per cent premium, thinking they would not give it.

77. Phillips not further identified.

Questions by Pltffs Counsel

1. Was the subject of the Union's being bound to Jamaica discussed by the Directors at the time you named the premium.

Ans: No, not a word said upon it, that I recollect—with any intention of taking the risk—something was said generally about the different passages in going there.

2. Is it the practice of your office to fill up your policies according to the memorandum or agreement made with the insured.

Ans: Always. The practice at our office is for the party applying to hand in his memorandum, and Mr Ashton[78] the President lays it before the Directors, and if they name a premium it is entered into a book and the premium is noted at the bottom—from this the Secretary fills the policy according to the terms of the memorandum. If any thing more is wanted than is in the memorandum it is a subject of after discussion, and Mr Ashton will not insert it without consulting the Directors. As soon as the agreement is made, the premium note is signed, and it is a rule of the office that the office is not holden until the premium note is signed. Sometimes it is agreed to fill a policy as another policy is filled, and then it is filled according to the terms of that policy—this applies to general liberty to India, most commonly.

3. If a mistake is made in filling the policy, is it your practice to rectify it by reference to the memorandum or agreement made with the insured.

Ans: Certainly—it would be done immediately.

4. Has your office taken risks on vessels engaged in illicit trade, or to prohibited ports.

Ans: Yes. We took one upon the Canton and another upon the Acorn—also a policy on the Mary. I was not present when the risk on the Mary was taken—in both the other cases I was—the Acorn's policy was copied from a policy on the same vessel in the Essex Fire and Marine Insurance Office.

Questions by Defdts Counsel.

5. Was there not a report at the time that Mr Shepard applied for insurance as before stated that Jamaica was open for trade.

Ans: I never heard a word about Jamaica being open—there was nothing said about it there—it was mentioned on the memorandum, but our objection was against taking West India risks at all.

6 Have your office ever written a policy with a knowledge, at the time, that you were rendering yourselves liable for risks of illicit trade.

Ans: No. I dont know that we ever have—we have written on vessels

78. Jacob Ashton, not further identified.

where the trade has proved to be illicit, but we did not know it at the time.

7. Is it not the practice of your office to refuse taking such risks.

Ans: Yes—when we knew it to be such.

8. Did not your office refuse to pay the loss on the Canton till the decree of condemnation was reversed, on the ground of her having been condemned for illicit trade.

Ans: I do not recollect that any demand was made, till after the decree was reversed—to the best of my recollection, the knowledge of the decree of condemnation being reversed, came with the news of her capture or condemnation.

9. Is it not common for the applicant for insurance to express either verbally or in the memorandum, the particular ports to which the vessel is bound when it is intended to have the policy filled up to the East or West Indies generally.

Ans: No—not one time in ten—it is very seldom the question is asked where she is bound as to the particular port—the policies are filled pretty much alike—round the Cape of Good Hope one or more times to one or more ports—pretty full, the liberty is.

10. Would or would not your office expect to make the policy conform to the understanding of the parties, whether it was contained in the memorandum or not.

Ans: We always make the policy conform to the memorandum—and that generally contains the meaning of the parties—and if any thing else is wanted it is put into the memorandum before the policy is filled—the memorandum always contains the risk which the office takes and the policy is filled conformably to it in every iota.

Questions by Pltffs Counsel

11. When the application was made for insurance on the Union, do you recollect who of the Directors were present.

Ans: No. I do not. I now recollect that Capt. Ichabod Nichols[79] was there, from the circumstances of his speaking about the different passages in going to Jamaica

12. After you had written upon the Acorn, did or did not your office ever call on the owners of her, to have any alteration made in the policy or in the orders of the owners.

Ans: No—not that I know of. I never heard of it.

13. If a loss happens and it is discovered that the risk described in the policy was erroneously copied from the memorandum, is it or is it not the practice of your office to rectify the policy by the memorandum

79. Not identified.

Ans: I do not recollect seeing a case of the kind, but in all cases that should happen I have not the least doubt it would be done.

14. Are you a private underwriter at the office kept in this town by Capt Lander.[80]

Ans: Yes. I have been an underwriter twenty two years.

15. Do the underwriters at that office take risks of illicit trade & prohibited ports, and are the premiums on such risks very different according to circumstances—sometimes very high and sometimes very low

Ans: Yes—sometimes high and sometimes low, on the same risk—they take all kinds of risks and at all rates of premium, and sometimes very different premiums for the same risk.

16. Is it not the practice for the offices to consider themselves holden on a policy after the Directors have agreed to the risk, and is it not taken for granted that the policy will be filled up conformably to the memorandum or agreement, without any particular examination to see if it is so conformable.

Ans: It is always understood that the memorandum is a guide for the policy—it is so in our office—they give the premium note upon the memorandum, the same as they would upon the policy, exactly—it is sometimes a week or more before the policy is taken away—the memorandum is considered the contract, & the note is given upon it.

17. Did not J. & T. H. Perkins offer a risk at and from Jamaica to port in the United States, and if so, what did the office say.

Ans: I think they offered such a risk, but the office did not take it.

Stephen Phillips

ADS. *Shepard et al.* v. *Essex Fire and Marine Insurance Company,* USCC,DMass, October 1822.

DOCUMENT 88. DEPOSITION

[May 6, 1822]

I, William Fettyplace of Salem in the County of Essex and Commonwealth of Massachusetts, of lawful age depose, that I am a Director in the Commercial Insurance Office in Salem, and have been one ever since that office was established—about four years—I recollect, that Mr John H. Andrews made an application at our office for insurance on the Brig Union, with general liberty of the West Indies and he stated that she was bound direct to Kingston in Jamaica. I do not recollect the time distinctly, but it was about the time the Union sailed on the voyage in which

80. Not identified.

she went to Kingston, and was either just before or just after the vessel sailed. We named to Mr Andrews a premium, I think of three and a half per cent, provided he would exonerate the office from any damage or expenses on account of any seizure at Jamaica. There was at that time a report that Jamaica was open for trade, but it was not certain. The memorandum now shown to me in the book of the Essex Fire & Marine Insurance Company, I think contains the purport of the one handed to our office by Mr Andrews. I well recollect that Mr Andrews stated that the vessel was bound to Kingston, and that fact was taken into consideration in naming the premium, and led to the request to be exonerated from seizure there, as before stated.

Questions by Plffs Counsel

1. Did your office in the case of the Brig Britannia agree to write as per memorandum handed in on saturday evening of 5th December 1818, and was she lost before the policy was executed.

Ans: We agreed to write on that vessel and did write. She was lost on sunday and the policy was handed on monday. It was in December of that year, but I do not recollect the precise day. She was wrecked but not totally lost—she was abandoned to the office and the abandonment was accepted—but there was afterward a compromise and she was received back again by the owners—the office paid fifty per cent or about that.

2. Did the owner apply on the following monday morning, or any other day, for the policy, after the loss was known, and did not the Directors agree unanimously to execute and deliver a policy agreeable to the memorandum, and did the assured abandon as for a total loss the same day.

Ans. Yes—the premium note was signed on saturday night and the policy and abandonment were on monday following, we always consider the office held as soon as a premium note is signed whether there be any policy or not.

* * * * *

Questions by Defdts Counsel.

5. Has it not been the uniform practice of your office to refuse writing upon risks of violation of the British Navigation Laws, or any other illicit trade

Ans: We have not been in the habit of doing it; and I dont know that any applications have been made to the office for that purpose. I do not know the practice of other offices, but my impression is that they do not write on risks against illicit trade,—unless an extra premium is paid. I have understood that insurance has been made on vessels round Cape Horn, but I do not know at what offices nor at what premiums. I mean those that are bound to Spanish ports round Cape Horn.

* * * * *

Questions by Pltffs Counsel

9. If your office had accepted the proposition of Mr Andrews for insurance on the Union in the terms in which it was offered to you, was it or was it not considered at the time that the office were to be held for a loss by seizure at Jamaica if any such loss took place. (objected to)

Ans: Had we taken the risk, I as one of the Directors should have considered the office liable for the loss. I cannot say what the other Directors would have said. I think that must have been their opinion or they would not have asked the exemption—there might have been heavy expenses without an actual condemnation

10. If your office had accepted the proposition contained in the memorandum of Mr Andrews would they or would they not have considered themselves bound to insert the risk in the policy, according to the tenor of the memorandum

Ans: Yes. We always consider the office bound to insert in the policy the terms of the memorandum offered by the insured. Sometimes verbal or written explanations are made which are not inserted in the policy.

11. Does or does not your office consider itself bound to insert in the policy every thing contained in the memorandum agreed to, which would affect the risk taken, so that the risk shall be fully described either by naming the particular ports and other things included in the risk, or by a general description which shall comprehend all such particulars.

Ans: yes.

12. When Mr Andrews made his proposition, as above, did or did not the Directors of your office decline accepting them, because Mr Andrews did not agree to exempt them from their liability in case of seizure in Jamaica.

Ans: Yes.

13. Is it, or is it not the practice of your office to rectify policies when any errors exist, by reference to the memorandum or agreement in the case

Ans: It is unquestionably the practice. I should expect it myself, and as a Director should feel the office bound to do it especially if the Secretary, in filling the policy should make an error or omission of that sort, and I was satisfied it was a mistake.

Wm. Fettyplace

Extract. *Shepard et al.* v. *Essex Fire and Marine Insurance Company*, USCC,DMass, October 1822.

DOCUMENT 89. AMENDED ANSWER

May 15th. 1822

Massachusetts ss. Circuit Court of U. States
John H. Andrews & al. Libellants
against
The Essex Fire & Marine Insurance Company.

And now the said Insurance Company file this further answer according to the agreement of the Parties filed in the case in the District Court, and by leave of the Court here first had & obtained.

The said Respondents appearing, to avoid all contumacy contempt & default & reserving to themselves all exceptions to the insufficiency of said libel & protesting against the Jurisdiction of this Court, because it is not a case of Admiralty or Maritime Jurisdiction, nevertheless for the reasons aforesaid, & as a cause why said Libel should be dismissed, they propound & say; that the said Shepard & Andrews before the twelfth day of January 1819, being owners of the said Brig Union & cargo they were about sending the same on a voyage to the Island of Cuba; but on the said twelfth day of January, when said Brig was about sailing on said voyage, an account appeared in one of the public newspapers, in the words following, to wit—

"Trade of Jamaica

A Committee of the Legislature of Jamaica have reported that the November storm destroyed the principal articles for the labouring classes in the western parishes, and recommended that the Governor be requested to open the ports of the Island to all Nations for the importation of those articles of provisions required to support the population generally; and in return, to allow payment in produce, or otherwise. But we have not heard that the Duke of Manchester (the Governor) had acted on it"

And in consequence of said account and in expectation or belief that said ports were or would be opened, said Shepard & Andrews were induced to alter the destination of said vessel & cargo, & ordered the master thereof to proceed with the same direct to Kingston in Jamaica. And on the evening of the same day, the Libellants applied for insurance on said vessel & cargo to the office of the Respondents, it being then expected that the ports of Jamaica were to be opened to American trade. And the Libellants or one of them then handed to the Secretary of said Insurance Company a memorandum in writing in the words & form following, viz.

"3000 on Brig Union & App[ur]t[enance]s } Allen Putnam master
8000 on effects on board said Brig }
From Salem to port or ports in the West Indies, one or more times

for the purpose of selling outward & procuring a return cargo, & at & from thence to port of discharge in the United States.

& what return if said vessel trades to but one port & arrives safe without loss.

The Union is bound to Kingston (Jamaica) if not allowed to sell there will proceed to Cuba."

And the said Libellants or one of them then informed the said Secretary of the age & tonnage of said vessel upon which he wrote at the bottom of said memorandum the words following,

"2 years old, sheathed last voyage 129 tons"—

And the said memorandum was afterwards on the same evening presented by said Secretary to Nathaniel Bowditch the President of said Insurance Company & by him laid before the Directors thereof; & they then and there consented to insure upon said vessel & cargo for a premium of four per cent; upon which the said Bowditch the President wrote at the bottom of said memorandum the words "4 per cent". Soon afterwards on the same evening the said Andrews or Shepard came to the office of the Respondents before the President & Directors had retired & was informed by the President that they would write for four per cent, but the said applicant retired without accepting said proposition. And afterwards on the same evening when the said President & Directors had retired, the said Shepard came to said office & informed the said Secretary, that he wished only one thousand dollars insured by the Respondents on said vessel & four thousand dollars on said cargo, because he expected to effect the rest of the insurance elsewhere for a less premium. And the said Secretary then wrote upon said memorandum the words "agreed for 1000 on vessel & 4000 on effects as above" which said Shepard signed for himself & said Andrews.

And the Respondents then understood, that the Libellants wished to have in the policy merely the words "from Salem to port or ports in the West Indies one or more times for the purpose of selling outward & procuring a return cargo & at & from thence to port of discharge in the United States," and that the subsequent clauses in the said memorandum formed no part of the description of the voyage to be inserted in the policy. And the Respondents aver that the names of ports to which the vessels are bound as well as various other particulars respecting the risks are frequently mentioned in the memoranda signed by the persons applying to them for insurance, without its being understood by either party that any of those particulars are to be inserted in the policies. And after the said Shepard had signed the memorandum as aforesaid, the said Secretary on the same evening called at the house of the said Bowditch the President & informed him that the said Shepard & Andrews had agreed to have insured only one thousand dollars on said vessel & four thousand dollars on said cargo by the respondents, to which the said President consented, & he thereupon directed the said Secretary to fill up the policy on the next day, but he gave the said Secretary no directions as to the form in which said policy was to be filled, or the particular words to be inserted therein. And on the next day the said Secretary did fill up the policy according to what he understood was the agreement of the parties and without any direction from the said President or any of the Directors. And after the said policy was so filled up, the said President came to said office & after reading said policy signed the same; and the same was afterwards on the same day presented to said Shepard, who then signed the premium note for himself & said Andrews. And the said Bowditch the President believes, that he either then read said policy to said Shepard or that said Shepard then read it himself. And the Respondents aver that the risk described in said policy is strictly conformable to what they understood was the risk which they had consented to insure, & that the clause "the Union is bound to Kingston (Jamaica) if not allowed to sell there will proceed to Cuba" was not omitted to be inserted in said policy by any mistake or misapprehension, but because it was never understood by the Respondents that it was to be so inserted, or that the risk of seizure for proceeding to or attempting to trade there was to be taken or borne by the Respondents. And the Respondents further aver, that they had never any intention of insuring the Libellants against the risk of illicit trade, and that the Libellants never requested them so to do. And they submit that neither said policy nor any act of the Respondents ought to be so construed as to include such risk. And they further aver, that it is against the well known usage of the office of the Respondents & of all other incorporated offices in Salem & Boston to insure against such risks, and that the premium named in said policy was the common premium which the Respondents received at that time for risks similar to that mentioned in said policy, not including illicit trade, & that they asked no extra premium on account of said vessel's being represented to be bound to Kingston as aforesaid.

And the Respondents further aver, that on the same day on which said policy was presented to said Shepard as aforesaid, the Libellants effected further insurance on said vessel & cargo to the amount of six thousand dollars at the office of the Union Marine Insurance Company[81] in Boston for the same risks as are specified in the policy aforesaid of the Respondents at a premium of three & an half per cent; but they did not inform said Union Insurance Company that said Vessel was bound to Jamaica or request them to insert a clause to that effect in their policy, as appears by the depositions of the President & Secretary of the

81. Called the "Union Insurance Company" in subsequent references.

same Company. And the Libellants by their Agents have represented that the risks in both said policies were the same, & have requested said Union Insurance Company to consent to abide by the event of this suit on that account, without intimating that there was any mistake or omission in the present policy. And the Libellants abandoned said vessel & cargo to said Union Insurance Company so far as they were insured by them, & claimed of them a total loss not on the ground that they had taken the risk of seizure at Jamaica for illicit trade but solely because as they pretended the said vessel was seized at Jamaica in consequence of going in there in distress, as appears by the depositions of the said President & Secretary.

And the Respondents further aver that the said vessel & cargo proceeded from Salem aforesaid direct for Jamaica, and arrived at Port Royal in Jamaica, & was there seized & condemned for an alleged violation of the British Navigation laws, as they have been informed which was a risk that the Respondents never agreed or intended to insure against. And they do not admit that there was any seizure or condemnation of said vessel & cargo for which they are liable, and they pray that the Libellants may be required to prove the seizure & condemnation thereof as alleged in their libel, with all the other allegations in said libel which are not admitted in this answer.

And the Respondents expressly aver that after the said policy was delivered to the Libellants, they retained it in their possession and never pretended to the Respondents that there was any mistake in it, till after they heard of said supposed seizure. And when they first informed the said Bowditch the President thereof, he replied to them that it was a risk for which the Respondents were not accountable. And the Libellants did not then suggest that there was any mistake or ommission in said policy, nor did they suggest it till a meeting on a subsequent day.

And the Respondents further aver that when the supposed seizure of said vessel & cargo took place, it became the duty of the master thereof to have informed & shewn to the officers of the Government at Jamaica, that he had come into Port Royal by mistake & misinformation, and with a full belief that it had been permitted by the Government there & was lawful, by doing which the said vessel & cargo as your Respondents believe would have been immediately discharged. But instead of so doing, the said master stated to the Government there and endeavored to prove in Court that the said Brig sailed "from the port of Salem aforesaid bound for the port of St Jago de Cuba and that the sole reason of the said Brig's coming into the harbour of Port Royal was merely to obtain a supply of water and with no other view or intention whatsoever; that at the time of the said vessel sailing from the said port of Salem it was well known and perfectly notorious that the ports of that Island were shut to the

American trade, and he submitted & insisted that had it been otherwise, or had there even existed any *reasonable hope or expectation* of the opening of the said ports to American vessels generally (which he most *positively denied* there did, to the best of his knowledge & belief) yet that it was perfectly obvious to every person acquainted with the trade to the British Co[lony] and well known both to him & to the shippers of the said [car]go that such a cargo as that of the said Brigantine was [and] must be wholly inadmissible into the ports of that Island at any time or under any circumstances whatsoever"; which allegations and assertions were not true and were proved to the satisfaction of the Government there to be false; whereby just cause was given as the Respondents submit, for the condemnation of said vessel & cargo.

Wherefore inasmuch as the said policy of assurance includes all the risks which were agreed & understood between the parties to be included therein & there was no omission therein by mistake or misapprehension; and inasmuch as the supposed loss of said vessel & cargo was occasioned by a violation of the British Navigation laws, and by the false statements of the said master, which were risks not insured against by the Respondents, they pray that the said Libel may be dismissed with costs.

In Witness whereof the said Insurance Company have hereunto caused their corporate seal to be affixed.

Nathl Bowditch Prest

I Nathaniel Bowditch President of the Essex Fire & Marine Insurance Company do swear, that what is contained in the above answer, as far as concerns my own acts & deeds is true of my own knowledge, & what relates to the acts & deeds of others, I believe to be true.

Nathl Bowditch

Essex ss Septr. 2d. 1822. Then Nathl. Bowditch Esq made oath as above Before me Benj. R. Nichols Justice of the Peace

ADS. *Shepard et al.* v. *Essex Fire and Marine Insurance Company*, USCC,DMass, October 1822.

DOCUMENT 90. DEPOSITION

Boston May 23. 1822

Thomas Perkins of Boston [in] the County of Suffolk, & Commonwealth of Massachusetts Esquire, of lawful age, [duly] produced, sworn & examined deposeth as follows that he is President of the Union Insurance Office, in Boston. In January 1819 Mr John H Andrews of Salem, got insurance effected, at said Office on the Brig Union, for himself & Michael Shepard, as appears by the Policy.[82]

* * * *

Quest by Respondents.[83] Did Mr Andrews inform you of the vessels being bound to Jamaica, when the insurance was made?
Answer. No. Not to the Deponents recollection.
By same. Did you ever know that she was bound to Jamaica, previous to the news of the vessels being seized there?
Answer. The deponent never heard it, untill about a fortnight ago, that he recollects. The first time he heard of it; was from Mr Bowditch.

* * * *

By same. Did not Mr Baker[84] apply to you, in behalf of Mssr. Shepard & Andrews, to agree to abide by the decision, in the case against the Essex Fire & Marine Insurance Company, upon the ground, that the policies in both cases, were the same? If so, when was this application made?
Answer. He did. It was a day or two, after Mr Bowditch told the Deponent, that it was intended, the vessel should go to Jamaica. The deponent asked Mr Baker, if the defence was grounded upon any thing except the language of the Policy. Mr Baker replied, that he did not know of any thing else, upon which, the deponent observed that he knew of some thing else, & did not choose to sign the paper. In this conversation, Mr Baker read an extract from a letter of Mr Andrews, by which Mr Andrews wrote Mr Baker, he wished him to get the deponent to sign an agreement, to abide the decision, in the case abovementioned; as Mr Baker had written him (Mr Andrews) some time before, that the deponent was willing to do. The deponent expressed his surprize, at hearing this extract, as he had never expressed his willingness to make any such agreement to his recollection nor did he know till a few days before said conversation happened, that Insurance on the Union, had been effected, at the Office, in Salem. Mr Baker observed, that he did not recollect having written Mr Andrews, to that effect, but as Mr Andrews said, he had written so, he presumed it must have been the case.

* * * *

By same. Is it, or is it not, common, to have a difference of one half per cent, on the same risk, at different Offices?
Answer. It is sometimes the case.

* * * *

82. The policy was annexed to the deposition. Union insured the ship for $2,000 and the cargo for $4,000 at 3½%. Thomas Perkins (1763?–1836), U.S. loan officer for Massachusetts (1802–1803), president, Union Insurance Company (1812–1835).

83. Essex Fire and Marine Insurance Company.

84. Not identified.

By same. Is it not the usage of all the Offices, in Boston, to refuse insuring against illicit trade?
Answer. It has been the practice of the Union Office, ever since the Deponent has been President of it, not to insure against any act, which contravenes the laws of any government or state. And the deponent believes, this is the practice of all the incorporated Offices in Boston.
By same. Do you not object putting into any policy, a clause of exemption of illicit trade? If so, on what ground?
Answer. The said Company do so object; for the reason, that if once omitted, by accident, it might be thought, the company allowed illicit trade.

* * * *

By same. Are not some thousands of applications for insurance made at your Office, in the course of a year, & are not a large proportion refused.
Answer. There are a great many, the deponent cannot state the number, & many are refused, the deponent could not say that more than one half are refused.
By same. Did you write at your Office, five policies, on the 8 Jan. 1819?
Answer. Yes, they were all for one house.
By same. Are not proposals for Insurance, at your office, usually made in writing, & if so, is it your practice to preserve them?
Answer. They are not commonly made in writing. A memorandum is made in the Companys book, of the proposal. The applicant examines it, & if it is found correct, a policy is made from it. It is more common, for persons out of town, to hand written proposals, when they personally appear than for residents, in town, as the former usually wait, untill their policies are completed.

* * * *

By same. Are you positive, that the first information you had, that the Union was bound to Jamaica, was from Mr Bowditch, about a fortnight ago?
Answer. He is.
By same. May not Mr Andrews have given you the information by reading a memorandum, to that effect, & you not recollect it, at this distance of time?
Answer. It is possible that the information might so have been communicated by Mr Andrews, but the deponent has no doubt, that the first information came from Mr Bowditch. As it was four or five months only, after the insurance, that the deponent heard of the vessels being in Jamaica, he thinks that he could not have forgotten the information, if it had ever been communicated to him. The letter from the Captain, was produced, to the deponent, & at that time, the deponent did not remember, that he had ever heard the vessel was going to Jamaica.
By same. Will you state, what conversation you had, with Mr Andrews,

concerning the proposal for insurance, on the Union, at the time he made it?
Answer. The deponent cannot recollect any thing special, except that Mr Andrews said, he wished a policy on a voyage, to the West Indies, & back. A memorandum was made in the companys book, & a policy filled accordingly. He cannot recollect whether Mr Andrews read the policy, or not, when it was delivered to him? Policies are usually delivered, by the Secretary, but the deponent does not know when the policy in question was delivered or who delivered it. Policies are usually read by the assured, before they are taken, from the Office.

* * * *

By same. Have not the libellants a claim, now pending, against your Office upon their policy on the Brig Union & effects?
Answer. They make a claim, but have not instituted any suit.

* * * *

Thomas Perkins

Extract. *Shepard et al.* v. *Essex Fire and Marine Insurance Company*, USCC,DMass, October 1822.

TO LEVERETT SALTONSTALL

Dear Sir, Sandwich Aug. 22 [1822]

Your letter followed me here.[85] It is my intention to be at Salem on *Thursday* next, to consult abt. Messrs Shepherd & Andrews' cause; or any subsequent day in the week, which may suit you better. I have recd a line from Mr. Prescot, desiring to know whether it would not be well to *put off* this adjourned term.[86] For myself, I shall not set up my own convenience or inconvenience, in the case, & shall at once acquiesce in any thing, which others may agree to; altho' the necessity of going to Washington naturally induces me to wish to do as much of my business, in September, as I can. Nevertheless, my personal accomodation need not all be considered, not being much affected, either way. In reference to the Argonaut,[87] the parties are all near you, & in Mr Andrews case, you represent him, & he is also at hand. In short, this adjourned Court was so much on account of the Salem business, that I think you must settle it altogether among yourselves. You may say to the Judge, that Mr. [George] Blake & myself shall make no difficulty about the case of the Portugal *Vessel*,[88] altho' Mr. Stockton will probably be on, at the time of the expected adjournment. Yet it may go over, if other causes do.

85. Letter not found.
86. The continuation of the previous May term.
87. See *Peele et al* v. *Merchants' Insurance Company*, pp. 474–489, below.
88. A reference to the *Marianna Flora*, 3 Mason 116 (1822), and 11 Wheaton 1 (1826), argued by DW.

My own opinion is, in honesty, that we shall not have so good a chance for the full hearing of these causes, at any time, as at the time of the proposed adjournment; and that if the weather should be tolerably temperate, it would be a real convenience, upon the whole, that the Court should sit, as proposed. This is, however, opinion merely, and I shall readily acquiesce in whatever is done. Please show this to Mr. Nichols. I am just setting out for home, and shall be glad to find there a line from you. Yr's always D. Webster

ALS. NhD. Leverett Saltonstall (1783–1845; Harvard 1802), Salem lawyer, studied with Ichabod Bartlett and William Prescott, admitted to the Essex bar in 1806, state senator, U.S. representative (1838–1843).

c. *Jurisdiction and Abandonment: Willard Peele et al.* v. *Merchants' Insurance Company*

In 1815 Justice Story ruled on circuit in *DeLovio* v. *Boit* that the federal district courts had admiralty jurisdiction over marine insurance policies.[1] On the basis of an elaborate review of the history of the English admiralty court, he concluded that federal admiralty jurisdiction extended to all maritime contracts wherever made or executed. The sole jurisdictional test for contracts was their subject matter. This broad view of federal judicial authority over maritime commerce contrasted sharply with the contemporaneously narrow jurisdiction of the English admiralty. That court had jurisdiction of only those maritime contracts made and executed on the high seas.[2] Story's justification for this expansive view of federal jurisdiction lay in his belief that the commercial interests of the coastal states needed uniform rules on maritime questions in order to conduct international trade. By making the federal courts the principal forum for maritime commercial disputes, a contested question would eventually reach the Supreme Court. Its decision would resolve the problem, and a uniform national commercial law would emerge. Furthermore, by bringing suit in the federal admiralty courts, litigants could evade unpopular state court decisions. The prestige of a Supreme Court decision might even persuade the state courts to follow federal precedents.[3]

1. 2 Gallison 398 (1815). For a critical evaluation of Story's evidence, see David W. Robertson, *Admiralty and Federalism* (Mineola, N. Y., 1970), pp. 65–94. Story did not claim an exclusive federal jurisdiction.

2. Admiralty jurisdiction over maritime torts was tested by the place where the tort occurred. A federal court had jurisdiction over torts that occurred only on the high seas or within the ebb and flow of the tide. Admiralty courts did not use juries.

3. In 1810 MassSJC Justice Theodore Sedgwick wrote: "There seems to be a peculiar propriety in respecting the decisions of the supreme court of the *United States* upon this subject [marine insurance]: because there is delegated to the national government an authority to regulate commerce: and because it is highly interesting to commerce, that the same rule of decision, in this respect,

Apparently, Story did not expect the merchants of the first circuit to applaud the *DeLovio* decision. When they did, he attributed it to a dislike for juries. "They declare that in mercantile causes, they are not fond of juries," he wrote, "and in particular, the underwriters in Boston have expressed great satisfaction at the decision."[4] But the merchants did not flock into federal court. Between 1815 and 1821, when Webster brought the *Shepard* case (above), there are no reported marine insurance cases on the admiralty side. Morton Horwitz has speculated that Story took a position that favored the insurance companies over general mercantile interests.[5] Yet, as Webster's strategy in *Haven et al.* v. *Holland* (above) demonstrates, a merchant might choose to litigate in federal court because it enhanced his chance of a recovery. In fact, as that case and the one discussed below demonstrate, Story's decisions could favor the insurance claimants. The companies preferred to keep litigation in the MassSJC, where favorable precedents gave them more control over the scope of the risk. In the case discussed below, the insurance company argued against Story's expansive view of the admiralty jurisdiction. It seems more likely that Story pursued an enlarged federal jurisdiction in the interest of rule uniformity and predictability. Whether this favored one commercial interest over another did not seem to concern him. For Story, admiralty jurisdiction meant an open door for Supreme Court decisions that would create a national commercial law.[6]

---

should pervade the whole country. It would indeed be inconvenient, embarrassing and disreputable, that in different actions, depending at the same time, in the national and state courts, brought on the same policy, and governed by the same facts, contrary judgments should be rendered." *Baxter et al.* v. *New England Marine Insurance Company*, 6 Mass. 277, 299–300 (1810).

4. As quoted in Horwitz, p. 251. While merchants disliked juries generally, it seems curious that they would criticize them in insurance litigation given the jurors' predilection in favor of claimants. Story's reference to underwriters probably meant both companies and private underwriters. It is possible, of course, that his statement was self-congratulatory. But see DW's cryptic reference to Story's position vis-à-vis the insurance companies. DW to Leverett Saltonstall, December 24, 1823, printed below.

5. Ibid. Horwitz acknowledges that the companies were not in a position to benefit from *DeLovio*, since they did not initiate litigation (p. 251, n. 140). It must also be kept in mind that the structure of the Massachusetts insurance business is unclear. In 1822 Boston had nine marine insurance companies and one private underwriter. See *The Boston Directory* for 1822, pp. 278–280, and *The Massachusetts Register* for 1826, pp. 176–181. Some companies seem to have been no more than incorporated private underwriters. Although underwriters had no love for juries, they might still prefer to litigate in the MassSJC, where the judges remained sympathetic to their interests.

6. Horwitz, p. 252, seems correct in pointing out that *Swift* v. *Tyson*, 16 Peters 1 (1842), represented Story's attempt to federalize commercial law through the diversity

For seven years Story's assertion of a broad admiralty jurisdiction went unchallenged in the first circuit and untested in the Supreme Court. Then in 1822 Webster initiated two cases in admiralty involving insurance contracts, each of which prompted a challenge by the insurance company to the court's jurisdiction. The first, *Shepard et al.* v. *Essex Fire and Marine Insurance Company*, is presented above. The second, the subject of this section, saw the jurisdiction question carried to the Supreme Court. The *Peele* case also became renowned for Story's exposition of the law of abandonment. The litigation involved four suits, one of which became the stalking horse for the other three.[7] Four Salem merchants insured the ship *Argonaut* and her cargo with two insurance companies and eight private underwriters for a voyage to Leghorn, Italy, and back. The ship completed the outward part of the voyage, but on her return a storm drove her onto the rocks outside of Portsmouth, New Hampshire, around three o'clock in the morning on March 24, 1821. Although the storm moderated, the crew was unable to get the ship off the rocks. By the afternoon, it became apparent that the ship's bottom had broken and water had entered the hold. The next day the storm resumed its intensity, and the master left the ship. The owners considered her wrecked. On March 26 they abandoned the ship to the insurance companies and underwriters and claimed a constructive total loss.[8]

The Merchants' Insurance Company followed the customary practice of Massachusetts insurers and neither accepted nor rejected the offer of abandonment. Instead, they appointed an agent to investigate the situation and, if possible, to get the ship off the rocks. A private company memorandum advised the agent that if the ship could be repaired for less than 50 percent of her value, the company would reject the abandonment.[9] Using forty or fifty men, the agent refloated the *Argonaut*, and on March 30 a fleet of twenty boats towed her into Portsmouth for repair. The *Argonaut* owners took no part in these actions. On April 2 the

jurisdiction. Of course, to the extent that Story took an actuarial approach, his decisions would, in the long run, favor the interests of the insurance business.

7. *Peele et al.* v. *Merchants' Insurance Company*, USDC,DMass, April 1822; USCC,DMass, May 1827 ($30,000); *Peele et al.* v. *Suffolk Insurance Company*, USDC,DMass, April 1822; USCC,DMass, May 1827 ($7000); *Peele et al. v. Forrester*, USDC, DMass, June 1827 ($500); *Peele et al.* v. *Peirce*, USDC,DMass, March 1822 ($500).

8. In order to claim a constructive loss, the insured had to notify the underwriter of the loss (called an *abandonment*). Once the underwriter accepted the abandonment, title to the insured property passed to the underwriter. In the case of an actual total loss, the law did not require an abandonment.

9. This reflected the 50 percent rule. If the repairs came to less than 50 percent of the ship's value, the law did not consider a constructive loss to have occurred.

insurance company offered to compromise but the owners made no response. Repairs began on April 20 and were completed in June. The underwriters then offered the repaired ship to the owners. They rejected the offer on the grounds that the insurance company had accepted the abandonment in March, and that this established the owners' right to claim a total loss. In the belief that their legal positions would suffer, neither side would give its permission to sell the ship. For the next seven years, the *Argonaut* would sit at a Portsmouth wharf.

Peele and his co-owners first brought suit in state court. Following a trial which left the dispute undecided, the parties appealed to the MassSJC. Before that court considered the matter, however, the plaintiffs took the unusual step of becoming nonsuit. Litigation strategy had dictated a change in forum. The plaintiffs now turned to Webster to begin an action in federal court.[10] On March 25, 1822, Webster and his co-counsel Benjamin R. Nichols filed a libel (Document 91) in federal district court under the court's admiralty jurisdiction. It is most likely that Webster chose this course in order to avoid the impact of the 1810 MassSJC decision in *Wood* v. *Lincoln and Kennebec Insurance Company*. That decision permitted Massachusetts underwriters to delay accepting an offer of abandonment until they determined the actual condition of the vessel. Chief Justice Theophilus Parsons said that in a case of a stranded vessel the court would not consider it to have been lost or the voyage defeated if the vessel was brought into port: "if the underwriter will himself undertake, at his own expense, for the owner, the recovery of his ship, and shall succeed, and offer to restore her to him, so that he may seasonably prosecute his voyage, the owner cannot abandon, for neither the ship nor the voyage is lost."[11]

While some factual differences existed between the *Wood* decision and the wreck of the *Argonaut*, it was clear that the MassSJC favored giving the underwriters the authority to wait and see how a situation would be resolved before requiring them to accept or reject an abandonment. This reflected the view that insurance was an indemnity for actual loss and not a means of making a profit. It also represented the pre-actuarial approach in insurance law. The court considered each individual accident as an isolated event. In a situation where it was unclear whether the ship could be saved, the insurer could wait to see how things turned out. On the other hand, if an event occurred which clearly de-

10. It is not known if DW participated in the state court trial, but his presence in the federal litigation from its beginning indicates his involvement in the planning of the *Argonaut* owners' strategy. For a full account of the case from the insurance company's perspective, see Joseph Balch to Leverett Saltonstall, December 13, 1826, in Robert E. Moody, ed., *The Papers of Leverett Saltonstall, 1816–1845* (3 vols., Boston, 1978–), 1: 200–203.

11. 6 Mass. 479, 484 (1810).

feated a voyage, such as a capture, the MassSJC did not give the underwriter the authority to delay action on the abandonment. This reflected a competing policy that sought to establish rules of law that would settle legal rights at the earliest possible moment.

The *Peele* case thus raised the question whether a court should adopt the perspective of the owners at the time they made the offer of abandonment or take the *Wood* position and evaluate the underwriters' action by subsequent information.[12] Parsons had chosen the latter position, because he did not want to discourage owners and insurers from saving ships that went aground on New England shores. He noted that although ships often became beached for a time in bad weather, the crew successfully refloated them once the weather improved. He focused on whether the ship completed the voyage. If so, the underwriter was responsible for only the owner's actual expenses (partial loss). The law favored insurers who made an effort to preserve the property. A court motivated by an actuarial view, on the other hand, might be more concerned with establishing legal rights than with saving insured property. When the Merchants' Insurance Company's lawyers answered Webster's libel (Document 92), they adopted two strategies. First, they protested the jurisdiction. Then they raised their defense that since the company repaired the ship and offered her to the owners, no constructive total loss took place. Webster replied that the alleged total loss had occurred.

In April 1822, the USDC entered a pro forma decree for the defendants and Webster appealed. In October the circuit court heard the evidence and the arguments, and Story rendered his judgment. First, he upheld his court's jurisdiction on the basis of his *DeLovio* decision. He did say, however, that he would accept a revision of his position by the Supreme Court. He expressed surprise that a marine insurance case had come before the admiralty court "presuming that from private convenience, the benefit of a trial by jury, and the confidence that is so justly placed in our state tribunals, the insured would almost universally elect a domestic forum."[13] It was true that most plaintiffs preferred to sue in state court, where juries sympathized with them. In this case, however, Webster must have feared the adverse effect of the *Wood* decision. The

12. The Massachusetts rule allowed the insurer to present evidence of the situation up to the date of his decision to reject the offer of abandonment. The English rule was even more favorable to the insurers. There the jury examined the facts as of the date of the suit. If the reason for abandonment no longer existed, there could be no constructive loss.

13. 3 Mason 27, 29 (1822). Story may have feigned surprise. The tendency for Massachusetts judges to control juries by overturning verdicts contrary to the weight of the evidence was well known among lawyers. William E. Nelson, *Americanization of the Common Law: The Impact of Legal Change on Massachusetts Society, 1760–1830* (Cambridge, Mass., 1975), p. 170.

events surrounding the wreck of the *Argonaut* looked too much like a simple stranding.

Story then upheld Peele's claim. He rejected the Massachusetts rule that the court tested the right to abandon by the true state of facts that existed at the time the insured made the offer of abandonment. The company had argued that any relaxation of the rules regarding abandonment as administered in the state common law courts would allow the claimants to take advantage of the underwriters. Story replied that the rules regarding abandonments were in fact so uncertain that they "encouraged expensive suits."[14] He would therefore seek to settle the matter on general principles. As he had done in *DeLovio*, he canvassed the precedents. When he found them hopelessly conflicting, he turned to "general principles" to try to cast the rules in a form which he hoped other courts would adopt.[15]

His method exemplified how federal judges could bring forth a national commercial law through the power of reason. Story pursued a quest for certainty in the rules of commercial law. Courts could reach this goal by defining the rights of the parties as early in a dispute as possible. His elaboration of the law of constructive loss showed the effect of an actuarial approach to insurance. He held that in cases of abandonment the law did not require destruction of the ship but only the probability of its loss. In the *Wood* case Parsons had put the risk of waiting on the insured. The insured's claim attended the underwriter's decision. Story shifted the risk to the insurer. Once the insured believed that the ship was in extreme danger (judged by the standard of a reasonable man) or could not be restored at an expense less than 50 percent of its value, the abandonment became effective. The insured's decision could not be evaluated by later evidence of the facts (the *Wood* case) or by subsequent events (the English rule). With this test, once the insurer accepted the abandonment, the insured's legal rights became established. "[T]he assured is to act, not upon certainties but on probabilities, and

14. Ibid., p. 38. Story's biographer speculates that Story prepared his long academic opinions in advance. Gerald Dunne, *Justice Joseph Story and the Rise of the Supreme Court* (New York, 1970), p. 129. Insurance company counsel Leverett Saltonstall and William Prescott had little faith in their ability to sway Story. On September 17, 1822 Prescott wrote to Saltonstall: "I told the Judge you would give him your Brief in the case of the Argonaut and I hope you have done it, altho I have but little hope in the cause. I fear its not in the Briefs to save us" (Moody, *Saltonstall*, 1: 103).

15. "The *American* cases then may be dismissed without further commentary, since they furnish no new rule. . . . We are therefore driven back upon general principles. . . . New cases, as they arise, must be settled . . . by general reasoning applied to the nature of the contract, and the general convenience and policy of the commercial world" (3 Mason 27, 64–66).

that if he should wait until an unfavorable result, he will not then be entitled to turn the loss into a technical total loss. . . . It appears to me . . . to be introducing a new element of discord into the law of insurance, to allow the right of abandonment to be a shifting right, dependent upon the will of both of the parties, and to be defeated by any act of one, after it has rightfully attached by the act of the other."[16] Story completed his reconstruction of the law of abandonment by altering several other rules. First, in determining constructive loss, the damage to the ship had to exceed 50 percent of the ship's value. Story held that this meant the ship's present value and not its policy value. Since a ship's policy value usually exceeded its current value, this ruling favored the claimants. Second, Story ruled that the jury could not deduct one third new for old from the cost of repairs.[17] He went on to rule that acceptance of an abandonment could be inferred from the acts of the insurer which related to ownership; and that an acceptance once made was irrevocable. These last two rulings also aided claimants.

The underwriters lost no time in responding to Story's decision. They drafted a new clause, soon called the "Boston clause," which began to appear in their policies. It read: "the acts of the Assured or Assurers in recovering, saving, and preserving the property insured in case of disaster, shall not be considered a waiver or acceptance of an abandonment."[18] The Merchants' Company also decided to appeal to the Supreme Court. In February 1823 they filed the case but too late for argument that term. On December 24, 1823, Webster wrote a letter to opposing counsel Leverett Saltonstall, printed below.[19] Webster wanted to know whether the insurance companies really intended to try to overturn the admiralty jurisdiction. Webster suggested that it would be in the companies' interest not to divest Story of his authority to rule on commercial questions. In a letter of January 9, 1824, printed below, Saltonstall responded that the jurisdictional question should be settled, although he doubted if the Supreme Court would hear it that term. A year later, on January 9, 1825, Webster sent another letter to Saltonstall, printed below, seeking to delay the argument until after March 3, 1825. Even

16. Ibid., pp. 61, 63. Under Story's approach neither side could delay making its decision.

17. The underwriters had been allowed to deduct one third of the value of the new materials used for repairing the vessel from the estimated cost of repairs, on the theory that the owner would get something better than his original ship. This ruling also benefited the insured.

18. See Policy of Assurance, case file, *Ruggles* v. *General Interest Insurance Company*, USCC,DMass, October 1825.

19. Interestingly, DW appeared as co-counsel with Saltonstall in the *Shepherd* case above. Benjamin R. Nichols appeared in that case for the insurance company; in *Peele* he teamed with DW.

then, Webster correctly predicted, it would be too late in the term for the Court to hear a case of such importance.

In anticipation of the argument in 1826, Benjamin R. Nichols, Webster's co-counsel, filed a brief on the jurisdictional question. Asserting that all maritime contracts came within the constitutional grant of admiralty jurisdiction, Nichols urged the court to affirm Story's assertion of jurisdiction in order to promote uniformity of decision. "Nothing can be more embarrassing than the conflicting decisions which now exist in the different states with respect to some of the most important points of commercial law."[20] But again, the parties put the case over a term.

Finally, in January 1827, the matter was resolved, though hardly as Story had expected. Instead of arguing the case, counsel for both sides agreed to a judgment reversing and annulling the decision of the USCC for want of jurisdiction. The insurance company had defeated Story's jurisdiction. Since the Court never heard argument or delivered an opinion, the judgment went no further than the instant case.[21] As a result, it remained unclear for the next forty-three years whether the federal courts had admiralty jurisdiction over marine insurance. In the first circuit, however, the federal judges did not consider their admiralty jurisdiction at an end. Those federal courts still heard an occasional libel, but counsel for the plaintiffs took care not to demand more than the statutory $2000 required for an appeal. They did not wish to become the test case for which Story yearned. In the 1850s the judges of the first circuit said they followed *DeLovio* even though its authority had never been affirmed. Finally, in 1870 the Supreme Court decided that the federal courts had admiralty jurisdiction over marine insurance.[22]

The *Peele* reversal, of course, did not settle the fate of the *Argonaut*. That question now moved back to the state courts. Webster turned the case over to Jeremiah Mason. On January 9, 1828, Mason reported:

> Since I saw you at Boston I have been twice to Salem to attend the

20. *Argument for Plaintiff's Counsel in Peele v. Merchants' Insurance Company* (Boston, 1826), p. 16.

21. Why Peele's attorneys, DW included, chose not to push the case to a decision is not clear. Some years later Story said that Justices Marshall and Washington would have voted to sustain the jurisdiction. *Hall* v. *Washington Insurance Company*, 2 Story 176 (1842). Evidently DW and his co-counsel had no faith in the other four judges. That same term Justice Johnson wrote an attack on the admiralty jurisdiction in *Ramsay* v. *Allegre*, 12 Wheaton 612, 614–640 (1827).

22. *New England Mutual Marine Insurance Company* v. *Dunham*, 11 Wallace 1 (1870). For the first circuit's decision see *Younger* v. *Gloucester Marine Insurance Company*, 1 Sprague's Admiralty Decisions 236 (1854) and 2 Curtis 322 (1856).

> trials of the Argonaut. We have had two tedious jury trials, & have obtained two successive verdicts much against the wishes of Judge [Samuel] P[utnam] He seemed to think it his duty to obstruct the Pl[aintif]fs course as much he could, but I believe we have got our verdicts on such grounds as must end the litigation, though not on the ground we ought to have had them. I left Salem immediately after the last verdict was given. I have no doubt the judge has in some way reserved the cases for the whole Court.[23]

Mason was correct. Putnam wanted to repudiate Story's *Peele* holdings on the abandonment issue. In November counsel argued the various points before the full SJC bench.[24] Ironically, Putnam had instructed the jury that if the insurance company had been unnecessarily slow in effecting repairs, the jury must find for the plaintiffs. The jury's verdict on this factual issue made the other aspects of the case irrelevant to a decision. Had the defense counsel moved to set the verdict aside as against the weight of the evidence, it would have allowed the SJC to examine the entire case. But since the defense had not done this, Chief Justice Parker wrote, the jury's finding bound the court, and it had no choice but to affirm the judgment. In his argument for the defendant, Saltonstall had launched a full-scale attack on Story's *Peele* opinion. Parker agreed with Saltonstall. In dicta he reasserted the correctness of the Massachusetts rules that subsequent events may be examined to determine whether a constructive loss in fact occurred, and that the insurance policy established the value of the ship.

In future decisions the MassSJC continued to criticize Story's rulings. Judge Putnam, in particular, urged the courts to keep a tight rein on the constructive loss concept. In *Hall et al.* v. *Franklin Insurance Company*,[25] decided in 1830, he rejected Story's rule that imminent danger of a technical total loss justified an abandonment. In 1835 Putnam put himself among those judges who favored restricting abandonments for technical total losses. "We are among those, who think that this part of the law of insurance, as it is now administered, is a clear departure from the great principle of indemnity upon which the contract of insurance should rest."[26]

23. *Correspondence*, 2: 275.

24. *Peele et al.* v. *Suffolk Insurance Company*, 7 Pickering (Mass.) 254 (1828).

25. 9 Pickering (Mass.) 466 (1830).

26. *DeBlois et al.* v. *Ocean Insurance Company*, 16 Pickering (Mass.) 303, 313 (1835). He also restated the Massachusetts rule that allowed insurers to deduct one third new for old. See also *Commonwealth Insurance Company* v. *Chase*, 20 Pickering (Mass.) 142 (1838); *Orrock et al.* v. *Commonwealth Insurance Company*, 21 Pickering (Mass.) 456 (1839); and *Hall* v. *Ocean Insurance Company*, 21 Pickering (Mass.) 472 (1839).

DOCUMENT 91. LIBEL

Boston March 25. 1822

To the Honble. John Davis, Judge of the District Court of the United States for the District of Massachusetts.

The Libel of Willard Peele, Richard Wheatland, James Silver and Benjamin Dodge[27] all of Salem in said District Merchants, humbly sheweth —that your Libellants at Boston in said District on the sixth day of December in the year of our Lord one thousand eight hundred and twenty according to the custom of merchants, caused to be made a certain maritime contract in writing commonly called a policy of assurance, of the tenor following to wit

No. 4921 Merchants' Insurance Company.

This Policy of Assurance witnesseth, That the President and Directors of the Merchants' Insurance Company, do by these presents cause Willard Peele, Richard Wheatland, Benja. Dodge & James Silver of Salem to be assured, lost or not lost, thirty thousand dollars on the Ship Argonaut and on property on board said ship viz $4000 on the vessel $26000 on the property on board at & from Leghorn to her port of discharge in the United States—whereof is master for this present voyage Gaml Hodges[28] or whoever else shall be master in the said vessel, or by whatever other name or names the said vessel or master thereof, is or shall be named or called; beginning the adventure upon the said Ship & property as aforesaid, and to continue during the voyage aforesaid, on the vessel, until she shall be arrived & moored at anchor twenty four hours in safety and on the cargo or effects, until landed. And it shall be lawful for the said vessel, in her voyage, to proceed and sail to, touch & stay at any ports or places, if thereunto obliged by stress of weather, or other unavoidable accidents, without prejudice to this assurance. Touching the adventures & perils which the said Insurance Company are contented to bear; & take upon them in this voyage, they are, of the seas, fire, enemies, pirates assailing thieves, restraints & detainments of all Kings, Princes or People, what nation or quality soever, barratry of the master (unless the assured be owner of the vessel) & of the Mariners; and all other losses & misfortunes which have or shall come to the damage of the said ship & property or any part thereof, to which Assurers are liable by the rules & customs of assurance in Boston. And in case of any loss or misfortune, it shall be lawful for the assured their factors servants & assigns, to sue labour & travel for in & about the defence, safeguard & recovery of the said ship & property or any part thereof, without prejudice to this assurance; to the charges whereof the said Insurance Company will contribute

27. Wheatland was also a ship captain. The others have not been further identified.

28. Gamaliel Hodges has not been further identified.

in proportion as the sum assured is to the whole sum at risk. And so the President & Directors aforesaid are contented, & do hereby bind the capital stock & other common property of the said Insurance Company to the assured, their executors or administrators, for the true performance of the premises confessing themselves paid the consideration due unto them for this assurance by the assured, at & after the rate of one & a fourth per cent. And it is hereby agreed that if the assured shall have made any other assurance upon the ship & property aforesaid, actually prior to this, then the said Insurance Company shall be answerable only for so much as the amount of such prior assurance may be deficient towards fully covering the property at risk; and the said Insurance Company shall return the premium upon so much of the sum by them assured, as they shall be exonerated from by such prior assurance excepting half per cent, which shall be retained in all cases of return premium. And in case of any assurance upon the said ship & property subsequent to this policy, the said Insurance Company shall nevertheless be answerable to the full extent of the sums by them herein assured, without right to claim contribution from such subsequent assurers; and shall accordingly be entitled to retain the premium by them received, in the same manner, as if no such subsequent assurance had been made. And in case of loss, the assured is to abate one per centum; and such loss shall be paid in sixty days after proof thereof, the amount of the premium note if unpaid & all sums due to the Company from the assured, when such loss becomes due, being first deducted. And it is also agreed between the parties, that the assurers are not liable for any partial loss on sugar flaxseed, bread, tobacco & rice unless the loss amount to seven per cent; nor for any partial loss on other goods or freight, or on the vessel, unless the loss amount to five per cent; but the assured shall recover on a general average. And it is further agreed between the parties, that the assurers are not liable for any partial loss on salt, grain, hemp flax fish, fruit, hides, skins, or other goods that are esteemed perishable in their own nature, but the owners of such goods shall recover on a general average, & on a particular average when the damage happens by stranding or bilging, provided such damage amount to seven per cent. And it is further agreed, that if any dispute shall arise, relating to a loss on this policy, it shall be submitted to the judgment & determination of arbitrators mutually chosen, whose award in writing shall be conclusive & binding on all parties. In witness whereof the President of the said Merchants' Insurance Company hath hereunto subscribed his name, & caused the same to be countersigned by their secretary, at their office in Boston this sixth day of December one thousand eight hundred and twenty.

Of which said writing or policy of assurance made as above set forth the said President & Directors of the Merchants' Insurance Company afterwards to wit on the said sixth day of December at Boston in said District had notice, & thereupon, there afterwards on the same day in consideration that the Libellants had paid to the said Company the sum of three hundred and seventy five dollars as a premium for the insurance of thirty thousand dollars on said ship & property and had then & there promised the said Company to perform all things on the part of the assured to be performed, they the said Company then & there undertook & faithfully promised the Plaintiffs that they would become Insurers to the Libellants of the sum of four thousand dollars on said vessel and twenty six thousand dollars on the property on board the same and would perform and fulfill all things on the part of the said Company to be performed and they accordingly then & there became Insurers [of the] vessel & twenty six thousand dollars on said property on board then & there caused their President Joseph Balch to sign & Secretary Moses L. Hale[29] their Secretary to countersign said policy[.] Now the Libellants say that there afterwards to wit, on the second day [of] February in the year of our Lord one thousand eight hundred and twenty one the said ship departed & set sail from Leghorn on her voyage aforesaid; and before her arrival at Salem which was her port of destination and intended discharge in the United States, to wit, on twenty fourth day of March in the year last aforesaid the said vessel was by & through the danger of the seas & the force of [illegible] & tempestuous winds & weather cast and stranded upon certain rocks near the harbour of Portsmouth and upon a placed called Gerrish's Island, whereby the said vessel became & was then & there wrecked, broken to pieces & totally lost to the Libellants, to wit at Salem aforesaid, and they also then & there sustained a general average loss of one per cent, of all which the said Company afterwards to wit on the twenty sixth day of the same March at Boston aforesaid had notice and proof.[30] And the Libellants aver that at the time of making said Insurance as aforesaid and also at the time of the loss aforesaid they were interested in said vessel & property to the amount insured, and they have performed all things in said policy of insurance on their part to be performed, whereby the said company then & there became liable to pay to the Libellants the whole sum insured by them upon said vessel as aforesaid together with a general average loss of one per cent upon the sum insured by them on said vessel & effects in sixty days from that day. Yet though often requested since said sixty days have elapsed the said Company have never paid the same but have neglected and refused so to do

To the end that your Libellants may obtain satisfaction in the Premises, they pray, that Admiralty Process may issue against the said Com-

29. Not further identified.
30. The plaintiffs' offer of abandonment.

pany, that they may be compelled to pay to your Libellants the amount due from them the said Company to them as above stated together with such other sums for damages, as to your Honor may seem just. And as in duty bound will ever pray.

D. Webster Proctor for Libellants.

ADS. *Peele et al.* v. *Merchants' Insurance Company*, USDC,DMass, April 1822. DW's name was signed by another.

DOCUMENT 92. PROTEST, ANSWER, AND REPLICATION

The Protest[31] of the Merchants' Insurance Company named in the libel filed by Willard Peele, Richard Wheatland and James Silver & Benjamin Dodge, appearing here to avoid all contumacy contempt and default under this their Protest against said Libel.

These Protestants reserving to themselves all exceptions to the insufficiencies of said Libel, and also liberty to make in the Circuit Court any more formal plea to the jurisdiction of this Court and any answer to said Libel; and protesting that said Company ought not in any wise to be required to appear and answer thereto as is therein prayed. Nevertheless for the reasons aforesaid, and as a cause why said Libel should be dismissed without further appearance or answer, said Company avers propounds & says; that they admit that said Ship during the voyage described in said libel by the winds & seas was driven upon the shore of Gerrish's Island in said Libel mentioned, & thereby damaged; but said Company avers that she was afterwards & within days got off & afterwards within a reasonable time viz: on or before the day of was well and sufficiently repaired by the said Company at their expense, and that said Company thereupon offered to restore & deliver her so repaired to the Libellants at Portsmouth in the District of New Hampshire where she was repaired or at Boston aforesaid, but said Libellants then refused to accept or receive her either at said Portsmouth or at said Boston; and the said Company now & ever since have been ready to cause said Ship so repaired to be delivered to the Libellants. And the said Company avers that the damage done to said Ship & her appurtenances by the winds & seas & by her being driven on shore as aforesaid was only a particular average or partial loss,[32] and that the said

31. A challenge to the court's jurisdiction.

32. If the ship was a total loss, the company had to pay the full amount of the insurance. As a partial loss they need only indemnify for the damage. Since the cargo had been off loaded, the repair costs would be less than a total loss.

Company caused the same to be fully & completely repaired as aforesaid, and they wholly deny that the said Ship was thereby totally lost to the Libellants as they in their Libel have alleged. Wherefore the said Company prays that said Libel may be dismissed with Costs.

Wm. Prescott Proctor for Said Company by S. Dexter

And the said Libellants consenting to the above reservation, & reserving to themselves a right to make any other replication, say said Ship was totally lost to them as they in said Libel have alleged

D. Webster & Nichols for the Libellants—by A. Bliss

ADS. *Peele et al.* v. *Merchants' Insurance Company*, USDC,DMass, April 1822.

TO LEVERETT SALTONSTALL

My Dear Sir Washington Dec 24. [1823]

I rec'd your letter, several days ago, & am very willing to be associated with you, in the causes which you mention.[33]

What is to be done with the Argonaut? Do your clients think it is for the interest of Insurance Companies to break up, if they can, the Judge's jurisdiction? If you expect to come on & argue that matter, let me know pretty soon, if you please, that I may have the law looked up.[34] My own wish—I may say my own *opinion*—is at present inclined towards avoiding the question of jurisdiction. Taking the whole of the Judge's decisions together, there is no doubt which way they tend.[35] But this is matter which your clients have a right to judge of for themselves. Yours with true regard Danl. Webster

ALS. NhD.

FROM LEVERETT SALTONSTALL

My Dear Sir, Salem Jany 9, 1824

I take the liberty of writing to you concerning our famous Argonaut case. Will it probably come on for argument at the approaching term? Mr. Ogden, who is retained in the case, thinks there is very little chance of it. Judge Story is of the same opinion—but you probably have better

33. Letter not found. Cases not identified.

34. Perhaps DW was bluffing. Henry Wheaton had written to him on November 30, 1823: "I am to argue with you for the Jurisdiction of Admiralty in Insurance but presume it will not come on this term" (mDW 3671).

35. Did DW mean that Story's decisions favored the insurance companies? Certainly, Story's penchant for uniformity and predictability in legal rules operated in the companies' long-term interest.

means of knowing than either of them, & I should esteem it a great favor if you will drop me a line on the subject. It would be very convenient for me to know, on account of other engagements.

If I were not engaged in the cause, I think I should visit Washington this winter for the sake of seeing the Country & the great men in it, but I do not like to go on, under the pretence of business, & for a single cause & then not have it tried. The question of jurisdiction certainly ought to be settled, but it never could come up under more unfortunate circumstances. The vessel is still at Portsmouth wharf & will be utterly lost, & besides is constantly at great expence. The owners will make no arrangement for the sale. It is painful to think of the horrible winding up there must be of the cause—if it is ever finished.

There is nothing new here, except the removal of Mr [John] Pickering & Mr. [Benjamin] Nichols to Boston. It will be a great loss to Salem, Mr. P. particularly. His going is a subject of universal regret here. I shall feel it deeply, having had the habit of daily intercourse with him for many years. While I have been *talking* & *thinking* of the same step, they have decided & are acting. Success attend them.

The most general subject of consideration is the *Greek cause*, & all are looking to the expected Debate upon your motion.[36] I am most truly & respectfy Yr. Friend & Ob. Servt Leverett Saltonstall

ALS. DLC.

TO LEVERETT SALTONSTALL

My Dear Sir, Washington Jan 9. 1825

I have yours of the 3rd. Inst.[37] It would give me great pleasure to oblige you, personally, in regard to the Argonaut; but, under present circumstances I cannot agree to the arrangement you propose.

In the first place, another Gentleman has yet *to prepare* for the argument, if it is to come on; & he will naturally want all the time he can get, after the Court begins. In the next place, my other engagements will incline me to postpone, if possible, all *important* discussions till after the 3rd of March.

This *Jurisdiction*-question will take at least four days; and as I shall find difficulty in being absent from the H. R. for so long a time at once, at a late period of the session, I shall be obliged should it come on early, to ask for *delay* or to give my brief to another. In the third place, I doubt,

36. In the early 1820s DW became a proponent of American support of the Greeks in their struggle for independence from Turkey. On December 8, 1823, he moved in the House of Representatives that the U.S. send a special commissioner to Greece. See *Correspondence*, 1: 332 et seq., and *Speeches*, 1.

37. Not found.

very much, whether the case will come on *at all*; as I hear it said that it is uncertain whether there will be a full Court; and I presume, on a Constitutional question of this magnitude the Court would naturally wish all its members to be present. Subject to these contingencies, and as far as is consistent with these views, we shall seize the earliest opportunity to comply with your wishes, & your clients, & to bring the cause to prompt decision.

We have no news here, likely to be interesting to you. I am passing rather a dull & solitary winter. It will do me good to see the Judge's face,[38] & quite revive me to see you with him. The misfortune of our family affects me, I think, much more than it would do at home, or else it is that I am older than I was ten years ago, & for that reason feel such loss now, more heavily than I did then[39]

Does it ever occur to you, that you & I are *old men*? Such, depend upon it, the boys consider us; & such in truth we are. I thank you & Mrs. S., truly, for your kind sympathy. I know how much, & how severe, has been your experience of similar affliction. Yr's mo. truly D. Webster

I will look tomorrow at the docket—see the No. of the *Argonaut*; & if any thing occurs write you farther.

ALS. DLC.

d. Allocation of Loss

i. Nathaniel S. Ruggles v. *General Interest Insurance Company.* In insurance cases the decisions of the courts often determined who would bear the loss. In the case presented in this section, the court dealt with the relationship between the insurer, the captain, and the insured, Nathaniel Ruggles, a Newport, Rhode Island merchant. Ruggles had purchased the sloop *Harriet* for use in coastal trading. Early in January 1824 he assembled a cargo of staples for shipment to the South. Unable to get insurance for a six-month voyage,[1] he sent the ship uninsured on January 12, 1824. Reports of severe weather along the Carolina coast had made the Rhode Island underwriters reluctant to insure southern voyages. Unknown to Ruggles, on January 19, 1824, the *Harriet* ran aground near Cape Hatteras (Document 93). After the master, Benedict Dayton, and the crew escaped, the *Harriet* washed back into the sea. Dayton knew the *Harriet* had left Newport without insurance. He instructed the crew not to reveal her identity to anyone. He then wrote a letter, dated January 20, to Nathaniel Ruggles's brother Henry, printed below, "suggesting" that Henry tell his brother to obtain insurance as

38. Possibly Story.

39. DW's son Charles died on December 19, 1824, his daughter Grace Fletcher on January 23, 1817.

1. Called a *time policy*, as opposed to insurance for a voyage between specified ports.

quickly as possible. Dayton enclosed this letter in an envelope addressed to his wife.

Meanwhile Nathaniel had continued trying to obtain insurance, but without success. On February 6, 1824, the following report appeared in the Boston *Daily Advertiser*, a newspaper read by Ruggles:

> A schr from the West Indies, with a cargo of molasses, and a coasting sloop from the Northward, were cast away on the night of the 26th. Part of the cargo of the schr was saved and her crew. The crew of the sloop abandoned her the same night—the wind shifted and she was blown off to sea. Nothing could be seen of her the next morning.[2]

Had the date of the wreck in the report been accurate, Ruggles might have become alarmed. Though the *Harriet* seemed overdue, he believed she was well past the Carolinas. On February 8 he sent his brother to Providence to seek insurance once more, while he journeyed to Boston on the same mission. Nathaniel had more luck this time. On the ninth, the General Interest Company agreed to insure the *Harriet* for $3000 at 4.5 percent. A day later, Henry obtained $2000 insurance at the very high rate of 25 percent.[3] That evening Henry received Dayton's letter (Documents 94, 95 and 96). On February 12 Nathaniel learned of the loss of the *Harriet* and abandoned her to the company, printed below.[4] The company, however, refused to pay.

Nathaniel Ruggles hired Webster and Bliss to collect the insurance. They brought suit in federal court at the May 1825 term under the diversity jurisdiction. The principal questions in the case involved the legal effect of the captain's action in concealing the shipwreck and whether Ruggles knew of the wreck when he applied for the insurance on February 9. Both Ruggles and the company's attorney examined several Newport residents in an effort to discover whether word of the wreck had reached Newport before the 9th. The attorney continued the case to the October term.

In preparation for the trial scheduled for October 25, 1825, Ruggles took several more depositions in Newport. He had to provide Webster

2. *Ruggles* v. *General Interest Insurance Company*, USCC,DMass, October 1826. The same report also appeared in New York, see Nathaniel S. Ruggles to General Interest Insurance Company, February 12, 1824, printed below.

3. See p. 498, below.

4. Technically, Ruggles did not have to make the offer of abandonment, since there was an actual wreck. He may not have known the details of the loss or he may have used the language of abandonment to put in his claim. One of the witnesses claimed he read a report of the loss on the tenth (see Document 97, below).

with evidence that the loss of the *Harriet* had not been common knowledge before he left for Boston to purchase the insurance. One of these witnesses almost ruined his case (Document 97). On October 15, 1825, William Gibbs testified that he had been with Ruggles and a group of people on February 8, 1824. He recalled a conversation in which some newly arrived sailors spoke of the wreck of the *Harriet*; after hearing the news, Gibbs continued, Ruggles set out for Boston. On October 20 the insurance company subpoenaed Gibbs. When Gibbs's health prevented his making the trip, the company tried to delay the trial (Document 98). Webster must have resisted this move, because a few days later both sides submitted questions for Gibbs to answer (Documents 99 and 100). On the 24th Gibbs answered the interrogatories (Document 101). His new testimony did not aid the company's case. His recollection grew hazier. It appeared that he had pieced his story together after Ruggles had insured the *Harriet*. To further impugn Gibbs's story, Ruggles took a deposition from the editor of a Newport newspaper. The editor testified that the first credible accounts of the wreck reached Newport on February 10 (Document 102). For the trial, the insurance company's lawyer sought all of Ruggles's papers regarding his relationship with Dayton (Document 103). If the company could establish that Dayton had had a financial stake in the ship or its insured cargo, the captain's actions would bind Ruggles.

After the attorneys presented their evidence, Story summed up the case for the jury.[5] Did the captain's willful omission to communicate the fact of the loss to the owner, with the intent to allow the owner to get insurance, and with innocence on the owner's part, discharge the policy? If it did, it would have to be on the theory that the captain served as the owner's agent, and that his concealment of the information operated as a concealment by the owner. Under the concealment doctrine, this would void the policy. Story told the jury they faced a situation where two innocent parties, the owner and the insurer, sought to shift the loss to the other. Story instructed them that if they found that Ruggles had had no prior knowledge of the wreck, the law would place the risk of loss on the underwriters. When an actual total loss occurred, the law did not require the insured to make an offer of abandonment. At the moment of such loss, the law transferred the insured property (or what was left of it) to the insurer. The captain no longer served as agent of the insured but became the underwriter's agent. Consequently, any action by the captain after that moment would not prejudice the rights of the insured. As in the *Peele* case, above, Story sought to use a precise point in time to determine legal rights.

5. 4 Mason 74 (1825).

The company argued that the master owed a duty to his owner to inform him of the wreck, irrespective of any agency relationship. If a third party was injured because the captain failed to perform that duty, the law should hold the owner responsible. Story resisted this strand of the company's argument. "For what reason should the law interfere between two innocent persons to change a loss, which, by contract, one has engaged to bear?" he asked. The direction of the law of insurance was away from the use of implied warranties to control the risk. "Is it a good public policy to endanger the interests of commerce by new implied warranties? The underwriter can require a warranty, or except the master's acts, or require his negligence to be fatal."[6] The position taken by the courts that men were free to order their relationships by contract meant that courts were less likely to intervene and upset bargained-for expectations.

The second part of the case involved the concealment and misrepresentation. In his argument Webster stressed the facts known at the time. Story instructed the jury that without proof that general news of the wreck existed, or that Ruggles had had specific knowledge of it, no concealment occurred.[7] The burden of proving fraud rested on the underwriters. The jury considered the evidence and then rendered a verdict in favor of Ruggles.

The company did not give up. Its lawyers filed a bill of exceptions (Document 104) for an appeal by writ of error to the Supreme Court. They challenged Story's instruction that if the owner had no knowledge of the loss or the captain's concealment, the law would not bar him from a recovery. Webster apparently did not expect to argue the case if the Court heard it that term. In a letter of January 15, 1826, printed below, he asked to have the record sent to Washington. On the 26th he docketed the case.[8] When the case was carried over a term, Webster decided to argue it with Bliss as co-counsel. In February 1827 the company's lawyers, Henry Wheaton and David Bayard Ogden, recited the same arguments the company had made in the USCC. On March 12, 1827, the Court announced its decision upholding Webster's client.[9] Webster immediately wrote to Bliss, in a letter printed below, with word of the good news.

6. Ibid., pp. 78–79.

7. The defense also raised the issue of misrepresentation over the way Ruggles had applied for the insurance. He pretended that he had mailed a letter of application from Newport. In reality, he had sent it by messenger.

8. Since DW was in Washington, he probably did this as a favor to the company.

9. 12 Wheaton 408 (1827). Justice Smith Thompson also saw it as a case of which innocent party should bear the loss. He rejected the company's argument that favored expanding the concept of agency and implied knowledge.

DOCUMENT 93. DEPOSITION

Boston August 11. 1824

I John J Greenman[10] of Newport in the State of Rhode Island, Mariner, of lawful age, do testify & say, that I was a seaman on board the Sloop Harriet, of Newport, on a voyage from Newport to Charleston, thence to Havanna, and elsewhere. We sailed from Newport, about the tenth day of January last. Benedict Dayton was master, Thomas Lawton mate, Allen Barlow & myself foremast hands, & Thomas Williams a mulatto was cook.[11] Nothing happened of note, untill the nineteenth day of the same January, just a week after we left Newport. At four A. M. the wind blowing from the northward or the northward & eastward, I was called on deck. The wind was fair, with flowing sheets, we went on our course, about two hours, when the Capt. took the helm, & told me to go aloft, to try if I could see Hatteras light, or the land. I came down, not being able to see either. A short time after, the wind increased so much, that we were obliged to call all hands to take in sail. We reefed the main sail, & took the bonnet off the jib. The wind increased so that we were obliged to take in the mainsail & beat the trysail, already for hoisting. After taking in the sail, I went aloft, & saw the light. The Capt steered right for it. He directed us to go into the hold, & get some strong rigging for sheets, for the square sail in case we should have occasion to hoist it to scud under. After we came up, I looked ahead & saw breakers. I also saw the light house & the beach. I sung out to the Capt, that there were breakers ahead, & so did Allen Barlow. The Capt. said never mind my boys, she does not draw but six feet of water, & she will go through it. We were going directly before the wind, & the sliding keel was chock up. All hands cried out Keep off! Keep off! The Captain said, he could not keep off any more, for the jib would not stand. Soon after this, we struck. Allen Barlow said, he would be damned if she was not stuck fast & we should not get off. He hove the lead & found the vessel was fast. A sea struck her, & she struck the bottom again, which threw the Captain off his feet at the helm in the lea becket.[12] The Captain cried out, "what shall we do"? The mate said hoist up the head of the mainsail. The Capt replied you may hoist it, but it will do no good. We hoisted up the head of the square sail. The crew kept singing out. She was fast but the Captain said she will go over boys. The Captain again sung out, what shall we do, the mate said, "get the boat out," & the Capt ordered it to be got out, & went down the Cabin. We launched the boat & the mate & myself went down the Cabin. The mate got out his trunk, & all his things of any value,

10. Not further identified.

11. Not further identified.

12. A becket is a loop of rope, large hook, or wooden bracket used for holding together ropes, oars, spars, etc., and for securing the tacks and sheets of sails.

& put them into the boat. I got out a shirt & pair of trousers only. The Capt saved two trunks. Allen Barlow saved a small bag of clothes. I got into the boat & took the things into it. The Capt & mate got in. The Cook was below, helping Barlow get up his chest. The Capt & mate kept singing out to Barlow, to come up as the boat would leave him. They sung out, we are gone & cut or cast off the warp. The Capt & myself got hold of the bobstays,[13] & Barlow & the Cook came running on deck & got out on the bowsprit, dropped into the boat, & we pushed off. At the time we struck, it was thick & snowing a little. It was from fifteen to twenty minutes not to exceed half an hour, from the time she struck, until we left her. We did not try the pumps, after the sloop struck. We were amongst the breakers, & the sea was washing over us. We were six hours in the boat, steering for the land. We saw the light untill nearly daylight. When we arrived at the beach, at ten o'Clk A.M. about six miles south of the light, we found two or three fishermen, on the beach. Mr Brady[14] & his company, who had come to hawl the seine. He assisted us to haul our boat up, & gave us some refreshment. I staid two or three days with Brady, after which, I went with Barlow & the Cook, to Mr Jennetts.[15] On the afternoon we went ashore, Mr Brady was going to the beach, to look after a Schooner, which went ashore there, & the Capt asked him if he would look for the sloop. When Brady returned, he said he could see nothing of her. Next morning, we all went down to the lighthouse to look for the sloop, but could see or hear nothing of her. It was clear weather. On Wednesday, we went down again, but saw nothing of her. The mate & Captain remained at Bradys, about ten days. We then concluded to give Mr Brady the sloops boat to carry us all to Elizabeth City, & he carried us all there. We started in the morning, & arrived at Elizabeth City, the next day. After we landed, we separated & the cook Barlow & myself remained in the boat, to get dinner & the Capt & mate went together. I shipped on that afternoon, on board the Schooner Rover of Boston Capt Cooper Master.[16] On the same afternoon, we were all together. I parted with the mate, Barlow & the Cook, about eight oClock that night. I left the Captain at sunset, he told me, that they were all going to Norfolk in a horse cart, at day light next morning, & that on his arrival home, he would give an account of the loss of the vessel, & if he did not go home he would write.

Quest by W D Sohier Esq. Counsel of Gen Int Ins Co.

Do you know that any letters were written home from Elizabeth City, giving an account of the wreck of the vessel?

Answer I do not.

By same. Did you write yourself or were you dissuaded from writing?

13. A rope used to draw down the bowsprit of a ship and keep it steady.

14. Not identified.

15. Not identified.

16. Not identified.

Answer. I was going to write, to my mother & sister, but the Captain told me, I had better not, as it would worry them, & they would suppose it was worse than it was.
By same. Do you know whether any protest[17] was made at Cape Hatteras?
Answer. A man who kept school at Cape Hatteras, & acted as a magistrate, one day when we were at the light house, called Capt. Dayton upstairs & said the paper was ready. I do not know what it was. The mans name was Midget.[18]
By same. On your arrival at Elizabeth City, were any enquiries made of you, or the Capt. in your presence, by any printers, or others, where you came from?
Answer. A printer of a Newspaper, called on us & asked us if we belonged to the sloop which was cast away, & wished to know the circumstances. We told him we were requested by the Capt., to say nothing about it. The Captain told Mr Jennett, in the presence of the Crew, that the printer met him in the street, & asked him if he was the master of the sloop, which was cast away, on Cape Hatteras, & that he told the printer he was not the Captain, & that the Captain was somewhere about the town.

John J Greenman

ADS. *Ruggles* v. *General Interest Insurance Company*, USCC,DMass, October 1825.

BENEDICT DAYTON TO HENRY RUGGLES

Dear Sir Hatteras Tuesday Jany. 20th 1824

The object of this is of great *importance* to your brother Nathl[19]—and will not admitt of my writing it to him. It is enough for me to say he should be insured as quick as possible for the value of the Harriet her cargo, outfitts, and freight.

Sloop	4000.—	
Cargo	190.—	shipped by me
Outfitts	112.—	provisions and advance
Freight	180.70	# oil 795 qts @ 30 cts to add
	$4482.70	
	#238 50	
	4721 20	

delays are dangerous and in the event of the abscence of your brother

17. A written statement by the captain to the effect that damage suffered by the ship was caused by storms or other perils of the sea.

18. Not identified.

19. Newport merchant and owner of the *Harriet*.

you had better make insurance as abouve. I have said nothing here which will prevent your doing it with propriety. I will write particulars as soon as I think it wil [torn] & remain Yours truly B. Dayton

NB the oil I forgot to esti[mate]

Copy. *Ruggles* v. *General Interest Insurance Company*, USCC,DMass, October 1825. Henry Ruggles, Nathaniel S. Ruggles's brother.

DOCUMENT 94. DEPOSITION

Boston May 19th. A.D. 1825

I Henry Ruggles of Newport in the State of Rhode Island, Merchant, of lawfull age to give evidence, depose & Say, that I have lived in Newport, R. I. for the last nine or Ten years and have done business in the Same compting house with Nathl. S. Ruggles on my own account & have also assisted him occasionally when he was hurried with bussiness. He bought the Sloop Harriet in the Spring of 1823 and owned the whole of her at the time of her loss; She went on her first voyage to New York the last of May or first of June 1823. Capt. Dayton helped rig her & went master of her from the time She was built untill She was lost in Jany. 1824. She was loaded with Iron, Oil, Rum, Soap, Apples, Potatoes &c taken in for Charleston or Savannah & Sailed for Charlestown the 12 Jany 1824. My Brother Nathl. told me that he applied to the Warren Inse Comp'y to get her Insured for 6 Months, with General Liberty, but they declined unless he would define the voyage She wod. go which he could not do. He then applied to the Marine Inse. Comp'y at Newport for the Same thing & after a week or more time having elapsed, the Secretary told him that they declined taking the risk, as the weather had been so Severe on the Southern Coast after She left Newport. This answer he said was given him Thursday Feby 5, 1824. He then wrote to the Washington & Union Insurance Offices of Providence for Insurance & they replied on Saturday Feby 7. 1824 that they declined taking the risk on account of the severe weather on the Southern Coast after the Harriet Sailed. He Shew me the letters he recd. from Providence the Same evening he got them, viz. Saturday Feby 7. 1824 & told me at the same time that he had wrote to Mr. Thatcher[20] for Insurance but had limited him to Six pr Cent for Six Months and was afraid he should have the same reply from Boston that he had received from Providence, he also Said that the New York paper—which he took, which I believe is the Daily Advertiser gave an account of an arrival at New York on Wednesday or Thursday in four days from Charleston, which gave no account of the Harriet at all. He expressed great fears about her Safety & Stated that

20. David Thacher, Boston merchant.

She was a very fast Sailer & had almost new Sails & rigging & had had good wind to Make a Short passage & what had become of her he could not conceive. He Said that there had been almost continual gales of wind ever Since She Sailed & that the accounts of damage to Coasters was greater than he recollected to have ever seen before. He said he did not Suppose he could get her insured in Boston without giving a very great premium & that he wished me to go to Providence & try to get her Insured, Stating to the Offices that from the time She had been out from Newport, to the last accounts received from Charleston, was so long, that he considered it an extra risk & that he should be willing to pay an extra premium rather than risk the whole of her himself—& in my applications for Insurance I did so. He said that he was in hopes that they might do it for a high premium & that he should be willing to give as high as fifteen or even as twenty or twenty five per cent rather than not have it done at all. Although he hoped I cod. get it done for ten or twelve pr. ct. He Said he wished me to go to Providence the next Monday & try it & that he should go to Boston the next day & be there on Monday & get her Insured if he could & Said that he Should not be obliged to pay but for one premium, as but one Policy could attach to the Same risk & that he was willing to pay the half per cent for filling the policy, in case we both got Insured. He went to Boston the next day which was Sunday & I on the Monday following went to Providence. I stoped at the Warren Insurance Office on my way to Providence & applied for Insurance & they replied that they considered her out of time & shod. decline the risk. I then asked them if they wod. take her at an extra premium. They said no & Stated that they made it a rule to take no risk on a Vessel that they considered out of time. I then went on to Providence and on my arrival there made application to the Washington, the Marine, & the Union Insurance Offices, for Insurance on the Sloop & Stated that as this was the Second application to them for Insurance on the Same risk, that I considered the Vessel out of time & Shod. be willing to pay a premium in proportion to the risk. This was on Monday afternoon Feby 9. 1824 & that evening I received an answer from each of them that they declined. The Union & Marine said they wod. not take her on any terms.

Mr. Jackson the President of the Washington Office[21] Said that he wod. mention it to Some of the Gentlemen of the Office when they came in that evening & perhaps they might be willing to write If I would give them a high premium & added that If I would come in the next morning that he would let me know what they said. The next morning I went to the Office & after some conversation upon the subject, he shew me in one of the papers an account of an Eastern Sloop that had ran on Shore & that the crew had left her & that she had drove to Sea, & also an ac-

21. Richard Jackson, not further identified.

count in the Boston Palladium of an other Vessel that had met with a dissaster on the Southern Coast, which he Said Might be the Harriet. In addition to which he Said that there had a Vessel arrived at Bristol in a Verry Short passage from Charleston (I forget the number of days) which did not report the Harriet. After much talk on both Sides upon the probability of the risk, I think that he Said that they would take the risk at 33 p Ct. which I declined. I am not possitive however that he named 33 p Ct. though I have an indistinct recollection of that premium being named. After further talk I Said that I shod. prefer Insuring $2000 If I had to give so high a premium & Mr. Jackson finally Said that they would take the risk at 25 pr Ct.—& that that was the lowest that they wod. do it at. I told him that I could not give that premium and soon after left the Office with a determination to go home; but after I returned to Hortons Hotel & considered of all the objection that Mr. Jackson had Made against the risk—and also that if my Brother got Insured at all in Boston that it wod probably be on Monday, and that he would there give such a premium as he wod. agree to himself on the Spot. I concluded to go back & get $2000 Insured knowing that If he affected Insurance in Boston that this policy would be void as it wod. be made one day later than his, & that the only expence would be the half per Cent for cancelling the policy and I further considered from *his great anxiety* at Newport, before he left there for Boston, that he would be willing to get this much done even at the high premium asked, rather than run the risk of the Whole of her himself & with these impressions I went back to the Office & after ascertaining to my Satisfaction that they would not do it for any less, I agreed to the terms & the policy was filled accordingly & given to me & I gave a Note for the premium. This was on Tuesday Feby 10. 1824 about Eleven o,clock in the forenoon. I then returned home & about dark that evening I was standing at the foot of King Street in Company with three or four gentlemen, when Mr. Anthony V. Taylor came up and said that Mrs. Dayton had received a letter from her husband by that evenings mail which contained a Note for me & handed it to me, after reading it I concluded that some misfortune must have befell the Sloop.[22] I then walked up Street with Mr. Taylor & soon met Mr Barber[23] the printer of the Mercury who told us that he had just got a paper out of the Mail, the Philadelphia Aurora which gave an account of the Sloop Harriet being Seen at Sea without any body on board of her & that a Seamans chest was seen open on deck. I considered her after all this information as lost beyond doubt, and as my Brother was still absent I considered it my duty to abandon the Sloop to the Office; which I did the next day &

22. Anthony V. Taylor, Newport trader; Catherine Dayton, Benedict's wife. The letter is reproduced above.

23. John H. Barber, at this time publisher of the *Mercury* in partnership with his brother, William.

stated the information that I did it upon. I received a letter from Mr. Jackson asking for a copy of Capt. Daytons Note to me which I furnished him with.

Capt Daytons Note and the News by the Aurora was the first and the only information that I had or any one else to my knowledge about the Harriet, up to the time of my abandonment, and it came to me as before Stated Tuesday evening Feby 10. 1824 after sunset. When my Brother returned from Boston I gave him the policy & have had nothing to do with the business Since.

Question by William D. Sohier Esquire, Counsel for the General Interest Assurance Company.

1 For what purpose was the Sloop Harriet built, and for what purpose was she used previous to her said voyage to Charlestown and Savannah?

Answer. She was built for the coasting and packeting trades, and had not been employed previous to her said Voyage to New York. I do not recollect distinctly how many trips she made. She returned from New York to Newport remained there a while, she then went south, I believe as far as Charlestown, from Charlestown to Richmond, and then to New York with wheat and from New York to Newport. I do not recollect the exact order of the voyages. She was built with a center board or sliding keel. She was built by John A. Saunders,[24] of (I believe) South Kingston R. I.

2 Question by same. In what parts or portion of the Cargo of the Harriet on her last voyage, was Nathaniel S. Ruggles interested and to what amount?

Answer. The oil, potatoes and apples he was interested in. The oil he owned wholly. The potatoes and apples were bought under a particular contract—to be paid for in case of their arrival out in safety. The particulars of this contract I learned only from conversation with Capt. Dayton. The oil I knew to be his. Ten Hogsheads of rum belonged to John G. and Lemuel Whitehorne;[25] about twenty seven tons of iron belonged to a Mr. Rogers[26] of Providence. There were some other articles on board; the owners of which I do not know.

3 Question. Do you know, or have you heard that Capt. Dayton had any interest directly or indirectly in the said Sloop or cargo in her last voyage?

Answer. I am positive he did not own any part of the Sloop, And believe he had no interest in the cargo. I understood at the time, but how, I do not recollect, that he was interested in the freight, but to what extent I do not know.

4 Question by Same. Did you ever see, or do you know the existence

24. Not further identified.

25. Not identified.

26. Not identified.

of any writing or agreement between said Dayton and your brother Nathaniel S. respecting the cargo of said Sloop on the voyage aforesaid?
Answer. No—I understood, but from whom I do not remember, that there was not a written contract—but a verbal one.

5 Question by same. Do you know, and have severally known all the dealings transactions and concerns, in which your brother Nathaniel S. has been engaged for two or three years last past?
Answer. I have a general knowledge of his business—but not a very minute knowledge. He keeps no clerk, and I assist him when he needs assistance.

6 Question by the Same. Who were the persons, with whom you were conversing in King Street, when Taylor delivered you the letter from Dayton.
Answer. Capt. Robinson Potter, Robert Robinson & I think Capt. James B. Phillips.[27]

7 *Question by same.* Have you the letter you then received from Benedict Dayton?
Answer. I have not. I gave it to my brother Nathl. S. soon after his return from Boston, and have not had it since.

8 Question by same. Did you transmit to Richard Jackson, President of the Providence Washington Insurance office, on or about the 14th day of February 1824 a true and accurate copy of said letter?
Answer. I did.

9 Question by Same. Had you any instructions, as to the amount of premium, from your brother, before he left Newport for Boston, on the 8th. day of February 1824?
Answer. He said he expected to give a high premium, that I might go as high as 25 Per cent, and if I found it necessary to go above that sum to use my own discretion.

10 Question by Same. When did your brother Nathl S. return from Boston, and were you the first person to communicate the loss of the Harriet to him?
Answer. He returned in the course of the same week that I got Insurance at Providence. I think the latter part of the week. I do not know whether I was the first to communicate the information. I now recollect that he told me that he heard of it on the Island on his return from Boston.

11 Question by Same. Did you ever see any letters from Capt. Dayton, addressed to any person, after he left Newport on the last voyage—except that delivered you by Mr. Taylor?
Answer. I saw a letter from Capt. Dayton to his wife, I think dated at Norfolk, which was shown to me the same evening that I received the

27. Newport merchants.

note from Capt. Dayton said to have covered the one received by me. The date of said letter I do not recollect. I never saw any other letter. I heard there was another letter but did not see it.

12 *Question by same.* Do you know whether your brother Nathaniel S. received any letter from Capt. Dayton during his last voyage?
Answer. I do not.

13 *Question by Same.* Who remained in charge of your brother's business or your own while you were both absent as above mentioned?
Answer. My brother's wife remained at Newport, but whether there was any business left in charge with any one I do not know. I left no business in charge of any one.

14 Question by same. With whom did you transact the business at the Washington office?
Answer. The contract was made with Mr. Jackson. The Secretary filled out the policy.

15 Question by same. Was there any other application to any other office, than those above mentioned for Insurance on the Harriet.
Answer. My brother made application to the Bedford office. I saw him writing a letter, w[hich] he said was an application to the Bedford offi[ce.]

[16 Question by same. To whom was the letter addressed?]
[Answer] The letter was addressed to Mr. Coggeshall of Newbedford. The letter was written Saturday evening February 7th. 1824. I saw the answer of Mr. Coggeshall[28] to my brother informing him that the office declined taking the risk.

17 " By same. Did you exhibit written proposals to the offices, where you applied for insurance.
Answer. I did. They were in my own hand writing.

18 Question By Same. Have you any connexion in business with your brother, or had you at that time?
Answer. No.

19 Question by Same. Which was the first application, to your knowledge, for Insurance, and when did you first know of any intention, on the part of your brother, to apply for insurance?
Answer. I never heard any thing on the Subject 'til. Saturday the 7th of February. I had supposed, up to that time, that insurance had been obtained. It was his usual practice.

20 Question by Same. What Newspapers printed in Boston, are usually taken in Newport?
Answer. The Palladium, Daily Advertiser, Centinel, Gazette and some others.

28. John Coggeshall, Jr. to Nathaniel S. Ruggles, February 10, 1824, *Ruggles* v. *General Interest Insurance Company*, USCC,DMass, October 1825. Coggeshall has not been further identified.

Ques. by same. Has your brother Nathl. S. ever been President of an Insurance Company?
Answer. Yes. He was President of the Ocean Insurance Company.

Henry Ruggles

ADS. *Ruggles* v. *General Interest Insurance Company,* USCC,DMass, October 1825.

DOCUMENT 95. DEPOSITION

Little Compton [Rhode Island] 4 March 1824

Newport (SC) State of Rhode Island &c &c

Anthony V. Taylor of Newport Trader being duly cautioned & sworn in answer to the following interrogatories deposeth & sayeth.
Interrogatories on the part of the Gen. Assurance Company in Boston.
1st. Did you early in feb. last take a letter or a piece of paper addressed to Henry Ruggles from Capt. Benedict Dayton. If so, on what day did you do so & what did that paper contain as well as you can recollect.
Ansr. I took a paper wearing the appearance of a sealed letter from Mrs. Dayton wife to Captn Benedict Dayton & delivered it to Mr. Henry Ruggles the contents I did not know—& delivered sd. letter to Mr. Ruggles on the tenth day of February last.

Anthy. V. Taylor

ADS. *Ruggles* v. *General Interest Insurance Company,* USCC,DMass, October 1825.

DOCUMENT 96. INTERROGATORIES

Newport 13th, October AD 1825

Catharine Dayton of the Town & County of Newport & State of R. Isd, of lawful age to give evidence on solemn oath, in answer to the following interrogatories, declares and says
Intg 1st. by Pltffs. Are you Wife of Capt Benedict Dayton
Answer—I am
Intg By same. Did you receive one or two Letters from your Husband on Tuesday Feby 10. 1824, and if so who brought them to you.
Answer—I recd. two Letters from my Husband on that Day: brought to me by John Tillinghast.[29]
Intg By same. Did you receive any other Letters or any intelligence from him of any sort or kind from the 12th Jany 1824 until you received the Letters by the Tuesday evenings mail Feby 10th. 1824.
Answer. I did not from my Husband or any one else.

29. Not identified.

Intg. by Defts. What became of said Letters? were they destroyed? If so how long after you recd them? in what manner, by whom, in whose presence, and why were they so destroyed.
Answer. I burnt them the next Day after I received them; there was no one present when I burnt them. I have been in the habit of destroying the Letters I receive from my Husband. My Husband has always been in the habit of writing to me very frequently, and if I did not some time destroy them, they would be in the way.
Intg by same. Did both or either of said Letters contain a Letter or Letters for any other person or persons: If so please to name the person or persons?
Answer. In one of these Letters there was, a Letter for Henry Ruggles—the other Letter had none in it.
Intg by same. At what time and where, were these letters respectively dated.
Answer. I do not recollect the date or the place.
Intg by same. When and by whom was the Letter directed to Henry Ruggles sent to him.
Answer. The same Day I received it; about half past seven in the evening, by my Brother.
Intg by same. Were all the Letters which came to your hands and were written by your husband in Feby 1824, addressed on the outside to you by your proper name? Were any such Letters directed to the care of any one.
Answer. They were all addressed to me in my own name and not to the care of any one.
Intg by same. Have you seen or ever heard of one or more Letters written by your husband at or after the time of his being at Cape Hatteras in Jany or Feby 1824 which was addressed to any other person than yourself.
Answer. I have not.
Intg by same. Did you ever hear your husband say or do you know that he has said that he had written any other Letters from Cape Hatterass, Elizabeth City, Norfolk or any other place respecting the situation of himself, the Harriet or her Crew, except the two Letters received by you as above stated. (waived, being objected to as an improper question).
Intg by Same. Is or are there in Newport any person or persons surnamed Dayton except yourself, husband & immediate family, and do you know or have you reason to believe that your husband directed any Letter to either or any of such persons in the months of Jany or Feby 1824.
Answer. I know of only one person except our family of the name of Dayton; and he John Dayton,[30] is Crazy and in the Asylum; his mother

30. Not further identified.

is in New Bedford I have no reason to believe that my husband directed any Letters to either of them.
Intg by same. Did any person or persons at any time after you received said two Letters the 10th Feby 1824 inform you that doubts respecting the situation and safety of the Harriet had been previously entertained; If so declare fully upon this particular subject.
Answer. Not that I recollect.
Intg by same. Did you at any time and when and where state that before you received said Letters your friends looked strange and as if they had news of the Sloop Harriet, or make any remark of like import.
Answer. I do not recollect of ever having said any such thing.
Intg by same. Did you ever shew to any person or persons or permit any person to read or see both or either of said two letters, recd by you the 10th. Feby 1824.
Answer. Not any one
Intg by same. Was Mr Nathl S Ruggles at your House during your husbands absence, on that voyage
Answer. He was not, nor has not been since, until this Evening.

Catherin Dayton

ADS. *Ruggles* v. *General Interest Insurance Company*, USCC,DMass, October 1825.

TO DAVID THATCHER FROM NATHANIEL S. RUGGLES

Sir New Port Feby 12, 1824

For will you be so good as to carry the above abandonment to the Mr Otis[31] Prest of the Gen Int Ins Co. & leave it with him. I have not heard one word from Capt Dayton & know no more about it than I see in the newspapers which I presume you have seen I am verry sorry for the loss of the favourite vessell but I presume it was owing to some event that no human power could controul as I know Capt Dayton would do all that any man could do—In haste N S Ruggles

[Enclosure]
TO THE GENERAL INTEREST INSURANCE COMPANY FROM NATHANIEL S. RUGGLES

Genn. Newport Feby 12, 1824

Having read in a Newyork paper this day the loss of the Sloop Harriet Capt Dayton Insured at your office induces me to abandon her to

31. Joseph Otis, not further identified.

you & I hereby abandon to you all my interest in said Sloop & Cargo as far as you insured on the same & claim of you the ammount insured in Policy No. 111 written at your office on the ninth instant

Nathl S Ruggles

Copy. *Ruggles* v. *General Interest Insurance Company*, USCC,DMass, October 1825.

DOCUMENT 97. DEPOSITION

Newport 15th October AD 1825

I William C Gibbs[32] of the Town & County of Newport & State of Rhode Island &c Esq. of lawful age to give evidence on solemn oath declare and say, That on the Evening of the Day Mr Ruggles left Newport, being Sunday Evening; I was at Townsends Corner, where there was a large collection of people; some one observed that Mr Ruggles had gone to Boston to effect insurance on his Sloop. It was then stated, that there was a Sloop on shore at Cape Hatteras which was supposed to be Mr Ruggle's Sloop. My impression is that the question was asked, how the news came which was answered, that it was brought by some sailors from Newyork. I have since enquired of those whom I supposed held this conversation, but they one and all positively deny having heard it, and some do not even recollect being there, except Mr Potter, who observed, if the loss of the Sloop had been known on that Evening, he should recollect it, and that it would have been known to all the commercial men in the Town; but that there were many things said at their occasional meetings in their loose way of conversing which if taken literally might effect the character or interest of any individual. I am still, however, confident there was conversation held on that Evening respecting Mr Ruggle's Sloop; but whether it was made up to amuse spectators, I am unable to say. As the conversation was held nearly two years since, it is possible, I may have been deceived or mistaken as to some of the facts as I took no minutes at the time, and I have since heard much conversation respecting the loss of the Sloop and it is probable I may have connected some of the facts together.

Interrogatory by Nathl. S. Ruggles. How did you know what Day Mr Ruggles left Newport; what Day and year was it?

Answer. I did not know what Day he left Town until I went to Townsends Corner on Sunday Evening, where I learnt from some one I think Capt Potter, that Mr Ruggles had that Day left Town; as to what Day of the month it was I do not recollect; but it was in the month of February 1824.

32. Not further identified.

Intg. by same. Who said Mr Ruggles had gone to effect insurance on his Sloop.
Answer. I do not recollect.

* * * *

Intg. by same. You say you are confident there was conversation about the Sloop Harriet on that Evening; did not that conversation arise out of the Sloops being supposed to be out of time. Have you not doubts in your mind now as to what was precisely said, and what its import was.
Answer. The conversation did not so arrise to my knowledge. I do not pretend to give the conversation precisely—as to the import of the conversation I have already stated my impressions.

* * * *

Intg. by same. Do you believe from all you have seen & heard that Mr Ruggles knew the loss of his Vessel before he went to Boston in February 1824.
Answer. From all I have seen and heard I do not believe that he knew or had heard of the loss of his Vessel.

* * * *

Intg. by same. Who was the individual that supposed the Sloop said to be on shore was Mr Ruggles'?
Answer. I do not know
Intg. by same. Is it your impression, and was it then, that the news had come on that Day viz the Day this conversation was held?
Answer. It was then my impression that the news arrived on Sunday, but I have learnt to the contrary since.
Intg. by same. Do you mean by the word "deny" that the persons who you went to for information and correction felt themselves accused of withholding any fact in their knowledge, as that they did not recollect what you thought you did.
Answer. I only mean by that word, that they had no recollection of any such conversation having taken place at Townsends Corner, and as they told me they thought no such conversation could have been had there in their presence without their recollecting it.
Intg. by same. Do you not think it very probable you are correct in facts but mistaken in dates.
Answer. I think not.
Intg. by same. You say it is possible you have connected some of the facts together; do you mean by that, that some of the facts you heard since that time have formed the idea in your mind, and that you have erroneously thought you heard it at the period you fix viz the Sunday Evening before named.
Answer. I have heard a good deal of conversation relative to this subject, and am sensible how difficult it is to disconnect in ones mind the cir-

cumstances which happened and the conversation that passed at the time, from that which has occurred since but I am not sensible of having done so in this case.

* * * *

Intg. by R K Randolph, Esq.[33] on the part of the Defendants

* * * *

Intg. by same. Are you confident that you heard a conversation at Townsend corner at the time you mention in which it was stated by some one that Ruggles Sloop of which Dayton was master had been lost or cast away.
Answer. I am confident there was conversation about the loss of Mr Ruggles Sloop; whether it was an actual or supposed loss, I am not able to say.

* * * *

Intg. by same. Have you been summoned to attend the Circuit Court of the United States at Boston as a Witness on behalf of the Defendants in the case of N S Ruggles against the General Interest Assurance Company? And is it your intention to be there or not.
Answer. I have been summoned; it will depend on circumstances whether I go or not.
Intg. by same. Will you state those circumstances.
Answer. I think it very doubtful whether my health will admit of my going.

Wm C Gibbs

Extract. *Ruggles* v. *General Interest Insurance Company,* USCC,DMass, October 1825.

DOCUMENT 98. AFFIDAVIT

Boston 20th. Octr. 1825.

I Joseph Otis, President of the General Interest Assurance Company doth depose & say that William C Gibbs of Newport in the State of Rhode Island Esquire, & Bendict Dayton of said Newport Master Mariner, are material witnesses in the trial of the Case of Nathaniel S. Ruggles against the said Company upon a policy of Insurance upon the Sloop Harriet & her Cargo—that he expects to prove by the said Gibbs & he verily believes that if said Gibbs is produced on the stand he will swear, that on Sunday Evening of the eighth day of February in the year of our Lord eighteen hundred & twenty four, he was at a place in said Newport called Townsends Corner, where a number of persons were assembled, & he there heard it stated that Mr Ruggles—the Plf—had

33. Richard K. Randolph, Rhode Island lawyer, state legislator.

that day gone to Boston to effect insurance on his Sloop called the Harriet—& that he also at the same time & place heard it stated that there was a Sloop on Shore at Cape Hatteras, which was supposed to be the Sloop belonging to Mr Ruggles—& that on the enquiry being made, in what manner the News came, it was stated, according to his best recollection that the news was brought by some sailors from New York—that he will swear that he is certain as to the fact that he heard this news on the Sunday Evening of the very day that Mr Ruggles went to Boston to effect insurance on his Sloop the Harriet & that it was not at a later period, not having been out of his house for ten days after said Sunday evening—but that he will not be able to swear with certainty who was or were the person or persons that mentioned the news in his hearing;—that the grounds of this Deponent's expectation of being able to prove the said facts by Mr. Gibbs are derived from reports made to this Deponent by individuals to whom said Gibbs communicated the same, and also from being apprised that said Gibbs has in fact deposed in substance to the facts above stated at the instance of the plaintiff;[34]—that the endeavors which have been made to procure his attendance on the trial of the cause are these—that he caused him to be duly summoned to attend as a witness on the trial of this cause on the nineteenth and twentieth days of this present month & did cause his fees for his travel and attendance to be tendered and paid to him—and that this summons was served upon him on the twenty sixth day of September last—& that on yesterday the said subpoena was returned to Boston, & there was received this day from Mr. Gibbs a certificate of his physician, stating that with his complaints it will not be proper for him to ride at this time under the course of medicine he is pursuing—and this deponent believes that his attendance can be procured at the next term of this Court, & he is advised that without such testimony he cannot safely proceed to trial.

* * * *

Joseph Otis

Extract. *Ruggles* v. *General Interest Insurance Company*, USCC,DMass, October 1825.

DOCUMENT 99. DEFENDANT'S INTERROGATORIES

October 22, 1825

Circuit Court U S. Masstts District Oct 1825

Nathl S Ruggles vs The General Interest Assce Co

Interrogatories to be administered to William C Gibbs Esquire of New-

34. See Document 97, preceding.

port in the State of Rhode Island a witness to be produced sworn & examined on the part & behalf of the General Interest Assurance Company defendant in a certain cause now depending in the Circuit Court of the United States Massachusetts District, in which cause Nathaniel S Ruggles is Plf

1 Do you know the parties Plf and deft in the title to these interrogatories named or either & which of them And how long have you known them or either & which of them?

2 Do you reside in Newport? If so, how long have you resided in that place?

3 Were you or not in any & what day, in the month of February in the year 1824, at a place, in said town of Newport, called "Townsends Corner" If you were, state on what occasion you were at that place & by what circumstances are you enabled at this time to recollect the time of your being present there

4 Did you on the Evening of Sunday the 8th of Feby 1824 or at any other time in said month & when hear any & what conversation respecting the loss or stranding of any Sloop or vessell of which Nathaniel S. Ruggles was the owner; or in which he had any interest? If so, state what you heard upon the subject of this enquiry & all the particulars of such conversation fully & at large according to the best of your knowledge

5 Did you or not in the even'g of Sunday the 8th of Feby 1824 or at any other time in said month, & when for the first time, hear any rumour or report in Newport, aforesaid that any Sloop or vessell belonging at Newport to said Ruggles had been cast-away wrecked or stranded at any & what place and did you or not at the same time learn or hear through what channel or by what means such rumour or report reached Newport? Declare the several matters inquired after by this interrogatory fully & at large according to the best of your knowledge & belief

6 Do you or not know that the Ptf did or did not leave Newport on Sunday the 8th. of February 1824 for the purpose of going to Boston to effect insurance? or for any other & what purpose?

7 Did you or not hear the rumor or report above enquire after, on the evening of the same day, on which said Ruggles went to Boston?

8 Do you know, or can you state any other matter or thing, or circumstances which can aid the defendants in this suit? If so declare the same fully & at large, as if you had been particularly interrogated thereunto.

W. D. Sohier for Defts

ADS. *Ruggles* v. *General Interest Insurance Company*, USCC,DMass, October 1825.

DOCUMENT 100. CROSS INTERROGATORIES

Ruggles v Gen Int Ass Co.
Cross ints to be proposed to Wm. C. Gibbs.

1. Have you, before this time, given a Deposition for this cause? If yea, does that deposition contain all you know relative to the subject for which that Deposition was taken? If not, what do you wish now to add?—and when, & before whom, was that Deposition taken?
2. Do you now undertake to swear, that you distinctly remember to have heard of the loss of the Sloop Harriet, on the Sunday Evening, of which you have spoken in your former Deposition?—or is this only an impression, or vague belief, resting on your mind?
3. Are you confident, that you have not in your statement referred to Sunday Evening, conversations which happened afterwards; or may not the conversations & discourses which you have heard on this subject have confused your recollection?
4. Can you state the day of the month, and the year, in which you think you heard this consideration?[35]
5. Who was present, at the conversation which you think you heard respecting the loss of the Harriet, on the Sunday Evening?—please name all persons who were present?
6. When did you first mention that you heard such a conversation on the Sunday Evening? To whom did you first mention it, & on what occasion?
7. Did you, in the course of Sunday Evening, or Monday, or on Tuesday before Evening, mention to any one that Mr. Ruggles had gone to get an insurance, after hearing of the loss of the Vessel? Did you know for what purpose Mr. Ruggles had gone to Boston? If you did, & had heard of the loss, should you not naturally have mentioned it?
8. At the time you say you heard conversation about the loss, was any thing said of Mr Ruggles' going to Boston to get insurance?
9. Will you please to state, in regard to this matter, distinctly, what you distinctly remember; and distinguish what you can positively swear to, as facts, from what you think you have an impression of, or a vague or indistinct notion of recollecting?
10. Have you had any conversation with Mr. Christopher Fowler,[36] on this subject? If yea, when & where was that conversation had—

35. DW meant "conversation."

36. Fowler testified that he heard on Sunday the 8th that Mrs. Dayton had received a letter. He had then formed an impression that the *Harriet* was lost. Fowler's testimony could be easily contradicted since the letter arrived on the 10th. If Gibbs had spoken with Fowler, that could account for Gibbs's story. (*Ruggles* v. *General Interest Insurance Company*, USCC,DMass, October 1825.)

and what was it?—please to state it all. State, among other things, whether you asked Mr Fowler to keep that conversation, or any part of it, private?

D Webster for N. S. Ruggles

ADS(DW). *Ruggles* v. *General Interest Insurance Company*, USCC,DMass, October 1825.

DOCUMENT 101. ANSWERS TO INTERROGATORIES

Newport 24th October AD 1825.

William C Gibbs of the Town and County of Newport & State of Rhode Island and Providence Plantations, Esqr, a witness adduced by the Defendants, in the case Nathaniel S Ruggles vs General Interest Assurance Company, who being by me, duly examined cautioned and sworn, in answer to the annexed Interrogatories on solemn oath declares and says—

In answer to the first Interrogatory he declares and says, that he knows but one of said parties viz Nathl. S Ruggles, and him he has known about seven years.

In answer to the Second Interrogatory he declares and says that he was born in Newport and has always resided there except about seven years of the time he was absent; that he returned to Newport in 1817 and has remained there ever since.

In answer to the third Interrogatory he declares and says that he was at Townsends Corner on the Sunday Evening Mr N S Ruggles went to Boston in February 1824; that it was not on any particular occasion that he was there at said Corners; that he was taking a walk and accidently stopped there. The circumstances which inable him to recollect the time were in particular, an application he made about that time to Mr Ruggles to purchase some window glass for him in Boston; that application he made as aforesaid the Friday previous, on which Day he went to Mr Ruggles' House and examined a specimen of the glass; that on that day, Friday, Mr Ruggles said he should go to Boston the following week; that this Deponent then said to Mr Ruggles that he would give him an answer about the glass before he went to Boston, and Mr Ruggles said he would make the purchase for him; that when this Deponent found or learnt at Townsends Corner, that Mr Ruggles had that day gone to Boston he was disappointed; that he was confined at home, by indisposition, the whole of Sunday, but took a walk in the Evening as far as Townsends where he remained only a few minutes; that he was confined to his House the succeeding ten days or thereabouts; that in March 1824 he had a conversation with Christopher Fowler, Eq. relative to what passed at Townsends Corner on said Sunday Evening: He was induced to speak to Mr

Fowler on that subject, in consequence of said Fowlers appearing to be very much depressed in his spirits on account of his not being able to find any one else that was at Townsends Corner on said Sunday Evening; this Deponent then stated to Mr Fowler that he also was there at that time: That in the month of March 1824 he had a conversation with Capt Robinson Potter at Newyork on the subject of what passed at Townsends Corner on said Sunday Evening.

In answer to the fourth Interrogatory he declares and says; that on the aforesaid Sunday Evening in February 1824 whilst at Townsends Corner as aforesaid he heard some one say or state that there was a Sloop on Shore at Cape Hatteras, supposed to be Mr Ruggles, that his impression is, that the question was then asked, how the news came, and that some person then present observed that it was brought by some Sailors from Newyork.

In answer to the fifth Interrogatory he declares and says, that he knows nothing in relation thereto, further than what he has stated in his answer to the fourth Interrogatory, excepting, that the first of his hearing any thing about the loss of the Sloop mentioned as aforesaid, was at Townsends Corner on said Sunday Evening in February 1824.

In answer to the Sixth Interrogatory he declares and says, that he does not know that Mr Ruggles left Newport on that day for the purpose of going to Boston to effect insurance; but he heard, as he has already said, on the Sunday Evening in February 1824 at Townsends Corner, some one say, that Mr Ruggles had that Day gone to Boston to make insurance on said Sloop.

In answer to the Seventh Interrogatory he declares and says, that he knows nothing in relation thereto other than what he has stated in his answer to the fourth Interrogatory.

In answer to the Eighth Interrogatory, he declares and says that he knows nothing further that can aid the Defendants in said suit.

In answer to the first Cross Interrogatory he declares and says that he gave his Deposition on Saturday fifteenth of October 1825 to be used in the case referred to, said Deposition was taken before Henry Y Cranston[37] the same person who is now administering interrogatories to the Deponent, and that Deposition contains all that this Deponent knows in relation to the subject for which it was taken, and that he does not wish to add anything further thereto.

In answer to the Second cross Interrogatory he declares and says that he does not now undertake so to swear, but he distinctly recollects to have heard a conversation relative to the loss or supposed loss of a Sloop said to have been Mr Ruggle's, as he has stated in his answer to the fourth interrogatory.

37. Henry Cranston, Rhode Island lawyer.

In answer to the third cross Interrogatory he declares and says he is confident or feels confident that he has not in his statement, referred to Sunday Evening, conversations which happened afterwards, nor is he aware that his recollection has, on the subject referred to been confused, although it is possible it may have been.

In answer to the fourth cross Interrogatory he declares and says, that it was in February 1824 and on Sunday Evening as he has before stated.

In answer to the fifth cross Interrogatory he declares and says he does not distinctly recollect any one that was there, but thinks that Capt Robinson Potter and Robert Robinson were there.

In answer to the Sixth cross Interrogatory he declares and says that he first mentioned the conversation to Mr Fowler as stated in his answer to the third Interrogatory and on the occasion as therein stated.

In answer to the Seventh cross Interrogatory he declares and says that he never did mention to any persons, as asked, that Mr Ruggles had gone to get insurance, after he had heard of the loss of his Vessel; that he did not know for what purpose Mr Ruggles had gone to Boston, except as he has already stated; that if he had known for what purpose Mr. Ruggles had gone to Boston, and had heard of said loss, he thinks it doubtful whether he should have mentioned it or not.

In answer to the Eighth cross Interrogatory he declares and says that at the time he heard the conversation about the loss, he heard something said about Mr Ruggles going to Boston to get insurance as he has before stated.

In answer to the ninth cross Interrogatory he declares and says he distinctly remembers that there was a conversation at Townsends Corner the Sunday Evening before referred to relative to the loss or supposed loss of Mr Ruggle's Sloop, and that he cannot further distinguish.

In answer to the tenth and last cross Interrogatory he declares and says that in March 1824 he had a conversation with Mr Fowler, and he thinks it was at said Fowlers Store; that he does not particularly recollect the conversation which took place at that time, and that he did request Mr Fowler to keep said conversation private.

Wm C Gibbs

ADS. *Ruggles* v. *General Interest Insurance Company*, USCC,DMass, October 1825.

DOCUMENT 102. DEPOSITION

Newport 17th. October 1825

John H Barber of the Town & County of Newport & State of Rhode Island &c of lawful age to give evidence on solemn oath declares and says in answer to the following Interrogatories

Intg. 1st. by Nathl. S Ruggles. Are you Editor of the Newport Mercury? If yea, are you in the habit of collecting marine news for said paper?
Answer. I am one of the Editors of said Paper; and am in the habit of collecting marine news for the same.
Intg by same. At what time did you first hear of the loss of the sloop Harriet, Benedict Dayton Master.
Answer. We first received it on Tuesday the 10th February 1824, in the Philadelphia Freemans Journal.
Intg by same. Do you keep a Reading Room in your office where Gentlemen resort to tell and hear the news of the day, particularly marine news.
Answer. We keep a reading Room where Gentlemen resort to read and hear the news of the Day.
Intg by same. Could the news of the loss of the Harriet have been in Town two or three Days without your having heard it.
Answer. I think not.
Intg by same. Would news or rumours of such an event as the loss of a Vessel belonging to this Town have escaped your hearing for two or three Days
Answer. I think it could not.
Intg by same. Do not the same people as many of them who resort to Townsends Corner on Sunday Evenings as well as other times also visit your office at all times of Day.
Answer. Yes many of them.
Intg. by same. If a report had circulated or any rumour of the loss of the Sloop Harriet at Townsends Corner on Sunday Evening 8th February would it not have reached you before Tuesday night 10t Feby 1824.
Answer. I think it would
Intg by same. Are you not in the habit of visiting Townsends Corner yourself on Sunday Evenings, and were you there on Sunday Evening 8th Feby 1824.
Answer. I seldom visit that corner on Sunday Evenings or any other; I was not there on the Evening of 8th Feby 1824.
Intg by same. Do you know or believe that there was any Vessel arrived here from Norfolk within the space of ten days before Sunday Evening 8th Feby 1824, excepting the Sloop Massachusetts Capt Sanford.[38]
Answer. I do not recollect
Intg by same. Do you know or believe that any Vessel or Vessels arrived here with Sailors as passengers from Norfolk direct or by the way of any port within ten days of the 8th Feby 1824, except the Sloop Massachusetts which arrived Monday 2d Feby, and the Sloop George Washington

38. Not identified.

Capt Swaine,[39] who arrived here on Wednesday 4th or Thursday 5t Feby by the way of N York.
Answer. I do not recollect.
Int by same. Did not most all the Citizens you conversed with know of the loss of the Harriet before Wednesday noon after the news of her loss came on Tuesday night, or do you not think it was very generally known by all classes throughout the Town in a few hours after the news arrived on Tuesday evening.
Answer. It was.

Intg. by R K Randolph, Esq on the part of Defendants. Who are the persons who are in the habit of visiting Townsends Corner on Sunday Evenings name as many as you can.
Answer. Robinson Potter, Nicolas Geffray, Ths R Gardiner, David M Coggeshall, Robert P Lee, Nathaniel Ruggles, John Dunwell, Henry Bull, George Hale,[40] William Barber and many others.
Intg. by same. Name also such of them as are in the habit of visiting your Reading Room
Answer. Geffray, Coggeshall, Lee, Ruggles & Dunwell, William Barber is always there being my Brother and partner.
Intg by same. you say you are not in the habit of visiting Townsends corner on Sunday Evenings or at any other time; how do you know who are in that habit.
Answer. I am frequently in the habit of passing there on Sunday Evening and notice who are there.
Intg. by same. Do you recollect ever to have heard any false reports which were circulated as truth, from the persons who assembled at Townsends Corner.
Answer. I do not recollect.
Intg by same. Did you hear no rumour of the loss of the Harriet until the Tuesday Evening you mention.
Answer. I never did.

J H Barber

ADS. *Ruggles* v. *General Interest Insurance Company*, USCC,DMass, October 1825.

DOCUMENT 103. INTERROGATORIES AND ANSWERS

28 October 1825

Interrogatories exhibited to Nathaniel S Ruggles in relation to his books

39. Not identified.
40. Newport merchants and residents.

papers &c he is required to produce at the Trial of the cause between him & The General Interest Assurance Company

1 Do your books of account, any or either of them, contain any entry or entries of your purchase of the Sloop Harriet, of the monies or other consideration paid for her, or of the Cargo shipped by you in that Sloop on her last voyage, its price, of whom it was bought or of what articles or merchandise it consisted?

2 Have you at this or had you at any former time, the orders instructions & agreement, any or either of them, by which Benedict Dayton took command of said Sloop on her last voyage—by which a compensation for his services as master was established, or by which his conduct & proceedings in relation to said Sloop, or her cargo were to be governed on her last voyage?

3 Is there now, or has there been in your hands or possession any paper or writing touching or in relation to said Dayton's interest in said Sloop Harriet or her cargo, or is there now or has there ever been any agreement in writing, in or by which, said Dayton might either absolutely or conditionally obtain an interest or share in said Sloop, or the cargo laden on board of her in her last voyage

4 Have you any Contract, note obligation or security for money given you by said Dayton for or on account any interest or share in the Sloop Harriet, or her Cargo in her last voyage or had you any such instrument in paper on the twelvth day of January (AD 1824) Eighteen hundred & twenty four or on the ninth day of February in the same year?

[5] Have you any bill of Sale of said Sloop?

[6] Have you now or had you at any time since the twelvth day of Jan'y AD 1824, any account or accounts shewing your dealings & transactions with said Dayton in relation to said Sloop or her Cargo on her last voyage.

Answers by N. S. Ruggles.

To the first Int.

1st my books do not contain any entry relating to the purchase of the Harriet, my books contain charges against the man I purchased the Sloop of. I have no entry of the purchase of the Cargo[,] the oil I imported in my own vessel

2 I had no written contract with Capt Dayton on this voyage or the one preceeding nor any written orders, other than a verbal agreement as to what part of the vessels earnings he was to have for going in her, he was ordered to do the best he could with the Cargo shipped & also to employ the vessel in freighting as well as he could

3 There is not now nor has not been any paper in writing touching or relating to Daytons interest in said Sloop he having none, neither as to Cargo

4 I have not now nor never had any such paper
5 I have a bill of sale of said Sloop
6 I have no account with said Dayton since Jany 12, 1824

Nathl S Ruggles

AD. *Ruggles* v. *General Interest Insurance Company*, USCC,DMass, October 1825.

DOCUMENT 104. BILL OF EXCEPTIONS

[November 3, 1825]

Circuit Court of the United States
Massachusetts District. October Term 1825
Nathaniel S. Ruggles vs. The President & Directors of the General Interest Assurance Company

And now the issue joined in this case between the parties, came on to be tried by a Jury duly empanelled. The Defendants admitted the making of the policy; mentioned in the declaration, and the plaintiff gave the usual evidence to prove that he was the sole owner of the Sloop, and had an interest also in her cargo at the time of the loss. It was also admitted by the Defendants that the Sloop with her cargo was wrecked on Cape Hatteras on the nineteenth day of January, 1824 and both wholly lost: and that the plaintiff, in due time, afterwards, made an abandonment to the defendants for a total loss.

The Defendants, thereupon gave evidence, which proved that the master of said Sloop immediately after the loss, for the purpose and with the design, that the owner, not hearing of the loss of the vessel, nor of her arrival at her port of destination, might effect insurance upon vessel and cargo did express his intention not to write to the owner, and took measures to prevent the fact of the loss from being known; and, that by the fraudulent conduct of the master in this particular and in consequence of the measures adopted by him to suppress the intelligence of the loss aforesaid, knowledge of the loss was so long suppressed, as that it was not known at the date of this policy; and that, by means thereof, the plaintiff, although wholly ignorant of what had befallen the property, and wholly ignorant also of the design and objects of the master in this respect, and acting bona fide, was yet enabled to obtain the insurance before the news of the loss became public through the ordinary channels of information.

Whereupon the Counsel of the Defendants did then and there insist before the said Court, that the said several matters so given in evidence on the part of the Defendants were sufficient to vacate the policy aforesaid, and bar the plaintiff of his action thereon; And the Defendants by their Counsel, did, then and there, request the Judge before whom said cause was tried, to instruct and declare to the Jury, that it was the duty of the master of a vessel, resulting from his situation, to use reasonable and ordinary diligence to communicate to the owner information of the loss of his vessel or cargo & that all acts and attempts of the master to suppress or withhold intelligence of such loss were fraudulent and unlawful; that the master of said sloop was, under the circumstances of this case, exclusively the Agent of the plaintiff so far as the Defendants are concerned, and, that for his wrongs and neglects, in suppressing the intelligence of the loss of said Sloop, and her cargo, for the fraudulent purpose of enabling the plaintiff to procure the insurance aforesaid, the policy declared on was void. And, further, that notwithstanding the plaintiff might be ignorant of the loss, at the time of effecting the said insurance, yet the fraudulent conduct of said master in omitting to give his owner due notice of the loss, and his acts in fraudulently suppressing intelligence of said loss as proved in the defence, furnished a sufficient answer to the plaintiff's demand;

Which direction so far as respected the duty and conduct of the master the Court accordingly gave.

But the Court further directed the Jury that, although it was the duty of the master to give information of the loss to his owner, as soon as he reasonably could, yet that in the present case where there had been an abandonment in due time for a loss really total, if the owner at the time of procuring the insurance, had no knowledge of the loss, but acted with entire good faith in procuring the insurance, he is not precluded from a recovery, nor is the policy void by the omission of the master to communicate, or by his acts in suppressing intelligence of the loss although such omission and acts were wilful and resulted from the fraudulent design to enable the owner to make insurance after the loss, the owner not being conversant of such act or design at the time of such insurance.

And with this direction the Court left the said issue to the Jury who found a verdict for the plaintiff.

Whereupon the Defendants Counsel in Court did except to the said direction of the Court as contrary to law. And inasmuch as the said several matters do not appear of record, the said Defendants by their Counsel did then and there offer and propose their aforesaid exception and prayed that the Judge who gave such direction would put his seal to such Bill of Exceptions. And thereupon said Judge did allow the same and put his seal thereto this third day of November in the year of our Lord one thousand eight hundred and twenty five

Joseph Story the Judge before whom the foregoing Issue was tried & one of the Justices of the Supreme Court of the U. States.

ADS. *Ruggles* v. *General Interest Insurance Company*, USCC,DMass, October 1825.

TO [?]

Dear Sir Washington Jan. 15. 1826.

I do not think you need employ Counsel at present in Mr. Ruggles cause. If you will send the record on to me, I will have the case entered, & if it should seem probable that the case will be reached this session (which is hardly possible) I will give you seasonable notice. The case cannot be entered till the record arrives; & that must be here within the first 6 days. I will see that nothing amiss takes place. Yours very sincerely Danl. Webster

ALS. Robert and Richard Upton, Concord, New Hampshire.

TO ALEXANDER BLISS

Dear Bliss Sup: Court. Mar. 12 [1827]

The *Genl. Int. Ass Co.* v. *Ruggles* is this moment decided, and the *Judgment* below is (not) *Reversed*!!![41]

If the above has sufficiently frightened you, know, that the opinion was delivered by Judge Thompson.[42] It went fully over all the ground, & treated the topics ably, confirming Judge Story, in all things. As far as appears, the opinion is unanimous.

I have written to Mr. Ruggles, to tell him the good news. Yrs D.W.

ALS. DLC.

ii. Oliver Jordan et al. v. *Warren Insurance Company.* In 1838 the Warren Insurance Company insured the freight (i.e., the compensation paid for the transport of goods) on the ship *Franklin*, jointly owned by Oliver Jordan of Maine and several others. At New Orleans the *Franklin* loaded a cargo consisting mainly of cotton (worth about $60,000) and tobacco ($10,500) for transport to France. In June 1838, as another boat towed the *Franklin* down the Mississippi to the sea, the current caught the *Franklin* and swung her into the river bank. The eddy then took the tow boat and smashed her into the *Franklin*. Water poured into the hold soaking most of the cotton. After the *Franklin* was towed back to New Orleans for repair, local merchants surveyed the cargo. In their opinion the wet cotton could not be safely transported until it had dried. This would take six months. On his own initiative, the captain decided to

41. 12 Wheaton 408 (1827).

42. Smith Thompson (1768–1843), New York lawyer and judge, studied with James Kent, admitted in 1792, state legislator (1801), judge, New York supreme court (1802–1819), secretary of the navy (1819–1823), justice, USSC (1823–1843).

sell the damaged cotton and to ship the remainder of the cargo to Havre in another ship while the *Franklin* underwent repair.

The auctioned cotton brought almost $20,000. Had the *Franklin* completed the voyage as planned, Jordan and his associates would have earned almost $10,000 freight money. When they learned of the captain's action, they turned to their insurer for payment on the policy. When the company refused, the owners hired Webster to sue for a constructive total loss of freight. John Plummer Healy, Webster's associate, prepared the initial papers for the May 1839 USCC term.[43] After a delay of a year, the court heard the case. The parties agreed on the formal elements of proof and arranged to share the basic documentary evidence of the case (Document 105). The key questions were, first, did the master, as a question of fact, perform his duty in selling the cargo, and, second, as a matter of law, did the sale bind the insurer to pay the lost freight, even though the captain could have reshipped the cotton after a six-month delay? The jury heard the evidence and in a special verdict decided that the master had an "absolute duty" to the owners of the cargo not to carry it forward. His decision to sell it had been properly made, and therefore the insurance company was liable for the loss of the freight money.

This did not end the case. The attorneys at the trial had reserved for the court the question whether in the eyes of the law there had been a constructive loss of the freight money and, if so, who should be entitled to the proceeds of the substitute voyage. In their reported argument (Document 106), Webster and Healy said that the owners of the vessel were under no duty to repair her and carry forward a damaged cargo. Webster had two problems. First, he had to distinguish New York and English precedents which held that in a policy on freight the insurer was liable only if the cargo was physically destroyed. Second, the captain's action did not appear to have been absolutely necessary. Webster tried to maneuver around these difficulties by arguing that a decision in favor of the insurer would cast an unfair burden on the ship owners. Webster contended that the captain, as agent of the ship owners, had acted as a prudent owner of both vessel and cargo would have acted. All the court should require of a captain, therefore, was such prudent behavior. Under that circumstance, the insurer should be held to make good on his policy.

Judge Story, however, remained unconvinced. He preferred to examine the case in terms of the different interests involved.[44] First, the freight had not been lost because of one of the insured perils. The ship had been repaired, and the captain could have waited for the cotton to dry. The loss of the freight was therefore due to the captain's decision.

43. *Jordan et al.* v. *Warren Insurance Company*, USCC,DMass, October 1840.

44. 1 Story 342 (1840).

Even though the jury found as a matter of fact that the captain had performed his duty to the owners of the cargo, Story would not recognize in the captain the power to elect which party would suffer the loss.

The law allocated the risk of loss of freight between the various interests. Between a shipper and a ship owner the latter earned full freight regardless of whether the goods arrived damaged or were off-loaded at an intermediate port at the shipper's request. The shipper could not shift a loss onto the ship owner. Likewise, the ship owner could not throw the loss of freight onto the underwriter if the captain decided to auction off the damaged cargo. Only in cases of necessity would the law make the captain the agent for all the parties and bind them by his decision. Story limited the claim of Jordan et al. to the general average and the loss of freight on those goods physically destroyed in the accident. He turned the case over to an auditor to assess damages (Document 107). Instead of the $7000 awarded by the jury, the auditor gave Jordan et al. only $1650.

DOCUMENT 105. PRETRIAL AGREEMENT

United States of America
District of Massachusetts ss.
Circuit Court of the United States, First Circuit.
Oliver Jordan[45] & al. v. The Warren Ins. Company.

It is agreed that upon the trial of this case both the Plaintiffs & Defendants may use as evidence, in the same manner as if they had been authenticated & proved by the depositions, regularly taken, of the proper witnesses, the following documents, to wit—

1. The copy of the Protest of J. S. Burgess, master of the Ship Franklin & others, taken before Carlisle Pollack,[46] Notary Public, July 16, 1838.
2. The copy of the surveys of the Ship Franklin, made by R W. Spedden & Charles P. Johnston, assisted by Peter Marcey, dated July 4, & July 10, 1838, & certified by Chas. P. Johnston, Deputy Warden.[47]
3. Bills of expenses in general contribution respecting said Ship Franklin, & the vouchers therefor, verified by Joseph S. Burgess, under the notarial certificate of Carlisle Pollack, Notary Public.
4. Bills of expenses in particular average respecting the said Ship Franklin, & the vouchers therefor, verified by Joseph S. Burgess, under the notarial certificate of Carlisle Pollack, Notary Public.
5. Account of Auction sales of the damaged part of the cargo, & the old

45. A resident of Thomaston, Maine. There were six other co-owners, all residents of Maine.

46. Neither further identified.

47. None of these has been further identified.

materials of said Ship Franklin, made by Joseph Le Carpenter,[48] Auctioneer, returned under the notarial certificate of Carlisle Pollack, Notary Public.

6. The copy of the freight list for said Ship Franklin on her voyage commenced from New Orleans for Havre in June 1838, signed by Levi H. Gale,[49] & dated June 6, 1838, whereby it appears that the freight & primage[50] on said voyage, if it had been performed, would have been Ten Thousand four hundred & twelve dollars & fifty nine cents ($10,412.59) to which the owners of said Ship would have been entitled, to wit for freight $9916.76 & for primage $495.83

It is also agreed that the Plaintiffs in this action were the owners of the said Ship Franklin; that the Policy of Insurance, made by the Defts. on the thirtieth day of May, 1838, whereby the Defts. caused Oliver Jordan, for whom it concerns, to be insured, lost or not lost, Seven Thousand dollars on the Freight of the Ship Franklin, at & from New Orleans to Havre, was made for the benefit of the Pltfs.

All the facts & documents above mentioned, are to be considered as in the case, & to be used by either party.

Theophilus Parsons[51] for Defts.
J. P. Healy for Pltfs.

ADS. *Jordan et al.* v. *Warren Insurance Company*, USCC,DMass, October 1840.

DOCUMENT 106. REPORTED ARGUMENT

The argument for the plaintiffs was in substance as follows:

There is no decision of authority here which would impose upon the owners of the vessel the duty of carrying forward the damaged cargo, under these circumstances. The cases cited for the defendants, from the New York Reports,[52] do not reach this question, even though the doctrines, there laid down, should be admitted. In all those cases the ship-owners endeavored to excuse themselves for not proceeding on their respective voyages, either because the vessel had been slightly injured, or because the cargo had been so damaged, as to render its reshipment

48. Not identified.

49. New Orleans merchant.

50. Sometimes called a master's "hat money." It was an extra sum paid to the master and mariners for loading and unloading the vessel.

51. Theophilus Parsons, Jr. (1797–1882; Harvard 1815), Boston lawyer, studied with William Prescott, admitted in 1819, author of several legal treatises, Dane professor of law, Harvard Law School (1848–1870).

52. *Herbert* v. *Hallett*, 3 Johnson's Cases (N.Y.) 93 (1802), *Griswold* v. *New York Insurance Company*, 1 Johnson (N.Y.) 205 (1806), same 3 Johnson (N.Y.) 321 (1808). These cases established the rule that the owners of the ship had a duty to repair the vessel and to carry the cargo, damaged or not, to its destination.

merely inexpedient. In every instance, the performance of the voyage was practicable, and would have been attended with no danger to life or health.

But the principle, which seems to have been adopted in New York, that it is the duty of ship-owners to carry forward every cargo, when its carriage is possible, in order to protect the underwriters on freight, even though they should thereby sacrifice the interests of the shippers to any amount, is unjust. It finds no support in reason, and can never receive the sanction of an enlightened commercial community. There are parties, having interests at stake, which are usually much larger than those of the underwriters on freight, and which are equally with theirs deserving of protection. It is the duty of ship-owners, in all cases, to act as a prudent man would act, who should be the owner of both vessel and cargo, without insurance on either; that is to say, it should be their object to save the greatest possible amount of property, without stopping to inquire to whose benefit it would enure. *Green* v. *Royal Exchange Ass. Co.* 6 Taunton, 68.[53]

The case of *Mordy* v. *Jones*, 4 Barn. & Cresw. 394, which, so far as it is entitled to weight, goes against the plaintiffs in this action, is happily answered by Mr. Phillips in his Treatise on Insurance, vol. 2, p. 190.[54]

The case of *Whitney* v. *N. York Fireman's Ins. Co.* 18 Johns. R. 208,

53. In this 1815 English decision a captain unloaded his cargo from his damaged ship and then sold the ship and most of the cargo. He brought the residue home on a second ship. Meanwhile, the purchaser of the damaged ship repaired her and sailed home with a new cargo. The court ruled that although the captain's actions should be judged by the standard of the prudent man, he should not be allowed to throw the loss of the freight on the insurer. DW wanted the court to adopt the prudent man test but not the result reached in the *Green* case.

54. This 1825 English case was the defendant's strongest English precedent. The facts were almost identical to *Jordan*. In *Mordy* the wet cargo could not have been reshipped without waiting for it to dry. The master sold it and sailed on with the rest of the cargo. The arbitrator found this to have been the decision of a prudent man, but the court reversed, holding that the underwriters were not liable for loss of the freight. All that the insurer of the freight insured was that the ship would not be reduced to such a state that the cargo could not be carried. The judges said that they did not want to give ship captains the authority to make this kind of decision. Thus if the master decided to sell part of the cargo, the ship owner would bear the loss of the freight. Phillips questioned the grounds of the decision. He said the test should be whether the master acted prudently. The judges in *Mordy* rejected the prudent man test, adopting instead a rule of law which made the ship owner responsible for the loss whenever the captain disposed of part of the cargo and then completed the voyage. Willard Phillips, *A Treatise on the Law of Insurance*, 2 vols. (Boston, 1823, 1824).

is precisely in point. All the circumstances in that case are similar to those in the case now before the Court; and if the decisions of New York were to govern here, this one would be decisive of the question in issue.[55]

The damage or loss of cargo, whereby the ship is prevented from earning freight, is a loss of freight. 1 Phil. Ins. 290; *M'Gaw* v. *Ocean Ins. Co.* 2 Law Reporter, 363.[56]

But it is unnecessary to cite authorities further on this part of the case. We consider, that the question, as to the duty of the ship-owners to have carried forward the cargo, or to have attempted to carry it forward, was disposed of by the finding of the jury.

(2d.) The authorities cited, for the defendants under this head, are not applicable to this case. A policy on freight does not attach to a cargo, which there is merely an intention to ship, but which is never taken on board. The risk cannot commence, until something is put at hazard. But when a cargo is once received, and the voyage commenced, the policy attaches to that specific cargo, and does not shift to another cargo for the same voyage; much less to another cargo for another and a different voyage. 6 Taunton, 68; *Everth* v. *Smith*, 2 M. & S. 278.[57]

(3d.) There are cases in which underwriters on freight, who have become liable to pay a loss under their policy, may avail themselves of the subsequent earnings of the ship, by way of salvage. But there are some limits to this right. The right remains with the underwriters, only so long as the ship continues under the protection of their policy. They can-

55. In this 1820 decision the ship went down, and the rescued cargo was too wet to reship. The court said the voyage had been defeated. Therefore the master could sell the cargo for the benefit of all the parties. The court allowed the insurer to deduct the pro rata freight charges from the origin of the voyage to the place of sale. This case was factually distinguishable from DW's, since in *Whitney* there was no way for the cargo to be reshipped and none of the other cargo ever reached its destination.

56. A direct quotation from Phillips. *M'Gaw* was an 1839 decision of the MassSJC, more fully reported in 23 Pickering (Mass.) 405, on facts similar to the instant case. The ship ran aground; the cotton was saved but the tobacco was lost. The shippers demanded that the captain deliver up the cargo instead of waiting for the repair of the ship. He did so, and the ship owner sought to recover for a total loss of freight. The court held that the ship owner could recover the freight only on the goods destroyed. He lost the freight on the cargo given up by the captain. The court decided that the insurer was not liable for the freight of those goods which might have been reshipped. Given the facts, this precedent favored DW's opponents. He cited it for the general proposition that loss of cargo is a loss of freight.

57. Besides the *Everth* case which DW cited, the defendant cited *McCarthy* v. *Abel*, 5 East 388 (1804). *Everth* was an 1814 English decision in which Lord Ellenborough held that the detention of goods did not justify an abandonment for a constructive total loss of freight when the cargo, in fact, eventually reached its destination.

not claim the earnings of the ship, when they would disclaim all responsibility for any losses or accidents, that might happen to her. In the present case we contend, that if the ship, when she was ready for sea, had taken another cargo at New Orleans for Havre, it would have been an entirely new undertaking, and an entirely new voyage, which would not have been protected by this policy. The policy surely did not cover the risks incurred by the voyage, which the ship did perform.

The cases cited for the defendants are not analogous to the present one.[58] If a ship, having received no injury, loses a part of her cargo, and procures other in its stead, and completes her voyage, the freight earned with the new cargo, is taken to be salvage on that, which was lost by the old one. But there is not a case on record, where the earnings of a ship on one voyage are treated as salvage on another and a different voyage. In the case of *Green* v. *Royal Ex. Ass. Co.* 6 Taunton, 68, the jury found a verdict for the plaintiffs; and the only ground, upon which the Court ordered a new trial, was, that the jury might inquire, whether the master had acted in good faith, as a prudent man would act, under like circumstances, who had no insurance. That question settled in the affirmative, the case would be with the plaintiffs. The broad and equitable principle, that the master should act prudently, without reference to the parties, that are to be affected by his action, is recognized in all the cases. This is a principle so just and reasonable, that all parties should be willing to abide by its operation; and it is a principle, which, if admitted, settles this case in favor of the plaintiffs.

Reprinted from *Jordan et al.* v. *Warren Insurance Company*, 1 Story 342, 345–348 (1840). The reporter apparently combined DW's and Healy's arguments.

DOCUMENT 107. AUDITOR'S REPORT

District of Massachusetts
C. C. U. S.
Oliver Jordan & al. v. The Warren Ins. Co.
In this case, pursuant to the order of Court hereto annexed,[59] I have heard the parties, & assessed damages for the Plfs on the following principles:—

The general average is thus stated:—

Loss, per statement in N. Orleans	$8517.98
Add wages & provisions 22 days	317.53
Total amot. of loss	$8835.51

58. Besides the *Green* case (note 53 above), the defendant cited *Brocklebank* v. *Sugrue*, 1 Moody & Robinson 102 (1831).

59. See the case file.

Contributory property		
Ship—valued at—$13,000 pays		$3996.62
Cargo— 19.043.93		
less freight 9.916,76 = 9.127.17—pays		2805.93
Freight—9.916.76. 2/3 is 6.611.21—pays		2032.43
	fraction	53
		$8835.51

Of the loss thus borne by the freight, the proportion to be borne by the underwriters is $1434.45.

The property physically lost consisted of two bales of cotton, on which the freight would have been	$11.82
& two sticks of cedar the freight on which is *supposed* to be about the same value	11.82
	23.64

I therefore assess damages for the Plfs in the foregoing sums of	$1434.45
and	23.64
amounting to	$1458.09
with interest from Nov. 11. 1838, when the loss was payable, being 2 years 2 months & 10 days	191.98
Total damages	$1650.07

The Plfs further claimed a proportional loss of freight on 100 hds tobacco. This tobacco, when taken out of the ship at N. Orleans, was, in the language of the surveyor, "badly damaged, rapidly deteriorating, & wholly unfit for shipment." The freight was $1489.80. It was all sold in N. Orleans, for account of whom it may concern, producing only $1279.30.

This amount is chargeable with brokers comn.	31.98	
& the sum it contributes in genl. average	393.20	425.18
leaving in the Plfs hands a net bal. of only		854.12
which being deducted from the gross freight		1489.80
leaves a deficit of		635.68
of which the Plfs claim a proportional share from Defts—which proportion, settled by the above rule, is		$448.27
to which add interest as above		58.91
Total claim		$507.18

This item of claim I have disallowed; in order that the opinion of the Court may be distinctly taken thereon; the parties being desirous of adjusting the residue without further delay.

The Defts contended that the *primage* ($495.80) ought to be made to contribute to the loss: but as this is a private perquisite of the master, & his wages do not contribute in general average, I rejected this claim & took no notice of the primage, in making up the average.

From the evidence of experienced underwriters in Boston, to whom the parties referred me for information, it appears that the usage there, & generally in this country, is, in cases like the present, to *add* the wages & provisions accruing after the disaster, to the loss; (instead of deducting them from the freight;) & to put the contributory value of the freight, in all cases, at 2/3 of its gross amount, instead of ascertaining it in each case by deducting wages, provisions &c. as in England. I have therefore adopted this usage, in the foregoing estimation.
Fees $75.

Simon Greenleaf

ADS. *Jordan et al.* v. *Warren Insurance Company*, USCC,DMass, October 1840.

4. BANKING AND THE LAW

a. Introduction

By the early nineteenth century commercial banking in New England had become an integral part of the business scene. Most commercial towns had their own country bank whose notes, moving from hand to hand, eventually wound up at the large banks of Boston, the major business center. Bank note issues provided the circulating medium for the regional economy. Before 1814 merchants ran most of the banks. As bankers, they adopted the conservative lending practices associated with mercantile credit. They favored short-term loans of thirty or sixty days and would not accept real estate as security. They saw their banks primarily as a service to the merchant community. During the War of 1812, however, the banks came under increasing pressure to make long-term loans to manufacturing enterprises. Entrepreneurs successfully demanded that banks become less conservative in their lending policies. As trade between the coast and the interior grew, banking operations also increased in scope and volume. This in turn led to the specialization of functions within the banks themselves.[1]

At its simplest level, a bank's board of directors, composed of mer-

1. Bray Hammond, *Banks and Politics in America from the Revolution to the Civil War* (Princeton, N.J., 1957) pp. 75–88, and George Rogers Taylor, *The Transportation Revolution, 1815–1860* (New York, 1951), pp. 311–320.

chants, met and made banking decisions once a week (on what was called the "discount day"). A cashier and one or two tellers handled the daily transactions. The men who filled those positions were little more than bookkeepers. The growth in the banking business after the War of 1812 and the competition between banks made the practice of banking more complex. A standing committee of directors which made daily decisions whether to accept notes for discount soon superseded the weekly directors' meeting. Divorced from decision-making, the board of directors turned into a policy-making body. The bank president, formerly often a figurehead, became the chief executive officer. The authority of the cashier and tellers also steadily grew.[2] With this enlarged authority, however, came greater opportunity for theft. Economic crime became a threat to the public's faith in the security of its banks.

The legal rules that governed the practice of banking also came under scrutiny. As banking became a separate function in a commercial society, litigants asked the courts whether general commercial law doctrines should apply to banks. With more banks in operation, the specter of bank failures soon menaced the financial security of the community. While the community at large turned to the state for statutory regulation of banking, the largest Boston banks created a private mechanism to control the excesses of the irresponsible banks by monitoring the circulation and redemption of country bank notes.[3] When the courts accepted bank notes as money rather than as promissory notes, they had to distinguish between the general common law right of borrowing and a bank's right to lend by issuance of obligations that circulated as money. The courts now faced a situation in which the informal and personalized transactions of the merchant-oriented banks were no longer the norm. When banks and note holders dealt with each other at long range, unconventional banking practices became snares for the unwary. Banking had become a business. Early in his Boston practice Webster had three cases that raised some of the legal problems of banking.

In the first case Webster defended the Dedham Bank, a country bank whose note-issuing practices caused public concern.[4] To make redemption of its notes difficult, the bank engaged in an elaborate subterfuge. First, the bank deposited specie in the Middletown Bank some one hundred miles away. Then the Dedham Bank printed up small denomination bills of exchange drawn on the Middletown Bank. The Dedham Bank

2. Fritz Redlich, "Bank Administration, 1780–1914," *Journal of Economic History*, 12 (1952): 438–453.

3. Massachusetts enacted supervisory legislation in 1829. Laws, Mass., c. 96 (1829). Boston bankers created the Suffolk system in the 1820s, Hammond, pp. 551–556. See also Edwin Merrick Dodd, *American Business Corporations until 1860, with Special Reference to Massachusetts* (Cambridge, Mass., 1954), pp. 201–217.

4. *King* v. *Dedham Bank*, 15 Mass. 447 (1819).

made these bills look just like bank notes. It intended the camouflage to serve two purposes. First, the bank would evade an 1809 statute that made any bank which refused to redeem its notes or bills liable for a penalty of 2 percent a month for the period of nonredemption.[5] The law of bills of exchange required the holder to present the bill to the payee before the holder could turn to the maker for payment. Here, although the payee (the Middletown Bank) was fictitious, the holders of the bills would still have to travel to Middletown before they could redeem the bills in Dedham. The holder of a bank note on the other hand, could present it directly to the maker. Secondly, by designing the bills to look like notes, the Dedham Bank hoped to fool its customers into accepting them as notes. In this the bank succeeded. When Samuel King presented for redemption what he believed were bank notes, the Dedham Bank pointed out that he would have to take them to Middletown first. King refused, and brought suit in 1818 to force the Dedham Bank to pay them.

The sort of deception practiced by the Dedham Bank had led the Massachusetts legislature in 1816 to pass legislation prohibiting banks from issuing bills, notes, and other negotiable paper with a face value of less than $100 payable at any place other than the bank that issued the paper.[6] The law applied the 2 percent penalty to such paper already issued (such as Dedham's). At the March 1818 trial the judge agreed with Webster's objection that the evidence was insufficient to maintain either count of the plaintiff's declaration. Following a directed verdict for the bank, the plaintiff appealed.[7]

The appeal presented Webster with two issues. First, he had to convince the court that the 1816 law was unconstitutional insofar as it applied to bills already in existence. Arguing along the lines of the *Dartmouth College* case, Webster asserted that a bill of exchange amounted to a contract between the Dedham Bank and the plaintiff that could not be retroactively altered by statute. The second issue involved whether the court would treat the bills as notes and thus not require their presentment in Middletown. Would the court place the risk of accepting these craftily designed bills on the note holders? Or would the court, as urged by the plaintiff's attorney, look through the fiction that the paper looked like bills of exchange, and, instead, adopt the understanding of the innocent noteholder that he had received notes.[8] On the latter point Web-

5. Laws, Mass., c. 38 (1809).
6. Laws, Mass., c. 91 (1816).
7. *King* v. *Dedham Bank*, Mass-SJC,S, March 1819. DW received $10 for his appearance; in June Dedham paid him $20 before the appeal, and in April 1819 $100 after he argued the appeal. See pp. 130, 131, and 136, above.

8. The plaintiff's attorney said: "Thousands of them [the bills] were issued of the denomination of one dollar, and drawn on a place a hundred miles distant, and all of the same date, and in favor of a fictitious payee. They were, in fact, paid out . . . as current money . . . engraved in close imitation of bank bills or

ster argued that his client had done nothing unlawful. The burden, Webster insisted, rested on "the public to discriminate between bank notes payable on demand, and these bills, so very distinct in their nature and properties."[9] Webster would later have occasion to argue the other side of this question.

The court agreed with Webster's position. First, the court ruled that the law of 1816 could not change the legal effect of the bills. The court warned note holders that they could not trust a bank's paper simply because the state chartered the bank. Banking was to be treated like any other business.

> The mistake of the plaintiff, and perhaps of others who received bills of this description, seems to have arisen from the belief that, when a bank was incorporated, all their bills and notes, of whatever tenor, were to pass as money, and were redeemable by the bank at the pleasure of the holder. . . . If the banks were not incorporated, and were dealing like any other private company or association, this would be the course of business; and it would probably, in general, give sufficient security to the public; as no notes would circulate where the ability and integrity of the members or partners of the banking company were not well known, and of established credit. Experience seems to have proved that the incorporation of banks gives but little, if any, additional security to the holders of their bills; and that no legislative acts which can be passed will supply the want of prudence, skill, or integrity, in those who administer the concerns of a bank.[10]

The second case, *Benjamin Foster et al.* v. *Essex Bank*,[11] gave the MassSJC further opportunity to discuss the standard of care which banks owed the public. On July 1, 1799, the state chartered the Essex Bank of Salem for a twenty-year period. In 1812 Israel Foster, a wealthy old merchant, brought a chest full of gold bullion to the bank for safekeeping. Sometime in 1818 the cashier and clerk entered the vault and helped themselves to most of the bank's specie, including Foster's gold.

Foster died in 1818. His executors hired John Pickering to recover the value of the stolen gold. Pickering filed suit at the MassCCP in November 1818. The bank demurred the case to the SJC April 1819 term, and then continued it to the November term, when Webster joined Pickering. In the interim, the bank's noteholders had become fearful that the expiration of the bank's charter on July 1, 1819, would wipe out

notes." *King* v. *Dedham Bank*, 15 Mass. 447, 448 (1819).

9. Ibid., p. 451. DW's argument is also printed in *W & S*, 15: 268–270.

10. Ibid., pp. 452–454.

11. MassCCP,E, March 1819, 16 Mass. 245 (1819), and MassSJC,E, October 1821, 17 Mass. 479 (1821). See also 9 American Decisions 168.

their claims. The legislature responded by passing an act on June 19, 1819, which extended the life of all corporations for three years following the expiration of a charter for the purpose of winding up a corporation's affairs.[12] At the opening of the trial the bank's attorneys, William Prescott and Leverett Saltonstall, informed the court that the expiration of the bank's charter had dissolved its existence and with that all liability for Foster's gold. Pickering and Webster pointed to the extension statute. The court heard arguments on the issue of the statute's validity at the March 1820 term. The bank's lawyers attacked the statute as retroactive legislation in violation of the contract clause. Webster now found himself in the position of having to distinguish not only *Dartmouth College* but *King* v. *Dedham Bank* as well. Webster pointed to a distinction between rights and remedies. He argued that the plaintiff in this case had an existing right for which the statute only gave a remedy.[13] The statute did not alter the plaintiff's rights. The court agreed with Webster and Pickering and upheld the law.

At the April 1820 term the case came to trial. The jury returned a special verdict on the facts. They found that Foster had delivered his gold to the bank, and that the bank had taken the same care of Foster's gold as it did its other special deposits. Given these facts, the legal question remained whether the court would hold the bank liable for its employees' theft. The case raised the fundamental problem of the responsibility of banks for special deposits, i.e. bailments. The attorneys again asked the MassSJC to examine the standard of care banks owed the public at large.

At the October 1820 term Webster and Pickering argued on behalf of their clients. In this case a bailment clearly existed. But because the bank received no compensation for the deposit nor had treated the gold as a general deposit on which the depositor might draw, the law considered the bank a gratuitous bailee. The common law made such a bailee responsible for the loss of the property only if the bailee could be charged with gross negligence, a legal concept with little definable content. Recognizing the weakness of their position under the rules governing bailments, Webster and Pickering urged the court to look at banking either

12. Laws, Mass., c. 43 (1819).

13. "In the case of *King* vs. *Dedham Bank*, this court held that an act of the legislature could not have the effect of altering a private contract, subsisting and unbroken between the parties at the passage of the law, by varying the terms, or imposing new duties on either party, in regard to the sum to be paid, or the place or time of payment. Or in other words, it could not *enact* that the parties had made a contract, which they never had made. The present case is like none of these. It is but a general provision, giving new remedies prospectively, for cases in which corporations might expire by the limitation of their charters, leaving their affairs unsettled." 16 Mass. 245, 269 (1819). DW's argument is also printed in *W & S*, 15: 271–274.

as a profession or in the same category as common carriers and innkeepers. The law imposed a higher duty of care on both these classes of occupation.

> The negligence of the defendants is not to be measured by the standard of a common individual, who does not make it his business to take charge of money, and similar valuable articles: for what would be only slight neglect in one, would be gross and highly reprehensible in the other. The defendants are bankers by profession: they provide themselves with secure vaults, and thus give the publick an assurance of the great care, which will be taken of the property deposited. An extraordinary degree of care is also expected by the publick from banks, because they are in some sort invested with a trust of public nature, and under the sanction of government: their exclusive privileges are for the convenience of the publick, as well as for their own emolument: they are in some degree publick agents, and even exercise one of the rights of sovereignty, that of regulating, to a certain extent, the currency of the state.
>
> The publick in return for these extraordinary privileges, expect of the banks extraordinary care in the exercise of them. For this reason the government guards the privileges of banks, by imposing such extraordinary penalties for the forging of their notes, and for having in possession bank paper and other implements for committing frauds, as are not known in the case of private persons.
>
> Considerations of publick policy therefore demand, that banks should be held to a degree of responsibility, little or nothing short of that which belongs to the class of bailees, under which common carriers, innkeepers and others are ranked: especially when it happens, as here, that the property entrusted to them has been lost by the fault of their own servants.[14]

Webster and Pickering did not persuade the court. In a leading decision on the law of bailments, Justice Parker held that a bank that received a special deposit was a gratuitous bailee. If the bank used due care in storing the deposit, it was not liable for its loss. Moreover, the bank would not be liable for any loss due to an act of its employee outside the scope of the employee's authority.

> If it be asked, for what acts then of a cashier or clerk the bank would be answerable; I should answer, for any which pertain to their official duty; for correct entries in their books, and for a proper account of general deposits; so that, if by any mistake, or by fraud, in these particulars, any person be injured, he would have a remedy. If they should rob the vaults of the property of the bank, the company would necessarily lose; as must have happened in this case to a great amount: and if the bank have become debtors to

14. 17 Mass. 479, 486–487 (1821).

> those who have deposited otherwise than specially, their debts will not be diminished by the fraud; so that in this form they are answerable to depositors: and for the correct conduct of all their servants, in their proper sphere of duty, they are answerable. They may also possibly be answerable for notices to endorsers upon bills and notes left with them for collection, if there should be a failure, by the neglect of any of their servants; because they have undertaken to give the proper notices. But even in that case it may admit of a question, whether they would be liable any further than attornies, who undertake the collection of debts, would be. But they are not answerable for special deposits, stolen by one of their officers, any more than if stolen by a stranger; or any more than the owner of a warehouse would be who permitted his friend to deposit a bale of goods there for safekeeping and the goods should be stolen by one of his clerks or servants.
>
> The undertaking of banking corporations is that they shall be skilful and faithful in their employments: they do not warrant their general honesty and uprightness.[15]

The court thus continued to treat banking as a business. In deciding that the bank's responsibility for its employees' acts did not extend beyond the employees' normal duties, the court kept the burden of care on those who dealt with banks. In many instances Parker's position would protect the bank's reserve fund and its ability to redeem its notes. Losses would fall on the note holders or special depositors.

In the third instance of bank litigation, the MassSJC heard a dispute between two country banks over who should bear the loss for forged bank notes. The Gloucester Bank's cashier kept a large number of bank notes in his desk. He filled in all the blanks except for the bank president's signature. In 1816 the president died but the notes remained in a desk drawer. In October 1817 someone stole nearly $25,000 of the notes, forged the president's signature, and began circulating them in eastern Massachusetts. On January 30, 1818, the Salem Bank put together a package of Gloucester notes. The Salem cashier asked his Gloucester counterpart to exchange the Gloucester notes for Essex or Boston bank notes. On February 7 the Gloucester cashier drew a check for $8500 on a Boston bank, which the bank's messenger delivered to Salem on the ninth. The next day the Salem Bank turned over its Gloucester notes, among which were many forged ones.

On February 16 the Salem Bank sent an employee to the Gloucester Bank with another batch of notes. By then however, Boston note brokers had alerted the Gloucester Bank that counterfeit Gloucester notes had appeared in circulation. The bank directors paid the older notes but returned the newer ones. The Gloucester Bank then closed for a month

15. Ibid., pp. 511–512. Joseph Story, *Treatise on the Law of Bailments*, 2nd ed. (Boston, 1840), p. 65.

while its directors tried to locate the bogus notes. The bank notified the public that it would redeem only notes which holders had received directly from the bank. On February 26 the Salem Bank cashier personally appeared at the Gloucester Bank and demanded payment. The Gloucester Bank's refusal set the stage for a suit by the Salem Bank. Meanwhile the Gloucester Bank asked the Salem Bank to take back the counterfeit bills Gloucester had paid. When Salem refused this request, Gloucester sued Salem. The Salem Bank hired Webster, Pickering, and Benjamin R. Nichols to handle both cases.[16]

In their action against the Gloucester Bank, the Salem Bank's attorneys filed two suits in September 1818, one in contract and the other in tort. The trial took place later that year. In the contract action the jury returned a special verdict that the deceased Gloucester president had not signed the notes. Chief Justice Parker directed a general verdict for the Gloucester Bank. Webster and his co-counsel moved for a new trial on grounds of misdirection of the jury. They had asked Parker to instruct the jury that the bank was responsible for the cashier's carelessness, and that in accepting the notes for examination, the bank had adopted them as valid. In the tort action the attorneys based their case on the theory that the Gloucester Bank was responsible for the negligence of the cashier. In this action the parties produced the same evidence. Parker directed a nonsuit subject to a hearing by the full bench on both actions.

In November 1819 the attorneys argued both actions. Webster and his co-counsel focused on two issues: (1) whether the Gloucester Bank had adopted the notes, and (2) whether Gloucester was responsible for its cashier's negligence. On the latter point, they started from the broad proposition that a principal was answerable for the acts of his agent. They again urged the court to adopt a higher standard of conduct for banks in the handling of bank notes. The argument resembled the one made by Webster and Pickering in the *Foster* case.

> Banks are bound to exercise an extraordinary care and diligence in the conduct of their affairs. This is implied in their profession or business: public policy demands it of them; and the nature of the property, being always money, requires it. The publick have a right to claim of them such a degree of care as will prevent any general injury, in consequence of the privileges given them by their charters. The commonwealth, in authorizing them to issue notes, which were to become the circulating medium, parted with a portion of its sovereignty. This was a privilege, which no individuals, nor any number of men could exercise, without the permission of the gov-

16. *Salem Bank* v. *Gloucester Bank*, MassCCP,E, September 1818, MassSJC,E, October 1820; *Gloucester Bank* v. *Salem Bank* MassSJC,E, October 1820. DW received a $30 fee in August 1818 and $70 in November, pp. 132 and 133, above.

ernment. The public good therefore requires of them, that they exercise this power carefully. . . .

It was said by Lord *Mansfield*, that bank notes are money, as much as guineas, or any other current coin that is used in common payments as money or cash. If this be so, ought not the makers of them to take care of their materials, that the public may not be imposed upon by receiving them as genuine when they are spurious. The great security of the community is in the quality of the paper, and the stereotype plates, which all the banks are required to use, and which has hitherto completely eluded the skill of counterfeiters. The paper and plate being genuine, the public have a right to presume, and do presume, that the signatures are also genuine: and much more, if the signature of the cashier is genuine, have they a right to rely on the truth of that purporting to be the president's.

The carelessness of the defendants in the present case was gross. It was in evidence that other banks preserve their unfinished notes with as much care as those finished, by placing them in their vaults. An unsuccessful attempt was made, to enter the vault of the defendants. Had this paper been deposited there, the mischief could not have arisen. But the defendants exposed it in a common desk in the public room for three years; and their only apology for not destroying it, after the death of the president, was, that it was forgotten.[17]

As he had done in the *Foster* case, Judge Parker (writing for the court) rejected this higher standard for banks. Though he acknowledged that the bank had been careless in its keeping of the unsigned notes, the mismanagement, he asserted, appeared too remote and indirect from the consequence. The act of theft was the immediate cause of the forgery; for this he could not hold the bank liable. This use of the distinction between direct and indirect consequences appeared in other areas of tort law.[18] It allowed the judges to limit the liability of certain economic interests whose importance to the economy outweighed a call for justice in individual cases.

Although he had lost Salem's case, Webster had reason to be optimistic about his defense of the Salem Bank in Gloucester's action. Parker heard that case at the November 1818 term. After he refused to accept Gloucester's offer of evidence that Salem had presented forged bills, he directed a nonsuit. Gloucester moved to set the nonsuit aside. A year later the attorneys argued the point. Webster and his co-counsel now found themselves on the side of decisions that favored the innocent note holder who had received value for what later turned out to be forged notes. They argued that in this situation the court must require a bank

17. *Salem Bank* v. *Gloucester Bank*, 17 Mass. 1, 17, 18 (1820).

18. See for example Horwitz, p. 235.

to give immediate notice if it wished its customer to take back spurious notes.

> What safety would there be in commercial negotiations, were the principle admitted, that a banking company, who had once received what they considered their own notes, should at any subsequent period have a right to call upon those, of whom they had received them, to take them back, on the ground that they were counterfeit.[19]

The attorneys focused on the distinction between bills and notes similar to the one Webster had presented in the *Dedham Bank* case. The law prevented the acceptor of a forged bill from recovering back the money paid to its innocent holder. They argued that if the law protected the holders of bills, even more reason existed to favor the holder of notes who had less occasion to question the notes' authenticity.

> It would seem that, as it respects bank notes, the law should be more favorable to persons receiving them, than to the receivers of bills of exchange. Bank notes are considered as the common currency. Persons receiving them rely more on the appearance of the paper and impression, than on the signatures. In bills of exchange, reliance is wholly upon the signatures. If then a bank suffers its own paper and plates to get into circulation, when they want nothing but a signature to make them good notes; if the signature is afterwards forged, and the bank receives them of a *bonâ fide* holder, it would be extremely unjust, if they could compel him to take them again.[20]

The court agreed. Parker stated that between two innocent parties, neither of whom were negligent, the loss would stay where the "course of business" placed it. To allow the Gloucester Bank to recover back its lost notes after it had accepted and held them for fifteen days, he said, would not be in the interest of secure dealings.

> The consequences of making the *Salem* bank answerable under such circumstances, would be very mischievous. Men would never feel safe in suffering bank notes to pass through their hands, if they were liable to be called upon, several weeks after, to make good such as might be discovered to be spurious. Even when passing a bad note, in the ordinary course of business, to pay a debt, a delay of a month or a week, in making the demand, would throw a suspicion upon the case, and make it difficult to recover. . . . [T]here must be some limitation to the right [to call back notes] in point of time, or the whole community would be in commotion. And the true rule is, that the party receiving such notes must examine them as soon as he has opportunity, and return them immediately. If he

19. *Gloucester Bank* v. *Salem Bank*, 17 Mass. 3, 41 (1820).

20. Ibid., pp. 41–42.

does not, he is negligent; and negligence will defeat his right of action.[21]

b. Economic Crime: Private and Public Remedies for Embezzlement

The law of embezzlement, as a species of theft, was a product of the commercial society of the eighteenth century. As business relations became based on paper transactions, the opportunity for what today would be termed white collar crime grew. Although the English enacted the first embezzlement statute in 1799, Massachusetts did not criminalize bank embezzlement until 1824. Up to that time, banks protected themselves by bonding their employees. When embezzlement became more widespread and the sums taken began to exceed the amount of the bonds, criminalization of these breaches of trust occurred. The cases presented in this section involved Webster in defending the consequences of two alleged embezzlements.[1]

i. Bonding: State Bank v. *Titus Welles, Executor.* In 1811 Massachusetts incorporated the State Bank, Boston's largest bank. Its charter required the bonding of each employee.[2] In January 1817 Edward Vose Baxter became the bank's second (receiving) teller. As required by the bank's charter, Thompson Baxter, a relative, and Abraham Touro, a merchant, signed a $7500 bond as sureties for the faithful discharge of Edward Baxter's duties. Shortly thereafter a stage coach driver observed Baxter gambling, losing heavily, and borrowing from others (Document 108). Word of Baxter's activities eventually reached the bank. On November 19, 1818, the cashier closed Baxter's books and fired him. The cashier soon reached the conclusion that Baxter had embezzled bank funds to finance his gambling and had stolen $4770 from the drawer of the first teller to cover the loss. The bank directors ordered the cashier to notify Touro and Thompson Baxter.

> Voted, That the Cashier be directed to address Letters to the Bondsmen of Edward V. Baxter second Teller of this Bank informing them, "That as the Directors of this Bank have reason to believe that the said Edward V Baxter has forfeited his Bonds to this Bank, we give the earliest notice that as his Bondsmen you may take such measures as you may deem expedient, for the Directors must look

21. Ibid., p. 45. Parker ruled that since the unreasonable delay was negligent as a matter of law, a new trial would be fruitless. He denied the Gloucester motion to set the nonsuit aside.

1. Jerome Hall, *Theft, Law, and Society*, 2nd ed. (Indianapolis, 1935), pp. 37–67. The statutory crime of embezzlement is the conversion to the embezzler's use of property that was legally in his possession. Since the common law considered theft (larceny) to entail the taking of property from another's possession, it could not bring embezzlement within the crime of theft.

2. Laws, Mass., c. 84 (1811).

> to you to make good any defalcation or other loss which may be found on further investigation to be sustained by this institution.[3]

Massachusetts had no bank embezzlement statute, and the common law did not regard embezzlement as larcenous. The bank's sole recourse was to sue Edward Baxter for conversion of bank property (which, of course, had been gambled away) and for recovery of the bond. The bank commenced the latter action in the CCP. Before the trial, however, Edward Baxter died. The bank then impleaded Touro and Thompson Baxter. The defendants demurred the case to the November 1820 SJC and continued it to November 1822. Touro then died. The bank's attorney suggested Touro's death on the record and proceeded against Baxter alone. At the close of 1823 the bank filed a separate suit against Touro's executor, Titus Welles (Document 109). Welles hired Webster and Bliss.

In their first move, Webster and Bliss filed a plea in abatement (Document 110) against the bank's declaration. The attorneys' theory was that since the original action had been against all the obligors jointly, the bank could not bring a second suit against the executor of one of the obligors before the conclusion of the first suit. The bank demurred. In March 1825 the court heard the arguments (Webster did not attend).[4] The court ruled that though the bank's right of action survived Touro's death, the court could not have summoned Welles in the first action because a common judgment could not have been issued. T. Baxter and Welles each acted in a different legal capacity—the one in behalf of his own property, the other in behalf of the property of a testator. Therefore, Touro's death worked a severance of the actions, and the bank had to sue Welles separately. The court ordered Welles to plead anew.

At the November term Webster and Bliss filed their pleadings (Document 111). In three separate pleas they alleged that E. Baxter had performed his duties in accordance with the bond and had accounted for all monies received by him in the course of his employment except for $3.06. The bank's attorneys, Daniel Davis and James T. Austin, filed their replication (Document 112). They set forth Baxter's duty to settle with the first teller, his receipt of bank notes in the course of his duties, his failure to pay them over to the first teller, his theft of the first teller's bank notes, and his consequent failure to account satisfactorily for the monies received by him. Webster and Bliss then filed a rejoinder (Document 113). They alleged that there had been no first teller in November 1818, and reasserted that Baxter had accounted with the bank and had paid what the cashier claimed Baxter owed the bank. The bank's attorneys filed one last pleading (Document 114), which denied that Baxter

3. The directors met on November 21, 1818, *State Bank* v. *T. Welles*, MassSJC,S, March 1826.

4. *State Bank* v. *T. Welles*, 3 Pickering (Mass.) 15 (1825).

had paid the bank what he owed them. Special pleading had focused the case on the issue of payment.

At the trial the bank's cashier testified that when he and Baxter went over the books, it appeared that Baxter owed the bank $27,211. Baxter then handed over that sum in several parcels. The bank offered to prove that Baxter had used notes stolen from the first teller to pay the cashier. Webster objected to the evidence. If he kept this testimony out of the trial, he might win the case on the pleadings. With the evidentiary point at issue, the lawyers for both sides agreed that if the evidence of Baxter's theft was admissible, judgment should go in favor of the bank. They also agreed that the full SJC bench would use the trial judge's report of the facts in making its decision.

In February 1826 Bliss sent Webster a copy of the judge's report. It shocked Webster. The judge had written that Webster's side admitted that Baxter embezzled bank funds and reimbursed them by theft. In his reply to Bliss, printed below, Webster denied ever making any such admission. If the case went up on those facts, he predicted, Welles's case was lost. He asked Bliss to check with James Austin and to examine the agreement Webster had signed.

On March 10, 1826, with Webster still in Washington, the court heard arguments on the evidentiary question. The trial judge's report, apparently, had not been changed. This forced Webster's stand-in, Richard Fletcher, and Bliss to use another strategy. Instead of arguing whether the court should admit the evidence of theft, they asserted that theft did not furnish a sufficient answer to Webster's plea of payment. Bliss and Fletcher argued that the theft could not violate the bond, since the theft was not an official act within the scope of Baxter's duties. They urged the court to treat the bank's acceptance of Baxter's payment as conclusive. Since the bank had the sole means of detecting fraud, the court should hold it responsible for the failure to detect it.

In a *per curium* decision, the court simply held that Baxter's delivery of money stolen from the first teller did not constitute a payment.[5] When Bliss informed Webster of the decision, Webster wrote back on March 18, 1826:

> I do not see what can be done for Mr. Welles in the Bank case. The truth is, the merits of the case are flatly agt us; *& that makes it difficult*. Baxter spent the Bank's money; & then paid the *debt*, by the Banks' <own> money. That is the real case; and it is "past surgery."[6]

On March 23 Bliss agreed on behalf of Welles to pay the bank $6081.

5. *State Bank* v. *T. Welles*, 3 Pickering (Mass.) 394 (1826).

6. mDW 5367.

DOCUMENT 108. DEPOSITION

Suffolk ss. Jan 25 1822.

I Charles Sargeant[7] of Gloucester, in the County of Essex Gentleman, of lawful age do testify & say that some time in the early part of the year 1817, in the month of February, I think, I saw Mr Baxter formerly a Clerk in the State Bank, at the Exchange Coffee House, in Boston. He was in a room in the third story, of that house, & was playing at a Faro Bank.[8] I saw Mr Baxter at the Faro Bank frequently, about this time, & saw him lose & win money; but on the whole I should think he lost considerably more, than he won. At one time, in particular, I saw him lose several hundred dollars. He took from his pocket Book, several Bills of one hundred dollars, which he staked on the table. This same Mr Baxter is now dead. He was receiving teller at the State Bank, where I often saw him, when I went to the Bank. For about a fortnight in the early part of 1817, I was at the Faro Bank at the Exchange Coffee House every other night; & almost every night, I was there, Baxter was there, playing at the Faro Bank. I mean nights of week days. At that time, I drove a Stage between Boston & Gloucester, & was in town every other night. There was a billiard room adjoining the one in which the Faro Bank was kept. I often saw Baxter at the Billiard Table. These rooms were frequented by people, who were constantly engaged in play. Baxter played very high[.] I have seen him bet sixty or seventy Dollars, on a card, at the Faro Table. When he lost several hundred Dollars on one night, I saw him take out of his pocket Book, two or three bills, of one hundred Dollars each, & several other bills, & when his own money was exhausted, he borrowed of another person. I went from Boston in March 1817 & I never saw Baxter after that time

Charles Sargent

ADS. *State Bank* v. *T. Welles*, MassSJC,S, March 1826.

DOCUMENT 109. SUMMONS

Suffolk, ss. Commonwealth of Massachusetts.
To the Sheriff of Our County of Suffolk, or his Deputy, Greeting.

We command you to Summon Titus Wells of Medford in the County of Middlesex Esquire as he is Executor of the last will & testament of Abraham Touro late of said Boston Gentleman deceased (*if he may be found in your Precinct*) to appear *before Our Justices of Our Court of Common Pleas, next to be holden at* Boston, *within and for Our said*

7. Not further identified.

8. A gambling house where faro is played. *Faro* is a card game in which the players bet on the order in which certain cards will appear when taken singly from the top of the pack.

County of Suffolk, *on the* first Tuesday of January next: *Then and there, in Our said Court, to answer unto* The President Directors and Company of the State Bank in a plea of debt for that said Abraham at said Boston on the thirtieth day of January in the year of our Lord eighteen hundred and seventeen then being in full life together with one Edward V. Baxter then alive but since deceased and one Thompson Baxter[9] by their writing obligatory of that date by them signed and sealed with their seals and here in Court to be produced bound and obliged & acknowledged themselves to be indebted jointly & severally unto the Pltfs in the sum of Seven thousand five hundred dollars to be paid to Pltfs on demand Yet tho often requested the said Abraham in his life time never paid said sum to Pltfs nor hath the said Titus since the decease of said Abraham tho often requested nor any other person but said Titus detains it
To the Damage of the said President, Directors & Company (*as they say*) *the Sum of* ten thousand *Dollars, which shall then and there be made to appear, with other due damages. And have you there this Writ, with your Doings therein. Witness,* Artemas Ward,[10] *Esquire, at* Boston, *the* Eleventh *Day of* December *in the Year of our Lord One thousand eight hundred and twenty*-three.

Jno. Callender,[11] *Clerk.*

APDS. *State Bank* v. *Welles*, MassSJC,S, March 1826.

DOCUMENT 110. PLEA IN ABATEMENT

And the said Titus Welles comes & defends &c when &c—& prays oyer of the condition of the said writing obligatory & it is read to him, as follows, to wit,—

Whereas on the tenth day of January in the year above written, the above bounden Edward V. Baxter was duly appointed Second Teller of the said Bank, & signified his acceptance of that trust. Now the condition of the present obligation is such, that if the said Edward V. Baxter shall faithfully discharge the duties of said office of Second Teller until he shall be legally discharged by the Directors of the said Bank, then this obligation to be void otherwise to be & remain in force.

Which being heard the said Titus Welles executor as aforesaid of the said Abraham Touro deceased prays judgment of the Plaintiffs writ and declaration, because he saith that the said President Directors & Company of the State Bank heretofore, to wit, at the Boston Court of Common Pleas holden at Boston within & for the County of Suffolk on the first

9. Not identified further.

10. At this time chief justice of the MassCCP.

11. John Callender (d. 1833; Harvard 1790), studied law with Christopher Gore, admitted in 1793, clerk of the MassSJC.

Tuesday of April one Thousand eight hundred & twenty impleaded the said Abraham Touro and the said Thompson Baxter as survivors of the said Edward Vose Baxter, who was then deceased, in a plea of debt, & for the same cause mentioned in the declaration aforesaid. And that upon the plea aforesaid in the said Boston Court of Common Pleas judgment was rendered for the said Abraham Touro & Thompson Baxter & that the said Touro & Baxter recover their costs of suit, as by the record thereof in said Court remaining fully appears,—from which judgment the said Plaintiffs duly appealed to the Supreme Judicial Court holden at Boston in the County of Suffolk, & for the Counties of Suffolk & Nantucket, on the first Tuesday of November eighteen hundred & twenty, when & where both parties appeared, & the said plea was duly continued from term to term in said Supreme Judicial Court, till the term thereof which commenced on the first Tuesday of November Eighteen hundred twenty two, when the said Touro having deceased, it was suggested on the record that said Touro was dead. And the said plea has since been prosecuted in said Court against said Thompson Baxter as survivor of the said Touro & the said Edward Vose Baxter & yet remains undetermined, and is now pending as by the record thereof in said Supreme Judicial Court will appear. And this the said Welles is ready to verify. Wherefore he prays judgment if he ought to be compelled to answer to the writ & declaration aforesaid &c.

by his Attorneys D Webster & A Bliss.

ADS. *State Bank* v. *T. Welles*, MassSJC,S, March 1826.

DOCUMENT III. PLEA

Supreme Judicial Court November Term 1825
The President Directors & Co of the State Bank
vs
Titus Welles Executor of Abraham Touro

And the said Titus Welles Executor as aforesaid comes and defends the wrong and injury when &c and craves oyer of the condition of the said supposed writing obligatory and it is read to him in these words namely "whereas on the tenth day of January in the year above written the above bounden Edward Vose Baxter was duly appointed second Teller of the said Bank and signified his acceptance of that trust: Now the condition of the present obligation is such that if the said Edward Vose Baxter shall faithfully discharge the duties of said office of second teller until he shall be legally discharged by the Directors of said Bank then this obligation to be void, otherwise to be & remain in force" which being heard the said Titus Welles waiving the plea by him in the Court of Common Pleas herein pleaded says that the Plaintiffs their action aforesaid thereof against him ought not to have or maintain because he says, that the said Edward Vose Baxter from and after his appointment to and acceptance of the office of second Teller of said Bank, as mentioned in said condition did from time to time and at all times faithfully discharge the duties of said office of second Teller until he was legally discharged therefrom by the Directors of the said Bank, according to the tenor & effect true interest & meaning of said condition & this the said Titus Welles is ready to verify. Wherefore he prays judgment if the plaintiffs their action aforesaid thereof against him ought to have or maintain &c by his attorneys.

D. Webster & A Bliss

And for another & second plea in this behalf by leave of the Court for that purpose first had and obtained the said Titus Welles says that the plaintiffs their actions aforesaid thereof against him ought not to have or maintain because he says that on the tenth day of January 1817 at Boston aforesaid the said Edward Vose Baxter was appointed to and accepted the office of Second Teller of said Bank, and that he the said Edward Vose Baxter continued in said office & in discharging the duties thereof until the Nineteenth day of November eighteen hundred and eighteen when he retired therefrom with the consent and by the request of the Directors of the said Bank & so was then & there legally discharged from said office and the performance of the duties thereof. And the said Titus Welles further says that during all the time of his continuance aforesaid in the said office and in discharging the duties thereof, he the said Edward Vose Baxter did at all times faithfully discharge the duties of said office of second Teller of said Bank according to the true intent and meaning of the said condition to wit at Boston aforesaid, and that at the expiration of the time of his continuance aforesaid in said office &c the said Edward Vose Baxter accounted with the Plaintiffs of and concerning divers sums of money, notes, bills, and other things by him received for and on account of the plaintiffs in discharging the duties of said office of second Teller during all the time of his continuance therein as aforesaid &c and then and there paid over and delivered to the plaintiffs all such sums of money, notes, bills and other things as were thereupon found to have been received by him in his said office of second Teller for and on account of the Plaintiffs; saving and excepting, however, the sum of three dollars and six cents, found on said computation & appearing to be due from said Edward Vose Baxter to the Plaintiffs; which said sum of three dollars and six cents the said Edward Vose Baxter forebore and failed to pay over and deliver to the Plaintiffs at the time aforesaid, and the defendant has ever been ready & willing to pay the same, & thereafterwards, before the commencement of said action, namely on the twentieth day of November aforesaid offered & tendered to the

Plaintiffs the said sum of three dollars & six cents which the said plaintiffs, then and there refused to accept, and the defendant now brings the same sum into Court ready to be paid to the plaintiffs if they will accept the same, and this he is ready to verify wherefore he prays judgment if the Plaintiffs their action aforesaid thereof against him ought to have or maintain &c

D. Webster & A Bliss

And for another & third plea in this behalf by leave of the Court for that purpose first had & obtained said Defendant says the plaintiffs their action aforesaid thereof against him ought not to have or maintain because he says that on the tenth day of January AD 1817 said Edward Vose Baxter was appointed to and accepted the office of second Teller of said Bank, & continued in said office until the nineteenth day of November AD 1818 when he was legally discharged therefrom by the Directors of said Bank. And the Defendant further says that during all the time aforesaid the said Edward Vose Baxter did from time to time and at all times faithfully discharge and perform the duties of the said office of second Teller according to the true intent and meaning of the said Bond & the condition thereof and this he is ready to verify: wherefore he prays judgment if the Plfs their action aforesaid thereof against him ought to have or maintain &c.

By his Attorneys D Webster & A Bliss

Copy. *State Bank* v. *T. Welles*, MassSJC,S, March 1826.

DOCUMENT 112. PLAINTIFF'S REPLICATION

Suffolk ss. Supreme Judicial Court
Term 1825. Replication.
The President Directors and Company of the State Bank vs. Titus Welles Executor of Abraham Touro.
And the Plaintiffs say that by any thing in the first plea of the said Titus Welles contained, they ought not to be precluded from having and maintaining their said action against him: because they say; that the said Edward Vose Baxter in the condition of the Bond aforesaid named, remained and continued in the service of the Ptfs in the office of such second teller of the Bank aforesaid as in the condition of the said writing obligatory is mentioned, for a long space of time, to wit from the tenth day of January in the year of our Lord one thousand eight hundred and seventeen untill the nineteenth day of November in the year of our Lord one thousand eight hundred and eighteen; and that it became and was the duty of the said Edward Vose Baxter, in his office of such second Teller as aforesaid, to account and settle with the first teller of the said

Bank, for all monies by him received in his said office of such second teller as aforesaid, and to deliver and pay over the same to said first teller of said State Bank for the use and benefit of the Pltfs. And the Pltfs further say that during the said time that he the said Edward Vose Baxter continued and remained in the service and employment of the Ptfs in the said office of such second teller as aforesaid, to wit on the said tenth day of January in the year of our Lord one thousand eight hundred and seventeen and on divers other days and times between that day and the nineteenth day of November in the year of our Lord one thousand eight hundred and eighteen at Boston aforesaid, he the said Edward Vose Baxter, as such second Teller as aforesaid had and received for and on account of the Pltfs divers sums of money and Bank Notes, amounting in the whole to the sum of ten thousand dollars, which he the said Edward Vose Baxter tho often requested during the life of him the said Edward did not account and settle for with the said first teller of the Bank aforesaid, and which he the said Edward did not deliver and pay over, either to the said first teller of the said Bank or to the Pltfs; but both wholly therein failed and made default and that the said sums of money and Bank notes so as aforesaid had and received by the said Edward Vose Baxter are wholly unsettled and unaccounted for with the said first teller of said Bank—and are wholly unpaid, either to said first teller of said Bank or to the Pltfs, contrary to the form and effect of the condition of said writing obligatory and this the Pltfs are ready to verify; wherefore they pray judgment if they shall be precluded from having and maintaining their said action thereof against him the said Titus Welles and for their debt and costs.

By [Daniel] Davis & [James T.] Austin their Attys

And as to the second plea of the said Titus Welles above pleaded the Plfs say, they ought not to be precluded from having and maintaining their said action against him the said Titus Welles by reason of any thing in said second plea contained, because they say that during the time that the said Edward V. Baxter was in the service and employment of the Plfs in the said office of such second teller of said Bank as is mentioned in the condition of the Bond aforesaid and in the said second plea of the said Titus Welles, to wit on the said tenth day of January in the year of our Lord one thousand eight hundred and seventeen, and on divers other days and times between that day and the said nineteenth day of November, in the year of our Lord one thousand eight hundred and eighteen, in the said second plea mentioned, he the said Edward Vose Baxter in his said office of such second teller as aforesaid had, and received for and on account of Pltfs divers sums of money and Bank notes amounting in the whole to the sum of ten thousand dollars which he the said Edward Vose Baxter tho requested during his life time never accounted for or paid over to the Pltfs, but which he the said Edward Vose Baxter then and there at Boston aforesaid wasted and converted to his own use, without this that he the said E[dward] Vose Baxter then and there paid over and delivered to the Pltfs all such sums of money notes bills and other things as were found to have been received by him in his said office for and on account of the Pltfs and this Pltfs are ready to verify. Wherefore they pray judgment if they shall be precluded from having and maintaining their said action thereof against him the said Titus Welles, and for their debt and costs.

By Davis & Austin their Attys

And as to the third Plea of him the said Titus Welles above pleaded the Pltfs say, that they ought not to be precluded from having and maintaining their said action against him the said Titus Welles; by reason of any thing in that plea contained because they say that the said Edward Vose Baxter in the condition of the Bond aforesaid named remained and continued in the service of the Pltfs in the office of such second teller of the Bank aforesaid as in the condition of the Bond aforesaid is mentioned, for a long space of time to wit, from the tenth day of January in the year of our Lord one thousand eight hundred and seventeen until the nineteenth day of November in the year of our Lord one thousand eight hundred and eighteen; and that it became and was the duty of said Edward Vose Baxter in his office of such second teller as aforesaid, to account and settle with the first teller of said State Bank for all monies by him received in his said office of such second teller as aforesaid and to deliver and pay over the same to the said first teller of said State Bank for the use and benefit of the Pltfs, and the Plfs, further say that during the said time that the said Edward Vose Baxter, continued and remained in the service and employment of the Pltfs in the said office of such second teller as aforesaid, to wit on the said tenth day of January in the year of our Lord one thousand eight hundred and eighteen at Boston aforesaid, he the said Edward Vose Baxter as such second Teller as aforesaid, had and received for and on account of the Ptfs divers sums of money and bank notes amounting in the whole to ten thousand dollars, which he the said Edward Vose Baxter tho often requested during his life time, did not account and settle for with the said first teller of the Bank aforesaid, and which he the said Edward did not deliver and pay over, either to the said first teller of the bank aforesaid or the Pltf, but hath wholly therein failed and made default; and that the said sums of money and bank notes &c, as aforesaid had and received by the said Edward Vose Baxter in his said office of such second teller as aforesaid are wholly unsettled and unaccounted for with the said first teller of said Bank, and are wholly unpaid either to the said first teller of said Bank or to the Pltfs; contrary to the form and effect of the condition of said writing obligatory, and this the Pltfs are ready to verify, wherefore they pray judgment if they shall be precluded from having and maintaining their said action thereof against him the said Titus Welles and for their debt and costs.

By Davis & Austin their Attys.

Copy. *State Bank* v. *T. Welles*, MassSJC,S, March 1826.

DOCUMENT 113. DEFENDANT'S REJOINDER

State Bank vs. Titus Welles Executor of Abraham Touro.

And the said Titus Welles saith that the plaintiffs by reason of any thing by them in their replication to the First plea in bar alleged ought not to have & maintain their said action, because he saith; that at the expiration of the term of time during which said Edward Vose Baxter is in said replication supposed to have been in said office of second teller of said Bank & in the service & employment of the plaintiffs & before the time when the pretended breach of said condition is therein supposed to have been committed, to wit, on the Nineteenth day of November aforesaid, the office of first teller of said Bank became & was vacant so that the said Edward Vose Baxter did not & could not account & settle with the first teller of said Bank for the monies of the Plaintiffs in his said office & in discharging the duties thereof by him had & received; they the said Plfs having then and there discharged & dismissed the said first teller from the said office of first teller of said Bank. And the said Titus Welles further saith, that thereafterwards, & on being discharged from said office of second teller of said Bank, to wit on the day last aforesaid at Boston aforesaid, said Edward Vose Baxter & the plaintiffs accounted together of & concerning divers sums of money notes bills &c theretofore had & received by him for & on account of the Plaintiffs, in his said office & in discharging the duties thereof as such second teller. And thereupon the sum of twenty seven thousand two hundred and eleven dollars & thirty cents and no more was found to be due & owing to the Plaintiffs as the balance of all such sums so received by him during the time aforesaid in discharging the duties of said office—which said sum of twenty seven thousand two hundred & eleven dollars & thirty cents the said Edward Vose Baxter then & there paid over & delivered to the plaintiffs & the same was thereupon received by them & the Cashier of said Bank. And the said Titus Welles further saith that in the computing & finding of the balance aforesaid all & every sums & sum of money & Bank notes, therefore, or then had & received by said Edward Vose Baxter, for & on account of the plaintiffs in discharging the duties of said office, & not before accounted & settled for, were included & accounted for. And that no money, bank notes &c,

ever after came to the hands or possession of said Edward Vose Baxter for or on account of the Plaintiffs in his said capacity. And this the said Titus Welles is ready to verify; wherefore he prays judgment if the plaintiffs their action aforesaid thereof against him ought to have & maintain

By his Attorneys.

And as to the replication to the second plea in Bar said Titus Welles saith that by reason of any thing therein contained the plaintiffs ought not to have and maintain their said action because he says that the said Edward Vose Baxter did pay over and deliver to the Plaintiffs all such sums of money notes bills and other things as were found to have been received by him in his said office for and on account of the Plaintiffs in manner and form as the said Titus Welles in his said second plea in bar alleged, and of this he puts himself upon the Country by his Attorneys

D Webster & A Bliss

And the plaintiffs do the like by their attorneys

Austin & Davis

And the said Titus Welles saith that by reason of any thing by the plaintiffs in their replication to the third plea in bar of said Titus Welles alleged, the plaintiffs ought not to have and maintain their said action, because he saith that said[12]

Copy. *State Bank* v. *T. Welles,* MassSJC,S, March 1826.

DOCUMENT 114. SURREJOINDER

Supreme Judicial Court.
November Term 1825.
State Bank vs Titus Welles Executor
And the said Pltfs say that they ought not to be precluded from having and maintaining their action thereof against the said Deft by reason of any thing by him in his said rejoinder to the replication of said Pltfs to the first plea of the Deft set forth because the said Pltfs Protesting that in the computing and finding of the ballance aforesaid (as set forth in the Defts rejoinder to the Pltfs replication to the first plea aforesaid) all and every sums and sum of money and Bank notes, thereto or then had and received by the said Edward Vose Baxter for and on account of the Pltfs in discharging the duties of said office and not before accounted and settled for were not included and accounted for, say that the said

12. The rest of this document is missing from the court records. It must have alleged settlement and payment of Baxter's account.

Edward Vose Baxter did not pay over and deliver to the Pltfs the sum of twenty seven thousand two hundred and eleven dollars and thirty cents as the said Thompson Baxter in his rejoinder to the replication to his first plea has alleged and this they pray may be enquired of by the Country

By Austin & Davis their Attys

And Deft likewise by his Attorneys D Webster & A Bliss

ADS. *State Bank* v. *T. Welles*, MassSJC,S, March 1826.

TO ALEXANDER BLISS

My Dear Sir Washington Feb. 26. [1826]

I do not find the Judge's Report, in the case of S[tate] Bank v Welles, to be just as I expected. I fear, that, as it stands, we have small chance. It says, *we admitted that Baxter embezzled* the property of the Bank, &c; & reimbursed it by *theft*; now, I supposed, all we admitted, was the *theft*;—& according to my recollections, *we did not mean to admit a previous embezzlement.* I may not be accurate, in my recollections, & must refer to the original paper, which I believe I *signed.*[13] Indeed I am sure, or feel so, that Mr [James T.] Austin and myself *signed* a statement. By that we must be bound, & I cannot help thinking it was differing from what you send me; alltho, such a number of things pass my mind, I cannot undertake to say absolutely. Pray search the records & files; & if this *case* be not stated right, have it corrected. *Look to the paper which I signed.* Yrs D. Webster

P.S. On a re-perusal of the statement, I feel very confident I never agreed to it.

ALS. DLC.

ii. The Crime of Embezzlement: Commonwealth of Massachusetts v. *William Wyman.* In October 1842 the Phoenix Bank of Charlestown suspended payment on all its outstanding notes. Under a recently passed statute, the Massachusetts banking commissioners appointed receivers to oversee the collection and distribution of the bank's meager assets.[14] A shocked Charlestown pointed the finger of accusation at bank president William Wyman, cashier Thomas Brown Jr., and Boston merchant

13. Not found.

14. Laws, Mass., c. 14 (1838); *Hubbard et al.* v. *Charlestown Branch Rail Road Company*, 11 Metcalf (Mass.) 124 (1846), and *Commonwealth* v. *Phoenix Bank*, 11 Metcalf (Mass.) 129 (1846). For a report of the proceedings in the *Wyman* case, see "The Phoenix Bank Cases," *The Law Reporter*, 6 (1844): 385–392, and 8 (1846): 337–344.

William Skinner. Wyman, indeed, admitted responsibility for the bank's failure. A few years earlier he had, on his own initiative, made a large loan to Skinner's mercantile firm. The company's subsequent difficulties forced Wyman to lend it more and more of the bank's assets. Finally when the company went bankrupt, it dragged the bank down with it. Although Wyman had not benefited financially from his lending practices, the community demanded his punishment. Citing Wyman's mismanagement and other questionable acts, the district attorney decided to seek an indictment against Wyman and his two associates for the embezzlement of the bank's capital. In June 1843 a grand jury indicted them for embezzlement and theft.

Massachusetts had criminalized embezzlement in 1824. Although an earlier 1791 statute had made it a crime for anyone employed in the state treasury to commit embezzlement, no apparent need existed until the 1820s for more stringent legislation. The 1824 statute made it larcenous for any "cashier, or other officer or servant" of any incorporated bank to take for his own use money (notes, bills, etc.) belonging to the bank or any of its depositors.[15] When the state enacted its comprehensive statutory scheme to regulate banks in 1829, it reenacted the 1824 bank embezzlement statute, but added "president and directors" to the list of those covered.

In 1834 the legislature addressed the problem of thefts by clerks from their own companies. Section 1 made embezzlement of any money or thing of value by a servant from his master a crime. It thus overcame a loophole in the common law of crimes, which said a clerk did not commit larceny if he took property left in the custody of his employer. In effect, the statute treated the employer's custody as constructive possession. This brought an employee's appropriation within the common law's traditional requirement that criminal theft be a taking out of someone else's possession. To further buttress the legislation, section 2 altered the traditional method of proof. Instead of having to allege and prove the embezzlement of a specific thing, the state could indict a suspect for up to three unspecified acts of theft of a general sum of money within a six month period.[16] The state then needed to prove only that the servant had taken something of value sometime within the period charged in the indictment. If the servant could not account for property entrusted to him, the jury could convict him of embezzlement.

In 1834 the legislature appointed a commission to revise the state's laws. In their revision the commissioners considered the several em-

15. Laws, Mass., c. 59, s. 5 (1791); c. 51 s. 1 (1824).

16. Laws, Mass., c. 186, s. 1 and 2 (1834). This was a transcript of 7 & 8 Geo. 4, c. 29, s. 47 (1827) enacted to close loopholes in 39 Geo. 3, c. 85 (1799).

bezzlement statutes.[17] First, they dropped "president and directors" from those who could commit bank embezzlement. This became section 24 of their chapter 126. Then they took the 1834 servant embezzlement law and broke it apart. Section 1 (with slight modification) became section 26 of chapter 126. Section 2, and its easier method of proof, found its way into chapter 133. The commissioners rewrote it to apply to any "prosecution for the offence of embezzling the money, bank notes . . . of any person or corporation, by a clerk, an agent or servant." When the legislature adopted the revisions, it dropped the reference to corporations.[18] By splitting the 1834 statute apart and placing sections 1 and 2 in different parts of the revised statutes, the revisors had set the stage for the Wyman trials.

The clamor for the state to prosecute Wyman as an embezzler reflected public frustration with incorporated businesses that failed through mismanagement and then left their creditors without remedy. One law journal commented that "these outrageous frauds have of late gone almost entirely unpunished even in Massachusetts, and there has seemed to be no law whatever for the swindling transactions of moneyed corporations."[19] In the *Wyman* case the state would try to use the embezzlement statutes to punish poor business judgment.

When the state indicted the Phoenix Bank defendants, the prosecutor assumed that the revised chapter 133 allowed him to make a general allegation of embezzlement during a succession of six-month periods. Proof of the theft, loss, or even, disappearance of any amount would win the case. The indictment therefore alleged a total theft of almost $300,000 (the bank's capital) and successive thefts of $50,000 in six-month periods from 1839 to 1842.

In August 1843 the case came to trial at the criminal common pleas in Concord. Wyman retained Webster and Franklin Dexter; Skinner hired Rufus Choate, Sidney Bartlett, A. W. Austin, and Ebenezer Rockwood Hoar. Choate and Bartlett also appeared for Brown. First, Skinner, successfully, moved to have his case tried separately. Then the jury heard the evidence against Wyman and Brown. The bulk of the testimony came from the bank's directors, who testified that they had trusted Wyman and had given him free rein. It also appeared (probably on cross examination) that they themselves had borrowed heavily from the bank. Webster and Dexter did not deny Wyman's breach of trust. They focused their attack on whether he had committed any crime. They asserted that not only did the state have to prove that Wyman had had a fraudulent intent

17. *Report of the Commissioners Appointed to Revise the General Statutes of the Commonwealth* (Boston, 1835), c. 126, pp. 13–14, and c. 133, p. 37.

18. Revised Statutes, Mass., c. 126, s. 24–27, and c. 133, s. 10 (1834).

19. *The Law Reporter*, 6: 392.

in making the loans but that the loans had been for his own benefit. But trial judge Charles Allen ruled against Webster's proposed jury instruction. Allen told the jury that if Wyman simply took the money without the knowledge of the directors, and contrary to the bank's interest, it amounted to a fraudulent taking and constituted an embezzlement. Webster reportedly made "a most able argument, and argued with great ingenuity and zeal to the jury, that the defendant Wyman, although not free from blame, was not guilty of the crime charged."[20]

Ralph Waldo Emerson attended the trial and recorded his impressions of the first part of Webster's summation to the jury.

> Mr Webster loses nothing by comparison with brilliant men in the legal profession: he is as much before them as before the ordinary lawyer. At least I thought he appeared among these best lawyers of the Suffolk bar, like a schoolmaster among his boys. His wonderful organization, the perfection of his elocution, and all that thereto belongs, voice, accent, intonation, attitude, manner, are such as one cannot hope to see again in a century; then he is so thoroughly simple & wise in his rhetoric. Understanding language, & the use of the positive degree, all his words tell, and his rhetoric is perfect, so homely, so fit, so strong. Then he manages his matter so well, he hugs his fact so close, & will not let it go, & never indulges in a weak flourish, though he knows perfectly well how to make such exordiums & episodes & perorations as may give perspective to his harangue, without in the least embarrassing his plan or confounding his transitions. What is small, he shows as small, & makes the great, great. In speech he sometimes roars. And his words are like blows of an axe. His force of personal attack is terrible, he lays out his strength so directly in honest blows, and all his powers of voice, arm, eye, & whole man are so heartily united & bestowed on the adversary that he cannot fail to be felt.[21]

After deliberating for several hours, the jury acquitted Brown. They could not, however, agree on Wyman's guilt or innocence. Judge Allen ordered a new trial for Wyman in Lowell in November.

At the second trial district attorney Daniel Wells outlined his proof along the lines of chapter 133. Either Webster or Dexter asked the court to decide whether the state must prove a single distinct act of embezzlement to make its case. As he had in the first trial, Judge Allen ruled that the state could prove that Wyman had made loans without the permis-

20. *The Law Reporter*, 6: 387. Webster also commented on the character of the directors who, he said, hoped to see Wyman convicted and thereby prevented from testifying against them in a civil suit by a bank stockholder against the directors.

21. William H. Gilman, et al., ed., *The Journals and Miscellaneous Notebooks of Ralph Waldo Emerson* (10 vols., Boston, 1960–1978), 8: 357–358.

sion of the directors, and that Wyman had loaned the embezzled property to the merchants without needing to show a specific theft. When the state closed its case, Webster and Dexter pressed the issue of proof once more. They moved the court to instruct the jury that it must find a distinct act of embezzlement. Judge Allen refused. Again, he told the jury that they could find Wyman guilty even if Wyman had not benefited from taking the bank's funds. The jury retired and then returned a verdict of guilty. Webster and Dexter filed a bill of exceptions (Document 115) setting forth their disagreement with Allen's rulings. If they could convince the full SJC bench that the state had to prove a bank officer guilty of a specific act, it would seriously weaken the state's case.

In the fall of 1844, prior to the argument on the bill of exceptions, Dexter learned from two witnesses that before the Lowell trial two of the jurors had expressed opinions adverse to Wyman's innocence. One of them had reportedly said that Wyman "ought to be shot or go to the State Prison" (Document 116). Using one of these accounts as evidence, Dexter drafted and filed a motion for a new trial (Document 117). In January 1845 he filed a second affidavit (Document 118). The district attorney sent word to Essex County to send the two jurors down to Boston (Document 119), where both denied the charges (Documents 120 and 121).

In January 1845 the MassSJC heard Webster and Dexter argue the bill of exceptions. Immediately thereafter the attorneys filed a motion in arrest of judgment (Document 122), alleging three defects in the state's indictment: first, that the indictment failed to allege a specific item embezzled by Wyman; second, that it neglected to identify the money taken; and third, that it did not describe Wyman's position with the bank.

The court sustained Webster and Dexter's exceptions and ordered a new trial.[22] In his opinion Justice Hubbard started from the premise that the court must construe penal statutes strictly. He then addressed the question whether bank presidents were "officers" within the meaning of the bank embezzlement statute, and, if so, whether the state could proceed against them as set forth in chapter 133. On the first point he held that the term "officer" included bank presidents. The revisers intended to apply the criminal sanction to all those properly entrusted with a bank's property. Turning to the second question, he examined the history of the statutes. Although chapter 133 contained general language, the legislature did not intend to apply the more general mode of proof to bank officers. When the revisers split the 1834 statute into two parts, they had not clearly indicated that it did not alter the requirement that the state must charge bank officers with a specific act of fraud. Given this

22. *Commonwealth* v. *Wyman*, 8 Metcalf (Mass.) 247 (1844).

interpretation of the statutes, the trial judge had erred. Wyman must be retried. By closing off the easier method of proof, Hubbard made Wyman's conviction impossible. The case, however, did not end here.

In March 1845 the legislature amended chapter 133. It now made the easier mode of proof applicable in prosecutions against "presidents, directors, cashiers and other officers of banks."[23] The district attorney then obtained a new indictment against Wyman. Wyman's third trial began on September 1, 1845, in Concord. Webster, Choate, and E. R. Hoar represented Wyman. In a preliminary move they sought to quash the indictment on the ground that it failed to set forth any specific offense. The attorneys focused on the effect of the 1845 amendment. Choate and Webster argued that the new statute either applied solely to prospective criminal acts, or if the legislature intended to apply it to Wyman, it was an ex post facto law in violation of the United States Constitution. Trial judge Emory Washburn denied the motion.[24] He held that since an indictment was only a "written accusation of a crime" the state could excuse the government from having to specify the precise acts of embezzlement. The statute therefore did not affect the ultimate proof of the crime charged.

Wyman's counsel then moved the court to require the state to prove a single substantive act of embezzlement. After the lawyers argued this point, the court again denied the motion. Judge Washburn told the acting district attorney J. P. Rogers that he need only prove the taking of part of the bank's capital within a six-month period. Choate and Webster then picked up on a suggestion in Washburn's opinion and moved for a bill of particulars of the acts of embezzlement. Washburn directed the state to produce a general statement of the larcenous transactions it intended to prove. When Rogers gave the defense a list of ten specifications, Webster asked the court to restrict the government's proof to the theft of metal coins, i.e. things. Webster intended this motion to save the point for an appeal. The court duly denied Webster's motion.

With these preliminaries over, Rogers spent the next six days presenting the government's case. He focused on the transactions with the Boston merchant firm. The evidence showed that Wyman had lent them large sums, had accepted bogus checks, and had discounted worthless notes. Altogether these transactions resulted in a transfer of over $300,000 to the merchants. Choate opened for the defense. He spoke for four hours, mainly on the law of the case. He focused on a critical aspect of the state's indictment and proof. Nowhere, he observed, had the state shown that Wyman had been entrusted with the actual money of the bank. The money had been in the custody of the cashier, the cashier had made the payments, and the cashier had been acquitted. Wyman could

23. Massachusetts Acts and Resolves, c. 215, p. 546 (1845).

24. His opinion is reported in *The Law Reporter*, 8 (1846): 392–402.

not have been guilty of an embezzlement, therefore, because he had never literally handled the money. Choate read to the court the bank's bylaws. They required the cashier to keep the money "in his possession" and to deposit the money in the vault at the close of each business day. Then Choate turned to Hubbard's opinion at the second Wyman trial. He read Hubbard's discussion of bank operations. Hubbard had written that the president and directors held a supervisory power; they entrusted the active management to the officers from the cashier on down. Only where the president and director was "charged as intrusted with the property of the bank" could they "be punished for the crime of embezzlement." Moreover, Hubbard applied the same requirement to the operation of chapter 133. The indictment must aver that the bank entrusted the defendant with its funds. Wyman's indictment said that he did "then and there have, receive, and take unto his possession certain money . . . and was then and there intrusted by said president, directors and company . . . with the money aforesaid."[25] But the government, Choate pointed out, never proved this.

Rogers must have been surprised by this turn of events. First, he said that Hubbard's opinion was only dicta. When this failed to sway the court, he argued that the directors had never released control of the funds to the cashier, and that Wyman had acted on behalf of the directors. The bylaws and testimony of the directors contradicted this. Finally, Rogers said that embezzlement did not require physical custody of the thing taken.[26] Webster then responded, briefly reiterating Choate's point.

Choate had mortally wounded the government's case. Judge Washburn said he considered it a question for the jury whether the directors had entrusted Wyman with the funds. Rogers asked Washburn to clarify the meaning of "intrusting" funds. Washburn then laid out his understanding of the law:

> If the president and directors of an ordinary country bank, at a regular meeting of the board, with a fraudulent intent to get possession of the moneys of the bank, were to discount notes and direct the cashier to pay out the money upon them, knowing them to be worthless, it would be a conspiracy and not an embezzlement, unless the cashier was privy to the fraud. If the cashier participated in the fraud, it would be embezzlement on his part, and the president and directors would be accessories. If the defendant, acting as president and directors, did the same thing and no more, and the cashier innocently paid out the money, could it be any more an embezzlement in the defendant than in the president and directors in the case supposed? To test this—if the cashier was party to the

25. Ibid., 8: 342.

26. Obviously, Rogers was ahead of his time. The judge's view of embezzlement was still controlled by the common law notion of a physical taking of another's property.

> fraud he clearly would be liable for embezzlement. Why? Because intrusted with the funds. Could the defendant in that case be otherwise indicted than as an accessory? Clearly not unless he and the cashier had joint possession of the funds. If they had not joint possession, one must be principal and the other accessory. If then the cashier was so intrusted with the funds as to render him liable for embezzling them, can the same funds at one and the same time be regarded, within the meaning of the Supreme Court,—as intrusted to the defendant, so as to render him liable for embezzling them by an act in which the cashier did not partake?[27]

Rogers rose and told the court that on the evidence presented he could not ask the jury for Wyman's conviction. He could not prove that the bank had intrusted Wyman with the lost funds. The court directed a verdict in Wyman's favor and ordered him discharged.

DOCUMENT 115. BILL OF EXCEPTIONS

Commonwealth of Massachusetts.
Middlesex ss. Criminal Court, of Common Pleas October Term 1843
Commonwealth v. { William Wyman,
Thomas Brown Junr
William H. Skinner[28]

This Indictment came on to be tried before a Jury empannelled for the purpose, at the June term of this Court, and the said Defendants, having all severally pleaded *not guilty*, the said Skinner by his Counsel moved the Court, that he should be tried separately from the said Wyman, and Brown, which motion was granted by the Court, and the said Wyman and Brown were then put upon their trial together, when said Brown was acquitted, and the Jury having disagreed as to said Wyman was by consent of the prosecuting officer,[29] and said Wyman discharged without a

27. *The Law Reporter*, 8: 343–344. Emerson attended this trial also. In the intervening two years the acrimonious debate over the annexation of Texas had made him less enamored of Webster. Shortly before the trial's conclusion he recorded in his journal: "There was Webster the great cannon loaded to the lips: he told Cheney that if he should close by addressing the jury, he should blow the roof off. As it was, he did nothing but pound. Choate put in the nail & drove it; Webster came after & pounded. . . . Ah if God had given to this Demosthenes [i.e., Webster] a heart to lead New England! What a life & death & glory for him. Now he is a fine symbol & mantel ornament —costly enough to those who must keep it; for the great head aches, & the great trunk must be curiously fed & comforted." (*Emerson's Journals*, 9: 250–251.) John Milton Cheney was cashier of the Middlesex Institution for Savings in Concord.

28. Brown, Jr., cashier of the Phoenix Bank; Skinner, a Boston merchant.

29. The prosecution was handled by district attorneys Asahel Huntington and Daniel Wells. Huntington

verdict; and now at this term this Indictment came on to be tried before a Jury empannelled for the trial of said Wyman, the Counsel for the Government, opened by stating that the Defendant was the President of the Phoenix Bank and as such Officer had controul and custody of the property of the Bank; that on the first day of October, 1842, it was ascertained that the whole Capital of the Bank $300,000, was lost, the Bank until that time, being in good credit, its Directors as well as the Public, supposing it to be good and its capital entire; that at some time or times unknown, but within six months after the day stated in the Indictment, the Capital of the Bank, was embezzled by the Defendant, and thereupon the Counsel for the said Defendant, Wyman moved the Court to decide that in point of law, the Commonwealth was restrained to the proof of some one single, and distinct act of embezzlement as a substantive offence, committed within six months from and after the day stated in the said Indictment and that no other distinct act of embezzlement could be proved except for collateral purposes, as for showing the intent with which such single substantive act, was committed or the like, but the Court expressed an opinion that the Government might prove any acts of embezzlement, committed within six months next after the day named in the Indictment and permitted the Counsel for the Government, to give evidence of the abstraction within said period of six months of a large amount of promissory notes, money & Treasury notes, without proof that the same were taken from the Bank or abstracted at the same time, and evidence was given upon the said trial, among other things, tending to shew that the Defendant had authority to lend money of the Bank without consulting the Directors; and also evidence tending to shew that the Defendant had lent the property mentioned in the Indictment to Stanley, Reed & Co,[30] and after the evidence was closed, the Counsel for the Defendant, made the following motion to the Court, in the terms following to wit:

> "The Counsel for the Defendant move the Court to instruct the Jury, First, That under this Indictment the Defendant cannot be found guilty of embezzling any description of property, mentioned in the Indictment except Treasury notes.
> Second; That to support the Indictment the Government must prove to the satisfaction of the Jury one or more distinct acts of embezzlement committed within six months from and after the day charged in the Indictment and that it is not sufficient to prove that within

(1798–1870; Yale 1819), Massachusetts lawyer, admitted in 1824, practiced in Salem until 1851 when he was appointed clerk of courts, Essex County, state legislator; Wells (1792–1854; Dartmouth 1810), Massachusetts lawyer and judge, district attorney, western district (1837–1844), chief justice, MassCCP,M (1844–1854).

30. Not further identified.

> that period, uncertain sums at uncertain times have been embezzled, although the aggregate of the same may be a sum certain
>
> Webster & [Franklin] Dexter for Wyman"

But the Court refused to instruct the Jury, according to the prayer of said motion. And respecting the legal character & meaning of the crime of embezzlement the Court instructed the Jury, that the crime of embezzlement with which the Defendant was charged consisted in the fraudulent conversion by him to his own use of the property of the Bank, described in the Indictment, but that it was not necessary to his conviction, that the Jury should be satisfied that it was appropriated to his own pecuniary or other personal advantage: It was equally an act of embezzlement if the motive for the conversion of the property was to benefit another person, for instance, a friend of the Defendant & funds fraudulently converted by him were thus applied. And the cause having been committed to the Jury, the Jury returned a verdict of guilty against the Defendant the said Wyman.

Whereupon the Counsel of said Defendant excepted to the said refusal and instructions of this Court and tendered this, their bill of Exceptions which being found to be true, the Judge of the said Court before whom the cause was tried has allowed the same this twenty fifth day of November in the year Eighteen hundred and forty three.

Charles Allen[31]
Presiding Judge

Copy. *Commonwealth* v. *Wyman*, MassSJC,M, October 1844.

DOCUMENT 116. AFFIDAVIT

[October 31, 1844]

I Miles F. Griffin of Methuen in the County of Essex and Commonwealth of Massachusetts shoemanufacturer[32] do testify and say that I went to Edward Young[33] of Dracutt (in the County of Middlesex and said Commonwealth, one of the jurors who tried William Wyman at Lowell before the C. C. Pleas for said County of Middlesex at the October Term thereof A.D. 1843) early in the autumn of said year 1843 either in the month of September or October and asked said Young to loan me, I think, ten dollars. Said Young replied that he had no money but had nineteen dollars of the Phoenix Bank of Charlestown and he did not know as that was

31. Charles Allen (1797–1869; Yale 1811), Massachusetts lawyer and judge, studied with Samuel M. Burnside, admitted in 1818, state legislator, judge, MassCCP,M (1842–1844), U.S. representative (1844–1853), judge, superior court, Suffolk County (1858–1859, chief justice, 1859–1867).

32. Griffin has not been further identified.

33. Not further identified.

good for anything, but he said there was a place in Boston or Charlestown where they allowed something for it in payment for clothing. I made the remark to Mr Young that I understood that the Bank had failed through the mismanagement of the President and Directors; he said he believed that it had so failed through their mismanagement and that they all ought to be shot or go to the State Prison, which last words were very angrily spoken by said Young who appeared to show much feeling by reason of his loosing the nineteen dollars. I do further testify and say that while the trial of said Wyman was going on, Mr Sawyer,[34] my neighbor said to me, "Griffin, they will acquit him because he is rich"—I replied no—there is one man that will not agree to a verdict to acquit him that is Young. I then stated to Mr Sawyer what Young had stated to me in relation to the nineteen dollars &c; whereupon Sawyer replied to me that the loss of the nineteen dollars would go further with Young than all the evidence in the case.

Miles F Griffin

ADS. *Commonwealth* v. *Wyman*, MassSJC,M, October 1844.

DOCUMENT 117. MOTION FOR NEW TRIAL

[November 21, 1844]

Commonwealth of Massachusetts
Court of Common Pleas
Middlesex ss
Commonwealth, by Indictment
v
William Wyman

And now the said William Wyman after a trial in said cause had at the October term of said Court A.D. 1843. comes and moves for a new trial therein for the causes following, to wit

Because Edward Young, one of the Jury that tried the said cause had before he was sworn and empannelled expressed an opinion therein and did not stand indifferent therein, which the said Wyman failed to discover, although said Young was examined by the Court on the Voire Dire,[35] and the requisite enquiry made of him, and which said Wyman was ignorant of until a long time after the verdict in said Cause was rendered

Because Luther Holden,[36] one of the Jury that tried the said cause, had before he was sworn and empannelled expressed an opinion therein and

34. Not identified.

35. Preliminary examination of a juror or witness by the court to determine competency.

36. Not identified. See William C. Gray's affidavit, Document 118, following. Dexter read both this motion and Gray's affidavit.

did not stand indifferent therein, which the said Wyman failed to discover, although said Holden was examined by the Court, on the Voire Dire, and the requisite enquiry made of him, and which said Wyman was ignorant of until a long time after the verdict in said Cause was rendered.

By Franklin Dexter *his attorney*

ADS. *Commonwealth* v. *Wyman*, MassSJC,M, October 1844.

DOCUMENT 118. AFFIDAVIT

Janr. 10. [18]45

I William C. Gray[37] of Lowell, make oath and say that since July in the year eighteen hundred and thirty six, I have been an express man between the cities of Lowell and Boston; that in one of my express trips in the year eighteen hundred and forty two, I met in the cars Luther Holden of Woburn, whom I had known for several years, and who was a passenger that day from Boston to Woburn, it was about the time of the commencement of the proceedings against William Wyman, President of the Phoenix Bank in Charlestown, before the examining magistrate in Middlesex.

The conversation in the cars turned on that subject and Mr Holden took part in it, it was brought about by the newspapers which we had in the cars in which this subject was commented on, and a conversation between Mr Wyman and his Directors was reported.

In that conversation the conduct of the President and different Directors of the Bank was discussed. Mr Holden expressed himself very violently against said Wyman; I stated that it might not turn out so bad as it now looked. Mr Holden replied that there could be no doubt about it and repeated this several times. He said that Wyman ought to be hung and that one half of the Bank Directors and Presidents—were in the same predicament that he was; He said also that the Laws were so made that the rich were shielded by them and that Wyman no doubt had the money and friends and that by means of these he would get clear. The conversation to which I refer commenced soon after we got into the cars and lasted till we got to the turn out at Woburn, which distance takes generally from twenty minutes to half an hour and Mr Holden was engaged in conversation throughout the whole of it. I should not have thought of this again had I not been called in the way of my business into the Court Room at Lowell, and there was said Holden sitting on the Jury that tried said Wyman. I was so surprized at seeing him there after the expression of opinion which he had made in the cars, that I mentioned it in a Hotel in Lowell at the time and then stated that I had no doubt Wyman would be

37. Not further identified.

brought in guilty, if it depended on Holden. I mentioned this conversation to several persons, but never to the Counsel of Mr Wyman or to Mr Wyman himself, till application was made by him to me within a short time previous to this day.

Wm C. Gray

ADS. *Commonwealth* v. *Wyman*, MassSJC,M, October 1844.

DOCUMENT 119. INSTRUCTION TO SHERIFF

[January 11, 1845]

I wish to have Messrs. Holden and Young come down in the 1st train of cars Monday morning, and report themselves to me at the Court House in Boston, if the Court is there, otherwise at East Cambridge, if the Court is there. I am not *certain* at *which place* the Court is held tomorrow.

An attempt is making to get a new trial in the case of Wyman, on the ground that Mess. Holden & Young expressed *strong opinions* agt. Wyman *before* the trial, two depositions have been taken to prove that fact. But I will explain further when I see the jurors. I do not *know* that it will be necessary to examine them, but it may be, & we must be prepared.

A Huntington

N.B. Mr. *Reed*[38] will shew this note to both the *gentlemen*

ADS. *Commonwealth* v. *Wyman*, MassSJC,M, October 1844.

DOCUMENT 120. AFFIDAVIT

Suffolk ss. Jany. 13. 1845.

I Edward Young, of Dracutt, on oath depose and say, that I was on the Jury, that tried the case of the Comwlth agt. Wm. Wyman, at the C. C. Pleas Oct. Trm. 1842—that I am acquainted with Miles F. Griffin, of Methuen—that I recollect his applying to me for the loan of small sums of money, in one or two instances—that I do not now remember when such applications were made—that I remember having had some eighteen or nineteen dollars of the Phoenix money on hand at the time of the failure of the Bank—that I had none of said money on hand at the time of the trial of said Wyman—having previously disposed of it at a discount part of it, at a discount of 25 per cent, and part of it at a discount at 33 per cent.

The Dis. Atty has read to me several times the affidavit of said Griffin, and its contents, as to certain expressions alleged to have been used by me in relation to the failure of the Phoenix Bank, another agency of the

38. Not identified.

Directors in producing the same, are fully understood by me. I have no recollection whatever of having held any such conversation with said Griffin or any conversation on the subject. I am sure I never said to him —that said Directors ought to be shot or to be sent to the State Prison, and that I never used words of equivalent import to him, said Griffin, or any one else. I am not in the habit of using violent language or strong expressions of that kind. I know, if I know myself, that when I took my seat as one of the Jurors to try the case of Wm. Wyman, I had formed no opinion on the question of his guilt or innocence—and that I was not conscious of any bias or prejudice in the case. I had then known or heard but little about the case, or any of the circumstances attending it. I had no personal knowledge of Mr. Wyman, never having seen him before said trial. I had never seen or read or heard any account of the former trials or examinations, taking but one newspaper myself, viz. "Zions Herald," and not ordinarily reading any others. I am sure that I had no other desire or aim in the trial of that cause, than to do my duty faithfully and impartially. I am certain further, that when I was examined on oath, touching my opinion formed or expressed in the case &c. before the commencement of the trial, that I *then* answered all questions put to me truly and conscientiously. However the fact may be, I was not *then* conscious of having *expressed* any opinion in the case. If in a loose or casual conversation I may have appeared to others to have expressed an opinion—it was not an *opinion* on the question of the guilt or innocence of the defendant in any just and true sense of that term, for I know that before the trial, I had *formed no such opinion.*

I have no recollection now of having expressed such an opinion to any person before the said trial, and I am sure that I never could have used the violent and vindictive language attributed to me by said Griffin, because I never harboured or cherished the feelings or sentiments, which the use of such language would imply. I had no knowledge of any of the Directors of said Bank before said trial.

Edward Young

ADS. *Commonwealth* v. *Wyman,* MassSJC,M, October 1844.

DOCUMENT 121. AFFIDAVIT

Suffolk ss. Jany. 13. 1845.

I Luther Holden of Woburn in the County of Middlesex make oath and say, that I have carefuly read the affidavit of Wm. C. Gray, relating to an alleged conversation with me in regard to the case of Wm. Wyman, Prest. of the Phoenix Bank, and that the contents of said affidavit are fully understood by me. I am well acquainted with said Gray, and have often had conversation with him on various subjects, in the cars, on my passages between Woburn and Boston—that I do not now recollect ever having conversed with him in relation to the case of Mr. Wyman, although I will not say, that I have not conversed with him on that subject. I am entirely certain that I never said to him or any other person, either before or since the trial of Mr. Wyman—that said Wyman ought to be hung, and that I never used words of equivalent import or character. I am also entirely certain, that I never said to him, that "one half of the Bank Directors and Presidents were in the same predicament that he was, or that the laws seem so made that the rich were shielded, and that Wyman no doubt had the money and friends, and that by means of them he would get clear." I am sure I never said this or any thing of equivalent import, because I never entertained such a sentiment or opinion. On the contrary, I believe, and always have believed that our laws are impartially administered. If I ever expressed such a sentiment, I expressed a sentiment which I did not and do not entertain. I am certain further, that I never said that I had "no doubt about Wymans guilt," and that I never used words of equivalent import. I might have expressed myself hypothetically on the subject, or I might have expressed myself ironically. If any expression like that imputed to me, about one half of the Bank Directors and Presidents, and the laws being so made as to shield the rich, was ever used by me, it must have been in an ironical sense, and not as expressing my real opinion, for I know that I never entertained such an opinion.

When I was examined on oath at the empannelling of the Jury, in the case of Mr. Wyman, touching my opinions, entertained or expressed in that case, or any bias or prejudice in the case, I answered all the questions put to me truly and conscientiously. At that time, I was not conscious of having formed or expressed any opinion in relation to the guilt or innocence of the defendant. I was not sensible of any bias or prejudice whatever in the case. At that time I had no personal knowledge whatever of the defendant. I had never seen him before that trial. I am sure <that> whatever I may have said in casual conversation in relation to his case—that before that trial, I had never formed an opinion on the question of his guilt or innocence and if to others at any time, I may have seemed to express an opinion, it was not an *opinion* in any true sense of that term. If I can judge at all of my own motives and feelings, I had no other desire or aim in the trial of that cause, than to discharge my duty, as a juror, faithfully and impartially. I know that was my earnest and sincere desire.

Luther Holden

ADS. *Commonwealth* v. *Wyman*, MassSJC,M, October 1844.

DOCUMENT 122. MOTION IN ARREST OF JUDGMENT

[January 8, 1845]

Middlesex ss.
Supreme Judicial Court
October term 1844

Commonwealth vs William Wyman

And now after the hearing upon the Defendant's bill of Exceptions the Defendant, said William Wyman, moves the Court here to arrest judgment in the said cause for the reasons following:

1st. Because the indictment in said cause does not set forth with sufficient legal certainty any particular thing with the embezzlement of which the said William Wyman is charged in said indictment.

2d. Because the said indictment after charging the said Defendant with the embezzlement of certain money to a large amount, to wit, to the amount and of the value of two hundred and twenty thousand dollars, also charges the Defendant in the same count thereof with the embezzlement of divers bills called bank bills, amounting in the whole to the sum and of the value of one hundred and twenty thousand dollars, and of divers notes called Treasury notes amounting in the whole to the sum and of the value of seventy five thousand dollars, but without any specification of any particular kind or denomination of money or bank bills or Treasury notes, whereby the said indictment is bad and insufficient whereon to found any judgment against the Defendant either at the common law or by any of the Statutes of this Commonwealth.

3d. Because the said indictment does not so describe the office and capacity in which the said Defendant is therein alleged to have received and taken the things therein charged to have been embezzled by him so that by law any judgment can be rendered thereon against the Defendant.

D Webster & F Dexter
Counsel for Wm. Wyman

ADS. *Commonwealth* v. *Wyman*, MassSJC,M, October 1844.

5. PROPERTY LAW

Our proper business is improvement. Let our age be the age of improvement. In a day of peace, let us advance the arts of peace and the works of peace. Let us develope the resources of our land, call forth its powers, build up its institutions, promote all its great interests, and see whether we also, in our day and generation, may not perform something worthy to be remembered.[1]

1. Daniel Webster, "Address delivered at the laying of the Corner Stone of the Bunker Hill Monument —June 17, 1825," in *Speeches and*

a. Introduction

Judges and legislators of early nineteenth-century Massachusetts agreed that the economic development of the country was crucial to its survival as an independent nation. Although the latter group encouraged the development of transportation and manufacturing through the state's power to grant economic privileges, the former undertook to subsidize private investment by decisions that held down the costs of development. Shifting the burden of loss away from entrepreneurs and onto other groups made the initial steps toward the industrialization of New England possible. By franchising turnpikes, canals, and mills, and granting to them the power to take by eminent domain the private property needed to construct such facilities, the legislature intervened in private property relations on the side of the manufacturing interests. Although the Massachusetts constitution required the payment of just compensation to the land owner whose property was taken by the state or incorporated bodies, the owner recovered only the land's current value. The courts also eroded the compensation principle when they made the state liable only for direct damage to private property. Any damage labeled "consequential" received no compensation.[2] Moreover, other judicial decisions narrowed the protective features of eighteenth-century strict liability for injury to another's property. When negligence began to displace both trespass and nuisance around 1840, it emerged as a limitation on the strict liability basis of the older common law categories. The plaintiff now had to prove the defendant's lack of care. Consistent with their effort to aid manufacturing, the courts also expanded the common law concept of public nuisance and thereby prevented private plaintiffs from suing for damage caused by manufacturing unless they demonstrated an injury different in kind from that suffered by the general public.[3]

The use of the eminent domain power by governmental bodies and corporations was the most visible manifestation of state intervention in private property relationships. In its eagerness to develop water power resources, Massachusetts enacted a series of mill acts that gave developers of water power the upper hand over nearby agricultural users. Under the acts the manufacturers built dams that flooded out nearby land owners without fear of having to pay large damage awards. The evident disparity in power between the mill operators and nearby land owners made the mill acts and the eminent domain power itself the subject of intense criticism.[4] Beginning in the 1820s, the use of the eminent domain power began to call forth opposition. The two letters printed below, one from Massachusetts and the other from New York, illustrate the begin-

---

Forensic Arguments (New York, 1830), p. 70.

2. The familiar legal expression was *damnum absque injuria*, i.e., damage without legal injury.

3. Horwitz, pp. 62–114.

4. Ibid., pp. 47–53.

nings of the attack on the power of eminent domain. This effort would not bear fruit until the 1840s.[5]

b. The Power of Eminent Domain

i. Faneuil Hall Market. In 1823 Josiah Quincy, the mayor of the newly chartered city of Boston, proposed an extensive reconstruction of the city's market adjacent to the harbor. In Quincy's view the area had become so congested that farmers could not get their goods to market. The activities of a group of middlemen (forestallers) had resulted in higher food prices. Quincy proposed that the city purchase the nearby land, enlarge the market, and construct six new streets and wharfs. The landowners, however, refused to sell at the current price. They realized that the value of their property would rise if the city undertook the project. Consequently many of them demanded the increased value of the land after development. After some negotiations, most agreed to a lower price and signed conditional contracts; but the owners of one key tract refused to sell. Undaunted, Quincy decided to seek legislative authorization to take by condemnation the errant parcels.[1] He prepared a memorial to the legislature in which he presented the traditional view that as part of its sovereignty the state had the right to take private property for public purposes. Private owners, he argued, held their land at the sufferance of the government. Quincy set forth the legislative view of property:

> In the nature of things, property is the creature of the social state. Where there is no society, there is no property; at least none except that which the strength of each individual enables him to maintain. It follows that property is in relation to society, a dependent interest. It follows also, that the exigencies or necessities of society are paramount to the rights of property.[2]

He pointed to the turnpike laws, which gave companies the authority to take land. Ironically, he pointed out, some of the opponents of the market project were businessmen who had previously gone to the legislature for eminent domain authority to develop water power sites.

In January 1824 John Codman, one of the threatened owners, solicited Webster's aid, in a letter printed below. Codman pointed out that the city intended to pay as compensation only the current value of his land. He wanted the city to pay the postdevelopment price. This request threatened the subsidization of economic growth through the eminent

5. J.A.C. Grant, "The 'Higher Law' Background of the Law of Eminent Domain," *Wisconsin Law Review*, 6 (1931): 67–85.

1. Josiah Quincy, *A Municipal History of the Town and City of Boston* (Boston, 1852), pp. 75–134. See also Robert A. McCaughey, *Josiah Quincy, 1772–1864* (Cambridge, Mass., 1974), pp. 111–113.

2. Josiah Quincy, *Remarks on the Constitutionality of the Memorial of the City Council for an extension of Faneuil Hall Market* (Boston, c. 1824), p. 1.

domain power. Calculating compensation on the basis of future value would have crippled the eminent domain power. Codman sensed that he would bear a burden greater than that borne by the other citizens. It was this perception of the redistributive potential of the eminent domain power that pushed the holders of property to press for limits on its exercise.[3]

Webster did not take Codman's case. He was too occupied with the Spanish claims. As it turned out, however, Codman did not go to court. In February 1824 a statute was passed giving Quincy the leverage he needed.[4] In March the council authorized purchase of the lands owned by Codman and five others. They rejected the city's offer. In June, however, they sold their lands for $286,000.[5] Three other owners held out. In 1826 the city took their land.

FROM JOHN CODMAN

My dear Sir, Dorchester, Jany. 22d. 1824.

I cannot express to you how much I regret your absence, not only on account of the deprivation which Mrs. C[6] & myself suffer in the loss of your & Mrs Webster's society, with which we were favoured last summer, but also in not being able to avail myself of your professional services in a case, in which my patrimonial Estate is involved.

You have, doubtless, been informed thro' our public prints, of the contemplated improvements in the vicinity of Faneuil Hall Market & of the application of the City authorities to the Legislature to extend their powers in obtaining the Estates necessary to the project. It is the object of the Mayor &c to obtain these Estates by an appraisement, predicated on their present income—than which, in my opinion, nothing can be more unjust. My Estate, in particular, has great *capabilities* of improvement, & is rising & must rise every day in value.

I am unwilling to sell it unless I can obtain a price, predicated on its *capability* of improvement rather than its present income. Whether this measure, wh[ic]h appears to me so arbitrary, will be sanctioned by the legislature is doubtful—but if such a law should be passed I have thought that the Damages to which I should be entitled might be a Jury question, in which case I wish to *retain* you as *my counsel.*

I am induced to make this early application, not only from the circumstance of your having assisted me very essentially, on a former occasion,[7] but from the repeated testimonies of your good wishes, which I assure you I highly appreciate.

3. Horwitz, p. 66.

4. Laws Mass., c. 147 (1824).

5. Quincy, *Municipal History*, p. 125.

6. Mrs. Codman not further identified.

7. We have not found a case in which DW represented Codman.

The kind interest which, as a parishioner, you have been pleased to take in my concerns, will excuse me in asking your sympathy, under a painful affliction with which I have been visited, since you left us.

My life has been again jeopardized by a fall from my horse which dislocated my right shoulder, & injured my left arm to such a degree that I am yet unable to use it.

I have now been confined to the house for two months, & have preached but one half day since you left us.

I hope you & Mrs. Webster enjoy uninterrupted health & happiness & are passing this winter not only with increasing usefulness, but with much domestic comfort.

Mrs C unites with me in aff[ectiona]te regards to Mrs. W. I am, Dear Sir, with sentiments of respectful consideration & personal esteem Your friend & servt. John Codman

ALS. NjR. John Codman (1782–1847; Harvard 1802), minister, Dorchester, Massachusetts (1808–1847).

ii. City Street Construction. In 1828 Webster received a letter from Peter Lorillard of New York City, printed below. The wealthy tobacco manufacturer sought Webster's help to prevent the taking of his property by the city for use as a street. Charging that speculators were behind the plan, Lorillard portrayed property as a natural right. It could only be taken for public "necessity," not for public use. This challenged the view expressed by Josiah Quincy in the previous section that the eminent domain power was an unlimited sovereign power. Apparently Webster did not take this case.[8]

FROM PETER LORILLARD

Sir New York June 26. 1828.

In consequence of a recent decision of the Common Council of this City to extend Cedar Street through an improved Block of Property from William Street to Pearl Street, I applied to Ambrose Spencer Esqr.[9] to be my counsel to oppose the measure before the Supreme Court of this State.

Mr Spencer declines appearing at Court any more, but recommends me to apply to you, & to engage you as Counsel in my Case.

Presuming you have access to the Laws of the State of New York, I beg leave to refer you to the Several Acts passed by the Legislature at the

8. In 1839 Lorillard lost a case which may have involved the property mentioned in his letter: *In the matter of William and Anthony Streets in the City of New York*, 19 Wendell (N.Y.) 678 (1839).

9. Ambrose Spencer (1765–1848), Albany lawyer, New York attorney general (1802), justice, New York supreme court (1804–1819; chief justice 1819–1823), mayor of Albany (1824), U.S. representative (1829).

request of the Corporation of this City for the opening extending & regulating Streets—viz

An Act passed 1813. 2 Vol. Revised Laws pages 408 to 422.

An Act passed	3 April 1816	p. 77
do	16 April	p. 172
do	10 April 1823	p. 146
do	13 Apl 1826	p. 155
do	14 Apl 1827	p. 249

These Laws were intended to apply to the improving of the *Grounds* in the outer part of the City & N York Island—but the laws have been made use of by Speculators to the cutting up Blocks of Improved property in the Lower part of the City, and the manner in which Commissioners have been named by the Common Council & appointed by the Sup[reme] Court has become so obnoxious & the effects of their appraisements of Damage & Benefit so obnoxious & ruinous to hundreds of persons here, that I have determined to try the Constitutionality of the Law & the Power of the Common Council to ask & receive of the Legislature a Law so unjust in its operations.

I contend that my property is sacred & ought not to be taken from me except for Public <purposes> Necessity—this is the point I shall contend at any reasonable expence—the late decision of the Common Council takes away my property, altho' I am one of the remonstrants—those who have petitioned for the measure are speculative individuals, who have stuck at nothing to get a Vote of the Council for that measure—the Public do not require my property, the measure is a speculative one altogether.

Should you take the subject in hand for me, the following points present themselves to me.

1st. Do, or can you appear in the Sup Court of this State?

2d. Can the matter be taken to the Sup. Court of the U States? as I am now a resident of the City of New York.

3d. Will any relief be gained by this appeal to the US. Court in a matter like this, apparently local?

4th. What course will be deemed expedient to pursue to assert this measure?

By the operation of the Law, the Attorney of the Corporation [of the City of New York] will apply to the Sup. Court at its next term held in Utica in August next for appointment of Commissioners for Estimate & assessment—there I think is the place & time to arrest the proceedings & bring up the constitutionality of the Law—*this point* has *never* been brought before the Court.

What I mean by taking away Property for Public Necessity in this case is, that Public Necessity does not require the use or the occupancy of my Grounds.

Another objectionable feature in the Law is, the manner of taking away & paying for property by the estimate of *three Commissioners* who are generally selected for the purpose *by the Street committee* of the Common Council & the names handed to the Court who appoints of course.

This mode of taking away property is unconstitutional, because owners of Land *cannot compel* witnesses to appear before the Commissioners or Sup Court, to state the value of the property—they the Commrs. judge of themselves solely, entirely & arbitrarily.

Property ought only be taken away, (If it can be taken at all) by a Jury of Twelve Freeholders before whom Evidence can be lawfully brought & their Verdict to shew the Value of the Property.

By examining the several Laws you will find several unconstitutional acts & clauses affecting contracts & taking away the Power & control every man has under the constitution over his own property.

As there is no time to be lost in this business, I must beg your early attention to it, & wait for your reply to know your determination in the matter.

Enclosed is a check for Retaining Fee[10]—as to my responsibility for your further services I refer you to A. Spencer Esqr. respy yr ob st

Peter Lorillard

Please address your reply to care of my Son in Law Thomas A. Ronald,[11] —as I am residing during the summer at my Country Place in West Chester 12 miles from the city. I only spend one day in the week in the City & that is Monday. Mr Ronald is always in the City & will attend to my letters.

ALS. NhHi. Peter Lorillard, New York tobacco and snuff manufacturer. The Lorillard family owned 7000 acres in New York's Orange County.

c. Adverse Possession: Tisdale Drake v. *John Curtis*

Since its founding, Massachusetts officials had followed a policy of encouraging the private development of the colony's (and then the state's) natural resources. As early as 1640 the colony acted to encourage owners of tidal shoreline to build wharves and other commercial facilities. Under the English common law, private ownership of seacoast land extended only to the mean high water line. From that point ownership remained in the crown subject to the public's right to fish and navigate coastal waters. Shortly after settlement, Massachusetts Bay officials granted the shoreline owners ownership in the tidal flats to the mean low water line. In conformity with English practice the colony prohibited them from hindering the passage of boats. Later, courts interpreted this reserved public right to include fishing as well as navigation. Once the shoreline

10. Not found.

11. Not further identified.

owner built wharf facilities on his portion of the flat, however, he could exclude the public.[1] For most of the Massachusetts shoreline, this colonial grant had little effect, but in the nascent seaports title to the flats promised great future value. In the case presented below, the plaintiff discovered that the defendant had built a wharf on the plaintiff's portion of the flats. His suit to oust the defendant brought the policy of granting shoreline property rights into conflict with another policy designed to encourage development by occupants.

This second policy—title by *adverse possession*—operated to quiet titles to land held openly for long duration. It also protected occupants with questionable titles from harrassment by speculators. The concept of adverse possession (alternatively called title by *disseisin*) came into Massachusetts law from the English statutes of limitation. These laws barred legal action by the true owner to regain possession from an occupant who had been on the land for a specified period of time—by the nineteenth century, usually twenty years. The period of occupation would be lengthened if the true owner had lacked the capacity to sue at the time the occupant made his entry. The recognition of such possessory titles added stability and security to land titles and thus supported the marketing of land. But because the true owner had a moral claim, the courts required the occupant to prove not only his entry and possession for the statutory period, but also that he had believed himself entitled to ownership and that his possession was open and publicly known. This would put the true owner on notice and give him the time to assert his superior title.[2] Webster's client on the appeal, John Curtis, the occupant, claimed title by adverse possession not only to the land under the wharf he had built, but to the open tidal flats as well.

In the first decade of the nineteenth century Curtis's predecessor, Jabez Hatch, putative owner of the upland bordering a portion of Boston harbor, built Cobb's wharf out over the flats. He later sold the wharf and title to the unenclosed flats to Curtis. In the early 1840s Andrew Drake, the owner of the adjoining land, discovered that he also held title to the upland bordering Curtis's wharf. In 1844 Drake brought suit to recover possession of the flats. In fact, Drake's title was better than Curtis's. The latter could keep the wharf and flats only if he could prove title by adverse possession.

Before the MassCCP,S heard the case, Andrew Drake died. His heir, Tisdale Drake, petitioned the court to substitute him as plaintiff. Due

1. Colonial Ordinance, 1641–1647, *The Book of General Lawes and Libertyes*, p. 50. See also *Opinion of the Justices*, 365 Mass. 681 (1974).

2. Percy Bordwell, "Disseisin and Adverse Possession," *Yale Law Journal*, 33 (1923): 148–151; Henry Ballantine, "Title by Adverse Possession," *Harvard Law Review*, 32 (1918): 135–144; Laws, Mass., c. 13 (1786) and c. 74 (1807).

to an ambiguity in the inheritance statute, the CCP denied Tisdale's petition. In order to expedite a decision on the merits, the parties agreed: (1) to prosecute the cases in both Andrew's and Tisdale's names until the SJC decided who was the proper plaintiff; (2) to submit the question of title to the court on the basis of the documents held by each side; and (3) to allow the court to determine the boundary lines of the property (Document 123). Curtis reserved the right to have a jury decide the question of his adverse possession and Drake's liability for the value of the improvements made by Curtis if the court awarded possession to Drake.

In 1846 a jury trial on the question of Curtis's adverse possession took place. Under Massachusetts law Curtis had the burden of proving that he had entered and used the wharf area in the belief that he owned the flats. Although Curtis could show that since 1806 he and his grantor had used the wharf and a small area at its end for vessels to turn around, he faced a problem with regard to the larger unenclosed portion of the flats.[3] The future growth of the harbor promised to make such undeveloped open areas more valuable. The parties thus focused on this aspect of the case. Would the trial judge allow proof of Curtis's use of part of the flats (in the vicinity of the wharf) to establish an adverse possession of the entire area? Curtis's trial attorney requested the court to instruct the jury that if they found that Curtis had used part of the claimed flats (and as to the rest had demonstrated ownership by sending ships over it), a verdict should be reached in his favor. The trial judge declined to make the instruction. Instead, he told the jury that as against the true owner the disseisin extended no further than the wharf and the flats occupied by vessels lying there. The jury, he said, might allow Curtis enough space at the wharf's end for vessels to turn around and for three vessels to lie at anchor. The jury returned a verdict for Curtis for possession of the wharf and the adjacent flats; Drake received the rest.

The verdict did not please Curtis, who filed a bill of exceptions to the judge's instruction. Pending the appeal to the SJC, Curtis hired Webster to assist Rufus Choate and Sidney Bartlett in the March 1848 argument. Webster, however, arrived too late to study the case and prepare a rebuttal to Drake's attorney, Benjamin R. Curtis. Instead, Webster put together a set of notes (Document 124) from which he prepared a written brief. In May he sent the brief and a note of explanation, printed below, to Chief Justice Shaw. He asked Shaw to show it to the other judges. Webster notified the other side, and Drake's other attorney, Richard Fletcher, filed a reply brief.

In the oral argument Benjamin Curtis had taken the position that the

3. Adding the time of possession of one's predecessors to one's own in order to meet the statute is called *tacking*.

law of adverse possession required the tenant (Curtis) to have taken possession by ousting the true owner. Sailing over the flats, Curtis argued, did not constitute an ouster or act of ownership, since use of the flats was open to the public. Therefore as to the property in question, Drake had possessed part (some of the upland), Curtis possessed part, and the remainder, most of the flats, was vacant. Under the legal rule, Curtis argued, the true owner had a paramount right to the vacant land.

In his argument Webster admitted that if John Curtis had not possessed any of the flats, title would go to Drake. Here Webster sought to convince the court to apply to shore lines the rule applicable to non-seacoast land: that an actual possession of part under a deed was possession of all against any one except the true owner. And that if the true owner did not possess any part of the land and acquiesced in the apparently valid claim of the adverse possessor for thirty years, the law barred the true owner's suit. In this case, Webster continued, Drake's ancestor had recognized Curtis's intent to possess all the property, as evidenced by the use of the flats by ships coming and going to the wharf. Here Webster reached the difficult part of the case for his client. Use of a public waterway, by itself, would not evidence possession; the assertion of Curtis's intent to possess the whole would not prove possession. But, wrote Webster, if the judges put these two facts together (Curtis's partial and Drake's non-occupancy) and added Drake's knowledge of Curtis's use and intent to possess, a case would be made for a title by adverse possession. Webster also argued that given the nature of tidal flats, the only way that a tenant could show an intent to possess them, short of enclosing the area, was by sailing over them.

In his reply brief Fletcher attacked the weakest part of Webster's case—the use of the open water. The evidence, he said, showed that Curtis had not used the flats in any manner different from the public in general. The exercise of the right of navigation was entirely distinct from a claim to the soil. Therefore, even if Curtis intended to possess the flats, his act of navigation did not evidence exclusive ownership of the flat. Such use, regardless of intent, would not put a true owner on notice.

In the fall the court announced its decision, affirming the verdict of the trial jury.[4] Chief Justice Shaw decided to treat the rules regarding the disposition of Massachusetts shoreline differently from the general case of adverse possession. He reviewed the instruction that Curtis had proposed to the court. It rested on the elements of Webster's argument. Shaw rejected them. To prove adverse possession, Curtis had to prove an initial trespass and ouster of Tisdale Drake's predecessor. But since Curtis had a right, as a member of the public, to sail over the flats, there

4. 55 Mass. 395 (1848).

was no trespass and hence no disseisin. Furthermore, since Curtis had a right to sail over the flats, Drake could not have sued to prevent him from doing so. The purpose of the doctrine of adverse possession, to force owners to defend their titles from late entrants, would not be achieved. After the decision, the court appointed referees to determine the value of the improvements made by Curtis (Document 125).

DOCUMENT 123. AGREEMENT BETWEEN PARTIES

Supreme Judicial Court.
Suffolk. November T. 1844.

Andrew Drake
vs.
John Curtis
Same vs. Ebenezer Francis.
Tisdal Drake vs. John Curtis
Same vs. Ebenezer Francis.[5]

These are real actions to recover parcels of wharves & flats near Sea Street in Boston. The two actions first named were brought by Andrew Drake in his life-time & he having died leaving a will which has been duly proved & which is made part of this case whereby he devised the lands & flats in question to the said Tisdale Drake, petitions were presented by the said Tisdale Drake to the Court of Common Pleas in which the said actions were pending for leave to appear & prosecute the said actions. The presiding Judge ruled pro forma that he had not a right to appear & upon exceptions to these rulings the cases have been brought to this Court. If upon the argument of the bills of exception this Court should be of opinion that Tisdale Drake is entitled to appear & prosecute the said actions originally brought by Andrew Drake then the said Tisdale Drake is to be admitted to prosecute the said actions & the title to the demanded premises is to be tried in those actions & the said actions brought by Tisdale Drake are to be dismissed with costs, but if the Court should be of opinion that the said Tisdale Drake has not a right to appear & prosecute the said first named actions they are to be dismissed and then the said titles are to be tried in the last named actions. The parties agree to submit the question of title to the Court upon such deeds wills &c. as they respectively rely on, each party agreeing to furnish to the other party a schedule of the documents he will offer

5. The case bore the names of Andrew and Tisdale Drake pending the decision whether Tisdale could succeed to Andrew's suit or would have to sue in his own name. The Drakes, Curtis, and Francis were all wharfingers. DW received as fee $500 from Francis, $300 from Curtis, see p. 172, above.

days at least before the time of trial. And either party or the Court shall be at liberty, to examine the surveyors employed by them, orally.

It is agreed that the Court may determine the course of the lines running between high & low water mark according to the legal rights of the parties upon the evidence, & to be at liberty to draw all such inferences of fact as a jury would be authorized to draw. If the Tenant in either action shall elect to do so he may afterwards submit to a Jury any question of adverse possession to bar the Demandant or any claim of tenants for betterments. If either of the said Tenants should not so elect, the Court is to render a judgment for the Demandant or Tenant according to the lines settled by the Court. If either of the Tenants should so elect a verdict is to be returned for the Demandant for all the land & wharf to which he is entitled according to the lines fixed by the decision of the Court except such part if any from which he is barred by adverse enjoyment—and subject to the amounts he ascertained & fixed for betterments—if any by verdict under the usual mode of proceeding when betterments are claimed—if any claim is made for betterments the deman[dan]t may make a claim for rents & profits.

S Bartlett for E. Francis
Choate & Crowninshield pr Curtis
B. R. Curtis for Drake[6]

ADS. *Drake* v. *Curtis*, MassSJC,S, November 1848.

TO LEMUEL SHAW

Sir Boston May 22. 1848

I arrived from Washington in March, just at the close of the argument in *Drake vs Curtis*. The Court was good enough to say, that I might have an opportunity, within a limited time, to present some remarks in writing, in reply to the argument of Plfs Counsel, on the motion for a New trial. The time limited has expired; & circumstances, not unknown to the Court, have placed it out of my power to prepare my remarks, until this day. I presume the Court has not yet taken up the case, for consultation,

6. Sidney Bartlett (1799–1889; Harvard 1818), Boston lawyer, studied with Nathaniel M. Davis and Lemuel Shaw, admitted in 1821, practiced with Shaw until 1830, state legislator; Francis Boardman Crowninshield (1809–1877; Harvard 1829), Boston lawyer, admitted in 1833, partner of Rufus Choate at the time of this suit, state legislator; Benjamin Robbins Curtis (1809–1874; Harvard 1829), Boston lawyer and judge, attended Harvard Law School, studied with John Nevers and with Wells & Alvord in western Massachusetts, admitted in 1832, moved to Boston in 1834, justice, USSC (1851–1859), counsel for Andrew Johnson at his impeachment trial in 1868.

& decision; & trust, therefore, that there will be no objection, on the part of the Judges, to receive the paper, which I now enclose.[7]

I shall give notice of this Communication to Counsel on the other side.[8]

With entire regard, Your ob. Sert Danl Webster

ALS. MHi.

DOCUMENT 124. NOTES FOR WRITTEN ARGUMENT

[c. May 1848]

Drake v Curtis

Notes, by D. W. in reply to Plff's Counsel

The importance of this question, as affecting other cases as well as this, may well require for it a careful consideration.

The Plfs suit is a writ of entry; the Plea is *null disseisin*;[9] &, no question of proper title being, for the present before the Court, the only point, at the trial was on the point of disseisin.

The defense was, in effect, that Plf had not been disseised, within thirty years, the Defdt, or those under whom he claims, having had for that time, an adverse possession, with notice to Plf, & those from whom he claims.

The Premises are partly solid & dry land, or wharf structure, & partly flats, covered by the tide.

<At the trial> In support of his defense, the Defdt introduced a great variety of proofs, documentary & by parol, as will be seen by reference to the report, & then submitted the following motion, or prayer; viz[10]

(here copy from the report—as marked)

But the Court declined so to instruct the Jury.

It was not suggested, at the trial, either by the Judge, or adverse Counsel, that the Defdt had not produced evidence sufficient to raise

7. This version of the brief has not been found. DW's notes appear as Document 124. A substantially similar brief is printed in *Drake* v. *Curtis*, 55 Mass. 395, 403–407 (1848), and probably was the one referred to by DW in this letter.

8. One of Drake's attorneys, Richard Fletcher, filed a reply brief.

9. The writ of entry alleged that the tenant disseised (i.e., dispossessed) the owner within 30 years of the date of the writ. Null disseisin was the general issue plea for writs of entry. It asserted that the tenant had not wrongfully disseised the claimant. The usual period of limitation was twenty years. Ten years was added if the demandant had received his title by descent (inheritance).

10. The prayer for instruction which the judge refused. The trial report has not been found.

this question; but the Judge ruled the point, simply as matter of law, and as supposing the alledged facts to be all proved.

This must, of course, be now so understood, because if the Judge had suggested deficiency of proof, to raise the question, his specific ruling on that proof, might have been objected to, & that question reserved.

The question, then, is on the propriety of the Prayer.

We submit, that this prayer offers to prove all that is necessary to show disseisin of the lower part of these premises.[11]

To make & prove, such disseisin, what is necessary?—Two things, & two only—

I. An exclusive possession & seizin, by Defdt, or those under whom he claims, adverse, & continued a sufficient length of time.[12]

II. Sufficient evidence of notice to the true owner, & of acquiescence by him.

We admit, there must be possession & seizin. Mere standing office, & claiming, is not enough.[13] We admit, also, that the possession & seizin must be exclusive; for if mixed, the seizin is according to the title.[14]

As to notice, possession itself is evidence of notice, according to its greater or less degree of notoriety; but actual notice is the best evidence in all cases.

We are then, to inquire first, whether Defdt offered to prove the first thing necessary, viz, adverse, exclusive possession, of the lower part of the premises.

1. We show possession of all, as distinct from mere claim to all.

An entry on part, as & for all under a deed calling for all, gives possession of all, against every body but the true owner.

This proposition will not be doubted. Upon such possession, all possessory remedies attach. It proves an averment of seizin. It is regarded by the law as a fixed right, *in re*; and is essentially different from mere

11. Here DW uses disseisin in another sense. The defendant must prove that he obtained possession by an ouster, i.e., a wrongful entry, more than thirty years before the suit began in order to make out a title by adverse possession.

12. By the various rules of law the possession had to be actual, adverse, notorious, exclusive, continuous, and under claim of right. Such open occupation and use would give the true owner notice and allow him to come forward to defend his title.

13. DW may have meant an office grant such as a tax deed. Payment of taxes did not establish adverse possession.

14. Meaning the title owner would be accorded precedence over a mere possessor.

claim, under color of title; for such claim supports no remedy, even against a stranger; & exposes the party to no action by the true owner, except it be for slander of tittle.[15]

But it is said, that this, as against the true owners, is no possession at all, but mere claim. This proposition we controvert. We maintain, that as against every body, it is something more than a claim; that it is a right, good, to all intents & purposes, as against strangers, <and good also as against the true owner, unless he has a different answer to it> and as against the true owner, it is a possession, tho not exclusive, nor efficacious, unless other ingredients be added, viz.

1st. Sufficient notice, that the party is in, claiming the whole;

2nd. A yielding up of possession, by the true owner, in recognition of the possession & claim of the other party.

But a possession it certainly, is, even against the true owner, as distinct from mere claim; and what proves this, conclusively, is, that the true owner may sue the party entering, in trespass; which he cannot do, against a party merely claiming. And this, he may do not on the ground of election to regard himself disseized,[16] but merely on proof the possession. It is a possession, therefore, which, on the one hand, gives possessory rights, & on the other exposes the party to possessory remedies by the true owner.

The confusion has arisen, from not distinguishing, between the facts of possession, & the different effects of that fact, on the rights of others. The fact of the possession is the same, whoever may controvert it; but its legal influence is one thing, on the rights of strangers, & another, on the rights of the true owner.

However this may be, it is irrevocably admitted, that an entry, on part, under a claim for all, gives seizin & possession of all, unless there be an actual adverse seizin, by the true owner[17]

Now, what we offered to show, was precisely that here was no such continued adverse possession of any part, by the true owner. Upon notice that we had entered, & taken possession, claiming the whole, he retired from the whole, & yielded up his own possession & claim, to the whole, in recognition of our possession & claim thereto.

Let the full import of the terms of the prayer be here examined.

To "yield" is; "to give as claimed of right"

15. An action for a false statement that disparaged a person's title to property.

16. *Disseisin by election* is where a person admits himself to be disseised when he has not really been so for purposes of trying title.

17. At the March argument Sidney Bartlett had urged the court to adopt this rule which the federal courts followed.

"to resign"
"to give up"
"to surrender to"
"to give way, to give place to."

To "recognize," is;

"to admit with a formal acknowledgment" so that, the words aver, that the Plf acknowledged the legal validity of Defdts possession, & yielded up his own thereto. In other words, they aver a complete transmutation of possession.

Thus far, I have been attempting to show, that Defdt offered to prove possession; & the same remarks show, that that possession was exclusive.

In other words, we offered to prove possession, founded on claim of right; & to prove, further, that in recognition of that possession under claim for the whole, the Plf abandoned <his own> the whole & left us alone, in the exclusive enjoyment of the property.

But the case goes farther. The Defdt offered to prove, not merely the visible & exclusive possession of part, & the exercise of acts of exclusive ownership therein; but, also, that <as to the residue, he used & enjoyed the same> this possession & exercise were taken, & had, with a definite & specific intent & purpose, notified to, and acquiesced in, by the other party viz, with intent, thereby <to take possession of the whole> to possess & hold the whole premises on a claim of right. This is exactly what the Defdt offered to prove. An entry on land is to be construed according to its intent; and it is particularly & directly alledged, in this case, that the entry on part was intended to be a taking possession of the whole, & was so understood by both parties. This we regard as a peculiarity in the case.

But the case goes farther still. The Defdt offered to prove, not merely the visible & exclusive possession of part, & the exercise of acts of exclusive ownership therein, with intent thereby to possess the whole, but, also, as to the residue, he used & enjoyed the same by passing over it, with vessels, with intent thereby to possess & hold the whole, on a claim of right.[18] And this use & enjoyment, together with the intent which accompanied & qualified it, were fully known & acquiesced in by the Plf.

Here, then, is a direct averment of possession & use, of all the parts, according to their several natures & capacities. Doubtless, the mere sailing over flats, without proof of any <intent> claim & possession, or intent to claim & possess, does not amount to nor evidence possession. All depends on intent & on the understanding, with which the thing is done;

18. In proving title by adverse possession in Massachusetts the defendant had to prove that he took possession as an owner, i.e., under claim of right, or color of title.

as the plucking of a twig from a tree, may be merely an wholly unimportant thing, or it may be the taking possession of a manor. And therefore one thing which distinguishes our case, from all other cases, connected with flats, is, that the acts of sailing over, as well as all others, done by us, were done, under claim of ownership, & so known to be done by the right owner. We offered to prove such passing over the flats, with vessels, to & from the Defdts wharf, as amounted to a use of the flats; now a use of flats, in modes & for purposes, far short of, & other than erections, or visible structures, may imply & evidence possession, for all purposes, against every body. Such is the use of waters, on flats, at the ends of wharves, for vessel to float, turn, or ground on. Such also would be the use of flats, between wharfs, or piers, over which vessels might sail. And it is to be kept constantly, & particularly, in mind that the plf yielded his own use, in this respect, to our possession, & our use; so that even if he sailed over the same flats, which does not appear, he did it in subordination to our claim & our acknowledged right.
The mere fact, therefore, that the use which we offered to prove, consisted only in sailing over the flats, to & fro, does not prevent its evidencing the requisite possession.

All comes at last, to intent, & the understanding of the parties.

Our case, therefore, presents these distinct facts & points.

1. The Defdts produced a deed, covering all the premises. This was not controverted.
2. An open entry under the deed, & visible & permanent possession taken of a part, with intention, by such possession of part, to take possession of the whole; & this particular intention known & acquiesced in, by the Plf
3. A use & occupation of the residue of the premises, according to its nature & capacities, with the definite intention thereby to possess the same; & this known to the Plf: thus making the legal possession thereof.
4. And, in general, that all the acts done by the Defdts, with the intent & purpose which accompanied & qualified them, were distinctly known to the Plf, thro the whole course of the thirty years.
5. That with such notice, he surrendered & abandoned all his own possession, in recognition of the fact, that the Defdt had the possession, & had it rightfully[19]

AD(DW). MHi.

19. Choate added two points that appear in his handwriting at the end of the manuscript and were incorporated in DW's argument as evidenced by the report of the case. First, that the statute of frauds did not make the tenant's parol evidence inadmissible. The question of who possessed real

DOCUMENT 125. RECEIPT

Sup. Jud. Court, Nov Term 1848

Tisdale Drake
vs
John Curtis

After Verdict in favour of the Demandant for a portion of the premises demanded, this cause was submitted to arbitration to determine the amount of rents & profits & the value of the improvements to which each party is entitled respectively, who awarded to the Demandt for his rents & profits $1317.98—& to the Tenant for his improvements $2274.80, now the parties unilaterally acknowledge satisfaction of the above sums respectively—and the Demandt acknowledged the receipt of the Costs of Court, taxed at $189.64—& Habere Facias to issue for the premises described in the Verdict.

C. P. & B R Curtis for Demdt
Francis B Crowninshield [for] Tenant

ADS. *Drake* v. *Curtis*, MassSJC,S, November 1848.

6. FEDERAL EQUITY JURISDICTION AND REMEDIES

a. Introduction

Massachusetts courts exercised only very limited equity powers. Unlike the federal Constitution, which specifically extended the judicial power "to all cases in law and equity," the Massachusetts constitution merely gave the legislature the power to create the courts and to define their jurisdiction.[1] The postrevolutionary MassSJC continued to exercise the jurisdiction of the colonial superior court of judicature. The legislature did not delegate to it a general equity authority. Instead, the SJC received piecemeal grants of equity authority as the need arose. But even then the SJC interpreted each grant as narrowly as possible.

---

estate was a question of fact to be proved by written or parol evidence. Second, that actual notice to the true owner was better than a constructive notice given by building a structure or by cultivation: "In conclusion, it may be observed, that when an actual possession has been taken of the whole, such as would be good against strangers, and going beyond a mere claim; then direct and actual notice to the true owner of such possession, and its acknowledgment by him, are as effectual to bar him, as if such notice had been given, by actual edifice or structure on or cultivation of the premises. Notice by structure, or enclosure, or cultivation, is constructive; but personal and direct notice, proved and acknowledged, is actual, and therefore higher and better than any constructive notice, and is conclusive." 1 Cushing (Mass.) 395, 407.

1. Edwin H. Woodruff, "Chancery in Massachusetts," *Boston University Law Review*, 9 (1929): 176–181; U.S. Constitution, art. III, sec. 2; Mass. Constitution, ch. 1, sec. 1, art. III (1780).

Both state and federal courts followed the general principle that equity would act only where no adequate remedy at law existed. In fashioning a test for this principle the courts of each jurisdiction took a different position. The federal courts tested the adequacy of the remedy at law by whether equitable relief had been available in England when the chancery was at its zenith. If the medieval chancellor could have intervened in such a situation, a nineteenth-century federal court could also act. The Massachusetts courts, however, interpreted "adequacy" to mean the availability of a legal remedy under current Massachusetts law.[2] This meant that the SJC narrowly construed grants of equity powers.[3]

At the beginning of Webster's practice, Massachusetts equity jurisdiction included only mortgage foreclosure and redemption, the administration of certain trusts, and the specific performance of written contracts.[4] Given the narrow scope of Massachusetts equity and the availability of equitable remedies in the federal courts, a plaintiff's lawyer faced with a case involving a Massachusetts resident and one from another state often opted for the federal forum. The existence of two judicial systems enabled attorneys to avoid a damaging precedent in one court by bringing suit in the other jurisdiction. Webster's expertise in practicing on the equity side of the federal court brought him legal work on referral from less experienced attorneys. The two letters printed below and the three cases following illustrate how lawyers used the federal and state systems to further the interests of their clients.[5]

FROM SAMUEL FESSENDEN

Dear Sir, Portland Decr. 13. 1823

Not having been acquainted with principles or practise on the Equity side, I have concluded to presume on your former kindness, and state a case. I will not say for your consideration, but for your opinion.

Thomas Robinson,[6] the elder, wishing to invest money in the purchase

2. The Judiciary Act of 1789 said that suits in equity "shall not be sustained in either of the courts of the United States, in any case where plain, adequate and complete remedy may be had at law": 1 U.S. Statutes at Large, c. 20, s. 16 (1789); *Bean* v. *Smith et al.*, 2 Mason 252, 270–271 (1821); John Norton Pomeroy (Symons, ed.), *Equity Jurisprudence* (5 vols., San Francisco, 1941), 1: 704–709.

3. For example, the SJC had equity authority to hear cases involving trusts created by will or deed. When confronted with a trust created by a foreign will, it refused to extend its authority by implication. (Pomeroy, p. 709).

4. Laws, Mass., c. 77 (1798) (mortgages) and c. 87 (1817) (trusts and specific performance).

5. We have not included in our examples the water power cases in which DW participated. These will appear in Volume 3 of the Legal Papers in a chapter on national economic development.

6. Thomas Robinson (d. 1806) served as a commander on the lakes

of real estate, contracted for certain houses &c to the amount of 20000. He paid the purchase money, and from some cause chose to have the deeds made to Arthur McLellan,[7] his friend, taking from McLellan an obligation to convey, on demand, the premises to himself, or to whomsoever he might appoint. Robinson subsequently made his will, by which he devised the said estates to his wife to hold for life, and after her death to be equally divided among his children, of whom Thomas Robinson the younger was one[,] Hannah, the wife of Stephen Codman another, and Mary, the wife of Robert Ilsley another and there were four other children.[8] Mr. Robinson, the elder, appointed Richd Cartwright[9] his brother in law, Executor, and died. The will was dully approved, and administration granted to Cartwright.

At the request of the Executor and the heirs, McLellan, for a consideration in the deed expressed of 25000, (although no money was in fact paid McLellan) conveyed the premises to Thomas Robinson the younger[,] Stephen Codman, and Robert Ilsley to hold to them and their heirs in fee, with the usual covenants. The deed is in common form, without any expression which would designate a use, or trust. At the same time Robinson, the younger, Codman and Ilsley, gave their personal bond to Cartwright the Executor, in the penal sum of 35000 conditioned to hold the estates subject to the provisions in the will of Robinson the elder, and to deed to the heirs, on demand after the death of the widow of the elder Robinson and in the mean time to account for rents to the Executor. The widow went into possession and is now living, and has received the rents, and still does receive them. In the Bond it is recited that the lands that day deeded to Robinson, Codman and Ilsley, by McLellan, were really and truly, at the time of his death, the property of Robinson the elder.

Robinson the younger has recently deceased—and deeply insolvent and intestate?

Now did Robinson the younger, Codman & Ilsley take an estate in trust, for the heirs of Robinson the elder, & the widow?

If so, does the trust survive in Codman & Ilsley? Can Codman & Ilsley legally convey the whole estate to hold agreeably to the provisions of the will?

Or can the Creditors of Robinson, the younger, get hold of one third of

---

during the Revolution, went to Portland in 1784 where he was engaged in distilling and general merchandising, and moved to Canada a few years before his death.

7. Arthur McClellan, a sea captain in Portland, Robinson's uncle by marriage.

8. Thomas Robinson, Jr., attained the rank of commander in the navy, Hannah married Boston merchant Stephen Codman in 1788, Mary was wed to Robert Ilsley (1772–1829), prominent Portland resident and politician, the other four children were Samuel, William, Jane, and Eliza.

9. Not identified.

these estates, or any part thereof except the reversion of one seventh?

How is this estate to be brought back to the heirs of Robinson?

Will you just drop me a line in answer to these questions? I presume they will not trouble you though they do me. Your friend & sert

Samuel Fessenden

ALS. NhHi. Samuel Fessenden (1784–1869; Dartmouth 1806), Maine lawyer, studied with Judah Dana, admitted in 1809, state legislator.

TO JARED COFFIN

Dear Sir, Boston April 20. 1838.

I have received your communication, & read & considered the two cases, in regard to which you desire my opinion. It seems to me there is very little question, in regard to either of them.

1. Mr. Easton,[10] most undoubtedly, holds the $135.54 in trust for you; & you can recover it, in a common action for money had & received.

2. This is a clear case of mortgage paid, but the land not reconveyed. Mr. Easton is unquestionably bound to give up the title, since the debt has been liquidated & paid; & he must surrender it to you, as the purchaser or assignee of the Gardners.[11]

Your remedy is by Bill in Equity, calling upon him to convey the title to you. Such conveyance will be decreed, of course, upon proof of the facts, & he must pay the costs of the proceeding. It will be proper, in the first place, to make a suitable demand on Mr. Easton to convey, & for you to offer to pay the expense of making the conveyance. This will render him liable to pay the cost of the proceeding, if he should decline.

Any good lawyer can draw the bill. As the evidence in the case may possibly be lost, by the death of the Arbitrators, or other cause, I should think you would do well to institute the proceeding, should any proceeding be found necessary, without delay.[12] Yours with regard,

Danl Webster

LS. ViU.

b. Probate: Mary Harvey v. *John Richards, Administrator*

In the 1790s James Mowry left Newport, Rhode Island and traveled to India. He changed his name to Murray and became a soldier of fortune in the employ of an Indian prince. By judicious investments in inland bills of exchange, he accumulated a large fortune. In 1806 he prepared to return to America. He took up temporary residence in Calcutta where

10. Easton was a member of a long line of Eastons on Nantucket Island, Massachusetts.

11. The Gardners belonged to the large Gardner family on Nantucket.

12. This suit would be brought under the limited Massachusetts equity jurisdiction.

he met George Dutch, the supercargo of a ship bound for Salem. Murray lent Dutch $10,000 and arranged for the shipment of about $20,000 in goods on Dutch's ship. On September 20, 1806, Murray fell from his horse; he died two days later. Before his death, however, he called in a business associate to draw his will (Document 126). In the will, Murray left legacies to three friends and to his common law wife.[1] Then in ambiguous terms he said: "All my property which has been remitted home by me from this Country to America, I desire may remain in the hands of those to whom I sent it to, for their own purposes. . . . the property now going to America I do not consider as belonging to any person."[2] He appointed as his executors the partners of the business firm which had handled his investments.

Shortly after Murray's death, George Dutch's ship sailed from Bombay with Murray's shipment on board. When the ship reached the United States, Dutch and his partner sold the goods for $21,000. They claimed the proceeds as legatees under the will. Murray's executors appointed Boston merchant John Richards to collect Murray's American assets. In August 1807 Richards filed Murray's will in Suffolk County and procured letters of administration. When Dutch refused to turn over the proceeds of the sale, Richards sued him for that amount and for repayment of the $10,000 loan. At the trial on the former matter, Dutch testified that Murray intended to name Dutch as a legatee but that they had not spoken to each other after Murray's accident. The jury returned a verdict for Dutch. Richards swore out a writ of review for a new trial. At the second trial, in the fall of 1809, Dutch changed his story. He now claimed that after Murray had signed the will, he, Dutch, had asked Murray how he intended to pay for the shipment of goods. According to Dutch, Murray had told him to keep the cargo on board the ship. Richards's attorney objected to the introduction of Murray's alleged statement as parol testimony and inadmissible evidence of Murray's intent. The trial judge overruled the objection, and the jury returned a second verdict for Dutch. Richards's attorney then obtained a hearing by the full SJC bench. In March 1810 the court heard the arguments and then decided in Richards's favor. The court ruled, first, that the trial judge should not have admitted Dutch's parol evidence, and, second, that a legatee had to go to the testator's former place of residence to collect a legacy. In preparation for the third trial, Richards obtained a detailed account of Murray's finances in India. No further record of these legal proceedings appears,

1. There was some confusion over Murray's true identity. Some of his friends in India believed his real name to be James Leathridge, a deserter from the British navy (see Document 126 below). The woman he called his "wife" was an Indian woman whom he never actually married. He left her 25,000 rupees.

2. The will is in the case file, *Harvey* v. *Richards*, USCC,DMass, May 1819.

and since Richards obtained the property, it seems likely that Dutch defaulted.

Through all these proceedings, Mary Harvey and John Mowry had been waiting in the wings. They claimed to be Murray's sister and brother, his heirs at law and residuary legatees. In November 1812 they proffered a petition in Suffolk County probate court asking the court to distribute to them the unbequeathed property in Richards's possession. In February 1813 Richards filed with the court an account of the estate and a denial of both the claimants' status as heirs and their entitlement under the law. When the probate judge decreed the distribution, Richards appealed to the MassSJC sitting as the supreme court of probate. His attorneys argued that the court should return the unbequeathed surplus to India, that the Indian assets were insufficient to pay the legacies, and that any residue should be distributed according to the law of Bengal. In March 1814 the MassSJC decided in Richards's favor.[3] The court reversed the probate court's decree and remitted the case to that court. At this point, Mary Harvey's attorneys, Samuel Dexter and William Aylwin, gave up on the Massachusetts courts and went into federal court seeking discovery and distribution of the unbequeathed estate to Mary alone. To their bill, filed in April 1814, Richards made an elaborate answer contesting not only her claim but the federal court's jurisdiction as well (Document 127).

In 1814 the attorneys argued the jurisdictional point before Judges Story and Davis. Did the federal court have jurisdiction if a competent state court had already heard the case? Richards's attorneys urged the court to consider Mary Harvey's decision to sue in state court as an election of the state court as her exclusive forum. They asked the court not to extend its jurisdiction over probate matters. This would only create a "clashing of jurisdictions."[4] That line of argument did not impress Judge Story, who overruled the plea and took jurisdiction. Story noted that the decision of the supreme court of probate had not decided the case on its merits.

In May 1815 Story directed the parties to hold a trial on the law side of the court to settle the question whether Mary Harvey was Murray's sole next of kin as claimed in her bill of complaint (Document 128). The jury decided that James Murray had been the legitimate son of Joshua

3. *Richards* v. *Dutch et al.*, 8 Mass. 506 (1812).

4. *Harvey* v. *Richards*, 2 Gallison 216, 224 (1814). Richards's attorney pointed out that if federal jurisdiction were available, any nonresident could stop a Massachusetts probate proceeding. "The complainant [Harvey] has arrested property, which was going to the executor in a foreign country. She has detained it here several years, and now that a decision has been pronounced against her, she comes into a court of chancery, to begin *de novo*, and still further to embarrass the proceedings of the defendant and executor" (224).

and Hope Mowry of Newport, and that Mary Harvey and John Mowry (who had left for Ohio) were his sole next of kin.[5] In light of this verdict, Harvey's attorneys amended their bill to include John Mowry (Document 129). Shortly thereafter, Mary Harvey received word of John Mowry's death, and his name was removed from the suit. Since many of the witnesses resided outside of Massachusetts, the parties used depositions—some of them received by Richards in his suit against George Dutch. The attorneys also agreed on the content of the testimony of one of the witnesses whose statement had not yet arrived (Document 130).

The attorneys continued the case to the May 1816 session. Harvey's attorneys moved the court to require Richards to disclose whether he had used Murray's funds in his business (Document 131). Richards told the court that he kept a separate account in his books for Murray's funds. At the October session the court ordered Richards to set aside funds to cover the payment of interest should he lose the case (Document 132). At this session Webster joined William Aylwin on the plaintiff's side. The parties then presented their evidence. Richards placed in evidence the deposition of the executor who had prepared Murray's will (Document 126), along with those of two of Murray's legatees (Documents 133 and 134). Webster and Aylwin offered evidence to prove that Murray had not had any children who might dispute Harvey's claim (Document 135). They also challenged two of Richards's depositions on the ground that as legatees those deponents were financially interested in the outcome of the case and therefore disqualified from testifying (Document 136).

Argument on the case did not take place until June 1818. The principal question was whether the court would distribute the property to the heirs at law or order it returned to India for distribution. Richards's attorneys pointed to *Richards* v. *Dutch* and another Massachusetts decision[6] for authority that the courts of Massachusetts required legatees of a foreign domiciliary to travel to that place to make their claim, and second, that the law required an ancillary administrator (in which capacity they claimed Richards acted) to send the personal property of the deceased to the place where the deceased's will had been proved. Since Harvey's attorneys had instituted the federal suit to get around these rulings, William Aylwin argued that although the law of the testator's domicile applied, Richards's administration represented an original one, not an ancillary one, and therefore a federal court could distribute the estate even if it had to follow Indian law. He passed off the language in the *Dutch* case as a comment by the reporter. When Webster's turn came, he reiterated Aylwin's argument on the choice of law issue and argued that on grounds of comity the court had authority to make a distribution

5. *Harvey* v. *Richards*, 2 Gallison 555 (1815).

6. *Stevenson* v. *Gaylord*, 11 Mass. 256 (1814).

(Document 137). He urged the court to take into account the international implications of its decision.

On June 29, 1818, an optimistic Webster wrote a letter to Jeremiah Mason, printed below. Webster expected Story to order Richards to distribute the fund in his hands. Story probably announced the court's decision at the October 1818 term.[7] In his decision he followed Webster's argument. He ruled that although the distribution had to follow the law of the testator's domicile, that did not mean that a United States court could not decree the distribution. He rejected the distinction presented by Richards's side between a principal (original) and an auxiliary (ancillary) administration. Nor did he find the citation of the two Massachusetts decisions persuasive. As a court of chancery, he ruled, Massachusetts decisions based on statutory authority could not constrain his equity powers. The question in this case, he observed, had national impact and could not be controlled by the case law of one state. Principles, not local usage, would guide him to a decision. He then pointed to a flaw in the argument of the defendant's counsel. They admitted that an American court could have decreed distribution to a creditor. But, Story noted, they had offered no good reason why a legatee might not also claim such distribution.

Before the court issued a final decree, Richards moved for a continuance on the grounds that he expected new evidence from India to show that the funds there were insufficient to pay the legacies (Document 138). Story overruled the motion. After a hearing in October 1818 Story ordered distribution of the estate in accordance with Harvey's bill (Document 139). He appointed two masters to make an accounting of Murray's assets. On January 12, 1819, they made their report (Document 140), to which Richards filed objections (Document 141).

Then, in another surprising turn of events, John Mowry's son and administrator, Tillinghast Mowry, appeared from Ohio seeking John Mowry's share. In January 1819 Webster and Aylwin filed Tillinghast's bill (Document 142). Following the introduction of this new party, Story decreed $11,000 to Mary Harvey and $9,000 to Tillinghast on proof of his affinity to John Mowry (Document 143). Webster and Aylwin received the money (Document 144) and turned it over to Mary Harvey's agent. At the May term Richards filed his answer to Tillinghast Mowry's bill (Document 145). He alleged that the Indian executors needed the funds remaining in his hands to pay the legacies. Webster filed a replication (Document 146) and Richards a rejoinder (Document 147). Story

7. 1 Mason 381 (1818). DW received $100 from Robert Lawton, Mary Harvey's agent in August 1817, probably as a retainer (p. 126, above), $550 from Lawton in January 1819, probably for arguing the case (p. 135, above), and $210 from Tillinghast Mowry in July 1819 (p. 137, above).

heard the parties and their witnesses and then issued a second decree confirming the payment of $9,000 to Tillinghast (Document 148). A few months later Richards's evidence must have finally arrived. In June Story adopted a final decree drafted by one of Richards's attorneys ordering $17,000 sent back to India (Document 149).

DOCUMENT 126. DEPOSITION

[February 21, 1811]

Be it known that on this twenty first day of February in the year of our Lord one Thousand eight hundred and Eleven—Before me The Honorable Sir William Burroughs Baronet[8] one of the Justices of the Supreme Court of Judicature at Fort William in Bengal duly commissioned and authorized to administer Oaths and affirmations in the Town of Calcutta in Bengal aforesaid Personally came Robert McClintock[9] of the said Town Agent a Partner in the House or Firm of MacKintosh Fulton and McClintock who being duly sworn according to Law on his Solemn oath deposes and says That in the month of September one thousand eight hundred and six and for a considerable length of time antecedent to that period he this Deponent was a Partner in the Banking and Agency House then carrying on Business in Calcutta under the Style or Firm of Alexander and Company and became well acquainted with James Murray[10] who had been a Major in the service of the Rajah of Jeypore an independent Prince in the East Indies on his arrival at Calcutta and who had an account with the said House and then resided in the vicinity of the said Town of Calcutta and lived as this Deponent believes in a very expensive manner. And this Deponent further saith that he understood and believes that Major Lewis Ferdinand Smith Captain Thomas Adkins Mr. William Hitchcock, Captain George Dutch[11] and several other Americans were constant Guests at the Table of the said James Murray while resident near Calcutta as aforesaid and that the said Captain George Dutch in return invited the said James Murray to an entertainment given by him upon one or two occasions but not more frequently as this Deponent verily believes. And this Deponent further saith that although he did not attend the Parties of the said James Murray (from a disinclination to mix with the Society of which they were principally composed) he was nevertheless very intimate with the said James Murray and when the accident occurred which occasioned the said James Murray's Death this Deponent was sent for at midnight to draw his Will, but in consequence

8. William Burroughs, created a baronet in 1804, Irish member of Parliament, advocate-general of Bengal.

9. McClintock was the principal executor.

10. Born James Mowry, not further identified.

11. None of these has been further identified.

of the messenger having gone to the office of business of the said Alexander and Company instead of to the House of this Deponent he did not hear of such accident until the next morning when this Deponent immediately repaired to the said James Murray's House and there found the said Major Lewis Ferdinand Smith Captain Thomas Adkins, Mr. William Hitchcock (who appeared particularly anxious that this Deponent should prepare the said James Murray's Will without any delay in the expectation as this Deponent believes that they would have considerable legacies bequeathed to them and insinuating that the said James Murray had never been married to the person who was his reputed Wife) Doctor Noskey and as the Deponent believes Doctor Loselt[12] in attendance upon the said James Murray who was in bed in violent agony, but perfectly sensible and collected in his mind. And this Deponent saith that he wrote the Will of the said James Murray on a Table by his bed side and in conformity with his instructions and read the same over sentence by sentence to him while writing and when finished and ready for signature repeated the entire reading of the said Instrument which was approved and executed by the Testator in the presence of this Deponent. And this Deponent further saith that after inserting in the said Will the several Legacies as directed by the Testator, this Deponent told him as there would probably be some surplus property after payment of the Legacies mentioned, he wished to know how the Testator meant to dispose of the same to which the said Testator replied "Keep it to yourself or to yourselves" or words to that effect, and this Deponent being the writer of the Will and one of the Executors answered "certainly not" and asked if the said Testator had no friend to whom he would bequeath such residue. But he declined making any disposition thereof, and directed that the Will should remain as it was or to that effect And this Deponent saith that to a question put by this Deponent to the said Testator whether the person who had the reputation of being the Wife of the said Testator was in reality married to him he replied with emphasis that she was his Wife. And this Deponent further saith that he has a perfect recollection of two passages in the said Will[13] which he hath understood were considered in America by the Court to require explanation and which this Deponent hath been informed were interpreted in a sense favorable to a Claim advanced by the said Captain George Dutch to certain property of the said Testator shipped for the United States on a Ship called the Boston Packet but which Claim this Deponent verily believes to be founded only in gross misrepresentation and falsehood And this Deponent saith that having heard the said James Murray was possessed of funds beyond those in the hands of the said Alexander and Company and had remitted such funds to America from Bombay this Deponent when writing the

12. Neither of these has been identified.

13. See p. 585, above.

said James Murray's Will enquired of him relative to the truth of this circumstance but he answered evasively. And this deponent adopted an indefinitive mode of expression when describing such property in the said Will, conceiving that if none had actually been shipped at Bombay (which this Deponent verily believes to have been the fact) that no inconvenience could be occasioned by the said Testators directing that the same should be left "to those to whom it had been sent" and with respect to the other passage in the said Will stating that the said Testator did not consider the property then going (meaning the goods going by the Boston Packet and Bills taken on America for Cash advanced in Calcutta) as belonging to any one. This Deponent deemed it necessary so to distinguish such property which he this Deponent knew to have been actually shipped and insured on the said Ship Boston Packet (and out of which and his other property known to this Deponent the Legacies bequeathed by the said Testators Will were to be paid) from that which was indefinitely as aforesaid stated to have been transmitted from Bombay And this Deponent further saith that on the twenty fourth day of September one Thousand eight hundred and six he this Deponent after returning from the funeral of the said James Murray took an Inventory of his Effects in conjunction with Mr. Frederick Hohler[14] a Partner in the house of Williams and Hohler auctioneers in Calcutta and upon that occasion the said William Hitchcock opened a Press and delivered to this Deponent a Pocket Book (stating that he knew not the contents) in which was found a Will regularly drawn and executed by the said James Murray whereby he had bequeathed the whole of his fortune to his Wife.[15] And this Deponent saith that at the funeral of the said James Murray he for the first time was informed by the said Major Lewis Ferdinand Smith that the name of the deceased was James Murray Leathridge or some such name and not James Murray he having deserted from one of His Majestys Regiments at Madras and therefore dropped his proper surname. And this Deponent further saith that he verily believes Captain George Dutch was present when the Will of the said Testator drawn by this Deponent was opened and read, and that the said Captain George Dutch spoke in general Terms of the said James Murray's affairs and made no observation whatever which could tend or be understood to insinuate that the said James Murray had made any verbal disposition or bequest of any part of his property a few hours before his decease contrary to or differing from the provisions in his said Will as drawn by this Deponent and afterwards read by him to the Party who returned from the funeral. And this Deponent verily believes that the said Testator never did make any such verbal disposition or bequest nor express a desire or intention so to do, or this Deponent would with the same readi-

14. Not identified.

15. Jane Murray, an Indian woman with whom Murray lived.

ness have written it as he did the Will made by desire of the Testator about Ten or eleven o'clock of the day of his decease this Deponent having no interest in the matter and being little acquainted with any of the Legatees and that if the said James Murray had afterwards expressed any desire to that effect such circumstance must have been known to Doctor Noskey and other persons who unceasingly attended the said James Murray during the short period between the execution of his Will and decease this Deponent never having heard of any such Idea until he saw two letters from Messrs Richards & Jones[16] dated Boston 14 Feby and 30th April 1810 in America stating that such was the declaration of the said Captain George Dutch. And this Deponent further saith that he hath understood the said Captain George Dutch has asserted that this Deponent stated after the death of the said James Murray that the said Alexander and Company had funds of the said deceased in their Possession amounting to Eighty Thousand Dollars which assertion this Deponent saith is utterly false and untrue the said Alexander and Company having in fact had at such period property of the said James Murray to a very inconsiderable amount only as will appear by their account current with the estate of the deceased filed by this Deponent in the Supreme Court of Judicature at Fort William in Bengal an authenticated Copy of which is hereunto annexed marked No. 1 and a continuation of the said account marked respectively No. 2 and 3.[17] And this Deponent further saith that he has not been a Partner in the House of Messieurs Alexander and Company since the first day of May one Thousand eight hundred and seven and that although he administered to the Estate of the said James Murray as being then a Partner in the said House of Alexander and Company the whole management of the said Estate has been in the hands of the said Alexander and Company and their Agents all along and this Deponent has no interest whatsoever in the decision of this matter,[18] but merely feels anxious that Justice may be done according to the true intent and meaning of the Will of the said Testator James Murray.

(sd) Robt. McClintock

ADS. *Harvey* v. *Richards*, USCC,DMass, May 1819.

DOCUMENT 127. ANSWER

Massachusetts District ss.

To the Honourable the Judges of the Circuit Court of the United States

16. John Richards and Stephen Jones, Jr., Boston merchants. Letters not found.

17. These documents are in the case file.

18. If McClintock were financially interested, he would be disqualified as a witness.

for the first Circuit in and for the District of Massachusetts
Mary Harvey[19] Petr. in Equity vs John Richards Admr.
The Answer of John Richards the Defendant to the bill of Complaint of Mary Harvey.
[Richards's attorney set forth the facts substantially as stated in McClintock's deposition, Document 126, preceding.]
And this defendant further answering admits, that he this defendant hath at sundry times after great labour and difficulty possessed himself in his said capacity of administrator of said testator, with the said will annexed of all the personal estate goods chattels and effects of said testator within this District, which he has been able to find. And this defendant further answering admits that the assets of the said testator, which have come to his hands after paying the charges of the administration up to the eighteenth day of April in the year of our Lord eighteen hundred & fourteen amount to the sum of thirty six thousand & thirteen dollars and two cents—and which said assets he this defendant is desirous to dispose of agreeably to law. But this said defendant doth wholly deny the right of the said Complainant to receive a distributive and proportional share of the estate goods chattels and effects of the said testator in the hands of this defendant[.] And this defendant doth wholly deny that the said Testator & James Mowry the person named in comp[lainan]ts said bill of Complaint are one & the same person, and in case the said Testator & the said James Murray are one & the same person he this Defendant says & he doth believe & insist that the complainant is not the next of kin to the said testator, but he this defendant doth believe and insist that the said testator was not born in lawful wedlock and by reason thereof as this defendant is advised and doth humbly insist he the said testator, could not have any lawful heirs & next of kin excepting those persons only who should be lineally descended from him And this defendant further answering says that in case the said testator was born in lawful wedlock, and in case the said complainant was his only next of kin, that he doth believe and insist that the said testator was not at the time of making his will aforesaid a resident of, nor had his domicile in the said town of Newport in said state of Rhode Island or in any other town or place within the United States and he is advised & doth insist that the said Testator was not a Citizen of the said State of Rhode Island and he doth also believe and insist that the said testator did not intend to return to and reside in said Newport or in any other place in said State of Rhode Island—but he this defendant doth believe and insist that he the said testator was at the time of making his said will a resident of, and had his domicile in or near the City of Calcutta in the province of Bengal,—and for a long time before had been a resident of, and had his domicile in one of the interior provinces of India called the Mahratta,

19. Mary Harvey has not been further identified.

and by means whereof as this defendant is advised and doth insist this Honourable Court has no power and authority to distribute any undevised surplus of the said testator's estate among his next of kin, but that all the personal estate goods chattels and effects of the said testator collected within this District by this defendant in his capacity of administrator with the said will annexed, after paying thereout the debts due from this testator, if any within this District, and the charges of administration ought to be transmitted to the executor or executors of the said will and testament of said testator in Bengal aforesaid to be there by him or them accounted for approbated, and distributed according to the will of the said deceased and the laws in force in said Bengal. And this defendant further answering says that if the said Complainant is the only next of kin of the said testator and as such entitled to the undevised surplus of his estate and effects he this defendant is advised and doth insist that the said complainant can only claim such undevised surplus of the said testator's estate and effects, after the payment of all debts legacies and charges of administering the said testator's goods and estate both in Bengal and within this District—and this defendant is advised and doth insist that the said complainant ought clearly to make it appear and fully to prove that the account of the said executor or executors to the will of the said testator has been settled approved & allowed by the Supreme Court of Judicature at fort William in Bengal aforesaid, or by such tribunal as hath jurisdiction of the same at said Bengal, and that nothing is now due in that Country for debts, legacies, and charges of administration there—for by the said account or otherwise clearly to show & fully to prove and establish that the said executor or executors of the will of the said testator in Bengal has or have in his or their hands & possession a sufficient sum of money within the Jurisdiction of the Court or tribunal having cognizance of the said will & the matters incident thereunto in said Bengal to pay all such debts legacies and charges of administration. And this defendant further answering says that in case the said complainant was the only next of kin of said testator, that the goods & estate of the said testator which have come to the hands and possession of his said executor or executors in Bengal are not as he this defendant doth believe & insist sufficient to pay the debts of the said testator together with the legacies given in and by his said will and the charges of administering his said estate in Bengal, but he doth believe & insist that they are insufficient for this purpose by the sum of fourteen thousand dollars and upwards exclusive of interest. And this defendant further answering says, that whether the said complainant is the next of kin to the said testator or not, in case there should be a surplus sum of money after the payment of all the debts & legacies of the said testator and after the payment of the charges of administration on his estate, both here and in Bengal, he this defendant is advised, & doth insist, that such surplus estate ought to be paid over and distributed according to the laws in force in said Bengal & this defendant admits that he doth not know whether by those laws the said surplus estate would be paid over to the next of kin of the testator, if any he had, or be given to the widow of the said testator, or whether the same would escheat[20] to the government of Bengal for want of heirs to the said testator, or be retained by the said executor or executors to his or their own use or be appropriated or distributed in any other manner but the said defendant doth humbly suggest, that by the laws in force in said Bengal, all such surplus estate ought to be retained by the said executor or executors to his or their own use. And the said defendant further answering says that he doth not yet know whether the said Jane Murray the wife of the said testator hath accepted the said sum of money bequeathed to her by the said will and in case she the said Jane Murray hath not accepted of the said legacy, this defendant is advised and doth humbly insists that she will then be entitled to receive a moiety of the estate and effects of her said husband, which may remain after the payment of the debts due by him & the other legacies given in & by his said will & the payment of the charges of administration, & notwithstanding the claim of the complainant or next of kin to the said testator—and this defendant believes & doth humbly insist that such election by the said Jane Murray would entitle her to a portion of the money remaining in his this defendants hands & possession but to what amount he is now unable to say. And this defendant further answering says that he believes & doth insist that the said Robert McClintock the acting executor of the said will of the said testator is materially interested in the premises & ought to have joined with the defendant as a party to the said complainant's bill. And this defendant further answering says that if the said complainant is the next of kin to the said testator, that she is not the only next of kin as in her said complaint she hath set forth, but this defendant doth believe & insist that one John Murray[21] late of Exeter in the County of Kent and State of Rhode Island is also one of the next of kin of the said testator & this defendant is advised & doth humbly insist, that by reason thereof the said John Murray ought to have been joined to & made a party with the complainant in her said bill. And this defendant further answering says & doth insist & believe that the said complainant has a full complete & adequate remedy at law to prosecute her claim to the monies or any proportional part thereof against him this defendant—and this defendant is advised and doth insist that the Courts of Common Law within this Dis-

20. A reversion of the property to the sovereign in the event that there is no one competent to inherit it.

21. John Mowry, Mary Harvey's brother. He died sometime in 1815.

trict have the same power & authority to grant commissions to procure testimony from parts beyond sea, or out of their respective jurisdictions as this Honourable Court has. And this defendant is advised & doth humbly insist, that this Honourable Court has no concurrent jurisdiction with the Courts of Common Law within this district in over & touching the premises set forth in the said complainants bill. And this defendant further answering says that he is advised & doth insist that the Courts of the United States have no jurisdiction in probate causes, or in things pending in the respective probate Courts in the several United States, & this defendant is advised & doth also insist that the Court of Probate within the County of Suffolk aforesaid & the Supreme Court of Probate in the Commonwealth of Massachusetts are Courts of Competent jurisdiction to try the claim of the said Complainant as alledged & set forth in her said bill. And this defendant denies all unlawful combination & confederacy in the said bill charged without that, that any matter or thing material or necessary for this defendant to make answer unto & not herein or hereby well & sufficiently answered unto confessed or avoided traversed or denied is true to the knowledge or belief of this defendant. All which matters & things this defendant is ready to aver maintain & prove as this Honourable Court shall direct & humbly prays to be hence dismissed with his reasonable costs & Charges in this behalf most wrongfully sustained.

[Harrison Gray] Otis & [Samuel] Hubbard Solicitors

ADS. *Harvey* v. *Richards*, USCC,DMass, May 1819.

DOCUMENT 128. RULE OF COURT

Massachusetts District.
Circuit Court May term 1815,
Harvey Compt. in Equity
vs
Richards Adr. of Murray.

Upon reading the bill and answer in this case, it is ordered that the said parties do proceed to trial, at law, upon this point;

Whether Mary Harvey is the sister and sole next of kin of the said James Mowry other wise called James Murray or not? Which trial is to be had at the bar of this Court by a jury for that purpose to be duly impannelled. And after the trial had the parties are to resort to the equity side of this Court for such further orders as shall be just. And at the trial either party is at liberty to make use of the depositions, taken in this cause, of such of the witnesses as cannot be brought to the trial, and also, by agreement, to make use of any other depositions filed in the cause which were taken to be used in the State Courts.

By the Court Wm S Shaw[22] Clk

ADS. *Harvey* v. *Richards*, USCC,DMass, May 1819.

DOCUMENT 129 AMENDED BILL IN EQUITY

Massachusetts District ss. [October 1815]

To the Honourable the Judges of the Circuit Court of the United States for the first Circuit in and for the District of Massachusetts begun and held at Boston; in said District, at the October term A.D. 1815.

Humbly complaining shews unto your Honours—your oratrix Mary Harvey of New Port, in the State of Rhode Island, Widow and a Citizen of said State as well on her own behalf as of John Mowry, formerly of Exeter, in said State of Rhode Island Yeoman, but whose place of residence is now unknown to your oratrix, which said Mary & sd John the only next of kin to James Mowry, otherwise called James Murray, late of said Newport, and a Citizen of said State of Rhode Island; that said James Mowry, otherwise called James Murray, having been a Captain in the Military service of Doulut Row Scindia a Mahratta Prince in the East Indies, did accumulate therein and was possessed of a large personal estate to the amount and value of two hundred thousand dollars at the least, and whilst on his return to said Newport, with said personal estate or a part thereof, at or near a place called Calcutta, in the Province of Bengal in said East Indies, on the twenty third day of September, in the year of our Lord Eighteen hundred and six, he said James Mowry, otherwise called Murray, duly made and published his last will and testament in writing, and among other things bequeathed therein and thereby to his wife Jane Murray, the sum of twenty five thousand Sicca rupees in full of all claims which she might have in any way whatsoever against his estate; and desired that all his property which had been remitted home by him from that country to America might remain in the hands of those to whom he sent it for their own use; and that the property then going to America he did not consider as belonging to any person; and of his said will he the said testator did nominate Messieurs Alexander and company his Executors. And your Oratrix further shews that the said James Mowry otherwise called James Murray thereupon departed this life without any lineal descendants surviving him, and without al-

22. William Smith Shaw (1778–1826; Harvard 1798), John Adams's private secretary, studied law with William Sullivan, admitted in 1814, editor, *The Monthly Anthology* (1803–1811), clerk, USDC,DMass (1806–1826).

tering or revoking his said Will; and upon his death one Robert McClintock one of the partners of said Alexander & Company and one of the Executors named in said Will, in the Supreme Court of Judicature, at Fort William in Bengal, proved said will, and administration was thereupon granted to him of all and singular the goods, chattels and credits of the said James Mowry otherwise called James Murray; and duly proceeding in administering said estate found in the Provinces of Bengal, Behar, Orissa and Zemindarry of Benares, he said Robert in his said capacity of Executor, as aforesaid, did pay and discharge thereout all the debts and legacies of said deceased, leaving a large surplus undisposed of.

And afterwards to wit, on the thirty first day of August in the year of our Lord one thousand eight hundred and seven John Richards of Boston within this District, Merchant, and a Citizen of the State of Massachusetts, did, before the Honorable Thomas Dawes,[23] Judge of the Probate of Wills and of granting of letters of Administration &c within the County of Suffolk in this District, file a copy of said will and of the Probate thereof; and thereupon solicited and procured from the said Dawes; in his said capacity, letters of Administration on the goods and estate of said James, by the name of James Murray, with the aforesaid will annexed, and thereupon possessed himself of all the personal estate of said James Mowry, otherwise called James Murray, within this District—to the amount of Forty thousand Dollars and upwards, by virtue of said letters of administration, by means of all which your Oratrix has become and is well entitled to a distributive and proportional share of the said James Mowry, otherwise called James Murray, estate and effects. And your Oratrix charges that since the said James's decease and the granting of the letters of administration last above mentioned, she has made frequent applications to the said John Richards, to come to a fair account with your Oratrix touching the said personal estate, and pay her a just and proportionable share thereof.

But now so it is, may it please your Honours, that the said John Richards having entered into a confederacy with divers persons to your Oratrix unknown whom, when discovered, your Oratrix prays may be made parties to this her bill of complaint with apt words to charge them, as Defendants hereunto, contriving how to defraud your Oratrix and defeat her right in the premises, having taken out the said letters of administration by virtue thereof hath gotten, into his possession all or the greater part of said deceased's Estate, to the value above set forth or some other great value, and absolutely refuses to come to any account with your

23. Thomas Dawes (1758–1825; Harvard 1777), Massachusetts lawyer and judge, studied with John Lowell, admitted in 1780, judge of probate, Suffolk County (1790–1792, 1802–1825), judge, MassSJC (1792–1802), judge, Boston Municipal Court (1802–1822).

Oratrix touching the distribution of the same; the said John Richards sometimes pretending that the personal estate of the said James Mowry otherwise called James Murray the testator, was insufficient to pay the debts, legacies and funeral expences; at others pretending that the said estate ought to be remitted to Calcutta aforesaid to be there distributed according to the laws of that place, and at others that your Oratrix and said John Mowry are not next of kin to said testator; Whereas your Oratrix charges, and so the truth is, that the said testator died possessed, of a very large personal estate much more than sufficient to pay all his just debts, legacies and funeral expences with a great overplus, your Oratrix charging that the said Robert McClintock hath, out of the monies arising from the personal Estate of the said Testator found in the East Indies, paid all the Testators just debts, legacies and funeral expenses and hath a great overplus in his hands; and that the Estate so received by the said John Richards ought not to be remitted to said Calcutta, to be there distributed and that she, your Oratrix and the said John Mowry are the sole next of kin to said testator.

All which aforesaid actings and pretences are contrary to equity and good conscience and tend to the manifest injury of your Oratrix.

In tender consideration whereof and forasmuch as matters of this nature are most properly cognizable and relievable in a court of equity before your Honours and your Oratrix cannot have a plain adequate and complete remedy at law by reason that many of the witnesses, who should make out the truth of several of the matters and things above charged are dead or in parts beyond seas.

To the end, therefore that the said John Richards, and his confederates when discovered, may full and perfect answer, upon their several corporal oaths, make to all and singular the premises, as fully and particularly as if the same were here again repeated and interrogated, and that the said John Richards may set forth, whether the said James Mowry otherwise called James Murray did not make such last will as is herein before set forth, or any other and what will after he had set out, on his return home, or otherwise; and whether the said Testator did not depart this life on or about the said twenty third day of September in the year of our Lord one thousand eight hundred and six without altering or revoking his said will, and whether upon his death, the said Robert McClintock did not alone prove the said will, and did not pay all the said testators just debts, legacies and funeral expences—and whether he the said John Richards, did not afterwards file a copy of said will before the said Honourable Thomas Dawes, Judge of Probate and so forth, and receive from him letters of administration with the will annexed as above set forth; and whether he the said John did not by virtue thereof receive and get into his hands, the custody possession or power of all or such parts of the Testator's Estate, as he could come by, and that he may set forth a true and perfect account of all and singular the estate of the testator which has come to his, the said John's hands, or to the hands, custody, power or possession of any other person or persons for his use, and how the same is disposed of, and what part remains unpaid or undisposed of and where and in whose custody all or any part thereof now is; And more especially whether your Oratrix and said John Mowry are not the sole next of kin to the said James, the testator aforesaid, deceased, in the manner above set forth, or how otherwise, and if your Oratrix and the said John Mowry are not entitled to some, and what share and proportion of his personal estate and effects, and if he the said James Mowry, otherwise called James Murray was not a citizen of the State of Rhode Island, and whether the said John Richards, did not, and for what reason, refuse to render or come to a general account with your Oratrix, touching the personal estate of said deceased. And that he may be decreed to pay her and to the said John when he comes in and contributes to the expenses of this suit what shall appear to be the share and proportion of your Oratrix and the said John according to law or otherwise; And that your Oratrix may have such other and further relief in the premises as the nature and circumstances of her case shall require and be consistent with equity and good conscience.

May it please your Honours the premises considered, to grant unto your Oratrix a writ or writs of Subpoena to be directed to the said John Richards and other, his confederates, when discovered, thereby commanding them and every of them, at a certain day, and under a certain penalty personally to be and appear before your Honours in this Honourable Court, then and there [to answer] all and singular the premises and to stand to perform and abide such order direction, and decree therein as to your Honours shall seem meet &c.

Selfridge & Aylwin Solicitors.

ADS. *Harvey* v. *Richards*, USCC,DMass, May 1819.

DOCUMENT 130. AGREEMENT

U. S. Circuit Court Oct T. 1815
C A No. Mary Harvey Petr in Eq v. John Richards

The parties agree that John Lathrop Jr[24] Esqr if present would swear, that in the year 1806 he was a resident in Calcutta & there knew Maj Murray, that Murray was there for the purpose of taking passage for America—that he had taken a house—but that there are no boarding houses there—that an American Captain takes a house, it being considered disreputable not to do it—that he had taken a passage for America

24. Not identified; see Document 135, below.

—that he came from the interior but he (Lathrop) dont know from what distance—that he had a wife who was the Widow of an English Officer, a half cast that he lived in great style his house was a garden house & that he had no town house—that he Murray told him (Lathrop) that he was born in America, that he was one of the boys in Philadelphia at the time of the adoption of the federal constitution and was one of the boys who went with the Ship—that he told him his real name was not Murray, that this reason of his change of name was a secret, but that he would tell him when he left Calcutta, and would write him by the Pilot—that when he knew Maj Murray in 1806, he appeared to be about thirty five years old, that he wrote an Epitaph upon him at the request of his friends who gave him the age of thirty five and that Maj Smith who knew him intimately mentioned to him, Lathrop, some circumstances as made him about thirty five years old.[25]

Selfridge & Aylwin for plt.
Prescott & Hubbard for Def

ADS. *Harvey* v. *Richards*, USCC,DMass, May 1819.

DOCUMENT 131. MOTION BY COMPLAINANTS

Circuit Court *May* term 1816. 21 May 1816.
Mary Harvey, Compt. in Equity v. John Richards Adm.

And now, on behalf of the said Comp[t.] it is moved that the Deft be ordered to state whether or not the money admitted by him in his answer in this cause to be in his hands—has been put out at interest or any gains made thereof since the same came to his possession. And further, that he be ordered to place the same out at interest under the direction of this Court.

Selfridge & Aylwin
Solicitors to Compt

ADS. *Harvey* v. *Richards*, USCC,DMass, May 1819.

DOCUMENT 132. ORDER OF COURT

Circuit Court October Term *A. D. 1817* 25 Octr. 1817.
Mary Harvey Compt. v. Jno. Richards adr

It is ordered by the Court, with the assent of parties, that the defendant in this cause do henceforth stand charged with interest on the sum admitted by him, in his answer to be in his hands, and in the event of

25. See Document 133, below.

the complainants obtaining a decree, the said Defendant shall account for interest accordingly.

Att[est] Jno W Davis Clk.

ADS. *Harvey* v. *Richards*, USCC,DMass, May 1819.

DOCUMENT 133. DEPOSITION

[October 18, 1810]

Lewis Ferdinand Smith late a Major in the service of Dowlut Rao Saindea and now an Inhabitant of Chinsurah in Bengal maketh oath and saith That he this Deponent in the year one thousand Eight hundred and six and for some time previous was well acquainted and upon terms of the most intimate friendship with one James Murray formerly a Captain in the service of the Rajah of Jeypore that this Deponent was frequently with him and knew his concerns and was present at his the said James Murray's decease at Calcutta on the twenty third day of September in the said year one thousand Eight hundred and six and this Deponent further saith that during three or four hours immediately preceding the Death of the said James Murray he this Deponent never quitted the House of the said James Murray who was there in a state of excruciating agony and pain from the violent effect of desease and sickness and totally incapable of giving any orders or directions respecting his Concerns and this Deponent further saith that he did not on the said twenty third day of September one thousand Eight Hundred and six or at any other time hear nor does he believe the said James Murray did ever express to George Dutch or any other person or persons whomsoever or relate any intention of bequeathing certain property which the said James Murray had caused to be shipped on Board of a Certain Vessel called the Boston Packet or any part thereof or any property monies or effects whatever to Messieurs Dutch and Deland[26] Merchants of Salem and owners of the said Ship Boston Packet or either of them and this Deponent Saith that it is not probable if the said James Murray had expressed or intimated any such intention or desire within three or four hours before his the said James Murray's decease that he this Deponent should not have heard and been aware of it he this Deponent having been generally present in the Chamber of the said James Murray as aforesaid and this Deponent further saith that he this Deponent was present about noon of the twenty third day of September one thousand Eight hundred and six when the said James Murray gave directions to Mr. Robert McClintock to draw his the said James Murray's will and the Deponent continued in the next room and saw the said James Murray dictating his will to the said Robert McClintock the doors between the two rooms being open the whole time it was preparing and until it was finished and executed

26. Thorndike Deland, not further identified.

by the said James Murray that the said James Murray did not during the whole time aforesaid or after this Deponent continued to remain with him from the time he executed the said Will until his decease and it is not likely that the said James Murray did a few hours before his decease send for the said George Dutch to his bed side and tell him that he had given by his will his property or any part thereof on Board the Boston Packet to the said Messieurs Dutch and Delande of Salem in compensation for the losses and expences sustained by them for his accommodation or any words to those or the like purport or effect or that the said James Murray had any conversation whatever relative to the supposed bequest with the said George Dutch from the time the said Will was executed until he the said James Murray expired and that if the said James Murray had in contemplation to bequeath any property or effects to the said Messieurs Dutch and Delande this Deponent conceives the said James Murray would have directed such bequest to have been mentioned and inserted in the said Will but which he this Deponent expressly asserts was not the fact nor did the said James Murray express any desire or intention whatever to that effect within the hearing of this Deponent and this deponent further saith that from his intimacy with the said James Murray he is certain it is not true that the said George Dutch or any other person maintained the said James Murray—and his suite or any or either of them or any part of his family for six weeks or any other time previous to his death but that the said deceased lived in his own house was attended and Supplied with all necessaries by his own servants and from his own funds and that the said George Dutch was merely a frequent visitor at the House of the said James Murray and that he the said George Dutch and his friends lived on the hospitality of the said James Murray and this Deponent further saith that he does not believe that the said James Murray did bequeath or intend to bequeath any part of his property on Board the said Boston Packet or any other property belonging to him to the said Messieurs Dutch and Delande as a compensation for or in consideration of any losses or expenses they or either of them were at or sustained by the said James Murray for this Deponent saith that independant of the absurdity that the said George Dutch should have refused freight upon the chance of the said James Murray's making his will and leaving property to the said Messieurs Dutch and Delande and afterwards immediately dying to give it.—Operation this Deponent heard from the said James Murray shortly previous to his decease and which the Deponent believes to be true that the freight given by the said James Murray to the said Boston Packet did exceed and was more than that offered by one Joseph Quieros[27] then of Calcutta and now of Lucknow merchant

27. Not identified.

and which freight was actually Shipped by the said James Murray before he made his said Will or gave any directions for preparing the same and this Deponent further saith that he was on board the Betsey commanded by the said George Dutch and which was a Vessel of one hundred and fifty tons or thereabouts at the time she was at Calcutta and shortly previous to the decease of the said James Murray that this Deponent saw the alterations that were made in the Cabin for the accommodation of the said James Murray and verily believes the same could not at the utmost have cost more than sicca Rupees five hundred or thereabouts and this Deponent further Saith that he and one William Hitchcock and one Thomas Adams [Adkins] were the most particular and intimate friends the said James Murray had in India and were well acquainted with all his Concerns and were to have proceeded to america with him in the same Vessel that this Deponent never heard from the said James Murray nor does he believe he ever intended to give any part of his property whatever to the said Messieurs Dutch and Delande or either of them or to any other person whatever in america and this Deponent further saith that he saw and conversed with the said George Dutch in Calcutta immediately after the decease of the said James Murray upon the affairs of the said James Murray but the said George Dutch did not then state having had any conversation with the said Deceased in which the said Deceased had declared that he had given or intended to give any part of his property to the said Messieurs Dutch and Delande nor did the said George Dutch set up or pretend to have any claim thereto and this Deponent further saith that from the intimate knowledge this Deponent had of the fortune and of the state of the affairs and Concerns of the said James Murray at the time of his decease he verily believes the same did not at the utmost exceed in Value Sicca Rupees one hundred and twenty thousand of which ninety thousand or thereabout was then gone or going to america aforesaid and this Deponent further saith that the said James Murray did leave a Widow him Surviving who is named in his said Will and that he lived and cohabited with her and acknowledged her as his wife and as such She was always acknowledged reputed taken and esteemed by the friends and neighbours of the said James Murray.

(sd) Lewis F Smith

ADS. *Harvey* v. *Richards*, USCC,DMass, May 1819.

DOCUMENT 134. ANSWERS TO INTERROGATORIES AND CROSS INTERROGATORIES

[March 28, 1817]

Thomas Adkins of Adderbury in the County of Oxford Esquire but now residing at the Bell Inn in Holborn in the County of Middlesex in that part of the United Kingdom of Great Britain and Ireland called England but late a Captain in the Service of the Honorable the East India Company aged forty three years and—upwards a Witness produced Sworn and Examined on the part and behalf of the Defendant deposeth and saith as follows.

First. To the first Interrogatory this Deponent saith that he doth not know the parties Complainant or Defendant in the Title of the Interrogatories named or either of them.

Second. To the second Interrogatory this Deponent Saith that he knew Major James Murray formerly an officer in the Mahratta Service in the East Indies now deceased and that he so knew him for about twelve years before his decease That he died at Calcutta on the twenty-third of September one thousand eight hundred and six.

Third. To the third Interrogatory this Deponent saith that the said James Murray was in the Mahratta Service several years with different Chiefs but the particular time he this Deponent cannot state And this Deponent further saith that he left that Service in the year One thousand eight hundred and three on the occasion of a proclamation being made by the Governor General in Council calling on all European and American Officers serving with the Mahratta Army to join the British Forces

Fourth. To the fourth Interrogatory this Deponent saith that the said James Murray when he quitted the Service of the Mahratta's entered into the Service of the Honorable the East India Company That he entered into the last mentioned Service in or about September one thousand eight hundred and three and received pay from the East India Company during the then War which continued about two years That he was not in the actual Service of the East India Company at his death but he received a pension from the said company at the time of his death

Fifth. To the fifth Interrogatory this Deponent Saith that the said James Murray died at Calcutta in the province of Bengal in the East Indies and this Deponent believes he was about forty years of age at the time of his decease and further to this Interrogatory this Deponent cannot depose.

Sixth. To the sixth Interrogatory this Deponent saith he believes that the Laws in force in Bengal in relation to wills and Testaments are the same or similar to those in England and he also believes that the Laws on these Subjects in Bengal are the same with those over all other parts of the Territories of the East India Company and further to this Interrogatory this Deponent cannot depose.

Seventh. To the seventh Interrogatory this Deponent saith that the said James Murray had a House and was domiciled in Calcutta at the time of his decease or near there in some of the Territories of the East India Company And this Deponent further saith he understands and believes that persons admitted into the Service of the East India Company and who are in India acquire a domicil in India by force of such admission into the said Service

Eighth. To the eighth Interrogatory this Deponent Saith—he does not know and cannot set forth whether the said James Murray had an Estate in Bengal but he believes he had not And this Deponent further saith that the said James Murray made a Will before his decease and that the Legatees have been paid in part, and the reason why the Legacies were not paid in full is because his property in India would not extend to pay them in full.

Ninth. To the ninth Interrogatory this Deponent Saith that the said James Murray a few hours before his Death declared to this Deponent that it was his intention that his agents should have the remainder of his property after his Legacies were paid And further to this Interrogatory cannot depose.

T. Adkins

Thomas Adkins a Witness already Sworn and Examined on the part and behalf of the Defendant and now again Sworn and Cross Examined on the part and behalf of the Complainant deposeth and Saith

First. To the first Interrogatory this Deponent Saith that it was not the intention or declared intention of the said James Murray in coming to Calcutta from the interior of India solely to procure a passage home to the United States, for when he came to Calcutta he hired a large House and furnished it in an expensive stile in which he lived, and it was not as this Deponent believes until about six weeks before his death that he had an intention of returning to America and the reason for such his belief is because this Deponent who was on very intimate terms of friendship with the said James Murray never heard him intimate or express any such intention before that time And this Deponent further saith that he was not in fact on his return home (if the United States are to be considered his home) at the time of his death, because his death was so sudden as not to permit him to put his intention of returning to the United States into execution

Second. To the second Interrogatory this Examinant Saith he doth know that the said James Murray had Shipped to the United States a part of his property but a short time before his decease and had then engaged his passage with the residue on board an American vessel bound to the Port of Salem in the said United States

Third. To the third Interrogatory this Deponent saith that the said James Murray did remain in Calcutta or in its Neighbourhood a longer period prior to his decease than was necessary to procure a Vessel with suitable accommodation to transport himself and Family to the United States at a fair or reasonable price.

Fourth. To the fourth Interrogatory this Deponent Saith that it is not a general Custom with Gentlemen who arrive at Calcutta and have the means to take a House hir[e] Servants and form a separate Establishment although they do not contemplate making it a permanent abode.

Fifth. To the fifth Interrogatory this Deponent saith that what he means by a domicil, is, the having acquired the protection of the Laws or Customs of the particular place in which a person resides but he is not particularly acquainted with what acts constitute one further or otherwise than he has before stated in his answer to the Interrogatories exhibited to him on the part of the Defendant.

Sixth. To the sixth Interrogatory this Deponent Saith that he never heard and does not believe that the said James Murray had a large or any Estate in the Province of Bengal and further to this Interrogatory this Deponent cannot depose.

Seventh. To the seventh Interrogatory this Deponent cannot depose.

Eighth. To the eighth Interrogatory this Deponent saith he is informed and believes that Interest is allowed by the Laws of Bengal or Hindostan on the payment of Legacies similar to those contained in the said James Murrays Will.

Ninth. To the ninth Interrogatory this Deponent cannot depose

Tenth. To the tenth Interrogatory this Deponent saith that he is a Legatee named in the Will of the said James Murray and has not compromised with the Executor, who has paid him in part only the remainder to the extent of one half or thereabouts being still due to him with Interest and further to this Interrogatory cannot depose.

Eleventh. Twelfth and Thirteenth. } To the eleventh twelfth and thirteenth Interrogatories this Deponent cannot depose.

Fourteenth. To the fourteenth Interrogatory this Deponent saith that he is a Legatee named in the Will of the said James Murray part of which Legacy still remains unpaid, that he is not fully acquainted with the objects of this suit, but as he has been informed that the will of the said James Murray has been proved both in India and America, he is not as he believes interested in the event of this cause and shall not gain or lose thereby

Fifteenth. To the fifteenth Interrogatory this Deponent cannot depose.

T. Adkins

ADS. *Harvey* v. *Richards*, USCC,DMass, May 1819.

DOCUMENT 135. DEPOSITION

May 8, 1816

7. I know of no issue of the said Major Murray. The female who passed

for his wife was a half cast, a native of Pondicherry. Whether he was married to her or not, [I am not] informed. She was a decent woman, and presided at his table. Concubinage is not esteemed so disreputable in Asia as in America. He never expressed any intention of bringing this female to America; but, on the contrary provided for her decent maintenance in India, as is usual with Gentlemen who have cohabited with females who are natives of the Country. I always understood that he executed a will in his last illness. One of the witnesses, Mr William J Edgar[28] informed me of the fact. I know nothing of the value of his estate. The amount was said to be large. I never heard any thing respecting the amount of his estate from either of his Executors. Nor do I know whether he died free of debts. Major Murray died in consequence of a fall from his horse. I attended his funeral, and afterwards, at the request of some of his military friends, composed an epitaph, which [w]as inscribed on a monument which they erected to his memory in the Burying ground in Calcutta.

* * * * *

Murray did not intend to bring his wife to America. She preferred a proper support in India which he told me he should make for her. I never heard of their having any children. I firmly believe Murray had no child living with him at the time of his death.

* * * * *

John Lathrop

[Cross interrogatory]
3. I know nothing of Major Murray's fortune, or how he acquired it, of my own knowledge. He told me that he had gained a very handsome fortune in the Mahratta service. I presume that he invested his salary and other acquired property in the inland Bills of exchange of the country, or in company's paper, and transmitted them to his agents in Calcutta. This is the customary way of transacting business between gentlemen in the interior of India, and their agents.

Extract. *Harvey* v. *Richards*, USCC,DMass, May 1819.

DOCUMENT 136. EXCEPTION TO TESTIMONY

[November 6, 1817]

Circuit Court October Term 1817

Exceptions exhibited by Mary Harvey complainant in a certain cause now depending & at issue in this Court wherein she is complainant and John Richards Administrator with the will annexed of James Murray deceased, is defendant, to the reading of the testimony of Thomas Ad-

28. Not identified.

kins and William Hitchcock two witnesses examined before Thomas Aspinwall[29] Esqe a commissioner duly appointed for that purpose on the behalf of the defendant.

First. The said Mary Harvey doth allege that the said Thomas Adkins & William Hitchcock are legatees named in the will of said Murray

Second. That the said Adkins and Hitchcock as appears by their answers are directly interested in the event of this suit—in as much as they severally testify that their legacies are unpaid from the want of sufficient funds in the hands of the Executor of said will—and do depose to facts to enable the Defendant in this cause to procure a jud[gment?] from which they may

AD. *Harvey* v. *Richards*, USCC,DMass, May 1819. Only this portion of the document has been found.

DOCUMENT 137. REPORTED ARGUMENT

Webster, in reply. This argument proceeds on the ground, that no debts or legacies remain unsatisfied in *India*; and that the executor, there, has no beneficial interest under the will. The case is presumed to be such, that if the plaintiff were before the proper court in *Bengal*, with this bill, such court would be bound to decree distribution.

It is no answer to the plaintiff, that her bill calls on the Court to apply the laws of another country. Courts apply those laws in many cases. The sessions did this in *Bruce* vs. *Bruce*. The master of the rolls did the same in *Kilpatrick* vs. *Kilpatrick*. The court of *Pennsylvania* applied the law of *Delaware* in *Guier* vs. *O'Daniel*.[30] So far there can be no difficulty or doubt in the case.

A decree for the plaintiff must be resisted, if it can be resisted at all, on the ground, that there being an existing administration, in *loco domicilii*, the effects collected elsewhere, must, in all cases, be remitted to the hands of the administrator or executor there, to be by him distrib-

29. Thomas Aspinwall (1784–1876; Harvard 1804), studied law with William Sullivan, active in the War of 1812, U.S. consul, London (1816–1854), thereafter a resident of Boston.

30. In these three cases the court distributed property of a person who died in another jurisdiction. In *Bruce* v. *Bruce*, 2 Bosanquet and Puller 229 (1790), the court ruled that the law of England would govern distribution of the property of an intestate who died in India. On p. 584 of 6 Brown's Cases in Parliament (1792) there is a reference to *Kilpatrick* v. *Kilpatrick*, as a case where Lord Kenyon, as master of the rolls, decreed distribution according to Scottish law of money in England belonging to a Scottish estate. In *Guier* v. *O'Daniel*, 1 Binney (Pa.) 349 (1806), the court presumed the deceased to be domiciled in Delaware, the place of his last residence, and distributed his personal property according to the law of the domicile.

uted. This is contended for as an universal rule; subject however to one exception, which is, that creditors here, have a right to be paid here, out of the funds.

Is there any such universal and inflexible rule? The plaintiff contends there is not. The law on this subject may be considered as of modern origin. It arises from comity, and from the regard, which courts of one country pay to the private rights of the citizens or subjects of another country. But a rule, in the extent contended for, is not required by any of the reasons, in which the general doctrine or general practice is founded. The property is to be remitted, when any purpose of substantial justice requires it. But if the rightful owner be here, why should it be sent abroad for no reason, but to send him after it? The case under discussion supposes the plaintiff entitled to this property, and that if sent to *India*, and she were to follow it thither, it could not be refused to her. If the fund were wanted in *India* for any purpose of the will; or if any persons there had rights in it, or claims upon it, the case would be different. But as the fund is here, and as the plaintiff, a citizen of this country, is entitled to it; and as this Court is competent to distribute it, comity cannot require from this Court the compliment of deferring the cause to the jurisdiction of the court in *India*. This is not required by that regard to the rights of individuals, subjects of other countries, which has governed the decision of courts in these cases. And, that regard to these rights, is the foundation, upon which courts proceed in such cases, is proved perhaps by the circumstance, that no case is mentioned, probably none exists, in which the government of one country claims property in another, as escheating to itself. The courts of this country would remit this property to *England* or to *India*, to answer the claims of legatees or next of kin there. But they would not remit it for the benefit of the British exchequer, if there were no legatees or next of kin.

If, then, the question be not a technical one about the jurisdiction of the Court, but of justice and private right, should it not appear, that some purpose of right or justice is to be answered by remitting the property to *India*?

If there is no known and fixed principle, requiring the rule to be carried to the extent mentioned, the Court will look to the consequences of adopting it in that extent. Many cases of inconveniences have been stated on the other side, which might happen, if the Court should distribute personal property, found here, and belonging to one dying abroad.[31] And no doubt there are cases, in which convenience, as well as justice would

31. Richards's attorneys argued that if the deceased had property in several states a decision for Harvey would make settlement of an estate very complicated. "What endless confusion would here be created! What a variety of accounts! What opportunities for fraud and embezzlement!" 1 Mason 381, 395.

require the fund to be remitted. But the question is, whether this must be done, and in all cases? Or, on the other hand, whether the Court may not do that, in each case, which the justice of that case shall require?

A man might die in India, domiciled there, leaving the bulk of his property, and all his creditors, next of kin and legatees, here. There may be nothing to be done in *India*, but collect debts due to the estate. Those may be here, who are entitled to the whole. Shall it all, nevertheless, be sent to *India*? If not, then there is no such universal rule as has been supposed.

There are many cases, in which decisions have been made inconsistent with the existence of any such rule. One is, where persons dying abroad leave executors, both abroad and in *England*. The executor in *England* is bound to distribute what comes to his hands. He is not merely to collect the effects, and remit them to the executor acting in *loco domicilii*. *Brooks* vs. *Oliver*, appears to be a case of this sort. So is *Chetham* vs. Lord *Audley*.[32]

Another case is, where the will is proved in both countries. *Cooper* says, "The municipal courts of this country will also, by a principle of the law of nations, in the case of strangers leaving property here, distribute that property, in the case of death, by the laws of their own country, provided such stranger is not domiciled here."[33] He makes no exception for the case of there being another administrator or executor in *loco domicilii*. All these cases and opinions seem to be wrong, if the law be, as stated in one of the cases relied on by the other side, viz. that all effects and choses in action, wherever collected, must be accounted for and finally administered in the country, where the deceased had his domicil.[34] The rule is not laid down to that extent, in any other case, or by any writer. The administration in *loco domicilii* may be, and in cases arising in the East and *West Indies*, very often is, considered as a mere agency. In *Chetham* vs. Lord *Audley*, Lord *Loughborough* says, "I think the appointment of an executor in *India*, no legacy being given to him, is the appointment of an agent for the management of the estate. They give them the character of executors."[35] In such a case, the creditors and

32. In *Brooks*, Ambler 406 (1761), the court ordered the English executor to make an annual accounting of the deceased's real and personal property, then located in Antigua, and to place the surplus in a bank. The court did not consider the testator's domicile an issue. In *Chetham* v. *Lord Audley*, 4 Vesey Jr. 72 (1798), the testator died in India. By his will he appointed executors in India and England. One of the executors in India claimed that the estate owed him a commission under Indian practice. The chancellor ruled that the court would follow Indian custom. The residuary legatee resided in England, and all other pecuniary legacies had been paid.

33. George Cooper, *Treatise of Pleading on the Equity Side of the High Court of Chancery*, 1st American ed. (New York, 1813), p. 121.

34. *Dawes* v. *Boylston*, 9 Mass. 323 (1812); see note 40, below.

35. p. 75. Loughborough meant

legatees, or next of kin being in an other country, the *India* administration should, from the nature of the case, be considered as auxiliary to the uses of the property and the interest of those concerned. It should be accessary to that administration, which exists, where those are, who have a right to the property.

In *Jauncy* vs. *Sealy*,[36] there seems to be no objection to calling the administrator *loci domicilii* to account to the administrator in *England*, provided there had been effects in *England*. *Tourton* vs. *Flower*[37] is to the same point. These cases are incompatible with the existence of a rule, which renders the administration in *loco domicilii* in all cases the leading one, and treats the other as entirely subordinate. Indeed there will hardly be found to be any such rule, as that where there are two administrations on one estate, existing in different independent countries, one must be considered in all cases as principal, and the other as merely auxiliary and subordinate. Strictly speaking, no such relation can exist between authorities derived from different sources. Each administration is independent of the other; the power of administering issues from different and independent origins. Courts of law and equity will compel administrators, who act in an official capacity, so to act as to answer the ends of justice; and for this purpose they will, if necessary, hold an administration in one country to be trustee of an executor or administrator in another country. But then a case must be made out, in which justice and equity require this. There may be administrations with equal claims to be considered, single and independent. Suppose a man domiciled in *England*, to make his will there, leaving property both there and here. He may give a legacy to a person here, charged on the property here, and a legacy to a person in *England*, charged on the property there; and he may appoint executors in both countries. Should the legatee here be referred in such case to *England* for payment? Or suppose that there were, in such case, only the English executor, and he should come here, prove the will, and obtain the property by the aid of the laws of this country, could he not then be compelled to pay the legacy here? If we go one step further and suppose, that instead of coming with the will, he should send it, and it should be proved, and administration granted, at his re-

---

that unless Indian executors received some compensation they would not collect the assets for English legatees.

36. 1 Vernon 397 (1686). The court held that a will of personal estate which lies in a foreign country may be proved in that country. But if the will disposes of goods located in England, it must be proved in England. The reporter referred to *Tourton* v. *Flower*; see note 37, below.

37. In *Tourton*, 3 Peere William 369 (1735), the English court refused to take notice of an administration granted in the French ecclesiastial court. The plaintiff, who sought an accounting of assets situated in England, had to take out an English administration.

quest, to some one, with the will annexed, and then suppose further, that instead of a legatee applying for a legacy, the next of kin apply here for a surplus, we have the present case. A will might be made abroad, which could be only executed here. It might charge annuities or the maintenance of infants or relatives on the funds in this country, and be made payable on contingencies, which could be known and ascertained no where else. It might direct property to be invested in stock here, for the purposes of the will. A testator in *England*, having property here, might bequeath it to charitable purposes here. Such a trust must be enforced here or no where; because the English court of chancery has declined to enforce the execution of a charity in favour of objects existing under a foreign government.

A principal case relied on by the counsel for the defendant is *Pipon* vs. *Pipon*.[38] As to that case, it may be remarked 1st. That the plaintiff there had clearly no right. 2dly. That the plaintiff did not ask for distribution according to the laws of *Jersey*. Lord *Hardwicke* seemed to think something remained to be done in *Jersey*. Nothing can be proved by that case, except that the succession is to be governed by the law of the domicil.

It has been said, that from an expression of the master of the rolls in *Somerville* vs. Lord *Somerville*, it may be inferred, that he would remit the funds for distribution to the court of the domicil, instead of distributing them himself. "The country," he says, "in which the property is, would not let it go out of that, until it knew by what rule it is to be distributed."[39] But this expression cannot warrant the inference drawn from it. And in the very cases in which it was used, the master of the rolls appears to have decreed distribution according to the laws of *Scotland*.

In *Dawes* vs. *Boylston*[40] it is said, that creditors here are to be paid before the fund is to be remitted. This is stated without qualification, and

38. In *Pipon*, Ambler 25 (1744), the intestate died in Jersey. The plaintiffs brought suit in England for distribution of a bond-debt due in London. The court ruled that personal estate must be distributed according to the law of the intestate's domicile under which the plaintiffs were not entitled to part of the distribution. The court stressed that the general administration of the estate was not before the court.

39. 5 Vesey Jr. 750 (1801). The master of the rolls ruled that the succession to the personal estate of the intestate is regulated by the law of the intestate's domicile. The quotation appears on p. 791. It is clearly a dictum. The master hypothesized a case where the deceased held two contemporaneous and equal domiciles. In that event the law of the place where the property was located would govern its disposition.

40. 9 Mass. 323 (1812) held that the rights of residuary legatees and next of kin depended on the laws of the country where the deceased had his home. All the deceased's personal effects were to be finally administered and distributed where the will was probated. The implication was that when the will was probated in England, the Boston administration was ancillary to the English one.

without reference to the case of other creditors existing abroad. This exception opens a door to all the inconveniences, which have been stated, and to great injustice, in many cases; because the greater part of the property might be here, while the greater amount of debts might be abroad, and the whole estate insufficient to pay all. And it is not easy to see, why the next of kin, there being no debts, have not as well founded a right to the property, as creditors, where there are debts. So also of legatees. It is not matter of favor, in courts of equity, to compel the payment of legacies, or to decree distribution; nor have they any broader discretion in such cases than in the payment of debts.

It is difficult to perceive the reason, why debts are to be paid, and legacies not paid, or the surplus not distributed. By the law of *England* assets are to be marshalled, and judgments and bond debts are to be paid before debts by simple contract. If a simple contract creditor be found here, his debts having been contracted in *India*, and with reference to the laws of that country, may he obtain satisfaction out of the funds here, and leave judgment creditors and bond creditors unpaid in *India*? It would seem at least to be equitable, that debts contracted in *India* should be paid according to the laws of India, wherever the fund might be found. A general rule, that all debts asserted here, wherever contracted, should, in all cases, be paid out of the funds here, would seem to be as objectionable, as the supposed rule, that legatees and next of kin must, in all cases, resort to the forum of the domicil. It is possible, that the judges in *Dawes* vs. *Boylston* might have felt themselves restrained by the nature of the jurisdiction, which they were exercising. They might not consider themselves as possessed of all the power of a court of equity. If there were no inconvenience of that sort, and if the merits of the case had required it, I am not able to see, why a decree might not have been made in that case in favour of the inhabitants of *Boston*. A conclusive reason in favour of such decree would seem to be, that if the will of the testator could not be enforced in that particular, by the court here, it could not be enforced at all, and the testator's object would be wholly defeated.

In the subsequent case of *Stevenson* vs. *Gaylord*, the same court appear not to have considered any rule established in *Dawes* vs. *Boylston*. The court in that case says, "If it should appear upon due examination in our probate court, that *Tilbalds* had his home in *Connecticut*, we should cause the balance, remaining in the hands of the administrator here, to be distributed according to the laws of *Connecticut*, or transmitted for distribution by the administrator in *Connecticut*, under the decree of the Court there."[41] This language is not consistent with the sup-

41. 11 Mass. 256, 264 (1814). In an action of assumpsit by the Massachusetts administrator against a citizen of Connecticut, the defendant pleaded his appointment as administrator in Connecticut and

position, that the Court had either found or made a rule, requiring a transmission of the fund in all cases. I consider, therefore, that the decisions in the supreme court of this state, taken together, have established no such rule as the defendant contends for.

If no settled rule has been shewn, by which the plaintiff must be referred to *India* for distribution, there is no principle of equity opposed to granting her relief here. The defendant professes to be trustee for the executors in *India*; and the case is such, that if the executors in *India* shall receive the money, they will be trustees for the plaintiff. Then why may not the plaintiff treat the defendant as her trustee, and claim the money directly from him. There is no question about sufficient parties. The executors in *India* have had notice of this suit, and the defendant represents them in it. A decree here will protect him against them. He has collected this fund through the assistance of the judicial tribunals of this country; and if he shall now distribute under their decree, he cannot be made further answerable to any body.

Printed in *Harvey* v. *Richards*, 1 Mason 381, 399–407 (1819).

TO JEREMIAH MASON

Dear Sir Boston June 29th 1818

Mrs. Webster has a letter from Mrs. Mason this morning, in which she says nothing as to the *time* of being this way. I have a little occasion, partly of business, & partly for the ride, to go to the Western Counties—say, the first of next week, to be gone 10 or 12 days. I would not go, however, if your arrangements are to be here within that time, as I prefer, very much, our Sandwich expedition & would not let this ride, if I take it, interfere with it. Mrs. W. will not go with me. Be good enough to let me know how you are, & whether you have fixed any plan & time &c.

I see that P is chosen Senator and [Samuel] Bell to be Govr. This I think, much better than could have been expected. Plumer[42] seems to have been *laughed* out of the whole.

We have no news. Judge Story's Court was here three days last week. We argued the question of law which I mentioned to you. The Judge gave

---

his inventory of the property. The quotation is substantially correct. The difference between *Stevenson* and *Harvey* v. *Richards* was that in *Stevenson* the court held the Massachusetts administration ancillary.

42. John Fabyan Parrott (1767–1836), Portsmouth resident, state legislator, U.S. representative (1817–1819), U.S. senator (1819–1825); William Plumer (1759–1850), New Hampshire lawyer and politician, studied with Joshua Atherton and John Prentice, admitted in 1787, state legislator, U.S. senator (1802–1807), New Hampshire governor (1812; 1816–1818). Plumer, a Republican, had decided not to seek reelection.

no opinion. I think we shall get a favorable decision, viz. to this effect that if the next of kin of one domiciled in India & dying there, be here; & funds be found here, which are an undevised surplus (a will having been made in India) and such funds, here be in the hands of an admr. with the will annexed; and the funds be not necessary for any purpose of the will in India, nor to pay debts—the Court will decree the admr. here to distribute;—it being a clear case, that the Plf would be entitled to distribution in India, if she were to follow the fund there.

Nothing else of importance was done. The Judge promised to come & spend a day with me when you should be in town. Let me here from you. Yrs D Webster

Copy. NhHi.

DOCUMENT 138. MOTION FOR CONTINUANCE

[October 21, 1818]

United States of America
Massachusetts District } Circuit Court of the United States

Oct T[erm] A D 1818

C A No. 2. Mary Harvey in Eq vs. John Richards Admr.

And now the said John Richards being duly sworn maketh oath & saith that he hath not yet received back the Commission[43] which was granted in this Cause to procure testimony in Calcutta, tho' he confidently did expect it before the present time—but that he now confidently expects to receive the same by the first arrivals from India—& from the Interrogatories annexed to said commission he verily believes that among other documents there will be returned with the said Commission true copies of the Executor's account with the Estate of the late James Murray—by which it will satisfactorily appear that there is a large balance due from the said Estate to the said Executor; besides large sums due to the Legatees of said James Murray—that the facts on which he grounds his belief that the said Commission will shortly be returned executed, are contained in a letter bearing date Calcutta February the tenth in the year of our Lord eighteen hundred & eighteen written by the House of Alexander & Co. of Calcutta to the Deponent & by him received on or about the tenth day of August last past—& in a Copy of a letter, accompanying that from said Alexander & Company—written by W. H. Smoult[44] to the said Alexander & Company both which are herewith exhibited—that the facts on which he relies to prove that the Estate of the

43. Authority from the federal court directing the taking of a deposition.

44. Not identified. Letters not found.

said James Murray is indebted to the Executor thereof & to the Legatees under the will of said Murray, are contained in a certified extract from a Decree in the Supreme Court of Judicature at Fort William in Bengal, made in an action therein pending between Nyan Ling[45] Executor of the last will & testament of Genevieve Murray, the widow of the said James Murray complainant; Robert MacClintock Executor of the last will & testament of James Murray deceased Defendant & received by the Deponent with the letters aforesaid—& also from certified copies of the accounts of said MacClintock as executor of the said James Murray, which with sundry documents relative to the said James Murray & his Estate were received by the Deponent a long time since from Calcutta[46] —and which with the Certified Extract aforementioned are herewith exhibited all the facts contained in which the Deponent verily believes to be true. And the Deponent verily believing that there is a large balance due to the Executor of the said James Murray in India for monies advances by him & for the payment of legacies is advised by his Counsel that it is not safe for him to proceed to trial until the said Commission is returned from India, or unless the Documents now exhibited are admitted & received by the Honourable Court as sufficiently proving the facts therein set out as true.

John Richards

Oct. Term (21. Oct.) 1818
Sworn to in Court. Att. Jno. Davis Clk.

Moved, that for the Causes set forth in the foregoing affidavit of the Respondent, that said action stand continued to the next term of this Court & that the same may not be sent to a Master until the Return of the Commission from Calcutta which has issued in this Case

By Prescott & Hubbard Counsel for Respondent

ADS. *Harvey* v. *Richards*, USCC,DMass, May 1819.

DOCUMENT 139. DECRETAL ORDER

Circuit Court of the United States October 28th. 1818
October AD. 1818
Mary Harvey Compt. in Equity
v.
John Richards, Administrator &c

This cause being at issue, divers witnesses were examined therein and their depositions, duly taken and published, as by the bill, amended bill, answers, replication and depositions in the said cause—all of them remaining duly filed and of record in this Honorable Court appears: And

45. Not identified.

46. See the case file.

the said cause being thus ready for hearing—a day was afterwards appointed for the hearing thereof: On which day being the twenty eighth day of October instant—this cause coming to be heard before this Court in the presence of counsel on both sides—the substance of the complainant's bill being for an account and distribution of the personal estate of the said James Murray deceased, which had come to the hands of the defendant; and which the defendant, in his answer insisted ought not to be distributed by this Court, in as much as the domicil of the said Murray, at the time of his death, was in Bengal, a province in the East Indies, under the government of the King of the United Kingdom of Great Britain and Ireland. Whereupon the Court—admitting the fact of domicil to have been, as alleged by the Defendant in his answer, did order, adjudge and decree that the personal estate of said James Murray deceased, in the hands of the defendant—should be distributed according to the prayer of the complainant's bill, and to that end—did further order—that the said Richards, the defendant, should come to an account before Warren Dutton and William P. Mason Esquires,[47] appointed to act as Masters in chancery in this behalf, for the personal estate of the said Murray, received by him the defendant or any other person or persons for his use; and of all gains, interest and profit by him made of said personal estate. And for the better discovery thereof, the said Richards is directed to produce before the said masters, upon oath, all books, accounts, papers, and writings in his custody or power relating thereto and to be examined upon interrogatories as said Masters shall direct. And in taking said account, the said masters are to make unto the said defendant all just allowances. And the said Masters are also directed to take an account of, and state the debts, legacies, and funeral charges of the said Murray, if any, which shall be proved to remain unpaid, by proper evidence and vouchers, to be produced before them by said Richards. And, if any be unpaid, they are likewise to state whether the estate, in the hands of the Executor of the last will of said Murray, is proved, by proper evidence and vouchers to be produced by said Richards—to be so far insufficient for the payment of such debts, legacies and funeral charges as to require that the money found in the hands of said Richards at the taking of said account, or any part thereof, should be remitted to said Executor for the purpose of discharging the same. The said masters are to make their report, in Court, or file the same in the Clerk's office on or before the seventh day of December next. And on the coming in of said report, the parties are to resort to the Court for further directions in this matter.

ADS. *Harvey* v. *Richards*, USCC,DMass, May 1819.

47. William Powell Mason (1791–1867; Harvard 1811), Boston lawyer, admitted in 1814.

DOCUMENT 140. REPORT OF MASTERS

[January 12, 1819]

Circuit Court of the United States for the
First Circuit and District of Massachusetts.
October Term 1818.
In Chancery
Mary Harvey Complainant vs. John Richards, Adm

In pursuance of a decretal order, made at the October Term of the said Court, in the year aforesaid, by which among other things, it was ordered, adjudged, and decreed, that it be referred to Warren Dutton and William P. Mason, Esquires, appointed by this Honorable Court Masters in Chancery in this behalf to take and state an account between the parties Complainant and Defendant, in the above cause, touching and concerning the personal Estate of James Murray in the hands of the Defendant, as Administrator, together with all gains, interest and profit by him made thereof: That in taking said account, all just allowances be made to the said Defendant. That the said Masters appointed as aforesaid, take an account of, and state the debts, legacies, and funeral charges of the said Murray, if any, which shall be proved to remain unpaid, by proper evidence and vouchers to be produced before them by the said Defendant, and if any be unpaid, to state whether the Estate in the hands of the Executor of the last will of the said Murray is proved, by proper evidence and vouchers, to be produced by the Defendant, so far insufficient, for the payment of such debts, legacies and funeral charges, as to require that the money found in the hands of the Defendant, at the taking of said account or any part thereof, should be remitted to said Executor for the purpose of discharging the same.

Now therefore we the Subscribers being appointed Masters of this Honorable Court, in this behalf, do Report that we have been attended by the Defendant and his Counsel and by the Counsel of the Complainant in the above cause, and having heard their allegations and the proofs thereon, have stated an account between the Parties—touching the matters referred to us in the above recited decretal order, as will appear by the Schedule marked A hereunto annexed.[48] By which it appears that there was in the hands of the said Defendant as Administrator, on the seventeenth day of April in the year of Our Lord eighteen hundred and fourteen the sum of $36,016,2 it also appears by evidence produced before us that $12000, part of this sum, had been before the commencement of this suit deposited with Jonathan Amory Junior[49] as a pledge and indemnity to the said Amory on his becoming the surety of the Defendant as Administrator of the estate of the said Murray, in whose hands it has hitherto remained without any profit, gain, or advantage to

48. See case file.

49. A Boston merchant.

the Defendant, no interest is therefore charged by us in this sum up to the 25th of October 1817.

It also appears by evidence produced before us, that the sum of $15000 part of the principal sum was remitted by the Defendant to England and was placed in the hands of the Messrs Baring & Co. on the 23d of July in the year 1814. On this sum we have charged an interest of three per cent per annum, being the interest received by the Defendant after deducting Bankers commissions for receiving and paying, up to the said 25th day of October in the year 1817. It also appears by evidence produced before us, that the balance of the principal sum, being $9016.2, remaining in the hands of the Defendant was not set apart or specially deposited by him, but partially mingled with his own property and employed in his commercial concerns, but that he constantly kept a balance to his credit at the Banks, of a much larger sum, than he should have done if he had not expected from Term to Term of this Court, that a judgment would be rendered against him; and that he was at all times prepared to satisfy such Judgment as might so be rendered against him, within fifteen days from the rendition thereof; that the portion of said balance, employed by him as aforesaid in trade, was unsuccessful, and that he did not make or receive any interest profit or gain thereby. It also appears, that from the said 17th day of April 1814 to the said 25th day of October 1818 a suit was pending in the Supreme Judicial Court of this State. The papers herewith connected and marked B. C. D. E. F. G. H. were returned into Court with this Report and made a part of this case.

W. P. Mason

ADS. *Harvey* v. *Richards*, USCC,DMass, May 1819.

DOCUMENT 141. EXCEPTIONS TO THE MASTERS' REPORT

Jany 16. 1819

United States of America } Circuit Court of the United States
Massachusetts District } Oct Term AD 1818

In chancery between

Mary Harvey Compt vs John Richards admin &c Deft.

Exception taken by the said Deft. to the Report made by Warren Dutton & William P. Mason Esquires two Masters in this Case, bearing date Jany 12. 1819.

Exception For that the said Masters have in & by their said Report stated that "no sufficient evidence having been produced before us to enable us to state an account of the debts, legacies & funeral charge of the said Murray; nor whether the Estate in the hands of the Executor of the last will of the said Murray, is or is not sufficient to pay the same, we have not allowed any portion of the principal sum in the hands of the Deft. to be retained by him for these purposes, but have charged him with the whole sum"—in which particulars the said Deft doth except to the said Masters Report & humbly appeals therefrom to the judgment of this Honourable Court

By his Counsel Prescott & Hubbard

ADS. *Harvey* v. *Richards*, USCC,DMass, May 1819.

DOCUMENT 142. SUPPLEMENTAL BILL AND PETITION

[January 16, 1819]

Mary Harvey
vs
John Richards, Adr
of
Jas. Murray.

To the Honorable the Judges of the Circuit Court of the United States for the first Circuit, held within and for the District of Massachusetts at the October term A.D. 1818.

In Chancery
October Term 1818.

Humbly shews Tillinghast Mowry[50] of Milton township, in the State of Ohio, yeoman, and a Citizen of said State, as he is Administrator of the goods and estate which were of John Mowry, late of said Milton township, yeoman deceased, intestate, and formerly of Exeter, in the State of Rhode Island, that on the twelfth day of April, in the year of our Lord one thousand eight hundred & fourteen, Mary Harvey, of Newport, in said State of Rhode Island, widow & a Citizen of said State, did exhibit her original bill of complaint in this honorable Court against John Richards, of Boston, in said District of Massachusetts, Merchant, in his capacity of Administrator with the will annexed of the goods & estate of James Mowry, otherwise called James Murray, late of Newport aforesaid, deceased, (amongst other things) for an account, discovery & distribution of the personal estate of said James deceased, the said Mary then claiming the same as the sister & sole next of kin of said James: And the said Defendant being duly served with process for that purpose, did appear & put in his plea and answer thereto & among other things insisted that if the said Mary was one of the next of kin of said Mowry that she was not the only next of kin, but that John Mowry late of Exeter, in the county of Kent, in said State of Rhode Island was also one of the next of kin, as by said bill and answer relation thereto being had, will more fully and at large appear. And your orator further shews that afterwards it was ordered by this Honorable Court that the said parties to said original bill should go to trial at law, upon this point—to

50. Not further identified.

wit whether said Mary Harvey was the sister and only next of kin of said James Mowry deceased or not. And at the October term of this Court held in the year of our Lord one thousand eight hundred & fifteen a jury having been duly impannelled and sworn to try the said issue returned their verdict that the said Mary—together with John Mowry, then in full life, were the sole next of kin of the said James deceased as by the record thereof will more fully appear; And thereupon, said Mary Harvey by leave of this Court amended her said original bill, by alleging and charging among other things that she together with said John Mowry, late of Exeter, in said State of Rhode-Island—but whose place of residence was then unknown—were the sole next of kin of said James deceased, & praying for an account, & distribution on behalf of herself and of the said John Mowry: to which said amended bill—said Richards put in his answer and said Mary replied thereto. And afterwards the said parties being at issue divers witnesses were examined & their depositions duly taken & returned, all of them remaining filed & of record in this honorable Court, relation thereto being had, may more fully & at large appear. And on the twenty eighth day of October last, the parties being so at issue—the said cause came on to be heard—and it was ordered, adjudged & decreed by this honorable Court, that the goods & estate of the said James, deceased, in the hands of said John Richards, should be distributed as prayed for by said Mary in her said Amended bill and for that purpose it was referred to Masters to take an account of said personal estate. And your Orator further shews that the said John Murray named in said answer & the said John Mowry named in said verdict and amended bill are one and the same & not divers nor other; and that on or about the first day of August, in the year of our Lord one thousand eight hundred & sixteen, the said John Mowry died, at Milton township aforesaid intestate; & afterwards on the twelfth day of October last your Orator being a son of the said John Mowry deceased, did apply, to the Judge of the probate of wills & of granting administrations within the County of Suffolk, in this District, for letters of Administration upon the estate of said John deceased, which might be found therein—and the same were thereupon granted to him by the said Judge of sd. probate Court, under the seal thereof which he now here produces: By reason of all which he is become well entitled to have, in his said capacity the same benefit of said suit, proceedings, & decree and relief against the said John Richards, as if the said John Mowry had been an original complainant therein; and he the said Richards ought to admit assets of the said James, deceased, in his hands—to be distributed among the next of kin and the legal representatives of such next of kin or else set forth, a particular & true account thereof & how the same have been applied & disposed of since the same came to his hands as Administrator aforesaid. To the end therefore that he, said Tillinghast, in his said capacity, may be admitted a party to the aforesaid suit—and that he may have all benefit & advantages of the testimony proceedings and decree therein taken, had & made as if said John Mowry had been a party to said original bill & that the said Richards may admit assets, & that your Orator may have such other & further relief in the premises as the nature of his case requires. He prays your honours to grant a writ of subpoena, or other proper process, directed to said John Richards, commanding him to appear before this Honorable Court—to answer the premises—and shew cause, if he can, why the said Tillinghast, in his said capacity should not be admitted to have all benefit & advantage of said testimony proceedings & decree as above prayed for & that he may be relieved in the premises as aforesaid, & that the said Richards further stand to & abide such orders & decrees in the premises as to your Honours shall seem meet &c.

D Webster
Wm. C Aylwin } Solicitors

ADS. *Harvey* v. *Richards*, USCC,DMass, May 1819.

DOCUMENT 143. DECREE

Massachusetts Jany 16. 1819
District ss—Circuit Court Oct Term AD 1818.
Mary Harvey Compt
& vs John Richards adm
Tillinghast Mowry admin Compt

Upon reading & filing the Report of Warren Dutton & Wm P Mason Esqrs. appointed to act as Masters, made in this Cause, & bearing date the twelfth day of January instant, by which report it appears that pursuant to a decretal order made in this Cause on the twenty eighth day of October last, they had pursued the directions of the said order & that upon taking & stating the accounts directed by the said order to be taken & stated it was found that there was a balance of thirty six thousand four hundred & seventy three dollars & ninety six cents of the personal Estate of said James Murray deceased in the hands of him said Richards on the twenty fifth day of October in the year of our Lord eighteen hundred & seventeen—& certain exceptions to the Masters Report on the part of the said Richards having been read & overruled, it is thereupon ordered adjudged & decreed & this Court doth order adjudge & decree upon the motion of the Counsel of the said Mary Harvey & Tillinghast Mowry that the said Report be confirmed in part to wit so far as to the taking of the accounts & balance found due: And the supplemental bill of the said Tillinghast Mowry praying for the distributive share of John Mowry of the personal Estate of said James Murray deceased as one of his next of kin, & the answer of the said Richards thereto having been read & informal testimony having been produced by the said Tillinghast Mowry to prove the affinity of the said John Mowry to the said James Murray & the decease of the said John Mowry which testimony could not be admitted: And the Attorney & Counsel in Court of the said Mary Harvey together with Robert D. Lawton her Agent & Attorney, in fact, here present—thereupon consenting to a decree for eleven thousand dollars in part of her distributive share of the balance in the hands of the said Richards, instead of the whole thereof to be paid to her at this time provided it should also be ordered & decreed that the further sum of nine thousand dollars should be paid at the next term of this Court to the said Tillinghast Mowry as administrator of the said John Mowry as part of his distributive share of the personal Estate of the said James Murray deceased upon his then procuring & exhibiting the testimony aforesaid.

It is thereupon further ordered by consent of parties that the sum of eleven thousand dollars be forthwith paid over to the said Mary Harvey out of the funds in the hands of the said Richards as a part & towards her distributive share of the personal Estate of said James Murray deceased as one of his next of kin & that the costs of the suit of said Mary Harvey now taxed at the sum of six hundred & twenty seven dollars & fifty four cents be charged on the funds in the hands of the said Richards & be forthwith paid thereout by him; And it is further ordered by consent of parties that the sum of nine thousand dollars be paid over to the said Tillinghast Mowry out of the funds in the hands of him the said Richards as a part & toward the distributive share of the said John Mowry of the personal Estate of said James Murray deceased as one of his next of kin at the next term of this Court upon publication of testimony formally taken under Commissions from this Court proving the affinity of the said John Mowry to the said James Murray & the decease of the said John Mowry And that the Report of the said Masters stand over for further directions & that the Causes be continued with liberty to the said Defendant Richards to take out new Commissions to India or elsewhere upon Interrogatories to be duly filed directed to any judge of a Court of Record or Master in Chancery or any Counsellor at Law to be appointed & designated by any judge of a Court of Record as aforesaid, not of Counsel for any party or person interested in this Cause.

AD. *Harvey* v. *Richards*, USCC,DMass, May 1819.

DOCUMENT 144. RECEIPT

Jany 16th. 1819.

Recd. of John Richards Adr. of James Murray decd. eleven thousand dollars—and also the sum of six hundred & twenty seven dollars & 54/100 the costs taxed in the cause Harvey v Richards—pursuant to the order this day passed by the Circuit Court of the United States in said cause & have given duplicate receipts

D Webster } Solicitors
Wm C Aylwin }

ADS. *Harvey* v. *Richards*, USCC,DMass, May 1819.

DOCUMENT 145. ANSWER

[May 22, 1819]

Mary Harvey vs John Richards Admr. of James Murray Tr Chancery Oct T 1818	To the Honourable the Judges of the Circuit Court of the United States for the first Circuit held within & for the District of Massachusetts at this October Term A D. 1818.

The Answer of John Richards the Defendant to the bill of complaint of Tillinghast Mowry filed in the cause of Mary Harvey against the said Richards pending In this Honourable Court.

The defendant now & at all times hereafter saving & reserving to himself all manner of benefit & advantage of exception to the manifold errors & insufficiencies in the Complainant's said Bill of complaint contained for answer thereunto or unto so much & such parts thereof as this Defendant is advised is material for him to make answer unto he answers & says that he admits it to be true that the said Mary Harvey did exhibit her original bill of Complaint in this Honourable Court against the defendant in his capacity of Administrator with the will annexed of the goods & estate of James Murray late a resident in Calcutta in the British India deceased Testate to which bill of complaint this defendant did put in his plea & answer—relation thereto being had will more fully & at large appear. And this Defendant doth also admit the facts stated by the said Tillinghast Mowry relative to the proceedings from time to time in the said cause of Mary Harvey against this Defendant to be in substance true. But this Defendant doth wholly deny the right of the said Complainant to receive a distributive & proportional share of the estate goods chattels & effects of the said Testator James Murray in the hands of this Defendant because he doth wholly deny that the John Mowry mentioned in the Complainants bill was the brother & next of kin of the said James Murray—& if it were clearly proved that the said John Mowry was the brother & next of kin of the said James Murray—the Defendant doth deny that the said John is deceased & if deceased he doth also deny that the complainant is Administrator of the goods & estate which were of the said John Mowry & as such lawfully entitled to claim & receive his goods chattels & effects from the hands of any person whatsoever or entitled to an account of the goods & estate of the said James Murray in the hands of this Defendant on the ground that said John Mowry as his brother and of his next of kin is entitled to a distributive share thereof.

And this Defendant further answering says that in case the said John Mowry was one of the next of kin of the said James Murray & that the said John is deceased & the said Complainant is his Administrator lawfully appointed & as such duly entitled to an account of the personal estate & effects of the said James Murray in the hands of this Defendant that the goods & estate of the said James Murray which have come to the hands & possession of his Executor or Executors in Bengal are not as this Defendant doth believe & insist sufficient to pay the debts of the said James Murray together with the legacies given in & by his said will & the charges of administering his said Estate in Bengal, but this Defendant doth believe & insist that they are insufficient for this purpose by the sum of thirty two thousand dollars & upwards that is to say that the amount justly due to sundry legatees or their legal representatives under the will of the said James Murray exceeds as this Defendant doth believe & insist the sum of eighteen thousand dollars—and that the amount of money justly due from the estate of said James Murray to the Executor of his will in Bengal exceeds the sum of fourteen thousand dollars—and that the monies in the hands of this Defendant do not differ materially from the sum of twenty eight thousand dollars the whole of which is required as the Defendant doth believe & insist by the said Executor in India for the purposes aforesaid—by reason whereof this Defendant cannot admit assets of the said James Murray deceased in his hands to any part of which the said complainant is in any event entitled to a distribution

All which matters & things this Defendant is ready to aver maintain & prove as this Honourable Court shall direct & humbly prays to be hence dismissed with his reasonable costs & charges in that behalf most wrongfully sustained.

AD. *Harvey* v. *Richards*, USCC,DMass, May 1819.

DOCUMENT 146. REPLICATION

Mary Harvey vs John Richards Adr. of Jas. Murray & Tillinghast Mowry Adr v said John Richards Adr	In Chancery—Oct. Term 1818 Circuit Court—Massachusetts District— Between—

The replication of said Tillinghast Mowry to the answer of said John

Richards. This replicant reserving to himself all manner of advantage and exception which may be taken to the manifold errors uncertainties and insufficiencies of the answer of the said defendant, for replication thereunto saith, that he doth and will aver, maintain and prove his said petition & supplemental bill to be true, certain & sufficient in the law to be answered unto by the said defendant, and that the answer is very uncertain, evasive and insufficient in the law to be replied unto by this replicant without that, that any other matter or thing in the said answer contained, material or effectual in the law to be replied unto and herein & hereby well and sufficiently replied unto, confessed or avoided, traversed or denied, is true; all which matters and things this replicant is ready to aver, maintain and prove, as this honourable Court shall direct and humbly prays as in & by his said petition & supplemental bill he hath already prayed

AD. *Harvey* v. *Richards*, USCC,DMass, May 1819.

DOCUMENT 147. REJOINDER

[May 22, 1819]

Mary Harvey vs John Richards & Tillinghast Mowry Adm vs said John Richards Adm	In Chancery October Term 1818 Circuit Court Massachusetts District

The rejoinder of John Richards Defendant to the replication of said Tillinghast Mowry complainant

This Defendant reserving to himself all & all manner of benefit & advantage of Exception which may be had or taken to the many uncertainties imperfections & insufficiencies of & in the replication of the said complainant for rejoinder to the same doth say (in all & every matter & thing as in & by his said answer he has said) he will aver justify maintain & prove his said answer in all & every matter clause sentence article & allegation therein contained to be just & true & certain & sufficient in the law to be replied unto in such sort manner & form as in his said answer the same are set forth & declared & that the said replication is very untrue uncertain & insufficient in the law to be rejoined unto by this defendant without that that any other matter or thing in the said replication contained material or effectual in the law to be rejoined unto by this defendant & not herein & hereby well & sufficiently rejoined unto confessed or avoided traversed or denied is true. All which matters & things this defendant is ready to aver & prove as this Honourable

Court shall award and direct & this Defendant prays as in & by his said answer he has already prayed.

AD. *Harvey* v. *Richards*, USCC,DMass, May 1819.

DOCUMENT 148. SECOND DECREE

May 24, 1819

Circuit Court of the United States
May Term 1819
Tillinghast Mowry Admr
v } Between
John Richards Admr

This cause on the petition and supplemental Bill of the said Tillinghast Mowry, being at issue, divers witnesses were examined therein, and their depositions duly taken and published, fully proving the affinity of the said John Mowry to the said James Murray and the decease of the said John, as by the said Petition and Bill, answer, replication and depositions in the said Case, all of them remaining duly filed and of Record in this Honourable Court appears. Whereupon pursuant to a decretal order made at the last term of this Court, it is now further ordered, adjudged and decreed by this Court, that the Defendant pay over to the said Tillinghast Mowry as he is Administrator of the goods & Estate of said John Mowry deceased the sum of nine thousand dollars, towards the distributive share of the said John Mowry deceased of the personal Estate of the said James Murray deceased, named in said Petition and supplemental Bill, and at the times following to wit one thousand dollars on the 25th. of May current & eight thousand dollars on the twenty ninth day of June next ensuing and that this Cause stand over for further directions.

AD. *Harvey* v. *Richards*, USCC,DMass, May 1819.

DOCUMENT 149. FINAL DECREE

June 29. 1819

Circuit Court of the United States
Massachusetts District ss.

May T. A D 1819

In Chancery
June 20. 1819

Mary Harvey
&
Tillinghast Mowry Admr Complainants
vs
John Richards Admr &c

These causes being again at issue in the presence of Counsel on both sides divers witnesses were examined therein & their depositions duly taken & published as by the bill, amended bill, suplemental bill, answers replications & depositions in the said Causes all of them remaining duly filed & of record in this Honourable Court appear. And it appearing to the Court that the former orders made in these causes the one on the 16th. day of January last directing the said Defendant Richards to pay to the said Mary Harvey the sum of eleven thousand dollars in part of her distributive share of the said Estate & the costs of suit up to that time taxed at six hundred & twenty seven dollars & fifty four cents—& the other passed twenty fourth day of May last directing the Defendant Richards to pay to the said Tillinghast Mowry administrator of John Mowry deceased the sum of nine thousand dollars in part of the distributive share of the said John Mowry deceased, of the said Estate have been complied with by the said Richards: And that the further costs of the clerk of this Court taxed at $209.86 be also paid by said Richards out of the funds in his hands and it further appearing from the Report of the Masters heretofore made in this Cause bearing date the 12th day of January last that the whole Estate & effects of the said James in the hands of the said Richards as administrator as aforesaid amounted to thirty six thousand four hundred & seventy three dollars & ninety six & a half cents, and an accruing interest of six per cent thereon to be cast from the 25th. day of October A D 1817. And the balance thereof now remaining in his hands after deducting the aforesaid sums paid to the Plfs in the above named causes and all charges & allowances to said administrator and the costs of said defendant taxed as between client and Attorney being found to amount to the sum of seventeen thousand seven hundred ninety one dollars & 13½ cents and no more agreeably to the account of the said Richards as now allowed by this Honourable Court. And it being clearly proved by the depositions published as aforesaid that the whole residue of the monies, effects & estate of the said James Murray deceased ascertained to be in the said administrators hands as aforesaid by the said Masters' Report is needed by the Executors of the last will of the said James Murray in India to pay debts & legacies there due from the Estate of the said James Murray Thereupon it is ordered, adjudged & decreed & this Honourable Court doth order, adjudge & decree that the said John Richards do remit to the Executors of the last will of the said James Murray in India the said sum of seventeen thousand seven hundred & ninety one dollars & thirteen cents & a halfe being the balance of assets in his hands belonging to the Estate of the said James Murray deceased on or before the first day of September next.

AD. *Harvey* v. *Richards*, USCC,DMass, May 1819.

c. Reconveyance: James Otis v. *Elias Phinney*

In 1818 a Middlesex County court convicted James Otis, a Boston carpenter, of forgery. Before the court passed sentence, Otis fled across the border to New Hampshire. He was soon arrested and returned to Massachusetts. In April the authorities placed him in custody. When he applied for bail to John Soley, a Charlestown JP, Soley told Otis to find two sureties to sign the bond for his appearance at the October term. Otis turned to Elias Phinney, a Middlesex County attorney, to aid him in obtaining his release. Otis also asked Phinney to help him apply to the governor for a pardon. Phinney offered his assistance, but for a price. Otis owned a parcel of rental property in Boston. Phinney agreed to act on Otis's behalf if Otis would convey his Boston property to Phinney as security. In a document drawn up by Phinney (Document 150), he wrote that in return for a $500 advance (a fictitious payment) Otis had conveyed the property to him. Phinney agreed to reconvey the real estate when Otis paid him the $500 plus any expenses Phinney incurred in becoming Otis's surety. At the end of the agreement Phinney wrote that if Otis removed Phinney's name from the bail bond, he would deduct $400 from Otis's debt. Otis also appointed Phinney as his agent to collect the rent, and on the same day executed the deed to Phinney. Phinney then took possession of the property. This arrangement bore all the hallmarks of a mortgage transaction, although Phinney had cast it in the form of a conditional sale.

Phinney soon arranged for Otis's release on a recognizance executed by John Soley. Phinney's name appeared as one of the sureties. Sometime before Otis's scheduled October appearance, he contacted Webster.[1] When Webster examined the case, he must have realized that Soley had not had the authority to sign Otis's release. If the bail bond was illegal, then the state could not enforce the penalty. Phinney had not run any risk. Webster probably advised Otis to revoke Phinney's agency and not to appear at the October term. In February 1819 Perez Morton, the state attorney general, notified the clerk of the MassSJC,M (see letter below) to prepare a writ of scire facias against Otis and the sureties on the bond. At the November 1819 term Webster filed a general demurrer (Document 151) to Morton's declaration. Webster's demurrer raised the legal issue whether a JP had the authority to release a prisoner after a conviction. The court ruled in favor of Webster's demurrer.[2] A JP's authority extended only to pretrial matters. Chief Justice Parker noted that if the court interpreted the statute to allow a JP to bail Otis in this case, JP's would then have the authority to bail anyone convicted and sentenced. The appropriate procedure was for the trial court to hold the convicted prisoner in jail until it passed sentence.

Otis was released and eventually received his pardon, but when he

1. In his fee book DW noted a $50 payment from Otis on October 25, 1818 (p. 132, above).

2. *Commonwealth* v. *Otis*, 16 Mass. 198 (1819).

asked Phinney to reconvey the real estate, Phinney refused because Otis had not paid him the $500. Otis's actions at this point are uncertain. Faced with Phinney's obdurate stand, Otis may have stopped trying to obtain return of the property. If Otis still lived in Massachusetts, he may have been advised that since Massachusetts lacked a court with broad equity authority to look into the transaction and its fictitious consideration, he would be bound by the agreement which called on him to pay $500 before he could redeem the land. He may have been told, also, to move back to New Hampshire to set up diversity of citizenship. A federal equity court, which might be persuaded to examine the entire transaction under a bill for reconveyance, would not be bound by the three-year Massachusetts statute of limitations on the right of redemption.[3]

In May 1825 Webster and Bliss filed a bill of complaint in federal circuit court (Document 152) seeking a reconveyance of the land. The attorneys contended that the $500 mentioned in the agreement signed by Phinney represented only a nominal consideration, that when Otis won his case on the bond, it released Phinney from his obligation, and that Phinney should have then reconveyed the real estate. Webster's theory was that the deed and not the repayment of $500 secured the costs of the suretyship. Phinney filed his answer (Document 153) at the next session. He claimed that in fact he had not only advanced Otis $500 but had incurred various expenses in maintaining the property. He professed his readiness to reconvey the property as soon as Otis repaid him.

Webster and Bliss filed exceptions to Phinney's answer (Document 154). They sought to force Phinney to disclose (1) whether he claimed the $500 as an agreed price (which would have been exorbitant) or as just compensation (which might have been unreasonable), (2) what work he had actually done for Otis, and (3) what charges he had incurred in managing Otis's property. Phinney filed an amended answer at the May 1826 term. He admitted he never advanced Otis $500. He now claimed that he offered Otis $500 and that Otis agreed to pay him $500 for becoming his surety and seeking Otis's pardon. But Phinney denied that it represented a nominal consideration. Phinney also claimed that Otis assured him that Otis would take his name off the bond to prevent a scire facias from being issued against Phinney, and that if he did not do so, Otis would pay Phinney a reasonable compensation. In fact, Otis had not removed Phinney's name, but when Webster won the case, Phinney suffered no loss. Phinney also pointed to his services in obtaining Otis's pardon, and to the fact that he had only charged Otis a $10 fee.

Phinney's answer still did not please Webster and Bliss. They renewed

3. Laws, Mass., c. 77 (1798) and c. 85 (1821).

their exceptions. They alleged that Phinney had failed to state whether he said he would deduct $500 if his name came off the bond, that Phinney had not spelled out his expenses in maintaining the property, nor had he set forth an account of the professional fees and services he had rendered to Otis. On May 24, 1826, Phinney filed a third answer. This time Webster was satisfied. Phinney annexed a statement of his account with Otis, and he admitted that he had drawn the agreement with Otis and that $500 had been agreed to be deducted if Phinney incurred no expenses.[4] Two days later Bliss filed a pro forma replication, and the two sides joined issue. At the October term Story heard the evidence and then ordered Phinney to reconvey the property to Otis, less $100 for Phinney's expenses. Webster drafted the decree (Document 155).

DOCUMENT 150. AGREEMENT TO RECONVEY

[April 8, 1818]

In consideration that I have this day become surety and entered into a recognizance before John Soley Esqr in the sum of five hundred Dollars, for James Otis[5] of Lime in the state of New hampshire, who was this day arrested, and ordered by said Soley to find Surety in the said sum of five hundred Dollars, and in further consideration of five hundred Dollars by me this day paid advanced to said Otis:—he the said Otis has conveyed to me a certain parcel of real estate, situated in Pinkney Street, in Boston in the County of Suffolk—being the same estate now occupied by Andrew Homer, and bounded as follows, viz. southerly on Pinkney Street, westerly on land late of Joseph Barnes, and easterly on land of Joseph Batson.[6] Now if the said Otis shall completely indemnify and save me harmless from said Recognizance, and from all costs & damages that may arise to me in consequence thereof, and shall pay & refund the said five hundred Dollars this day paid by me as aforesaid, then & that case, I hereby covenant & agree to reconvey said estate conveyed to me as aforesaid,

In witness whereof I have hereunto set my hand and seal this eighth day of April in the year of our Lord Eighteen hundred & Eighteen. It is

4. There is some discrepancy here. Phinney's agreement (Document 150) states that $400 would be deducted. A copy of this agreement in the case file mentions the sum of $500. DW and Bliss probably used the latter in preparing their pleadings. Since Story eventually awarded Phinney $100, the $400 figure is probably the accurate one.

5. John Soley, Charlestown JP; after Otis received his pardon, he apparently returned to Lyme, New Hampshire, his place of birth.

6. Neither Homer nor Barnes has been identified, Batson was a stucco worker. Homer's rent was $300 a year.

understood if said Otis shall cause my name to be taken off from said Recognizance, I am to deduct four hundred Dollars from the above

Elias Phinney[7]

ADS. *Commonwealth* v. *Otis*, MassSJC,M, March 1820.

FROM PEREZ MORTON TO ABRAHAM BIGELOW

Sir. Feby 10th. 1819

A few days since I informed Mr Webster, that I should direct the Scire fac[ia]s to issue against James Otis and his sureties—in order to try the regularity of his being held to bail, in the manner he was.

I now, Sir, request you to issue them, as soon as you can make it convenient.

With great respect, I am yr hm Servt Perez Morton Atty Genl

ALS. *Commonwealth* v. *Otis*, MassSJC,M, March 1820. Abraham Bigelow was clerk of the MassSJC,M.

DOCUMENT 151. DEMURRER

[November 1819]

Middlesex ss.
Supreme Judicial Court
Novr. Term 1819
Commonwealth vs James Otis.

And the said James comes and defends the force and injury, when &c & where &c and prays oyer of the said Recognizance and it is read to him &c. and he also prays oyer of the condition of the said recognizance, and it is read to him in these words, to wit. The condition of the above-written recognizance is such that if the above-bounded James Otis, shall personally appear before the Justices of the Supreme Judicial Court next to be holden at Cambridge within the said County of Middlesex on the last Tuesday of October next; then and there to answer to such matters and things as shall be objected against him on the behalf of said Commonwealth, more particularly for absconding from the Court aforesaid on the last Tuesday of October in the year of our Lord one thousand eight & ten, after being duly convicted of the crime of forgery and before sentence was rendered against him, and shall do and receive that which by the said Court shall be then and there enjoined upon [him] and not depart without licence, then the above-written recognizance to be void and of none effect; otherwise to abide in full force, power and virtue.

John Soley Jus of the peace

7. Elias Phinney, lawyer, later clerk of the MassSJC,M.

which being read and heard the said James says that the declaration aforesaid of the said Commonwealth thereof against him and the matters therein contained are not sufficient in law for the said Commonwealth to have or maintain the said action or writ of scire facias thereof against him; and that he is not obliged by law in any way to answer thereto; and this he is ready to verify: wherefore for want of a sufficient declaration in this behalf the said defendant prays judgment that the Commonwealth aforesaid may be precluded from having or maintaining the said action thereof against him &c. &c by his attorney

D. Webster

Copy. *Commonwealth* v. *Otis*, MassSJC,M, March 1820.

DOCUMENT 152. BILL OF COMPLAINT

Boston. May. 6. 1825

To the Honorable the Judges of the Circuit Court of the United States, for the first Circuit, holden at Boston within and for the District of Massachusetts.

Humbly complaining sheweth unto your Honors, your Orator, *James Otis* of Lyme in the State of Newhampshire, and a citizen of said State, that on the first day of April in the year of our Lord one thousand eight hundred and eighteen, your Orator was seized of a certain parcel of real estate, situated in Pinkney Street, in Boston, in the State of Massachusetts, being the same estate then occupied by Widow Homer, and bounded as follows, to wit, Southerly on Pinkney Street, westerly on land late of Joseph Barnes and easterly on land of Joseph Batson; and your Orator further sheweth, that on the eighth day of the same April, your Orator was arrested at Charlestown in the County of Middlesex, and ordered by John Soley Esquire, a Justice of the peace within and for said County, to enter into a recognizance with surety in the sum of five hundred dollars for your Orators appearance before the Supreme Judicial Court of Massachusetts, then next to be holden within and for the said County of Middlesex, and your Orator further sheweth, that *Elias Phinney* of Lexington in the State and District of Massachusetts and a citizen of said State, became surety for your Orator, and entered into the recognizance aforesaid for your Orator's appearance as aforesaid, and your Orator further sheweth that in consideration thereof, and to indemnify the said Elias Phinney and save him harmless from the said recognizance, your Orator afterwards, on the same eighth day of April, did convey to the said Elias Phinney the aforesaid parcel of real estate situated and being in Boston as above described, and your Orator further sheweth unto your Honors, that on the same day, to wit on the eighth day of April in the year of our Lord Eighteen hundred and eighteen, the said Elias Phinney at Boston aforesaid, entered into an obligation,[8] under his hand and seal, whereby, after reciting the premises, and that he had entered into a recognizance and become bound for your Orator in the sum of five hundred dollars, and that he had further advanced unto your Orator and paid him the sum of five hundred dollars in consideration whereof your Orator had conveyed to him the aforesaid parcel of real estate, the said Elias Phinney acknowledged himself bound upon condition that in case he was saved harmless from said recognizance, and indemnified for all costs and damages, that might arise to him therefrom, and your Orator would repay to him the said Elias Phinney the five hundred dollars recited as aforesaid to have been by him advanced to your Orator, or cause him to be discharged from said recognizance at any time then, in such case, that he would reconvey your Orator the real estate as aforesaid, as by the said obligation herewith to be exhibited and to which your Orator begs leave to refer, will more fully appear, and your Orator further sheweth that the five hundred dollars recited in said obligation to have been paid to your Orator, was a mere nominal consideration,[9] and that it never was advanced and paid to your Orator, or any part thereof by the said Phinney, and your Orator further sheweth that the said Elias Phinney afterwards, to wit on the aforesaid eighth day of April entered into possession of the aforesaid real estate, and into the receipt of the rents and profits thereof, which he has received ever since that time to a great amount, and your Orator further sheweth that he did appear at said Supreme Judicial Court holden within and for the County of Middlesex, as aforesaid, and was there afterward discharged from his said recognizance, and that consequently the said Elias Phinney being discharged and saved harmless from his obligation as surety for your Orator and from all costs and damages arising therefrom, was bound according to the tenor and effect of his obligation aforesaid, to reconvey to your Orator, the parcel of real estate aforesaid, to account for the rents and profits, and to pay over the balance thereof to your Orator, and your Orator further sheweth unto your Honors that he has at various times, since his discharge by the said Court from his said recognizance, requested the said Elias Phinney to convey your Orator the said real estate, to account for the rents and profits, and pay over to him the balance thereof, and your Orator well hoped that he would comply with such request as in conscience and equity he ought to do.

But now so it is, may it please your Honors, that the said Elias Phinney

8. See Document 150, above.

9. One bearing no relation to the real value of the exchange; in this case a nonexistent consideration.

combining and confederating to and with divers persons as yet unknown to your Orator (but whose names when discovered your Orator prays may be inserted herein as defendants and parties to this your Orator's suit, with proper and sufficient words to charge them with the premises,) in order to oppress and injure your Orator does absolutely refuse to convey to your Orator the said real estate, or to account with your Orator for the rents and profits thereof: for reason whereof the said Elias Phinney and his confederates sometimes pretend that such obligation was never made by the said Elias Phinney, to the intent and effect as aforesaid, and at other times they admit the existence of such obligation, but pretend that the sum of five hundred dollars therein recited to have been advanced by the said Elias Phinney, was well and truly advanced and paid him to your Orator, and that it was not a nominal consideration, and that the said five hundred dollars has never been repaid to the said Elias by your Orator, and at other times the said Elias Phinney and his confederates say that he has been put to great trouble and expense in the management of the said real estate, and that he has been further put to great trouble and expense respecting the arrest and recognizance of your Orator as aforesaid, and that the value of the said real estate and of the rents and profits thereof is extremely small and not sufficient to pay and satisfy the said Elias Phinney for his expense and trouble aforesaid, and at the same time the said Elias Phinney and his confederates refuse to discover and set forth the value of the said real estate and of the rents and profits thereof and how and for what the said Elias has applied them, and they likewise refuse to set forth and discover the particular manner in which the said pretended expense and trouble were incurred and the items thereof

Whereas your Orator chargeth the truth to be that the said five hundred dollars recited in the said obligation was never advanced and paid to your Orator, or any part thereof; and that the said real estate is of great value; and that the rents and profits thereof were much more than sufficient to pay any trouble and expense, which the said Elias Phinney and his confederates have incurred; and that the said Elias Phinney and his confederates have converted the same to their own use, without rendering any account to your Orator; All which actings, pretences, and doings of the said confederates are contrary to Equity and good conscience, and tend to the manifest injury and oppression of your Orator

In tender consideration whereof, and for that your Orator is remediless in the premises by the Strict Rules of the Common Law and releivable only in a Court of Equity, where matters of this nature are properly cognizable.

To the end therefore that the said Elias Phinney and his confederates may respectively file true and perfect answers make upon their respective corporal oaths, according to the best of their knowledge, information, and beleif, to all and singular the charges and matters aforesaid; as fully, in every respect, as if the same were hereagain repeated, and they thereunto particularly interrogated; and more especially, that they respectively set forth and discover, according to the best of their knowledge, whether the said Elias Phinney did enter into the recognizance as aforesaid, whether the real estate as described aforesaid was not conveyed to the said Elias Phinney by your Orator, whether the said Elias Phinney did enter into the obligation conditioned as above, whether he ever paid to your Orator the sum of five hundred dollars as in the said obligation expressed, and whether he was not discharged from the before mentioned recognizance in the manner and at the time aforesaid; and whether the said Elias Phinney has in fact been put to any expense in consequence of the arrest of your Orator, and said Phinney's recognizance as aforesaid, and the amount of such expense, and whether the said Elias Phinney has been put to any trouble and expense in the management of the real estate as they the said confederates pretend, and the amount thereof; and whether the said Elias Phinney has not received the rents and profits of the said estate and converted them to his own use, or to what purpose he has applied them, and what is the value thereof; and that the said Elias Phinney and his confederates may respectively set forth whether your Orator has not since the said Elias Phinney was discharged from his said recognizance often requested the said Elias to reconvey the said real estate, and to account with your Orator for the rents and profits thereof and to pay him the balance, and whether the said Elias Phinney and his said confederates have not refused and neglected to comply with such request and for what reasons, and whether such refusal was grounded upon the pretences herein before charged, or any, and which of them, or any other, and what pretences particularly; and that the said Elias Phinney and his confederates may convey to your Orator the real estate situated in Boston aforesaid, and also render an account of the rents and profits, and of all monies in his hands recd for the Complainant and pay over the balance thereof to your Orator, and that your Orator may have such other and further releif in the premises as the nature of the case shall require, and as to your Honors shall seem meet. May it Please your Honors to grant unto your Orator the most gracious writ of Subpoena of the Circuit Court of the United States issuing out of and under the seal of this Honorable Court, to be directed to the said Elias Phinney and his confederates when discovered, thereby commanding him and them, at a certain day, and under a certain pain, therein to be specified, personally to be, and appear, before your Honors in this Honorable Court; and then and there to answer all and singular the premises aforesaid, and to stand to perform and abide such order, direction and decree therein as your Honors shall meet; and your Orator shall ever pray.

by his solicitors D Webster & A Bliss

ADS. *Otis* v. *Phinney*, USCC,DMass, October 1826. The bill was probably drawn by a student; Bliss made some interlineations and signed it for DW and himself.

DOCUMENT 153. ANSWER

5. Septr. 1825.

Circuit Court of the United States
Massachusetts District ss.

James Otis in Equity
v
Elias Phinney

Answer of Elias Phinney to the bill of Complaint filed in this Court by James Otis.

The said Defendant saving & reserving now, and at all times hereafter, all and all manner of benefit and advantage of exception to the manifold uncertainties & imperfections in the Complainant's said bill of Complaint, contained, for answer thereto, or to so much thereof as it concerns this Defendant to answer, he answers and says, that he doth admit that the said Complainant, on or about the day mentioned in his said bill, did make and execute a Deed, conveying to this Defendant certain real estate, situated in Boston aforesaid, a Copy of which deed, (Marked A)[10] he doth hereto annex & pray may be taken as a part of this answer, that the same was executed & recieved in good faith and upon consideration hereafter mentioned and set forth, and that this Defendant did on the same day execute and deliver to the Complainant a certain obligation or instrument of defeazance under his hand & seal, a Copy of which is annexed (Marked B.)[11]

And this respondent further answering Saith that he has been informed and fully believes that the said Complainant before the said time mentioned in his said bill of Complaint, had been convicted before the Supreme Judicial Court of the Commonwealth of Massachusetts, holden in and for the County of Middlesex at a former Term thereof, of the crime of forgery, that before sentence was passed upon him pursuant to said conviction, he avoided and went into the State of New Hampshire, beyond the jurisdiction of the said Supreme Judicial Court; that shortly before the time mentioned in said bill in pursuance of the Application & request of the Executive Government of the Commonwealth of Massa-

10. See case file.

11. See Document 151, above.

chusetts to the Executive Government of the State of New Hampshire, the said Complainant was arrested and brought under legal custody to Cambridge in the County of Middlesex in order to be further proceeded against upon the conviction aforesaid; that at the time aforesaid, and ever since, this respondent hath been and still is a Counsellor and Attorney of the Supreme Judicial Court aforesaid, practising as such, and having his place of business at Charlestown in said County of Middlesex, that a few days prior to the execution of said deed, the said Complainant being in custody as aforesaid, applied to & retained this defendant for the purpose of affording him such legal counsel & professional aid, assistance and services as his situation required, that in pursuance of such application, this defendant did immediately attend the Complainant in custody at Cambridge as aforesaid, for which service on the night of the sixth day of April aforesaid this Defendant charged him the sum of ten Dollars, that he did pass the greater part of that night & of the two ensuing days and nights, in getting information from the Complainant and in consultation with him relative to his affairs. And this defendant further answering saith that afterwards the Complainant made application to John Soley Esquire, a Justice of the peace for said County, and thereupon the said Complainant was ordered to find bail with two sufficient sureties for his appearance at the Supreme Judicial Court, then next to be holden in said County of Middlesex, and to enter into a recognizance accordingly, whereupon the said Complainant after fruitless applications to several other persons, earnestly requested & solicited this defendant to become bail & surety for him, and to procure some other sufficient person to become bail & surety for him & in his behalf to allow such other surety a reasonable compensation and satisfactory indemnity therefor. And he further saith, that the said Complainant, representing to this defendant that there were many mitigating circumstances in his case, relative to the offence for which he stood convicted as aforesaid, and that he was desirous of making an application for a pardon, did request and retain this defendant to make an application in his behalf to the Executive Government of the Commonwealth for the pardon of his said offence, and by all lawful, fair and honorable means to aid and promote such application, whereupon the said Complainant did voluntarily offer, *and it was ultimately agreed by the parties, that in consideration of the services thus performed*, and of the further services to be done for the benefit and at the request of the Complainant as aforesaid, by the defendant, the Complainant *would* pay this defendant the sum of five hundred Dollars and give him security to indemnify him from all loss and damage arising from his said Suretyship. And this defendant further answering saith that he did in fact become surety for the Complainant in the sum of five hundred Dollars, and enter into the said recognizance for that purpose, that he did procure one Cotton Curtis[12] a sufficient person to become surety in a like manner, in consideration that this defendant would pay him thirty five Dollars therefor and indemnify him, that this defendant did so indemnify him and has paid him the said sum of thirty five Dollars, on account of the Complainant, that the Complainant did not afterward cause the name of this defendant to be taken off from said recognizance, but on the contrary the same was returned to the said Supreme Judicial Court, and suits were commenced thereon by the Commonwealth against said Complainant & his sureties.[13]

And this defendant further saith that in pursuance of the said retainer and agreement he did in behalf of the Complainant, make application to the Executive Government of the Commonwealth for a pardon, and he further saith, that a pardon for the said offence was afterwards granted. And this defendant further answering saith, that the deed aforesaid given by said Complainant to this defendant, and recited in the instrument of defeazance aforesaid, given by this defendant to the Complainant, was given and accepted in good faith, pursuant to said agreement, as well to secure to this defendant the payment of the said sum of five hundred Dollars, as to secure and indemnify him from any loss damage and expense which might arise or happen to this defendant in consequence of his becoming surety and procuring said Curtis to become surety as aforesaid.

And this Defendant further answering denies that the sum of five hundred Dollars mentioned in the obligation or instrument of defeazance, given by him to the Complainant, was a mere nominal consideration, but on the contrary he alleges that it was a sum of money justly due from the Complainant to this defendant, *pursuant to the agreement aforesaid*, and the payment of which was there foreborn upon the agreement of the Complainant to give and upon his actually giving the said mortgage security therefor. And this defendant further answering denies that he did on the said Eighth day of April or at any time afterward enter into possession of the aforesaid real estate or any part thereof, under and by virtue of the deed aforesaid, or collect or recieve the rents and profits thereof to his own use, in virtue of said deed, but he doth say that long prior to the time of the execution of said deed, viz some time in the month of April in the year of our Lord, one thousand Eight hundred and seventeen, the said Complainant did by his letter of Attorney, constitute this defendant his agent and reciever to collect & recieve the rents and profits of the said real estate, together with sundry of the parcels of real estate belonging to the Complainant and situated in the town of Boston

12. Not identified.

13. 16 Mass. 198 (1819), discussed above, p. 630, above.

& elsewhere, that by virtue of said Special authority and not otherwise, he did recieve the rents & profits of the real estate in question, together with the rents of other parcels of real estate, untill the month of October in the year of our Lord one thousand Eight hundred and eighteen, at which time the said power was revoked by the said Complainant, and that from and after the revocation of the said power, this defendant hath not collected or recieved the rents & profits of the said real estate or any part thereof, but he hath been informed and believes that the same have been collected and recieved by the Complainant. He further saith that between the Eighth day of April 1818 the day of the execution of said Deed and the day of the revocation of said power in October 1818 he did collect & recieve the rents and profits of said real estate, to the amount of One hundred & ninety Dollars, (some part of which had accrued previous to the Execution of said deed) and no more, and he paid for repairs on the said real estate, between the said April & October the sum of five Dollars & seventy five Cents; the said amount of rents he credited in a general account with the Complainant. This defendant further answering doth admit that the Complainant has requested him to reconvey said real estate to him, but denies that the Complainant hath ever paid or tendered the said sum of five hundred Dollars, or any part thereof or consented to allow the same in the settlement of their general account; on the contrary this defendant avers that he hath at all times been ready & willing to reconvey said real estate, pursuant to the terms of his said obligation or instrument of defeazance, and hath accordingly made & executed and offered to deliver to the Complainant a deed of reconveyance of the same, according to the tenor & effect of his said obligation or instrument of defeazance, if the Complainant would pay the said sum of Five hundred Dollars, or consent to allow the same in a settlement of a general account, which is still open and unsettled between the parties, but this the Complainant hath refused and still refuses so to do. And this defendant further answering doth admit that he hath been duly discharged from the obligation of said recognizance after a suit commenced thereon in the said Supreme Judicial Court, & that he hath been put to no cost or trouble by reason thereof, except the service & trouble, of defending himself against the said prosecution previous to the discontinuance thereof, and some small costs incurred therein. And this defendant further answering denies that he hath ever pretended to hold said real estate, or withhold a reconveyance thereof, on account of any charges or expenses incured, or services performed, in the care and management thereof, or for any other cause than as above stated, and he denies all & all manner of combination and confederacy with any person or persons in any matter of thing relating to the premises, and wherewith he stands charged in & by the said bill of Complaint. Without that, that there is any matter or thing material or necessary for this defendant to make answer unto, and not herein & hereby well and sufficiently answered unto, confessed or avoided, traversed or denied, is true.

All which matters & things this defendent is ready to aver & prove as this Honorable Court shall direct & award, and respectfully prays that he may be hence dismissed, with his reasonable costs & charges in this behalf wrongfully sustained.

Elias Phinney.

ADS. *Otis* v. *Phinney*, USCC,DMass, October 1826.

DOCUMENT 154. EXCEPTIONS TO RESPONDENT'S ANSWER

[October 1825]

Circuit Court of U. S. First Circuit
Massachusetts District
In Chancery
Between James Otis, Complainant, and Elias Phinney, Respondant
Exceptions, taken by the said Complainant, to the answer; put in by the said Phinney, to the Complainant's bill of Complaint in this cause

First. For that the said Respondent hath not, in his said answer, set forth and discovered, altho' interrogated thereto, whether the said sum of five hundred dollars, mentioned in the said obligation to have been paid and advanced by said Phinney to the Complainant at the time of executing said deed, was, in truth and reality, paid and advanced by him to said Otis; but only saith that said sum was justly due to said Respondent from said Otis; on an agreement relative to certain services which had been, and were to be, rendered to the Complainant by said Phinney as a counsellor at Law & without mentioning whether said sum was an agreed price for said services, or was merely a just compensation, in his estimation, for said services.

Second. For that said Phinney in his said answer, hath not, according to his best knowledge and beleif, declared and set forth for what purpose and to what end, the said sum of five hundred dollars, which, he saith, was the sum in which said Complainant stood indebted to him for services, was described and mentioned in said obligation as a sum paid by said respondent to said Otis, and, again, as a sum to be deducted in case the name of said Phinney should be taken from said recognizance.

Third For that said Respondent hath not disclosed his account against said Complainant containing copies of his original charges for said services, nor declared certainly the amount thereof; or whether the same was exhibited to said Otis at the time of executing said deed, and the amount thereof made known to him; nor whether any acquittance of said account was delivered to said Otis or demanded by him.

In all which and divers other particulars the said Complainant is advised, and humbly insists, the answer of the said Phinney is altogether imperfect, and insufficient: Wherefore the said Complainant doth except thereto, and humbly prays that the said Phinney may be compelled to amend the same, and put in a full and sufficient answer to the Complainant's said Bill

James Otis by his solicitors
D Webster & A Bliss

ADS. *Otis* v. *Phinney*, USCC,DMass, October 1826.

DOCUMENT 155. DRAFT DECREE

Circuit Court U. S. Mass: District } October Term 1826

James Otis plf vs Elias Phinney Defdt.

And now this cause came on to be heard on the Bill, Answer & exhibits in the cause; and thereupon, after full hearing & consideration thereof, the Court doth order and decree, that the said Phinney do forthwith reconvey the said house and land mentioned in said Bill to the said Otis, the Plf, by good & lawful conveyance, with warranty against all persons claiming under him.

And the Court doth further order and decree, that the account rendered & stated by the said Defendant, & annexed to his answer,[14] of the rents & profits of said house & land, & of divers other matters of account between the parties, be reformed as follows, viz, that the sum of one hundred Dollars be added to the said amount of charges therein agt. the said Otis, as compensation for the services & agency of the said Phinney, in regard to the said recognizance & becoming bail for said Otis, according to the provision of the said Instrument of defeazance; so that instead of nine hundred & fifty nine dollars, eighty one cents, the balance of said account be taken & established, & the same is decreed to be established at the sum of eight hundred & fifty nine Dollars eighty one cents. And all further claim for allowance or deduction from said account is hereby disallowed. And the Court doth further order & decree that the said sum of eight hundred & fifty nine Dollars & eighty one cents, with interest thereon from the day of the filing of the Bill, at the rate of six per cent, being seventy nine Dollars, & seventy two cents; amounting, together to the sum of Nine hundred & thirty nine Dollars & fifty three cents be forthwith paid by the [said] Phinney the Defendant, to the said Otis the plf.

Draft (DW). *Otis* v. *Phinney*, USCC,DMass, October 1826.

14. See the case file.

d. Problems of Equitable Title: Archibald McNeil v. *James Magee*

In 1808 Archibald McNeil, a Charlestown ropemaker, and James Magee, of Boston, entered into a transaction of apparent mutual benefit. McNeil owed several creditors a total of almost $20,000. Magee agreed to become responsible for payment of these debts. To secure this arrangement, McNeil conveyed certain Charlestown lands to Magee. The latter gave McNeil two $20,000 notes. By a separate document (not recorded for over a year) the two men agreed that either one could end the arrangement by notification to the other. In the event of such cancellation, Magee promised to reconvey the lands and to account with McNeil for any money he received from their sale. McNeil in turn agreed to credit Magee for any sums Magee had paid to McNeil's creditors. McNeil had not mortgaged his lands; he had made a conditional sale to Magee. The agreement gave Magee absolute power of sale.[1]

McNeil gambled that Charlestown land values would increase. If they did, the real cost of meeting his obligations would decline. But after three years McNeil became nervous. He had put a great deal of authority into Magee's hands. He decided to cancel the arrangement. When he asked Magee to reconvey the lands, Magee refused. Unable to settle their dispute, McNeil and Magee agreed to submit it to arbitration. They agreed that the arbitrators would adjust the accounts between them and then divide the lands accordingly. Magee promised to reconvey the lands awarded to McNeil, and the latter agreed to release his claim to the portion retained by Magee. When the arbitrators awarded Magee $27,100 and proceeded to set off land worth that much, McNeil was shocked. This left him with land worth only $2,832.

The referees ordered the two men to execute mutual deeds to each other within twenty days. In August 1811 Magee tendered his deed to McNeil, and asked McNeil to release his claim to the larger parcel (Document 156). When McNeil refused, Magee sued to enforce the award. McNeil countered with a suit against Magee on the two $20,000 notes. McNeil's action raised the question whether the arbitration award foreclosed a lawsuit based on the original agreement. Both suits came before the MassSJC in March 1814. In an unreported decision the court dismissed Magee's case on a procedural point and held that the award barred McNeil's suit on the notes. Following this decision, Magee sold the land the arbitrators had awarded to McNeil and mortgaged the land awarded to himself.

McNeil had run out of remedies in Massachusetts. When he moved to New Hampshire he created a diversity of citizenship between Magee,

1. Justice Story categorized the transaction as a conditional purchase. Since it was not a mortgage, the only avenue open for McNeil to recover the property was to assert an equitable title in a bill for reconveyance.

Magee's grantees, and himself. McNeil hired Webster and Bradford Sumner, a Charlestown lawyer, to try to get his land back. In May 1823 the lawyers filed a bill of complaint for a reconveyance against Magee and Margaret Magee, one of the grantees. The attorneys based the bill on the deed from McNeil to Magee and the conditional sale agreement. Without mentioning the arbitration award, they charged that McNeil had requested a reconveyance in accordance with the agreement, but that Magee had refused and instead had conveyed the land to his confederates, who now claimed it as their own. McNeil thus asserted an equitable title which a court of equity could enforce.

By May term 1824, both defendants had died. Sumner filed a bill of revivor against Margaret's administrator. In January 1825 Sumner amended the bill to include all of James Magee's other purchasers (Document 157), thereby putting their titles in jeopardy. This time the amended bill recited the arbitration award but averred that the arbitrators had conditioned McNeil's giving Magee a release on Magee first making the reconveyance. Webster and Sumner also alleged that Magee's grantees had known both of his dispute with McNeil and the existence of McNeil's title.

In January 1826 Webster and Sumner amended their bill once more. They added new defendants and continued to attack the validity of the arbitration award. The case dragged on for almost two more years. Then at the September 1827 rules term, Sumner filed a bill of revivor against James Magee's administrator, Simon Green.[2] In preparation for the trial, counsel for both sides examined a great many Charlestown residents. If the plaintiff could prove that the Magee-McNeil dispute had been common knowledge in 1811, then the defendant-purchasers could be held to have bought with notice of a competing claim. The defense prepared a memorandum summarizing the results of these labors (Document 158).

At the October 1827 term, Green filed his answer. Sumner followed with his replication in September 1828. During the initial phase of the argument in October 1828, Judges Story and Davis indicated that they believed themselves bound to follow the MassSJC decision which validated the award. This undercut Webster's case completely. If the court would not examine the validity of the award, then it would not overturn the titles of those of Magee's vendees who had purchased the land awarded to Magee. Webster therefore moved to amend McNeil's bill to seek only recovery of the lands the arbitrators awarded to McNeil. Webster thereby conceded defeat on the larger amount of property. Although the judges noted the irregularity of Webster's motion, they granted it. Green filed another answer and Sumner a new replication.

2. At the May term 1828 the court dismissed the suit against Margaret Magee's administrator.

In preparation for the trial, Sumner prepared an abstract of all the testimony he had gathered (Document 159). The problem facing Webster was that although McNeil had been awarded the land, he had never taken any steps to assert his rights. The key question was whether McNeil would be entitled to relief against Magee if he were alive, and, if so, was he entitled to relief against the purchasers of Magee. In a fragment of Webster's brief that exists (Document 160), he argued that the award gave McNeil an equitable title to his share, and thereby gave notice to Magee's purchasers of McNeil's title. Sumner, too, prepared a trial brief (Document 161).

At the May term, 1829, Story announced the decision.[3] First, he examined the nature of the transaction. It had been conditional until the referees' award gave Magee absolute title to the land awarded to him. As to the residue in his possession, he became McNeil's trustee. He could not give good title to anyone with notice. But beyond this, McNeil's actions raised a serious question of his entitlement to equitable relief. Story went through the effect of McNeil's failure to complete his part of the award. Lacking a release from McNeil, Magee had not been able to sell the land at its full value. He had died insolvent. McNeil's delay in asserting his rights damaged his case. Twelve years had elapsed from the date of the award till the moment when McNeil changed his bill of complaint and accepted the arbitrators' award. On these facts, Story said, no court of equity would have decreed specific performance against Magee.

Turning to McNeil's position vis-à-vis the other defendants, Story noted that McNeil had to prove that Magee's purchasers had clear notice of the award, not merely a suspicion regarding the validity of their titles. McNeil had not recorded the 1808 agreement until a year after he signed it, and the deed he executed to Magee did not mention it. The agreement was neither a defeasance nor an encumbrance, and McNeil had given Magee the power to make lawful transfers. Magee's authority to sell could have been canceled at McNeil's election, but such notification did not require recording. Without such a requirement, Magee's purchasers could not be bound by constructive notice of the revocation of the power to sell.

Although Sumner had presented evidence of the public's awareness of the McNeil-Magee dispute and the arbitration, Story pointed out that the evidence came from the 1820s; there was virtually none from before 1814 when Magee sold the last contested parcel. An even greater problem for McNeil was the evidence that he had taken no steps to stop the defendants from improving the land. Legal title, Story said, was sufficient protection for the defendants unless McNeil proved notice. More-

3. *McNeil* v. *Magee et al.*, 5 Mason 244 (1829). Mason incorrectly identified the plaintiff as Archdeacon McNeil.

over, since Magee was dead, a decision in McNeil's favor would leave the defendants high and dry. They could not recover on their covenants of warranty. After taking all the circumstances into account, and noting that the case presented a difficult question, Story held in favor of the purchasers and dismissed the bill.

DOCUMENT 156. DEPOSITION

[October 14, 1828]

I Thomas Welsh Junior,[4] of Boston in the County of Suffolk Esquire, of lawful age, do testify and say that on the eighteenth day of August in the year 1811 I went with Captain James Magee, now deceased, to Charlestown, and there called upon Mr Archibald McNeil,[5] to whom Capt Magee tendered a deed of release, of certain lands in that town which I identified by writing on the back of the Deed, "18 August 1811 T. W" after having read to Mr McNeil the contents of the Deed, which Capt Magee tendered to him, Capt. Magee produced to Mr McNeil another deed of release which Capt. Magee requested him to execute. The deed was read to Mr McNeil, who refused to execute it. Mr McNeil asked Capt Magee whether he would reconvey the land in question, upon the payment of twenty thousand dollars. Capt Magee said he would not for that sum, but that he would for twenty two thousand Dollars, or for twenty per Cent, less than the amount of the award, of certain Referees whom they named, but whose names, I do not recollect.[6] Mr McNeil refused this offer. The Deed which Capt. Magee requested Mr McNeil to execute was indentified, by my writing on the back of it as follows "18 August 1811. T. W" in pencil marks. Mr McNeil refused to accept the Deed which Capt Magee tendered him.

I have examined the two papers annexed marked A. B.[7] They have my initials in pencil marks, of the date 18 August 1811 & I have no doubt they are the identical papers which were tendered by Capt Magee to Mr McNeil as above stated.

Thomas Welsh Jr

ADS. *McNeil* v. *Magee et al.*, USCC,DMass, May 1829.

DOCUMENT 157. ABSTRACT OF PLAINTIFF'S BILL AND AMENDED BILL

Archibald McNiel vs James Magee & al

Complainant's bill: sets forth that on 13th. Feb'y 1808 McNiel con-

4. Thomas Welsh, Jr. (d. 1831; Harvard 1798), Boston lawyer.

5. Magee (d. 1823) has not been further identified; nor has McNeil, spelled variously McNiel or McNeill.

6. The referees were Benjamin Weld (d. 1828), Boston lawyer, Oliver Holden, and Lemuel Shaw.

7. See the case file.

veyed to Magee by two Deeds lands at Lynde's point in Charlestown—that on the same day an Indenture was made between McNiel and Magee reciting the above conveyances—that Magee gave to McNiel as a consideration for them promissory notes for $40000, & that McNiel was indebted to sundry persons as by schedule annexed to said indenture; in which Indenture Magee covenanted that whenever McNiel should feel dissatisfied with the security of the purchase money, or should require a reconveyance & give notice thereof he (Magee) would reconvey the whole or so much of said lands as he should then hold McNiel giving up the notes & would transfer & pay over to him the proceeds of such of sd lands as he should have sold & which he had not applied to the payment of McNiel's debts—& McNiel was to account with him for any sums which might have been paid upon his (Magee's) notes.

McNiel further avers that on 15 Oct. 1810 he required a reconveyance from McNiel[8] and did all the acts which by said indenture was required of him to be done to entitle him to such reconveyance.

That Magee confederating with the other defts refused to reconvey or to account with McNiel, but conveyed to the other defts who have entered upon said lands and still retain possession thereof claiming title under Magee

In the amended bill the said McNiel sets forth that the sd Indenture was recorded in the Registry of Deeds for the County of Middlesex on 25 Sept. 1809—that Magee had no right whatever to the said land except under the said Deeds of Indenture—that he conveyed the sd lands to the sd defts for other purposes than those mentioned in sd Indenture & did not apply the proceeds of the sales according to the provisions thereof

That on 13th. April 1811 McNiel & Magee submitted their respective claims and demands against each other to Benj.Weld, Oliver Holden & Lemuel Shaw who published an award 21st. May 1811.—that by the said submission it was agreed that the arbitrators should determine what sum was due from McNeil to Magee should appraise all the said lands & should award to Magee a portion thereof equivalent in value to the sum they should find to be due from McNiel to Magee, & to McNiel the remainder of said land—& when the necessary deed should be executed. And it was agreed in sd submission that Magee should convey to McNiel free from all incumbrances by him made the land which the said arbitrators should so award to the said McNiel and on receiving such conveyance the said McNiel was to release to Magee the land which shd be awarded to him.

That the said arbitrators awarded certain parcels of the said land to the sd Magee appraising them at certain sums amounting in the whole

8. Magee.

to $27100 the balance they found to be due from the sd Magee to McNiel—& that they set off another portion of the sd lands to McNiel appraising them at $2832.—they further awarded that McNiel should within 20 days make to the sd Magee sufficient deeds of release & quit claim of the parcels set off to Magee in fee with warranty against all persons claiming and or himself:—And that Magee should within 20 days make to McNiel a deed of quit claim of the portion of land awarded to him with covenants of warranty against all persons claiming under him,—that Magee never made or offered such a deed as was prescribed by the referees to McNiel nor were the lands ever after the award free from incumbrances brought upon them by Magee—that the delivery [of] such a deed of the land awarded to McNiel free from all such incumbrances was a condition precedent to any thing to be performed by McNiel & McNiel ought to have the lands awarded to him.

That the defendants had notice & knew at the time of taking conveyances to them of the trusts upon which Magee held the land—of the award—of McNiels title under it and that Magee conveyed without title:—that they lived in Charlestown in the vicinity of the lands & of the office of the Registry of Deeds that McNiel & Magee were well known in the neighbourhood—that all the facts charged in the bill and amended bill were topics of common conversation among the neighbours of the defts with whom they were on intimate terms. That the Defts bought the land at prices much below their true value [illegible] the insufficiency of the title of Magee & that they refused to give [warranty] deeds to those who wished to purchase of them—& that they have taken security for the repayment of the purchase money paid by them in case their title prove bad

That Magee had no right to mortgage to Elliot,[9] that that mortgage did not include any considerable portion of the land in question and that that mortgage has been discharged

As to the mortgage set up by Jaques to Margaret Magee[10] that the mortgage money was paid & if it had not been paid the legal steps to foreclose the mortgage had never been taken

That the release by Magee to Margaret Magee was without consideration & with a knowledge on her part of the nature of his title—tho she was the mother of Magee & lived in the same house with him and the writings between him & McNiel relating to these lands were well known to her & was the subject of frequent conversation in the family,—Jaques knew the imperfection as such in the title of Margaret Magee as in that of James Magee

9. Not identified.

10. Samuel Jaques, a Charlestown merchant, mortgaged some of the land to Margaret Magee, James's mother. McNeil alleged that it was a sham transaction.

The last amendments limit McNiel's claim to the lands awarded by the referees.

Webster & Sumner[11] for Plff

AD. *McNeil* v. *Magee et al.*, USCC,DMass, May 1829.

DOCUMENT 158. MEMORANDUM OF DEPOSITIONS

Thanksgiving day

The Pllf has examined 10 witnesses—citizens of Charlestown. They are asked—Did you [know] of suit—that it was refered—that it resulted in award of land

7. answer they knew of suit—

3 —did not—

Show how little reliance—before award, no suit—They generally concur in knowing report of land awarded to Mc.N. situate near Baptist M[eeting] H[ouse].

none of them describe particularly what land—

Heard report at different times—respectively—and one (Sawyer)[12] before Mc.Neill conveyed.

Heard *q*[uit] *c*[laim] necessary from Mc.N.

This report if it existed implies that the legal title was in Magee, and that at most Mc.N. had an equitable title.—

The claim of Mc.N. extended to all he had ever owned. Whether reports applied to one part or another not stated.

Pllfs witnesses concur in this. That Defts said Mc.N. had no claim—and that their title was good.

3 of Pllfs witnesses say that he claimed while that he ever conveyed to Magee—Notice not brot home to any one of Defts—unless it be to Adams.[13] No one of witnesses bring home knowledge to him at any time before his purchase.

On the other hand we produce 15. Witnesses. The most prominent men—and likely to know—2 of [them] are professional men—None carry back reports to a time earlier than March 1820—many to a much shorter time

There must be some general rule which governs the principle of notice founded in vague reports—if such rumours are any evidence. They are evidence because *They would put the party on inquiry*

To what would inquiry lead?

To any record? The county record disclosed nothing.

11. Bradford Sumner (1782–1855; Brown 1808), Massachusetts lawyer, admitted in 1813.

12. William Sawyer, the only deponent who indicated that he had heard doubts about Magee's title.

13. Nathan Adams, one of Magee's vendees.

To the *award*? It was no where recorded, it was only in poss. of parties
To McNeill? He claimed *all*—as well on the covenant as the award.
To Magee—? He insisted he had a good title—and was willing to Warrant it.

AD. *McNeil* v. *Magee et al.*, USCC,DMass, May 1829.

DOCUMENT 159. ABSTRACT OF TESTIMONY

Began an abstract of the Plfs. testimony but omited it, under an apprehension that it would serve the court very little if any trouble, and that it might be better that the whole should be seen.
General opinion that a quit claim from McNeil was *necessary*. Heard such report ever since the award was made. It was a common report about the town. Dunkler[14]
Heard that McNeil claimed an interest in these lands *many years ago 12 or 14 years ago*. The report *related* to the lands *awarded* to McNeil. It was thought *necessary* as long ago as that to *purchase a quit* claim of *McNeil* in order to be *safe*. Has heard *many persons* say they would not *purchase* and take a *quit claim* only of Adams. Heard of the award *in 1811*—from *Magee himself*. It was a *common talk immediately* after the reference. Conversed with *many persons* who appeared to be *perfectly acquainted* with the report. Could fill a *volume* if he *could state* all the *conversations* he has had with the *great number* of persons he has conversed with on the *subject* from *1811* down to the present *time*. From the *currency* of the report, and from his *conversations* with the persons who *purchased* should think they *must have known* at the time they purchased, of *McNeils claim* J Hallett
It was *currently* reported among the people in *Charlestown* that the dispute between McNeil *and Magee* was *settled* by a *reference* and that a part of the land in *dispute* was awarded to McNeil. Became acquainted with this report 12 or 15 *years ago*. Should think before *Magee sold any of the lots* of *land referred to*. I Kendall
It was generally reported in Charlestown that the dispute between McNeil & Magee was settled by a reference & that a part of the land was awarded to McNeil.

Testimony of Defendants Witnesses

Abstract.

Heard of the award and McNeils claim *before Magee sold out the lots* which was *15 years ago*, and understood *then* that the land *awarded* was the land claimed in this suit. I Kendall

McNeil & Magee both *claimed the land* McNeil told him it was his;

14. J. P. Dunkler; the other witnesses mentioned in this document were all Charlestown residents.

cannot say how long *but y[ear]s ago.* The *neighbours* said it was not *safe* to buy without a quit claim deed from McNeil. McNeil said he meant to have his land *back.* C. Drew

McNeils *claim reported many years ago.* It was the *common* report. Never heard of the reference or the award. G. Barrett.

Heard of McNeils claim *10 years ago.* It was a *current report* in Charlestown, that it was *best* to get a quit claim deed from McNeil. D. Fosdick

Heard report of McNeils claim *8 or 10 ys ago.* Heard of the *award.* Heard that he claimed under the *award.* Some thought it best to get a quit claim from *McNeil.* His claim was *currently reported* as long ago as when Bailey *& Wheeler purchased* which was *15 or 16 years ago.* Obtained a quit claim 8 years ago of McNeil of *lands not awarded. B. Edwards.*

Heard of McNeils claim to those lands as many as *8 or 10 ys* ago and perhaps *more. John Levertson.*

Heard of McNeils claim *as long ago as Magee sold these lots.* As long ago as when the *Batist meeting house was built, 15 ys ago.* It was currently *reported that McNeil* had a claim. Said as many as *15 ys ago* that it was not *safe* to purchase these lands without *a quit claim* from *McNeil.* A. B. Thompson.

Heard of McNeils claim as long ago the *winter of 1821.* Thinks it was *generally known* in the neighbourhood that McNeil made such claim. J. Tufts.

Has been in Charlestown about *5 or 6 years* and has heard of McNeils claim *5 years.* J. Smith.

Heard of claim made by McNeil to the lands as long ago as when he went *to N. H. in 1821*, and *heard* of *reference* at *same time.* N. Austin

So that it is brought down &c.

AD. *McNeil* v. *Magee et al.*, USCC,DMass, May 1829.

DOCUMENT 160. WEBSTER'S TRIAL BRIEF

[c. May 1829]

McNeil has no way interfered with the parts assigned to McGee.

Therefore McGee could not resist this claim.

These Defdts—

have they notice—that depends on notice—proof

Denial of notice, insufficient—

as to time—

It might be they improved[?], on contract

It might be, they knew before they paid consideration money.

They cannot rely on the vendor's title.

These Defdts claim by quitclaim deeds

McNeil might resist the award, & yet claim under it.

Case of legacy

Original agreement—

It was not a conveyance in trust, with power to sell,—in common form. A sort of mortgage, with power to sell. The clear title was in McGee.

The submission was to put an end to the trust; & receive the unexhausted <pro> portion of the fund.

The award, in all that was material, was merely the reconveyance to McNeil.

This, the main thing.

After this award, the land assigned to McNeil was his in Equity.

This land, we seek to reclaim, from him & his vendees, with notice. This notice of record.

As to McGee—what could he object?

1. He has offered a deed.

1. Suppose he had—he must offer it again.

A tender, for once, is no bar, in Equity.

2. He has offered no deed, in effect; because he had disabled himself to do so.

3. We wd. not give him a deed—not bound to, till he gave his deed, & a good deed.

Submission construes award.

AD(DW). *McNeil* v. *Magee et al.*, USCC,DMass, May 1829.

DOCUMENT 161. BRADFORD SUMNER'S TRIAL BRIEF

1. The counsel for the plff, are not aware that any principle has been advanced by the counsel for the Dfts, which they are disposed to controvert. But their answer is that the testimony produced, on the one side and the other, does not bring the case *at all* within these principles, and this they think will fully *appear from the evidence*.

2d. It is said that the subject must be considered in the same manner, as if Magee was in court, and if the plf, could not recover against him, he cannot against the Dfts. This is *our* view of the subject.

3 It is said further, that McNeil has never performed his part of the award; that it was his duty to give a deed of quit claim to Magee, when Magee gave, or offered, his deed to him, but that McNeil was disabled to do so.

4 We say that at the time of the award, *McNeil* was *able* to perform his *part* of it, but that *Magee was not.* The lands awarded to McNeil, were at the *time* of the award as appears by *copies of the deeds* in the case as well as by the Defts *answer* under a mortgage,

made by James Magee himself, to Henry Cory[15] for $3000. and there is no evidence that Magee ever discharged this mortgage in his life time. It is not therefore for *him* to say, that *McNeil* has neglected to perform his part of the award, in not offering him a deed under these circumstances.

5. It is said that McNeil has disabled himself, to perform the award. But how? He has given several quit claim deeds, but in *every instance* as we believe of lands *previously* occupied by Magee; and a quit claim from him, to persons holding under *Magee*, and by which Magee was *protected from* any call by his *grantees* for *breach of covenant*, had the same beneficial effect, in regard to Magee, as a quit claim from McNeil to him, *before* his sale to his several grantees. So far as McNeil has made any *conveyances* then, they have been virtually in performance of the award.

6 We say that the land awarded was McNeils, as to Magee, his trust having terminated, and he having no right what ever, under the circumstances of the case, to intermeddle with lands awarded.

7. The lands awarded were also McNeils, as to all *persons* who *had a knowledge* of the circumstances which made them *all* [torn] as to Magee.

8 We say further, and, which we consider but a modification, or different application (at most) of the same principle, that the lands awarded were *McNeils* as to all those persons who *might have known*, who had the *means of knowing*, and whose duty it *was made* under the peculiar *circumstances of the case* to know those *facts* and transactions, which made the lands McNeils, at [as] to Magee. These principles we do not propose to discuss, but merely to see whether the testimony on the one side & the other brings the case within them.

9 The reason why McNeil is not now in the quiet enjoyment of these lands, and has not been, from the date of his award, to the present time, is wholly owing to the conduct of those, who have from time to time, dealt in those lands, and under such circumstances, as should have detered them from engaging in such negotiations.

Proof—

10. *The deed from McNeil, to Magee and the writing from Magee, both which, taken together, constituted the estate a conditional one, to be reconveyed to McNeil, on the happening of interim events, and contingencies, therein mentioned, were spread upon the record. The information was given where it should be given—the place appointed by law, for all men to learn the condition of estates.*

11. Purchasers should have examined, and if they had, they would have

15. Not identified.

found such information, as would have left them without excuse for purchasing.

12. Others did inquire, and were detered from purchasing, and with no other knowledge, than those had or might have had, and ought to have had, who bought.

13. The plf says in the next place, that the reasons why those purchased who did purchase, are found in the facts, that the lands were sold cheap, as in the case of those purchased of N. Adams, and that it was considered that McNeil could not see counsel, to bring his claim before a court as appears by the declaration of E. Wheeler.[16]

14. The issue is not, whither these Dfts and occupants, of the land, shall loose their lands, and the plf get them, but whither they shall loose the money, they have *improvidently paid* to one who *had no right* to *receive it*, or the plf shall loose his lands, when he had not been even the occasion, of such loss.

15. The Dfts. may have the lands now by paying the *owner*, what they are worth, and will therefore suffer no hardship.

16. But the Dfts *did actually know the circumstances* which made these *lands* McNeils as to Magee

Proof. Depositions
on both sides.

Nathan Adams said in *particular* that he *knew all about McNeils title.* This was said by him *unequivocably*, at the *time when Magee was selling out these lots*, and this too, when his attention was drawn to the subject by Wm Sawyer & others whose depositions are in the case. These declarations of Adams, together with corroborating circumstances we hold to be conclusive against him. And that he cannot now escape from what he has thus *voluntarily* said.

17. Reference lasted 30 days, and occasioned 20 sittings, one of the referees from Charlestown; the witness from thence, one of the parties lived there, lands lay there, one of the referees inquired, of winning the title, to these lands. Must have been a matter of notoriety.

18. Testimony, comes down all the way from 1811—to the present time.

19. McNeil gave the following quit claim deeds.

To Barker	June 1823.
To Carpenter[17]	May 1821.
To Binney	1819.

20. Purchasers of Bailey & Wheeler[18] about the same time & with the same means of knowing the tittle with those who bought of McNeil.

16. Not identified.

17. Barker and Carpenter have not been identified.

18. We are indebted to Linda A. Golden for our reading of this line.

Nichols	Nov. 1821.
Davis	" 1821.
Cutter	" 1821.
Deblois[19]	Feby. 1822.

21. McNeil always *kept up continual claim*, from the time of the award to the present time. *Proof in depositions.*
22. Claimed the lands awarded, and said he meant to have them back. *proof as above*
23. Magees tittle to lands now declared good, excepting in connection with McNeils claim. *Proof as above.*
24. McNeil never denied the validity of the award, nor said he did not mean to abide by it, so far as I recollect the testimony.
25. *The public registry of his tittle and his continual claim*, enough, to put every man on his inquiry, which could not have fail[ed] to have resulted, in a knowledge of facts, that would have detered him from purchasing, as in many instances it did.

    The counsel for the Plf. have made no remarks on the subject of foreclosure by Binney, as stated in Dfts amended answer, both because no evidence was offered to that effect, and because such evidence as could have been produced, applied not to the lands awarded, but to lands lying between Richmond and Washington Streets.

AD. *McNeil* v. *Magee et al.*, USCC,DMass, May 1829.

19. These have not been identified.

APPENDIX: LAWYERS IDENTIFIED IN LEGAL PAPERS, 1.

Samuel Bell (1770–1850; Dartmouth 1793), New Hampshire lawyer, studied with Samuel Dana, admitted in 1796, state legislator (1804–1808), executive councillor (1809), justice, NHSCJ (1816–1819), New Hampshire governor (1819–1823), U.S. senator (1823–1835), first president of the Hillsborough Bank.

George Blake (1769–1841; Harvard 1789), Boston lawyer, studied with William Caldwell and James Sullivan, admitted in 1792, U.S. attorney (1801–1829), and state legislator.

Edward Cutts, Jr. (1782–1844; Harvard 1797), Portsmouth, New Hampshire lawyer, studied with Jeremiah Mason, admitted in 1804.

John Davis (1761–1847; Harvard 1781), Massachusetts lawyer, member, U.S. Constitutional Convention (1788), state legislator, U.S. comptroller of the currency (1795), appointed U.S. attorney in 1796, judge, USDC,DMass (1801–1841).

Caleb Ellis (1776–1816; Harvard 1793); New Hampshire lawyer, studied with John Davis of Plymouth, Massachusetts, admitted in 1796, U.S. representative (1805–1807), state legislator, justice, NHSJC (1813–1816).

Timothy Farrar, Jr. (1788–1874; Dartmouth 1807), New Hampshire lawyer, admitted in 1810, DW's partner (1813–1816), judge, NHCCP,G (1824–1833), cashier, Exeter Bank (1833–1844), moved to Boston in 1844.

Peyton Randolph Freeman (1775–1868; Dartmouth 1796), New Hampshire lawyer, studied with William Gordon and Benjamin J. Gilbert, practiced in Hanover (1799–1803) and then Portsmouth, clerk, USDC, DNH (1817–1821).

Nathaniel Pierce Hoar (1784–1820; Harvard 1810), Portsmouth, New Hampshire and Massachusetts lawyer, studied with his brother Samuel Hoar of Concord, Massachusetts.

Daniel Humphreys (1739–1829; Yale 1757), Portsmouth, New Hampshire lawyer, admitted in 1774, member, New Hampshire Constitutional Convention (1791–1792), U.S. district attorney (1804–1829).

Jacob McGaw (1778–1867; Dartmouth 1797), Maine lawyer, studied with Thomas W. Thompson, admitted in 1801.

Jeremiah Mason (1768–1848; Yale 1788), New Hampshire and Massachusetts lawyer, studied with Simeon Baldwin of New Haven, Connecticut and Stephen R. Bradley of Westminster, Vermont, admitted in 1791, New Hampshire attorney general (1802–1805), state legislator, U.S. senator (1813–1817), president, Portsmouth branch, BUS (1825–1829), moved to Boston in 1832.

Harrison Gray Otis (1765–1848; Harvard 1783), Boston lawyer, studied with John Lowell, admitted to the Suffolk bar in 1786, variously U.S. representative and senator, U.S. district attorney, state representative and senator, judge, MassCCP,S, mayor of Boston.

Theophilus Parsons (1750–1813; Harvard 1769), Massachusetts lawyer and judge, admitted in 1774, chief justice, MassSJC (1806–1813).

John Pickering (1777–1846; Harvard 1796), Massachusetts lawyer and linguist, studied with Edward Tilghman, secretary to the U.S. ambassadors to Portugal (1797–1799) and England (1799–c.1804), Boston city solicitor (1829–1846).

William Prescott (1762–1844; Harvard 1783), Massachusetts lawyer, studied with Nathan Dane, admitted in 1787, practiced in Beverly and Salem, Massachusetts, before moving to Boston in 1808; judge, Mass CCP,S (1818–1819), delegate, Hartford Convention (1814), member, Massachusetts Constitutional Convention (1820).

Thomas Oliver Selfridge (1777–1816; Harvard 1797), Boston lawyer, studied with Robert Treat Paine, admitted in 1800.

Jeremiah Smith (1759–1842; Queen's College [Rutgers] 1780), New Hampshire lawyer and judge, studied with Shearjashub Bourne and William Pynchon, admitted in 1786, state representative (1787–1790), delegate, New Hampshire Constitutional Convention (1791–1792), U.S. representative (1790–1797), U.S. district attorney (New Hampshire, 1797–1800), judge of probate, Rockingham County (1800–1802), appointed midnight judge by President Adams, chief justice, NHSCJ (1802–1809), New Hampshire governor (1809), chief justice, NHSJC (1813–1816).

Joseph Story (1779–1845; Harvard 1798), Massachusetts lawyer and judge, studied with Samuel Sewall and Samuel Putnam, admitted in 1801, state and federal representative, associate justice, USSC (1811–1845), Dane professor of law, Harvard Law School, author of many legal treatises.

William Sullivan (1774–1839; Harvard 1792), Boston lawyer and author, admitted in 1795, state legislator.

Peter Oxenbridge Thacher (1776–1843; Harvard 1796), Boston lawyer, admitted in 1801, judge, Boston Municipal Court (1832–1843).

Thomas W. Thompson (1766–1821; Harvard 1786), New Hampshire lawyer, studied with Theophilus Parsons, admitted in 1794, U.S. representative (1805–1807), state legislator (1807–1808 and 1813–1814), state treasurer (1809–1811), U.S. senator (1814–1817), Dartmouth College trustee (1801–1821).

Index

Numbers set in boldface type indicate pages where individuals are identified.

LIBRARY OF CONGRESS CATALOGING IN PUBLICATION DATA (REVISED)

Webster, Daniel, 1782–1852
The papers of Daniel Webster.

Includes indexes.
CONTENTS: ser. 1. Correspondence: v. 1, 1798–1824. v. 2, 1825–1829. v. 3, 1830–1834. v. 4, 1835–1839. v. 5, 1840–1843. ser. 2. Legal papers: v. 1, The New Hampshire practice. v. 2, The Boston practice.
1. United States—History—1801–1809—Collected works. 2. United States—History—1809–1817—Collected works. 3. United States—History—1815–1861—Collected works. 4. Webster, Daniel, 1782–1852. I. Wiltse, Charles Maurice, 1907– II. Moser, Harold D. III. Dartmouth College. IV. Title.
E337.8.W373 973.5′092′4 [B] 73-92705
ISBN 0-87451-240-9 (ser. 2, v. 2) AACRI